Human Trafficking

In *Human Trafficking: Interdisciplinary Perspectives*, experts from a wide range of disciplinary and professional backgrounds provide a uniquely comprehensive understanding of human trafficking in the twenty-first century.

Chapter authors consider historical, sociocultural, legal, public health, human rights, and psychological aspects of this issue. New chapters address important topics such as racism, child soldiers, organ trafficking, and the role of technology and the banking industry in trafficking. The third edition also explores the ways in which institutionalized oppression of people of color, Native Americans, and those in the LGBTQ+ community can underlie vulnerability of these populations to being trafficked.

Human Trafficking is essential reading for professionals in law enforcement, human services, and health care, and for concerned citizens interested in human rights and making a difference in their communities. This book is also intended for use in undergraduate and graduate interdisciplinary courses in human trafficking.

Mary C. Burke is a Professor of Psychology in the Department of Psychology, Counseling and Criminology at Carlow University in Pittsburgh, Pennsylvania, where she is Director of the Doctoral Program in Counseling Psychology. She has been involved in anti-human-trafficking efforts since 2004 and is the founder of the Project to End Human Trafficking.

Criminology and Justice Studies

Series Editor: Shaun L. Gabbidon, Penn State Harrisburg

Criminology and Justice Studies publishes books for undergraduate and graduate courses that model the best scholarship and innovative thinking in the criminology and criminal justice field today, but in a style that connects this scholarship to a wide audience of students, researchers, and possibly the general public.

For more information about this series, please visit: www.routledge.com/Criminology-and-Justice-Studies/book-series/CRIMJUSTSTUDIES

Human Trafficking

Interdisciplinary Perspectives

Third Edition

Edited by Mary C. Burke

Routledge
Taylor & Francis Group

NEW YORK AND LONDON

Cover image: © Getty Images

Third edition published 2022
by Routledge
605 Third Avenue, New York, NY 10158

and by Routledge
2 Park Square, Milton Park, Abingdon, Oxon, OX14 4RN

Routledge is an imprint of the Taylor & Francis Group, an informa business

First edition published by Routledge 2008
Second edition published by Routledge 2018

Library of Congress Cataloging-in-Publication Data
Names: Burke, Mary C. (Mary Cecilia), editor.
Title: Human trafficking : interdisciplinary perspectives /
  edited by Mary C. Burke.
Description: Third edition. | New York, NY : Routledge, 2022. | Includes bibliographical
  references and index.
Identifiers: LCCN 2021034235 (print) | LCCN 2021034236 (ebook) | ISBN 9780367644741
  (hardback) | ISBN 9780367644727 (paperback) | ISBN 9781003124672 (ebook)
Subjects: LCSH: Human trafficking.
Classification: LCC HQ281 .H8765 2022 (print) | LCC HQ281 (ebook) |
  DDC 364.15/51—dc23
LC record available at https://lccn.loc.gov/2021034235
LC ebook record available at https://lccn.loc.gov/2021034236

ISBN: 9780367644741 (hbk)
ISBN: 9780367644727 (pbk)
ISBN: 9781003124672 (ebk)

DOI: 10.4324/9781003124672

Typeset in Bembo
by Apex CoVantage, LLC

CONTENTS

AUTHOR BIOGRAPHIES

Nour Alabase, M.S., as an Iraqi-American, became interested in helping children and their families with trauma and attachment disturbances. She completed her master's degree in clinical mental health counseling and Bachelor's of Science in Psychology in Fargo, North Dakota. Her research interest lies in childhood sexual abuse and disturbed attached styles. Nour hopes to integrate marginalized and underserved populations within her research and is currently pursuing her doctoral degree in counseling psychology at Carlow University in Pittsburgh, Pennsylvania, in the United States.

Elizabeth Bowman, Ph.D., LICSW, LCSW-C, is full-time faculty in the Master of Social Work Program within the Social Work Department at Gallaudet University. She is a minor sex trafficking survivor and advocate for victims' rights. As a clinician, she provided nearly 10 years of trauma-informed care, crisis, case management, and supervision in the District of Columbia's child welfare system. She currently works in private practice for children and adolescents in D.C. and Maryland, is a certified yoga instructor, and mother of two teenagers.

Mary C. Burke, Ph.D., is a Professor of Psychology at Carlow University in Pittsburgh, Pennsylvania, where she is the director of the APA -accredited doctoral program in Counseling Psychology. Her scholarly interests include minority mental health in the context of oppressive systems, gender-based violence, trauma and human trafficking. She has been active in the anti–human trafficking movement since 2002 and has been involved regionally, nationally, and internationally on work to address this issue. Dr. Burke has begun antitrafficking coalitions in Pennsylvania and Virginia and consulted on the development of coalitions in other regions. In addition, she has spoken to various state and regional elected officials in Pennsylvania and Virginia regarding this issue and has worked on legislation in these states in support of strengthening human trafficking laws. Current international efforts are focused in Uganda, where she and her team work collaboratively with citizens to prevent trafficking through school- and community-based programming. Access to education and therapeutic services for women and child sex trafficking survivors is also part of the focus in the Soroti and Lira areas of northern Uganda, a region traumatically impacted by armed conflict for over 20 years. Dr. Burke was a member of the American Psychological Association Task Force on the Trafficking of Women and Girls and is working to advance knowledge about current best practices regarding therapeutic work with survivors.

Lynsie Clott, M.P.I.A., specialized in human security studies at the Graduate School of International and Public Affairs, University of Pittsburgh. Since 2012, Lynsie has served as the program director for the Project to End Human Trafficking, a Pittsburgh based nonprofit. In this role, she initiated and implemented public awareness and prevention programming locally. Simultaneously, she served as a co-chair, first responder, and a survivor services navigator for the Western PA Human Trafficking Coalition. Today, Lynsie resides in north Idaho and heads leadership programming for students at the University of Idaho. She continues to educate the public and advise emerging antitrafficking nonprofits and coalitions in the U.S. and abroad.

Marci Cottingham, Ph.D., is a tenured assistant professor (universitair docent 1) of sociology at the University of Amsterdam, a senior researcher at the Amsterdam Research Centre for Gender and Sexuality, and a former fellow at the Hanse-Wissenschaftskolleg Institute for Advanced Study, Delmenhorst, Germany. Her research examines emotion and social inequalities broadly and in the context of healthcare, biomedicine, and risk. Her work has been funded by the National Science Foundation and published in sociological (*Social Problems*, *Theory & Society*, *Gender & Society*) as well as interdisciplinary journals (*Social Science & Medicine*, *Qualitative Health Research*, *Qualitative Research*). More about her research can be found here: www.uva.nl/profile/m.d.cottingham.

Terri Collin Dilmore, Ph.D., is an Assistant Professor and clinical director of the Counseling Psychology program in the Department of Psychology, Counseling and Criminology at Carlow University. She also holds specialty certification in group psychotherapy from The National Group Psychotherapy Institute of the Washington DC School of Psychiatry.

Sandi DiMola, J.D., a former Fulbright awardee, is chair of the Department of Analytical, Physical, & Social Sciences and director of the Center for Experiential Learning at Carlow University (Pittsburgh, PA, USA). Dr. DiMola is a founding member of Mediators Beyond Borders, an

NGO engaged in capacity building in postconflict societies. She has served as a consultant to the Pittsburgh Public Schools on the design of a mediation plan for resolution of ethnic violence and as a project advisor in the Heinz College of Carnegie Mellon University for a graduate student capstone entitled "Developing a Tool for International Mediators by Modeling Conflict Ripeness," which was undertaken for the U.S. Institute of Peace.

Michael J. Frank, J.D., is an Assistant United States Attorney in the U.S. Attorney's Office in the Eastern District of Virginia. He has prosecuted a number of labor- and sex trafficking cases. The views expressed in his chapter are solely those of Mr. Frank and are not those of the U.S. Department of Justice or the U.S. Attorney for the Eastern District of Virginia.

Laura Gooding is a graduate student pursuing a Master of Public and International Affairs with a concentration in security and intelligence at the University of Pittsburgh Graduate School of Public and International Affairs. She holds a graduate assistantship with the Vira I. Heinz Program for Women in Global Leadership and serves on the leadership team for Pitt's chapter of Women in International Security, an international organization dedicated to increasing the presence and leadership of women in the international security arena. Laura has worked as an editor for graduate journals at both The University of Pittsburgh and Princeton University and has previously participated in graduate research focusing on the issue of human trafficking in global supply chains in partnership with the U.S. Department of State. She is also completing research focusing on issues of COVID-19-related fraud in partnership with the FBI Pittsburgh office. She holds a B.A. in anthropology and a certificate in transatlantic studies from the University of Pittsburgh.

Judy Hale, J.D., is dedicated to improving the lives of women and children and to combating trafficking in persons. For more than two decades, she has been working to improve gender equity and promote safety for vulnerable people. She has focused on addressing these issues through partnerships and cooperation between government and civil society and building professional capacities by teaching and training a variety of professionals and students on human trafficking and related matters. Ms. Hale served as a Peace Corps volunteer in the Republic of Moldova. She returned to Moldova to work on social service system development and then on national coordination and capacity building for antitrafficking in persons work with the OSCE Mission to Moldova. She is a licensed attorney with a Juris Doctor, a Master of Public Administration, and a Bachelor of Arts in sociology and women's studies. Ms. Hale currently works with the

Women's Center & Shelter of Greater Pittsburgh as the legal advocacy manager and participates on their Refugee, Immigrant, and Limited English (RIL) team to improve the agency's capacity to serve all victims. She teaches a human trafficking social sciences course at Chatham University, and serves on a variety of boards and commissions related to social justice, gender equity, and human rights.

Lisa C. Huebner, Ph.D., is a sociologist of gender and Professor in the Department of Women's and Gender Studies at West Chester University of Pennsylvania. For more than 25 years, Dr. Huebner has studied, taught, applied, and published in the areas of qualitative research methods, intersectionality theory, and sociology of gender, specifically as these relate to the experiences of women of color college students, care work, immigration, and intimate violence. Dr. Huebner's publications include the book (under the name Lisa Ruchti), *Catheters, Slurs, and Pickup Lines: Professional Intimacy in Hospital Nursing* (2012, Temple University Press), which uses intersectionality to introduce the concept "professional intimacy" to demonstrate how nurses negotiate care as part of social and economic life and how "being caring" changes according to the intersections of race, gender, sexuality, and nationality. Her other publications include "Fear, Fraud, and Frank Complexities: The Influence of Gender on Human Trafficking" and "It Is Part of the Job: The Impact of Work Culture on How Waitresses and Nurses Perceive Sexual Harassment." Dr. Huebner presents on a wide array of issues related to sociological explanations of inequality as they occur in institutions, culture, and between individuals. She has appeared on Aljazeera America to discuss racism in hospitals and discussed the #metoo movement and sexual harassment as a live guest expert on NPR *Radio Times* and in NPR *All Things Considered*, *NBC News*, and *USA Today*. Dr. Huebner's current ethnographic research study explains the successes and obstacles faced by women of color college students. She is currently writing a six-chapter book from this project to contribute to the sociological literature and to help higher education professionals best achieve diversity, equity, and inclusion on college campuses nationwide. Dr. Huebner is also currently co-PI on a mixed-methods and policy-oriented study that explains the often-invisible experiences of student parents on a college campus. Dr. Huebner regularly teaches two upper-level undergraduate courses that she developed from her research expertise: Violence: Intimate, Group, and State-Sanctioned and Gender, Labor, and Globalization. She has also taught Feminist Research Methodologies; Sociology of Gender; Sex and Society; Social Theory; Sociology of Medicine; Feminist Theory; Introduction to Women's and Gender Studies; and Women and Self Representation. Dr. Huebner is the current chair of the West Chester University President's Commission on the

Status of Women. She has a Ph.D. in sociology with a doctoral certificate in women's studies from the University of Pittsburgh and an M.A. in women's studies from the University of Cincinnati.

June Kane, A.M., Ph.D., is an internationally respected expert in human rights, specifically in the fields of violence against children and women, child labor, sexual abuse and exploitation of children, and human trafficking. As an independent expert since 1996, Professor Kane has worked with governments, UN agencies (particularly the ILO and UNICEF), regional bodies and grassroots organizations on a wide range of initiatives. Her work has covered research and writing; strategy, program and policy planning; capacity building; evaluation and monitoring. She has a profound understanding of current issues in child labor/trafficking and in 2008 developed the first anti–child trafficking training manual and resource kit for UN.GIFT, the UN's global initiative to fight human trafficking.

In the past two decades, Professor Kane has written more than a dozen books in the areas of child labor, human trafficking, domestic labor and violence against children. From 1996 to 2004, she was the European Commission Daphne Programme's Expert on Violence against Children, Young People and Women and in 2006 was an advisor to the UN Secretary-General's Study on Violence against Children. In 2019, while also continuing to work on UN assignments, Professor Kane was appointed Adjunct Professor at RMIT University, Australia, where she has taught global governance and international law. On Australia Day 2007, Professor. Kane was made a Member of the Order of Australia in recognition of her work. She is also a recipient of the Albert Schweitzer Medal for Humanitarian Action and in 2016 was the inaugural recipient of the Freda Miriklis Award for Women's Empowerment. June Kane has her own website for sharing lessons and publications on human trafficking, child labor, and violence against women and children: www.kaneinternational.com.au.

Emily Kennedy is president and founder of Marinus Analytics, a social impact company spun out of Carnegie Mellon University that creates AI tools to fight human trafficking. Their flagship software, Traffic Jam, leverages big data and AI to identify and locate victims of sex trafficking sold online and dismantle organized criminal networks. Traffic Jam operates in the United States, Canada, and the United Kingdom, with continued global expansion in progress. Ms. Kennedy greatly enjoys telling the stories of impact that Marinus has made in the global community, showcasing the team's innovative spirit in the realm of AI for good, and bringing life to the company's core goals and long-term strategy. She routinely advises stakeholders—such as attorneys general, prosecutors, law enforcement agents, and NGOs—on use of technology to enable data-driven, proactive impact. Ms. Kennedy is a social impact entrepreneur, Forbes 30 Under 30, Toyota Mother of Invention, one of Entrepreneur's Most Powerful Women, and keynote speaker. She also hosts *The Empower Podcast* and coaches founders on how to build businesses that change the world.

Anne Kielland, Ph.D., is a researcher at the Oslo-based Fafo Institute for Applied International Studies, where she works with African child protection issues. Kielland holds a Ph.D. in sociology; the topic of her thesis was child mobility in West Africa. Alongside several papers and research articles, she has published a book on child labor migrations in Benin and another on child labor practices in Sub-Saharan Africa with her former World Bank colleague Maurizia Tovo. Kielland was involved in research and supervision following the Harkin Protocol on child labor in coca farming in West Africa. Her academic focus is the design and implementation of fertility-based household surveys aimed to quantify and identify the determinants of child mobility in the region.

Tina Krolikowski, M.S., is currently completing a doctoral degree in Counseling Psychology at Carlow University in Pittsburgh, Pennsylvania, in the United States. In 2018, she earned her Master's degree in experimental psychology from Bucknell University. Coming from a low-socioeconomic background herself, Krolikowski has a passion for understanding societal issues that influence low-income populations. She hopes that knowledge of these issues will encourage the development of unique solutions that positively influence individuals experiencing systemic barriers.

Allyson M. Lowe, Ph.D., is Vice President for Academic Affairs at Trocaire College. Prior to joining Trocaire, Dr. Lowe served as Dean of the College of Leadership and Social Change at Carlow University, where she was a tenured faculty in the political science department. She was awarded a Fulbright and holds membership in the American Council on Germany based on her study of the EU and marginalized groups. Dr. Lowe has led multiple grant-funded study abroad trips for college students and has served as a program reviewer for nonprofits and universities.

Veronica M. Lugris, Ph.D., is a licensed psychologist and consultant. An active member of the New York State Psychological Association and the Society for Consulting Psychology, Dr. Lugris received her doctorate from the University of Illinois, Urbana—Champaign. She also holds a postdoctoral certificate in organizational development and consultation from the William Alanson White Institute in NYC. Throughout her career, Dr. Lugris has specialized in issues of diversity, interpersonal relationships, organizational assessment, training and development, group and leadership dynamics, and trauma management.

Kimberly A. McCabe, Ph.D., is a Professor of Criminology at the University of Lynchburg in Virginia. She has served as a US Fulbright Specialist as well as the series editor for Roman and Littlefield's Theory and Practice in Criminal Justice. Accomplished through her research are more than 50 publications to include seven books on the topics of child abuse, human trafficking, and school violence. In addition, she has served as a special consultant in UK, Canada, Serbia, and Albania. Her most recent book, *Acts of Violence in the School Setting* (2020), was published through Rowman and Littlefield.

Brooke N. Newman, Ph.D., is an Associate Professor of History at Virginia Commonwealth University. She specializes in the history of slavery in the British Atlantic world and is the author of *A Dark Inheritance: Blood, Race, and Sex in Colonial Jamaica* (Yale University Press, 2018) and the co-editor of *Native Diasporas: Indigenous Identities and Settler Colonialism in the Americas* (University of Nebraska Press, 2014).

Thomas Nowak, Ph.D., is Professor Emeritus of Sociology at Indiana University of Pennsylvania. He has published widely in journals such as the *American Political Science Review*, the *Journal of Marriage and the Family, Comparative International Development*, and the *Journal of Applied Social Psychology*. His research interests include technology, mass media, globalization, and postindustrial societies.

Mary Onufer is a university professor, author, and speaker. She teaches Cybercrime in the Master of Fraud and Forensics program at Carlow University and works as a Cybersecurity curriculum teaching consultant. She is part of a team that developed The Master of Fraud and Forensics program at Carlow, a unique graduate program that prepares students to prevent, detect, and remediate financial crime. Working in conjunction with the National Cyber Forensics Training Alliance (NCFTA) in Pittsburgh, Mary added a graduate certificate in Cyber Threat Research and Analytics certificate to the program and developed an internship in Human Trafficking at NCFTA for Carlow students. Cybersecurity has been her research agenda for the last 8 years and she worked as a research associate at the NCFTA in 2020. Her writing credits include articles and blogs on Cybersecurity. Mary has been called on for commentary by news agencies and speaks on cybersecurity and cyberfinancial crime topics.

Bradley W. Orsini, joined the Secure Community Network (SCN) as the Senior National Security Advisor in January 2020. SCN is the official safety and security organization for the Jewish community in North America, formed under the auspices of The Jewish Federations of North America and the Conference of Presidents of Major American Jewish Organizations. In his role, Mr. Orsini provides security consultations, training, and direct response to critical incidents to Jewish communities across North America. From January 2017 to January 2020, Mr. Orsini served the Jewish Federation of Greater Pittsburgh as its first Director of Community Security. Prior to joining the Jewish Federation of Greater Pittsburgh, Mr. Orsini was a Special Agent (SA) of the Federal Bureau of Investigation from September 1988 until his retirement in December 2016. SA Orsini spent more than 16 years investigating violent crimes, gangs, drug organizations, public corruption and civil rights cases. After the terrorist attacks of September 11, 2001, SA Orsini was selected to supervise the New Jersey response, in which he led all searches and arrests with a group of federal, state, and local law enforcement officials. In 2004, SA Orsini was transferred to the Pittsburgh Division, where he was assigned to the Public Corruption/Civil Rights Squad. In September, 2007, SA Orsini was promoted to Supervisory Special Agent (SSA), where he supervised the Public Corruption/Civil Rights Squad. SSA Orsini also supervised the training and community outreach programs and was the crisis management coordinator for the Pittsburgh Division. Prior to joining the FBI, Mr. Orsini was on active duty as an officer in the United States Marine Corps, attaining the rank of captain. Mr. Orsini earned a Bachelor of Science in Administration of Justice from the Pennsylvania State University.

Gabrielle Sinnott is a graduate student pursuing her Master of Public and International Affairs at the University of Pittsburgh, Graduate School of Public and International Affairs. She is also pursuing an Asian Studies certificate as a Foreign Language and Area Studies (FLAS) Fellow for Mandarin Chinese. Gabrielle is originally from Lockport, New York, and attended Daemen College for her undergraduate degree in history and political science. Her prior research with the Ford Institute for Human Security and Department of State, Office to Monitor and Combat Trafficking in Persons (J/TIP), titled "Human Trafficking in Palm Oil Supply Chains," was the result of group collaboration with 12 graduate researchers to assess best practices of combating human trafficking in global supply chains. Her contributions to the report involved assessing the Modern Slavery Acts of the United Kingdom and Australia, corporate liability, supply chain transparency, public-sector legislation, and revising labor inspectorate enforcement.

Gabrielle's interests are in anti–human trafficking, human rights, sustainable development, and climate change.

Kay Snyder, Ph.D., is Professor Emeritus of sociology at Indiana University of Pennsylvania. She has published in a range of journals such as the *Journal of Marriage and the Family*, the *American Political Science Review*, *Comparative International Development*, and the *Journal of Applied Social Psychology*. Her research interests include gender, class, and racial inequalities, the intersection of family and work, and teaching sociology.

Melissa Swauger, Ph.D., is a Professor of Sociology at Indiana University of Pennsylvania. Her research interests include family sociology, public sociology, and ethical feminist qualitative research practices with "vulnerable" populations. Her most recent research examines the experiences of families with adult children suffering from substance use disorder. She has published in a range of journals such as *Qualitative Sociology*, *Symbolic Interaction*, and *Sociological Focus*. Melissa also volunteers and consults for several youth-empowerment organizations in the Southwestern Pennsylvania region.

G. Zachary Terwilliger, J.D., is an Assistant United States Attorney in the U.S. Attorney's Office in the Eastern District of Virginia. He has prosecuted a number of labor- and sex trafficking cases. The views expressed in his chapter are solely those of Mr. Terwilliger and are not those of the U.S. Department of Justice or the U.S. Attorney for the Eastern District of Virginia.

Patrizia Testaì, Ph.D., earned her doctoral degree in the area of slavery and the Italian sex industry at the Institute for the Study of Slavery (ISOS) (University of Nottingham, School of History) in July 2008. Her research interests have focused broadly on migration and related issues of ethnicity, identity and gender, while her recent scholarly publications and work touch more specifically on questions about consent, choice, violence and victimhood in the field of migration and trafficking. She is currently collaborating with the University of Nottingham (UK) and with the Stein Rokkan Centre for the Studies of Social Sciences in Bergen (Norway) in a series of seminars focusing on the politics of victimhood, with papers elaborating on and discussing slavery and debt as concepts related to policies and public discourse on trafficking. Dr. Testaì has also been involved in the voluntary sector, for the prevention of HIV and other sexually transmitted diseases (STDs) among prostitutes, within the Italian NGO LILA (Italian League for the Fight Against AIDS).

Shannon White, M.A., is currently completing a doctoral degree in Counseling Psychology at Carlow University in Pittsburgh, Pennsylvania, where she also serves as an adjunct faculty member in the Department of Psychology, Counseling, and Criminology. In 2019, she earned a Master of Arts degree in psychology from Carlow University. Her current scholarly interests include gender-based violence, childhood trauma, and the trafficking of women and children. She hopes to contribute further research to bolster culturally congruent interventions that will properly address survivor-victim trauma-informed care.

Candence Wills (she/her) is currently in the Criminology and Justice Policy doctoral program at Northeastern University. She focuses her research primarily on institutional responses to human trafficking and marginalized populations, including racial/ethnic minorities, gender, and sexual minorities. While at Northeastern, Candi has served on several research projects with Dr. Amy Farrell including NIJ funded US Citizen Labor Trafficking and most recently the Office of Victims of Crime Grant: Improving Outcomes for Children and Youth Victims of Human Trafficking and a project funded by the NIJ, Understanding the Trafficking of Children for the Purposes of Labor in the United States, in collaboration with Dr. Meredith Dank at John Jay in New York City. As a member of the Institute on Race and Justice, Candi has also helped to create "Hate Crimes Resource Guide" for MA public schools and the Douglas County Police project. Ms. Wills worked on a correction officer well-being project to understand the mental health and well-being in their high-stress and dangerous profession. In the fall 2019 semester, Ms. Wills was awarded the Experiential Learning Fellowship and had the extraordinary opportunity to conduct research at the United Nations Office on Drugs and Crime in Vienna, Austria. While at the UNODC, she contributed to the 2020 Global Report on Trafficking in Persons (GLOTIP).

SECTION I
HUMAN TRAFFICKING EXPLAINED AND COMMON FORMS

1

INTRODUCTION TO HUMAN TRAFFICKING

MARY C. BURKE, TINA KROLIKOWSKI, SHANNON WHITE, & NOUR ALABASE

The purpose of this chapter is to introduce the reader to the complex issue of human trafficking. A definition is offered and trafficking in its various forms is explained. Characteristics of victims are described, and the right to work is provided as a context in which to understand the relationships between poverty, migration, and trafficking in persons. The extent to which human trafficking occurs is discussed, as well as some of the limitations related to relevant data. The process of trafficking people is reviewed, and the chapter closes with an introduction to the issue as it exists in the United States.

Chapter Learning Objectives

- Be able to define human trafficking according to the Protocol to Prevent, Suppress and Punish Trafficking in Persons, especially Women and Children of the United Nations Convention against Transnational Organized Crime and the US Trafficking Victims Protection Act of 2000 (TVPA).
- Understand the differences between human trafficking and other related phenomena such as immigration, emigration, smuggling, and prostitution.
- Understand the underlying causes of human trafficking.
- Understand the ways in which human trafficking constitutes a violation of fundamental human rights.

3

DOI: 10.4324/9781003124672-2

> • Understand the difference in viewing human trafficking as an issue of human rights, crime, migration, and labor.

Human trafficking has received increased attention over the past 15 years in both political and public arenas. "Human trafficking" or "trafficking in persons" and "modern slavery" are terms often used interchangeably to refer to a variety of crimes associated with the economic exploitation of people. Human trafficking has been associated with transnational organized crime groups, small, more loosely organized criminal networks and local gangs, violations of labor and immigration laws, and government corruption (Channing, 2017; Richard, 1999; U.S. Government Accountability Office, 2006; Väyrynen, 2005). At the international level, the United Nations Convention against Transnational Organized Crime, which was adopted by UN General Assembly resolution 55/25, is the primary legal instrument used to combat transnational organized crime.[1] The Convention is supplemented by three Protocols, each of which focuses on specific types of organized crime and are as follows: the Protocol to Prevent, Suppress and Punish Trafficking in Persons, Especially Women and Children; the Protocol against the Smuggling of Migrants by Land, Sea, and Air; and the Protocol against the Illicit Manufacturing of and Trafficking in Firearms, their Parts and Components, and Ammunition. Article 3 of the Protocol to Prevent, Suppress and Punish Trafficking in Persons, Especially Women and Children defines human trafficking as follows:

> Trafficking in persons shall mean the recruitment, transportation, transfer, harboring or receipt of persons, by means of the threat or force or other forms of coercion, of abduction, of fraud, of deception, of the abuse of power, or of a position of vulnerability or of the giving or receiving of payments or benefits to achieve the consent of a person having control over another person, for the purpose of exploitation. Exploitation shall include, at a minimum, the exploitation of the prostitution of others or other forms of sexual exploitation, forced labor or services, slavery or practices similar to slavery, servitude, or the removal of organs.
>
> (Europol, 2005, p. 10)

The definition of trafficking noted here was intended to facilitate convergence in approaches to the issue by member states of the United Nations around the world. The hope was to enhance international cooperation in addressing trafficking in a manner that would support the end goal of the protocol: to end human trafficking as it exists today. While there have been disagreements about and variations on the definition of human trafficking among practitioners, scholars, activists, and politicians (Clawson & Dutch, 2017; Laczko & Gramegna, 2003; Richard, 1999), this definition is commonly used and has indeed provided the foundation for a legal framework for dealing with the issue. For the purpose of this text, the definition will be used.

The definition comprises three essential parts: recruitment, movement, and exploitation, all of which point to critical aspects of the trafficking process. It is important to note that it is not necessary for "movement" to include crossing from one country into another; an individual can be trafficked within the borders of her or his own country or town and can even be trafficked from the home in which she or he lives, in which case movement is not even relevant. As an example of an in-country situation, it is not uncommon for a girl or woman to be trafficked from the rural areas of Costa Rica to the coastal regions, where the commercial sex industry is thriving. Also critical to understanding human trafficking is understanding what is meant by **coercion**. The term "coercion" in this context specifically refers to (a) threats of harm to or physical restraint against any person; (b) any scheme intended to cause a person to believe that failure to perform an act will result in harm or physical restraint against any person; or (c) the abuse or threatened abuse of the legal process. However, it is essential to take other factors into consideration with regard to coercion, in particular when working with victims of sex trafficking and prostitution, such as whether the individual had any legitimate alternatives to support her basic needs (Hernandez, 2001) when approached by the pimp (trafficker). If not, then the thinking is that desperation to perform responsibilities such as support a child, and feed and keep oneself safe, can be a form of coercion. Types of coercion found in human trafficking include isolation, near-constant surveillance, forced exhaustion, threats, providing limited forms of kindness, demonstrating extreme power, degradation, and the enforcement of frivolous demands (Baldwin et al., 2015). These methods of coercion guide individuals towards becoming victims of trafficking.

Technically, people are trafficked into a slavery-like situation; however, that distinction is not often made in reference to these terms, meaning the terms "human trafficking" and "slavery" are sometimes used interchangeably. This leads to an incomplete and therefore inaccurate representation of human trafficking. Coercive and sometimes forcible exploitation of one human over another has occurred in a variety of forms throughout history, as you will learn more about in Chapter 2 of this text. The primary characteristics of this phenomenon have remained the same over time and include one person exercising fear- and sometimes violence-based control over another for economic gain. What is typically different in the 21st century is that it is far less expensive to purchase or otherwise secure a person today than previously. For example, costs as low as 10 U.S. dollars have been reported in places like South East Asia and 13 to 25 U.S. dollars in groups such as The Islamic State of Iraq and the Levant (Channing, 2017; Free the Slaves, 2021) The average cost for a person is approximately 90 U.S. dollars (Free the Slaves, 2021). A second difference is that the relationship between the trafficker and the victim is shorter in duration. This is primarily a consequence of the large number of individuals vulnerable to trafficking (i.e., available to be exploited) and the care and health care costs associated with a lifelong or longer-term relationship (i.e., it's easy and less costly to find a healthy replacement). A trafficker would rather purchase another person for 90 U.S. dollars than invest hundreds or thousands of dollars into maintaining the health and profitability of a victim.

Forms of Human Trafficking

Categorization of trafficking by the nature of the work performed is a common, although misleading, practice. Categories of labor and sex trafficking are most often used; however, concerns have been raised that this separation may serve to make invisible the sexual exploitation that occurs for most women in this situation, even if they are involved in what might be described as a labor trafficking situation. In other words, a woman may be trafficked primarily for domestic servitude, though it is likely that she will be forced to engage in sex acts, too. This speaks to the unique vulnerabilities of women and girls, which Chapters 4, 7, and 9 explore in more detail.

While the type of labor performed by victims is varied (with regard to both labor and sex trafficking), some of the most common *forms* of human trafficking are noted in what follows.

Bonded labor or **debt bondage** is a form of human trafficking that most closely parallels slavery, in which a person takes or is tricked into taking a loan. The person must then work to repay the loan; however, the nature of the work and the amount of time necessary to repay the loan are undefined and often remain that way. Individuals in debt bondage may receive food and shelter as "payment" for work, and in some cases, victims will not be paid monetarily at all, and their debt may increase to account for costs associated with food and shelter. A debt can be passed down for generations, which means that the child or grandchild of the person originally taking the loan is left to pay off the debt. It is important to note that not all instances of work-based debt are human trafficking, as someone may willingly enter into this type of arrangement and actually be fairly compensated for her or his labor.

Chattel slavery is characterized by ownership of one person by another, and individuals in this form of slavery are bought and sold as commodities. It is the least common form of human trafficking today; however, it was the most prevalent in the United States until the 1865 passage of the Thirteenth Amendment to the United States Constitution.

Early and forced marriage primarily affects girls and women who are married to men without any choice. They then live as servants to the men and often experience physical and/or sexual violence in the home environment.

Forced labor is characterized by an individual being forced to work against her or his will, without compensation, with restrictions on freedom, and under violence or its threat. This term is also sometimes used in reference to all forms of human trafficking.

Involuntary domestic servitude is a form of forced labor in which an individual performs work within a residence such as cooking, cleaning, childcare, and other household tasks. This becomes trafficking when the employer uses force, fraud, and/or coercion to maintain control over the individual and to cause the worker to believe that she or he has no other options but to continue in the position. This type of environment puts the individual at increased risk because she or he is isolated, and authorities are not able to easily gain access to inspect the workplace.

Sex trafficking is an extremely traumatic form of human trafficking in which a commercial sex act is induced by force, fraud, or coercion; or a sex act in which the person induced to perform is under 18 years of age. Victims of sex trafficking can be girls, boys, women, or men—although the majority are girls and women. It is not uncommon for traffickers to employ debt bondage as an attempt to legitimize their confiscation of the victim's earnings. Sex traffickers use a variety of methods to control and "break in" victims, including confinement, physical abuse, rape, threats of violence to the victim's family, forced drug use, and more. Victims of this form of trafficking face numerous psychological and physical health risks, which are covered in depth in later chapters.

Slavery by descent occurs when individuals are born into a socially constructed class or ethnic group that is relegated to slave status.

Child trafficking involves displacing a child for the purpose of economic exploitation. In the case of children, force, fraud, and coercion do not need to be demonstrated. It is estimated that 152 million **children** are presently victims of trafficking, about half in its worst forms, primarily hazardous work (ILO, 2017). Like adults, children are trafficked for the purpose of labor and sexual exploitation.

Worst forms of child labor is a term that refers to child work that is seen as harmful to the physical and psychological health and welfare of the child. The International Labor Conference in 1999 adopted Convention No. 182 concerning the Prohibition and Immediate Action for the Elimination of the Worst Forms of Child Labor. The sale and trafficking of children is noted in this convention as one of the "unconditional" worst forms of child labor.

Other unconditional worst forms noted in the Convention include "the use, procuring or offering of a child for prostitution, for the production of pornography or for pornographic performances" and "the use, procuring or offering of a child for illicit activities."

Child soldiering is a form of human trafficking that involves the use of children as combatants; it may also involve children forced into labor or sexual exploitation by armed forces. In this case, traffickers may be government military forces, paramilitary organizations, or rebel groups. In addition to being used directly in armed conflict, children may be used for sexual purposes or forced to work as servants, cooks, guards, messengers, or spies. Approximately 250,000 children from more than 20 countries are in a forced-combat scenario (Theirworld, 2017).

Maslow's Hierarchy of Needs

Individuals whose basic needs are not being met are most vulnerable to exploitation and as such are targeted by traffickers (Perkins, 2015). Maslow's Hierarchy of Needs provides a schema for understanding the context in which the survivor/victim exists. Maslow's model is designed as a pyramid to exhibit the significance of how an individual's needs must be met to achieve optimum wellness (Meshelemiah & Lynch, 2019). The lower level of the pyramid represents physiologic/basic needs of human existence—food, water, air, sleep, sex; one must have these essential needs met to survive. The next level addresses the next most fundamental needs, which Maslow identifies as safety and security—avoiding harm, physical safety, and freedom from fear (Perkins, 2015). The experience of love and a sense of belonging—friendship, intimacy, healthy relationships, group identification—represent the next-most-essential experience. Only then, after all of these primary needs are

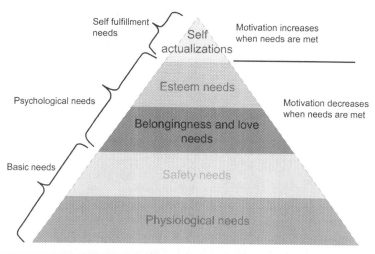

Figure 1.1   Maslow's hierarchy of needs

Source: Adapted from Maslow, 1943

fulfilled, can an individual experience self-esteem—self-respect, self-efficacy, respect of others, and work-related achievements. The uppermost level of the hierarchy is self-actualization—the feeling of self-fulfillment, which further signifies the realization of the highest potential (Perkins, 2015).

Those struggling to meet basic needs are at increased risk of exploitation by traffickers due to feelings of desperation and the need to survive. As one trafficking ring leader stated, "Always make them need and depend on you so you have power over them. Power is control" (Polaris Project, 2021a). Although Maslow's model may not fully address all underlying factors of vulnerability, it can serve as a model for better understanding the context in which victim/survivors exist that predates victimization by traffickers (Gambrel & Cianci, 2003; Meshelemiah & Lynch, 2019).

Organ Trafficking

Advances in the medical field have led to improvements in the identification and treatment of a wide range of illnesses and injuries to the human body. In part, advances include increases in organ transplantation, which is the use of viable organs from either healthy or recently deceased individuals to support the physical wellness of those with compromised functioning. The demand for organs is in excess of organ availability, and perhaps not surprisingly, this imbalance is being met through the criminal industry of organ trafficking. That is, the illegal procurement and sale of healthy organs for use in medically fragile patients.

Current research does not fully recognize the extent of the problem or the relationship between immigrants and organ harvesting (Gonzalez et al., 2020). Approximately 10% of all transplants utilize organs obtained by illegal means (Channing, 2017). The most commonly illegally harvested and transplanted organs are kidneys, followed by livers, hearts, lungs, and pancreases (Channing, 2017). Organ trafficking generates an estimate of $840 million to $1.7 billion of profits every year (Channing, 2017). Many individuals contribute to the maintenance of organ trafficking systems.

Vendors are those that have their organs harvested and tend to live in poverty. **Recipients** purchase the organs and tend to be of higher economic standing. **Brokers** or **scouts** locate vendors, recipients, and/or doctors to foster organ trading and tend to have the greatest financial benefit from these transactions. **Transplant teams** are responsible for determining if the vendor's organs will be an appropriate match for the recipient and performing the medical procedures. **Public- and private-sector services** contribute to organ trafficking in a variety of ways.

Medical centers, airlines, law enforcement officers, translators, and other services and individuals, sometimes unknowingly, aid in the successful organ trafficking systems (Channing, 2017).

Organ trafficking generally occurs through four types of tactics: traditional, mirroring, killing, and conflict. Traditional methods involve a network in which a vendor is located and supplies the organ to the recipient. Mirroring involves similar methods to those found in other forms of human trafficking. For example, they may promise a new job abroad but instead force the individual to sell the desired organ upon arrival. It is less common to kill the vendor, though when killing is used, it tends to occur to ethnic minorities. Areas of the world experiencing conflict, especially war, are a prime target for organ traffickers. Many refugees choose to sell organs due to their dire circumstances and limited financial resources (Channing, 2017).

Organ trafficking is an internationally recognized problem. The Declaration of Istanbul was originally formed in 2008. This declaration is updated regularly, with the most recent version being developed in 2018 with more than 250 people contributing from countries around the globe. The definitions for organ trafficking are provided, along with outlines of policy and procedure suggestions (DICG, 2018). Such documents and organizations provide insight into the issue and will hopefully lead policy in directions that decrease or eliminate the organ trafficking trade.

The Trafficked Person

In popular stereotypes, victims of human trafficking are often portrayed as innocent young girls who are lured or kidnapped from their home countries and forced into the commercial sex industry (Bruckert & Parent, 2002; Richards & Reid, 2015). While this is not necessarily an erroneous depiction, girls are by no means the only victims of trafficking. Women, men, and children of all ages can be trafficked for sex and labor. Those at risk of trafficking most often come from vulnerable populations including undocumented migrants, runaways, LGBT and other at-risk youth, females, and members of other oppressed or marginalized groups, and the poor. Traffickers target individuals in these populations because they have few resources, limited social support, and limited work options. This makes them easier to recruit through deception or force, and they tend to be easier to control.

At-risk youth and runaways are targeted by traffickers and by pimps for labor exploitation, begging, and very often for commercial sex (Estes & Weiner, 2002; Fedina et al., 2019; Finkelhor & Ormrod, 2004). Pimps and sex traffickers manipulate child victims and are known to make use of a combination of violence and affection in an effort to cultivate loyalty in the victim, which can result in **Stockholm Syndrome**, a psychological phenomenon wherein hostages experience and express empathy and positive feelings for their captors. This is more likely to develop with children than with adults. This psychological manipulation reduces the victim's likelihood of acting out against the trafficker.

A combination of factors makes undocumented immigrants extremely vulnerable to being trafficked (Human Rights Watch, 2018). Some of these factors include lack of legal status and related protections, poverty, few employment options, immigration-related debt, limited language skills, and social isolation. It is not uncommon for undocumented immigrants to be trafficked by those from a similar ethnic or national background, which may play into the victim's trust in a way that makes her or him more easily deceived.

Regions impacted by political instability and war create an environment that fosters trafficking (Channing, 2017). In particular, long-term military occupation as well as the presence of "peacekeepers" feed the commercial sex industry in these areas and facilitate the sex trafficking of women and girls (Mendelson, 2005; Morris, 2010). Another situation that promotes trafficking is that of a natural disaster. Natural disasters can destroy communities in a matter of minutes and create physical and economic insecurity. Children can be separated from their caregivers, making them prime targets for traffickers. The December 2004 Indian Ocean earthquake and ensuing tsunami is an example of one such natural disaster, where the lives of close to a million children were placed in jeopardy. In this situation, seemingly for the first time, a concerted effort was made to stop human trafficking before it could begin. Another example, although with a bleaker outcome, is the 2007 severe drought in Swaziland during which ECPAT International (End Child Prostitution and Trafficking) found increases in the trafficking of children; specifically, there were reports of parents trading the bodies of their children for food and water. Diseases also contribute to the increased risk of exploitation, such as the Ebola outbreak that struck West Africa in 2014, which left thousands of children vulnerable to potential human trafficking attempts (Worsnop, 2019) as well as the COVID-19 pandemic that began in 2020. Natural disasters not only impact children, they increase adult vulnerability to trafficking as well. The kind of devastation imposed by disasters of this type can create extreme poverty and make it very difficult to meet basic needs. This, for example, may lead to immigration that, as demonstrated above, can lead to victimization at the hands of a trafficker.

Human Rights and Human Trafficking

Most commonly, a criminal justice lens is used to frame the issue of human trafficking. Consideration of trafficking from the perspective of human rights allows for identification of points of prevention and intervention that may not otherwise be clear. In particular, this view highlights where larger sociocultural structures create vulnerability in large populations of people. What follows is a list of some of the human rights most relevant to human trafficking. These violations occur at different stages of the trafficking process, and often, more than one right is in violation at a time. For more information about human rights visit www.un.org/en/about-us/universal-declaration-of-human-rights.

Human rights most relevant to trafficking:

- The right to life
- The right to liberty and security
- The right not to be subjected to torture and/or cruel, inhuman, degrading treatment or punishment
- The right not to be submitted to slavery, servitude, forced labor or bonded labor
- The right to be free from gendered violence
- The right to freedom of association
- The right to freedom of movement
- The right to the highest attainable standard of physical and mental health
- The right to just and favorable conditions of work
- The right to an adequate standard of living
- The right to social security
- The right of children to special protection
- The right to not be subjected to discrimination on the basis of race, color, sex, language, religion, political or other opinion, national or social origin, property, birth, or other status

Globalization, the Right to Work, and Human Trafficking

Globalization has had an enormous impact on the trade in people, widening the gap between rich and poor and making it easier for traffickers to recruit and move victims. In fact, it can be said that those involved in transnational crime have benefited significantly from globalization. Current global conditions have created an increased demand for cheap labor, thereby increasing migration and, consequently, human trafficking and smuggling (Naim, 2006; Raigrodski, 2015). Increased supply of individuals vulnerable to exploitation is present because globalization has contributed to an increase in economic disparities between more developed and developing countries. Tourism has also grown because of globalization, which makes it easier for consumers of the sex industry to travel and engage in sex tourism.

The right to work is the concept that every human has the right to work and to be fairly compensated. The term was coined by French socialist leader Louis Blanc in the early 19th century. The right to work is articulated in the *Universal Declaration of Human Rights* (1948) and elaborated upon in the International Covenant on Economic, Social, and Cultural Rights (1976). The right to work is also recognized in international human rights law. Article 23.1 of the *Universal Declaration of Human Rights* states: "Everyone has the right to work, to free choice of employment, to just and favorable conditions of work and to protection against unemployment."

Despite Article 23.1 in the Declaration, millions of people around the world work in inhumane conditions for little or no compensation. Corporations from countries with more developed economies intentionally produce goods in countries with fewer resources because it is better for their bottom line. Products that are commonly used, ranging in value from goods such as coffee and chocolate to cell phones and televisions, are too often made by people who are struggling to survive. By utilizing these workers, corporations are exploiting the low cost of labor and lack of environmental and community protections that are characteristic of developing countries. Workers, including children, pay the price by toiling long hours, often in unsafe environments, for wages that barely afford the basic necessities, or in slavery conditions for no compensation at all. The result is corporations and consumers who reap the benefits of this unlawful "employment."

The disproportionate availability of resources worldwide creates conditions of vulnerability to labor exploitation and slavery. Before addressing this issue, it is important to understand the nuances of the different terms involved. The term **migration** is used to describe the movement of people from one country to another. **Immigration** is when a person moves *to* a country, and **emigration** is when a person moves *from* a country. The primary reasons for immigration remain constant—immigration is typically fueled by the need to escape poverty, political instability, or warfare. The possibility of finding work that will better enable one to be self-sufficient and meet the basic needs of family members is also a driving force. Human smuggling is one method by which a person may immigrate to a country. According to the US Department of State (2021), **human or migrant smuggling** is the facilitation, transportation, attempted transportation, or illegal movement of a person across an international border. This usually refers to crossing an international border either secretly, such as crossing at unauthorized locations, or deceptively, such as with the use of falsified or counterfeit documents. Human smuggling is generally a voluntary act, with the person being smuggled paying a significant amount of money to the smuggler. Two common terms in human smuggling are "coyote" and "snakehead" (Kung, 2000; Walters & Davis, 2011). Coyotes and snakeheads perform the same function, which is to smuggle people into the United States. Coyotes transport individuals from Mexico, and snakeheads transport people from China. An individual being smuggled may be subjected to unsafe conditions during the smuggling process including physical and sexual violence. It is not uncommon for the smuggled person to be held by the smuggler until her or his debt is paid off by someone (often a family member) in the destination country. It is important to note that at any point in the smuggling process, the person may become a trafficking victim.

Traffickers who actively recruit victims use traditional immigration as a way to conceal their criminal intentions. With the false promise of compensated work in another country, traffickers are more easily able to get people to cooperate with illegal border crossing. For example, a woman may knowingly agree to be smuggled into a country to work in the sex industry or as a nanny, but she may be unaware that the traffickers will keep all of the money she makes, restrict and control her movement, and subject her to physical and sexual violence. In other instances, an individual may migrate on her or his own, legally or illegally, identify a work opportunity upon arriving in the destination country, and become a victim of trafficking due to the illegal practices of an employer.

Table 1.1   Human Trafficking Compared to Migrant Smuggling

	Human Trafficking	*Migrant Smuggling*
Action	Recruitment, transportation, transfer, harboring, or receipt of a person by means of threat or use of force, fraud, coercion	Facilitation of illegal entry of a person into a country of which the person is not a citizen or legal resident
Transnational Border Crossing	Not required	Required
Consent	If other elements of definition present, consent not relevant, not relevant for minors	Required
Outcome	Economic exploitation of the individual, which may include sexual exploitation and/or forced labor	Illegal border crossing

It has been suggested that more stringent border entry regulations force migrants to use illegal channels more often, which can increase their risk of being exploited (Salt, 2000). Another perspective is that there is a need for additional antitrafficking legislation and that the enforcement of the laws that are in place is inconsistent across points of entry, thereby reducing the effectiveness of these antitrafficking laws.

Temporary Visas and Human Trafficking

Some of the characteristics of the temporary work visa program in the United States, in particular for low-wage workers, create conditions that are similar to those that underlie vulnerability to trafficking.

The two most widely used temporary work visa programs in the United States are the H-2A and the H-2B visas. These programs are intended to help employers fill positions that they report being unable to fill with U.S. citizens. The H-2A allows for those from other countries to work in agricultural positions and the H-2B allows for those from other countries to occupy other manual labor positions, such as construction, cleaning, meat/seafood processing, etc. Those coming to the U.S. using these visas do so to work in order to provide for the basic needs of their families at home. Many sacrifice quite a bit to be employed in this economy, leaving family and other communities behind and often incurring significant debt to secure U.S.-based employment.

One of the most problematic and dangerous elements of both the H-2A and H-2B visa programs is that for the duration of the visa, the individual can only work for the employer whose name appears on the visa paperwork. If for whatever reason the individual decides to leave the position, their legal immigration status is revoked. This may result in being deported, which would make it extremely difficult to regain legal status in the U.S. at a future point. This is especially problematic for the seasonal worker whose family depends on her or him being permitted to work in the U.S. each year.

This element of these visas creates quite a bind, in particular for those who are being mistreated or trafficked by the employer yet have incurred debt in order to work in the U.S. that may take generations to pay down in a less robust economy. This all too often pushes the immigrant visa worker to stay in an exploitive and/or trafficking situation. It is easy to see how this specific criterion plays into the issue of trafficking, yet changing this stipulation continues to be overlooked by legislators as a relatively simple way to create a safety net of sorts for vulnerable workers. Following is a list of visas that are commonly linked to trafficking and whether the visa is tied to a specific employer.

Visa Type	Visa Description	Tied to Specific Employer
A-3/G-5	Personal attendants to diplomats & employees of international organizations	Yes
B-1	Business visitors	No
F-1	Students	No
H-1B	Specialty occupations	Yes
H-2A	Agricultural workers	Yes
H-2B	Temporary non-agricultural workers	Yes
J-1	Participants of cultural and educational exchange programs	No (however, in most instances, the sponsor must approve the employer, so can present similar vulnerability)

Source: Adopted from the U.S. Department of State—Bureau of Consular Affairs

Prevalence and Profits

According to the United Nations Office on Drugs and Crime (2008), human trafficking is the fastest-growing criminal industry in the world and is considered relatively low risk and one of the most profitable (Haken, 2011; Interpol, 2002; Raigrodski, 2015). However, despite its magnitude, there are a variety of reasons this crime and its included human rights violations are so difficult to quantify. Some reasons include variation in the operational definitions used by researchers, methodological flaws such as those related to sampling techniques, and the difficulty and potential risks involved for researchers wishing to engage in primary versus secondary research. Also, and perhaps most challenging in the quest to obtain accurate statistics on the prevalence and geography of human trafficking, is that traffickers work to keep their crime undetected. Victims are difficult to identify since they often work in businesses or homes or behind the locked doors of a factory. They are closely monitored by the traffickers and often not permitted in close proximity to those who may be of assistance. These and other similar factors make human trafficking particularly difficult to accurately quantify and describe. Therefore, all reports regarding prevalence should be interpreted with caution. What follows are popular estimates in the field today.

Case Study 1.1: Thailand Farm Workers

A recruiting agency in Thailand was looking for men to work in the United States as farmers through the H2A visa program. The men were to pay recruiting fees totaling 20,000 U.S. dollars, an amount that, if repaid in the Thai economy, would take approximately three generations to eliminate. Many of the men secured high-interest loans using their family home and land as collateral. They believed that being paid 9.42 U.S. dollars hourly (as specified in their contract) would mean that they could make the loan money within a year and spend the next two years earning enough money to bring their families out of poverty. However, when the men arrived in the U.S., things were quite different to their expectations. Their passports and visas were taken by the traffickers. They lived in a rural area and had no access to transportation or to U.S. citizens. Forty-four men were housed in one five-bedroom, two-bathroom house. There were not enough beds in the house, so some of the men slept on the floor. They woke each morning at 4 a.m. so that there was time for everyone to shower. They were driven to work at 6 a.m. in a produce truck with a vertical sliding door and no windows. They had inconsistent access to food. They were not paid the hourly wage they were promised, and oftentimes they were not paid at all.

Question: Was this a case of smuggling or human trafficking?

Answer: The men in this situation were victims of human trafficking. They were transported for the purposes of labor exploitation through the use of fraud and coercion, which resulted in their being subjected to involuntary servitude. Confiscation of their passports by the trafficker led the workers to believe that they had no other choice but to stay with the company.

- According to the International Labour Organization (ILO), there are at least 24.9 million people in forced labor (including sexual exploitation) worldwide, as well as more than 40 million people in modern-day slavery (ILO, 2016).
- Data suggest that women and girls comprise more than 70 percent of detected individuals trafficked over the past 15 years (UNODC, 2018).
- Approximately 62 percent of victims are trafficked for forced labor exploitation (ILO, 2016).

- UNICEF (2020) estimates that 152 million children are engaged in child labor. This is equal to 1 in 10 children worldwide.
- The ILO (2016) estimates that children comprise 25 percent of the total enslaved population.
- In countries with the fewest resources, 29 percent of all children are engaged in child labor that often interferes with their education, robs them of childhood pleasures, and has a negative impact on their physical and psychological (UNICEF, 2020).

It is similarly as difficult to assess profits as it is to assess forced labor and human trafficking. Globally, it is estimated that annual profits from forced labor are equal to 150 billion U.S. dollars. It is further estimated that of the 150 billion U.S. dollars, 35 percent is generated for Asia and the Pacific, 8 percent is generated for Latin America and the Caribbean, 8.6 percent is generated for Africa, 5.7 percent is generated for the Middle East, and 31.3 percent is generated for developed economies including the U.S. and the EU (ILO, 2014). The ILO (2014) also estimated that 66 percent of the money made was from forced sexual exploitation, 5.3 percent of the profits were from domestic work and nearly 30 percent of the profits were from non-domestic labor.

Native Americans and Human Trafficking

Native American women have been subjected to rape, genocide, conquest, and war for the last 500 years and continue to deal with the effects of these traumatic experiences to this day (Deer, 2010). Native American women and children are easily targeted for sex trafficking within their tribal communities due to poverty, history of family substance abuse, histories of childhood sexual abuse, homelessness, generational trauma, and lack of educational resources (Mandeville, 2015; Deer, 2010). In the United States, Native American women are overrepresented in sex trafficking, as they suffer disproportionately from associated risk factors (Deer, 2010).

Native American women experience rape and sexual assault at a rate of 2.5 times more frequently compared to all women in the United States (Finn et al., 2017). This means that about 1 in 3 Native American women report being raped during their lifetime (Finn et al., 2017). Oftentimes, Native American women describe their perpetrators as non-Native American men (Finn et al., 2017). It has been found that "American Indian and Alaskan Native women were at a higher risk for rape, prostitution, physical abuse, and racist verbal abuse" (Farley et al., 2016, p. 6). Both American Indian and Alaskan women are vulnerable to sexual exploitation. These groups tend to experience homelessness, poverty, physiological and psychological health problems and lack financial resources to address these issues. Native women identifying as Anishinaabe (Ojibwe or Chippewa) were a significant majority (81%) subjected to sexual exploitation (Farley et al., 2016). Moreover, women identifying as Anishinaabe typically were involved in commercial sex by the age of 14 and before turning 18, were sold for sex (Farley et al., 2016). These women reported being involved in commercial sex in exchange for shelter, food, drugs, or a combination of these resources. Family history of substance abuse, generational trauma, and homelessness were strongly correlated with a higher risk of children running away, placing them at a higher risk of sexual exploitation (Mandeville, 2015). The overrepresentation of Native women trafficking in the United States remains a paramount concern and calls for further research and support.

The Trafficking Process

The business of human trafficking is carried out by individuals, small, loosely organized criminal networks, or by traditionally organized crime groups. It includes both small "mom-and-pop"–type operations, as well as larger, well-organized businesses that operate in a competitive international arena. Some involved in trafficking may assist with a single border crossing, while others may work in an ongoing manner with a larger trafficking organization. These larger trafficking organizations often function on a more permanent basis and are involved in the entire trafficking enterprise, from the recruitment of victims to the selling and reselling of victims to employers. **Organized crime groups** or **criminal organizations** are local, national, or transnational groupings of centralized enterprises with the purpose of engaging in illegal activity for financial gain. **Transnational organized crime** refers to the planning and execution of unlawful business ventures by groups or networks of individuals working in more than one country (Reuter & Petrie, 1995). Those involved in both national and transnational organized crime systematically use violence and corruption to achieve their goals (Albanese, 2004). Transnational organized crime undermines democracy and impedes the social, political, economic, and cultural development of societies around the world (Channing, 2017; Voronin, 2000). It is multifaceted and can involve a variety of different illegal activities including drug trafficking, trafficking in firearms, migrant smuggling, and human trafficking. In addition to human trafficking being carried out by organized crime groups, it is also carried out by more loosely organized **criminal networks**. These criminal networks are decentralized and less hierarchical, and according to international securities expert Phil Williams, they can be as effective as and more difficult to detect than traditional organized crime groups (2001).

The processes through which people are trafficked are varied. Because trafficking is a moneymaking endeavor for the trafficker, all exchanges are made in an effort to maximize financial gain while minimizing costs and financial loss. Traffickers engage in numerous individual and small-group transactions, the characteristics of which are situation dependent. Common roles traffickers assume in the process are described in what follows; keep in mind that not all roles are relevant for all trafficking situations.

Trafficker Roles

Recruiter: The recruiter identifies, makes contact with, and brings the victim into the first phase of the trafficking process. Depending on the situation, the recruiter sells the victim either directly to the employer (e.g., brothel owner, bar manager, farmer, etc.) or to the broker. The recruiter does not always know that the person she or he recruited is going to be enslaved. Some common recruitment methods include:

- use of the internet to advertise for employment opportunities, study abroad, or marriage;
- in-person recruitment in public places such as bars, restaurants, and clubs;
- in-person recruitment through community and neighborhood contacts including families and friends;
- purchase of children from their parents or legal guardians.

Broker (agent): The broker is the middle person between the recruiter and the employer.

Contractor: The contractor oversees all of the exchanges involved in the trafficking of the victim.

Employment agent: The employment agent takes care of securing "employment" for the victim; this sometimes includes making arrangements for identification paperwork such as visas and passports.

Travel agent: The travel agent arranges for the transport of the victim from her or his point of origin to the destination. This can mean arranging for travel within one country or across country borders.

Document forger/thief: The document forger/thief secures identification documents for cross-border travel. In some instances, this may include creating false documents, and in others, it may mean illegally modifying actual government documents.

Transporter: The transporter actually accompanies the victim on the journey from point of origin to destination. Transportation may be via boat, bus, car, taxi, train, plane, or on foot. Delivery of the victim is made either to the broker or directly to the employer.

Employer (procurer): The employer purchases and then sells or otherwise exploits the human trafficking victim.

Enforcer ("roof" or guard): The enforcer is responsible for ensuring victim compliance, protecting the business, and, at times, ensuring that outstanding debt is paid by the customer (e.g., payment by a john in a sex trafficking situation).

Pimp: A pimp is a sex trafficker who directly or indirectly controls a person who is prostituted. He or she takes the profit made from the sex act and may or may not dole out a portion of this to the person being prostituted. The notion exists that the pimp provides protection for those being prostituted; however, the pimp himself often presents the most danger to the individual through threats, physical abuse, rape, and the introduction or maintenance of drug use by the person being prostituted.

"Bottom Bitch": The prostitute who is most trusted by a pimp and will frequently help the pimp with training new women, collect money from other prostitutes for the pimp, and only have sex with the pimp.

In order for human trafficking to work, the traffickers have to either force or somehow convince victims to leave their homes and to accompany the trafficker to the destination point. While coercion was defined earlier, what follows are common means of ensuring victim compliance with departing from her or his point of origin:

- abduction or kidnapping;
- purchasing of a child from her or his parents or legal guardians;
- deception through the promise of legitimate employment and/or entry into a country;
- deception about working conditions;
- deception about compensation and other benefits (e.g., school attendance for children);
- deception through a seemingly intimate/romantic relationship (i.e., trafficker pretends to be romantically interested in the victim).

Traffickers will use a combination of methods to control victims. Methods used to depend on a variety of factors including, for example, the personality of the trafficker, the culture of the group in which they are working, the gender and age of the victim, and the behaviors of the victim while in the situation. Examples of control methods follow:

- violence (including rape and murder) and the threat of violence against the victim and her or his family;
- deprivation of agency or the sense of control over self;
- isolation;

- confiscation of identification and/or travel documents;
- religious beliefs and practices (e.g., threat to use voodoo to harm the family member of a victim whose religious beliefs include voodoo).

Also, a commonly employed strategy of control is for traffickers to tell victims that law enforcement and immigration officials are not trustworthy or will treat them harshly if they are discovered. Obstacles to seeking assistance on the part of the victim are many; for example, in many instances of international trafficking, victims are unaware that they have rights and often do not know that contracts they may have signed are not legally binding. Other obstacles to seeking assistance can be related to family loyalty (i.e., desire to protect family from the trafficker), cultural practices, language barriers, and political suppression in countries of origin.

Snapshot of International Efforts to End Trafficking

Nongovernmental organizations and activists assumed a grassroots role in the fight against human trafficking and have been instrumental in bringing the issue to the attention of governments around the world. At the international level and largely consequent of international agreements reached at the UN, the United Nations Global Initiative to Fight Human Trafficking (UN. GIFT) was initiated in March 2007 to support the global fight on human trafficking.

The Global Initiative is based on the idea that the crime of human trafficking is of such magnitude that it requires an approach to eradication that is implemented globally and by a variety of relevant stakeholders. In order for this to happen, according to UN.GIFT, stakeholders must "coordinate efforts already underway, increase knowledge and awareness, provide technical assistance; promote effective rights-based responses; build capacity of state and non-state stakeholders; foster partnerships for joint action; and above all, ensure that everybody takes responsibility for this fight."[2] UN.GIFT sees its role as that of facilitator of coordination and to "create synergies among the anti-trafficking activities of UN agencies, international organizations and other stakeholders to develop the most efficient and cost-effective tools and good practices."[3] Efforts to address human trafficking are further addressed in Chapter 13 of this text.

Human Trafficking in the United States

Like most countries with well-developed market economies, the United States plays a role in fueling the international trade of people. Also, as is the case with most if not all countries affected by human trafficking, the United States is faced with the trafficking of its own citizens within country borders. Sex trafficking of women and children, in particular girls, is the most significant form of domestic trafficking in the United States. Children targeted in these situations by traffickers, who are commonly referred to as "pimps," are most often runaways or homeless youth. The Williams Institute (2012) conducted a study and found that as many as 40 percent of runaways and homeless youth are members of the lesbian, gay, bisexual, and transgender (LGBT) community (Choi et al., 2015). A similar study was conducted by the Williams Institute in 2015, finding homeless populations with median percentages of 20 percent identifying as gay or lesbian, 7 percent as bisexual, 2 percent as questioning, 1 percent as transgender male, and 1 percent as genderqueer (Choi et al., 2015). Labor trafficking is also an issue within the United States; however, many of these cases involve individuals trafficked into the country to perform a variety of what are characterized as low-paying jobs. An example of labor trafficking of U.S. citizens appears in the textbox that follows.

Case Study 1.2: A Federal Case of Domestic Labor Trafficking

Labor camp owners recruit homeless African-American addicts from shelters throughout the Southeast, including Tampa, Miami, Orlando, and New Orleans, to work at labor camps, promising food and shelter for only $50 a week. The camp owners picked up prospective workers in vans and transported them to isolated labor camps in North Florida and North Carolina. Once on site, the workers were supplied with crack cocaine. The cost of the drug was deducted from their paychecks. Every evening, camp owners gave workers the opportunity to buy crack, untaxed generic beer, and cigarettes from the company store. Most workers spiraled into debt. On average, workers were paid about 30 cents on the dollar after deductions. The case broke in 2005 after a federal raid on the North Florida camp. Advocates were stunned that the camps could so easily exploit American citizens.

Source: Naples Daily News, September 23, 2006.

At the federal level in the United States, Congress passed the Victims of Trafficking and Violence Protection Act (TVPA) of 2000 (P.L. 106 386), the Trafficking Victims Protection Reauthorization Act of 2003 (H.R. 2620), the Trafficking Victims Protection Reauthorization Act of 2005 (H.R. 972), the Trafficking Victims Protection Reauthorization Act of 2008 (H.R. 7311), and the Trafficking Victims Protection Reauthorization Act of 2013 (H.R. 898). Prior to the passing of the TVPA in 2000, no comprehensive federal law existed to address human trafficking in the United States. Other federal legislation that relates to human trafficking includes the Trade Facilitation Act of 2015 (H.R. 644) and the Executive Order on Strengthening Protections Against Trafficking in Persons in Federal Contracts of 2012.

In the United States TVPA, severe forms of trafficking in persons are defined as:

> Sex trafficking in which a commercial sex act is induced by force, fraud, or coercion, or in which the person induced to perform such act has not attained 18 years of age; or
>
> The recruitment, harboring, transportation, provision, or obtaining of a person for labor services, through the use of force, fraud, or coercion for the purpose of subjection to involuntary servitude, peonage, debt bondage, or slavery.
>
> (8 U.S.C. §1101)

Much like the United Nations Trafficking Protocol, the TVPA focuses on the "three Ps" of trafficking to guide antislavery efforts: *prevention* of the crime, *prosecution* of the trafficker, and *protection* for victims. Recently, a fourth "P" standing for "*partnerships*" was added to the framework. Partnerships are intended to take place across all levels of society—local, regional, national, and international—and are to involve both government and civil society organizations. In addition to providing a comprehensive definition of human trafficking, this legislation gave law enforcement tools to enhance the extent to which traffickers are prosecuted and punished. The TVPA also called for the establishment of a global Trafficking in Persons (TIP) Report, which is published annually, and the President's Interagency Task Force to Monitor and Combat Trafficking in Persons.

The TIP Report documents and evaluates the antitrafficking efforts of foreign governments. Countries are ranked in tiers depending on the extent to which they are compliant with minimum standards established by the TVPA. Countries on the lowest tier may be subject to economic sanctions enacted by the United States. While the TIP Report is thought to be a useful tool, it has been criticized for presenting incomplete information, for not including evaluation of the United States, and for being biased and "politicized." Three primary concerns are as follows: how the minimum standards are applied, what methods are used to justify tier placements, and how information for the report is collected and analyzed. Recently, efforts have been made to address some of these concerns, the most visible of which is the inclusion of analysis of U.S. efforts in the 2010 publication of the report.

Under the TVPA, the US Department of Health and Human Services can "certify" international human trafficking victims as such in the eyes of the law. After being certified, victims are then qualified for physical and psychological health services, housing, food stamps, and educational and vocational programs, as well as support for legal services. Victims of international trafficking may also be granted a T Visa, which allows them to live and work in the U.S. for up to three years, after which application for permanent resident status may be made. Criticisms of the TVPA have included that eligibility requirements for the T Visa are too rigid and enforcement is deficient, leaving many deserving victims unprotected. Others have noted that there are unnecessary barriers to obtaining the benefits afforded through the TVPA. These include victim identification, difficulty qualifying as a "severe trafficking" victim, and the time it takes to certify a victim. Victims are often left for long periods of time, waiting for assistance to meet the most basic of needs such as shelter, food, and clothing. Communities in which grassroots antitrafficking coalitions are established often step in to provide support at this critical time. The TVPA has been most strongly criticized by victims' rights activists and social service providers for its requirement that victims participate in the prosecution of the trafficker prior to releasing funding in support of their basic needs (e.g., shelter, food, clothing, access to health care, and counseling). This requirement is tantamount to requiring a rape victim to press charges against her rapist before giving her access to medical attention and counseling.

As of August 2014, all U.S. states have developed laws that address sex and labor trafficking. The distinction now comes with regard to how states institute safe harbor protections, provided access to civil damages, and vacating conviction for sex trafficking victims. The Polaris Project, a nonprofit agency working against trafficking nationally, has a rating process through which it tracks the presence or absence of 10 categories of state statutes they deem essential to a comprehensive antitrafficking legal framework (Polaris Project, 2021b). Currently, 39 states qualify for Polaris Projects top tier, 9 states are in the second tier, and 2 states are in tier three (Polaris Project, 2021b). Safe harbor laws ensure victims are provided with resources. Thirty-four states currently have safe harbor laws, most of which allow the state to intervene and provide state assistance to the child (Polaris, 2015).

Safe Harbor Laws

Safe harbor laws implement change in the way systems of care respond to juveniles exploited in sex trafficking in the United States (Cole & Sprang, 2020). The Safe Harbor Law is necessary to protect potential victims of trafficking, such as homeless youth and children who report abuse or neglect (Williams, 2017). New York was one of the first states to pass the Safe Harbor Law for Exploited Children Act. Since 2016,

Safe Harbor Laws have passed in 28 states, allowing the enactment of 51 bills addressing the trafficking of minors (Williams, 2017). These laws provide immunity for certain crimes and services to protect children from sex trafficking. Twenty states, including the District of Columbia, have legislated "prosecutorial immunity" for trafficked youth, indicating that these youth cannot be charged with specific crimes (William, 2017). However, many other states continue to neglect the importance of protecting children from exploitation. Further research addressing a necessary set of rules and applying safe harbor law is essential for all states.

There has been little research on how safe harbor laws impact juveniles' exploitation, yet there is an increasing rate of referrals to the child welfare system, as it is mandated by law (Cole & Sprang, 2020). Research by Alexandra Russell (2019) said that safe harbor laws focus on "mandated care and rehabilitation after a victim is identified" (p. 1). In addition, health care professionals are unique in identifying child abuse suspects and address the possibilities of child sex trafficking (Russell, 2019). These efforts improve the chances that trafficked children will be identified and protected from further harm.

The following chart includes the states that address the trafficking of minors:

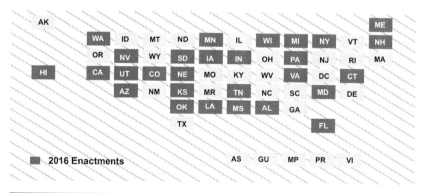

2016 Enactments

Figure 1.2   The current states that utilize safe harbor laws

Source: Adapted from NCSL, 2017

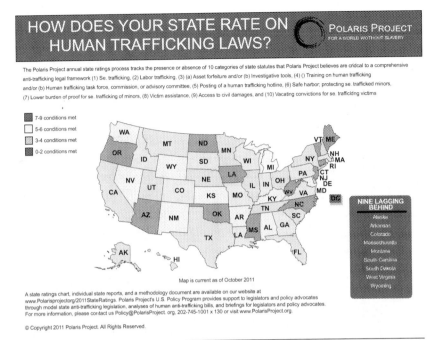

Figure 1.3 Polaris project sample state ratings chart

Closing

While the United States has made progress with regard to the extent to which labor and sex trafficking is addressed, there is still much to be done. While much of this text provides in-depth, discipline specific perspectives on the issue of human trafficking, Chapter 20 "Addressing the Problem: Community-Based Responses and Coordination," explains some ways in which anti-trafficking efforts can be augmented both in local communities and nationally.

Discussion Questions

1. How is human trafficking defined by the United Nations Protocol to Prevent, Suppress and Punish Trafficking in Persons, especially Women and Children?
2. What are the differences between human trafficking and other related phenomena such as immigration, emigration, and smuggling?
3. What are some of the underlying causes of human trafficking?
4. Name some of the ways in which human trafficking constitutes a violation of fundamental human rights.

Notes

1. It was signed by member states of the UN at a conference in Palermo, Italy, on December 15, 2000, and was entered into force in 2003 on September 29 (www.unodc. org/unodc/en/treaties/CTOC/index.html).
2. See www.ungift.org/knowledgehub/en/about/index.html.
3. Ibid.

References

Albanese, J. (2014). *Organized crime in our times* (6th ed.). New York: Taylor & Francis.

Baldwin, S. B., Fehrenbacher, A. E., & Eisenman, D. P. (2015). Psychological coercion in human trafficking: An application of Biderman's Framework. *Qualitative Health Research, 25*(9), 1171–1181. https://doi.org/10.1177/1049732314557087

Bruckert, C., & Parent, C. (2002). *Trafficking in human beings and organized crime: A literature review.* Research and Evaluation Branch, Community, Contract and Aboriginal Policing Services Directorate, Royal Canadian Mounted Police. https://www.corteidh. or.cr/tablas/r28012.pdf

Channing, M. (2017, March). Transnational crime and the developing world. *Global Financial Integrity.* www.gfintegrity.org/wp-content/uploads/2017/03/Transnational_Crime-final.pdf

Clawson, H., & Dutch, N. (2017, February 21). Identifying victims of human trafficking: Inherent challenges and promising strategies from the field. *ASPE, Office of the Assistant Secretary for Planning and Evaluation.* https://aspe.hhs.gov/report/identifying-victims-human-trafficking-inherent-challenges-and-promising-strategies-field

Cole, J., & Sprang, G. (2020). Post-implementation of a Safe Harbor law in the US: Review of state administrative data. *Child Abuse & Neglect, 101.* https://doi-org.carlow. idm.oclc.org/10.1016/j.chiabu.2019.104320

Declaration of Istanbul Custodian Group (DICG). (2018). *The declaration of Istanbul.* Retrieved March 9, 2021, from www.declarationofistanbul.org/the-declaration

Deer, S. (2010). Relocation revisited: Sex trafficking of native women in the United States. Faculty Scholarship, Paper 157. http://open.mitchellhamline.edu/facsch/157

Estes, R. J., & Weiner, N. A. (2002). *The commercial sexual exploitation of children in the U.S., Canada and Mexico.* Center for the Study of Youth Policy, University of Pennsylvania. https://abolitionistmom.org/wp-content/uploads/2014/05/Complete_CSEC_0estes-weiner.pdf

Europol. (2005). *Legislation on trafficking in human beings and illegal immigrant smuggling.* https://ec.europa.eu/anti-trafficking/sites/default/files/europol_2005_legislation_en_4.pdf

Farley, M., Deer, S., Golding, J. M., Matthews, N., Lopez, G., Stark, C., & Hudon, E. (2016). The prostitution and trafficking of American Indian/Alaska Native women in Minnesota. *American Indian and Alaska Native Mental Health Research, 23*(1), 65–104. https://doi.org/10.5820/aian.2301.2016.65

Fedina, L., Perdue, T., Bright, C. L., & Williamson, C. (2019). An ecological analysis of risk factors for runaway behavior among individuals exposed to commercial sexual exploitation. *Journal of Child & Adolescent Trauma, 12*(2), 221–231. https://doi-org.carlow.idm.oclc.org/10.1007/s40653-018-0229-5

Finkelhor, D., & Ormrod, R. (2004). *Prostitution of juveniles, patterns from nibrs* (Ser. Juvenile justice bulletin). U.S. Department of Justice, Office of Justice Programs, Office of Juvenile Justice and Delinquency Prevention.

Finn, K., Gadja, E., Perin, T., & Fredericks, C. (2017). Responsible resource development and prevention of sex trafficking: Safeguarding Native women and children on the Fort Berthold Reservation. *Harvard Journal of Law & Gender, 40*(1). https://scholar.law.col orado.edu/articles/629

Free the Slaves. (2021). Retrieved March 10, 2021, from www.freetheslaves.net/

Gambrel, P. A., & Cianci, R. (2003). Maslow's hierarchy of needs: Does it apply in a collectivist culture. *Journal of Applied Management and Entrepreneurship, 8*(2), 143–161. https://carlow.idm.oclc.org/login?qurl=https%3A%2F%2Fwww.proquest. com%2Fscholarly-journals%2Fmaslows-hierarchy-needs-does-apply-collectivist%2Fdo cview%2F203916225%2Fse-2%3Faccountid%3D38069

Gonzalez, J., Garijo, I., & Sanchez, A. (2020). Organ trafficking and migration: A bibliometric analysis of an untold story. *International Journal of Environmental Research and Public Health, 17*(9), 3204. https://doi.org/10.3390/ijerph17093204

Haken, J. (2011). *Transnational crime in the developing world.* Global Financial Integrity. https://www.gfintegrity.org/wp-content/uploads/2014/05/gfi_transnational_crime_ high-res.pdf

Hernandez, M. D. P. (2001). A personal dimension of human rights activism: Narratives of trauma, resilience and solidarity. *Dissertation Abstracts International: Section B: The Sciences and Engineering, 61*(7-B), 3846.

Human Rights Watch. (2018, July 5). *Immigrant crime fighters.* Retrieved March 10, 2021, from www.hrw.org/report/2018/07/03/immigrant-crime-fighters/how-u-visa-program-makes-us-communities-safer

International Labour Organization (ILO). (2016). *Forced labour, modern slavery and human trafficking.* Retrieved March 11, 2016, from www.ilo.org/global/topics/forced-labour/ lang--en/index.htm

International Labour Organization (ILO). (2017). *Global estimates of modern slavery.* International Labour Office. https://www.ilo.org/wcmsp5/groups/public/---dgreports/--- dcomm/documents/publication/wcms_575479.pdf

Interpol. (2002). *The effective administration of criminal justice in tackle trafficking in human beings and smuggling of migrants.* Lyon: Interpol.

Kung, C. J. (2000). Supporting the snakeheads: Human smuggling from China and the 1996 amendment to the U.S. statutory definition of "refugee." *The Journal of Criminal Law and Criminology (1973–), 90*(4), 1271–1316.

Kyu Choi, S., Wilson, B. D. M., Shelton, J., & Gates, G. (2015, June). *Serving our youth.* Williams Institute. https://williamsinstitute.law.ucla.edu/publications/serving-our-youth-lgbtq/

Laczko, F., & Gramegna, M. A. (2003). Developing better indicators of human trafficking. *The Brown Journal of World Affairs, 10*(1), 179–194. http://www.jstor.org/stable/24590602

Mandeville, G. (2015). Sex trafficking on Indian Reservations. *Tulsa Law Review, 51*(1), 28. https://digitalcommons.law.utulsa.edu/tlr/vol51/iss1/5

Maslow, A. H. (1943). A theory of human motivation. *Psychological Review, 50*(4), 370–396. https://doi-org.carlow.idm.oclc.org/10.1037/h0054346

Mendelson, S. E. (2005). *Barracks and brothels: Peacekeepers and human trafficking in the balkans* (Ser. Csis report). Center for Strategic and International Studies.

Meshelemiah, J. C. A., & Lynch, R. E. (2019). *The cause and consequence of human trafficking: Human rights violations.* Columbus, OH: The Ohio State University Pressbook.

Morris, C. (2010). Peacekeeping and the sexual exploitation of women and girls in post-conflict societies: A serious enigma to establishing the rule of law. *Journal of International Peacekeeping, 14*(1/2), 184–212.

Naim, M. (2010). *Illicit: How smugglers, traffickers, and copycats are hijacking the global economy.* Anchor eBooks.

Perkins, A. (2015). The truth about human trafficking. *Nursing Made Incredibly Easy, 32–40.* NMIE1115_Cover_Puneet.indd (ceconnection.com)

Polaris. (2015). *Human trafficking issue brief: Safe harbor.* https://polarisproject.org/wp-con tent/uploads/2019/09/2015-Safe-Harbor-Issue-Brief.pdf

Polaris Project. (2021a). *Human trafficking.* www.polarisproject.org/human-trafficking/overview

Polaris Project. (2021b). *Sex trafficking in the U.S.* www.polarisproject.org/human-trafficking/sex-trafficking-in-the-us

Raigrodski, D. (2015). Economic migration gone wrong: Trafficking in persons through the lens of gender, labor, and globalization. *Indiana International & Comparative Law Review, 25*(1), 79–114. https://doi-org.carlow.idm.oclc.org/10.18060/7909.0006

Reuter, P., and Petrie, C. (Eds.). (1995). *Transnational organized crime; Summary of a workshop exit notice.* Washington, DC: National Academy Press.

Richard, A. (1999). *International trafficking in women to the United States: A contemporary manifestation of slavery and organized crime.* Center for the Study of Intelligence.

Richards, T. N., & Reid, J. A. (2015). Gender stereotyping and sex trafficking: Comparative review of research on male and female sex tourism. *Journal of Crime & Justice, 38*(3), 414–433. https://doi-org.carlow.idm.oclc.org/10.1080/0735648X.2014.1000560

Russell, A. B. (2019). Finding a safer harbor: Mandating health care clinics to intervene in child sex trafficking by amending the Safe Harbor Act. *Family Court Review, 57*(1), 136–150. https://doi-org.carlow.idm.oclc.org/10.1111/fcre.12401

Salt, J. (2000). Trafficking and human smuggling: A European perspective. *International Migration, 38*(3), 31–56. https://doi-org.carlow.idm.oclc.org/10.1111/1468-2435.00114

Theirworld. (2017, December 15). Child soldiers. *Theirworld.* Retrieved March 10, from https://theirworld.org/explainers/child-soldiers#:~:text=There%20are%20an%20estimated%20250%2C000,%22wives%22%20by%20male%20fighters

UNICEF. (2020, September 3). *Child labour.* Retrieved March 11, 2021, from www.unicef.org/protection/child-labour

United Nations. (1948). *Universal declaration of human rights.* Retrieved October 1, 2021, from https://www.un.org/en/about-us/universal-declaration-of-human-rights

United Nations Office of Drugs and Crime (UNODC). (2008). *Human trafficking: An overview.* Retrieved March 11, 2021, from www.unodc.org/documents/human-trafficking/2008/HumanTrafficking-AnOverview.pdf

United Nations Office on Drugs and Crime (UNODC). (2018). *Global report on trafficking in persons.* www.unodc.org/documents/data-and-analysis/glotip/2018/GLOTiP_2018_BOOK_web_small.pdf

U.S. Department of State. (2021, January 10). *About human trafficking—United States Department of State.* Retrieved March 11, 2021, from www.state.gov/humantrafficking-about-human-trafficking/

U.S. Government Accountability Office. (2006). Human trafficking: Better data, strategy, and reporting needed to enhance U.S. antitrafficking efforts abroad. *Trends in Organized Crime, 10*(1), 16–38. https://doi-org.carlow.idm.oclc.org/10.1007/s12117-006-1023-6

Väyrynen R. (2005). Illegal immigration, human trafficking and organized crime. In G. J. Borjas & J. Crisp (Eds.), *Poverty, international migration and asylum. Studies in development economics and policy.* London: Palgrave Macmillan. https://doi.org/10.1057/9780230522534_7

Voronin, Y. (2000). *Measures to control transnational organized crime.* Retrieved from www.ncjrs.gov/pdffiles1/nij/grants/184773.pdf

Walters, J., & Davis, P. (2011). Human trafficking, sex tourism, and child exploitation on the southern border. *Journal of Applied Research on Children: Informing Policy for Children at Risk, 2*(1). Retrieved from https://digitalcommons.library.tmc.edu/childrenatrisk/vol2/iss1/6

Williams Institute, University of California Los Angeles. (2012, July). *Serving our youth: Findings from a national survey of service providers working with lesbian, gay, bisexual, and transgender youth who are homeless or at risk of becoming homeless.* Retrieved from http://

williamsinstitute.law.ucla.edu/wp-content/uploads/Durso-Gates-LGBT-Homeless-Youth-Survey-July-2012.pdf

Williams, P. (2001). Transnational crime networks. In J. Arquilla & D. Ronfeldt (Eds.), *Networks and netwars: The future of terror, crime, and militancy* (pp. 61–98). Pittsburgh, PA: RAND.

Williams, R. (2017). *Safe harbor: State efforts to combat child trafficking*. National Conference of State Legislatures. www.ncsl.org/Portals/1/Documents/cj/SafeHarbor_v06.pdf

Worsnop, C. Z. (2019). The disease outbreak-human trafficking connection: A missed opportunity. *Health Security, 17*(3), 181–192.

2

HISTORICAL PERSPECTIVE

SLAVERY OVER THE CENTURIES

BROOKE N. NEWMAN

Overview

Human trafficking for the purposes of forced labor, commercial sexual exploitation, or reproductive slavery is often seen as a modern phenomenon. However, the trafficking and enslavement of men, women, and children is one of the most ubiquitous and pervasive features of all human civilizations across time and space. While the nature and extent of slavery and the international trade of human beings, both legal and illegal, have changed dramatically over time, today's global slave trade is by no means a novel or recent development. Acquiring trafficked individuals for labor or sexual exploitation has remained one of the principal concerns of human societies for centuries, and cases of severe exploitation continue to be found on every continent.

The discovery and conquest of the Americas, rise of capitalism, and emergence of a global economy, among other key developments over the past 500 years, have merely intensified and transformed forms of human trafficking and bondage long present across most cultures worldwide. With its many variations and conceptual ambiguities, contemporary slavery may not always be easy to recognize, but it is continuing to evolve and adapt to modern conditions, just as slave systems did in the past (Quirk, 2011; Bales, 2005).

This chapter provides a brief overview of various forms of human bondage, touching upon several important characteristics of slavery and slave trading present throughout documented history, from the ancient period to the early twentieth century. It will highlight the common attributes of the institution of slavery across cultures and describe the contexts in which the enslavement and trafficking of men, women, and children has persisted over the centuries. Beginning with some of the core characteristics associated with human

DOI: 10.4324/9781003124672-3

bondage, the chapter then moves to slave holding in the ancient world, specifically the societies of ancient Mesopotamia, Greece (particularly Athens), and Rome. After a discussion of ancient slave ownership as it varied from place to place and over time, the chapter provides an assessment of slavery and servitude during the medieval and early modern eras (*c*.1450–1800 CE), in Europe, Africa, and the Islamic world. The next section traces the emergence of African slavery in the Americas and the transatlantic slave trade and its legacies. The chapter concludes by surveying the rise and origins of global antislavery movements in the late eighteenth, nineteenth, and early twentieth centuries. Attention is directed throughout to the uniquely exploitative situations in which women and girls found themselves in the worldwide history of slavery in its premodern and modern manifestations and to the importance of legal definitions of slavery.

As a concise summary of the history of human bondage and slave trading across a select range of societies and cultures worldwide, this chapter serves as a springboard for an in-depth analysis of modern human trafficking patterns and characteristics. Engaging with historical forms of enslavement allows scholars, students, and activists interested in combating the illegal trade in human beings today to make connections between what is known about slave systems in the past and the continuance of forced labor, sexual exploitation, and slave trading in the modern era. Studying the past also demonstrates how slavery has helped to define notions of freedom by serving as a counterpoint.

Chapter Learning Objectives

- Describe the basic features of the institution of slavery, from ancient history to the present.
- Recognize important periods and significant players in the history of slavery and human trafficking.
- Explain how slave systems have enabled the sexual exploitation of women and girls.
- Sketch out milestones in global efforts to criminalize and eradicate slavery and the global trade in human beings and assess their long-term impact.
- Recognize and compare ancient, premodern, and contemporary forms of human bondage.
- Recognize the differences between historical forms of slavery and human trafficking in the modern world.

Common Features of the Institution of Slavery

Slavery has existed in many places and in multiple forms for thousands of years and is one of the most extreme forms of human domination. The institution of slavery is also one of the few truly omnipresent institutions in human experience. Since the beginning of recorded history, virtually every "advanced" world civilization has been touched by slavery, and many societies have seen a robust presence of slaves employed for a number of different purposes within them.

Surviving inventories of items bought and sold in the ancient Middle Eastern civilization of Sumeria (4000–2300 BCE), the first culture to leave written records, indicate that merchants bought and sold human beings 5,000 years ago along with other commodities deemed valuable (Watkins, 2001). The earliest known written legal code, the Hammurabi Code, composed in approximately 1780 BCE by Hammurabi, a Babylonian ruler in ancient Mesopotamia, officially recognized slavery. In every major civilization since, ancient and modern, human beings have engaged in the coercive recruitment of individuals for sexual exploitation or forced labor, with many civilizations viewing slavery as both advantageous and acceptable. Indeed, until the modern era, unfree labor was the norm throughout the world rather than the exception. The pervasiveness of slavery in human history has prevented the institution from dying out completely, even during periods when slaves were of minimal economic significance. Understanding the historical dimensions of slavery is thus essential to comprehending its role and meanings in the modern world (Engerman, 1999; Rodriguez, 1997; Davis, 1966).

Slavery and slave trading are fundamental, though unsavory, aspects of human history, deeply embedded in our past as well as our present. For centuries, human beings have served as one of the chief commodities of localized and global trade, and many economies have been dependent upon unfree labor and the brutal exploitation of individuals. The continual search for cheap and plentiful sources of labor has motivated the capture, purchase, and transport of millions of men, women, and children throughout the world. It has contributed to the emergence of multiple slave systems designed to assist slave owners to extract the maximum amount of profit from unwilling laborers and to use the enslaved—particularly young women and girls—for sexual and reproductive purposes against their will. Since the ancient period, masters have utilized their slaves in a wide range of tasks including agriculture, mining, domestic service, manufactures, military defense, and even business and administration, and many have exposed their slaves to sexual abuse and forced them to live as concubines (Rodriguez, 1997; Meltzer, 1993; Patterson, 1982; Davis, 1966).

As a long-standing worldwide phenomenon, the institution of slavery has impacted millions of lives, and the pervasiveness of slavery throughout human history makes it difficult to generalize about the experience of bondage for the individual. Still, while the work conditions, legal status, and daily lives of individuals subject to bound labor within differing slave systems have varied dramatically from century to century and place to place, basic similarities have emerged across specific societies and historical periods. Historians, economists, sociologists, anthropologists, and psychologists, in their speculations about slavery's origins, have identified several common characteristics underpinning differing manifestations of the institution of slavery (Lovejoy, 2004; Meltzer, 1993; Winks, 1972).

First, societies that have practiced slavery have tended to dehumanize workers of the lowest and most degraded social status by classifying them as human **chattels**, or items of personal property capable of being bought, sold, hired, mortgaged, bequeathed to heirs, and moved from place to place. In slave societies, chattels remained property for life and held no legally recognized personal or property rights of their own. At its most essential level, then, slavery consists of an unequal balance of power between two or more people that is designed to benefit the master rather than the slave. In the master–slave relationship, it is the slave who lacks power, honor, and an independent social existence; the slave is perceived as unworthy, and in many cases incapable, of possessing human rights, autonomy, or dignity. Throughout recorded history, most slaves have been codified as human chattel by dehumanizing legal codes that prioritized the rights of property owners over those of their human property. Although particular societies legislated differing levels of freedom and mobility for the enslaved, slaves generally remained bound to their owners for life as a form of animate property, sanctioned as such by social and cultural norms and enforceable legal codes. To slave owners, a slave's capacity to labor and produce a surplus over the cost of his or her upkeep—or submit to sexual or reproductive exploitation in lieu of manual labor—was of central importance. The slave was perceived as essentially a disposable, economic creature without a social identity, although some societies recognized slaves as subordinate members of kin groups who could potentially become less marginalized members of the community. In premodern Africa, for instance, many tribal communities used enslavement as a means of recruitment for the kinship group. Slaves were expected to labor and could be sacrificed or exploited at any time for the benefit of the group but could eventually enter into full membership in the community (Lovejoy, 2000; Eltis, 2000; Rodriguez, 1997).

Second, most societies with slaves marginalized the enslaved population by ensuring that chiefly persons considered "outsiders" to the community—such as foreigners, criminals, war captives, and those of different religious or ethnic backgrounds—were subjected to the indignities of slavery. A wide variety of determinants, ranging from culture and ethnicity to religion, were used to determine insider or outsider status in early societies that practiced slavery. Most communities relied upon the influx of outsiders, whether through warfare and capture or purchase at market, to maintain their supply of slaves (Eltis, 2000). The word *slave* comes from *Slav*, a term used to describe people sold into slavery to the Muslims of southern Spain and North Africa during the Middle Ages who originated in the Slavic regions of eastern Europe. The use of this terminology is illustrative of the way in which a particular group of outsiders could become intimately associated with the condition of bondage over time (Watkins, 2001). Both ancient and premodern slave societies prized group identity and tended not to subject one of their own to involuntary enslavement, although exceptions were sometimes made for those individuals accused of unacceptable, antisocial behavior. There is also a long record of voluntary slavery in human history, often known as debt bondage. Desperately indebted individuals could sell themselves or their dependent family members into slavery during periods of economic hardship, working without compensation until their creditors deemed their debts paid off. Debt bondage could be temporary in some cases or inherited by the debtor's family; failure to repay a debt, for example, could shift a bondsperson's status into hereditary slavery. Societies that have permitted this practice usually placed restrictions on the nature and extent of voluntary enslavement among their own members (Ishay, 2008; Engerman, 1999).

To meet the increasing demand for involuntary bondspersons to serve as human chattels, most slave systems have relied overwhelmingly upon captives of war who, rather than being killed or left to die of starvation or exposure, were moved to a new community and subjected to the authority of an unknown master. In this foreign environment, with the connections to their own ancestry and people severed, slaves experienced what the sociologist Orlando Patterson has termed "social death," living publicly on the margins of another society with no social identity, rights, or privileges (Patterson, 1982). By primarily enslaving persons outside the core group, societies with functioning slave systems ensured that their bondsmen and -women owed their continuing survival to the mercy of their owners and to the new community in which they found themselves. Chattel slavery could then be perceived as an act of benevolence on the part of captors who had spared the lives of their former enemies. The enslavement of persons outside the community also ensured, moreover, that the most repressive form of human domination was reserved for those who did not belong. Debt slaves were commonly held in higher esteem than and not identified with foreign-born slaves; chattel slavery was not something done to one's own people (Eltis, 2000; Rodriguez, 1997).

A final shared characteristic of ancient and modern slave systems is that chattel status is typically a **heritable condition** passed from mother to child. In the eyes of the law, a slave possesses no recognizable male parent. If one's mother is a slave, then one is automatically subject to the same fate. This feature sharply distinguishes slavery from other forms of coerced labor, as forced labor typically involves a loss of citizenship or community rights but does not necessarily imply ownership of one person by another and an inherited status. Hereditable status also keeps slave systems functioning by providing owners with a steady stream of human property (Bradley & Cartledge, 2011). The frequency of **manumission**, or formal emancipation, for individual slaves has varied widely, with the highest rates of manumission to be found in urban slave systems. In the slave society of ancient Rome, where manumission was widespread, expanding numbers of emancipated slaves meant that the slave population had to be continually replenished with new war captives. In other slave systems, including eighteenth-century Jamaica, the antebellum American South, South Africa, and Iraq, manumission rates remained very low, and slavery was, for most, a permanent condition (Mouritsen, 2011; Grusky, 2008).

Slavery in Ancient Societies

From the objects and texts unearthed by archeologists, we know that slavery existed as early as 4000 BCE in the world's oldest known civilizations in Mesopotamia, between the Tigris and Euphrates Rivers (now modern Iraq). When farming techniques improved enough to produce settled communities with growing populations and surplus food, it became increasingly clear that whoever owned the land and possessed the human beings who worked it could gain both property and free labor. It then became pragmatic to take captives after a battle rather than kill them; as valuable human tools, slaves could work the fields, labor in mines, tend flocks, and assist in the production of the food supply that would keep them and their captors alive. In this way a system of slavery developed in ancient Mesopotamia in which the condition of bondage generally existed in one of two forms: either as a method of organizing marginalized laborers to perform tasks critical to the survival of the community or as a form of punishment imposed on outsiders who had either taken up arms against the community or transgressed important laws or customs. Slaves also became regarded as status symbols, demonstrating the might of victors over their enemies (Watkins, 2001; Rodriguez, 1997; Meltzer, 1993).

King Hammurabi, who ruled Babylon, the world's first metropolis (*c.*1792–1750 BCE), consolidated most of Mesopotamia politically during his reign and established one of the first complete written legal codes in history. The **Code of Hammurabi** combined diverse traditions present throughout the newly unified polity and assembled them into a collection of 282 laws, inscribed on a large stone pillar and placed in a public temple for display. Many of these laws related to slavery. Hammurabi's code deemed slaves merchandise rather than human beings but acknowledged the right of male slaves to own property, marry free women, and potentially purchase their freedom. Female slaves possessed none of these rights. The Code of Hammurabi also made distinctions between debt slaves and all other slaves: persons in debt bondage were to be released by their owners after a period of three years; chattel slaves recruited by capture, sale, or punishment for criminal misbehavior would remain enslaved for life (Horne, 2007). Across Mesopotamia, slaves were employed in public buildings, temples, and private homes, and they faced harsh punishments if they tried to escape or disobeyed. Yet members of every level of society were expected to follow the rules. Ordinary citizens who harbored or detained a runaway slave would be put to death (McKeon, 2002; Rodriguez, 1997; Meltzer, 1993).

Just as slaves worked in the fields and households of Mesopotamia, so too did they toil a thousand miles west of Mesopotamia, in Egypt, during the same period and then later, in the same region, among the Hebrews. Both Mesopotamia and Egypt contained river valleys with rich soil capable of sustaining growing populations through high crop yields. However, due to the great mass of peasants in Egyptian society, who lived like serfs bound to the

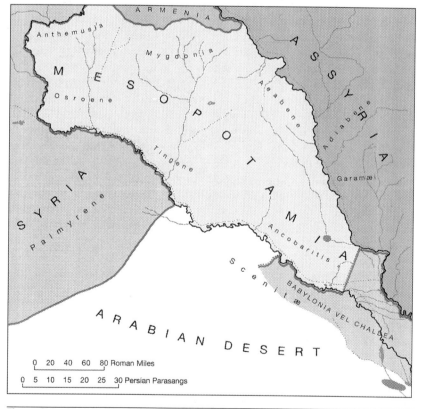

Figure 2.1 Map of ancient Mesopotamia

soil, working the lands of the pharaoh or nobles, slaves were generally of less importance in Egypt. Some slaves submitted to bondage voluntarily in lieu of a debt payment, but most were foreigners or prisoners of war put to work in palaces or temple estates, in royal quarries, in the fields, or in the building of great construction projects. Certain ancient groups, such as the Hebrews, practiced slavery but only attached a stigma to those among the enslaved whom they deemed "heathens." While there was no prospect of release for heathens, slaves of Hebrew origin were not kept in bondage in perpetuity. A formal process of manumission helped to facilitate their transition from slavery to freedom after a period of approximately six years (Meltzer, 1993). Similarly, many early West African societies incorporated slaves and their off-spring into the community as freemen and -women after their manumission (Heuman & Burnard, 2011; Lovejoy, 2000). Thus, while slavery was a fact of life in the majority of ancient societies, the actual conditions and terms of enslavement and the prospect of eventual release varied enormously from place to place.

Even though the presence of trafficked and enslaved individuals was nearly ubiquitous in the ancient world, slaves formed a relatively small percentage of the total population in early civilizations. Slavery represented only one of several systems of labor. Consequently, in most ancient societies, the economic significance of slave labor remained relatively minor for several centuries, but this did not prevent the institution of slavery from spreading. Slavery appears

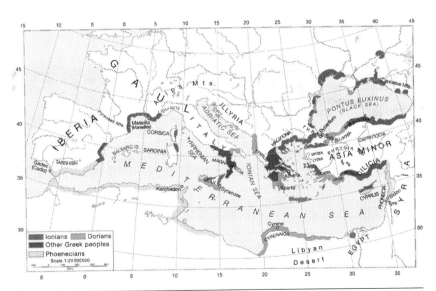

Figure 2.2 Helas: The ancient Greek World c.550 BCE

Source: Adapted from William R. Shepherd, Historical Atlas, 1926

to have helped ancient civilizations to absorb outsiders and benefit from their labor, as most slaves were completely isolated from their kin and communities and dependent on their owners (McKeon, 2002). It was not until sometime between the fifth and third centuries BCE that the autonomous city-states of Ancient Greece, particularly **Athens**, became dependent on slave labor and hence fully fledged slave societies. In **slave societies**, as the historian Ira Berlin has observed, "slavery stood at the center of economic production, and the master—slave relationship provided the model for all social relations"; Berlin opposes this to **societies with slaves**, where "slaves were marginal to the central productive processes" (Berlin, 1998).

At its height, around the middle of the fifth century BCE, Athens contained a greater proportion of slaves than free citizens, with an estimated population of 100,000 slaves and 40,000 free adult males. The growing demand for enslaved laborers to perform a wide range of tasks, from farming and producing goods for sale to making tools and tending to the sick, prompted Athenians to utilize human capital to an unprecedented extent. Although most Athenians worked as peasant farmers, Athenians generally viewed chattel slavery as a necessity because it allowed the most privileged class of free citizens to turn their attention to political and cultural matters rather than to unsavory tasks associated with manual labor. Even those at the lower end of the social scale enjoyed a higher status than that possessed by slaves. Although all occupations were open to slaves, excepting those of politician and soldier, the majority of slaves were employed in domestic, agricultural, and industrial labor. Greeks tended to enslave foreigners and immigrants, known as "barbarians," but also subjected marginalized and desperate members of their own polities to bondage as well (Heuman & Walvin, 2003; Blundell, 1995; Phillips, 1985).

In Athens, sharecroppers were frequently enslaved as debtors because they could not produce enough shares to satisfy the demands of the nobles whose lands they occupied. The practice of enslaving other Greeks for nonpayment, however, was outlawed in 594 BCE; thereafter, slaves had to be noncitizens born in foreign lands—generally captives of war purchased at market. Greeks purchased most of their slaves from non-Greeks around the Aegean Sea, and slave trafficking emerged as a highly lucrative business. Warfare, kidnapping or banditry, piracy, self-mortgaging, and child exposure were the most likely means by which merchants acquired men, women, and children to trade at market. Women and girls in particular were perceived as spoils of war, available to the highest bidder and commonly exploited for sexual purposes (Watkins, 2001; Rodriguez, 1997; Meltzer, 1993).

As the Athenian economy and social order became increasingly reliant upon slave labor, it became commonplace for Athenian citizens to assume that slaves, and "barbarians" in general, were inferior and hence not capable of attaining full citizenship or enjoying the fruits of freedom. In time, the condition of bondage became closely associated with perceived differences of mind and soul rather than a matter based on the legal distinction between freedom and slavery. This redefinition of enslavement as a moral and spiritual issue is evident in the Greek philosopher Aristotle's concept of slavery. **Aristotle** (384–322 BCE) envisioned slavery as a natural component of a hierarchical social and political structure in which every individual plays a prescribed role suited to his or her innate capabilities. For Aristotle, non-Greeks were "natural slaves," who lacked the higher qualities of mind and spirit necessary for freedom and were marked out by nature as capable of belonging to and being ruled by their intellectual superiors (Garnsey, 1996). Studying the emergence of slavery in ancient Greece is critical because concepts of freedom and liberty still influential today developed at the same time that Greek philosophers and statesmen attempted to justify their use and acceptance of slavery. Social practices, legal patterns, and attitudes and philosophical notions established in ancient Greece had an important impact on the civilizations that came after, particularly the **Roman Empire** (*ca.* 27 BCE through 476 CE), an ancient empire centered around the Mediterranean Sea and containing most of modern Western Europe (Bradley & Cartledge, 2011; Heuman & Burnard, 2011; Meltzer, 1993).

Slavery existed in ancient Rome from its earliest stage of development, and as the Roman Republic expanded into a vast empire over a period of several centuries, it became the largest slave society in the ancient world. Historians argue that slaves constituted roughly 30 to 40 percent of the population of Italy and perhaps 10 to 15 percent of the entire Roman Empire. The Romans transmitted their conception of slavery to subsequent civilizations through their system of law, codified in the sixth century CE under the emperor Justinian and rediscovered during the medieval period by European scholars. Roman legislation concerning slavery, slave trading, and manumission offered a concrete example of a slave system in an earlier period and served as an intellectual basis upon which medieval societies could draw as they created their own methods of bondage (Phillips, 1985). Roman slaves came from a variety of sources, including the offspring of existing slave women; free children exposed to the elements for a variety of reasons by their parents and raised as slaves; and men, women, and children purchased at markets or captured elsewhere and then transported into the empire. Most slaves were probably owned by the elite and engaged in domestic and agricultural work or urban trades. Scholars stress that female slaves of childbearing age were rarely freed; their children made up three-fourths of Rome's total population of enslaved laborers. Masters expected their female slaves to produce offspring to replenish the slave supply (Heuman & Burnard, 2011; Bradley, 1994).

Legal texts offer the greatest source of information about the lives of slaves in the Roman Empire. Per Roman law, slaves were considered property rather than people, human objects lacking kin, honor, or a social identity.

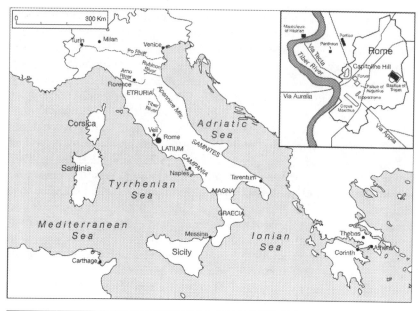

Figure 2.3   Map of ancient Italy and (inset) Rome

From the first century CE, the state intervened whenever possible to prevent the abuse of slaves by their masters, but shielding slaves from the actions of third parties represented an attempt to protect a master's property rather than the slave as a person. Although masters or third parties could not kill their slaves without just cause, the murder of a slave was not considered as serious of an offense as the murder of a free man or woman (Heuman & Burnard, 2011; McKeon, 2002). Like classical Athens, Rome, too, had to confront the fundamental dilemmas raised by slavery, particularly the difficulty of owning something deemed both a living person and an object; the impossibility of maintaining complete control over another human being; the reliance on coercion to maintain the slave system; and the moral implications of owning fellow humans (Rodriguez, 1997; Bradley, 1994; Phillips, 1985).

Medieval and Early Modern Slavery
Between the six and thirteenth centuries, slavery gradually died out in Western Europe as **feudalism** emerged as the dominant social system. The feudal system linked high-ranking members of the landed military elite—the lords—with other military personnel known as knights who possessed equipment necessary for warfare, such as horses and weaponry. In highly ritualized feudal agreements, lords offered knights a *fief*, typically the right to use or

govern lands and manors, in exchange for their loyalty and service in war. A knight who swore to serve a lord in exchange for a fief was known as a vassal. Central rulers (like English and French kings) could draw upon the personal line of contractual relationships stretching throughout their kingdoms to establish larger royal networks, ensuring that nobles at all levels owed allegiance to those of a higher rank and, ultimately, to the crown (Singman, 1999; Bush, 1996).

Lords and knights did not perform economically productive work; instead, they relied upon the toil of peasants, known as serfs or *villeins*, who lived on the estates of the elite and received protection, land they could work for themselves, and the right to graze their domestic livestock in exchange for unpaid agricultural labor. Subject to the will of their lord and legally bound to his manor, serfs held few legal rights; they could not carry arms, were obligated to sue for justice in the local manorial court, and could not appeal their lord's decisions. Everything they owned technically belonged to their lord. Serfs supported themselves and their families by working an individual plot on a lord's estate and then giving him part of their production as rent. They were also required to work on the lord's much larger plot of land. Serfs had to obtain their lord's permission and pay a fee in order to move, marry, learn a trade, sell goods at open market, or travel. Nonetheless, serfs were not slaves. They possessed rights and were bound in a reciprocal relationship with their lords that entitled them to protection, justice, and land (Engerman, 1999; Bush, 1996; Phillips, 1985).

The decline of slavery and weakened economy in medieval Western Europe did not prevent the flourishing of slavery and slave trading outside the region, particularly in the Islamic world, stretching from southern Spain to the Arabian Peninsula to North Africa. Although Europeans agreed not to allow the sale of fellow Christians to non-Christians as slaves, European countries participated in the slave trade to these foreign markets, relying on overland and sea routes from Italy and southern France as key transfer points for the sale and trafficking of slaves with the Islamic world. In the more economically advanced and urbanized Islamic world, across the Mediterranean from Europe, the population included a diverse array of ethnic groups including Persians, Berbers, Greeks, Syrians, and Egyptians, linked together through the religion of Islam. Slavery was a pervasive feature of Islamic society, and Muslims looked to markets in Europe, sub-Saharan Africa, the area of the Russian rivers, and India and Turkestan to meet the demand for bondsmen and -women (Lovejoy, 2004; Phillips, 1985).

Because free men carried out most of the production of agricultural and industrial products, Muslims utilized their slaves in nonproductive roles, especially artisan labor, military service, and domestic work. The Qur'an ordered masters to treat their slaves well, yet slaves did not possess legal rights and were considered morally and physically inferior to free Muslims. Masters could severely punish or even kill their slaves without fear of retribution. Male slaves performed a wide range of business tasks for their masters, but slaves in general were used as domestic servants. In a society in which men could maintain as many concubines as they pleased, female slaves were commonly subject to sexual exploitation and forced to work as prostitutes, dancers, and entertainers. Lighter-skinned women in particular were highly prized as concubines (Lovejoy, 2004; Phillips, 1985).

In Africa during this same period, the status of individuals subjected to slavery varied according to their ethnicity, the distance they had been removed from their homeland, and whether they had been born into slavery or enslaved during their lifetime through sale, capture, or kidnapping. Slaves were commonly acquired through violent means—seized from their farms and villages by means of warfare, kidnapping, and military raids. There was some continuity in terms of the slave systems and trafficking practices of sub-Saharan and northern Africa, and the Muslim regions of Africa, both north and south of the Sahara, overlapping with the Islamic world to the north. Slaves performed agricultural tasks for and traded on behalf of their masters, and women as well as men were exploited sexually. Pretty women and girls and eunuchs, or castrated males, fetched high prices in slave markets throughout Africa, and slaves were not allowed to engage in sexual relationships without their master's consent. Children produced by slaves were raised as the property of their master and could be removed at any time and sold, taken as a concubine, redistributed as part of a marriage arrangement, or trained for the army. Like many slave systems, masters held the power of life or death over their slaves, but some tribes, such as the Igbo and Yoruba, acquired slaves primarily for the purposes of human sacrifice. They were free to sacrifice their slaves at funerals or as an offering to the gods, as in Dahomey, where hundreds of captives were publicly killed at festivals for religious purposes (Heuman & Burnard, 2011; Lovejoy, 2004).

African Slavery and the Atlantic Slave Trade

While it is clear that slavery and slave trading predated European forays into West Africa and the New World in the fifteenth, sixteenth, and seventeenth centuries, the slave system and transatlantic trafficking network that developed during the early modern period was more brutal and exploitative than that which had previously existed in Europe, Africa, or the Middle East. The European conquest and settlement of the Americas ushered in an increased demand for agricultural laborers and a new era of global trafficking and enslavement. To produce labor-intensive crops such as tobacco, sugarcane, and cotton for distant European markets required a large and plentiful workforce. In the early phase of European colonial settlement, thousands of indigenous peoples were initially employed as laborers throughout the Americas, especially in the Spanish-operated silver and gold mines of

Mexico and the Andes. Bound laborers from Europe also toiled in the agricultural fields of the Americas as plantation laborers, particularly in the English and French mainland North American and Caribbean island colonies. The death of Amerindians from epidemic diseases, coupled with the emergence of large, integrative plantations requiring hundreds of workers, led to the rapid rise of a new system of slavery based on the labor of African men, women, and children.

What was once a means of domestic labor exploitation in Africa became a huge, intercontinental system based on the drive to provide an abundant and affordable supply of ready hands to cultivate crops. To feed the European need for slaves to labor in their plantation colonies, Africans began to enslave one another for judicial reasons and criminal misbehavior and to conduct raids with the explicit intention of bringing in captives for sale. Kidnapped in the interior and marched to European coastal forts, African captives of all ages were sold as slaves to European traders in exchange for guns, cloth, alcohol, and many other goods. They were then packed like cargo into overcrowded spaces between the decks of slave ships and forced to endure the lengthy, often lethal voyage across the Atlantic—known as the **Middle Passage**. Of those who survived this harrowing voyage, the final destination for the vast majority was South America, primarily Brazil, or the Caribbean islands; the rest ended up in Central America and North America, in the region that is now the United States (Berlin, 1998; Curtin, 1998; Blackburn, 1997).

Though the transatlantic African slave trade began rather slowly in the sixteenth century, by the seventeenth and eighteenth centuries, the trafficking of bound African laborers had blossomed into a large-scale enterprise capable of supplying slaves to labor in the sugarcane fields of the West Indies; the mines and coffee and sugar plantations of South America and Central America; and the tobacco, rice, and cotton fields of North America. During this period, Europeans grew increasingly unwilling to perform the grueling agricultural tasks that they demanded Africans perform under threat of physical and psychological violence.

The economies of European countries and their overseas colonies, as well as the emerging states in the Americas, were thus sustained by African slavery and the commodities produced by enslaved laborers. An estimated total of 11 million African slaves crossed the Atlantic for New World destinations during the era of slavery, and the labor of those who survived produced goods quickly and relatively cheaply for international markets, bolstering profits and manufacturing and increasing rates of consumption in Europe, in the Americas, and across the globe (Rawley & Behrendt, 2005).

Critically, the transatlantic slave trade and mass enslavement of Africans throughout the Americas gave rise to new racial classifications designed to bolster and justify the slave systems of the New World. While early colonists

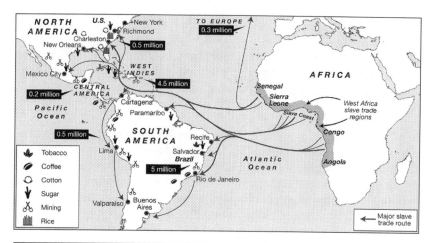

Figure 2.4   Map of the Transatlantic African Slave Trade, 1650–1850

Source: Adapted from www.slaverysite.com/Body/maps.htm#map5

had typically referred to themselves as "Christians" and their African and Amerindian slaves as "heathens," during the seventeenth century, this terminology was gradually replaced by the terms "white" and "black" or "Negro." In colonies as disparate as Brazil in South America, Barbados in the West Indies, and Virginia in North America, the term "Negro" meant being both a slave and inferior. Formal slave codes curtailed the rights of the enslaved and guaranteed that the status of a slave was reserved almost exclusively for persons of West African ancestry. The developing racial order, which degraded men and women of African descent to the lowest social positions, gave weight to the notion of African inferiority and served as further justification for their enslavement. Moreover, racial distinctions not only became the chief rationale for slavery in the Americas, they also helped to secure the hegemony of slaveholders by discouraging collusion between poor whites and enslaved blacks. But assumptions about African inferiority failed to prevent slaves from rebelling against their masters or forming ties with nonslaves, and New World racial slavery sparked some of the most intense rebellions, wars, and radical political and religious movements of the early modern era (Heuman & Burnard, 2011; Drescher, 2009; Davis, 1984).

Global Abolition and Emancipation Movements

The three centuries following the European settlement of the Americas were marked by a dramatic and devastating expansion of legal forms of slavery and human trafficking. European colonizing powers, particularly the British, French, Spanish, and Portuguese, exploited slave labor in far-flung corners of the globe, in Africa, Asia, and the Americas. Slave labor and the continual influx of slaves to European colonies provided the impetus behind the growth of plantation economies. The global increase of slavery occurred at the same time that the institution all but disappeared in Europe, as jurists ceased to sanction slavery within their jurisdictions, both for native-born residents and for foreign-born slaves who reached their range of legal authority. For Europeans living in the age of overseas expansion, slavery had become a critical, though distasteful, imperial institution necessary to secure economic growth, domestic prosperity, and international competitiveness.

But this notion of slavery as a necessary evil would change in the late eighteenth century. Starting in the 1780s, organized abolitionist campaigns cropped up on both sides of the Atlantic, spearheaded by reformers who sought to criminalize the transatlantic slave trade in Africans and end the practice of human bondage. British and French Enlightenment thinkers such as Adam Smith and Baron de Montesquieu argued that slavery was the antithesis to natural law and less productive than free labor. The primary goal for antislavery advocates was to effect the legal abolition of slavery and slave trading, and, following a number of setbacks, in this they were largely successful. In little over a century, from the 1780s to the 1880s, antislavery activists led by the British gradually put a stop to the transatlantic slave trade and dismantled slave systems throughout the New World. By the late nineteenth century, the same European countries that had for centuries relied upon slave labor to bolster their wealth and power now became committed opponents of human trafficking and the institution of slavery. At the dawn of the twentieth century, the near-universal legal status of slavery had eroded dramatically, with the trade in human beings increasingly perceived as an unlawful impediment to human rights and progress on a global scale (Drescher, 2009; Davis, 1984, 1966).

In the nineteenth-century Atlantic world, the site of so many deeply embedded, interconnected slave systems, the process of legal abolition and emancipation assumed a variety of forms and spanned most of the century. The declaration of immediate emancipation in Haiti (1804), as well as the United States' Emancipation Proclamation (1863) and Thirteenth Amendment (1865), were the fruits of prolonged, violent struggles. Spurred to action by the specter of revolutionary emancipation in Haiti, the British abolished the slave trade in 1807–1808 and then attempted a gradual transition to full freedom beginning in 1834—but this did not apply to India. Other nations soon followed in Britain's footsteps, with Denmark and France (1848), the Netherlands (1863), Puerto Rico (1873), and Cuba (1886) abolishing slavery as a result of international pressure, religious efforts and moral petitioning, legislative action, and, in some cases, bloody skirmishes. With the abolition of slavery in Brazil in 1888, the institution officially came to an end in the Americas. But for the formerly enslaved and their descendants, the process of emancipation had only just begun. Oppression, exploitation, racial conflict, and violence remained prevalent in former slave societies, and true freedom and liberty continued to remain the province of wealthy elites, and of whites. Politically, socially, culturally, and economically, many of the descendants of the enslaved remained marginalized and trapped in a state of continued exploitation throughout the Americas (Drescher, 2009; Davis, 1984, 1966).

In African and Asian regions formerly colonized by Europeans or under their domination beginning in the nineteenth century, reformers imposed a free-labor ideology on indigenous populations and pressured reluctant masters to emancipate their slaves. Slavery in these Old World societies, however, was extensive, vigorous, and diverse during this period, and the slave trade remained intact through interregional and long-distance trafficking and slave raiding. In addition to outright slavery, a range of forms of social, economic, and sexual exploitation existed in Africa and South and South East Asia, some hereditary and permanent, and some temporary. Men, women, and children could be subject to debt bondage or pawnship, contract slavery, forced labor for the benefit of the state, serfdom, or concubinage. Slave labor was still cheaper than wage labor and more widely available. Debt, famine, and poverty prompted parents to sell children, husbands to sell wives, and people to bind themselves to a master in exchange for sustenance. Slavery was also used as a punishment for certain types of crimes. The vulnerability of slaves and their detachment from kin and community allowed for their subjugation; slaves' rootlessness enabled masters to subject them to ever-greater levels of labor and sexual exploitation. This, in turn, increased productivity levels, generating profits that masters were unwilling to lose. In many areas of nineteenth-century Africa and India, for example, slavery was firmly rooted in the social order and flourishing rather than declining (Lovejoy, 2000; Klein, 1993).

During the late nineteenth and early twentieth centuries, European encroachments in parts of the Old World where slavery and the slave trade remained widespread were fiercely resented. For decades, European powers had avoided complicating their relations with local rulers and slave owners by choosing not to intervene in master–slave relations. In British India, Indian masters owned millions of slaves, and the institution of slavery remained robust despite the abolition of slavery in other parts of the empire. British officials in India, who relied heavily on the support of local Indian princes, soldiers, and subalterns to carry out their will, were hesitant to enforce an antislavery policy. Moreover, they had long engaged in the exploitation of Indian workers and women and girls to suit their own economic, political, and sexual purposes. It was not until 1860 that it became officially illegal to own slaves in British India. Fourteen years later, in 1874, the British governor of the Gold Coast of Africa forbade courts to recognize slavery as a legal institution. French imperial administrators also exercised restraint, enforcing the prohibition of slaveholding after 1848 only to French citizens in the colony of Senegal. Even with legal abolition, forced labor and other exploitative forms of contractual labor remained extensive in African and South and South East Asian societies, and European-sponsored laws and edicts releasing slaves were often enforced loosely or not at all. In many regions, former masters continued to maintain power over labor through debt bondage and control of job markets, land, and housing. The formerly enslaved and their family members also found it difficult to escape the stigma of slave origins. Young women and girls remained particularly vulnerable to sexual exploitation as the proportion of females trafficked by slave traders rose, especially in the Islamic world, at the end of the nineteenth century (Drescher, 2009; Miers, 2003; Klein, 1993).

In 1925, the League of Nations was determined to draw up a formal agreement on the abolition of slavery, and representatives of member countries willingly included other forms of forced labor and sexual exploitation under the general umbrella term of "slavery." At the League of Nations' Slavery Convention, held in Geneva on September 25, 1926, envoys from 40 countries agreed to prevent and suppress the slave trade and eradicate slavery in all its forms as soon as possible. Although they agreed that abolishing slavery was a worthy and important goal, they also acknowledged that extensive forced-labor systems still remained in existence in Africa—particularly the Sahara, the Sudan, and Ethiopia—as well as in the Arabian Peninsula, the Persian Gulf, and parts of South and South East Asia. Ethiopia's formal proclamation ending the slave trade in 1923 had closed the entire globe as a legal source of slave trading, but human traffickers continued to operate vigorously outside the law. The Geneva Convention thus carefully specified the various abuses that would no longer be tolerated and attempted to establish the international machinery necessary to eradicate these practices (Miers, 2003). Rhetoric associated with the antislavery efforts of the early twentieth century suggests that the United States and European nations generally believed that slavery, and the "white" slave trade of prostitution, was confined to non-Western areas of the world, beyond the line of modern, presumably enlightened civilization. They also shared an assumption that slavery's eradication was inevitable, tied to "the Western-led march of human and moral progress" (Drescher, 2009, p. 409).

Yet in the decades after the Geneva Convention, varieties of labor coercion and sexual exploitation continued to operate throughout the world under a wide range of designations other than "slavery." The widespread nature of these insidious practices became increasingly apparent to opponents of human trafficking over the course of the twentieth century. Of particular concern was the marked global increase of the illegal trafficking of young women and girls for sexual purposes. Indeed, it was clear that modern forms of sexual exploitation were far from new.

Only recently have international political leaders recognized that to combat the contemporary manifestations of forced labor and sexual enslavement requires the adoption of a more flexible legal terminology of slavery. "Under the auspices of both the League of Nations and the United Nations," Joel Quirk has explained,

> the range of problems that have been formally equated or associated with slavery has expanded markedly, reflecting a transformation away from strict equivalence and toward sufficient similarity. Instead of functioning as an analytical category, slavery has been increasingly evoked as an evocative concept.
>
> (Quirk, 2011, p. 162)

Slavery, then, is not "a historical relic which belongs in the past," as many still believe, but remains an issue of fundamental importance in the modern world (ibid.).

Discussion Questions

1. What are some of the common features linking different forms of slavery over time and from place to place?
2. Why have most societies tended to enslave outsiders?
3. What types of labor did slaves perform in ancient and premodern societies?
4. Describe the various motivations behind the practice of voluntary enslavement.
5. How have legal codes enabled us to learn about ancient slave systems?
6. In what ways does gender shape the experience of enslavement for the individual?
7. How did the transatlantic slave trade in Africans shape the development of modern understandings of race?
8. How successful were the antislavery efforts of the nineteenth and early twentieth centuries?
9. Why did European nations—especially Britain—support the eradication of slavery and the slave trade?
10. Did slavery end with the Geneva Convention of September 25, 1926?

References

Bales, K. (2005). *Understanding global slavery: A reader.* Berkeley, CA: University of California Press.

Berlin, I. (1998). *Many thousands gone: The first two centuries of slavery in North America.* Cambridge, MA: Harvard University Press.

Blackburn, R. (1997). *The making of new world slavery: From the baroque to the modern, 1492–1800*. London: Verso.

Blundell, S. (1995). *Women in ancient Greece*. Cambridge, MA: Harvard University Press.

Bradley, K. R. (1994). *Slavery and society at Rome*. Cambridge: Cambridge University Press.

Bradley, K. R., & Cartledge, P. (Eds.). (2011). *The Cambridge world history of slavery. Volume I: The ancient world*. Cambridge: Cambridge University Press.

Bush, M. L. (1996). *Serfdom and slavery: Studies in legal bondage*. New York: Longman.

Curtin, P. D. (1998). *The rise and fall of the plantation complex*. Cambridge: Cambridge University Press.

Davis, D. B. (1966). *The problem of slavery in western culture*. Ithaca, NY: Cornell University Press.

Davis, D. B. (1984). *Slavery and human progress*. New York: Oxford University Press.

Drescher, S. (2009). *Abolition: A history of slavery and antislavery*. Cambridge: Cambridge University Press.

Eltis, D. (2000). *The rise of African slavery in the Americas*. Cambridge: Cambridge University Press.

Engerman, S. L. (Ed.). (1999). *Terms of labor: Slavery, serfdom, and free labor*. Stanford, CA: Stanford University Press.

Garnsey, P. (1996). *Ideas of slavery from Aristotle to Augustine*. Cambridge: Cambridge University Press.

Grusky, D. B. (2008). *Social stratification: Class, race, and gender in sociological perspective*. Philadelphia, PA: Westview Press.

Heuman, G., & Burnard, T. (Eds.). (2011). *The Routledge history of slavery*. New York and London: Routledge.

Heuman, G., & Walvin, J. (Eds.). (2003). *The slavery reader*. New York and London: Routledge.

Horne, C. F. (2007). *The code of Hammurabi*. London: Forgotten Books.

Ishay, M. (2008). *The history of human rights: From ancient times to the globalization era*. Berkeley, CA: University of California Press.

Klein, M. A. (Ed.). (1993). *Breaking the chains: Slavery, bondage, and emancipation in modern Africa and Asia*. Madison, WI: University of Wisconsin Press.

Lovejoy, P. (Ed.). (2000). *Transformations in slavery: A history of slavery in Africa* (2nd ed.). Cambridge: Cambridge University Press.

Lovejoy, P. (Ed.). (2004). *Slavery on the frontiers of Islam*. Princeton, NJ: Markus Wiener Publishers.

McKeon, N. (2002). *The invention of ancient slavery*. London: Duckworth.

Meltzer, M. (1993). *Slavery: A world history*. New York: Da Capo Press.

Miers, S. (2003). *Slavery in the twentieth century: The evolution of a global problem*. Walnut Creek, CA: AltaMira Press.

Mouritsen, H. (2011). *The freedman in the roman world*. Cambridge: Cambridge University Press.

Patterson, O. (1982). *Slavery and social death: A comparative study*. Cambridge, MA.: Harvard University Press.

Phillips, W. D. (1985). *Slavery from roman times to the early transatlantic Trade*. Manchester: Manchester University Press.

Quirk, J. (2011). *The anti-slavery project: From the slave trade to human trafficking*. Philadelphia, PA: University of Pennsylvania Press.

Rawley, J., & Behrendt. S. (Eds.). (2005). *The transatlantic slave trade: A history* (Revised ed.). Lincoln, NE: University of Nebraska Press.

Rodriguez, J. P. (1997). *The historical encyclopedia of world slavery. Volume I*. Santa Barbara, CA: ABC-CLIO.

Singman, J. L. (1999). *Daily life in medieval Europe*. Westport, CT: Greenwood Press.

Watkins, R. R. (2001). *Slavery: Bondage throughout history*. New York: Houghton Mifflin Company.

Winks, R. W. (Ed.). (1972). *Slavery: A comparative perspective*. New York: New York University Press.

MAKING MONEY OUT OF MISERY

TRAFFICKING FOR LABOR EXPLOITATION

JUNE KANE

This chapter looks at the relationship between human trafficking and what is often called "the world of work." It aims to help readers to understand that at the end of most trafficking chains, there is a situation of exploitative labor and that, in many ways, human trafficking is a corrupt form of labor migration.

The chapter first establishes labor and labor migration as fundamental rights, enshrined in human rights law and at the heart of every person's desire to earn a living that will enable them to survive and promote the well-being of their family. It underlines that when people are deprived of the right to move to seek work, for whatever reason, they may seek out alternative avenues to legal channels, and that this puts them at high risk of falling into the hands of traffickers. The international definition of trafficking as comprising three essential parts—recruitment, movement, exploitation—is explained in the context of trafficking for labor exploitation, and there is a brief exploration of where "demand" for exploited labor occurs.

The chapter emphasizes the fundamental difference between forced labor and trafficking for labor exploitation. It emphasizes the imperative to differentiate between the two both in programming terms and in responses to the needs of victims. Finally, the chapter considers briefly how trafficking into sexual exploitation relates to the labor trafficking context and outlines some ways in which so-called labor actors can contribute to ending this heinous denial of human rights.

DOI: 10.4324/9781003124672-4

Chapter Learning Objectives

- Understand how human trafficking relates to labor migration and the desire for decent work.
- Know the principal relevant international labor conventions, in particular how they relate to human trafficking.
- Understand the specific case of child trafficking and the relationship between trafficking and child labor.
- Recognize the difference between trafficking into labor exploitation and migration that results in forced labor.
- Understand the three main elements of trafficking into labor exploitation (recruitment, movement, and exploitation) and how they fit together.
- Have gained an insight into the concept of sex trafficking as a variant of trafficking for labor exploitation (and why this concept is sometimes controversial).
- Appreciate the role that "labor actors" can play in combating human trafficking.

Approaches to Human Trafficking: The World of Work

Human trafficking is looked at in different ways by the various groups and individuals who work to put an end to it. For those working in law enforcement, it is primarily a **criminal problem**, cross-border or domestic, sometimes involving organized crime, sometimes just a series of criminal offences involving different individuals or groups who come together in a less structured, often temporary relationship.

Those whose work focuses on supporting victims of trafficking and people who may be at high risk of being trafficked see human trafficking as essentially a **human rights issue**, robbing people of their rights to live free from exploitation, in good health, with their families, and in charge of their own destinies. Some may additionally address it from the **health angle**, focusing on the physical and psychological impact on victims and their families.

Advocates for women's rights and gender equity approach human trafficking as a form of **violence against women** and emphasize the role played by gender inequalities in the family and in society at large. Similarly, some see trafficking as a heinous **derogation of children's rights**, especially the right to education and to a childhood free of the burden of child labor.

Increasingly, governments look upon human trafficking as a **threat to national security**, particularly when it involves irregular movements of people across borders and when it is linked to other forms of organized crime such as money laundering, the smuggling of contraband, or the trade in illicit drugs.

So which of these approaches is the right one? All of them. Human traf- ficking fits appropriately into each of these categories, and the fact that it is addressed from many different angles by people with different sets of skills and expertise is a positive thing. Human trafficking is such a complex process that it needs to be tackled on many different fronts at the same time, and it is clear that a multidisciplinary approach to solving the problem must be taken.

In the 2010s, first nongovernmental organizations and the media and eventually international agencies and governments started using the phrase "modern slavery" to denote human trafficking, perhaps because the public reacts more emotionally to this phrase. Some commentators reject this, though, explaining that "slavery" is defined in international law as an unequal relationship between two parties (with the stronger or more powerful party using this fact to impose submission on the weaker or more vulnerably party). Human trafficking, they argue, is much more complex than this.

The International Labour Organization (ILO) uses the phrase "modern slavery" nowadays, but specifically to refer to forced labor and forced marriage (which is more in line with the power relationship traditionally involved in slavery). The ILO says[1] that, on any given day in 2016, there were 40 million people who were victims of modern slavery: 25 million in forced labor and 15 million in forced marriage. This represents 5.4 victims of modern slavery for every thousand people in the world in 2016. Some 25 percent of victims were children.

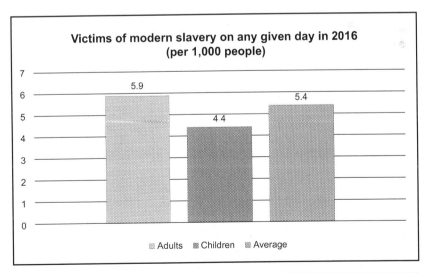

Figure 3.1   Victim of modern slavery on any given day in 2016 (per 1000 people)

Source: Global Estimates of Modern Slavery, ILO, Walk Free Foundation and IOM, 2017

For individuals and organizations like the ILO specializing in what is often called "the world of work," human trafficking is very much a **labor issue**, firmly rooted in labor market dynamics and the overwhelming need and desire of people to earn a living.

The Right to Decent Work

All people who have reached the legal minimum age for work have a right to work—without coercion, in decent conditions, for a fair wage—to ensure their economic well-being and that of their families. Alongside international and national laws relating to human trafficking, there exists a body of legislation that is designed to ensure that labor is regulated and policed so that people's labor rights are protected. These include, for example, the right to work in safe, nonhazardous conditions; to have set working hours with regulated time off and holidays; access to insurance that covers the worker who is unable to work because of sickness or injury; minimum guarantees including rates of pay, including for work done outside regular hours or at unsocial times; laws governing female workers' right not to be discriminated against on the basis of their sex; and laws that stipulate a minimum age for work so that children are free to complete their education and gain the skills that will prepare them not only for work but for life. Taken together, these elements are often called "decent work" and are enshrined in labor law.

Labor laws exist at international and national levels. International legal instruments are generally negotiated and adopted through the mechanisms of the ILO, the United Nations body that deals with all matters relating to the world of work. Member states of the ILO meet annually in conference to consider and adopt new instruments, and countries that then ratify these conventions undertake to report regularly on what they have done to translate the conventions into their national laws. Of vital importance to the effective implementation of international labor conventions is the fact that the ILO has a unique "tripartite" governing body and membership, bringing together with the ILO governments, workers' organizations (trade unions), and employers' associations. These "labor actors" are ideally placed not only to know and understand the realities of the world of work but also to act to turn the promises enshrined in international labor conventions into workplace realities.

International labor conventions cover, *inter alia*, workplace conditions (known as norms and standards), the rights of those migrating for work, gender equity, and the importance of fixing a minimum age for work and protecting children from premature entry into labor. There are also conventions relating to particular occupations such as road transport, seafaring and construction, and, since 2011, domestic work.[2]

Among the many conventions relating to labor rights, eight are considered "fundamental."[3] Consolidating the spirit of these fundamental conventions, in 1998 the International Labour Conference adopted a Declaration on Fundamental Principles and Rights at Work. This embodies what might be considered the most basic rights that must be protected and upheld at all times and in all circumstances, and all member states of the ILO—including those who have not ratified one or more of the conventions included in the fundamental conventions—are required to report on the progress they are making in implementing the Declaration.

Human trafficking is both directly and indirectly covered through these international conventions. Where people enjoy freedom of association and collective bargaining, for example, their rights as workers are protected and they are less likely to be exploited. Action against forced or compulsory labor is instrumental in breaking down the motives for trafficking and the means of profiting from it. Abolishing child labor and protecting children from exploitation directly addresses the problem of employers who see in children a cheap and easily exploitable source of labor and so thwarts the traffickers who provide such labor. Eliminating discrimination strikes at the heart of the exploitation of workers who are targeted because they are from another country, tribe, or caste, of a different color, culture, or religion, or are women whose position in family or community too often makes them subservient to those who wish to profit from their labor.[4]

At national level, labor laws are an important weapon in the antitrafficking legislative armory, especially where specific antitrafficking laws do not exist. They allow labor inspectors and regulatory authorities to take action against unscrupulous employers who accept and exploit trafficked people, for example. Identifying and bringing wayward employers to justice may subsequently help in investigations of other links in the trafficking chain. Laws

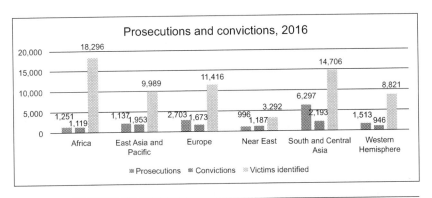

Figure 3.2 Prosecutions and convictions, 2016

Source: US State Department TIP Report 2017

against abduction, deception, extortion, forgery, fraud, assault, rape, and other crimes that traffickers may commit in the course of trafficking may also be used where specific laws against trafficking are not in place, and even when they are.

Despite efforts to identify and prosecute traffickers, convictions remain elusive, partly because it is difficult to prosecute trafficking, while convicting someone of assault, extortion or forced labor may be more successful. According to the US State Department's Trafficking in Persons (TIP) report in 2017, there were just 14,894 prosecutions and 9,071 convictions for trafficking in the world in 2016.

When People Are Excluded From Labor Markets

In addition to the laws that govern the conditions under which they work, people also have a right to move to find work if they wish or need to. A number of ILO conventions set out this right and the responsibility to guarantee it:

> The Migration for Employment Convention (Revised), 1949 (No. 97), aims to regulate the conditions under which the migration of workers and their families takes place, and the Migrant Workers (Supplementary Provisions Convention, 1975 (No. 143) contains specific standards to counter illicit and clandestine labor trafficking which disturbs orderly migration and creates negative social and human consequences. States ratifying this convention undertake, for example, to investigate illegal migratory movements on their territory that aim to facilitate substandard employment.

States have the primary responsibility to regulate migration. Regulating migration, though, is not the same as preventing migration. Regulating migration means making migration safe and regular so that people can exercise their right to migrate if they need or wish to. In fact, people may seek to migrate to find work for a number of reasons:

- In many developing countries, unemployment is linked inextricably to low rates of literacy. People simply do not have the basic skills that equip them for employment, except perhaps in casual manual work, which is often acquired in the "grey market" where workers have no contract, no security of employment, poor pay and conditions, and no power to negotiate.
- Skilled workers may find themselves unemployed if the skills they have do not coincide with the skills demanded in the labor market. This might occur suddenly, if a particular industry relocates, for example, or it could result from a mismatch between the training on offer and the jobs available.

- Unemployment can also result when markets are disrupted by financial crisis, natural or man-made disasters, conflict or just national policy shifts that cause changes in the labor "geography" of a country or region.
- Sometimes, people seek to move for work simply because they want to. In a world in which global communications allow people to see what life is like in other places (sometimes not necessarily accurately), people may believe that there are better opportunities "elsewhere." This is particularly true of young people, who are disproportionately affected by unemployment and who may be more mobile, unencumbered by family or debts.
- It may also be the case that there are geographical, social, or economic factors that result in a demand for workers in one place and a surplus of workers in another. For example, there may be a high demand for seasonal agricultural workers in one part of a country alongside low employment in another, which will result in unemployed workers looking to move temporarily to find seasonal work. This might also happen across a border, and there are known areas where seasonal workers have moved for generations to follow opportunities to earn a living. Sometimes this is done legally, but often, workers slip across borders that are not well policed.
- Women may find themselves excluded from labor markets because national policies discriminate against them or local customs mean they are not able to compete with men for jobs even where they are equally or even more qualified.

In short, there are many reasons—personal, structural, economic, geographical, societal, and even historical—that prompt people to consider relocating, permanently or temporarily, in order to find work.

What happens, though, when would-be labor migrants find migration channels closed (permanently or temporarily)? And what if migration channels are open but people do not know about them or cannot afford the costs involved? When migration channels are closed or inaccessible for some reason, people who need or want to move to find work seek other ways to do this and become highly vulnerable to falling into the hands of traffickers.[5]

Recruitment and Entry Points

All human trafficking begins with a process or event that entraps the victim and sets her or him on the path to being trafficked. In the case of would-be labor migrants, alongside the legitimate "entry point" into work, there is the risk of encountering parallel entry points that lead to trafficking.

For example, those wishing to find work in another place (not only in another country but perhaps in another part of their own country) often approach a recruitment agent to help them. In the cities of industrialized countries, recruitment may be done through an agency or via an advertisement in the newspaper or other media.

In recent years, the ILO has emphasized the importance of "safe recruitment" and has worked with governments to regulate and monitor recruitment agencies to ensure that they are not misleading would-be migrants with false information about jobs on offer in another country or acting as a front for trafficking operations.

For people who live in villages or small communities, though, the recruiter may be someone in the community who is known to have contacts who can find work or help with transport.

Regardless of the form, traffickers are known to set up parallel mechanisms that promise job placement, help with necessary documents, advice on transport or provision of the services themselves, and sometimes contacts that will provide accommodation. Each of the links in this "trafficking chain" may comprise a legitimate service (the transport, for example) or a crime (for example, document forgery, an illegal sweatshop), or the whole chain may consist of traffickers and intermediaries who knowingly break the law.

It is worth recalling here how the UN trafficking protocol (the Palermo Protocol) defines human trafficking:

> the recruitment, transportation, transfer, harbouring or receipt of persons, by means of the threat or use of force or other forms of coercion, of abduction, of fraud, of deception, of the abuse of power or of a position of vulnerability or of the giving or receiving of payments or benefits to achieve the consent of a person having control over another person, for the purpose of exploitation.

The first part of this definition relates to the links in the trafficking chain. It starts with recruitment—that "entry point" described earlier—then involves movement, described here as transport or transfer, and ends in exploitation.[6] This exactly parallels regular labor migration, which also begins with recruitment/entry into the process, involves temporary or permanent movement, but which ends in legitimate work. The difference between regular labor migration and human trafficking lies in the criminal nature of the different parts of the process and, importantly, in the exploitative outcomes of the trafficking, including forced labor, debt bondage (where the victim has entered into debt to finance what s/he believes to be legitimate and has to pay this off to the traffickers), or exploitative labor in dirty, dangerous, demeaning, often slavery-like conditions.

It is important to remember that, for trafficking to occur, the recruitment and transport must involve

> the threat or use of force or other forms of coercion, of abduction, of fraud, of deception, of the abuse of power or of a position of vulnerability or of the giving or receiving of payments or benefits to achieve

the consent of a person having control over another person . . . for the purpose of exploitation.

In other words, there has to be *ab initio* intent to exploit.[7] Although common wisdom (and Hollywood movies!) tend to emphasize the violent abductions that sometimes do take place at the beginning of the trafficking chain, trickery, deception, lies, and misrepresentation are more common. The promise of a job, exaggerated stories of the money to be made, and the sad misrepresentations that exploit a person's hopes and dreams are more likely to be used to lure people into the hands of traffickers.

A typical example of how this works is the young woman in a small town who cannot find work and who has heard about other women from the community who have moved to the "big city" and found well-paid work in restaurants and hotels. Tempted by an advertisement in the local paper for women to work in the city as waitresses, she pays a fee to the agent who placed the advert for help with transport and accommodation, believing his promises that the work, although it may involve unsocial hours, is well paid. He tells her she will work alongside other young women from her town and that he will try to find her accommodation in the same boarding house. When he quotes the cost of all these services, she does not have enough money, but he tells her that she will be able to pay him back from the money she earns. Soon, the young woman is on her way to the city, full of hope and having promised her family she will send money back to them as soon as she has repaid her debt.

When she arrives in the city, she finds things are very different. She is housed in dingy rooms with a group of other women she doesn't know. The "aunty" who looks after them locks the door at night and only opens it when someone comes to collect them to take them to work. This is not the restaurant that was promised but a nightclub where the "waitresses" are expected to provide sexual services to the customers. Our young woman wants to go home, but she is trapped by the debt she entered into and scared to voice her objections because of threats of violence not only to her but also to her family.

In situations like this, it is not surprising that some of the young women may accept the drugs that are often offered to them. It is surprising, however, that some will eventually return to their homes and work as recruiters for the traffickers. One explanation for this is that the young women's situation once they return home has not changed: they are still unemployed, have earned almost no money from their exploitation, and, having after all survived the trafficking experience, no matter how damaging it was, they may feel that other women will be able to survive it too and that they will therefore not do "too much harm" by earning money as a recruiter. Many women, on the other hand, do not survive the trafficking experience, or they emerge with long-term physical and psychological problems.

Trafficking victims—men, women, and children—often endure physical violence at the hands of traffickers and intermediaries who aim to subdue them and reinforce the power relationship that is so necessary to the success of the traffickers. Women and girls may be raped as part of this violence. Psychological trauma is also common, as victims are confronted with threats, isolation, feelings of helplessness, and verbal abuse. Trafficking is particularly pernicious because it involves moving the victim away from her/his normal environment, robbing them of known protection services and safety nets. When people are trafficked into other countries, additionally, they may not know the language of the people with whom they come into contact and find it impossible to even think of escaping because they do not know who to turn to or how to explain their situation. The fact that they are regularly told by traffickers that their documents are not legal or that their exploiters take away their documentation makes them even more unlikely to seek help.

The ultimate irony of trafficking into labor exploitation is that most trafficking victims never earn the money they were promised and that was one of the primary motivations for their desire to move in the first place.

Movement: The Difference Between Human Trafficking and Forced Labor

It will be clear from the example given that "movement" is at the heart of trafficking, because it is the means by which traffickers isolate victims from the environment in which they are safe and can seek help.

There is no defined extent of the movement; the essential point is that the victim is moved. Traffickers may move their victims within the country, for example, from rural area to city, from city to coastal resort, from periurban settlements to farms. When trafficking does not cross national borders, it is called "domestic" trafficking, and, despite what common wisdom often suggests, it is known that most of the trafficking in the world is domestic.

Traffickers who move their victims to another country are guilty of "cross-border" trafficking. They may move people on foot, by road, by sea, or by air. Often, these journeys are hazardous, involving, for example, dangerous mountain routes, leaky boats, or modified vehicles in which victims are hidden. Sometimes, people are moved in regular transport, on scheduled flights, in buses or taxis. In such cases, traffickers may provide forged documents to fool border authorities, or corrupt border or immigration officers might be working with the traffickers.

These complex mechanisms may suggest that trafficking is hardly worthwhile for criminals who, after all, are engaged in this crime in order to make money. Often, however, traffickers use processes and personnel already engaged in moving illicit goods (drugs, arms, stolen vehicles, contraband). Additionally, it is a sad fact that human trafficking is a low-cost and low-risk criminal activity since, if they are intercepted, trafficking victims are relatively easy to replace, and the "loss" of a victim does not cost as much as losing a consignment of drugs or contraband. Because of the nature of the trafficking chain, moreover, it is most likely that, even when police or migration officers identify one link in the chain, they will not be able to trace it back to the initiator, especially where the chain has been constructed of casual relationships, people who do not work regularly together but as "freelance operators" for one particular action in the chain.

It is the existence of these diverse elements and the complex nature of the trafficking chain that differentiates human trafficking from forced labor. Forced labor is a typical outcome of trafficking and occurs at the point of exploitation. Victims of forced labor, for example, may have migrated willingly and without help (legally or irregularly) and have then been unlucky enough to enter employment that is coercive and exploitative. They may also not have moved at all but be in forced labor in the place where they live. The essential difference between migration with forced labor and trafficking into labor exploitation is that, in the case of trafficking, the third parties involved at the beginning of the process—at the entry point—had the *intention* of leading the person involved into exploitation.

Case Study 3.1: Forced Labor in the Brick Industry in Nepal

In 2020, the ILO, in collaboration with UNICEF and the Central Bureau of Statistics of Nepal, published the results of the first ever survey of employment relations in the brick kilns of Nepal. The project, which was supported by the US Department of Labor, identified 103,548 individuals as "main workers" in the brick kilns and, since they were often accompanied by their family members who lived (and often worked) in the kilns, a total of 186,150 people were working in the brick industry—176,373 manual workers and 9,777 administrative workers.

Of the total manual workers (main workers and family members), 6,229 (3.5%) were found to be in forced labor (defined for this study as working involuntarily and also working under a threat or menace). Nearly all the workers in forced labor (97.5%) were unable to leave their job without negative repercussions or some risk. More than 8 in 10 (81.5%) had contracted a debt that could not be paid back without their job at the kiln, and 633 of them (15.3%) reported that they would lose all wages due to them if they left the kiln.

Only 1 in 5 (22%) of the main workers came from the districts where the brick kilns are located; 78% of the workers migrated to work in the brick kilns from other districts of the country or from another country.

Roughly 32% of the main workers were internal migrants. All the main workers who migrated from another country (46%) came from India.

The workers migrated by choice, and so even those who were in forced labor were not in fact trafficked. This shows clearly the difference between trafficking and migration into forced labor.

Source: Streamlined report on employment relationships in the brick industry in Nepal, ILO 2020

The Exploitative Outcomes of Human Trafficking

What is often called the "exploitative labor outcome" of trafficking can occur in many different labor sectors. The ILO has outlined the major areas of work that frequently harbor trafficking victims as: "agriculture, food processing, construction, textile and garment enterprises, retail, manufacturing, logging, mining, restaurants, domestic work and entertainment," and there are other sectors into which trafficking occurs.[8] To these also can be added begging and the commercial sex sector, on which there is more in what follows.

Across the globe, the majority of trafficking victims find themselves exploited in **agriculture**, not only in the fields but also in fishing, flower picking and packing, and related work. Because of the seasonal nature of agricultural work, trafficking victims are often moved from place to place as their traffickers undercut regular rates of pay for seasonal workers and offer teams of workers—sometimes entire families—as cheap labor. In this way, children are trafficked alongside their parents and enter into child labor.[9]

There is much debate over where the "demand" for such cheap labor originates. Some commentators place the responsibility firmly in the hands of the consumer, who seeks out the lowest possible prices on foodstuffs. However, the whole supply chain plays a part, from the supermarkets that put pressure on suppliers to keep costs low, to the suppliers who prevail on producers to cut prices, to the producers themselves who may knowingly recruit laborers from sources they know to be suspect or just turn a blind eye to offers of labor that really are too good to be true, all with the aim of maintaining their profit margins.

After agriculture, the next most frequent destination sector for trafficked people is the broad category of "**service industries**." This ranges from high-end hotel work to street-based trades such as selling small goods or cleaning shoes.

Alongside legitimate workers, trafficked people may be found working in hotel kitchens, as chambermaids, cleaners, and as tradespeople. They may work in restaurant kitchens or in retail stores or wholesale warehouses. They may be selling things on the street, for example, flowers, newspapers, cigarettes, candy, or shoelaces.

In some parts of the world, those working as street vendors may be under the control of "handlers." In a throwback to the times of the English novelist Charles Dickens, a "handler" will watch over trafficked street vendors to make sure they do not try to run away and that they earn enough money to satisfy the exploiter(s).[10] If they do not, they are regularly beaten or burned with cigarettes. Often linked to such street activity is petty crime, in particular pickpocketing and bag snatching.[11]

Many people, especially women, are trafficked into **domestic labor**. This has been a challenging sector for trafficking researchers and programmers because, until the adoption in June 2011 of the Domestic Workers' Convention, 2011 (No. 189), the private home was not considered a "workplace," and labor laws were both ignored and impossible to police. Working behind closed doors, the domestic worker is hidden away from labor inspectors and other observers and is readily exploited. Although men and boys may be trafficked into domestic labor, the majority of victims are women and girls. Typically, they will have to rise before the rest of the household to prepare breakfast and perhaps get children ready for school and take them there (a particular burden for children who may themselves be of school age but who are denied the right to education and have to wait and watch while the children of "their" family enjoy that right). Domestic workers do the cleaning (often with toxic chemicals), cooking (perhaps in extreme heat or using equipment unsuitable to their age), and other household tasks as necessary, and, in extreme cases, may be expected to provide sexual services to the men in the household. These workers may be beaten if they make a mistake or disobey, are often given a label to replace their own name, and may be deprived of food and made to sleep in the kitchen or outhouse.[12]

Case Study 3.2: The Gangmasters of Europe

For many years, the mosques and community centers servicing the ethnic South Asian population of England's second city, Birmingham, helped long-term and recent migrants to find work in the fruit and vegetable growing and packing business of the Midlands, the region of which Birmingham is the hub. The community leaders negotiated legal contracts and generally ensured the rights and well-being of the workers.

In the 1990s, though, they began to experience difficulties securing work for their community members because Eastern European "gangmasters" were undercutting the rates and had begun providing cheap labor, sometimes up to 200 men at a time, transported to the fields and packing plants in fleets of buses. The gangmasters not only owned the buses, they owned the accommodation the men lived in—and effectively owned the men themselves.

By 2001, the gangmaster system had become big business in the UK, with an estimated turnover of $45 million a year. Some of the gangmasters operate in compliance with labor laws; many do not. Some use undocumented workers who have been shipped in and are effectively locked into their accommodation when they are not working. They have no contracts, allowances, insurance or time off. They are charged high fees for transport and accommodation in substandard hostels. They are effectively in forced labor and, since they have been promised decent work before they set off, have been deceived and so are victims of human trafficking.

Trafficking into agricultural labor in Europe is not confined to the UK. Moroccan workers are trafficked to Spain; Switzerland and the Netherlands have large numbers of illegal migrant workers, among whom some will have been trafficked.

Source: Adapted from ILO, *Trafficking in Human Beings: New Approaches to Combating the Problem*, ILO SAP-FL, May 2003

When many people think of forced labor or human trafficking, however, the image that comes to mind is of rows of victims, generally women, heads down over a sewing machine or other piece of machinery, toiling in a warehouse-sized factory. In fact, "**manufacturing**" as a sector is a major receiver of trafficking victims, even if the common image is not always correct. Men, women, and children are trafficked to work in a broad range of manufacturing enterprises, and these range from large factories to cottage industry enterprises housed in a small apartment or basement room.

In recent years, the US government and other countries that are major importers of manufactured goods have researched and blacklisted goods coming from countries where there is a possibility that trafficked labor was used in their manufacture. Clothes, sports shoes, rattan and cane furniture, leather goods, jewelry, and a range of other items are routinely excluded from US markets following reports of forced labor or trafficking victims being exploited in source factories.

Men in particular may be trafficked into **heavy industries, including construction and mining**. Incredibly, however, children are also trafficked into mining, particularly smaller-scale operations where narrow tunnels are dug and exploiters look for children who are small enough to fit into them. Underground work of this kind, particularly in situations where safety is rarely a priority, is considered to be one of the worst forms of child labor.

Children are also trafficked into **begging**, although women and more rarely men are also exploited as beggars. As with those trafficked to work as street vendors, trafficking victims forced to beg are often under the control of a handler who will watch them from a safe distance. Different forms of trafficking into begging are known. In Thailand, for example, the government has run campaigns to discourage people from giving money to women they find begging with a baby on one of the many footbridges crossing the main roads in Bangkok. These women are most often Cambodian women who have paid a family to "borrow" their infant in order to take her/him across the border to Thailand to exploit. The women are traffickers. Dealing with this particular example of child trafficking is a challenge, because the women are known to simply dispose of the babies if they think they are going to get caught.

Case Study 3.3: Garment Factories in Jordan

The US National Labor Committee (NLC) has reported that Jordanian garment factories supplying major outlets like Walmart, Hanes, and Macy's run advertisements in Bangladeshi newspapers announcing jobs that pay high wages, provide health care and accommodation, serve food that is "like the West," and offer a chance to see the country.

The recruiters typically charge a fee of between 1,000 and 3,000 US dollars for arranging a three-year contract guaranteeing them work when they get to Jordan. Many would-be migrants go into debt in order to pay this fee, believing that they will be able to pay it off with wages they earn in their new job. When they arrive in Jordan, the Bangladeshi workers are immediately stripped of their passports. Typically, they also soon find that they will not even receive the legal minimum wage and are often cheated of half the wages owed to them. Factory owners commonly require them to work more than 100 hours a week without overtime pay, enforce seven-day working weeks, and provide only one or two days off a month. Workers told the NLC that they are beaten if they fall asleep. If they complain, they are beaten or threatened with deportation.

When their contracts expire, most of the workers are denied the return ticket promised them by employers and have to borrow money so that they can return to their homes. These workers are victims of human trafficking since, although they sought to migrate for work willingly, their recruitment into what amounts to debt bondage/forced labor was based *ab initio* on lies and misrepresentation—the deception required by the Palermo Protocol for trafficking to occur.

Source: Adapted from J. Kane, *People on the Move: Human Trafficking in Jordan, Lebanon and Syria*, Euro-Mediterranean Centre for Applied Research on International Migration and ITC-ILO, San Domenico di Fiesole, 2011

In the major capitals of Western Europe, conversely, women who are trafficked from Eastern Europe to beg with babies in tow do all they can to protect the children—because they are often not their own. Traffickers who move whole families across the borders of Europe are known to split them up, diverting the men toward various forms of labor exploitation and taking children from their mothers and giving them to other women. The women are told that if they ever want to see their own baby again, they must obey their traffickers.

Although begging is not exactly a form of labor, it is a way of earning money, and the traffickers who force their victims to beg are making a profit by exploiting their time and effort.

Case Study 3.4: Doing "Ngangendong" in Bali

Children are often to be found begging—or selling small goods or flowers—in resorts where there are tourists who can be trusted to respond sympathetically to requests for help. In Denpasar, the main town in the island resort of Bali, Indonesia, for example, children are tricked into begging with false promises.

One 14-year-old boy told the story of a man who had approached his parents, offering to take him to Denpasar to work, and to provide the finances to send him to junior high school in the evenings. The boy and his parents were happy, but the boy soon realized that he would not be going to school. Instead, he was forced with other boys to do *"ngangendong"*—begging for goods, not money—and was expected to bring back at least 5 to 10 kilos of rice a day. The man sold the rice and kept all the money himself.

This boy had been trafficked, and note that the lies the trafficker told the parents in order to "recruit" the boy are not relevant in this case, since the boy was under the age of 18. The fact that he had been moved in order to be exploited is sufficient to make him a trafficking victim.

Source: Adapted from J. Kane, *Unbearable to the Human Heart: Child Trafficking and Action to Eliminate It*, ILO-IPEC, Geneva, 2002

The Special Case of the "Sex Sector"

As is the case with begging, some commentators argue that sexual exploitation is not a labor issue and insist that prostitution is not a "sector" and that women exploited in prostitution should not be considered as "working in the sex sector" but as victims of human rights violations. This outrage at the sexual exploitation of women (and indeed of girls and boys) is understandable, but the truth is that in many countries, prostitution is legal and is regulated in the same way as less controversial occupations. Where prostitution is legal, it is in women's interests to enjoy all the protections that labor laws allow, including a negotiated contract, minimum pay, decent working conditions, access to sick pay, health insurance, holidays, and agreed time off. Regular inspection of premises by labor inspectors is also in the women's interest, and health and safety regulations must also apply to these premises.

Regardless of the moral arguments put forward for or against prostitution, the truth is that in countries where it is legal, prostitution is effectively a labor sector. Just as with other sectors that receive trafficking victims, the sex sector often includes trafficked women alongside those who have elected to work legitimately. Very often, of course, women and girls are trafficked into sexual exploitation in countries where prostitution is not legal and where they are put to work in clandestine brothels, massage parlors, or hotels or on the streets. Frequently, women who are trafficked into prostitution are fooled with promises of other kinds of work and only on arrival at their destination find that they are to be prostituted. Frequently also, however, women may agree to relocate in full cognizance of the work they are going to perform; rarely, however, do they have any idea of the conditions they will face. Reports of violence, coercion to have unsafe sex, threats against the victim and her family, forced administration of drugs, and slavery-like conditions are common. Since the women were thus effectively deceived when they agreed to move, they are also victims of trafficking.

The nature of "demand" for the services of women trafficked into sexual exploitation is much debated. In regions of the world where trafficking into prostitution is a major problem, governments and nongovernmental organizations frequently run campaigns targeting the "clients" of brothels and other venues where sex can be bought. However, research in Europe has suggested that most men express concern that the women providing sexual services to them might have been forced to do so or have been trafficked into exploitation.[13] Indeed, they suggest that it is important to them that the woman whose body they buy is selling herself freely.

So where does the "demand" lie? This is not an easy question to answer, because the truth is that many of the men interviewed also say that they prefer to buy services from "foreign" women. This has been described as "otherness," a means of distancing the person who is selling herself from the wife, mother, girlfriend, sister of the man who is buying. What it also means, however, is that the intermediaries involved in the prostitution "business"—pimps, brothel owners, and other operators—look for women who satisfy this preference and so recruit women from other countries or different ethnic backgrounds. It is therefore the intermediaries who are generating the primary demand for "other" women; the clients are generating secondary demand.

The Links Between Child Labor and the Trafficking of Children

Children are also trafficked into sexual exploitation. This is an extremely emotional topic that is often misrepresented.

Many people believe that child trafficking into sexual exploitation always involves pedophiles and so-called pedophile networks. In fact, the most common manifestation of child sex trafficking is the trafficking of adolescent girls and boys who have not yet reached adulthood (but are close enough for clients to tell themselves that they are "old enough") into brothels and other commercial sex venues. It is known that the prostitution of adolescents in the commercial sex sector is an extension of the adult sex market. Put bluntly, the adolescent girls and boys provide choice to those prostitute-users who are looking for someone younger. Often, these men argue that, although they prefer young girls, for example, they thought the girl had reached the legitimate age to be working.

There are, of course, instances in which the men involved not only know their victims are underage but specifically seek out minors for sexual exploitation. This is a very specialized "market," and there are intermediaries who make money from providing children for it. The men who buy sex from children are child sex abusers.

They may not, however, be pedophiles but men who have normal sexual relationships with adult women and may indeed be married. Pedophilia, on the other hand, is a recognized sexual deviance in which perpetrators (usually men but very occasionally women) have a preference for sexual relations with a child who has not yet reached puberty, which is generally under the age of around 12 years. This sexual deviance has very specific characteristics: for example, pedophiles demonstrate difficulty in maintaining normal adult relationships with women; the men like to collect photographs of very young children to "fix" the age of the child so that s/he does not grow older in their minds; they organize themselves into "clubs" by using the photos as "calling cards" to exchange with other pedophiles in order to build up around themselves a supportive group of like-minded abusers. This is what is often called a "pedophile network." With the enormous strides in technology, these networks and the exchange of images have gone online and given rise to a growing market in child pornography.

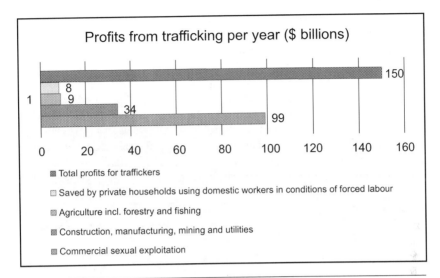

Figure 3.3   Profits from trafficking per year ($ billions)
Source: ILO, 2014

The commercial sexual exploitation of children, whether by pedophiles or by child sex abusers, does give rise to child trafficking, since traffickers will seek to supply children to these "markets" where there is a shortfall in supply. The use of these terms may seem harsh and inappropriate, but it is vital to stress that the traffickers and intermediaries who make money out of the misery of trafficking victims, whether adult or children, see what they do as "business." Indeed, the ILO estimated that in 2014 the profits from trafficking amounted to an incredible 150 billion US dollars a year. Looking at traffickers' actions in the same financial, entrepreneurial, and organizational ways that they do is one way to get to the heart of their activities.

This is one way of looking, also, at child labor. Child labor is defined through a number of international instruments but essentially it is often about people making a profit by exploiting the work of children.[14]

Links Between Trafficking and Child Labor

The UN Convention on the Rights of the Child (1989) stipulates that children have "the right to be protected from economic exploitation and from performing any work that is likely to be hazardous or to interfere with the child's education, or to be harmful to the child's health or physical, mental, spiritual, moral or social development" (Article 32).

However, two international labor conventions give us the most detailed understanding of what constitutes child labor: the ILO Minimum Age Convention, 1973 (No. 138) sets down the minimum legal age at which children can enter work, and calls on ratifying states to ensure that this is enshrined in national law. The age is set at 15 years, or 14 if a country's economic status requires this and then only until such time as this can be raised to 15. The convention also says that for the two years before they reach the minimum working age, children may perform "light work" as long as this is for a limited number of hours per week (notionally 14 hours, or 2 hours a day) and that it does not interfere in any way with their schooling. Additionally, no child under the age of 18 may at any time be engaged in work that is considered to be a "worst form of child labor."

These are clearly defined in the ILO Worst Forms of Child Labour Convention, 1999 (No.182). This says that the worst forms of child labor are:

(a) all forms of slavery or practices similar to slavery, such as the sale and trafficking of children, debt bondage and serfdom and forced or compulsory labour, including forced or compulsory recruitment of children for use in armed conflict;
(b) the use, procuring or offering of a child for prostitution, for the production of pornography or for pornographic performances;
(c) the use, procuring or offering of a child for illicit activities, in particular for the production and trafficking of drugs as defined in the relevant international treaties; and
(d) work that, by its nature or the circumstances in which it is carried out, is likely to harm the health, safety or morals of children.

The first three categories are considered to be "unconditional," that is, they cannot be negotiated. The fourth category, in paragraph (d), represents "conditional" forms that are specified by each nation following tripartite negotiations. Some countries compile what is called a "hazards" list of either tasks or occupations that fall into category (d), for example, lifting heavy loads above a certain weight, or working with specified toxic substances; or occupations such as textile dyeing or mining.

Note that category (a) includes the trafficking of children as a worst form of child labor. This means that in addition to labor laws and dedicated trafficking laws that can be used against traffickers, authorities may have at their disposal laws against the worst forms of child labor that can be used when the trafficking victims are under the age of 18. National Plans of Action to eliminate the worst forms of child labor will also include actions to address child trafficking in many cases.

Mobilizing the World of Work

The fact that trafficking is a complex problem that can be approached from several different angles means that the responses to it must be similarly multifaceted and undertaken by a wide range of different antitrafficking actors. Governments, law enforcement authorities (not only police but migration officers and labor inspectors), nongovernmental organizations (NGOs), researchers, and academics—all have a role to play.

When considering trafficking in the context of the world of work, it is also important to look at how labor actors—workers' and employers' associations especially—can also be active. They are, after all, ideally placed to know what is happening in labor markets generally and particular sectors specifically. The case study given above of the agriculture gangmasters, for example, first came to light when a UK trade union began to investigate complaints from employment agencies about the undercutting of rates of pay.

Actions to combat trafficking are frequently categorized into "prevention, protection, and prosecution" actions (there is also a specialized category related to victim support), and labor actors can and do contribute to all of these.

Employers and employers' associations, for example, are well placed to understand labor market dynamics and to know where there may be "grey market" operations and unscrupulous employers operating clandestine workplaces or employing trafficked labor. Employers' associations are also the primary body for policing and enforcing codes of conduct and labor agreements related to recruitment and employment.

Workers' organizations (trade unions) have a good idea of what is happening "on the ground." They closely monitor the conditions under which workers are employed and frequently learn of situations in which workers are being denied their rights. They are then able to investigate these reports with a view to uncovering breaches of contract or irregular situations.

Both workers' and employers' associations are engaged in education and awareness raising among their constituencies. Increasing understanding of what trafficking is and how it works means that more workers and employers are likely to identify trafficking in their midst. The ILO, in particular, has been instrumental in supporting workers' and employers' associations in putting in place reporting mechanisms and helping train managers, employees, and policy makers to understand and identify trafficking and respond to it.

Finally, workers' and employers' associations are able to provide short- and longer-term support to trafficking victims when they are identified. Employers may be able to guarantee regular employment if the victim wishes it or short-term employment while a victim is waiting to go home. Workers' groups may provide counselling or support, accommodation, or financial help.

In relation to child trafficking, employers' cooperation is crucial in ensuring that the whole supply chain is free of child labor (and potential trafficking linked to it). Employers are also, of course, vital to efforts to develop labor markets by providing investment and creating jobs. Skills training, apprenticeships, and on-the-job training will ensure that people who may otherwise be unemployed and so vulnerable to the tempting offers made by traffickers find decent work.[15]

Mobilizing workers and employers to contribute to antitrafficking efforts underlines the fact that trafficking is a labor issue. At its beginning is the desire to move to find decent work; at its end is exploitation in work that is often said to be akin to modern slavery.

Discussion Questions

1. Consider the different approaches to human trafficking and (i) how they complement each other and (ii) how they may hinder each other. Consider the roles and responsibilities of the different actors involved and how resources may be allocated among them to achieve the best possible outcomes.
2. Discuss the differences between human trafficking, legal and illegal migration, and people smuggling. Do you think that the general public can differentiate among them? Do you think they need to? Consider from the point of view of the legislator, relevant authorities, and the victims of human trafficking.
3. Think about the influence of the consumer who demands ever-lower prices and how this pressure is transmitted through the supply chain. Do you think that consumers would be willing to pay higher prices if they thought it would help close down the human trafficking business? Consider an example of a consumer good that you frequently use and map out the supply chain involved. Think carefully—a simple jacket, for example, can involve dozens of different suppliers (fabric, thread, buttons, zipper, dye, packaging, etc.).
4. Discuss media reports you may have seen about human trafficking. How many of these related to trafficking into sexual exploitation and how many into other forms of exploitation? Which sectors were mentioned in the reports? Were the trafficking events domestic or cross-border? Do you think that media reporting of human trafficking is well informed and balanced?
5. Look at the Recommended Principles and Guidelines developed by the Office of the UN High Commissioner for Human Rights and discuss them. To what extent do you believe these rights-based principles are embodied in national laws? If they are not, why is this?

6. Discuss what you know about child labor, including the worst forms. For background, you may wish to look at the section of the ILO website devoted to the International Programme on the Elimination of Child Labour (IPEC), where you will find general descriptions as well as sectoral and country publications and fact sheets.

7. Search the websites of companies and workers' organizations in your state and find out whether they are involved in combating human trafficking. Do they have corporate social responsibility policies? If yes, do these include the need to avoid child labor and the employment of trafficked people?

Notes

1. These figures are taken from the 8.7 Alliance's *Global Estimates of Modern Slavery*, Geneva 2017. The 8.7 Alliance comprises the ILO and the Walk Free Foundation, in cooperation with the International Organization for Migration (IOM).

2. The ILO Domestic Workers' Convention, 2011 (No.189) is seen as a major breakthrough, since domestic work has long been a subject of dissension, with some states insisting that it is not "real work" and should not be regulated and others arguing that it is a major sector of labor, especially for women, that is so often open to abuse. Accepting that domestic work is "legitimate" work and that those performing domestic duties have a right to the protections that labor laws provide is a vital step in ensuring workers' rights and women's rights.

3. These cover freedom of association and the right to collective bargaining (Conventions 87 and 98); the elimination of forced and compulsory labor (Conventions 29 and 105); the abolition of child labor (Conventions 138 and 182); and the elimination of discrimination in employment and occupation (Conventions 100 and 111).

4. This description is taken from: ILO: *Trafficking in Human Beings: New Approaches to Combating the Problem*, ILO SAP-FL, May 2003, p. 7.

5. This chapter does not look at illegal (irregular) migration, in which the would-be migrant knowingly contravenes labor laws and migrates without proper documentation; or people smuggling, in which would-be migrants (often asylum seekers hoping to gain refugee status on arrival) pay for illegal transport. Trafficking is differentiated from these by the victim status of the person who is caught in the traps laid by traffickers.

6. It should be noted that the US definition of human trafficking differs from the Palermo Protocol definition in that it does not require there to have been "movement." This can be problematic because it effectively looks only at the end result of trafficking: exploitation. It is important to differentiate trafficking victims from victims of "simple" exploitation because they may need specific services (for example, they may be in a country without legal documents). It is also vital to identify cases of trafficking in order to trace the whole trafficking chain and investigate all those involved from beginning to end, not only at the point of destination. In its work to eliminate human trafficking, the US approach emphasizes, instead, "action, means, purpose," which is a slightly different way to interpret the Palermo Protocol. As with most international instruments, ratifying parties will adapt the contents of the instrument to their national situation without compromising the underlying intent.

7. These conditions do not apply to people below the age of 18, considered to be children.

8. ILO: Fighting Human Trafficking: The Forced Labour Dimensions, background paper for the Vienna Forum on Human Trafficking, February 2008.

9. In fact, ILO Convention No.182 on the Worst Forms of Child Labour defines any form of child exploitation that also involves trafficking as an "unconditional worst form of child labour," from which children must be withdrawn immediately and that must be eliminated as a priority.

10. Reading the classic Dickens novel *Oliver Twist* gives a good insight into street gangs and their handlers and also into child labor. Although a masterpiece of fiction, the novel contributed to social awareness of these issues and to legislative change.

11. It is important to remember that, as laid out in the Recommended Principles and Guidelines on Human Trafficking developed by the Office of the UN High Commissioner for Human Rights, trafficked people should not be held responsible for crimes committed in the course of their being trafficked, or at least their victim status should be taken into account as a mitigating circumstance.

12. For more on child domestic labor, see J. Kane: *Helping Hands or Shackled Lives? Understanding Child Domestic Labor and Responses to It*, ILO-IPEC, Geneva 2004.

13. J. O'Connell Davidson, *Review of Evidence and Debates on the Demand Side of Trafficking*, unpublished manuscript supplied to the author, London 2002.

14. There are instances where children's labor is not exploited for profit but because it is a "tradition" or more properly a long-established "habit" to send children to work. A 2020 report on child labor in the vanilla sector in Madagascar, for example, noted that almost half (46%) of the children in child labor were unpaid family workers, undertaking a variety of tasks in family smallholdings. Some of the children also go to school, and there was very little difference between children from families identified as "poor" and those identified as "wealthy" (comparative measures). In these cases, it seems that children are put to work because that is what children do—but this does not, of course, make it right. See *Baseline survey of child labour in the SAVA region of Madagascar*, ILO, Geneva, August 2020.

15. For an overview of good practices involving employers' organizations, see *Human Trafficking and Business: Good Practices to Prevent and Combat Human Trafficking*, UN.GIFT, Vienna 2010.

4

SEX TRAFFICKING

YESTERDAY AND TODAY
KIMBERLY A. McCABE

Chapter Learning Objectives

- Be able to describe commonly used human trafficking terminology, including organized or transnational crime, sex trafficking, human trafficking, human smuggling, traffickers, sex tourism, mail-order brides, and the dark net.
- Understand the role of organized crime in human trafficking, including specific technologies that allow for trafficking to take place.
- Recognize common demographic features of victims of sex trafficking.
- Understand the structural conditions that foster trafficking and common techniques used by sex traffickers to locate, coerce, and traffic victims.
- Identify and explain relevant national and international legislation that has attempted to combat sex trafficking.

Human trafficking is one of the most profitable aspects of organized and transnational crime to date. The International Labour Organization (ILO) estimates suggests an annual profit of over $150 billion across the globe. Unfortunately, although the phrase "human trafficking" is widely recognized

DOI: 10.4324/9781003124672-5

from television drama, documentaries, and movies, the clarity of its definition, the profile and recruitment of victims, demographics and motivations for traffickers, and the dynamics behind human trafficking remains muddied and misunderstood. Today's influence of technology and the physical distancing mandates of COVID-19 has only increased the problem of human trafficking.

In the United States and across the globe, individuals are victimized through the criminal action of human trafficking. In fact, in 2019, the US identified approximately 12,000 cases of human trafficking as reported to police (World Population Review, 2020), which research suggests is only a fraction of the cases actually occurring (McCabe and Manian, 2010). Internationally, current estimates are between 20 and 40 million victims of human trafficking on an annual basis (Anti-Slavery International, 2019). Victims of human trafficking include men, women, and children from a variety of countries and a variety of cultures with factors such as poverty and gender inequality often accompanying the victimization (McCabe, 2018). In many cases, victims of human trafficking are deceived, coerced, and abused—all for profits to their perpetrators or traffickers. This chapter recognizes human trafficking as a transnational criminal enterprise that reaches far beyond geographic boundaries and flourishes with the victimization of a seemingly endless supply of potential victims.

This chapter is organized to provide an overview of human trafficking, to discuss some of the causes, victims, and offenders of sex trafficking, and to explain some of the reasons human trafficking continues to thrive. In addition, this chapter discusses the role of technology in the trafficking of adults and children. In a nutshell, through this chapter, readers will be provided clarity on the terms associated within human trafficking and, in particular, the issues surrounding sex trafficking.

Defining Human Trafficking Terminology

Human trafficking has been referred to as the *white slavery* of today; however, not all of the victims are white. Victims of human trafficking include individuals from all countries and with all skin colors. For decades, the United Nations has defined human trafficking as the recruitment, harboring, transportation, provision, or obtaining of a person for labor or services, through the use of force, fraud, or coercion for the purpose of subjection to involuntary servitude, peonage, debt bondage, or slavery. The U.S. State Department's *Trafficking Protection Act* (2000), in an attempt to provide a consistent definition across countries, further identified severe forms of human trafficking as: (1) sex trafficking in which a commercial sex act is induced by force, fraud, or coercion, or in which the person induced to perform such an act has not attained 18 years of age; or (2) the recruitment, harboring, transportation, provision, or obtaining of a person for labor or services through the use of force, fraud, or coercion for the purpose of subjection to involuntary servitude, peonage, debt bondage, or slavery. Hence, human trafficking, by definition, deprives its victims of the freedom of consent and control over their actions and locations.

Perpetrators of human trafficking, which also are from a variety of backgrounds and demographics, are referred to as *traffickers*. For the purpose of this chapter, the structure of the trafficking routes through which individuals are identified, acquired, and moved is referred to as the trafficking network or network. Sex trafficking is defined as human trafficking for the purpose of sexual exploitation to include forced prostitution, pornography, and, for children, sexual corruption and child sex rings.

Lastly, organized crime or transnational organized crime, often involved in sex trafficking, according to the US FBI, are groups who operate by illegal means and often without respect for geographic lines (FBI, 2020). Unfortunately, defining a criminal activity is only the first step in the attempt to reduce the activity of human trafficking, which flourishes and is often unrecognized by victims, the public, and even the criminal justice community. To begin to understand human trafficking, one must first recognize the uniqueness of the criminal activity and the rationale behind the trafficking of persons.

Human trafficking may occur in many forms as individuals are forcibly moved within countries or across borders. Although the international community came together in the late 1990s to improve and coordinate responses, oftentimes, the criminal activity of sex trafficking goes undetected as there exists the tendency to conflate sex trafficking with all sex work (Cockbain and Bowers, 2019). Individuals are victims of human trafficking for a variety of reasons to include prostitution, domestic work, pornography, farm labor, and organ transplants; however, the two main reasons are sex and labor, with the most common form of human trafficking classified as sex trafficking.

It is acknowledged that human trafficking is not exclusively tied to adult victims and that children are also trafficked for a variety of reasons in addition to sex and labor, such as adoption, soldiering, camel jockeying, child marriage, or for their internal organs (McCabe and Murphy, 2016). This chapter focuses only on the trafficking of individuals for commercial sexual exploitation.

In many cases, human trafficking is misidentified as human smuggling or people smuggling (McCabe, 2018). Whereas people smuggling implies enabling passage into a region (i.e. across a border) where the person is not a resident and is commonly recognized by Americans as across the US and Mexico border, human trafficking does not.

Specifically, with cases of human trafficking, although they involve exploitation, crossing a national border is not a requirement; thus, individuals may be trafficked within regions or US states where they are residents.

However, it should be noted that some cases of human smuggling may become cases of human trafficking if the initial consent for the victim to leave one country for another was achieved through deception or coercion (McCabe, 2008). In these cases, consent is irrelevant, and human trafficking has occurred.

Sex Trafficking and Organized Crime

Organized crime and transnational organized crime groups are comprised of individuals who operate by illegal means and often without the concern of geography or jurisdictional laws. Organized crime groups seek profit and power without concern for laws, policies, or victims. Research suggests that there is no single structure for organized crime; as they vary from hierarchies to networks, the groups are characteristically insular and operate through corruption and violence (FBI, 2020). However, the link between organized crime and human trafficking cannot be dismissed. As suggested by the UN's Office of Drugs and Crime (UNODC), sex trafficking and organized crime continues to be one of the most profitable industries in the world (McCabe, 2017).

Researchers who study sex trafficking suggest that the movement of these victims may be on a group or individual basis. These movements are generally based upon the relationship between the traffickers and the brothel owners, the size of the traffickers' networks, and the need for a certain type of victim. For example, in Central Asia, a blond female from Sweden is very profitable for her trafficker. Organized crime networks are aware of these preferences and capitalize on the knowledge.

Discussions on crime networks and human trafficking suggest that most sex trafficking organizations are small units of one- to five-individual-person networks (McCabe, 2008). In addition, also suggested by the UNODC, is the fact that these small criminal organizations maintain very high levels of secrecy often because of fear of community reactions more than fear of police reactions and that these small units continue to exist for long periods of time with flexible structures and simply change their products for consumption (i.e., drugs to people) based upon demands of the market. These small individualized groups are involved in the identification, transportation, housing, and victimization of the victims; thus, the criminal process is essentially invisible to observers.

With the increased use of technology, these small crime networks are supported, as group members now incorporate cybertechniques and web pages to facilitate their illicit activities. Thus, technology is enabling organized crime networks to engage in traditional criminal activities such as sex trafficking with a greater reach to expand their global impact (FBI, 2020). However, some of the original crime networks that have existed over the years are larger, with more than 50 individuals involved in the delivery of the human product, and continue to exist (Raymond and Hughes, 2001). Regardless of the size of the network, criminal networks are involved in much of the sex trafficking business.

Sex Trafficking Victims

It is impossible to document the first time sex trafficking occurred; however, in the 1980s, globalization and technology facilitated the movements of individuals across international borders. Often, victims of sex trafficking are subjected to more than one form of exploitation to include not only forced prostitution but also the forced production of pornography. Unfortunately, in many cases, victims of sex trafficking are viewed as simply as individuals involved in prostitution with their invisibility under the cloak of legalized or illegal prostitution. This is particularly the case in the US state of Nevada, which has legalized prostitution and the highest rate of sex trafficking (World Population Review, 2020). In response, police efforts and nonprofit organizations that help victims of sex trafficking have existed for over three decades (Guinn and Steglich, 2003). Research suggests that globally on an annual basis, there are over 5 million victims of sex trafficking, with at least 20% of these victims under the age of 18 (Toney-Butler and Mittel, 2020). In fact, in research conducted by Internet Watch Foundation (2020), approximately 30% of the pornography was from children who were groomed, deceived, or extorted into producing sexual image or videos of themselves. Thus, the popularity of technology and the internet has increased the popularity of sex trafficking.

Historically, the general demographic characteristics of the victims of sex trafficking are young and female (McCabe, 2008). Current research supports these general demographics, as further explorations suggest that victims of sex trafficking are twice as likely to be female and significantly younger (median age 22.8 years) than victims of labor trafficking (median age of 29.2 years) and domestic servitude (median age of 25.2) (Cockbain and Bowers, 2019).

Since sexual exploitation is the goal of the trafficking, the more 'attractive' the product, the higher the sale price. Although specific ages of sex trafficking victims are unknown, research suggests that the average age of a sex slave in the United States is around 20, while the average age outside of the United States is approximately 12 years old (McCabe and Murphy, 2016).

Unfortunately, those estimates on child victims may be conservative, as the prostitution of children is not always recognized as sex trafficking (Clawson et al., 2009). Given that sex trafficking is the most prevalent aspect of human trafficking and by far receives the most publicity, discussions on victimization are often provided from both a personal or individual perspective and an environmental or structural perspective. These perspectives of explanation provide those interested in combating human trafficking the baseline of information required to establish evidence-based efforts for prevention and law enforcement.

Researchers who attempt to provide generalizations from an individual perspective suggest that many adult victims are aware of their potential involvement in the sex industry prior to their commitments to the work (McCabe, 2018). Unfortunately, often, these adults become unable to control their activities or provide consent to sexual encounters for profit and, therefore, become victims of sex trafficking (McCabe and Murphy, 2016). Hence, in the majority of the cases of sex trafficking in the United States, victims are prostituted through force on the part of their traffickers, and the victims do not have the choice to decide to work or not. These adults, in many cases, are willing participants of smuggling efforts or willing participants in the sex industry with a desire to relocate; however, they become victims of sex trafficking when their authority over their free will is removed. Unfortunately, in the cases of victims who have agreed to prostitution but are then trafficked, assistance from law enforcement is extremely difficult to obtain. The victims have willingly agreed to participate in an illegal activity (prostitution) and are unlikely to report their victimization for fear of being arrested. It is also this group of victims that is perceived by the public as unworthy of legal assistance, as they voluntarily participated in criminal activities themselves.

In addition, regardless of the degree of victim involvement in sex trafficking, the destinations for most of the trafficking victims are cities with large commercial trade centers or areas with large military bases. It is within these densely populated areas that victims of sex trafficking and their traffickers easily blend in and function. Therefore, just as the criminal activity of prostitution occupies a central position in the development of national and international capitalism, sex trafficking flourishes within the same governmental structure (McCabe, 2018).

Child victims of sex trafficking, who by law do not have the authority of consent, are common in the United States and even more common outside the United States (Kangaspunta, 2006). For many of these child victims of sex trafficking, consent has been provided by their families (McCabe and Manian, 2010). In other instances, the child has participated in their sexual exploitation because of their attempt to satisfy another person (McCabe, 2017). In these cases, the child victims may not perceive themselves as victims. In fact, often, the child victim views their trafficker as their boyfriend and everyone else as an enemy; hence the child, isolated and controlled, is a victim of sexual exploitation through sex trafficking (Tennis, 2020). The United States government estimates that approximately 70% of the victims in the US are female, and approximately 50% of the victims are under the age of 18 (McCabe, 2018). Therefore, many children are involved in sex trafficking, as research suggests that one single trafficked child can net their trafficker up to $30,000 (Kangaspunta, 2006). However, across the globe, sex trafficking is not limited to prostitution. Victims of sex trafficking are forced into a variety of forms of sexual exploitation to include prostitution, pornography, bride trafficking, and sex tourism. The common element in all forms of sex trafficking is the total control of the trafficker over his victim, or the term 'forced'. Often times, victims of sex trafficking are not only abused by their clients, they are abused by their traffickers; therefore, victims of sex trafficking face multiple situations of victimization—all for another's profit or pleasure.

Language and culture are other individual-level risk factors for many victims of sex trafficking (Toney-Butler and Mittel, 2020). For some victims of sex trafficking, their language skills in the host country are nonexistent. For other victims, their culture has taught them to fear law enforcement, either as result of experience with corrupt officials or as a result of their traffickers' narratives regarding the police; thus, they are not likely to seek law enforcement help to end their victimization (Clawson et al., 2009).

Debt bondage is another individual reason for sex trafficking (McCabe, 2008). For some victims of sex trafficking, the perception that they owe a financial debt to their trafficker exists. These debts, perhaps for movement into the area, for rent, or food place the victim in the position of debt bondage to their trafficker, and for many, the debt is repaid through sexual exploitation.

Another explanation of human trafficking is family involvement. Just as a family member often perpetrates the abuse of a child, a family member is often responsible for a woman or child becoming involved in sex trafficking. In exchange for money or even a television set, a family member will sell or trade their loved-one into the world of sex trafficking (Farr, 2004). As the family member has allowed and even profited from the victimization of this person, the sex trafficking victim cannot return to the family for fear of punishment by their traffickers or that same family member.

In addition, children, as well as lesbian, gay, bisexual, and transgender populations, often face the additional dilemmas of parental acceptance or ignorance, their dependency for survival, and their desire to belong and be accepted. For these populations, the additional vulnerabilities of homelessness, depression, and lack of family support heighten their vulnerability for sex trafficking (Toney-Butler and Mittel, 2020). Therefore, just as there are a variety of individuals victimized through sex trafficking, there are a variety of individual reasons the victimization continues.

In attempting to explain how sex trafficking can occur from a structural perspective, one of the earliest theoretical explanations for human trafficking is founded in Lee's (1966) Push-Pull Theory of Migration. Just as with migration in general, characteristics of both the host and destination countries facilitate human trafficking. Specifically, characteristics of the host country push its natives out, and conditions of the destination country pull the immigrants into the country. One common method of recruiting women for sex trafficking is by placing an advertisement in local newspapers for nannies or waitresses in another country (sometimes the United States). Once the women have been recruited, they are transported to the destination country, where their travel documents are confiscated and they are imprisoned by their traffickers and forced to repay their debts (i.e. cost of their transportation, food, clothing, and shelter).

Another explanation for sex trafficking is military presence. Farr (2004) suggests that in areas with a strong military presence, there are often women engaging in prostitution. The prostitution serves both the military members and the prostitutes. When the military vacates the area, that demand for prostitution no longer exists; thus, prostitutes are in the area without work. It is these women who become the targets for traffickers interested in victims for sex trafficking. Research supports this finding that many sex-trafficked adults are simply aged prostitutes that have chosen to relocate for prostitution (Raymond and Hughes, 2001). Again, these women will endure the abuse of a trafficking victim and resist being arrested for fear of being sent back to a country where they cannot secure work.

Also, sex trafficking is related to the cultures of spousal prostitution and the mail-order bride industry. Cullen (2002) has reported that often, the mail-order bride becomes trapped in the climate of slavery and prostitution. A young woman who wishes to escape the poverty and depression of her home country may choose to become a mail-order bride to a man in a 'better' country. Of course, the mail-order bride feels that this decision will lead to a secure environment in which her basic needs will be met and she may even perhaps discover love. Unfortunately, this is rarely the case, as the mail-order bride business is essentially unregulated (McCabe, 2007). Instead, these women are perceived as any material purchase—replaceable or even disposable. To give some perspective on the magnitude of this problem, there are over 200 mail-order bride businesses operating in the United States, with over 5,000 women entering the United States each year as potential brides (McCabe, 2018). The brokers of mail-order brides are not considered traffickers; however, they are often regarded as frauds for not disclosing all of the facts of the transaction. In addition, McCabe's (2007) phrase *spousal prostitution* is also an element of sex trafficking and the mail-order bride business in that in these cases the husbands receive money or other goods in exchange for sex with their wives.

The structural conditions of poverty, inequality, and corruption all are related to sex trafficking and exist for both adult and child victims. The US Department of State, in an attempt to monitor human trafficking across the globe, produces an annual report that identifies countries and their efforts to address human trafficking. In the Trafficking in Persons (TIP) report, general information on enforcement efforts is provided at the country level as well as identified as source, transit, and/or destination countries for human trafficking. In addition, countries are categorized in tier classifications (1–3) based upon their documented legal and enforcement efforts. Through these sources of information, it is suggested that associations exist between poverty and sex trafficking (Deshpande and Nour, 2013), gender inequality and sex trafficking (McCabe and Murphy, 2016), and corruption and sex trafficking (Jonsson, 2018).

In particular, research suggests that human trafficking thrives on extreme poverty and is especially true for victims of inequality (McCabe, 2018). In many countries, women and children are seen as property and disposable. It is these persons that will be recruited for human trafficking. Researchers who have attempted to generate a profile of the child victims of sex trafficking suggest that the children come from families with four or more children, from families with few family members contributing to the household income, and from families that reside in extremely poor countries (Kang-aspunta, 2006).

Lastly, it is recognized that individuals are victimized in sex trafficking through their forced participation in the sex industry; however, sex trafficking is not simply prostitution, as it also involves pornography. In many cases, even women who enter the sex industry as strippers will eventually engage in prostitution as a victim of sex trafficking. Thus, one cannot discount the link between prostitution, pornography, and sex tours when attempting to explain sex trafficking.

Traffickers

Explanations of the conditions that facilitate sex trafficking are often global, with far less attention paid to the local environments and those who traffick victims (Kragten-Heerdink et al., 2017). Hence, those interested in studying sex trafficking, a for-profit action, must also consider the opportunities of the local areas and the traffickers that pragmatically and rationally operate locally (Cockbain and Bowers, 2019). The United Nations has recognized the distinction between sex trafficking and prostitution and advanced the notion of a participant-victim by their extension of the definition of sex trafficking to include payments or benefits to a person with control over another person for the purpose of exploitation, thus recognizing the role of the trafficker in human trafficking (McGinnis, 2004). Specifically, in the criminal activity of sex trafficking, the trafficker controls the type of sexual exploitation for his sex worker, his worker's 'decision' to work or not work, and his worker's location. Note that although in this narrative, the trafficker is referred to as 'he' there are many cases, especially in the cases of the sex trafficking of children, where the trafficker is a female not a male (McCabe and Murphy, 2016).

Research has suggested that with most crimes involving online networks, one of the best ways to identify the perpetrators is to identify the environment of the criminal action (McCabe, 2018). In cases of sex trafficking, environments prone to these crimes are usually those areas prone to heavy-security establishments, including bars on the windows and strong locks on the doors. Thus, due to the secrecy of sex trafficking, victims and traffickers are often hidden from public view, so environments may be misleading. Therefore, in an attempt to identify sex traffickers, one must consider the multiple aspects of the criminal activity and, in many cases, the relationship between the trafficker and the victim. In addition, as many cases of sex trafficking involve multiple individuals involved in the victimization, many researchers also consider the client of the sex trafficking victim as an offender as well as the others involved in the process of trafficking.

To identify the offenders (hereafter traffickers) involved in sex trafficking, one must first consider the individual who has introduced the victim to the criminal organization. As suggested in research, the individual that is often involved at the entry level of the victim is a family member, close family acquaintance, or boyfriend of the victim (McCabe, 2018). With child victims of sex trafficking, the individual most likely responsible for their entry into this type of victimization is a family member or family acquaintance who allows the child to enter into this arrangement of victimization (McCabe and Murphy, 2016). As discussed previously, some family members believe that their child will receive a better life and benefit from more opportunities in other locations and allow the movement of their child. Other family members, in need of money or in desire of some material good (such as a television set), may offer the child as trade (McCabe, 2008). Hence, it is difficult to provide demographic characteristics of family members involved in sex trafficking, with researchers suggesting that these family members are most often male as the family unit exists within a male-dominated culture. Others suggest it is the mother of the child who makes such arrangements for the good of the remaining children (McCabe and Murphy, 2016).

Another person who is often involved in the entry of young women into the arena of sex trafficking is the 'boyfriend' of the young victim. This boyfriend, much like a pimp in the arena of prostitution, begins to pursue the young woman with promises of love and security, when in actuality, he is a recruiter for the sex trafficking organization and will soon offer this young, unsuspecting female to the criminal world of sex trafficking (McCabe, 2018). In addition, and not to be overlooked, in many cases, the recruiters of young women for sex trafficking are other young women who are themselves victims of sex trafficking (McCabe, 2008). These victims, to continue their relationship with their traffickers, will bring other young women into the world of sex trafficking, and therefore the process of recruiting victims for sex trafficking continues.

Also involved as traffickers of sex trafficking are the so-called middlemen who are responsible for a variety of activities involved in the movement of victims. These activities include creating the documents for travel, arranging for the approval of travel, accompanying the victim from the source country (or area) to destination country (or area), and, in some cases, facilitating the entry process (usually with a bribe) with the customs officials who allow 'questionable' individuals to enter the destination country.

Similar to cases of counterfeiting and fraud, the individuals who arrange the travel documentation are experienced in this area, are often acquainted with local government employees, and are known through the criminal network (McCabe, 2018). In addition, the individuals who arrange for legitimate travel documents are often trained in law or in some other aspect of government-based regulations. Just as there exists some information on individuals involved in the smuggling of persons, there is some information on those individuals who travel with the victims of human trafficking to suggest that these individuals are often male and often posing as a family member of the victim (McCabe, 2018). However, as stated, with the trafficking of children, it is not unusual for the accompanying traveler to be a woman with the responsibility of childcare (McCabe and Murphy, 2016). In some extreme cases of child sex trafficking, these females travel with the very young children, care for the children until they are at an age to be profitable in the criminal activity, and then offer the children to the trafficker for a fee.

Nearly two decades ago, Bales (2004) suggested that one identifying characteristic of a trafficker is an individual involved in a 'respectable' business in addition to owning a brothel (perhaps through an investment club) and that the profits from sex trafficking are hidden under the red tape of legitimate business bureaucracy. In these cases, the traffickers are most often male, they are most often involved in some sort of entertainment business, and they may in some cases have friends in high government positions (sometimes law enforcement). Finally, as Kangaspunta (2006) suggested, it is not unusual for many of the members of the sex trafficking criminal organization to share the nationality of the victim, whereas the client does not share the nationality of the victim. In every case of sex trafficking, the motivation for the trafficker is profit, and the motivation for the client is pleasure (McCabe, 2018).

Facilitating Sex Trafficking

As with any type of criminal activity, there are multiple explanations for the success of sex trafficking. In particular, with sex trafficking realized as a multibillion-dollar industry with an endless supply of victims and traffickers, the action flourishes. Unfortunately, there will always exist poor countries with little opportunity for women and children, and there will always be individuals willing to exploit others for personal gain. Hence, until societies decide to address sex trafficking and its impact on individuals and societies as a whole, it will continue for a variety of reasons.

First, investigative efforts by criminal justice systems are one aspect of the problem of sex trafficking that remains a challenge (McCabe, 2018). Globally, resources for law enforcement and prosecutors to reduce sex trafficking or human trafficking are limited. With little training on the recognition of cases of sex trafficking and little experience in identifying or investigating cases of sex trafficking, few officers and even fewer prosecutors are able to distinguish cases of sex trafficking from cases of prostitution. Therefore, victims remain unidentified, and traffickers operate successfully. In addition, limited penalties for sex traffickers are yet another aspect fueling the problem of sex trafficking. In particular, in comparing cases of human trafficking with cases of drug trafficking or firearms trafficking, the maximum penalty for sex trafficking is perhaps 10 years, whereas distributing a kilo of heroin or stolen weapons could mean a life sentence (McCabe, 2010). Again, without the recognition of victims and without legislative penalties, sex trafficking continues.

Second, there are still limited reports of sex trafficking by the victims (McCabe, 2018). As suggested, many of the victims of sex trafficking are from countries outside of their destination country, and therefore, language is a barrier in reporting abuse. In addition, many of these victims have enter the destination country illegally or have had their travel documents taken from them by their traffickers. These victims are often from countries with negative perceptions of law enforcement and, in many cases, they fear law enforcement and are unwilling to speak with officers even to report their own victimization. For those victims who do not fear the corruption of law enforcement, the fear of being returned to their home country causes victims to resist reporting their victimization to law enforcement. In addition, for those victims of sex trafficking within their own countries, oftentimes, they are recruited into sex work as a result of a lack of social support in their homes or communities; hence, as they become involved in sex trafficking from those conditions that existed, they will likely not report the victimization, as those conditions still exist. Hence, without a victim to report an abuse, efforts by law enforcement to end that abuse are non-existent.

Finally, the emerging entrepreneurs in the area of sexual exploitation are those who utilize the internet. The internet is the newest avenue for those interested in sex trafficking. It can be used to distribute pornography produced with victims of sex trafficking or to arrange a sexual encounter. Just like with any online order, perpetrators interested in obtaining a victim for sexual exploitation may utilize the internet and email or a website to facilitate their desire. Unfortunately, this mode of communication is very difficult to monitor, and oftentimes, regulations go unenforced. Therefore, the use of technology is often critical in fueling sex trafficking. Specifically, in this environment, the victim is a product and a product worthy of much effort in its care and very profitable to its owner. In fact, a single victim may produce over $250,000 per year for their abuser (McCabe and Murphy, 2016). From the perspective that the victim is the product, the individual wishing for sexual exploitation is considered the consumer and the trafficker is simply the means of recruitment, production, and distribution for the product. Therefore, from a rational, objective perspective, online sexual exploitation is a business, and two of those businesses that further facilitate sex trafficking are sex rings and sex tours.

In considering child sex rings, usually within the category of extrafamilial (outside the family) abuse, multiple children and multiple abusers are involved (McCabe, 2017). Through this type of exploitation, there is sexual activity among multiple child victims and multiple adult offenders. Traditionally, in sex rings, there is communication (often online) among the offenders in terms of the desired demographic characteristic(s) of a child such as the age and/or gender of the child and the sex ringleader's ability to identify and locate a sought-after child. Historically, this line of communication involved either a phone call or email; however, today, those communications are much more likely to in private chat rooms, instant-messaging apps, and websites operated as 'discussion-only' forums from computer servers that are often based outside of the United States and, therefore, outside US regulations (McCabe, 2017). These forums, self-identified as discussion-only for individuals to share their thoughts on sexual activity, often lead to members moving to more private venues for sharing images and videos of child pornography as well as their plans for participation in a sex ring to abuse children. Hence, these crimes are able to operate without police knowledge, without police jurisdiction, and without intervention. In addition, with multiple law enforcement jurisdictions, varying laws, and few children identified by name, the prosecution of those responsible is extremely difficult and, therefore, an ongoing investigation (McCabe, 2017).

In considering the victims of sex tourism (or as our government defines it—the extraterritorial sexual exploitation of children), federal law prohibits any US citizen from traveling to a foreign country with the intent to engage in any form of sexual conduct with a minor as well as to help organize or assist another person in traveling for this purpose. However, each year, Americans are convicted of committing this crime, and in 2005, the convictions of a pediatrician, a dentist, and a university professor by the US government helped to dismiss the idea that those involved in these types of crimes were poor, uneducated, and feared criminals (Protect, 2016).

Historically, three of the most popular destinations for sex tourism are the countries of Thailand, Brazil, and Spain (Chawai, 2016). These are also countries that are often locations for educationally based study abroad trips for American high school and college students. Advertising for these child victims is often online through classified ad sites such as Craigslist, Back Page, and various dark net sites (Calder, 2004).

For clarity, the term *dark net* refers to a network that requires special access and is characterized by the anonymity of users and hosts to conceal illegal activities such as the production and distribution of illegal drugs, hidden financial accounts, or illegal sexual activities (McCabe, 2017). To avoid detection and facilitate child abuse, most dark net users utilize code words related to ordinary objects such as food to discuss the desired characteristics of children. For example, the food item *pasta* may represent a *young boy* and the food item *pizza* may represent a *young girl* (McCabe, 2017). Unfortunately, the relative ease and automation of international travel in today's society has led to an increase in sex trafficking. Thus, one cannot underestimate the impact of technology and the internet in the trafficking of persons for sexual exploitation.

Legislative Responses to Sex Trafficking

In response to cases of sex trafficking, legislative efforts have existed for over two decades. In addition, many nongovernmental organizations (NGOs) have been established to identify victims of sex trafficking and to provide assistance to those victims. However, when asked about the problem of sex trafficking, most individuals still have no idea that the criminal activity exists and especially that it exists in every country today.

During the 20th century, there was no single department or agency responsible for collecting data on sex trafficking (McCabe, 2008). Surprisingly, it was not the human rights groups or law enforcement that began to recognize this injustice, but rather, it was the business industry, concerned for the competition of labor, who prompted the awareness of the problem of human trafficking for labor (Bales, 2004). Later, when then-Secretary of State Colin Powell announced that monies acquired through human trafficking were used to support the activities of the 9–11 hijackers, legislative acts and law enforcement efforts began focusing on sex trafficking (McCabe, 2008).

In 2000, with an estimate of nearly 700,000 individuals trafficked annually worldwide, the United States Congress passed the Victims of Trafficking and Violence Protection Act of 2000, P.L. 106–386, commonly referred to as the Trafficking Victims Protection Act (TVPA). The TVPA mandated that the Secretary of State submit a report on severe forms of human trafficking to Congress on June 1 of that year. This report, which identifies countries as source, transit, and/or destination countries for human trafficking, has continued to be produced annually, citing a list of countries and their rankings in a tier classification system (McCabe, 2010). Specifically, those countries that fully abide by the TVPA's minimum standards for 'elimination of trafficking' are placed on Tier 1. Countries that do not fully comply but were making efforts to do so were placed in either Tier 2 or Tier 2 Watch categories, and Tier 3 countries are those countries not in compliance with the minimum of standards for the elimination of trafficking and appear to not be making any significant efforts to do so.

After the 2000 TVPA, other countries began antitrafficking efforts on a larger scale to address human trafficking as the United Nations Office on Drugs and Crime (UNODC) began focusing on strategies and policy development to prevent human trafficking and assist victims (UNODC, 2019). In 2003, then-President George W. Bush signed the amended Trafficking Victim Protection Reauthorization Act (TVPRA), which further supported government efforts to reduce human trafficking. In addition, and after the passing of the 2003 TVPRA, data began to be published in the annual Trafficking In Persons Report (on a limited basis) on cases of sex trafficking within various countries (McCabe, 2018). Legislative efforts from various countries have continued as more and more geographic locations attempt to identify and reduce cases of human trafficking. In the United States, the TVPRA has been reauthorized on multiple occasions, with the most recent in 2019 with its three-pronged approach of prevention, prosecution, and protection adopted globally. More specifically, during 2015–2019, an €11 million efforts by the European Union and the UN has provided resources to government authorities and civil organizations in 'hot spot' countries of Belarus, Brazil, Colombia, Egypt, Kyrgyz Republic Lao PDR, Mali, Morocco, Nepal, Niger, Pakistan, South Africa, and Ukraine (UNODC, 2019).

Summary

The United Nations has defined human trafficking as the recruitment, transfer, harboring, or receipt of persons by threat or use of force. The US State Department's Trafficking Protection Act (2000) identifies severe forms of human trafficking as (1) sex trafficking in which a commercial sex act is induced by force, fraud, or coercion, or in which the person induced to perform such an act has not attained 18 years of age or (2) the recruitment, harboring, transportation, provision, or obtaining of a person for labor or services through the use of force, fraud, or coercion for the purpose of subjection to involuntary servitude, peonage, debt bondage, or slavery. In most cases, individuals are trafficked for one of two main reasons: labor or sex. This chapter focused on the trafficking of individuals for sex or sex trafficking.

International estimates suggest that there are between 20 and 40 million victims of human trafficking annually, with many of these individuals victims of sex trafficking. Victims of sex trafficking usually become involved in sex trafficking through deception or coercion, with the destinations for many of the trafficking victims within urban areas or cities with large commercial trade centers. Unfortunately, it is within these densely populated areas that victims of sex trafficking and their traffickers can easily blend in and function unnoticed.

Explanation for sex trafficking include poverty, inequality, and family involvement. The United States is one of the most-reported destination countries for sex trafficking, as it is perceived by many of the poorer countries as the land of opportunity. Unfortunately, this appeal of the United States facilitates the criminal enterprise of sex trafficking.

The offenders of sex trafficking include those involved in the sex trafficking of the victim and the client of the sex trafficking victim. Due to the secrecy of this activity, little research exists on traffickers, and much of the information that does exist is based upon only a few cases (McCabe, 2018).

Poverty, inequality, corruption, and marketability all explain the consistency in cases of sex trafficking. In addition, an unwillingness by victims to report sex trafficking often results in the continued use of the virtual community to facilitate the criminal activity.

Finally, after the original 2000 TVPA (and ratified TVPRA), other countries began more focused antitrafficking efforts on a larger scale. After the passing of the 2003 TVPRA, data began to be published in the annual Trafficking In Persons Report on cases of sex trafficking within various countries. In addition, legislative efforts from various countries have continued in an attempt to identify and reduce cases of sex trafficking. However, the activity of sex trafficking is still often misunderstood and misidentified. Only though research and books such as this one will sex trafficking finally be understood, identified, and eliminated.

Discussion Questions

1. If human trafficking is a problem in essentially all countries, why are law enforcement efforts so limited?
2. Why is there often little public sympathy for adult victims of human trafficking?
3. Is it conceivable that a parent would allow one of their children to be a victim of sex trafficking to provide food for the others?
4. Why do you think sex trafficking continues and becomes even more profitable every year?
5. With so many crimes of concern in the United States, do we really have the time or the money to be concerned about a crime that largely occurs outside of the United States?

Postchapter Quiz

1. What are the two main the reasons for human trafficking?

    A. Sex and labor
    B. Adoptions and sex
    C. Human organs and sex
    D. Labor and human organs

2. What are two major US acts prohibiting human trafficking?

    A. TVPA and TIPs
    B. TVPA and TVPRA
    C. POLARIS and TVPA
    D. Protect Act and TVPA

3. How does technology facilitate sex trafficking?

    A. Promotes victims
    B. Connects victims and offenders
    C. Reduces the likelihood of detection
    D. All of the above

4. How is human trafficking different from human smuggling?

    A. Children are trafficked
    B. Only women are trafficked
    C. Force and coercion of victims
    D. They are the same

5. All of the following countries have been identified by the UN as 'hot spots' for sex trafficking except?

    A. Belarus
    B. Mali
    C. Niger
    D. USA

6. With severe cases of human trafficking, often _____ are victims.

    A. Wildlife
    B. Weapons
    C. Children
    D. Drugs

7. Transnational organized crime involves groups that _____.

    A. Are in Italy
    B. Operate without respect for geographic lines
    C. Are rarely involved in sex trafficking
    D. Operate within the boundaries of law

8. The term _____ was first used to identify human trafficking.

    A. white slavery
    B. black slavery
    C. smuggling
    D. immigration

9. All of the following except _____ are general characteristics of countries with significant problems with human trafficking.

    A. poverty
    B. inequality
    C. corruption
    D. equity among classes

10. In the US, addressing human trafficking is founded on the 3 P's, which include all of the following except:

    A. People
    B. Prevention
    C. Prosecution
    D. Protection

References

Anti-Slavery International. (2019). *Modern slavery factsheet*. Retrieved October 12, 2020, from www.antislavery.org/wp-content/uploads/2016/11/Modern-slavery-fact-sheet.pdf

Bales, K. (2004). *New slavery: A references handbook* (2nd ed.). Santa Barbara, CA: ABC-CL10.

Calder, M. (2004). *Child sexual abuse and the internet: Tracking the new frontier*. Dorset, UK: Russell House.

Chawai, A. (2016, December 18). The disturbing reality of human trafficking and children. *Huffington Post*. Retrieved October 19, 2016, from www.huffingtonpost.com/

Clawson, H., Dutch, H., Salomon, A., & Grace, L. (2009, December). *Study of HHS programs serving human trafficking victims*. Washington, DC: US Department of Health and Human Services (HHSP233200600001T).

Cockbain, E., & Bowers, K. (2019). Human trafficking for sex, labour, and domestic servitude: How do key trafficking types compare and what are their predictors? *Crime, Law and Social Change, 72*, 9–34.

Cullen, S. (2002). The miserable lives of mail order brides. *Women in Action, 3*, 6–9.

Deshpande, N., & Nour, N. (2013). Sex trafficking of women and girls. *Review of Obstetrics & Gynecology, 6*(1), 22–27.

Farr, K. (2004). *Sex trafficking: The global market in women and children*. New York: W.H. Freedman.

Federal Bureau of Investigation. (2020). *Transnational organized crime*. Retrieved November 3, 2020, from www.fbi.gov/investigate/organized-crime

Guinn, D., & Steglich, E. (2003). *Modern bondage: Sex trafficking in America*. Herndon, VA: Transnational.

International Labour Organization (ILO). (2014, May). *ILO says forced labour generates annual profits of US$ 150 Billion*. Retrieved October 12, 2020, from www.ilo.org/global/about-the-ilo/newsroom/news/WCMS_243201/lang--en/index.htm#:~:text=The%20ILO%20report%2C%20Profits%20and,work%2C%20agriculture%20and%20other%20economic

Internet Watch Foundation. (2020, November 9). Analyst's hunch leads to British schoolgirl's rescue from online child sexual abuse. Retrieved December 30, 2020, from www.iwf.org.uk/news/analyst-s-%E2%80%98hunch%E2%80%99-leads-to-british-school girl%E2%80%99s-rescue-from-online-child-sexual-abuse

Jonsson, S. (2018). The complex relationship between police corruption and sex trafficking in origin countries. *Journal of Human Trafficking, 5*(2), 109–129.

Kangaspunta, K. (2006, April). *Trafficking in persons: Global patterns*. Vienna, Austria: United Nations Office on Drugs and Crime.

Kragten-Heerdink, S., Dettmeijer-Vermeulen, C., & Korf, D. (2017). More than just "pushing and pulling": Conceptualizing identified human trafficking in the Netherlands. *Crime and Delinquency, 64*(13), 1–25.

Lee, E. (1966). A theory of migration. *Demography, 1*, 47–57.

McCabe, K. (2007). Spousal prostitution. In N. Jackson (Ed.), *Encyclopedia of domestic violence* (pp. 673–674). New York: Routledge.

McCabe, K. (2008). *The trafficking of persons: National and international responses*. New York: Peter Lang.

McCabe, K. (2017). *Protecting your children online*. Lanham, MD: Rowman and Littlefield.

McCabe, K. (2018). Common forms: Sex trafficking. In M. Burke (Ed.), *Human trafficking: Interdisciplinary perspectives* (2nd ed., pp. 122–138). New York: Routledge.

McCabe, K., & Manian, S. (2010). *Sex trafficking: A global perspective*. Lanham, MD: Lexington Books.

McCabe, K., & Murphy, D. (2016). *Child abuse—Today's issues*. Boca Raton, FL: Taylor & Francis.

McGinnis, E. (2004). *The horrifying reality for sex trafficking*. Washington, DC: Concerned Women for America. Retrieved November 12, 2006, from www.cwfa.org

Protect.org. (2016). *What is the magnitude of child exploitation?* Retrieved November 23, 2016, from www.protect.org/articles/what-is-the-magnitude-of-child-exploitation

Raymond, J., & Hughes, D. (2001). *Sex trafficking of women in the United States: International and domestic trends*. Amherst, MA: Coalition Against Trafficking in Women.

Tennis, T. (2020, June 9). Porn and human trafficking: The facts you need to know. *The Exodus Road*. Retrieved December 3, 2020, from https://blog.theexodusroad.com/porn-and-human-trafficking-the-facts-you-need-to-know

Toney-Butler, T., & Mittel, O. (2020, November 16). Human trafficking. *StatPearls*. Retrieved December 5, 2020, from www.ncbi.nlm.nih.gov/books/NBK430910/

UNODC. (2019). *EU-UNODC cooperation: Preventing and addressing human trafficking and migrant smuggling*. Retrieved December 30, 2020, from www.unodc.org/unodc/en/human-trafficking/glo-act2/Countries/eu-unodc-cooperation_-preventing-and-addressing-human-trafficking-and-migrant-smuggling.html

World Population Review. (2020). *Human trafficking statistics by state 2020*. Retrieved October 12, 2020, from https://worldpopulationreview.com/state-rankings/human-trafficking-statistics-by-state

5

COMMERCIAL SEXUAL EXPLOITATION OF CHILDREN

SPECIAL POPULATIONS AND SOCIOLOGICAL CONSIDERATIONS

ELIZABETH BOWMAN

Introduction

Certain populations of children and youth are at greater risk for being exploited by traffickers due to a lack of effective social safety nets that protect individuals with vulnerability to such exploitation. Sex trafficking, or the commercial sexual exploitation of children (CSEC), as defined by the TVPA, is any "commercial sex act induced by force, fraud, or coercion in which the person induced to perform such act has not attained 18 years of age" (Federal Victims of Trafficking and Violence Protection Act, TVPA, 2000) and annually impacts an estimated 10,000 children nationwide (Swaner et al., 2016). While human trafficking for the sexual commodification of human beings is an international concern, the current chapter will focus specifically on this issue in its domestic context, including cultural and economic factors unique to the United States that contribute to the problem. More specifically, this chapter will focus on the domestic CSEC of special populations including youth involved in child welfare systems, youth and adults who identify as LGBT, and those who are d/Deaf.

Through a review of the literature, this chapter will describe each population (i.e., child welfare involved, LGBT, and d/Deaf children and youth) in terms of demographics such as age, incidence of trafficking in the population, risk factors, and special considerations for intervention and prevention. The overall issue of trafficking risk within these special populations will be explored from a systems perspective, which conceptualizes vulnerability

DOI: 10.4324/9781003124672-6

within the context of societal supports such as mental health care, education and economic systems, and the accessibility of services to each group. It is important to note that children and youth who are in foster care or identify as LGBTQ and/or d/Deaf are not exploited because of their personal identities but rather that because of a lack of social acceptance, service accessibility, and overall support, these populations may become vulnerable to exploitation. Meaning this chapter will not emphasize the individual characteristics that make these populations easy targets but rather will focus on how social factors may allow CSEC to take place and what efforts can be made to reduce trafficking risk.

Chapter Learning Objectives

- Define vulnerability to exploitation within a social systems context that emphasizes societal accountability and service provision.
- Identify risk factors present in vulnerable populations that include children in foster care, children who are d/Deaf, and children who identify as LGBT.
- Utilizing relevant research in the field, recommend interventions and policies that support these populations and reduce exploitation opportunities.

Review of the Literature

While human trafficking can include forced labor, prostitution, and organ theft, the current chapter will focus on the commercial sexual exploitation of children (CSEC) of three identified vulnerable populations: persons who are involved with child welfare systems, those who identify as LGBT, and/or those who are d/Deaf. Human sex trafficking as defined by the United Nations (2004) Protocol to Prevent, Suppress, and Punish Trafficking in Persons is:

> the recruitment, transportation, transfer, harbouring or receipt of persons, by means of the threat or use of force or other forms of coercion, of abduction, of fraud, of deception, of the abuse of power or of a position of vulnerability or of the giving or receiving of payments or benefits to achieve the consent of a person having control over another person, for the purpose of exploitation. Exploitation shall include, at a minimum, the exploitation of the prostitution of others or other forms of sexual exploitation, forced labour or services, slavery or practices similar to slavery, servitude or the removal of organs.
>
> (p. 42)

It is important to note that in the United States, any person under the age of 18 who engages in any commercial sex act, such as prostitution, exotic dancing, or pornography, is a victim of sex trafficking (TVPA, 2000; Miller-Perrin & Wurtele, 2017; Nichols, 2016).

Estimates of trafficking victims in the United States and globally are a point of contention in research and practice. The exact number of individuals trafficked each year is unknown, though estimates ranged anywhere between 100,000 and 300,000 minor children. While the data suggests that the majority of trafficking victims are female, young adults or children, and/or have a history of homelessness (Nichols, 2016; Polaris Project, 2015), it is estimated that men and boys, particularly those who identify as LGBT or who have been coerced (i.e., trafficked) into nonconsensual homosexual prostitution, are less likely to report trafficking or ask for help because of a perceived social stigma as well as other issues related to reporting (Martinez & Kelle, 2013; Nichols, 2016; Polaris Project, 2015).

Studies have shown that there are particular risk factors for exploitation that may lead to individuals being trafficked. Specifically, these risk factors include: a person's identity as a female, sexual minority (i.e., LGBT), and/or Latinx or African American; lack of education; current or recent homelessness; a history of abuse (i.e., domestic violence, child abuse or neglect, sexual assault); and/or disability status (Choi, 2015; Fedina et al., 2019; Gibbs et al., 2018; Lalor & McElvaney, 2010; National Research Council [NRC], 2013). The common thread among many of these characteristics is the limited social or systems support available to those populations.

Because these victims are often targeted by traffickers due to a perceived vulnerability to exploitation, the common discourse focuses on this vulnerability. While this is not inherently wrong, this chapter seeks to emphasize social systems gaps that may enhance trafficking risk rather than focusing primarily on personal characteristics which make a person "at risk." In identifying factors relevant to consider in trafficking research and practice, vulnerability is relevant in terms of services (i.e., prevention and intervention efforts), but the presence of vulnerability (i.e., disability status, trauma history, mental health, gender identity, etc.) does not lead to victimization and exploitation in and of itself. Therefore, while discussing populations that may be more susceptible to trafficking victimization, vulnerabilities will be discussed as they relate to broader systemic issues.

In the sections to follow, the intersection of CSEC and populations experiencing child welfare system involvement and adverse childhood experiences; LGBT or sexual minority status, and hearing status will be explored.

Child Welfare and Child Maltreatment

Each year, 3.5 million children and teens come into contact with child welfare services in the United States (CWIG, 2017). Of these, approximately

415,000 are placed in out-of-home care (i.e., foster homes) due to various types of maltreatment in the home of origin (CWIG, 2017). Research has shown that there are disproportionately higher rates of African American and Latinx children removed from their homes when child welfare services investigate maltreatment allegations, and therefore, there is a higher percentage of these populations in out-of-home placements (CWIG, 2016). As previously discussed, children of color are more likely to be exploited by traffickers than white children, and children in foster care are much more likely to be trafficked than children not in care, with some studies showing that 50% to 90% of identified trafficking victims having a history of foster care placement (CWIG, 2017). The characteristics of children in foster care are relevant not because these populations are more predisposed to violence or sexual abuse but because the systemic marginalization of persons of color, girls, and low socioeconomic status suggests that the systems meant to protect these populations are inadequately responsive. It stands to reason, then, that the disproportionate representation of children of color in trafficking statistics may be related to this intersection of disproportionate representation in foster care rather than individual factors of race itself.

In fact, in a study of nursing care to trafficked children, Choi (2015) found that demographic characteristics and other individual factors were not significantly related to trafficking risk, while childhood maltreatment trauma and running away from home were the greatest predictors of trafficking victimization. Focusing on the individual demographic factors that may put a person at greater risk for exploitation is less appropriate here than focusing on the systems factors that may increase risk. Children and youth who are in foster care are at greater risk for being trafficked primarily due to:

- psychological monetization and foster care
- maltreatment and trauma history
- placement tracking and monitoring issues
- runaway status and/or homelessness.(Casey Family Programs, 2014; CWIG, 2017; Gibbs et al., 2018; Miller-Perrin & Wurtele, 2017; NRC, 2013)

While the argument can be made that trauma history or ACEs (adverse childhood experiences) are an individual characteristic, they are often the result of breakage in various community systems including mental health, substance abuse, child welfare, and economic systems.

Application of a conservation-of-resources theoretical framework can help to explain how experiencing trauma, maltreatment, and/or foster or group home placement can increase risk of CSEC. Certain materials, characteristics, conditions, and relationships—collectively called "resources"—are necessary to human life for an adequate sense of well-being. A lack of adequate resources can become a source of stress, as can the depletion of resources in the quest to maintain others (such as when emotional energy is depleted in the search for stable housing) (Hobfoll, 1989). Further, in order to maintain resources, some resources may need to be used, such as using emotional energy to seek out social support or financial resources to obtain stable housing. Children who have lost family members (either to death, abandonment, or child welfare removal), been maltreated, and/or had a lack of basic needs or a sense of love and attachment, have experienced a loss of resources. With each resource loss, it becomes more challenging to both maintain resources and to seek out and establish additional needed resources in the environment. Therapeutic intervention and environmental stability can reduce risk of exploitation and help to create internal (i.e., coping skills and resilience) and external resources (i.e., attachment figures, shelter, etc.) for children who have experienced trauma.

Using this theoretical framework, it is clear that children who have experienced trauma in the form of maltreatment or inadequate material or relational resources could be vulnerable to those who offer love and belonging, food and shelter, or other basic human needs. While this conceptualization of the issue does not address how to approach the exploiters directly, it does illustrate how children and youth become vulnerable to CSEC, how systems (criminal justice, child welfare, education, economic, etc.) can provide various resources to bolster protective factors, and how population needs and systemic gaps intersect to create the space in which traffickers thrive.

In discussing systems issues, the psychology of monetization for children in out-of-home care has also been shown to play a significant role in the transition from foster child to trafficking victim. Foster and group homes are provided monthly stipends ranging by state from $300 to $1,600 for the care of a single child (North American Council on Adoptable Children, 2016). Studies have shown that children and youth sometimes struggle to connect with their foster families when the youth feels like a commodity (Casey Family Programs, 2014). This foundation of relational distrust makes social support and connection challenging, both of which are protective factors that may reduce risk of trafficking. This is exacerbated by the presence of the check itself, which is attached to the relationship and the child's value in the home, meaning that the absence of genuine relationships in the foster home combined with the preconceived notion on the part of the child that his or her value is financial puts foster-care youth at an increased risk of CSEC.

Children who are in foster care have been shown to have varying degrees of trauma resulting from various forms of maltreatment including physical abuse, sexual abuse, and/or neglect (Franchino-Olsen et al., 2020; Landers et al., 2017). Trauma that stems from maltreatment in particular can result in a loss of resources such as self-worth, love and attachment, food and shelter, and/or personal safety and increases the potential for exploitation (Fedina et al., 2019; NRC, 2013; Reid, 2016). Specifically, sexual abuse can normalize sexual contact with adults and sexual activity at young ages (NRC, 2013; Lalor & McElvaney, 2010; Landers et al., 2017; Wilson & Widom, 2008) and often occurs in the context of neglect. Neglect, by definition, is characterized by a deficit in basic needs and/or safety in the home; children may not have access to food, shelter, education, or supervision when being neglected by their primary caregiver (CWIG, 2017). Therefore, both neglect and sexual abuse, which may overlap for a maltreated child, lead to an absence of resources, which makes it easier for a seemingly trustworthy adult to coerce the child into CSEC by meeting those basic needs. In fact, the most common traffickers who engage in CSEC are family members or romantic partners (Bigelsen & Vuotto, 2013; Murphy, 2016; Rosenblat, 2014), and it is not surprising that having a family member or close friend in sex work increases a child's risk of sexual exploitation (Fedina et al., 2019; Franchino-Olsen et al., 2020).

When a child is removed from the home of origin due to maltreatment and placed in a foster or group home setting, CSEC risk may actually increase for a number of reasons. First, the maltreatment history continues to be present and impacts the child's sense of safety, attachment, and other resource deficits, creating vulnerabilities that could be exploited (Fedina et al., 2019; Macias-Konstantopoulos et al., 2015; Murphy, 2016). Second, the development of resilience and protective factors that reduce the risk of exploitation after maltreatment have been shown to be influenced by having a connection with a caring adult (Bigelsen & Vuotto, 2013; CWIG, 2017), which may not always be present in foster or group-home settings. This lack of family-like connections and/or maltreatment in the foster care system may contribute to the risk of victimization and many other poor psychosocial outcomes (Franchino-Olsen et al., 2020; Hobbs et al., 1999).

Additional research has shown that youth placed in group homes may be at greater risk for CSEC than those in foster homes due to less supervision (supervisions is usually provided by an employed staff rather than a family-like caregiver), the lack of an attachment figure, and the presence of other trafficking victims who are required to recruit by their traffickers (Fedina et al., 2019; CWIG, 2017; Landers et al., 2017; Walker, 2013). Traffickers often rely on peer recruitment to find more victims, coercing their current victims into recruiting other children and youth into CSEC through peer pressure. The lack of supervision and number of children with various traumas in group home settings makes the environment ripe for further trafficking (Macias-Konstantopoulos et al., 2015; Reid, 2016).

Another added risk factor in child welfare system involvement for maltreated children is related to inadequate placement tracking and supervision by child welfare agencies. Each time a child moves from one foster or group home to another, federal law requires that the child welfare agency update placement information and ensure monitoring of the child in the new home. However, issues with monitoring are common due to heavy caseloads and inadequate agency resources, particularly as youth may not feel comfortable making disclosures when there is a limited relationship with the social worker and/or the caregiver is present for caseworker meetings (Manigault, 2020). It is critical that social workers who meet with youth in foster or group homes make efforts to do so outside the presence of the caregiver to ensure youth are able to feel safe making disclosures about maltreatment, including CSEC.

Physical and sexual abuse are commonly linked to runaway behavior for children involved with child welfare (Gibbs et al., 2018). However, youth who run away from the home are also much more likely to be victims of CSEC either through recruitment by a peer or romantic partner or through survival-sex exploitation (Biehal & Wade, 2000; Fedina et al., 2019; Gibbs et al., 2018; Murphy, 2016). Homeless youth have likely experienced maltreatment, and this resource deficit becomes more complex as youth struggle to meet basic needs such as food and shelter. Traffickers, those who coerce youth into sexual acts for financial gain, and solicitors, those who exploit youth for sexual gratification, both promise to meet these resource deficits including love, attachment, food and shelter, etc. (Casey Family Programs, 2014; CWIG, 2017; Gibbs et al., 2018; NRC, 2013; Reid, 2016). In a study of homeless youth in New York City's Covenant House program, Bigelsen and Vuotto (2013) found that half of homeless teens surveyed engaged in commercial sexual activity due to lack of a place to stay and that this need was exacerbated by a lack of income and/or a "caring supportive adult" in the youth's life. It is important to note that the sample in this case was primarily teenagers over the age of 18 due to the requirements of the program. However, homelessness has been shown in multiple studies to be a risk factor for exploitation in both children and adults (Fedina et al., 2019; Gibbs et al., 2018; Murphy, 2016).

Survival sex, which is exploitation in its own right and, for minor children, constitutes CSEC, is common for homeless youth as a means of meeting basic resource needs. The primary difference in survival sex compared to other types of CSEC is that the child is exploited only by the solicitor in the absence of a trafficker rather than by both trafficker and solicitor (Bigelsen & Vuotto, 2013; Miller-Perrin & Wurtele, 2017; Murphy, 2016), though there is some fluidity between survival sex and "being pimped," as one exploitative relationship has been shown to be related to the other (Bigelsen & Vuotto, 2013; Nichols, 2016). For LGBT youth, whom we will examine in the next section, survival sex is the most common type of CSEC exploitation described in the literature.

LGBT Children and Youth

Lesbian, gay, bisexual, transgender, and other non–heterosexual-identifying youth are at risk for CSEC at rates greater than heterosexual peers for a variety of reasons. LGBT youth are more likely: to be homeless; have experienced sexual abuse, sexual violence, and bullying; have limited social supports, economic resources, and employment opportunities due to social stigma and marginalization; and to lack access to equitable social services (Hogan & Roe-Sepowitz, 2020; Martinez & Kelle, 2013; NRC, 2013; Polaris, 2015; Tomasiewicz, 2018). Though additional research is needed on this understudied population, current numbers suggest that male youth are also less likely to report being trafficked and other types of sexual exploitation by male solicitors due to a perceived stigma (Goździak & Bump, 2008; Martinez & Kelle, 2013).

Homelessness alone is a significant risk factor for CSEC; however, youth who also identify as LGBT have been found to have higher rates of commercial exploitation including trafficking and survival sex than homeless peers who are heterosexual (Hogan & Roe-Sepowitz, 2020; Murphy, 2016; Polaris, 2015; Tomasiewicz, 2018). Conceptualizing this issue in terms of conservation-of-resource theory, LGBT youth are likely to experience bullying in school, sexual abuse and sexual violence, and social stigma all based on their sexual orientation, identity, and/or gender expression (Hogan & Roe-Sepowitz, 2020; Polaris, 2015; Xian et al., 2017), leading to reduced personal resources and increased stress. LGBT youth are also often victims of family rejection, sometimes then facing homelessness after being forced out of their homes by family members or by running away (Polaris, 2015; Xian et al., 2017), which leaves them with a resource deficit of both basic survival needs as well as of love and acceptance.

Despite these resource deficits, it has been found that LGBT youth, particularly those who are male, gender nonconforming (GNC), or transgender, are less likely than heterosexual female peers to have a trafficker but typically are exploited directly by solicitors through survival sex (Murphy, 2016; Nichols, 2016; Polaris, 2015; Tomasiewicz, 2018). The stigma of homosexual survival sex adds to the social perception that LGBT youth who engage in commercial sex acts are not "true victims" or "deserving of help" (Boukli & Renz, 2019), and therefore, LGBT youth who are sexually exploited may not identify themselves as victims and/or have less access to supportive services when help is sought. The presence of personal resource deficits (i.e., self-esteem, trauma, attachment, social capital) combined with environmental resource deficits (i.e., homelessness, poverty, inaccessibility of intervention services) creates a perfect storm of victimhood in which the individual is not seen as a victim by self or society, and therefore help is not offered or sought, leaving solicitors and/or traffickers with unencumbered access to exploit the child who has a lack of protective factors to prevent exploitation.

Among LGBT youth, transgender and GNC youth face particular social stigma such as a lack of homeless shelters and social services access, in addition to employment discrimination. This actual or perceived lack of employment options may lead to a sense of limited opportunities to meet economic needs (Bigelsen & Vuotto, 2013; Murphy, 2016; Nichols, 2016; Tomasiewicz, 2018). Multiple studies have found that homeless transgender youth are especially vulnerable to CSEC due to the intersectional discrimination by family and social supports, community service providers, employers, and society as a whole (Bigelsen & Vuotto, 2013; Nichols, 2016; NRC, 2013).

Complex and interrelated legal issues intersect in the CSEC experiences of LGBT youth. For example, LGBT youth are overrepresented in juvenile justice detention for prostitution charges, despite Safe Harbor laws that are meant to protect trafficked youth (Polaris, 2015). Safe Harbor laws have been established in a majority of states across the US and seek to prevent legal consequences for minor children who have engaged in any commercial sexual activity, instead connecting the child with supportive services including child welfare and/or mental health (NRC, 2013; Polaris, 2015). Because of the stigma associated with survival sex as a type of CSEC and the likelihood of LGBT youth to be exploited in this way, they are at greater risk of prosecution despite the presence of Safe Harbor laws.

d/Deaf Children and Youth

In the face of little empirical literature regarding CSEC of d/Deaf children and youth, the focus in this chapter shifts to risk factors for exploitation. Though homelessness is a significant risk factor for CSEC among youth, it has been shown that homelessness among d/Deaf youth is less common than among hearing youth (Crowe, 2019), suggesting that incidents of CSEC are more likely to take place in the family home by people known to the child.

Deaf children are disproportionately affected by sexual abuse and other types of maltreatment in the home compared to hearing children. Sexual abuse, in particular, is two to three times higher in populations of d/Deaf children and youth compared to hearing (Kvam, 2004; Sullivan et al., 1987; Wakeland, 2017). The impact of sexual abuse is exacerbated by challenges in reporting including communication barriers in disclosure, a lack of awareness with regard to what sexual abuse is, and a sense of guilt and/or shame. Often, service providers in child welfare, health care, law enforcement, and social service or mental health agencies are not fluent in ASL or able to communicate directly with d/Deaf children. While interpretation may be requested by providers who are knowledgeable about ADA requirements for communication access, children who have experienced maltreatment trauma may be hesitant to disclose, and both comfort and timing are critical (Jones, 2017; Kvam, 2004). Additionally, when sexual abuse takes place at the hands of a relative or other trusted adult, children may not be aware that the activity constitutes maltreatment (Job, 2004) and/or may feel a sense of guilt about reporting, particularly if there are limited other social supports (Kvam, 2004; Titus, 2010).

It has been shown that incidences of childhood neglect and physical and sexual abuse are higher in populations of d/Deaf adults than hearing peers (Titus, 2010; Wakeland, 2017). As there is an increased risk of commercial sexual exploitation of children and youth in the face of maltreatment, it is likely that d/Deaf children and youth experience CSEC at a rate higher than the general population. In a study of minor sex trafficking of girls with disabilities, Franchino-Olsen et al. (2020) found that girls with disabilities had a higher rate of commercial sexual exploitation than hearing peers; more severe physical disabilities were associated with significantly higher rates of trafficking.

It has been noted that internationally, d/Deaf women are disproportionally trafficked for both sex and labor (Withers, 2017). However, with little research on this topic and unclear estimates of commercially exploited children in the overall US population, it is unknown how many d/Deaf children and youth may be trafficking victims domestically. Given the presence of significant risk factors including social isolation, communication barriers, sexual abuse and maltreatment, and reporting barriers, d/Deaf children and youth are vulnerable to trafficking, and additional research is needed to determine the scope of this problem.

Service accessibility continues to be a significant barrier to prevention as well as intervention with trafficking victims of varying cultural and linguistic backgrounds. In the section to follow, practice implications for how to best serve these three special populations in CSEC work will be discussed.

Implications for Practice
Children and adolescents who are sexually exploited for commercial gain come from various demographic backgrounds, and much of the literature has focused on their shared personal characteristics that leave them vulnerable to this type of exploitation. This chapter has provided a review of both the factors that may contribute to this vulnerability such as lack of personal and societal resources. System and societal dysfunction should be heavily considered in the discussion around CSEC, as the social safety nets of juvenile justice, child welfare, healthcare, education, and family and economic systems often fall short, leading to exploitation vulnerability. Both individual issues in terms of personal factors as well as social systems issues are important to be factored into the discourse. In order to best serve minor children who may be vulnerable to CSEC, specifically those who are involved with child welfare systems, identify as LGBT, or are d/Deaf, certain considerations must be made.

Terminology, Stigma, and Self-Identity

The terms "victim" and "survivor" are both used within the literature on CSEC. "Victim" is often a term used to describe those who are currently being exploited, while "survivor" has traditionally been reserved to those who have in some way overcome this traumatic experience (NRC, 2013). Both terms are needed in practice, but further examination of these terms is needed in the empirical literature, particularly as it is conceptualized by victims/survivors themselves. Additionally, this chapter has briefly discussed the idea of more versus less deserving victims, but the deconstruction of the social ideas behind victimhood and vulnerability continues to be needed in trafficking literature and practice. Most cases of CSEC do not involve children who are kidnapped by strangers and held against their will but rather those who are taken advantage of by trusted adults and otherwise look and operate like typical children (Bigelsen & Vuotto, 2013; Murphy, 2016; NRC, 2013).

Research shows that many children and youth do not identify themselves as being sexually exploited even when their experiences meet TVPA definitions of commercial sexual exploitation (Murphy, 2016; Reid, 2016). There is significant social stigma attached to commercial sexual activity for both those who choose sex work as a profession and those who are exploited. This social stigma and identity, combined with the absence of social support, isolate exploited children, particularly those with histories of maltreatment, foster care involvement, LGBT identities, and/or who are d/Deaf. It is critical for practitioners and policy makers who focus on CSEC to address this stigma and raise public awareness of what criminal sexual exploitation really looks like so that youth are better recognized in situations in which they are being exploited.

Raising public awareness about CSEC would also challenge some of the justice system dysfunction that permits the prosecution of adolescents who are prostituted. While Safe Harbor laws protect youth in many states, approximately 14 states still do not have laws protecting youth who have been prostituted (Polaris, 2015). This means that adolescents in these states often face criminal prosecution for engaging in survival sex with adult solicitors or when prostituted by adult traffickers. It is critical that criminal justice workers and policy makers change this practice and ensure the safety of youth through diversion programs that address the mental and physical health, shelter and safety, and other needs of commercially exploited youth (Casey Family Programs, 2014; Martinez & Kelle, 2013).

The identification of certain risk factors by child welfare providers can also mitigate the rates of adolescents involved in CSEC. Risk factors for children who have been involved with child welfare systems include the experience of maltreatment, early childhood sexual abuse, and limited social support from caring adults (Choi, 2015; Gibbs et al., 2018; Fedina et al., 2019). Therefore, child welfare providers who work with children who are in out-of-home care or in either foster or group-home settings should:

- Engage both casework staff and foster/group-home caregivers in training to identify child sex trafficking and how to effectively provide support (Casey Family Programs, 2014; CWIG, 2017)
- Include screening and data collection in child welfare intake to ensure children are referred to treatment and incidence of CSEC is documented (CWIG, 2017)
- Refer to mental health and substance abuse treatment to address the presence of substance use disorders, depression, anxiety, trauma or PTSD, and suicidal ideation as needed for identified trafficking victims (Barnert et al., 2017; Le et al., 2018; Whaling et al., 2020)
- Partner with area clinicians and victim advocates who provide supportive services such as individual or group therapy (Casey Family Programs, 2014; Middleton et al., 2018)
- Ensure full medical evaluations that assess the presence of STIs, HIV, and/or pregnancy as well as rape and sexual assault (Barnert et al., 2017; Le et al., 2018)
- Refer to existing or develop programs that facilitate long-term connections with a trusted adult (i.e., mentoring, foster parent, teacher, etc.) to increase social support networks, which reduces CSEC risk (O'Brien, 2018; Reid, 2016)
- Address social stigma by raising public awareness of commercial sexual exploitation in all its forms, and work with youth to reduce stigmatized self-identity (Reid, 2016)

Cultural factors may also impact whether youth are deemed "deserving" of intervention and the accessibility of services. This chapter has focused on two cultural groups: LGBT and d/Deaf, each of which have different needs in service accessibility. Specific recommendations for provider engagement and policy work with LGBT victims of CSEC include:

- Providers (i.e., caseworkers, shelter staff, healthcare and juvenile justice workers, etc.) should engage multidisciplinary teams to ensure service equitability for youth who are LGBT including trauma-focused, culturally sensitive services.
- Staff training should take place in shelters, healthcare facilities, child welfare and juvenile justice agencies and include elements of gay and lesbian social norms and culture, as well as the specific exploitation considerations for male, GNC, and transgender youth (i.e., being exploited by solicitors more commonly than traffickers; survival sex; stigma for males) (Whaling et al., 2020).

- Outreach for commercially exploited youth should include:

  o Education about healthy sexuality and relationships including physiology, definitions of sexual assault and exploitation, and partner violence, as well as safety planning tips and how and where to get help for self or friends (Murphy, 2016; Polaris, 2015)
  o Confidential identification and tracking of LGBT youth in agencies
  o Job training that includes educational programs, financial education, supportive employment, and which incorporates how to avoid dangerous job listings or those that may be trafficking in disguise (Murphy, 2016; Reid, 2016; Whaling et al., 2020)
  o Homelessness prevention, which includes ensuring access to shelters for transgender and GNC youth (Greeson et al., 2019; Whaling et al., 2020; Murphy, 2016)

- Policy makers and advocates to engage in assessment of social institutions (i.e., education, economic support and welfare programs, mental health, healthcare, criminal justice, child welfare, etc.) to determine if there are service gaps and/or discriminatory practices that ultimately exclude or target LGBT youth, increasing susceptibility to exploitation (Nichols, 2016; Xian et al., 2017).

For providers and advocates working with d/Deaf children and youth involved in CSEC, additional considerations include:

- Providers in criminal justice, child welfare, education, and other social institutions should engage in training for providing services to d/Deaf children and youth that includes:

  o Education about the heightened risk of maltreatment including neglect and physical and sexual abuse (Titus, 2010; Wakeland, 2017)
  o Information about how to interview the child directly using interpreters rather than talking to a hearing parent who may be the abuser or trafficker (Bowman, 2018; Jones, 2017; Kvam, 2004)
  o Knowledge of community resources for support including agencies which work with d/Deaf victims of CSEC

- Education programs at schools for the d/Deaf and other providers of services for d/Deaf children and youth which, similar to LGBT programs:

  o Provide education about healthy sexuality and relationships including physiology, definitions of sexual abuse and exploitation, and partner violence, as well as how and where to get help for self or friends including community resources (Job, 2004; Murphy, 2016) o Confidential identification and tracking of d/Deaf children and youth who are connected to each agency and identified as CSEC victims (Franchino-Olsen et al., 2020)

o Linguistically accessible job training that includes educational programs (i.e., provided in American Sign Language), financial education, and supportive employment and that incorporates training in how to avoid dangerous job listings or those that may be trafficking in disguise (Murphy, 2016; Reid, 2016; Whaling et al., 2020; Withers, 2017)

Research clearly shows that the commercial sexual exploitation of children from vulnerable populations requires further investigation and shifts in practice. Finigan-Carr et al. (2019) proposed a traumagenic social-ecological framework for CSEC that outlines a synergistic model for understanding the intersection of individual vulnerabilities, social norms and societal factors, and various environmental conditions including interpersonal relationships in trafficking and exploitation. Children and youth may have personal and social conditions that increase vulnerability to exploitation, such as being in foster care, LGBT, or d/Deaf. However, social systems, beliefs, and supports are meant to protect children and youth, particularly those who are vulnerable. Providers should take a step back to see the broader picture of CSEC and understand that being a homeless or LGBT youth or a foster-care runaway or a d/Deaf sexual abuse survivor does not in and of itself create the conditions for exploitation. Social stigma, lack of service access, and many other factors turn vulnerability into victimhood. Intervention efforts focusing on the individual are not enough; social systems and societal conditions must be targeted in efforts to protect children and youth from exploitation.

Discussion Questions

1. How do specific social factors allow commercial sexual exploitation of children to take place?
2. What positive social changes could be developed based on our knowledge of access to resources in at-risk groups?
3. In what ways can we work to reduce social stigma surrounding individuals that were victims of sex trafficking?
4. What efforts can be made to reduce trafficking within the United States? Consider individual efforts and policy within your response.

References

Barnert, E., Iqbal, Z., Bruce, J., Anoshiravani, A., Kolhatkar, G., & Greenbaum, J. (2017). Commercial sexual exploitation and sex trafficking of children and adolescents: A narrative review. *Academic Pediatrics, 17*(8), 825–829. https://doi.org/10.1016/j.acap.2017.07.009

Biehal, N., & Wade, J. (2000). Going missing from residential and foster care: Linking biographies and contexts. *The British Journal of Social Work, 30*(2), 211–225. https://doi.org/10.1093/bjsw/30.2.211

Bigelsen, J., & Vuotto, S. (2013). *Homelessness, survival sex and human trafficking: As experienced by the youth of Covenant House New York.* Retrieved from https://humantraffickinghotline.org/sites/default/files/Homelessness%2C%20Survival%20 Sex%2C%20and%20Human%20Trafficking%20-%20Covenant%20House%20NY.pdf

Boukli, A., & Renz, F. (2019). Deconstructing the lesbian, gay, bisexual, transgender victim of sex trafficking: Harm, exceptionality and religion—Sexuality tensions. *International Review of Victimology, 25*(1), 71–90. https://doi.org/10.1177/0269758018772670

Bowman, M. E. (2018). The grand challenges of social work: Deaf children in the child welfare system. *Child and Youth Services Review, 88*, 348–353. https://doi.org/10.1016/j.childyouth.2018.03.034

Casey Family Programs. (2014). *Addressing child sex trafficking from a child welfare perspective.* Retrieved from www.casey.org/media/child-sex-trafficking.pdf

Child Welfare Information Gateway. (2016). *Racial disproportionality and disparity in child welfare.* Washington, DC: U.S. Department of Health and Human Services, Children's Bureau.

Child Welfare Information Gateway. (2017). *Human trafficking and child welfare: A guide for child welfare agencies.* Washington, DC: U.S. Department of Health and Human Services, Children's Bureau.

Choi, K. R. (2015). Risk factors for domestic minor sex trafficking in the United States: A literature review. *Journal of Forensic Nursing, 11*(2), 66–76. https://doi.org/10.1097/JFN.0000000000000072

Crowe, T. V. (2019). Deaf child and adolescent consumers of public behavioral health services. *The Journal of Deaf Studies and Deaf Education, 24*(2), 57–64. https://doi.org/10.1093/deafed/eny036

Fedina, L., Williamson, C., & Perdue, T. (2019). Risk factors for domestic child sex trafficking in the United States. *Journal of Interpersonal Violence, 34*(13), 2653–2673. https://doi.org/10.1177/0886260516662306

Finigan-Carr, N. M., Johnson, M. H., Pullmann, M. D., et al. (2019). A traumagenic social ecological framework for understanding and intervening with sex trafficked children and youth. *Child Adolescent Social Work Journal, 36*, 49–63. https://doi.org/10.1007/s10560-018-0588-7

Franchino-Olsen, H., Silverstein, H. A., Kahn, N. F., & Martin, S. L. (2020). Minor sex trafficking of girls with disabilities. *International Journal of Human Rights in Healthcare, 13*(2), 97–108. https://doi.org/10.1108/IJHRH-07-2019-0055

Gibbs, D. A., Feinberg, R. K., Dolan, M., Latzman, N. E., Misra, S., & Domanico, R. (2018). *Report to congress: The child welfare system response to sex trafficking of children.* Washington, DC: U.S. Department of Health and Human Services, Administration for Children and Families.

Gibbs, D. A., Henninger, A. M., Tueller, S. J., & Kluckman, M. N. (2018). Human trafficking and the child welfare population in Florida. *Children and Youth Services Review, 88*, 1–10. https://doi.org/10.1016/j.childyouth.2018.02.045

Goździak, E. M., & Bump, M. N. (2008). *Data and research on human trafficking: Bibliography of research-based literature*. Washington, DC: U.S. Department of Justice.

Greeson, J. K. P., Treglia, D., Wolfe, D. S., & Wasch, S. (2019). Prevalence and correlates of sex trafficking among homeless and runaway youths presenting for shelter services. *Social Work Research, 43*(2), 91–100. https://doi.org/10.1093/swr/svz001

Hobbs, G. F., Hobbs, C. J., & Wynne, J. M. (1999). Abuse of children in foster and residential care. *Child Abuse & Neglect, 23*(12), 1239–1252. https://doi.org/10.1016/s0145-2134(99)00096-4

Hobfoll, S. (1989). Conservation of resources: A new attempt at conceptualizing stress. *The American Psychologist, 44*(3), 513–524. https://doi.org/10.1037/0003-066X.44.3.513

Hogan, K. A., & Roe-Sepowitz, D. (2020). LGBTQ+ homeless young adults and sex trafficking vulnerability. *Journal of Human Trafficking, 1*(1). https://doi.org/10.1080/23322705.2020.1841985

Job, J. (2004). Factors involved in the ineffective dissemination of sexuality information to individuals who are Deaf or hard of hearing. *American Annals of the Deaf, 149*(3), 264–273. Retrieved from www.jstor.org/stable/26234671

Jones, S. (2017). Enablers of help-seeking for Deaf and disabled children following abuse and barriers to protection: A qualitative study. *Child & Family Social Work, 22*(2), 762–771. https://doi.org/10.1111/cfs.12293

Kvam, M. H. (2004). Sexual abuse of Deaf children: A retrospective analysis of the prevalence and characteristics of childhood sexual abuse among Deaf adults in Norway. *Child Abuse & Neglect, 28*(3), 241–251. https://doi.org/10.1016/j.chiabu.2003.09.017

Lalor, K., & McElvaney, R. (2010). Child sexual abuse, links to later sexual exploitation/highrisk sexual behavior, and prevention/treatment programs. *Trauma, Violence, & Abuse, 11*(4), 159–177. https://doi.org/10.1177/1524838010378299

Landers, M., McGrath, K., Johnson, M. H., Armstrong, M. I., & Dollard, N. (2017). Baseline characteristics of dependent youth who have been commercially sexually exploited: Findings from a specialized treatment program. *Journal of Child Sexual Abuse, 26*(6), 692–709. https://doi.org/10.1080/10538712.2017.1323814

Le, P. D., Ryan, N., Rosenstock, Y., & Goldmann, E. (2018). Health issues associated with commercial sexual exploitation and sex trafficking of children in the United States: A systematic review. *Behavioral Medicine, 44*(3), 219–233. https://doi.org/10.1080/08964289.2018.1432554

Macias-Konstantopoulos, W. L., Munroe, D., Purcell, G., Tester, K., Burke, T. F, & Ahn, R. (2015). The commercial sexual exploitation and sex trafficking of minors in the Boston metropolitan area: Experiences and challenges faced by front-line providers and other stakeholders. *Journal of Applied Research on Children: Informing Policy for Children at Risk, 6*(1), 1–21. Retrieved from https://digitalcommons.library.tmc.edu/childrenatrisk/vol6/iss1/4

Manigault, S. A. (2020). *Child welfare workers perceptions of their competencies at detecting and reporting abuse of foster children* (Walden dissertations and doctoral studies). https://scholarworks.waldenu.edu/dissertations/9180

Martinez, O., & Kelle, G. (2013). Sex trafficking of LGBT individuals. *International Law News, 42*(4), 1–7.

Middleton, J. S., Gattis, M. N., Frey, L. M., & Roe-Sepowitz, D. (2018). Youth experiences survey (YES): Exploring the scope and complexity of sex trafficking in a sample of youth experiencing homelessness. *Journal of Social Service Research, 44*(2), 141–157. https://doi.org/ 10.1080/01488376.2018.1428924

Miller-Perrin, C., & Wurtele, S. K. (2017). Sex trafficking and the commercial sexual exploitation of children. *Women & Therapy, 40*(1–2), 123–151. https://doi.org/10.1080/02703149.2016.1210963

Murphy, L. T. (2016). *Labor and sex trafficking among homeless youth.* New Orleans, LA: Loyola University Modern Slavery Research Project. Retrieved from https://nspn.memberclicks.net/assets/docs/NSPN/labor%20and%20sex%20trafficking%2 0among%20home less%20youth.pdf

National Research Council. (2013). *Confronting commercial sexual exploitation and sex trafficking of minors in the United States.* Washington, DC: The National Academies Press.

Nichols, A. (2016). *Sex trafficking in the United States: Theory, research, policy, and practice.* New York: Columbia University Press.

North American Council on Adoptable Children. (2016). *Summary of state adoption assistance programs.* Retrieved from www.nacac.org/help/adoption-assistance/adoption-assistance-us/all-states-at-a-glance/

O'Brien, J. E. (2018). "Sometimes, somebody just needs somebody—Anybody—to care:" The power of interpersonal relationships in the lives of domestic minor sex trafficking survivors. *Child Abuse & Neglect, 81,* 1–11. https://doi.org/10.1016/j.chiabu.2018. 04.010

Polaris. (2015). *Human trafficking issue brief: Task forces.* Retrieved from https://polarisproject.org/sites/default/files/2015%20Task%20Forces%20Issue%20 Brief%20Final.pdf

Reid, J. A. (2016) Entrapment and enmeshment schemes used by sex traffickers. *Sexual Abuse, 28*(6):491–511. https://doi.org/10.1177/1079063214544334

Rosenblat, K. (2014). Determining the vulnerability factors, lures and recruitment methods used to entrap American children into sex trafficking. *Sociology and Criminology, 2*(1), 1–15. http://dx.doi.org/10.4172/2375-4435.1000108

Sullivan, P. M., Vernon, M., & Scanlan, J. M. (1987). Sexual abuse of Deaf youth. *American Annals of the Deaf, 132*(4), 256–262. https://doi.org/10.1353/aad.2012.0614

Swaner, R., Labriola, M., Rempel, M., Walker, A., & Spadafore, J. (2016). *Youth involvement in the sex trade: A national study.* New York: Center for Court Innovation. Retrieved from www.courtinnovation.org/sites/default/files/documents/Youth%20Involvement%20 in%20the%20Sex%20Trade_3.pdf

Titus, J. (2010). The nature of victimization among youths with hearing loss in substance abuse treatment. *American Annals of the Deaf, 155*(1), 19–30. https://doi.org/10.1353/ aad.0.0127

Tomasiewicz, M. L. (2018). *Sex trafficking of transgender and gender nonconforming youth in the United States.* Chicago, IL: Loyola University School of Law Center for the Human Rights of Children.

United Nations. (2004). *United Nations protocol to prevent, suppress, and punish trafficking in persons.* Retrieved from www.unodc.org/documents/treaties/UNTOC/Publications/ TOC%20Convention/TOCebook-e.pdf

United States of America: Victims of Trafficking and Violence Protection Act of 2000 [United States of America], Public Law 106–386 [H.R. 3244], 28 October 2000. Retrieved from www.refworld.org/docid/3ae6b6104.html

Wakeland, A. (2017). What is the prevalence of abuse in the Deaf/hard of hearing population? *The Journal of Forensic Psychiatry & Psychology, 29*(3), 434–454. https://doi.org/10. 1080/14789949.2017.1416659

Walker, K. (2013). *Ending the commercial sexual exploitation of children: A call for multisystem collaboration in California.* Child Welfare Council. Retrieved from www.youthlaw.org/ fileadmin/ncyl/youthlaw/publications/Ending-CSEC-A-Call-for-MultiSystem_Col laboration-in-CA.pdf

Whaling, K. M., der Sarkissian, A., Sharkey, J., & Akoni, L. C. (2020). Featured counter-trafficking program: Resiliency Interventions for Sexual Exploitation (RISE). *Child Abuse & Neglect,* 1–4. https://doi.org/10.1016/j.chiabu.2019.104139

Wilson, H. W., & Widom, C. S. (2008). An examination of risky sexual behavior and HIV in victims of child abuse and neglect: A 30-year follow-up. *Health Psychology*, *27*(2), 149–58. https://doi.org/10.1037/0278-6133.27.2.149

Withers, M. (2017). *The underrecognized victims of trafficking: Deaf women*. Retrieved from www.psychologytoday.com/us/blog/modern-day-slavery/201709/the-underrecognized-victims-trafficking-Deaf-women

Xian, K., Chock, S., & Dwiggins, D. (2017). LGBTQ youth and vulnerability to sex trafficking. In M. Chisolm-Straker & H. Stoklosa (Eds.), *Human trafficking is a public health issue*. New York: Springer.

SECTION II
A CLOSER LOOK

6

SOCIOLOGICAL PERSPECTIVE

UNDERLYING CAUSES

MELISSA SWAUGER, KAY SNYDER, THOMAS NOWAK, AND MARCI COTTINGHAM

In this chapter, we use theory and research from sociology to better understand the complex ways that political, economic, and other sociocultural factors interact within and across country borders to cause human trafficking. First, we discuss how sociologists approach the study of social problems and phenomena using a sociological imagination, including macrosociological and microsociological perspectives. We then illustrate how using one's sociological imagination and the macro- and microsociological perspectives can inform our understanding of human trafficking. Using these analytical approaches, we present key sociological terms and apply these terms to the phenomenon of trafficking. Finally, we illustrate how applying sociological knowledge to trafficking can inform policies and practices established to eradicate this horrible crime.

Chapter Learning Objectives

- Explain the sociological imagination.
- Distinguish between macro- and microsociological approaches to studying social problems and phenomena.
- Discuss how macro- and microsociological perspectives offer complementary perspectives in understanding human trafficking.
- Apply sociological terms and concepts to the issue of human trafficking.

DOI: 10.4324/9781003124672-8

Sociology: Macro- and Microapproaches

Sociology is the scientific study of social behavior, human relationships, and social institutions. Sociologists employ what C. Wright Mills termed the "**sociological imagination**" as a way to understand how "to connect the most basic, intimate aspects of an individual's life to seemingly impersonal and remote historical forces" (Conley, 2011, p. 5). Using the sociological imagination to study human trafficking helps unravel the vast and complex factors that lead to buying, selling, and trading human beings in modern societies. The sociological imagination makes clear that historical, economic, and social trends inform the very real and intimate circumstances of trafficking, clarifying the connections between "normal" society and this devastating crime.

Sociologists are also interested in studying the relationship between the individual and her/his culture. Dalton Conley (2011, p. 73) defines culture as "a set of beliefs, traditions, and practices" embraced and often taken for granted by members of a society. In essence, culture shapes our behaviors, values, and attitudes in ways that we often do not realize unless we encounter a person from another culture. Culture is socially created by humans living in a given society. To understand human trafficking, one must consider the cultural context in which trafficking occurs. We might better understand why the sexual trafficking of women and girls occurs so frequently, for example, if we find that a society is highly patriarchal—that is, devalues women and girls over men and boys. We also might understand why young boys are forced into combat if we know about the culture's history of civil wars or the emergence of terrorist groups in the region.

Cultural values may also help us understand societal responses to trafficking. In cultures that value individualism (where individuals and/or their families are viewed as responsible for their plight), trafficked individuals or their families may be more likely to be blamed for the choices they made that led to them being trafficked. In societies with strong familial obligations and very limited economic opportunities, poor families may sometimes sell relatives to traffickers with the hope of providing for their families. The examples that follow may help illustrate how understanding culture helps further our understanding of human trafficking.

In employing our sociological imagination, we use macro- and microsociological levels of analysis to analyze the problem of human trafficking. **Macrosociology** seeks to understand systematic patterns of human behavior that underlie economic, political, and social systems. In the case of human trafficking, macrosociologists are interested in such topics as how and why specific groups of people become vulnerable to trafficking, which groups profit from trafficking, and why such mass and systematic exploitation is tolerated in many societies. **Microsociology** seeks to understand the local contexts in which individuals interact and make meaning. In the case of human trafficking, microsociologists examine the face-to-face encounters between victims and traffickers as well as others, the group networks established in trafficking, and an individual's sense of agency and meaning across situations. While a distinction between macro-and microlevels of analysis certainly exists, we propose that examining human trafficking from both perspectives helps us understand the complex and multiple circumstances in which trafficked individuals find themselves. In order to effectively address the issue of human trafficking, we need to focus on changes at both the micro- and macrolevels.

Macrosociological Approach

Focusing on the macrolevel, macrosociologists analyze the broad features of society such as systematic patterns of human behavior that underlie economic, political, and social systems. Next, we discuss some of the ways that macrosociology can inform our understanding of human trafficking. These include specific attention to globalization and the historical development of national economies, worker exploitation and vulnerable populations, and how trafficking organizations and networks are formed and maintained. Macrosociologists come from a variety of theoretical traditions, with important contributions coming from conflict and critical theories.

Globalization and the Development of National Economies

There are costs and benefits to **globalization**. Countries around the world exchange products through global markets, and cultural exchanges occur between individuals of various ethnicities and nationalities. While development and expansion have benefited both developed and developing nations, not all countries benefit equally from globalization (Ferraro, 2009). Instead, the gap between the richest and poorest countries continues to widen, as does the gap between rich and poor individuals within nations.

Since World War II, we have seen major breakthroughs in communications, technology, and industry. These advancements have resulted in a transformation of the global economy and changes in the way the world's labor is divided. Developed nations have shifted their industrial focus from manufacturing goods to service-based economies, while developing nations have taken on much of the production of goods such as textiles, electronics, automobiles, and steel. As a result, the division of labor and levels of specialization around the world have grown more complex not only within countries but also between countries. For example, workforces in developed nations include a primary labor market with educated workers holding high-paying, stable positions, whereas those in a secondary labor force face low wages, instability, and vulnerability. In developing nations, where industrialization has ushered in rapid urbanization, individuals respond by migrating to wealthier nations to try their hand at service work or moving into cities within their own countries to work in factories.

In this new global economy, old European colonial empires have been replaced by new institutions including **multinational corporations**, foreign aid agencies, and international monetary bodies that continue to practice exploitation and destruction in the form of **neocolonialism**. Examples of this process exist in many settings. In traditional Southeast Asian countries such as the Philippines, the family and "neighborhood" often served as an informal safety net for peasants before **colonization**. After colonization, first by Spanish and then by Americans, and subsequent integration into the world capitalist system, traditional systems of security and sustenance were eroded. Former colonial powers established economic systems in the form of plantation systems based on exporting commodities such as sugar and bananas to "developed" countries. While ostensibly free, peasants were often indebted and highly dependent on plantation owners and landlords to access resources, such as land and wages, which helped them survive. High birth rates, combined with a reduction in land ownership and the size of small farms, meant that many peasants migrated to cities in search of work, swelling the ever-growing ranks of the underemployed, urban underclass.

High demand for fossil fuels beginning with the Industrial Revolution and the discovery and exploitation of vast oil deposits in Saudi Arabia, Iran, Iraq, and other Middle Eastern countries changed tribal patterns in the Middle East. Western technology, consumerism, secularism, and other forces were highly disruptive in the Middle East, as was actual military conflict, such as the U.S. invasion of Iraq, the Arab invasion of Israel, Israeli conflicts with the Palestinians, the war between Iran and Iraq, and many others. Change exacerbated Sunni–Shia conflicts in Iraq, Yemen, Syria, and other countries. Military groups such as ISIS and Boko Haram kidnapped and enslaved girls and women, particularly females from one of the minority groups in Iraq, Syria, and Nigeria. Yazidi in Iraq and schoolgirls in Nigeria were captured and enslaved. Women captured by ISIS or Boko Haram were often given to soldiers or supporters of ISIS and Boko Haram as temporary wives. Such females were beaten and typically sexually exploited. Boko Haram soldiers often tried to impregnate these women to raise a new generation of soldiers (Nossiter, 2015, p. 1). Before being passed on to another man, a female might be temporarily married, raped, and then divorced. Forced marriages may involve victims who are girls or young women.

Worker Exploitation and Vulnerable Populations

According to Ferraro (2009, p. 410), "the high tech industries characteristic of the global economy depend on local infrastructures created and maintained by low-income, unskilled, and semi-skilled workers." Low-wage work in the global economy is fulfilled not only by individuals from developing nations but also by native-born people in wealthy nations with limited education and skills. While some of these workers are a part of the formal economy, many are part of the informal economy—made up of undocumented, untaxed, and unorganized workers. The work of informal workers is performed in homes, factories, or "illegal domains such as brothels" (ibid., p. 410). Indeed, much of this work is performed by women, many of whom are migrant workers from developing nations. While the informal economy has opened many employment opportunities, it has also left workers vulnerable to exploitation (ibid., 2009).

Worker exploitation and its connection to the trade in human beings are not new. While the poor have remained vulnerable under many different kinds of economic and social systems, the nature of competition over scarce resources has changed over time. Throughout history, tribes, clans, and societies in various types of economies have often competed for advantage and scarce resources. As societies became more complex, the nature of such competition took many forms—some violent and highly degrading of subjugated, conquered, and minority groups. Rises in productivity together with complex divisions of labor led to the development of caste and class systems, systems in which privileged groups emerged to control and extract labor from subordinate groups. The labor exchange between master and slave, landowner and peasant, manager and employee, owner and employee very much depended on the balance of power between groups and individuals. In societies with high levels of inequality, the potential for exploitation increased.

Slavery was a common form of such exploitation. Humans captured or conquered by others became an important asset used as slaves or serfs and often trafficked for profit through trade. Throughout the 1800s in the American South and the Caribbean, for example, plantation systems providing cotton, sugarcane, and other commodities relied heavily on slave labor. Slave women in the South not only picked cotton, cleaned houses, helped raise children of plantation owners, and bred more slaves but frequently were also coerced into providing sex for white male slaveholders.

While slavery in the United States was abolished in 1865, the legacy of slavery lived on in many forms of exploitation and racism including sharecropping, discrimination in the labor market, and Jim Crow laws. Poor young African American females also suffered from new forms of sexual exploitation including prostitution. Even though African American females are not now trafficked from abroad, they are trafficked in the United States by pimps (often also Black) who understand how to dominate and coerce girls in order to provide a steady stream of revenue from prostitution. Young African American females, as well as others who are particularly vulnerable, often fall prey to recruiters who promise a better life. African American women and girls in the United States have constituted surplus labor for many years, with high unemployment rates—particularly among the young. Poor schools, family problems, and cycles of abuse and drug use have handicapped many of these females in the labor market. In such cases, the promise of a "better" life—for higher wages abroad or in the United States, escape from an abusive family, or promise of a fictive family—is often used to lure women into settings such as a house or a camp where they can be isolated and controlled. Control occurs through the use of both positive rewards (such as clothes, jewelry, food, affection, attention, drugs) and negative sanctions (beatings, withholding drugs, threats of death to themselves or other family members, etc.). In these settings, young, poor, African American females may find themselves in webs of dependence and exploitation every bit as suffocating as those experienced by trafficked females from abroad (Lloyd, 2011).

While the division of labor involved in sexually trafficking females from poor countries abroad may be more complex than the process whereby poor young African American women become commercially sexually exploited, important similarities exist. The evolution of organized sex trafficking in the United States, for example, provides important parallels to the cases of Thailand and the Philippines. In both the United States and Southeast Asia, as in other countries, the lack of decent-paying jobs has contributed to the growth in new forms of human trafficking. The abolition of slavery in the United States created a large labor force of undereducated, economically vulnerable Blacks, many of whom left rural areas in the South in search of work. The migration of African Americans in the Southern United States to the rapidly industrializing North was not unlike the rural-to-urban migration in the Philippines and Thailand. In all three cases, impoverished groups (whether ex-slaves or rural peasants) sought work in urban areas that were unable to absorb the rapidly growing influx of migrants. While Black women in the United States were often employed as domestics and some Black men found wage employment in the rapidly growing auto industry and in the steel industry between 1920 and the 1960s in cities such as Detroit, Chicago, and Pittsburgh, others remained chronically underemployed or unemployed because of discrimination and a lack of skills.

In the second half of the twentieth century, changes in technology, globalization, and migration of capital to the American South diminished industrial employment opportunities for working-class men in many Northern cities. For example, the American auto and steel industries dramatically contracted in the latter part of the twentieth century, again placing an undue burden on African Americans and raising Black unemployment. Irrespective of the historical period, Black unemployment (particularly among younger African Americans) typically has been higher than white unemployment. Both automation and the export of jobs abroad in the global economy have contributed to high unemployment rates in the United States. While some of this unemployment may be cyclical, more unemployment now is structural or relatively permanent.

This new economy has created a dual labor market. The primary market is characterized by high-paying, stable jobs held predominantly by white men and increasing numbers of white women breaking into lower professional positions. But a higher percentage of job growth in the United States involves lowly paid service employment. For example, as domestic work becomes "commodified" or "turned into commercial products or activities," domestic work and caretaking are filled by documented and undocumented immigrant workers (Glenn, 1992, p. 6). Still others are forced to find alternative means of subsistence. Sexual services continue to fill some of this employment void among young, poor African American and migrant females.

Globalization has changed the structure of the global economy, resulting in millions of people migrating from poor to rich countries. What is different today is that many of these migrants are women looking for income and doing so by taking on the **reproductive labor** women in rich nations cannot or do not want to do (Ehrenreich and Hochschild, 2002). Some migrant women have legitimate jobs and provide substantially for their families; others come under the control of criminal employers and/or traffickers. These women are discounted because they are racial and ethnic minorities, their work is done in private, and they are often hidden.

Additional historical evidence documents the connections between exploited workers and the trafficking of humans, although not always for sexual or domestic services. In the 1800s, Chinese men were trafficked into California as semi-serfs to work on railroads and provide cheap labor. Today, the trafficking of poor immigrants desperate to improve their economic lot continues to contribute to economic prosperity and low-cost goods. The same patterns of labor trafficking occur both in the United States and abroad—whether among Hispanics in agriculture or slaughterhouses in the American Midwest, Africans and South or East Asians in textile sweatshops throughout the world, or domestic servants recruited into the richest nations. Although potential migrants are often promised a better life, trafficked laborers are organized for transit, passed off to labor "contractors" who may hold their passports, and then streamed into low-wage jobs, often in debt to the contractor and cramped in crowded apartments or camps. In debt and afraid, such migrants continue to be exploited by the labor contractors and companies offering them work.

In Southeast Asia, high birth rates combine with rural and urban poverty to create a "surplus" of individuals living on the edge of poverty. While the families of such individuals may be intact, strong kinship obligations may actually push women into sex trafficking or contract labor abroad to support the family. In Eastern Europe, similarly, the collapse of the Russian empire and socialism left many families vulnerable to capitalism's vagaries of surplus labor with no safety net.

Comparisons between the Philippines and Thailand are also illustrative. As a former Spanish and then American colony until its independence in 1946, the Philippines has been highly integrated into the global economy in the post–World War II era. American military bases (such as Clark Air Base and Subic Bay Naval Complex) remained in the Philippines, where demand for sex was high and lucrative. Young Filipinas at times were sold by impoverished families to pimps to work in the sex industry and earn hard currencies for their families. Such sex workers could be paid in hard currency held by American sailors and airmen. Many nightclubs dotted the landscape near bases, serving as convenient settings for buying and selling sex. Once the American bases were closed in 1991, the entrepreneurs of sex trafficking found new markets, sending commercially and sexually exploited Filipinas to Japan, Thailand, and other countries. Ironically, as protests against sex tourism in the Philippines and other countries emerged, organized crime groups such as the Yakuza in Japan imported females from the Philippines into Japan to work in the indigenous sex industry (Brock and Thistlethwaite, 1996, p. 56).

While Thailand was never colonized, it too was rapidly integrated into the world capitalist system following World War II. Like the Philippines, Thailand emerged in the post–World War II era as an important rest and recreation destination for American troops deployed to Asia, first as a result of the Korean War and later the Vietnam War. In both nations, the presence of American troops with large amounts of disposable income created a ready market of prostitutes and nightclubs catering to foreigners. The remarkable economic resurgence of Japan in the post–World War II era, combined with the Japanese tradition of women serving men for pay (as geishas, soap girls, prostitutes; see Allison, 1994), created a growing market for Japanese sex tourists in Thailand. This pattern illustrates Seager's (2009) observation that as wealth expands in particular countries, "men in those countries fuel an increased demand for trafficked women and girls" (ibid., p. 56).

As part of their heavy promotion of tourism, Thais also promoted sexual tourism. Thai military and government officials often owned and profited from nightclubs and brothels promoting sex. While the patterns of integration of Thailand and the Philippines into the global capitalist economy were different, the results have many parallels—including the development of thriving sex industries in both countries. In fact, estimates indicate that prostitution and sex trafficking represents 14 percent of Thailand's gross domestic product (GDP) (Seager, 2009). Sex trafficking is so lucrative that, as Seager notes, "hundreds of thousands of foreign women, most from Burma, China, Laos, and Vietnam, have been sold into the Thai sex industry since 1990" (ibid., p. 57). While sex trafficking is less essential to the GDP of the Philippines, remittances from Filipinos working abroad in the United States, the Middle East, and elsewhere are critical to the Philippines' GDP. Some of these remittances come from voluntary migration of skilled workers such as nurses abroad, but others come from individuals who have been coerced or semi-coerced through deceptive promises of bright prospects abroad. In some cases, labor recruiters have confiscated or "held" passports of Filipinos and tracked such individuals into work settings that are quite exploitative—e.g., nannies and domestic servants in the Middle East, nursing home employees in the United States.

As the global economy grows in sophistication and capital is mobile, the human trafficking industry keeps pace. Manufacturing and service firms develop extensive webs of subcontractors to keep fixed costs low and take advantage of low-cost labor in China, Southeast Asia, and other countries. Similarly, the global sex industry has shown itself equally adept. Young girls are the most important resource for the global sex industry. Whether because of dysfunctional families, extreme poverty, or lack of education, the young are often the most vulnerable. Clients particularly value younger females, creating a continual market for new and young recruits. As trafficked females age, which occurs quickly as a result of the rigors of commercial sexual exploitation, they lose their value in the commercial sex industry and may be "traded" by pimps to work in lower-wage sectors. Trafficked females may also be graded according to their earning potential and priced accordingly. Sexually exploited females also are moved from city to city, country to country, and neighborhood to neighborhood to keep them dependent as well as to meet the demands of clients in different areas. For example, nightclubs in Bangkok are not only able to offer many services but many kinds of prostitutes— indigenous, Eastern European, and Filipino, among others.

Sex trafficking is not the only type of activity that exploits the young. Abuse of child labor was common during the Industrial Revolution in the United States and continues in many Third World nations. Large families, combined with poverty, push all family members into the search for subsistence— which may include pressures on children to retrieve garbage from dumps, beg, work underage in textile mills, or illegally sell sex. In some cases, babies may become human commodities that are sold to unscrupulous adoption brokers by poor families. In Spain, thousands of newborn babies are thought to have been stolen from parents in hospitals and sold to other families, a practice that began during the Franco dictatorship in the 1930s. The baby trafficking business became so profitable that it continued for decades, perhaps as late as the 1990s, as doctors, nurses, and even nuns apparently colluded with organized crime (Minder, 2011). Many parents said that they were told by hospital staff that their children had died during or after childbirth, even though they were never shown the body. The practice especially preyed on vulnerable parents—those who were less educated, too poor to pay for funeral expenses, and less likely to question hospital authorities (ibid., 2011).

Conquest over rival groups is another way in which women and children become vulnerable to traffickers. Enslavement of women by ISIS (Syria, Iraq, and Yemen) and Boko Haram (Northern Nigeria) is largely a function of war and disdain for apostates by some Sunni groups. Captured women are given to warriors and other group members as a reward. At times, Boko Haram released Moslem students and "gave" young Christian women to warriors fighting for Boko Haram. While Islam is very diverse and supportive of women in many cases, religion has been used to devalue and oppress women in others. The Yazidis (from Northern Iraq) are considered infidels since they are a religious minority. Tales of rape, enslavement, and forced marriage are common among the few Yazidi women who escaped. Boko Haram has recently pledged allegiance to the Muslim Caliphate (ISIS) "and embraced its policy of religious cleansing, enslaving and impregnating female apostates" (Nossiter, 2015, p. 1). In these cases, trafficking of women is internal and used to both intimidate and reward members of the organization. Kidnapping and ransom provide ISIS and other groups with money. Men (rather than women) are typically kidnapped and at times beheaded if not ransomed. Children may be forced into action as child soldiers.

Organizational Structure

An **organization** includes a network of individuals that share a purpose and common membership. Understanding trafficking networks is often difficult because the networks of individuals within an organization do not follow typical organizational patterns, such as those in a formal association or club. Still, we can study organizational structures to examine hierarchies and power distribution within trafficking networks.

For example, sex trafficking now is more "free floating" than in the past. While brothels still exist, commercial sexual exploitation in the twenty-first century may take place in many settings (hotels, the back of nightclubs, etc.), and may be arranged over the internet, via cell phone messaging, and through other means. The decentralization of sexual trafficking makes it more difficult to track, which underscores the importance of understanding the complex coordination between different crime groups and individuals performing the multiple roles involved in human trafficking.

Human trafficking among criminal networks is well organized (e.g., the Yakuza in Japan, the Russian Mafias, the Italian Mafia, Mexican drug cartels, gangs such as the Crips in the United States, and Chinese Triads). While these crime groups sometimes compete violently with each other for control over territory and franchise, at other times, they cooperate when such cooperation is seen as mutually beneficial to all parties. The internet and cellular technology make such cooperation easier today than in the past. Typically, a group of agents recruits young females with promises of better employment. Females may be transported across borders by an agent and sold to a brothel, bar, or some other establishment. Passports and identity papers are often confiscated, and females may find themselves isolated, unable to speak the language of the host nation, and socialized into a life of commercial sexual exploitation through threats, coercion, rape, beatings, and deprivation of sleep and food. Because this is a high-profit business, traffickers are able to employ many assistants to control and watch over trafficked females. Sex trafficking is low-risk, high profit activity for global criminal networks. According to Kara (2009, p. 200), "laws against sex trafficking are overwhelmingly anemic and poorly enforced."

The extensive networks and subcontractors involved in human trafficking mean that we must move well beyond the hierarchical model of organization popularized by Max Weber to examine how networks are formed and reformed to perform the several tasks involved in human trafficking. As shown in Table 6.1, Farr (2005, p. 63) identified eight different roles that exist in the trafficking business around the world—which include recruiter, contractor, transporter, employer (procurer), and enforcer (guard). These roles may either be performed by the same individual or by different individuals, small cliques, or organized mafias. Commercially exploited females may be recruited by agents located in towns and villages, who might even know a relative of the trafficked woman. Promises of better jobs may entice young females to leave their town or village. In some cases, the individual recruiter provides across-border transportation; in other instances, a transporter is hired. The latter may also be responsible for procuring work visas and passports for the women. Once across a border, sexually exploited females may be confined in a holding area (for example, an apartment where they are closely supervised), until shipped to their final or temporary destination. At some point in this process, females are informed that they are working as prostitutes in part to pay the large debt accrued from their transport, food, lodging, documents, and so on. Those who resist are often beaten and raped until they comply. Pimps who profit may be part of a larger gang or syndicate, or they may work as small-time entrepreneurs. Since opportunity for theft (of the women and/or money) occurs at many points in this process, subcontractors who do not keep their commitments may suffer retribution by being beaten or even killed.

Some of these criminal networks are well established and have been in place for some time. Others emerge and develop as the opportunity presents itself (Farr, 2005). Smaller traffickers not affiliated with one of the more established criminal groups, such as the Russian or Italian Mafias, often must pay protection money to the larger crime groups. Farr argues that the higher-level Mafia profit largely through extortion, money laundering, club ownership, and other investments, while the mid- to lower-level Mafia groups are most actively involved in carrying out trafficking in several countries (ibid., p. 101). Alliances across borders among different criminal groups help sustain trafficking across borders, which is often both lucrative and important in keeping commercially, sexually exploited females isolated and dependent.

Table 6.1   Sex Trafficking Roles

Position	Role	Common Strategies
Recruiter	Finds, brings females into industry—usually by deception, sometimes force	Sells recruits to brokers or directly to employers
Broker (agent)	Go-between or middleman; may be more than one person	Typically buys females from recruiter and sells to employer
Contractor	Organizes, oversees entire trafficking transaction	Usually played by relatively professional criminal organization or group
Employment/travel agent	Arranges trip and alleged purpose (e.g., job, job training, tourism)	May serve as "fronts" for criminal trafficking activity
Document thief/ forger	Arranges for, obtains "legitimate" travel documents	May steal or illegally obtain legitimate documents or create false documents
Transporter	Accompanies females on trip	Usually delivers females to broker
(escort, "jockey")	to destination	at border or inside destination country but sometimes to employer
Employer	Purchases, then sells	Provides females with place to live
(procurer)	"commodity" to customer; provides place of business for sex	and work; explains conditions of work in sex trade to pay off debt
Enforcer (guard, "roof")	Provides protection for business and, to a lesser extent, trafficked females	Protects business from gangs, police raids, runaway females, nonpaying customers, etc.; may also extort on behalf of crime group

Source: Adapted and condensed from Farr (2005, p. 63)

The heavy use of subcontractors in human trafficking allows the business to expand and contract with fluctuations in the available opportunities. Since trafficking is illegal, subcontracting also allows trafficking organizations to disguise parts of their operation, escaping scrutiny from authorities by shifting location and subcontractors as needed. Shared kinship, region, ethnicity, and nationality all ensure greater trust among specific subgroups of traffickers than might be the case when traffickers do not have common bonds beyond being in the trafficking business.

In a recent report on "human smuggling," Sara Stillman (2015) of the *New Yorker* suggests that as Mexican/American border controls become tighter, organized crime groups have capitalized on moving individuals from South and Central America into the United States. In doing so, they are not only charging large amounts of money to help people cross the border, but "small-time smuggling operations—lone guides, in many cases, bringing migrants across the border—have been replaced with sophisticated, and increasingly brutal, transnational networks" (Stillman, 2015, para. 18). Stillman quotes interviewee and activist Michel Brane, who suggests, " 'Smuggling is not the same as trafficking.' Migrants pay smugglers to transport them; traffickers are in the business of moving or holding people against their will. 'But as the border becomes militarized the differences become blurred' " (Stillman, 2015, para. 18). The tighter the Mexican/American border becomes, the larger the profits made from vulnerable migrants who are robbed, kidnapped for ransom, and charged extraordinary fees for their safety.

As stateless people, minorities, and other marginal individuals flee their homelands, they are susceptible to trafficking. For example, the Muslim Rohingyas of Myanmar have been pushed out of their homes, and Bangladeshis seeking livable employment opportunities have fallen victim to trafficking as they attempt to migrate to Thailand ("The Rohingya Refugees Adrift," 2015). Similarly, refugee groups from Eritrea, Gambia, Somalia, and Syria attempt to flee violence and travel to Europe for asylum through Libya (Kirkpatrick, 2015). In doing so, humans are treated as cargo, with smugglers making huge profits to move their bodies. Thousands of refugees have died, numerous others are held in detention centers, and still others are sent back to the places they fled where they face persecution and death.

The macrosociological approach focuses on the broad features of society such as systematic patterns of human behavior that underlie economic, political, and social systems. Using a macrosociological lens to inform our understanding of human trafficking includes paying specific attention to globalization and the historical development of national economies, worker exploitation and vulnerable populations, and how trafficking organizations and networks are formed and maintained. Complementary to a macro understanding of the social causes, consequences, and processes surrounding human trafficking is the microsociological approach.

Microsociological Approach

Focusing on the microlevel, microsociologists look at the local context of a social phenomenon, particularly addressing how the social context shapes an individual and his or her perceptions as well as how assumptions about others shape who is defined as a victim or offender. Next, we discuss some of the ways that microsociology can inform our understanding of human trafficking and how the term has been applied. These include specific attention

to the predominant focus on girls and women as victims, socialization/
resocialization of trafficked victims, the impact of situational definitions on
individuals' perceptions of human trafficking, and the causes and consequences of trafficked victims' stigmatized identities. Microsociologists
come from a variety of theoretical traditions, one important tradition being
symbolic interactionism. Before applying this theoretical perspective to the
issue of human trafficking, we outline the general characteristics of the
theory and key concepts.

Symbolic Interactionism

Symbolic interactionism focuses on the universal processes of the self—an
emergent characteristic of humans—and how these processes impact behavior
and identity. Coined by Herbert Blumer ([1969] 1999) and extending the
work of George Herbert Mead (1934), social interactions are seen as the
"nexus" in which society and self have a "reciprocal impact" on one another
(Stryker, 1980, p. 52). Self and society are seen as mutually emergent phenomena, and the complexity of each must be accounted for, including the
self's active role in a collective interpretive process (Blumer, [1969] 1999).
Macroforces exist outside of individuals, but the effects of these forces are not
predetermined. While social structures constrain the situations and choices an
individual faces, they do not determine precisely how an individual will
respond. The interpretive aspect of social interaction rests on the assumption
that human beings do not simply react to each other; rather, symbols, objects
that have meaning, are exchanged and interpretations formed before action
takes place. As a key element of symbolic interactionist theory, social interaction of the symbolic type refers to interaction in which the individual interprets the other's gesture/action and then constructs action based on the
interpretation. Social interaction is where self and societies meet. Through
interpretive processes, the self assigns meanings in a manner that gives them
social significance. While the macrosociological approach highlights the economic, political, and cultural shifts that contextualize the human trafficking
trade, a microsociological approach highlights the emerging situations, interactions, and individual interpretations that color and shape the everyday lives
of individuals involved. Drawing from symbolic interactionism and particularly the work of Erving Goffman, we apply this perspective to the interactions
of actors implicated in human trafficking. We liken the resocialization of
victims to that experienced by individuals in total institutions, highlight the
multiple definitions that each actor brings to situations and the role of stigma
as a conceptual tool for making sense of individuals' attitudes and behaviors.

Meaning-Making and Defining Situations

Socialization heavily influences how a person views the self and the world
around him or her. Socialization refers to the ways in which individuals learn

how to behave, think, and feel within their social context. Primary socialization usually takes place in the family unit when a child is learning the many behaviors and attitudes expected of them. Perceptions of the world and others, though, also vary across contexts and situations. This variation in perception and meaning is captured in the phrase "the **definition of the situation**." Developed by William Isaac Thomas and Florian Znaniecki (1919), the concept refers to the important role that subjective meanings have for understanding behavior. In order to fully understand why people behave as they do, we must understand how they define the situations in which they find themselves.

Human trafficking is often equated with sexual exploitation of females, despite the substantial number of male victims and victims subjected to other types of trafficking. According to International Labour Office (2014) estimates, approximately 21 million men, women, and children are trafficked globally. Of these, 22 percent are victims of forced sexual exploitation, and 68 percent are victims of forced labour exploitation in the private economy. The remaining 10 percent involve state-imposed forced labour, such as prisons or work imposed by military or paramilitary forces—including the use of child soldiers. While the vast majority of victims of forced sexual exploitation and domestic work are women and girls, the majority of trafficking victims in other types of economic activities are men and boys. Yet as Hepburn and Simon (2013) found in their study of 24 nations, men face discrimination after being trafficked and, in many nations, are not considered victims. In Brazil and China, for example, neither the government nor the general population identify forced labor as human trafficking. Even governments of nations that recognize that men can be victims, such as Poland and Japan, lack shelters specifically designed for men. Hepburn and Simon argue that the issues facing trafficked men have not been prioritized, in part because of their gender but also based on the type of trafficking considered most offensive. Since forced labor has only recently been introduced into criminal codes as a form of trafficking, victims often go unrecognized and may be prosecuted for offenses (such as immigration violations) that occurred while being trafficked.

Just as socialization is ongoing, definitions of situations are continually in flux and changing. While situations involving traffickers and victims may be viewed by an outsider as manipulative, deceptive, and criminal, individuals within the situation may define the same behaviors differently and therefore may act in ways that an outsider would not anticipate. To understand why this is the case, we must look past our own assumptions and try to view these situations, as much as possible, through the lens of the individuals involved. Research that attempts to do so will rely on information directly from the victims and traffickers themselves and less so on authorities and advocates, who will likely have limited experiences in the situations under study.

Regardless of the type of trafficking, traffickers use similar deceptive, exploitative methods to lure potential victims and keep them from leaving (Hepburn and Simon, 2013). Traffickers often make false job offers or fake romantic relationships. Later, they may charge exorbitant fees (for visas, room and board, etc.) that keep victims continually in debt or fine victims for not meeting work quotas or behaving badly. In an effort to control victims' mobility, Hepburn and Simon found that " . . . traffickers frequently withhold victims' visas and other identifying documentation, isolate victims, threaten deportation, threaten to harm victims or families, and physically harm victims" (p. 1).

To better understand how victims of sex trafficking define their situation, Lloyd (2011) shares the stories of many girls who, like herself, have survived commercial sexual exploitation. As Lloyd notes, sexually exploited girls often view traffickers as their boyfriends, whom they typically call "Daddy," and may at first feel that these men are providing the love and family support that they did not receive at home. Traffickers and pimps (who are typically much older than the girls themselves) purposely use seduction and promises to lure young, vulnerable girls into commercial sexual exploitation. These men may befriend girls at the train station, for example, buying girls a meal or a cheap necklace, which many vulnerable girls interpret as signs of love. It may not be until much later, when the reality of the situation begins to sink in as the girls are threatened with increasing levels of violence, that girls may consider leaving the situation. For a homeless girl who is desperate for money and affection, she may only come to view her trafficker as a pimp after she has nearly died from his escalating levels of violence towards her. Based on Lloyd's experiences, as well as those of the many girls she has worked with at GEMS (Girls Educational and Mentoring Services) to meet the needs of girls who have experienced similar histories to hers, she found that leaving this type of life takes practice. Girls need to try to leave multiple times without someone giving up on them. Few resources are available to meet the needs of girls who try to leave, and few understand what they have experienced.

The challenge for trafficked victims is to redefine reality so that the economic and psychological rewards in the outside world are sufficient to sustain a life beyond the reach of traffickers. Trafficked victims may relapse and disappear from halfway houses for long periods of time, only sometimes to return with a better understanding of why the ways they were treated are highly exploitative. In some cases, only outside assistance can provide enough support that trafficking victims are able to escape their exploiters, who work very hard not to lose valuable resources under their control. Furthermore, those providing assistance need to make great efforts to try to understand the lived experiences of trafficking victims, including their differing cultural responses and the various effects of the trauma they have endured. As Kara (2009) found, many sex trafficking victims who escape end up returning to their original trafficker or are deceived by a new trafficker, since they have few options other than returning to the same conditions that led to their initial trafficking.

Resocialization in Total Institutions

Institutions in which individuals undergo extreme **resocialization**, uprooting a large amount of the "ways of being" learned in primary socialization, are considered total institutions. Erving Goffman uses the term "**total institution**" to refer to mental institutions as a place where individuals may be easily controlled because they are closed off from others, a place where "all aspects of life are conducted under a single authority [. . .] in the company of a batch of others, all of whom are treated alike" (Goffman, 1961, pp. 5–6). Extending beyond brick-and-mortar buildings, we can see that anywhere where these characteristics of control and exclusion are practiced could be considered a total institution.

Resocialization, the type most likely to occur among victims of trafficking, takes place outside the original family. The behaviors and attitudes learned in primary socialization are often overturned. During primary socialization, for example, children may learn some form of modesty, undressing and using the restroom in private or only around close family members. With this behavior comes a person's belief in their right to privacy. Resocialization in total institutions such as prisons or the military contradicts this basic behavior by demanding individuals perform such behaviors as undress publicly in front of strangers or use a public toilet. Over time, these behaviors may cause a person to question their right to basic privacy, as well as their sense of personal autonomy, reshaping the way an individual views him- or herself. One tenet of microsociological theory is that changes in conceptions of the self will impact future behavior and interactions with others. An individual who comes to view him- or herself as less deserving of privacy and autonomy will behave differently in future interactions than someone with a self-concept rooted in independence.

Individuals who are vulnerable to trafficking have often experienced an early form of socialization that primes them for exploitation. As Hepburn and Simon (2013) consistently found in all 24 nations they studied, persons who are marginalized are often the most vulnerable—whether defined by race, social class, gender, or citizenship. According to Estes and Weiner (2005), more than 90 percent of trafficked and exploited youth in the United States have experienced some form of abuse and neglect; the majority are runaways or homeless. Like their foreign counterparts, trafficked youth in the United States often are poor and minorities, which (along with being children) also puts them at greater risk for recruitment by traffickers. While some are kidnapped by force, many others have been primed for predatory adults as a result of their backgrounds and experiences.

The processes whereby commercially sexually exploited children and other trafficked labor are controlled are similar to the process of control and reso-cialization in total institutions such as prisons, the military, and concentration camps. Goffman (1963) and others describe resocialization as a series of steps designed to remake the personality of the individual in order to control him or her. First, an individual is isolated and deprived of any means for unsuper-vised movement. We have already noted that such isolation for some begins by shipping commercially sexually trafficked females across borders, holding passports and identity papers. Isolation also may occur by crowding many girls into a tightly supervised house or apartment. Sex traffickers may increas-ingly tell girls what to wear and how to act. Those who refuse are typically beaten and raped until they comply. Since some clients pay more for virgins, rape is not always the tactic of choice to resocialize a sexually exploited female, but it is common. Trafficked women and girls also find themselves highly dependent on their pimps, bar owners, and others who control their lives. Such females typically find themselves in debt bondage, where living expenses and transportation costs far exceed their earnings (Farr, 2005).

Pimps use a variety of types of control and coercion to keep the girls they sexually traffic in line. As Lloyd (2011) notes, American pimp culture is built on a language of humiliation and degradation. The many rules and codes are designed to break an individual's will. For example, girls may be punished for not earning enough money or for disagreeing with their pimp, and they may be beaten or harassed for even minor infringement of the rules. As has so often been the case historically in efforts to control others, pimps create hier-archies among the sexually exploited girls that they manage, with the head girl gaining certain privileges or perhaps less abuse, at least until they do something wrong. Girls may consequently compete with each other for the attention of their pimp or to avoid being beaten, even if they end up turning on each other in the process. Among the girls they have traumatized and humiliated, pimps leave behind damaged lives.

Stigma

The sociology of Erving Goffman (1961, 1963) follows the emphasis of other symbolic interactionists on individuals' interpretations and the meaning inter-actions and objects assume within situations. Just as Goffman's concept of total institution is helpful for understanding how controlled environments are experienced by victims of trafficking, a second important concept is stigma. **Stigma** refers to any quality or characteristic of an individual that discredits a person in the eyes of others.

Stigma is often associated with physical blemishes, such as deformities. However, it can be extended to other physical qualities such as being over-weight or abnormally short and even further extended to more social qualities that result from behaviors or experiences. As certain qualities carry a degree of stigma, the individual is treated differently by others and will come to view him- or herself in a different and usually negative light. Lepers or the disabled are examples of stigmatized people whose moral credibility is called into question by their blemish. They must have done *something* to deserve their lot in life, so the socially accepted logic goes. This can be further applied to social deviants of other types, such as juvenile delinquents, criminals, sex workers, and the victims and profiteers engaged in human trafficking.

In applying the concept of stigma to sex trafficking, microsociologists might consider who is most likely to be stigmatized in various situations involving sex trafficking. In a landmark case in Niger that released Hadijatou Mani Korao from sex slavery, for example, a court ruled improperly that a freed slave girl was still the wife of her master (Hepburn and Simon, 2013). As so often happens, traditional definitions of the situation based on custom prevailed, despite changes in the law.

Even though American girls who are trafficked domestically may be just as exploited as those trafficked into the United States from elsewhere, they tend to be viewed quite differently (Lloyd, 2011). Police and other authorities are more likely to perceive those who have been brought into the United States from other countries as trafficking victims who have been sexually exploited, whereas American girls (especially girls of color) are more likely to be viewed as willing participants who have "asked for it." As Lloyd notes, "It is difficult to view yourself as a victim, no matter what happens to you, when your pimp, the men who buy you, and even those who are supposed to protect you see you as incapable of being victimized" (ibid., p. 126). Even when they spend time in jail or in shelters, trafficked women and girls tend to be scorned and stigmatized, often treated as if they are on the lowest level of the social hierarchy.

How, we may ask, have some sexually exploited girls and women managed to overcome their stigmatization and transform their lives? As Lloyd (2011) notes, exploited girls need skills and tools so they can create a new sense of self. In creating GEMS, Lloyd "understood that they also need a place where they could feel like they belonged, where they could feel strong and empowered, a place where they could feel loved and valued, even as the struggles remained right outside the door" (ibid., p. 229). For long-term healing to occur, these girls must come to believe that they do not deserve to be exploited. Such a realization is difficult, since many of these girls, their family members, law enforcement officials, and human services workers view what these girls have experienced as their fault. Rehabilitation is particularly acute for Moslem women who have been enslaved and raped, since sexually exploited women in cultures that highly value virginity are often outcasts.

A number of those who have made the difficult journey from human trafficking victim to survivor play a key role in fighting human trafficking. According to the U.S. State Department (2014, p. 24), "Survivors run shelters, advocate before legislatures, train law enforcement officials, and meet with presidents and prime ministers to push for a more robust response to this crime." Survivors' voices are crucial not only to help victims become survivors but also for governments, advocates, and officials to design effective ways of addressing these issues.

The microsociological approach focuses on how the social context shapes an individual and his or her perceptions. Using a microsociological lens to inform our understanding of human trafficking includes examining how trafficking victims are defined and viewed by researchers, how they are socialized/resocialized, the impact of situational definitions on individuals' perceptions of human trafficking, and the causes and consequences of trafficked victims' stigmatized identities. Both macro- and microsociology inform our understanding of the causes and ways to combat human trafficking.

Applying Sociological Knowledge to Create Social Change

The Trafficking Victims Protection Act of 2000 (TVPA) defines children under 18 in the commercial sex trade as trafficking victims, regardless of whether they have experienced "force, fraud, or coercion" (Lloyd, 2011, p. 78). As a result of a double standard being typically applied, however, women and girls trafficked into the United States from abroad are provided with services through the TVPA, whereas American girls are typically arrested. Even though some police officers do not believe that sexually trafficked girls are criminals and that the traffickers should instead be prosecuted, Lloyd realized that she needed to work with others to change the state law so that girls would not be locked up for having been victimized. As she noted,

> I watched sexually exploited girl after girl arrested and charged with an act of prostitution and struggled with getting the cops, the courts, the families, even the girls themselves to believe that they were truly victims, when the law said that they were criminals.

(ibid., p. 139)

Partially as a result of her advocacy efforts, along with the impassioned testimony by a number of the formerly trafficked girls with whom she had worked, New York passed the Safe Harbor for Exploited Youth Act, making it the first state to protect rather than prosecute sexually exploited children.

According to the recommendations of the National Conference of Commissioners on Uniform State Laws (2013), all states should adopt safe harbor legislation, protecting all victims of human trafficking under the age of 18 from prosecution for nonviolent offenses and providing access to services.

Some safe harbor laws that have been passed only provide immunity for sexually exploited children under a specific age (typically 14 or 15) or first-time offenders. While current state safe harbor laws vary widely, all restrict immunity only to children who have been commercially sexually exploited, with protections only applying to prostitution-related crimes. The Polaris Project (2014) and many others recommend broadening the scope of protections to include child victims of labor trafficking. When child victims of labor trafficking are forced to commit crimes while being exploited, they should be provided with the same protections as victims of child sexual exploitation.

The fact that human trafficking laws are evolving and that some formerly trafficked victims have experienced remarkable transformations in their lives suggests that individuals can sometimes change their perceptions and definitions of the situation, as microsociologists would argue. Such examples also provide hope that some individuals who have been trafficked can become empowered, overcoming at least some of the incredible stigma and exploitation that they have endured. Not only is it important that victims of trafficking redefine their self-perceptions, but law enforcement, judges, and other authorities (who often treat victims the same as perpetrators) must also change their perceptions of victims. Too often, victims are subjected to punishment because they are viewed as willing participants (Stillman, 2015).

At the same time, these examples remind us of the importance of also working to address the types of broader social changes that macrosociologists examine. In order to begin to adequately address the issue of human trafficking, we need to change laws and social policies, as well as address the economic and social conditions that contribute to human trafficking globally. Responses also need to be adapted to the specific culture and situation in which they occur. Even though some trafficked individuals may overcome tremendous odds and escape their exploitation, macrosociologists argue that human trafficking will persist unless these broader social issues are addressed.

Understanding the macro- and microissues described earlier is vital for creating change in the justice system in order to deter traffickers, assist victims, and punish those who benefit from the exploitation of others. As actors and groups involved in human trafficking redefine situations with the interpretations and meanings of individual victims in mind, laws and norms may evolve to better deter this growing social problem. Such change is necessary, as the current system continues to revictimize individuals caught in the web of macro- and microlevel forces described here, particularly those individuals who are most vulnerable. The justice system can better serve the victims of trafficking by taking into account the nuances of the macro context and constrained agency. We need to stop stigmatizing and criminalizing trafficking victims, understanding how they instead need to be provided with a safety net.

Discussion Questions

1. What are the differences between the micro- and macroapproaches in sociology? What facets of human trafficking do these different approaches focus on?
2. What do you think are the most important contributions of a sociological perspective for understanding human trafficking?
3. What do you think law enforcement and government officials should be aware of in order to ameliorate the problem of human trafficking?
4. Describe the organizational structure of human trafficking.
5. Americans are socialized to believe that the United States is the "Land of Opportunity." In what ways does understanding trafficking in the U.S. demystify this belief?

References

Allison, Anne. (1994). *Nightwork: Sexuality, pleasure, and corporate masculinity in a Tokyo Hostess Club.* Chicago: University of Chicago Press.

Blumer, Herbert. ([1969] 1999). *Symbolic interactionism: Perspective and method.* Berkeley, CA: University of California Press.

Board, T. E. (2015, May 13). The Rohingya Refugees, Adrift. Retrieved from https://www.nytimes.com/2015/05/13/opinion/the-rohingya-refugees-adrift.html

Brock, Rita Nakashima, & Thistlethwaite, Susan Brooks. (1996). *Casting stones: Prostitution and liberation in Asia and the United States.* Minneapolis, MN: Fortress Press.

Cave, Damien. (2011, July 6). Better lives for Mexicans cut the allure of going north. *New York Times*, p. 1.

Conley, Dalton. (2011). *You may ask yourself: An introduction to thinking like a sociologist* (2nd ed.). New York: W.W. Norton.

Estes, Richard J., & Weiner, Neil Alan. (2005). *The commercial sexual exploitation of children in the U.S., Canada and Mexico.* Unpublished report. Philadelphia, PA: University of Pennsylvania.

Farr, Kathryn. (2005). *Sex trafficking: The global market in women and children.* New York: Worth Publishers.

Ferraro, Kathleen J. (2009). *Women's lives.* Boston, MA: Allyn and Bacon.

Glenn, E. N. (1992) From servitude to service work: Historical continuities in the racial division of paid reproductive labor. *Signs, 18*(1), 1–43.

Goffman, Erving. (1961). *Asylums: Essays on the social situation of mental patients and other inmates.* Harmondsworth: Penguin.

Goffman, Erving. (1963). *Stigma: Notes on the management of a spoiled social identity.* Englewood Cliffs, NJ: Prentice Hall.

Hepburn, S., & Simon, R. (2013) *Human trafficking around the world: Hidden in plain sight.* New York: Columbia University Press.

International Labour Organization (ILO). (2014, May). *ILO says forced labour generates annual profits of US$ 150 Billion.* Retrieved October 12, 2020, from www.ilo.org/global/about-the-ilo/newsroom/news/WCMS_243201/lang--en/index.htm#:~:text=The%20

ILO%20report%2C%20Profits%20and,work%2C%20agriculture%20and%20other%20 economic

Kara, Siddharth. (2009). *Sex trafficking: Inside the business of modern slavery*. New York: Columbia University Press.

Kirkpatrick, D. (2015, May 5). Young African migrants caught in trafficking machine. *The New York Times*. Available at: www.nytimes.com/2015/05/06/world/africa/migrants-libya.html?ref=topics.

Lloyd, Rachel. (2011). *Girls like us*. New York: Harper Collins.

Minder, Raphael. (2011, July 6). Spain confronts decades of pain over lost babies. *New York Times*, p. 2.

Mead, George Herbert. (1934). *Mind, self, and society*. Chicago, IL: University of Chicago Press.

Nossiter, A. (2015, May 18). Mass rape seen as way to build new generation of Boko-Haram. *The New York Times*. Available at: www.nytimes.com/times-insider/2015/05 /18/mass-rape-in-nigeria-reporters-notebook/?_r=0.

Polaris Project (2014). Human Trafficking Issue Brief: Safe Harbor, Fall 2014. Available at: www.polarisproject.org/storage/documents/policy_documents/Issue_Briefs/2014/ 2014_Safe-harbor_Issue_Brief_Final-1.pdf.

Seager, Joni. (2009). *Penguin atlas of women in the world* (4th ed.). New York: Penguin.

Stillman, S. (2015, April 27). Where are the Children. *The New Yorker*. Available at: www. newyorker.com/magazine/2015/04/27/where-are-the-children.

Stryker, Sheldon. (1980). *Symbolic interactionism: A social structural version*. Menlo Park, CA: Benjamin Cummings.

Thomas, William I., & Znaniecki, Florian. (1919). *The polish peasant in Europe and America: Monograph of an immigrant group*. Boston, MA: The Gorham Press.

US Department of State (2014). *Trafficking in persons report, June 2014*. Washington, DC: U.S. Department of State.

7

FEAR, FRAUD, AND FRANK COMPLEXITIES

THE INFLUENCE OF GENDER ON HUMAN TRAFFICKING

LISA C. HUEBNER

I show a movie in my Gender, Labor, and Globalization course to help me teach how the trafficking industry is invisible in mainstream globalization discourse. A colleague recommended it, and I imagine it is a film shown in women's and gender studies classes around the world. *Trading Women* (Slotar and Feingold 2002) is a documentary film that chronicles the relationship between the Thai sex industry and the destruction of Thai agricultural economies due to the spread of western capital and associated ideologies. In a voice leveled by doom and sadness, Angelina Jolie narrates a story of the rural hill tribes in Thailand, where young women and girls are vulnerable to sex traffickers due to lack of citizenship and poverty. A particular scene stands out in the film: two local men are identified as traffickers who are known for abducting young women in the Hill Tribes and selling them in the international slave trade. Several family members of such women are interviewed and express a range of emotions from anger to confusion. Although a major point of this film is to demonstrate the relationships between United States anti–drug lobbying, rural Thai economies that are dependent on the trade of the opium poppy plant, and the sex industry in Thailand; the film's name suggests it is solely about the trafficking of women.

The film, which I will revisit throughout this chapter, makes clear that women and girls are disproportionately impacted by the social and economic factors underlying human trafficking worldwide. What are the causes of and responses to trafficking? Do victims need to be rescued, and if so, how? Is

DOI: 10.4324/9781003124672-9

trafficking a form of labor exploitation, or is it a form of violence against women? These are questions that frame many debates about trafficking and its impact on women. Trafficking is gendered; that is, its meaning as a social and economic experience is shaped by gender ideologies, institutions, and interactions.

[handwritten: gender is a social construct]

Chapter Learning Objectives

- Understand the relationship between gender, work, and human trafficking.
- Understand feminist theory and how it can inform policy and advocacy response.
- Understand important women's studies and sociological concepts as they relate to human trafficking.

Historically, gender scholars have explained the relationship between gender and trafficking two ways: as cause and as effect. As a cause, trafficking results from gender inequality, which creates this vulnerability. We can see this is a women's issue in part because there are so many women who are trafficked. As an effect, trafficking affects women disproportionately more than men because women are more vulnerable to exploitation than men. But *why* are there so many women who are trafficked? In contrast to the transatlantic slave trade, modern human trafficking is characterized not by investing in free human labor via buying one individual but by coercion of extremely needy people living in overwhelming poverty. They do not care about the health and well-being of trafficked people. There is no ownership and no investment. There is no record keeping. Modern human traffickers prey on vulnerable individuals and treat them as disposable goods.

[handwritten margin note: women are targeted for sex, which is large in the HT world]

A primary goal of this chapter is to explain why a large proportion of trafficking victims are women, but to do this, I must first establish some of the issues with making claims that assert women are disproportionately victims of trafficking. Mary C. Burke speculates on one reason that women might seem to be the primary victims of trafficking: much of the public discourse on trafficking is about the exchange of women for sex. While there are other forms of trafficking in modern slavery, they are primarily labor related. She explains:

> We consistently hear that eighty percent of those involved in slavery are women and children. However, we also tend to hear more about sex trafficking which includes more women and children, so my thought is

that the eighty percent may be slightly inflated. If we get more of an understanding of labor trafficking which includes more men then that number might go down.

(Satalia 2010)

Although trafficking as modern-day slavery includes forced labor of all sorts, not just sex work, this may not guarantee a decrease in the numbers of trafficked women. Modern slavery does not distinguish sex trafficking from work trafficking because sex trafficking amounts to work for the victims. When not trafficked, women and other individuals are paid for sex and other commercialized intimacies in various forms: prostitution, massage, and exotic dancing. The difference between sex work and sex trafficking is the absence of money and fair work conditions, although one cannot assume that legal sex work guarantees fair wages and work conditions.

Since the 1980s, there has been a steady increase in women who migrate for work. Women who must leave their home countries for work seek all kinds of jobs, but most jobs available are those that include traditionally feminine tasks of serving and nurturing. Therefore, women migrate to do domestic work, service work, care work, and sex work and risk becoming trafficked in all these jobs. Indeed, the most common route to sex trafficking is fraudulent recruitment for other jobs (Hodge and Lietz 2007) and as such, migrant workers and trafficked victims share many of the same experiences and risks (Schwarz et al. 2017). It follows, then, that high numbers of women will continue to be trafficked as modern slaves if two conditions persist: first, the global economy requires women to migrate to take care of their families and, second, the global economy in advanced nations has available low-wage feminized work.

In this chapter, I introduce and define three forms of oppression that contribute to the influence of gender on human trafficking. Violence against women, commercialized intimacy, and the feminization of migration help explain why women are targeted for human trafficking and why they may be more at risk than men. It is well documented that women can and do commit intimate violence against men and other women. In the international arena, however, violence against women typically is defined by the male subordination of women. Using this framework in trafficking helps demonstrate the common patterns among several forms of intimate violence to detail the range and extent of violence in women's lives. The second and related condition is the kind of jobs in advanced nations that rely on the exchange of commercialized intimacy between worker and client. The third is the feminization of migration, which explains the increase of women who migrate from poor and developing countries to richer countries so they can support themselves and their families. After this, I will explain and use transnational feminist theory to contribute to the discussion on how we can respond to the modern slavery of women in these contexts of violence, migration, and work.

As noted previously, the learning goals for this chapter are twofold. The first is to make clear the relationship between gender, work, and human trafficking. The second is to demonstrate the use of feminist theory and how it can inform policy and advocacy response. In addition, the reader will learn the following concepts in the order that they appear in the text: oppression, social construct, gendered ideology, gendered institution, gendered interaction, violence against women, commercialized intimacy, feminization of immigration, transnational feminist theory, and intersectionality.

Oppression and Identity

Simply put: human trafficking is inhumane. It is a form of oppression that—like a fast-acting disease—attacks the most vulnerable and neediest of people. Vulnerability and neediness are not accidental, nor do they need to be permanent. These circumstances are, as feminist philosopher Marilyn Frye writes, set up as "a network of forces and barriers which are systematically related and which conspire to the immobilization, reduction, and molding of women and the lives we live" (1983, p. 7). Worldwide, women more than men are at risk for intimate violence, are sexually objectified virtually and in real life, and live in extreme poverty conditions.

targets groups rather than individuals

In the film I introduced earlier, *Trading Women*, a high-end massage parlor owner says, "[My employees] come for many reasons, but the main reason is their need to work, their need for money. This is the main reason. If they have enough to eat in the countryside, ok. But if they don't have enough to eat, they come here." Another massage parlor owner says, "The girls from the North are the best because they have white skin. They are beautiful. They are the best workers because they can charge the highest rates." In this section of this chapter, I will discuss how oppression functions as an invisible set of interrelated dynamics that harm people in part through normalization in society.

In our everyday lives, our gender, race, sexual, and national identities *feel* personal and natural. This means that many of us think our identities *are* personal and a part of us and do not impact the way we experience the world in any kind of political way. We tend to think of our identities as individual and unique. They do not affect whether we have opportunities or disadvantages in life. What is often true, however, is that social identities systematically offer or inhibit our opportunities to lead a successful, healthy life. Frye defines **oppression** as a systematic act intended against a targeted group of people. The systematic nature of oppression is what makes oppression distinct from human suffering. The targeting of a group rather than an individual is what makes oppression defined through what seem like personal identities but are actually socially constructed concepts that stratify groups (1983). In other words, identities are defined through hierarchy and in opposition to each other. Renowned feminist poet and essayist Audre Lorde writes:

> Racism, the belief in the inherent superiority of one race over all others and thereby the right to dominance. Sexism, the belief in the inherent superiority of one sex over the other and thereby the right to dominance. Ageism. Heterosexism. Elitism. Classism (1984).

Whether or not we pay attention, our identities shape our experiences in the world. These include how we access opportunities and resources as well as how we experience oppression and discrimination. Although we may experience gender, race, sexuality, and nationality as personal identities, feminist and gender scholars define identities as social categories, which are shaped by social ideologies, institutions, and interactions.

A **gendered ideology** is a set of values, beliefs, and/or ideas that reinforce our practices of gender socialization. Gendered ideologies suggest masculine characteristics are natural to men and feminine characteristics are natural to women. Gendered ideologies support the belief that men and women are naturally different and that this difference results in a hierarchy of men dominating women. In the film *Trading Women*, for example, a gendered ideology is the generally unquestioned belief that men biologically need to have sex whenever they feel desire. This belief helps to justify the gendered practice of the modern trade of women for sex.

Gendered practices are social interactions that are justified by ideologies and reinforced through institutions. A social interaction identifies how more than one individual relates to another through communication and other actions. A **gendered interaction** from *Trading Women* identifies how women are bought and sold by men for men in most sex trafficking scenarios. One group (men) buys another group (women). It is the act of purchase that is the interaction. Social ideologies and social interactions are systemized through institutions.

A social institution is a group, organization, or concept that makes and enforces social rules and ideologies. A **gendered institution** is the massage parlor that is owned by a man and buys and sells women in addition to the massage services it advertises. Two things happen when we name social identities **"social constructs"**: first, it distinguishes talking about identity in a social way from how identity is personally experienced; second, it indicates that as members of society, individuals and groups participate in constructing the meaning of social identities.

If we say people agree to meanings of social constructs—both events and identities—we can also argue that they disagree. The meanings of these categories are not fixed because they are based on the perceptions and experiences of individuals and groups. Social practices and ideas change over time, and these changes affect how meanings of events change. In other words, sometimes you know a social, cultural, political, or economic idea is socially constructed because it changes over time and by geographic region. Gender scholars study personal identities as social constructs to help explain how societal views on race, gender, sexuality, and nationality change over time and according to where we live.

Members of society continuously socially construct the meanings of identities by creating a relationship between an identity and specific values and beliefs for that identity. People then reinforce these meanings by practicing them in social interactions and regulating them through social institutions. In other words, we create social constructs; we express and perform them, we perceive them, and we identify with them. Over time and reinforced through various elements of society, people experience socially constructed identities as natural and normal. This makes the meanings of social constructs seem unchangeable. At the same time, when we analyze the social circumstances of "natural" experiences over time, we can see how the meanings of social constructs change. This analysis challenges "facts" we take for granted, such as the idea that women are inherently and always vulnerable to men or that most human trafficking is sex trafficking.

I have identified three distinct situations that contribute to the oppression of women in human trafficking. These are *violence against women*; the *commercialization of women's bodies*; and the *feminization of migration*. Understanding these issues will help the reader identify several related problematic social and economic conditions that support the phenomenon of a greater proportion of trafficked women than men in modern slavery.

Violence Against Women

Feminist scholars show how trafficking of women is a form of gender-based violence (van Niekerk 2018) and a violation of human rights (Gusta and Madera 2019). They promote gender equity because they position women as citizens who have a right to live free of violence and provide legislative pathways that support survivors, punish traffickers, and prevent trafficking. Framing trafficking as violence against women makes clear how those who are victimized are survivors, not criminals, which then acknowledges how trafficking is abusive and is connected to bodily and psychological harm (Mutter 2018). One scene in *Trading Women* shows a raid of a brothel, and approximately twenty girls are escorted out by the police. The narrator explains that rather than arrest the girls for breaking prostitution laws, Thai officials treat trafficked girls as victims of their circumstances. There is even a shelter created for survivors of trafficking to help the often very young girls get education and vocational training. As the former director of the United States President's Interagency Council on Women, Theresa Laur, remarks, "The real heart of this and the thing that drives people to get at this issue is that real girls and women and children are being affected. They are truly victims. And it's not on a small scale. It's on an enormous scale." In this section, I will discuss how human trafficking fits into a violence-against-women framework.

In 1995, the Fourth World Conference on Women characterized sex trafficking as an international human rights violation by naming it a form of violence against women. As a violation of human rights, violence against women instills fear and insecurity in women's lives and is an obstacle to the achievement of equality, development, and peace. This fear of violence is a permanent constraint on the mobility of women and limits women's access to resources and basic activities. The frame of trafficking as violence against women acknowledges that this behavior is abusive and is explicitly connected to bodily and psychological harm.

As a rhetorical frame, **violence against women** is defined as gendered: masculine bodies harming feminine bodies. It is viewed as a way for perpetrators to assert male dominance, power, and control over women. It is maintained through social and cultural tolerance of abuses that occur in both public and private lives. Behaviors include physical, sexual, and psychological violence that occur in the family such as battering, sexual abuse of female children in the household, dowry-related violence, marital rape, female genital mutilation and other traditional practices harmful to women, non-spousal violence, and violence related to exploitation.

Behaviors also include physical, sexual, and psychological violence occurring within the general community including rape, sexual abuse, sexual harassment and intimidation at work, in educational institutions, and elsewhere, and trafficking in women and forced prostitution (UN Division for the Advancement of Women Beijing Update, Retrieved December 9, 2003, from www.un.org/womenwatch/daw/followup/beijing+5.htm).

In March 2010, government leaders from all over the world met to celebrate the fifteenth anniversary of the 4th World Conference on Women and report on the status of recommendations produced at the original conference. One report from the United Nations' economic and social council from the Economic and Social Commission for Asia and the Pacific clearly positions trafficking as violence against women. It states:

> Many countries, including Azerbaijan, Cambodia, Georgia, India, Indonesia, Japan, Kyrgyzstan, Nepal, Philippines, Republic of Korea, Thailand, and Uzbekistan, have introduced anti-human-trafficking legislation in the last five years. There is also more focus on legal protection and support for victims, in contrast to earlier approaches that tended to treat the victim as a criminal while rarely prosecuting traffickers.
> (UN Division for the Advancement of Women Beijing Update, Retrieved May 11, 2011 from www.unescap.org/esid/GAD/Events/HLM-2009/download/BPA09_2E.pdf)

Thailand's and other countries' focus on antitrafficking legislation and support for victims likely occurred in response, at least in part, to legislation and required reporting that was mandated by the United States Victims of Trafficking and Violence Prevention Act of 2000. The act contains provisions to protect victims of trafficking from criminal charges and strengthens domestic laws against trafficking by trying perpetrators as rapists. The act also sets international standards with which governments must comply in order to continue receiving nonhumanitarian aid from the United States. Countries are ranked according to tiers. Tier one demonstrates a country's full compliance with the law. Tiers two and two-watch are countries that show effort but still need improvement. Tier three represents those countries that have shown no effort to comply.

Commercialized Intimacy

Throughout *Trading Women*, several clips from advertisement and film show how Asian women and girls are hypersexualized in film and other media. In one instance, the viewer of the film sees General William Westmoreland explain trafficking in Thailand by saying, "Well the oriental doesn't put the same price on life as the Westerner. Life is plentiful. Life is cheap in the Orient." "Cheap" can mean "disposable" or it can mean "inexpensive." Also consider this statement from *Trading Women* by Dr. Saisuree Chuticku from the National Committee on Combating Trafficking in Children and Women in Thailand: "The sight that I couldn't stand is when they have young girls put on numbers and sit in a glass window and they say I want number thirty-two and to me that is almost like animal and I couldn't take it." Putting girls in windows in a line treats them like objects to be considered, selected, purchased, and consumed.

   In this section, I will define *commercialized intimacy* and discuss the relationship between women workers and care and love as global commodities that contribute to the global economy but do so in invisible ways (Cohen and Wolkowitz 2018; Ehrenreich and Hochschild 2002). In **commercialized intimacy**, bodies or parts of bodies are the product, and to make someone a product or an object one must be dehumanized or as Dr. Chuticku says, one must be "like an animal." The relationship between money and intimacy helps illuminate how and why women migrant workers are more at risk than men migrant workers for entrapment into modern slavery. The consumption of intimacy primarily happens on and through women's bodies (Kang 2010).

   Feminizing paid labor helps remedy any cultural and economic problems that come from these intimate interactions (Cohen and Wolkowitz 2018).

   The study of commercialized intimacy reveals how emotions including love, sex, and care are bought and sold in the market as products or commodities (Zelizer 2005). In labor, slave or paid, commercialized intimacy is part of the increasing commodification of intimacy that permeates and sustains global capitalism (Parrenas 2005). This is to say that as our society advances economically, culturally, and technologically, intimacy and capital become more tightly linked (Boris and Parrenas 2010). Emotional, care, and service labor fulfills human desire and need and is available in several forms. In all these forms, commercialized intimacies are packaged as global products and exported and imported across national borders. Sex work and care work, including that which happens in the trafficking of humans, meet physical and emotional needs for sex and construct a mimicked intimacy for the purchaser. Domestic labor assumes and partitions the care of our young and the messy work of homemaking that creates a space for intimacy to occur between others. Beauty work, for example manicures and massages, provides comfort, rest, and relaxation and a feeling of closeness and consideration.

Emotion is not the only commodity in commercialized intimacy; the body is also a site of exchange (Cohen and Wolkowitz 2018). In the case of human trafficking, it is the body and not just the work that is exchanged. In her discussion of global domestic work, Bridget Anderson distinguishes between the body as personhood and the body as property (2000). She asserts, "with particular reference to the caring function of domestic labour, that it is the worker's personhood, rather than her labour power, which the employer is attempting to buy, and that the worker is thereby cast as unequal in the exchange" (2). In the trafficking of humans, it is clearly the personhood that is exchanged, not simply the work for which the person is bought and sold.

When the body is property, two things happen. First, the propertied body is dehumanized, and second, the employer feels entitled to this body. Because she is dehumanized and because she is paid for, an employer may feel a disproportionate sense of access to the care worker's body. Jobs in intimate settings exacerbate these violations because employers are not monitored. In some of these cases, harm becomes indistinguishable from job expectation. Care work is often sexualized because much of it involves intimate interaction, the meeting of physical and emotional needs. Sometimes, from an employer's perspective, care work is laced with sexual expectations. This has become so normative that live-in domestic workers try to prevent misunderstanding from the beginning by clearly stating in their newspaper advertisements, "no sex." But sexual abuse and harassment, embedded in normative terms, persist:

> A friend of mine went for a job and he opened the door and he was totally naked. She didn't want to show how she felt so she said, 'do you want me to clean your house or watch your body?' He said, 'What's wrong? It's only natural!' One worker in Paris was furious when her friend passed on a male employer who liked to watch her clean when he had no clothes on. When she complained, her friend told her that she had worked for him for years under these conditions.
>
> (Anderson 2000, p. 135)

Feminine bodies are objectified and commodified, whether through work or performance.

Recall the quote from the massage parlor in *Trading Women*, "The girls from the North are the best because they have white skin. They are beautiful. They are the best workers because they can charge the highest rates." Here it is not just the massage and/or sex that is being purchased; it is not just the woman's body that it is being displayed and sold; it is her light skin in particular that is marketed. Sociologist Evelyn Nakano Glenn explains how skin lighteners serve as symbolic capital to women who otherwise do not have any power available to them (2008). She argues:

> Skin lightening has been incorporated into transnational flows of capital, goods, people, and culture. It is implicated in both the formal global economy and various informal economies. It is integrated into both legal and extralegal transnational circuits of goods.
>
> (283)

Although Nakano Glenn refers to the illegal smuggling of lighteners, the same principle applies to bodies in the case of human trafficking. Lighter is ideological better, and this is what institutionally sells. Whether it is the product or the body being sold, commercialized intimacy depends on sexist and racist ideologies that objectify women's bodies and prefer whiteness over other skin tones. These ideologies support the institutionalized practices of human trafficking of women.

Despite dehumanizing work experiences, there continues to be a clear need for migrant women workers to do reproductive work or "women's work" to meet the needs of what Arlie Hochschild calls a "care crisis" in economically rich nations (Ehrenreich and Hochschild 2002). This is because in most families, all the adults work outside of the home, and no one is left to take care of the house or the children. Women's work includes domestic and care work and jobs that replicate personal characteristics traditionally associated with women such as serving, nurturing, and fulfilling one's needs. Women's work also includes what some gender scholars call performing femininity or doing the work of *being* a woman through makeup, plastic surgery, and diet and exercise (Banet-Weiser and Portwood-Stacer 2006; Dworkin and Wachs 2004; Ferreday 2008).

When General Westmoreland says "life is cheap in the Orient," what he really means is that the bodies of women, especially dark-skinned women, are cheap. The commercialization of intimacy reveals the connections between microlevel interactions such as those between traffickers, consumers, and slaves and macrolevel processes such as the relationship between human trafficking and the global economy. It shows how experiences of the intimate construct social relations and how social relations such as those that are raced and gendered construct intimate experiences. It also shows the connections between intimacy, violence, and purchase (van Niekerk 2018).

Feminization of Migration

For survival, women have migrated internationally for various types of domestic, care, and sex work throughout the twentieth century and into the twenty-first century (Chang 2000; Choy 2003; Ehrenreich and Hochschild 2002; Plambech 2017; Sharpe 2001). In *Trading Women*, three young women, two girls from Burma and a girl from Louse, tell how they were trafficked into sex work. Here, they serve as a composite to illustrate the reason women migrate for work: as a solution to economic crisis.

> I'm from the Hill Tribes. We don't have money so I have to send money to my parents. My relative came first and I followed. A woman came to see me at home and asked if I wanted to go [to Thailand]. I said I didn't. One day I said I would go . . . one day she turned up. My mother did not want me to leave . . . The owner asked me if I would like to stay with her to work as a waitress in her place. I then said ok. She gave me her telephone number. Later I called her to apply for a job. . . . My mother did not know what kind of work I was doing. She thought I was a waitress. If my mother knew I was working in this kind of job, she wouldn't have let me come.

These quotes illustrate the need for women to migrate as well as the risks they take when they do. Women who migrate for work do so because they are in extreme poverty. In most cases, a woman's poverty is inextricably connected to her country's economy and its relationship to the dominant global economy. In this section, I discuss research on **feminized migration** to demonstrate how women of color migrant workers are at risk of being trafficked through fraudulent recruitment strategies used by traffickers and vulnerable work conditions (Anderson and Li 2018; Parrenas 2006).

Today, women make up half of all migrants who move to places all over the world. These places include the United States and other advanced nations, but they also include developing countries. Essentially, we see migrations from less rich nations to richer. Rich nations remain rich and poor nations remain poor in part because poor nations are in debt to supranational organizations like the World Bank and the International Monetary Fund, which are dominated by rich nations. As a result of having loans with rigid structural conditions attached, there are fewer jobs in the home countries of women migrants. Unemployment persists in these developing and underdeveloped nations, which causes men to lose their jobs and governments to cut back on social assistance. Women, rather than men, must migrate because the jobs available outside of their home countries seem more suitable to women. Socially constructed gender ideologies and a systematic need for care in advanced countries construct opportunities for women rather than men.

Ideologically, women of color are hypervisible as natural nurturers (Chang 2000; Collins 2000; Hondagneu-Sotelo 2001). Sociologist Pierrette Hondagneu-Sotelo examines how United States employers of immigrant Latina domestic workers view domestic workers as more "naturally" loving than white women caregivers and how these ideologies contribute to their socially invisible and oppressive work conditions (2001). In her study, employers consistently thought of their domestic workers as naturally warm, patient, and loving. In other words, the care work of Latina domestic workers was so natural it was effortless. As such, employers negated domestic work and diminished its contribution to economic growth through low wages. Rather than emphasize how domestic work is work and also contributes to the economy, employers attributed the labor of domestic workers to their national or ethnic culture.

This ideology that associates women of color with hyperloving care abilities is not new to maintaining social and economic stratification. Sociologist Bonnie Thornton Dill's classic research on black women's work at the turn of the twentieth century demonstrates that the high proportion of Black women in household work was a direct product of residual ideologies that justified slavery (1983). Controlling images justified the presence of Black women in slavery by saying they were both inherently hypersexual and hyperloving. These same ideologies justified job discrimination and poor work conditions for Black women postslavery. Evelyn Nakano Glenn also demonstrates how stratification of paid care work has been historically structured by ideological and material inequalities in race, gender, and nationality (2010, 2002). Nakano Glenn reveals that the coercion of people of color and the denial of their freedoms as part of the historical construction of paid care work helped to define the meaning of care as altruism, a status obligation, or an extension of servitude.

Once migrant workers arrive, they are isolated in many variations of homes: personal homes, nursing homes, and brothel homes. As such, they are part of the informal sector, not protected with social security or labor legislation, and they have no legal recourse to protect themselves. They are exposed to harassment, intimidation, and threats to themselves and their families, economic and sexual exploitation, racial discrimination, poor working conditions, increased health risks, and other forms of abuse, including trafficking into forced labor, debt bondage, involuntary servitude, and situations of captivity. To ensure their compliance, employers often hold visas or passport papers. Domestic, care, and sex workers are part of an invisible economy and work unlimited hours for inconsistent wages and often under the threat of deportation.

*black wet nurses

Women are recruited through what sociologist Saskia Sassen calls "third party migrations" and often under misleading, fraudulent conditions. Women are told that they can earn much more money abroad than at home for the same work. Once they begin their new jobs, they are paid minimal wages for work that is less skilled than they expected (Parrenas 2006). For example, many immigrant nurses in the United States are first underemployed as nursing assistants before getting the chance to work the jobs they were promised. In the case of sex work, women may be told that they will be working in factories or as domestic workers only to be sold to a brothel when they arrive in the city. Despite promises for a better life, migrant women's expectations are often not met and they are in fact abused and exploited.

Employers and traffickers alike trick women into working in unfair conditions. Most trafficked people are not kidnapped but rather are solicited by known people (friends and family members) or agencies that promise them good jobs in prosperous countries but deceive them and sell them to traffickers. Traffickers rarely approach families and offer to exchange girls and young women for a "better life." More commonly, seemingly legitimate organizations recruit women under fraudulent conditions such as marriage, work, and modeling.

Traffickers and employers use remarkably similar methods to maintain control over women workers. These include inflicting physical and sexual violence, hiding passports and other documentation, and psychological threats to report them to immigration authorities. Abuse of migrant workers is more obvious in the industry of sex trafficking but still presents itself in other kinds of labor that depend upon commercialized intimacy. If emotional attachment is simultaneously couched as "natural" and paid labor, job expectations become more easily blurred. Long, indeterminate hours and unstable pay that depend not on fixed labor conditions but rather on a family's or individual's shifting needs are more easily justified. When public and private spheres merge, labor boundaries become less stable and offer more opportunity for mistreatment. Exploitation is further exacerbated for migrant workers because for many, their undocumented status makes them even more vulnerable to unfair, unsafe, and sometimes life-threatening work conditions (Anderson 2000; Ehrenreich and Hochschild 2002; Parrenas 2006).

Women do domestic, care, and sex work in other countries not because they seek a better life for themselves and for their families but for their families to survive. Whole families are often dependent on the wages of just one immigrant care worker. The home countries of immigrant workers benefit as well. Poor nations gain resources through the export of workers.

For example, Jamaica exports teachers and nurses in partnership with the United States, and in turn, the United States provides money to educate teachers and nurses in Jamaica.

Moreover, many countries require immigrant care workers to submit part of their paycheck back to their home governments in exchange for the "right" to work in the United States and other economically rich nations (Choy 2003).

Transnational Feminist Theory: Suggestions for Research and Activism

not a border issue

Women are trafficked more often than men. What is not always clear, however, is *why* women are trafficked so often. One common misconception in trafficking discourse is that women are trafficked more often than men simply because they are women in need of protection (from men). This might imply that women are trafficked because they are naturally weaker than men. To say women are naturally weaker than men may suggest that women are inherently inferior to men. On a global scale, we know this is not true. For centuries, transnational feminist scholars and activists consistently have demonstrated that women are just as physically, emotionally, and spiritually strong as men. It is a mistake to think that women are trafficked more than men because they are inferior to men.

In this chapter, we have learned that gender is socially constructed and, as such, impacts three major dimensions of the oppression of women: interpersonal violence against women, the commercialized intimacy of women's bodies, and the feminization of migration. These issues do not just manifest on a gendered level; they depend on national identity and are raced and classed. Who is sold and to whom that person is sold depends upon gender, yes, but they also depend on one's global national, racial and socio-economic class status. What seems clear, for example, is that the poorer you are *and* the more feminine you are the more likely you are to be trafficked. One cannot analyze trafficking without analyzing multiple social identities and their social and economic influences.

intersectionality

Transnational feminist theorists show that the export and import of care, service, love, and sex as commodified goods are integral to the functioning and spread of capitalism and western ideologies. At the same time, the labor that produces care and service remains invisible in discourse on globalization processes (Eherenreich and Hochschild 2002). While much of the discourse on globalization speaks in broad, sweeping terms, Saskia Sassan asserts that the global production of commodities occurs in concrete locations—global cities—that reflect real time and space. Like paid workers, trafficking victims move from place to place to ensure that they remain undetected by people who could help them and also—especially in the case of sex trafficking—to continue to offer clients a new "product" in the form of new bodies and faces.

With regard to human trafficking, transnational feminist theorists and activists are suspicious about the universalizing rhetoric used in the trafficking discourse, such as all women are at risk for trafficking in the same ways and need to be rescued. Feminists argue that we should always carefully interrogate the claims made about global sex trafficking and the rescue missions designed to solve the trafficking problem (Parrenas 2006; Sharma 2005; Soderland 2005). We should pay particular attention to any rhetoric or practice that reinforces a framework that positions some women in negative opposition to others (Collins 2000). There is no doubt that the United States' Victims of Trafficking and Violence Prevention Act (TVPA) has saved lives. At the same time, the rhetoric used to support saving women could be the same rhetoric used to subordinate them through a politics of fear (Parrenas 2006); a politics of fraud via anti-immigration work policies (Parrenas 2006; Sharma 2005), and frank, complex gender politics such as those that support anti–reproductive justice campaigns (Soderland 2005). For the latter, some scholars note: "the Bush administration's fight against global sex trafficking conveniently dovetails with its quest to dismantle public health efforts that support women's reproductive rights and champion condom use as a viable means to control pregnancy and the spread of HIV/AIDS" (Saunders 2004 quoted in Soderland 2005, p. 79). Indeed, as Audre Lorde famously said, "The master's tools will never dismantle the master's house" (1984).

It is important, then, to keep analysis of human trafficking away from moral concerns.

Trading Women features several United States politicians who initiated and supported the TVPA. As the film states and portrays, antitrafficking campaigns attract an "odd coalition that range between feminists and evangelicals; liberal Democrats and conservative Republicans." One TVPA initiator, Sam Brownback, a Republican Senator from Kansas, is shown saying the following about victims: "None of us are perfect. And we've all had problems or motivations that are impure." The word "impure" implies a false but deeply held and consistently reinforced ideology that makes women solely responsible for acts of unwanted sex or, in this case, acts of trafficking. Chris Smith, a Republican Congressman from New Jersey, is shown saying, "It's amazing how dismissive many people in government are, oh they're just prostitutes. Well my faith tells me that they are not just prostitutes, they are as valuable as anyone else on Earth." Although initially seeming generous to the viewer, Smith's portrayal of sex trafficked women as prostitutes is a negative one. He draws on familiar tropes that suggest, first, that all sex trafficked women are prostitutes and thereby criminals and, second, that they are less valuable than women who are not prostitutes. Whenever seemingly positive references of trafficked victims are evoked in this way, they are potentially positioned against others that do not deserve to be saved (Collins 2000). One more important note: all these rhetorical strategies strip women of any sort of agency or control over their circumstances and/or their bodies.

At another point in the film, UN Resident Coordinator Thailand Robert England says,

> I think everybody would agree that trafficking in human beings is morally reprehensible. On the other hand, it's a very, very complicated issue which cannot be solved easily and certainly cannot be solved by a purely moralistic approach which says: "Naughty. You mustn't do that."

At the same time that England warns the viewer of any approach based on totalizing moralistic views, Brownback's legislative aide is shown saying in frustration, "unless someone just says no (moves her hand in a wiping motion) it's going to keep going and it's going to get more and more perverse." Transnational feminist scholars would avoid using any kind of universal language.

As a framework, transnational feminist theory helps to analyze a problem without objectifying the subject of that problem or universalizing all women into one category.

Transnational feminist scholars use **intersectionality** as an analytical lens to explain how multiple and discrete social categories—race, gender, sexuality, class, and nationality—work together to create unique experiences of privilege and subordination (Crenshaw 1989, 1991). It maintains the subject's agency and helps to preserve her voice and perspective in policy and law (Desyllas 2007; Mohanty 2002; Sharma 2005). It considers how an individual's circumstances cause the problem without blaming the individual; it reveals previously invisible oppressions (Frye 1983). Transnational feminist theory seeks partnerships with other feminist movements that do not impose universalizing language that may not account for all women's experiences (Long 2004). It partners with other feminists without an "arrogant eye" that could unwittingly impose Westernization (Frye 1983; Gunning 1991; Mohanty 2002). These are the many features of transnational feminist theory, but here, I will focus on how to use intersectionality to respond to trafficking in women.

In 1989, renowned legal theorist Kimberle Crenshaw coined the term "intersectionality" to help explain how sexual harassment experienced by women of color is not captured by existing legal rubrics (Crenshaw 1989). Rooted in the writings of multicultural feminists and critical race theory, intersectionality is a conceptual and methodological framework that explains how discrete social categories—race, gender, sexuality, class, and nationality—work together to create unique experiences of privilege and subordination. For two decades, intersectionality has challenged the law and traditional research methodologies in various disciplines. Scholars have used it develop transnational and multicultural feminist theories (Collins 2000; Mohanty 2002).

Scholars who use intersectionality theory to study sociology must stay true to how and when their categories emerge in the analysis, or we run the risk of erroneously including categories simply for the sake of inclusiveness. A scholar's attempts to be inclusive could result in statements of false universals. They may conflate distinct effects or mask salient patterns in their data by attempting to analyze all possible relationships rather than the ones that specifically emerge from the subject being studied (McCall 2005; Welsh et al. 2006). One way to precisely analyze the influence of multiple social constructs on inequalities is to use intersectionality to inform conceptual strategies and research designs (Collins 1999).

As a framework that explains the dynamics of oppression in various contexts, intersectionality also challenges established meanings of social life. Patricia Hill Collins (1999) inspired gender and feminist scholars to use intersectionality to change how we conduct scientific research. Changing the production of knowledge requires scholars to look not just at the structural effects of the intersections of social identities but also at how these relations inform the process of meaning making. This is an integral component of intersectionality; if it does not connect knowledge making to structural practice and experience, then it is not intersectionality theory (Collins 1999).

In addition to those I've mentioned, several transnational feminist scholars discuss the importance in how we frame gender issues in human trafficking. First, the socially constructed categories of identities such as race and gender are not fixed. They are produced in specifically contextual ways that are shaped by region, economics, politics, religion, etc. (Collins 2000).

Next, although violence against women is a significant form of oppression faced by women worldwide, to combat human trafficking, we cannot just focus on violence against women as a gender issue. The meaning and experiences of violence against women change at the intersection of race, gender, and nationality (Crenshaw 1989, 1991, 1992; Ehrenreich and Hochschild 2002). In addition, whether "paid" or trafficked, the meanings of jobs that require commercialized intimacy also function specifically at intersections of race, gender, and nationality, for example, in nursing (Ruchti 2012) and in Korean-owned nail salons (Kang 2010). Finally, the meaning of femininization of migration changes at the intersection of race, gender, nationality, region, and class. There are multiple forms of trafficking (Parrenas 2006). As women move for work, women are trafficked within and across borders (Boxill and Richardson 2007; Tambe 2005).

Here, the concepts of nationality and citizenship are important because they intersect with race, gender, and other identities to construct experiences.

Proponents of intersectionality agree that intersectionality can be conceptualized many ways: as a theory, a methodological approach, a context to situate people's experience, and a lens to act. It is here that I will share my inspiration and my intention for the use of intersectionality in this chapter. Women's and gender studies scholars use intersectionality to capture the impact of multiple identities, develop research questions, shape designs, think through power dynamics, and explain the social, economic, and symbolic meanings of everyday life. To study human trafficking today, we cannot separate social constructs of race, gender, sexuality and nationality because individuals do not live—identify, perceive, and practice—these experiences separately.

End-of-Chapter Discussion Questions

1. How does each of the following inform and sustain the trafficking of humans: a gendered ideology, a gendered interaction, and a gendered institution?
2. Are *all* women at risk for trafficking? Why or why not?
3. What are the similarities between the system of trafficking of persons and the system of feminized migration of women? What are the differences?

A "Postchapter" Quiz for Students
1. How is oppression distinct from human misery?
2. What is the definition of commercialized intimacy?
3. How is immigration feminized?
4. Identify one feature of transnational feminist theory.

Reading/video suggestions (Compiled by Amanda Brooks, West Chester University)

Ursula Biemann. *Performing the Border.* Switzerland/Mexico, 1999, 42 minutes, Color www.wmm.com/filmcatalog/pages/c474.shtml

Ursula Biemann. *Remote Sensing.* 2001, 53 minutes, Color. www.wmm.com/filmcatalog/pages/c564.shtml

Ursula Biemann. *Writing Desire.* 2000, 23 minutes, Color. www.wmm.com/filmcatalog/pages/c537.shtml

Joan E. Biren. *Women Organize!* Union Institute Ctr. for Women & Women and Organizing Documentation Project. 2000, 32 minutes, Color. www.wmm.com/filmcatalog/pages/c536.shtml

Gillian Caldwell. *Bought & Sold: An Investigative Documentary About the International Trade in Women.* 2009, 42 min, Color.

Mimi Chakarova. *Price of Sex.* US, 2011, 73 minutes. www.wmm.com/filmcatalog/pages/c804.shtml.

Michael Cory Davis. *Cargo: Innocence Lost*. 73 min. color. www.cargoinnocencelost.com/home.html

Sharon Genasci and Dorothy Velasco. *Troubled Harvest*. 1990, 30 minutes, Color. www.wmm.com/filmcatalog/pages/c72.shtml

Larry Rich & Gayla Jamison. *Lives for Sale*. 2007.60 min, Color. www.livesforsale.com/index.html

Chris Ho & Greg Shapley. *Empire's New Clothes, The*. 2000, 9 min. Color www.fulfillmentwarehouse.biz/witness/default.asp?cat=328&pid=2764

ABC News Primetime, *Sex Trafficking in America*. 2006 http://abcnewsstore.go.com/webapp/wcs/stores/servlet/DSIProductDisplay?catalogId=11002&storeId=20051&productId=2003493&langId=-1&categoryId=100024

CBS News. *Halting Human Trafficking*. 2007 www.cbsnews.com/video/watch/?id=3261066n

References

Anderson, Bridget. 2000. *Doing the dirty work: The global politics of domestic labour*. New York: Zed Books.

Anderson, Jade and Annie Li. 2018. "Refugees or victims of human trafficking? The case of migrant domestic works in Hong Kong." *Anti-Trafficking Review* 11: 52–68.

Banet-Weiser, Sarah and Laura Portwood-Stacer. 2006. "I just want to be me again! Beauty pageants, reality television, and post-feminism." *Feminist Theory* 7 (3): 255–272.

Boris, Eileen and Rhacel Salazar Parrenas (Eds.). 2010. *Intimate labors: Cultures, technologies, and the politics of care*. Palo Alto, CA: Stanford University Press.

Boxill, Nancy A. and Deborah J. Richardson. 2007. "Ending sex trafficking of children in Atlanta." *Affilia: Journal of Women and Social Work* 22 (2): 138–149.

Chang, Grace. 2000. *Disposable domestics: Immigrant women workers in the global factory*. Brooklyn, NY: South End Press.

Choy, Catherine Ceniza. 2003. *Empire of care: Nursing and migration in Filipino American history*. Durham, NC: Duke University Press.

Cohen, Rachel Lara and Carol Wolkowitz. 2018. "The feminization of body work." *Gender Work and Organization* 25 (1): 42–62.

Collins, Patricia Hill. 2000. *Black feminist thought: Knowledge, consciousness, and the politics of empowerment*, second edition. New York: Routledge.

Collins, Patricia Hill. 1999. "Moving Beyond Gender: Intersectionality and Scientific Knowledge." In *Re-visioning gender*, edited by Myra Marx, Ferree, Judith Lorber, and Beth B. Hess. Thousand Oaks, CA: Sage Publications.

Crenshaw, Kimberle. 1989. Demarginalizing the intersection of race and sex: A black feminist critique of antidiscrimination doctrine, feminist theory and antiracist politics. *University of Chicago Legal Forum* 1(8):139–167.

Crenshaw, Kimberle. 1991. "Mapping the margins: Intersectionality, identity politics, and violence against women of color." *Stanford Law Review* 43: 1241–1299.

Crenshaw, Kimberle. 1992. "Race, gender, and sexual harassment." *Southern California Law Review* 65: 1467–1476.

Desyllas, Moshoula Capous. 2007. "A critique of the global trafficking discourse and U.S. policy." *Journal of Sociology and Social Welfare* 30 (4): 57–79.

Dill, Bonnie Thornton. 1983. "Race, class, and gender: Prospects for an all-inclusive sister-hood." *Feminist Studies* 9 (1): 131–150.

Dworkin, Shari L. and Faye Linda Wachs. 2004. Getting your body back: Postindustrial fit motherhood in Shape Fit Pregnancy Magazine. *Gender & Society* 18: 610.

Ehrenreich, Barbara and Arlie Russell Hochschild. 2002. *Global woman: Nannies, maids, and sex workers in the new economy*. New York: Metropolitan Books.

Ferreday, Debra. 2008. "Showing the girl: The new burlesque." *Feminist Theory* 9: 47.

Frye, Marilyn. 1983. *The politics of reality: Essays in feminist theory*. Freedom, CA: The Crossing Press.

Gunning, Isabelle. 1991. "Arrogant perception, world travelling, and multi-cultural feminism: The case of female genital surgeries." *Columbian Human Rights Law Review* 23: 189.

Gusta, Ana Laura Rodriguez and Nancy Madera. 2019. "When some rights matter more than others: Recent national legislation on women' human rights in Latin America and the Caribbean." *Canadian Woman Studies* 33 (1/2): 117–125.

Hodge, David R. and Cynthia A. Lietz. 2007. "The international sexual trafficking of women and children: A review of the literature." *Affilia: Journal of Women and Social Work* 22 (2): 163–174.

Hondagneu-Sotelo, Pierrette. 2001. *Domestica: Immigrant workers cleaning and caring in the shadows of affluence*. Berkeley, CA: University of California Press.

Kang, Miliann. 2010. *The managed hand: Race, gender, and the body in beauty service work*. Berkeley, CA: University of Berkeley Press.

Long, Lynellyn. 2004. "Anthropological perspectives on the trafficking of women for sexual exploitation." *International Migration* 42 (1): 5.

Lorde, Audre. 1984. *Sister outsider*. Berkeley, CA: Crossing Press.

McCall, Leslie. 2005. "The complexity of intersectionality." *Signs: Journal of Women in Culture and Society* 30: 1771–1800.

Mohanty, Chandra Talpade. 2002. "'Under western eyes' revisited: Feminist solidarity through anti-capitalist struggles." *Signs: Journal of Women in Culture and Society* 28 (2): 499–535.

Mutter, Alice. 2018. "From criminals to survivors: Recognizing domestic sex trafficking as violence against women in the District of Columbia." *American University Journal of Gender, Social Policy & the Law* 26 (1): 593–621.

Nakano Glenn, Evelyn. 2002. *Unequal freedom: How race and gender shaped American citizenship and labor*. Cambridge, MA: Harvard University Press.

Nakano Glenn, Evelyn. 2008. "Yearning for lightness: Transnational circuits in the marketing and consumption of skin lighteners." *Gender & Society* 22: 281.

Nakano Glenn, Evelyn. 2010. *Forced to care: Coercion and care giving in America*. Cambridge, MA: Harvard University Press.

Parrenas, Rhacel Salazar. 2005. *Children of global migration: Transnational families and gendered woes*. Stanford, CA: Stanford University Press.

Parrenas, Rhacel Salazar. 2006. "Sex for sale: Trafficked? Filipino hostesses in Tokyo's nightlife industry." *Yale Journal of Law and Feminism* 18: 145.

Plambech, Sine. 2017. "Sex, deportation, and rescue: Economies of migration among Nigerian sex workers." *Feminist Economics* 23 (3): 134–159.

Ruchti, Lisa C. 2012. *Catheters, slurs, and pick-up lines: Professional intimacy in hospital nursing*. Philadelphia, PA: Temple University Press.

Satalia, Patty (Senior Producer). 2010, December 16. Mary Burke—Slavery Not a History Lesson: *Conversations* from Penn State [Television broadcast]. State College, PA: Penn State on Demand.

Saunders, Penelope. 2004. "Prohibiting sex worker projects, restricting women's rights: The international impact of the 2003 U.S. Global AIDS Act." *Health and Human Rights: An International Journal* 7 (2): 179–192.

Schwarz, Corrine, Emily J. Kennedy and Hannah Britton. 2017. "Aligned across difference: Structural injustice, sex work, and human trafficking." *Feminist Formations* 29 (2): 1–25.

Sharma, Nandita. 2005. Anti-trafficking rhetoric and the making of a global apartheid. *NWSA Journal* 17 (3): 88–111.

Sharpe, Pamela. 2001. *Women, gender, and labor migration: Historical and global perspectives.* London: Routledge.

Slotar, Dean W. and David A. Feingold (Producers). 2002. *Trading women.* Ophidian Films.

Soderland, Gretchen. 2005. "Running from the rescuers: New U.S. crusades against sex trafficking and the rhetoric of abolition." *NWSA Journal* 17 (3): 64–87.

Tambe, Ashwini. 2005. "The elusive ingénue: A transnational feminist analysis of European prostitution in colonial Bombay." *Gender & Society* 19: 160.

Van Niekerk, Caitlin Jade. 2018. "Interrogating sex trafficking discourses using a feminist approach." *Agenda: Empowering Women for Gender Equity* 32 (2): 17–27.

Welsh, Sandy, Jacquie Carr, Barbara Macquarrie, and Audrey Huntley. 2006. "'I'm not thinking of it as sexual harassment': Understanding harassment across race and citizenship." *Gender & Society* 20: 87–107.

Zelizer, Viviana A. 2005. *The purchase of intimacy.* Princeton, NJ: Princeton University Press.

8

THE EXPLOITATION EQUATION

DISTINGUISHING CHILD TRAFFICKING FROM OTHER TYPES OF CHILD MOBILITY IN WEST AFRICA

ANNE KIELLAND

Introduction

When trafficking in women and children hits the headlines, prostitution and other forms of sexual exploitation is the first association that comes to mind. The second may be children abducted and forced to participate in armed conflict. This chapter is not about these most extreme forms of trafficking in children, nor is it about the use of children in smuggling and other illicit activities. They are indisputable and terrible crimes and should be fought by all means available. Instead, this chapter takes a closer look at the vast gray zone between what may constitute child trafficking and what could represent other types of child mobility that both normatively and politically should be treated differently. That way, the possibility for a more thoughtful process of defining the phenomenon is addressed.

The chapter starts by presenting three debates that are central in contemporary child research and explains how they are relevant to the analysis of child trafficking situations: childhood as a social construction, child agency, and the intergenerational contract that binds children to family and kin, especially in uninsured societies. In the second section, definitions of relationships of dominance are explored: when do we (ab)use power against a child? How is child slavery different from child trafficking? And what indeed constitutes child trafficking according to the international discourse? In the third section, I present the empirical setting of West Africa—a region where child mobility and child labor, two of the core indicators of child trafficking, are rampant.

DOI: 10.4324/9781003124672-10

Over the past decade, international agencies have struggled to sort out which parts of this labor-related mobility can be said to constitute child trafficking. I will argue that they have largely failed due to overly simplistic definitions and that this failure has had some undesirable consequences. I will focus on trafficking to domestic servitude, mainly because similar academic approaches to the other large issue in the region, trafficking to farm work, are excellently explored in other academic contributions (Castle and Diarra, 2002; De Lange, 2006; Akresh, 2009; Hashim and Thorsen, 2011). In the fourth section, I will suggest ways to organize the relationship of exploitation, the central term in defining child trafficking, into a social equation. How can we best identify the complexities of rights and duties and benefits and costs for each of the two parties tied together in an exploitative relationship in a given social setting? Exploitation would assume that this relationship—this equation—is seriously out of balance. The chapter concludes with some future considerations and discussion questions.

The main objective of this chapter is to provoke critical thought around the use of the "child trafficking" term. Although child welfare is always the ultimate concern, it matters greatly what label is used to define a given situation. A trafficking s3ituation requires legal interventions. Many mobile and working children may be in need of very different types of support. The intended learning goals are reached if the student is able to provide a complex discussion of a given child mobility case, where arguments for and against defining the situation as trafficking can be provided in light of the concepts and ideas presented here.

Chapter Learning Objectives

- Understand the meaning of the social construction of childhood and how this construction affects the way the international discourse addresses child labor and child mobility issues.
- Understand child agency and how the two main forms of agency are relevant to children in general and children in trafficking situations in particular.
- Understand the intergenerational contract and what possible implications of such social commitments are for children working away from home.
- Understand the difference between child trafficking and adult trafficking.

Core Concepts and Child Research Debates

In this first section, I will present some theoretical concepts that will be useful to the later discussion. I will argue that in spite of claims of childhood being a Western social construct, children are different from adults in terms of their relative developmental vulnerability, their more limited ability to recognize and negotiate their interests, and their high dependency on adult caretakers to meet their basic needs. I'll present the central scientific discourse on child agency and explain its constraints in the context of the social contracts and informal safety nets into which children in developed countries are often born.

The Construction of Childhood and the Differentness of Children

From a relativist perspective, the heading of this subsection could be contagious. Childhood has, in Western culture and in recent history, been defined in very deterministic terms as a period fundamentally different from adulthood. Notably, labor and sexuality were perceived to be adult activities and had no place in the lives of children. Constructivists have argued that such a perception is a Western social construction rather than nature given (Aries, 1960). Circumstantial conditions, such as the demand for highly skilled labor that requires a time-consuming education process, have created an artificial divide between citizens who qualify for adult work life and those still in training.

If childhood is indeed socially constructed, global generalizations about children should be avoided. While this observation is important and deserving of reflection, I will argue a more pragmatic position in this chapter. I claim that there are some central distinctions between children and adults that affect the way we should look at child victims of trafficking compared to adult victims of trafficking. These differences are (i) developmental, (ii) cognitive, and (iii) social.

Children are physiologically different from adults, and they are in a constant process of adaptation and development. These differences are quite evident in the relatively helpless infant. It takes six months to learn to grab an object and a year to learn to walk. Advances are then gradually made by growth and practice. The following two examples of developmental processes children undergo help to illustrate their physical vulnerability. Bones are soft and moldable—an unfortunate working position or the repeated carrying of heavy loads could affect the development of the bone structure and create malformations that may lead to chronic muscle problems later in life. The brain is the last organ to develop in a child's body—at birth, the brain is only partly wired, and external impulses contribute to defining its structure. Physiologically speaking, this means that a child growing up in a violent environment may experience brain development and structuring that prompts the release of adrenaline at minute cues that otherwise may not have caused such an intense reaction. Such sensitive developmental processes add an aspect of vulnerability to children victims of trafficking.

Childhood is a relative state that gradually merges into adulthood. From infant to adolescent, children develop the cognitive ability to relate to multi-faceted environments and complex social settings. Under sound conditions, maturity and experience gradually make children more self-reliant, both with regard to trusting their own instincts and with regard to assessing and responding to their environment. On such a background, they develop self-identity, self-respect, and the ability to recognize and negotiate their own interests in encounters with others (Giddens, 1991). Children do not mature at the same rate or along the same paths. Social factors and biological conditions interact to determine the speed and direction of development. Children growing up under unfortunate conditions risk developing a disintegrated self-identity and a poor ability to both recognize and negotiate their own interests.

Due to factors like these, children depend on adult (or adolescent) caregivers to have their basic needs met as they develop physically, mentally, and socially. This dependency is stronger for children than it is for adults and only gradually declines with age. The importance of this dependency, for the purpose of this chapter, is the fact that the situation and interest of children cannot be understood without consideration of the situation and interest of the child's parents, kin, or caretakers. The child is often vitally dependent on the welfare of the mother (Case et al., 2002); therefore, the interest of the mother becomes a crucial interest to the child. The child's reliance on the social interest structures of close family and kin is qualitatively distinct from that of many adult victims of trafficking.

Children Have Agency: Strategic Versus Tactical Agency

The previous section conveys a picture of the relative weaknesses and vulnerabilities of children compared to those of adults. It is important to stress that this vulnerability is by no means absolute. The term **child agency** has been central to contemporary debates around childhood and has been a part of breakthrough childhood theories that are based on the notion of **the competent child**. "The competent child" contrasts historical images of children as passive victims of other people's decision making. From birth, children's preferences are constantly negotiated against the interests of their caregivers. The infant screams for food. The toddler learns that it can distract parental fighting by acting out. The girl child learns to calm down a violent father by imaging adult flirtation. Gradually, children develop overt or covert social strategies to defend or to advance their interests within their particular social setting.

"Agency" is a term closely related to the concept of **power** (Honwana, 2006, p. 69). Giddens (1984) defines human agency as the *capability* of doing something. It involves responsibility, as the person in question either produces or prevents a certain outcome by not acting: it is in the power of the person to do differently. Drawing on De Certeau (1984), Honwana distinguishes between **strategic** and **tactical agency** in her book about child soldiers in Africa. In short, the distinction corresponds to Bourdillon et al. (2010), who distinguish a *proactive* form of agency from a *reactive* one. Honwana points out that strategy assumes situational normality of some sort, a social setting where relations are generated with some level of autonomy. Tactics on the other hand, are short term and assume the absence of situational normality. That is the lack of "a spatial or institutional locus under the subject's control" (Honwana, 2006, pp. 70–71). Quoting de Certeau:

> The place of a tactic is the space of the other . . . it must play on and with a terrain imposed on it . . . it is a maneuver within the enemy's field of vision . . . it takes advantage of opportunities and depends on them . . . accepts the chance offerings of the moment.

Tactical Agency Is Characterized as the Art of the Weak

The term "he had no choice" is still often used to explain incidences where children in extreme situations act in ways that seem to conflict with their self-interests. Yet within the current discourse, children are often seen as holders of agency (Iversen, 2002a, 2002b; Hashim and Thorsen, 2011). While children in certain cases literally act with a gun to their heads, the child agency discourse argues that in most cases, they have at least a restricted set of options (Bourdillon et al., 2010). The fact that there are constraints to agency does not mean it ceases to exist: agency is almost always restricted (Whitehead et al., 2005). It still seems meaningful to apply the definition of a reactive *tactical agency* rather than strategic agency to children who find themselves in extreme situations such as trafficking. It can further be argued that to some extent, all children play on the field of "others"—the playing field of the world is generally structured and ruled by adults.

Children Are Not Isolated: Informal Safety Nets and the Intergenerational Contract

The first spatial and institutional locus for most children is their immediate family and kin. Looking primarily at children in poor countries, families represent more than a home and a source of food and care. The less insured the society, the stronger is the role the family members play as the informal social safety net for one another. In uninsured societies, survival rates of children would fall substantially without such kinship networks. It is also important to recognize that adults in these societies depend on children as they age. Consequently, the social contract between parents and children tends to represent a substantial commitment in those societies (Whitehead et al., 2005).

In uninsured societies, there is no pension, no sick leave, and no unemployment compensation. If drought or locust kills the family's crop, there is no insurance company to cover the damage. If the father dies, the widow receives no allowance, and the children are not compensated by some governmental power. No one pays your hospital bill, and the decision of investing your own savings in your children's education requires thorough deliberation in an insecure formal labor market.

In these uninsured societies around the world, families play the role of insurance agents. Within the informal safety nets composed by families and kin, risk is pooled and costs are shared. Individual aspirations may be compromised against collective interests. A risky business investment, a marriage proposal, or relocation is ideally discussed within the group or left to the head(s) of family to decide or advise. What would a gain or a loss mean to the group? What will a prospective spouse bring to the unit—benefits or risks? What benefits or risks could be derived from sending a young son to Cote d'Ivoire? To the son? To the group? The clan leaders may not forbid a young girl to marry her infatuation from a dubious family, but if she does not follow their advice and her new husband lets her down, she often carries the costs alone. Disobedience cannot be encouraged; rewards are given to those who step up and make decisions that serve the interests of the group.

One social institution that supports this informal insurance arrangement is the intergenerational contract (Kabeer, 2000, p. 465).[1] In short, parents give life and care to their children. Children repay them with obedience and are obliged to take care of their parents when they are no longer able to work to sustain themselves. The intergenerational contract is in many places fortified by religious institutions: only by the parents' prayers can the children succeed in life, and parents pray for the children who cooperate and obey. This social structure puts a harsh constraint on individual freedom, but consider the options and consequences of any rapid dissolving of this arrangement without the gradual introduction of a tailored welfare state—the consequences could be catastrophic. Not surprisingly, people in poor countries tend to be more collectively oriented and less individualistic than in the Western hemisphere. A striking expression of this is the labeling of the article collection of the African Charter on the Rights and Welfare of the Child as "Rights and Duties." Linking rights to duties makes children's rights relative instead of absolute, as they appear in the UN Convention for the Rights of the Child. Concretely, Article 31 of the African Charter reads:

> Every child shall have responsibilities towards his family and society, the State and other legally recognized communities and the international community. The child, subject to his age and ability, and such limitations as may be contained in the present Charter, shall have the duty: (a) to work for the cohesion of the family, to respect his parents,

superiors and elders at all times and to assist them in case of need; (b) to serve his national community by placing his physical and intellectual abilities at its service.

(Organization of African Unity, 1999)

In conclusion, children are developmentally vulnerable, have limited bargaining powers, and depend heavily on adult caretakers. They are, however, in most cases, the competent holders of agency, at least a tactical agency, and promote their interests by overt or covert negotiations with their surroundings. Their agency is constrained by the social contracts they are born into, notably the social safety net arrangements of their family units, fortified by intergenerational contracts and religious practices.

The A's and the B's: The Social Relationships of Power, Slavery, and Exploitation

Both trafficking and slavery assume that an individual exercises power over somebody else. As this section will explain, trafficking in children is definitionally closely tied to the idea of exploitation. The concepts of *power*, *slavery*, and *exploitation* all define social relationships between two parties. Such parties are commonly labeled A and B in definitional work and follow the structure "the superordinate A interacts with the subordinate B," preferably in a nontrivial way. In this section, some central concepts related to the trafficking of children will be explored and clarified along this line.

Children and Power

The classical definition of power is credited to Robert Dahl (1961) and states that A has power over B to the extent that A can get B to do something B would not otherwise have done. The definition, and especially the way it was operationalized by Dahl, presupposes an overt, observable conflict between A and B. In a discussion of the use of power against children, it becomes relevant to know whether A and B's subjective interests also correspond to their "real" interest (Lukes, 2005. For example, is B, the child, both clear and right about what is good for him/her? Normative concerns over the use of interpersonal power differ if an altruistic A makes B do what is best for B in a case where B does not seem able to understand B's own best interest: some children clearly express that they would like to live on candy and never go to bed at night, while this would obviously cause ill health. An adult refusing them to do so exercises power in responding to what the children perceive to be a conflict of interest.

Lukes (2005) proposes an alternative definition of power: A exercises power over B when A affects B in a manner *contrary to B's interests*. Lukes stresses that although problematic to determine, subjective interest and "real" interest do not always correspond. For example, one may not know what is in one's own interest if information vital to the decision is withheld. Moreover, deliberate attempts can be made to manipulate B to believe that his interests in fact correspond to the interests of A. According to this definition of power, an adult (A) exercising power over a child (B) does not only force B to accept A's agenda but also violates B's "real" interests. As we will see, this definition of power borderlines a definition of *exploitation*; it represents an abuse of power, not simply the exercising of power.

In the first section of this chapter, human agency was defined in terms of power: a capability to shape outcomes. In a situation where A exercises power over B, B may still have agency, but B's understanding of his or her own interests may be limited by A's field of vision. It is likely that B's opportunity to exercise power is mainly of the tactical type: moving within the imposed space of A. This will often be the situation of a child in a trafficking situation.

Children and Slavery

Slavery is a state that occurs where there is little space left even for tactical agency. Inspired by the modern slavery definitions of Bales (1999), slavery assumes that A fully controls B and, by violence and threats, makes B work without pay and physically prevents B from leaving. There is a considerable inflation in the use of the slavery concept. People working for a very low salary with few other options are frequently labeled as working under slavery-like conditions. I support Bales in arguing that the slavery concept should be conservatively defined and reserved for the unambiguous cases. In a complex world, it is difficult to draw any absolute lines for what ought to be morally condemned, but slavery should be an issue that no one should have to morally debate. I have argued, however (Kielland and Tovo, 2006), that the definition of child slavery be slightly modified from the adult definition of slavery.

Three points are central to such a modification. First, it is a central point to the conservative definition of slavery that A does not pay B. In many countries, children work a lot, and most of their work activities are not remunerated. Child activities predominantly take place in the informal sector, where the employers are their own families or immediate caretakers. While adult workers generally expect to be paid unless they work for themselves, the practice is different for children, and social expectations change correspondingly. A child working is seen as a helper to his caretakers but also as a learner. The child learns to do the task well, and in addition, he or she learns about the hardship of life and incorporates the needed discipline to cope with it (Reynolds, 1991). Working without pay would clearly be an issue for an adult but is hardly out of the ordinary when it comes to a child, and the assumption is therefore less suitable to distinguish a relationship of slavery from another type of a child labor arrangement.

The second point relates to how a slave is controlled. The strict definition would require that A uses violence or the direct threat of such in order to make B work. Although violence is frequently used against child workers, it may not be necessary in order to keep the child producing a profit for the person in control. As explained in the previous section, children are easy to manipulate due to immaturity and lack of experience. A child who is constantly told that he or she is worthless, dirty, undeserving, or owing something will have his or her self-confidence seriously under mined. Traffickers might say, "You are so stupid! Not even your parents wanted you!"; "You are such a burden and should be grateful that I keep you here"; "You have done things (real or imagined) that make you socially unacceptable." In the end, B may come to believe that he is lucky to be exploited by A, as B comes to see himself or herself as disgusting and unwanted by everybody else: B comes to fully adopt A's strategic perspective.

The third point relates to possibilities to run away. Many children, especially the younger ones, do not need bars to be kept in captivity. Traditional definitions of slavery underscore the importance of distance to deprive the captives of networks and knowledge that could be used to escape (e.g., Lovejoy, 2000). Distance is an even higher barricade to children, and a shorter distance is needed to control an inexperienced child than is necessary for a more experienced adult. A (young) child needs not be very far away from parents or potential rescuers but would still know no way of getting there by themselves in a complex social environment like a city or a remote rural district. Yet the main obstacle to escape is often created within the mind of the child. An intimidating adult saying: "Wherever you go, I'm going to find you!" The use of religion or witchcraft can be scary and powerful: "Without my prayers, you'll go to hell!" "I have a lock of your hair and can put a spell on you." Moreover, urban legends circulate about the child who got away and was gruesomely punished. I have met many children who have heard them but no one who in fact knew the child in question. Finally, and quite significantly, breaking out of a situation, changing all coordinates in one's life, is extremely stressful to a mentally drained individual, as is often the case with abused children. Bales's (1999, p. 61) description of young prostitutes who run back to the brothels after their rescue is a stark example of this. There is a stage in the human psyche where people prefer the safety of the known to almost anything else, even though the person lives in absolute misery.

It should be noted that some of these limitations would also be true for adolescents and adults who have not enjoyed a safe and healthy childhood. Disorientation and lack of confidence in one's own judgment and perception of reality are common consequences of oppression and enslavement. Being removed from peer networks renders people vulnerable across the world. Although B may be free to walk out the door, she or he may in reality have no other place to go than back to A when the day is done.

Children and Trafficking

Leading international agencies currently apply some very broad definitions of child trafficking. Comparing those definitions to a Bales-inspired definition of slavery would indicate some important overlaps, but not all child trafficking would qualify as slavery. The three points discussed in the previous subsection are crucial here: children considered trafficked may be remunerated, they do not always work under threats or use of violence, and they may in some situations be in a position to choose and change employers.

As this book explores, definitions of human trafficking are elaborate.[2] According to the UN, a trafficker is someone who is part of the *act* of recruiting, transporting, or receiving of a person, through criminal *means* ranging from brute force and purchase of a person to taking advantage of someone in a vulnerable situation, and whose *purpose* is gross exploitation. The "trafficking" term in popular discourse tends to refer to criminally organized groups moving people across borders against their will, often women for sexual exploitation. The UN, however, stresses that trafficking also may take place within countries, organized crime groups need not be involved, and there are many types of exploitation that qualify as trafficking beyond sexual exploitation.

A main challenge becomes determining acts and practices that do not qualify as trafficking. The US State Department, probably inspired by the Palermo Protocol, has made an attempt at this by providing a practical guide to distinguish a trafficking victim from a person involved in human smuggling. In their definition, someone being smuggled is not a victim but the contrary: someone who willingly crosses a border and by that violates the law. An interesting aspect of their definition, however, is that they acknowledge that someone who agrees to be smuggled may turn into a trafficking victim if their situation transforms into one of captivity and exploitation.

Child trafficking was earlier defined within the same framework, but as practical challenges started to arise, many of the initial criteria were tossed out. To follow the structure of the UN: With regard to the *act*, it remains sufficient that the child has relocated somehow; by what *means* is no longer important, while the essence remains the *purpose*: someone's intent to exploit the child. In short, child trafficking comprises three elements: (i) relocation, (ii) evil intent, and (iii) exploitation.

Why did the international community decide to remove a range of specificities from the definition that applies to children? How did they see children as different from other human beings?[3] The current, broadened definition of what qualifies as trafficking a child is an expression of some of the claims made earlier in this chapter. Children are perceived as poor negotiators, immature, with limited experience and therefore limited ability to recognize what may seem to be their own "real" interest. Their dependency on adult guidance makes us prone to accuse their caregivers rather than the child for being in a situation that seems to conflict with the child's real interest. Children are less liable, that is, they are seen to have a constrained and mainly tactical agency, where knowledge about their options and potential is being severely restricted by the field of vision of their superordinate. In such a situation, a child may travel quite voluntarily into an exploitative situation, no abduction, force, coercion, or payment needed.

The broad definition of child trafficking makes it even harder to distinguish a trafficking case from a nontrafficking case, when acts and practices in a given situation would be similar. The International Labour Organization (ILO), after consultations with the United Nations Office on Drugs and Crime (UNODC) and the International Organization for Migration (IOM), has suggested distinguishing between *child trafficking* and *migration-related child labor* much along the lines of the State Department's distinction between the trafficking and smuggling of adults. However, while the latter suggests that an act of smuggling can turn into a trafficking situation, ILO concludes that if the relocation of a child was not motivated by exploitation, the exploited child will be a child laborer and not a trafficking victim (ILO, 2007). In conclusion, with regard to children, without movement there is no trafficking (this is not true when children are involved in commercial sex acts in the United States). Without evil intent, we have migration-related child labor. That is, if the child ends up being exploited. But what exactly is exploitation?

Child Trafficking as Exploitation

Most definitions of *exploitation* describe a social relationship out of balance. A exploits B when A takes unfair advantage of B (Wertheimer, 2008). Ethical definitions emphasize the way A treats B as an object and uses her or him instrumentally to cover their own needs. Economic definitions refer to A profiting from the labor of B to an unreasonable price.

Is exploitation slavery? Reiman (1987, pp. 3–4) claims that exploitative societies represent forms of slavery when they are structured in ways that force given groups of people to offer their labor to others at unfair rates. Taking the point of departure in a Bales-inspired, modern slavery definition, as I do here, slavery and exploitation should, however, be clearly distinguished from one another. While all slavery is exploitation, the opposite is not the case. In an exploitative relationship that is not slavery, B may be paid, although underpaid. B might also be able to leave to look for other, although not necessarily much more attractive opportunities. Moore (1973, p. 53) presupposes "a substantial degree of coercion" to take place in an exploitative relationship. There are two frameworks for defining exploitation, offering two different approaches to the coercion factor. First, in exploitative social relationships between individuals, coercion is exercised in the form of power where A forcefully imposes his will on B. The second approach (as exemplified by Reiman) focuses on how some societies are structured in ways that produce systems of individual exploitative relationships.

Similar to the slavery debate, Bourdillon et al. (2010) underscore how the "exploitation" term has become incorrectly inflated by central participants in the child labor debate. In some contexts, any child below a certain age entering into the labor market is automatically regarded as exploited (ibid., p. 176). ILO, for instance, regards child labor as exploitative per definition, and in Convention 138 Article 2, this includes all work done by children under the minimum age for admission to employment (ILO, 2007). Similarly, when the working child is of a foreign nationality, he or she is easily considered a victim of trafficking. I concur with these authors and stress that like "slavery," "exploitation" is a serious term associated with criminal action. It should consequently be reserved for serious cases deserving of physical intervention.

So, when is a child exploited? There is a series of challenges related to the identification of a child victim of exploitation. I have previously mentioned how considering the salary level of a child may be misleading in societies where children are socially perceived as the helpers and learners of the people with whom they stay. In real-life settings, we constantly run into children who insist on staying in situations that seem fundamentally intolerable to the Western eye. A common reason is the plain fact that they come from places that are even worse. They consequently see a potential return as a sure deterioration of their living and working conditions as well as their future prospects. The backbreaking agricultural work of the rural areas from which many relocating children depart is certainly not romantic. So when a technically speaking exploitative situation means a welfare improvement to the child, does it still make sense to talk about exploitation? What do "unreasonable" and "unfair" really mean in this context?

In his book *Exploitation* and in some more recently updated articles, Alan Wertheimer (2008) has collected an impressive list of exploitation definitions from both the systemic and microrelational academic debates. I'll make reference to some of them, as they may apply to children in particular ways. First, Hill (1994) argues that exploitation is a psychological rather than a social or an economic concept. For an offer to be exploitative, it must serve to create or to take advantage of some recognized psychological vulnerability that, in turn, disturbs the offeree's ability to reason effectively (p. 637).

The previous discussion has highlighted the particular and psychological vulnerabilities of children. The problem is that it is exactly this vulnerability that disturbs the child's "ability to reason effectively" and necessitates adult guidance. This adult guidance should ideally be fully altruistic if we are to say that advantage is not taken.

Are children exploited if they escape an even worse situation? Theorists do not agree on this point. Roemer (1986, p. 136) argues that a group "is exploited if it has some conditionally feasible alternative under which its members would be better off." Benn (1988, p. 138), on the other hand, claims that "Exploitation [in exchange] demands . . . that there is no reasonably eligible alternative [for the exploitee] and that the consideration or advantage received is incommensurate with the price paid." In the first case, the child is exploited because she or he would have been better off elsewhere. In the second case, the child would have no other place to go, and the exploiter takes advantage of this lack of options by treating the child unfairly.

The concepts "unfair" and "unreasonable" repeatedly come out as indicators in the identification of child exploitation. In this chapter, I argue that the social relationship of exploitation can be illustrated by an equation. On the one side of the equation, we have the benefits minus the costs of A. On the other side, the benefits minus the costs of B. Exploitation occurs when this equation is seriously imbalanced. I'll round off this theoretical section with two more definitions that may support the idea of an exploitation equation. Munzer (1990, p. 171) describes the relationship between A and B as one where A benefits and B is harmed: "Persons are exploited if (1) others secure a benefit by (2) using them as a tool or resource so as (3) to cause them serious harm." Importantly, he adds the element of instrumentality—A is treating B as an object; personal or emotional relations are excluded from his case, at least for B's part. This condition certainly simplifies the equation and appeals to a mathematical modeling of the relationship. Similarly, Levine (1988, pp. 66–67) says that "An exploitative exchange is . . . an exchange in which the exploited party gets less than the exploiting party, who does better at the exploited party's expense." Here, the equation becomes more complex than in the simple case where A profits and B suffers. B simply gets "less" than "A," but we do not assume he gets nothing. Empirical situations will help shed light on the real definitional challenges.

Child Mobility in West Africa

The previous section concluded that the two most important elements in the child trafficking definition are mobility and labor exploitation. This section presents an empirical setting in which extensive child mobility and endemic child labor practices define normality. West Africa is a place where international definitions and legal frameworks continue to meet considerable challenges: determining whether a given child presented to a police officer, courtroom, or child protection agency is indeed the victim of trafficking has turned out to be far from straightforward. The complex realities of West African children are simply difficult to fit with the one-dimensional definitions given by international conventions, charters, and declarations.

Child mobility is and has been common in the West African region ever since the establishment of sedentary societies. In the research literature, the phenomenon is most commonly treated under child fostering practices and

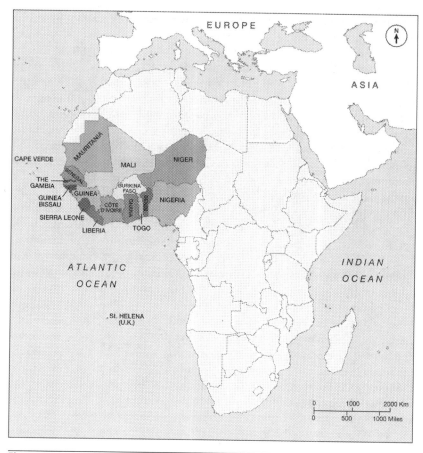

Figure 8.1   Map of West Africa

labeled the circulation of children (Goody, 1982) or child relocation (Isiugo-Abanihe, 1985) and more recently as child migration (Hashim and Thorsen, 2011; Kielland, 2008). In the classical work on the topic, *Parenthood and Social Reproduction*, Esther Goody (1982) presents the variation of the practice across cultures in the region and identifies some of its main motivations as (i) education and social mobility: for children to learn skills other than those of the parents; (ii) informal social protection: establish and consolidate reciprocal claims within families and between households (see also Bledsoe, 1990; Kielland, 2009); (iii) economic and social: distribute child labor and the joyful company of a child within extended families to the places where it is most needed (see also economic theorizing by e.g., Ainsworth, 1992; Akresh,

2009); and (iv) promoting character development: to prevent spoiling of the child (see also Isiugo-Abanihe, 1985).

Skills Diversification and Social Mobility

Childhood is the period for acquiring the technical skills needed for adulthood responsibilities and survival. Besides—or in the absence of schooling—children learn by imitating their caregivers. Goody (1982) emphasizes that one of the main functions of child circulation is to allow children to learn other skills than those mastered by their parents. In increasingly complex societies, differentiated and specialized adult roles are developed thanks to the outsourcing of child-rearing to households with different skills to teach (ibid., p. 5).

Both vocational and social skills are important. Vocational skills achieved by child mobility range from the farming of a different crop to the learning of a craft or an art. However, social skills could be just as attractive to an out-fostering family, as they allow for social mobility. If a child is allowed to stay with a family of a higher social standing, perhaps involving relocation from a rural to an urban area, this could represent the acquisition of social skills that could be marketable in both the labor and spousal markets. In Muslim areas, it is similarly still common to entrust children with religious teachers in the hope that they will obtain a spiritual quality from religious reading and interaction with knowledgeable true believers.

In my 2009 article in *Forum for Development Studies*, I have suggested that skills diversification within a family unit, obtained through out-fostering, can contribute to income diversification and thus a less vulnerable joint family portfolio. A household whose members are predominantly involved in agriculture will be utterly vulnerable to drought. If the household members operate as a mutual insurance unit, and they are all involved in the production of the same crop, no one will be able to support the others if that crop fails. If, however, skills and therefore income are diversified within the group, the unit will be much less vulnerable. While some markets may fail simultaneously, all seldom do. So-called apprenticeship fostering can therefore be useful and even a deliberate part of household efforts to develop social safety nets, as described in the next subsection.

Mutuality and Informal Social Safety Nets

In largely uninsured societies, informal social protection becomes vitally important. Families represent the natural insurance units, where mutual binding is represented by intergenerational contracts between parents and their children. Mutuality commitments are created and reinforced selectively also within the extended family structure and with kin, but the functioning of such additional ties depends on active maintenance and investment.

Goody (1982, p. 47) specifies that while skills training may be the main rationale for child mobility, its main function is to reinforce ties between kin. The same way that marriage binds two families together, child relocation from one household to another, as Bledsoe (1990) says, opens up a channel for the exchange of goods and services between the two households. That is, such a channel can be opened, or an existing, perhaps fading relationship may be renewed and reinforced, securing the same mutual commitments.

Children can be excellent network builders. They help reinforce the social networks of their parents while simultaneously starting to create future safety nets on their own. Being a good helper in and around a labor-intensive household, an obedient and pleasant child will often create a sense of grate-fulness toward the biological parents who gave him or her up. This gratitude converts into obligation, a feeling that is fortified by the emotional bonds children often invoke in their caretakers. In addition to this, Reynolds (1991) describes how children initiate the building of social protection on their own behalf. She explains how children strategically choose to allocate their labor to a favored older brother or uncle and that way begin the investment in a tie of obligation that can prove most useful to them in the future.

A More Effective Allocation of Child Labor . . . and Affection

West African households are labor intensive, and many of the everyday tasks required are technically simple and considered low-status jobs: that is, the typical kind of work that children do. Traditionally, farm production was limited more by the lack of labor force than land scarcity, and an additional, productive household member was generally welcomed by a family. Murray Last (2000) interestingly describes how parents in a rural farmstead in north-ern Nigeria simply did not corporally punish children, as the latter could eas-ily relocate and offer their labor to others if they were discontent.

Compared to children of the largely legally regulated Western world, African children, especially in rural areas, are often allowed a much greater agency with regard to who they want to live with (see also Reynolds, 1991). However, child relocation decisions are generally influenced by other family members, or the relocation decision is made by family leaders. Economic theory, not surprisingly, emphasizes the labor allocation aspect of child fos-tering practices. If child relocation is predominantly an efficiency concern, economic theory suggests that children are relocated away from households with a large child labor surplus and limited productive assets toward house-holds with a more limited labor supply and more productive assets (Ains-worth, 1992; Akresh, 2009; Serra, 2000). That way, children are able to be more productive in the households they are fostered out to and contribute to an increase in the joint production of the kinship group. As discussed, households that give up child labor can instead incur a social debt from the household where the child was placed. This debt could in turn be repaid in terms of skills acquired by the child, goods, or services—or as insurance, as earlier explained.

Both Ainsworth (1992) and Akresh (2009) look specifically at this in their doctoral work in economics. They both empirically demonstrate how households fill demographic gaps in their own membership structure: households will foster in children of genders and ages that are not yet represented in their family and conversely foster out children of a gender and age of which there is a surplus. Many labor tasks are gender and age specific, and they thus ensure a daily labor supply appropriate for the household demand.

Goody (1982, p. 44) is critical to the claim that child mobility is motivated by economic concerns. In her discussion from Gonja, she argues that if labor was indeed so attractive, stepfathers should be expected to make a greater effort to retain the children of their wives from previous marriages, the sons especially. The argument is interesting but again met by economist Bhalotra (2003), who points out that labor capability is clearly worth less without loyalty. In his classification of child fostering types in West Africa, Isiugo-Abanihe (1985) hardly refers to economic motivations. Education, child-rearing concerns, and strengthening of kinship dominates his argument. Even when debating crisis fostering situations, he predominantly refers to social crises rather than economic ones.

A final aspect of child redistribution within networks deserves mentioning in the context of this paragraph. Labor is not the only thing a child brings to her or his new household. Children are generally seen as affectionate and joyful, and perhaps the most important asset they bring to their new family is life and love. When children are placed with childless relatives or elderly family members, this aspect may be as important as the child labor provision. The child can most certainly contribute to the everyday work needed in the household, but to keep an elderly person company may be equally important. In some cases, the two functions may overlap: a child obliged to entertain an elderly relative may suffer a considerable constraint on his or her freedom of movement. Entertainment and caretaking easily becomes a round-the-clock occupation, as some elderly and singles resist being left alone, even for a few hours, and the child is expected to fill their void of loneliness.

Character Development and the Ethos of Sufferance

We have seen how child mobility can help children obtain social mobility or a profession, serve as investments in social safety nets, and help extended families distribute their productive capacity in an efficient way. A central concern, however, is the hardships faced by many of these children on the move when they leave their primary caregivers and guardians. They work hard and often, it seems, without being paid. They are frequently corrected, also corporally. However, those adhering to West African social traditions may not perceive these hardships as problematic in the same way as those in the international debate on trafficking. To the contrary: the hardship suffered by relocated children can be a goal in itself. It represents a path to true learning and to character development. Sufferance is an ethos: working so that your caregiver can rest will earn you his prayers. As Caroline Bledsoe puts it in the name of her well known article about foster children in Sierra Leone from 1990, there is "No success without struggle."

Life in Africa can be hard, and those who cannot cope with hardship may have poor chances for survival. Reynolds (1991) describes the ethos of womanliness as "the dull compulsion of daily work," explaining how the duty of a mother is to ensure that her daughter can take it and thereby become useful to the kinship network. Learning to suffer and take harsh treatment is by no means seen as a survival skill only for girls. Bledsoe (1990) describes how the unruly boy Munda is left in a slave-like existence at the teacher's house in order to get his act together. His father shows no compassion with his sufferance, because "to advance, children must work and study hard, endure beatings and suffer sickness, to mould their character and earn knowledge" (p. 71).

Goody (1982, p. 44) similarly stresses that fostering can be used as a disciplinary measure in itself: "difficult and proud children" risk being sent away to be taught respect and discipline by someone less lenient than their own parents. Ushe Isiugo-Abanihe writes:

> Children may be sent away at a very early age to homes where they are disciplined or where they learn a trade. Some parents are thought to spoil their children by not being firm with them, so sending them away is supposed to help the children develop better characters. It is generally believed, in many parts of Africa, that thrashing makes a child wise and helps it to learn quickly. A surrogate parent is believed to be in a better position to inculcate acceptable forms of social behavior, and to spank a child, or inflict other punishment, until the child learns to perform useful functions. Clearly, the motivation for this type of fostering is social mobility, and it is commonly believed that children raised under the supervision of surrogate parents, especially those socialized in superior or prestigious homes, are more sophisticated than those raised by their own parents.
>
> (Isiugo-Abanihe, 1985, p. 57)

Perpetue Dagba was a live-in domestic servant for some remote relatives (by marriage not blood) for many years. She was not paid and did not go to school. Yet a complex set of factors described in this chapter makes it difficult to say that this was simply a "purposely exploitative" relationship. Today, 10 years later, Perpetue is a skilled hairdresser. Her apprenticeship was paid for by the family she served and their acquaintances.

Many of the classical works about child circulation in Africa are 20 to 30 years old. Yet the social perceptions of the positive outcomes of hard ship are still very much alive today. A recent survey asked parents in rural Senegal if they would accept corporal punishment for children who were sent away to stay with others. Almost 60 percent of the parents said they accepted occasional slapping, while 52 percent found corporal punishment acceptable or conditionally acceptable (Kielland and Gaye, 2010). Religion plays an important role in the reinforcement and maintenance of the social obligations children have to their parents and employers—when you suffer for your parents or master, they will pray for you, and only with those prayers can you succeed in life and reach paradise.

Child Exploitation as an Equation: Factoring the A and the B Sides

In April 2001, the Nigerian registered bulk ship M/S *Etireno* went missing in the Bay of Benin. The cargo vessel had been refused docking in Gabon, as it was suspected to contain Beninese and Togolese children who were being trafficked. The incident caused enormous international attention. There was a reasonable suspicion of someone planning to profit from the children's labor. More than that, the image of African children being transported on a ship out of what is historically labeled the Slave Coast inevitably evoked some very unpleasant associations. Rumors were spinning. There were supposed to be as many as 250 trafficked children on board, children who were bought and paid for (BBC, 2001; CNN, 2001).

A week later in Cotonou, Benin, the ship was welcomed by the world press. The confused passengers included 23 children who had been on their way to expatriate Beninese families in Gabon. The children were taken into custody and placed in the care of the NGO Terre des Hommes. As it turned out, only one knew about a transfer of money having taken place, while two reported that a very small sum had been spent on a departure ceremony when they had left their home village.[4] Most likely, the M/S *Etireno*, like other cargo ships in the area, had been the vehicle for a number of similar relocations over the past five years.

The *Etireno* incident shed international light on the massive streams of independent child migrants in West Africa. The world discovered that children from the entire region, especially Mali and Burkina Faso, were moving toward the Ivory Coast for agricultural labor. Children from Ghana, Togo, Benin, and Nigeria went by sea to the wealthy in Gabon for domestic services. In addition, children were legally crossing borders all over the continent to work abroad. However, the foreign eye was relatively blind to the fact that not many of these children had been recruited by cunning middlemen, and few, if any, were heading for the households of complete strangers. Instead, they were travelling to family and kin for housing, work, and the hope of a better future. As anthropologist Dorte Thorsen put it in a presentation at the

University of Oslo: "[child] migration is not seen as a rupture with the family but perhaps rather as incorporation into the wider network of kin" (Hashim and Thorsen, 2011).

The children are moving away from their parents, and most of them will be involved in labor when they arrive at their destination. Along the way, they may get assistance from other travelers or locals—these people are not naïve and understand where the children are heading. Sometimes the children pay these people for the help that they get. But is this trafficking? Are their helpers traffickers? For a decade, the international community tried to convince national governments and local police that this age-old social practice was indeed trafficking.

The Socially Constructed Child Trafficking Case

If we were to take the international discourse and construct the perfect representation of child trafficking in a West African context, this is the story we would get: a young rural boy and his naïve parents are lured by a charming stranger who is recruiting children to work on a cocoa plantation in the Ivory Coast. After being brought to the plantation, the boy is locked up behind bars with no way to escape. The children work with bleeding backs and are maltreated and die. Taking an extreme risk, the little boy manages to escape the plantation and is taken in by the nice policeman, who brings him to a joyful reunification with his parents.

This is not an imagined story but the booklet *Chaga and the Chocolate Factory* (Hartman, undated), developed by a Western NGO to advocate for fair-trade chocolate. Had this been representative of the child trafficking situation in West Africa, identification of victims and perpetrators would not have been much of a problem. The story has everything: deception, control, violence, and a child who has no problem understanding his own real interests. Once the deception is revealed, his parents are happy to have him back. The implications of the story are clear: by buying fair-trade chocolate, you can help the thousands of children who, just like Chaga, are working as slaves on cocoa farms (ibid.).

In all my years working with child labor and child mobility issues in the region, I have never heard a story like Chaga's. That is, none of the stories I have been told fit the definitional blueprint of the international discourse. They are simply too complex, and all of them are full of surprising twists and turns. I cannot say that the Chaga story never happened, but I dare to claim that it would be rare and unusual if it did. Few cocoa farmers could afford to send recruiters into Burkinabe villages—the revenue produced by the children's labor is not enough to pay for something that financially taxing. Recruitment, when it takes place, goes through expatriate kin who are visiting their home villages, although it is important to keep in mind that recruitment is often not necessary. An expatriate leader may help with labor mediation, notably a process often taking place within an already established kinship network (see Akresh, 2009;[5] De Lange, 2006; Thorsen, 2007, 2009; Hashim and Thorsen, 2011). Locking the children up is normally not necessary. They tend to withstand tough working and living conditions to the end of the season when involved in agricultural work—for if they leave, all their potential salary would be lost. To me, Chaga seems to be the perfect cliché and not a real child.[6]

The Simple Equation: A and B Are Alone

The child mobility described in the previous sections may or may not qualify as trafficking. If we are to apply the going definitions of child trafficking as a combination of mobility and exploitation, the key to assessing the situation of relocated children in the region becomes the concept of exploitation. The basic definition of exploitation stated that A is exploiting B when the benefits that A gets from the relationship appear unreasonable compared to those of B. The idea of exploitation as an equation measuring the benefits and the costs of A versus B is suggested by Kielland and Bjørkhaug (2009). In the equation "The cons are subtracted from the pros on each side of the equation symbol, and, ideally, there is a cut-off point where the benefit/compensation ratio between the parties must be deemed to be unreasonable" (ibid., p. 238).

A striking feature in the international trafficking debate has been the isolation of A and B from their social and familial embeddedness. This again reflects a Western, individualistic approach to human rights—an ideological perspective that contrasts the strongly collectivist social norms of West Africa, as described in the first part of this chapter. The equation picturing the balance between A and B thus becomes very simple, with clear demarcation in both time and space: the costs and benefits included on each side are those borne or enjoyed by A and B alone. Others, with which their lives are intertwined, remain in the obscure outskirts of the picture. The image is static: it ignores the fact that the situation in question may be a springboard to future opportunities or, to the contrary, put constraints on such future possibilities. The equation reads: (benefits of A)—(costs of A) = (benefits of B)—(costs of B) + X. The X term expresses the absolute size of the difference in net benefit. The ratio ((benefits of A)—(costs of A)) ÷ ((benefits of B)—(costs of B)) may express the degree of unfairness. Exploitation requires this equation to be strikingly imbalanced; that is, X is substantial, or the ratio is much larger than 1.

Some children are indeed alone: boys and girls run away from abusive parents, driven by their own ambition, fleeing a forced marriage or the miserable conditions in some relocation arrangement staged by their parents or close relatives. The children need to work to live and are among the most vulnerable in the labor market, since their bargaining power and negotiation skills are both weak. Some of these children succumb to brutal labor conditions that may be their only apparent option at the time. In the simplest of real-life situations, X is larger than the net A-side of the equation as A has only benefits and B only losses, like in Munzer's (1990) definition of exploitation. Independent child migrants estranged from their families are often found in miserable jobs in the agricultural sector or as porters or water sellers in urban areas. Yet common for most of them is that they see this situation as a springboard—a necessary rung on the ladder to something better. "I'm going to work in agriculture to get a foothold in this country, but then I'll go to Abidjan and work in construction." "I'm going to sell water for this lady for a while, but then I'll save enough money to buy myself a sewing machine."

The Complex Equation: A and B Are Social Beings

The simple equation would require a comparison of the value of the child's labor services to the employer, to the pay the child receives, and how the child is fed and treated. Most West African children on the move, however, are not always free to operate outside their family and kinship networks, as described in the child mobility section. As Thorsen concludes, family relations are not likely to be broken by child mobility, even when the child appears to be running away without the permission of the parents (Thorsen, 2007). In fact, in most situations, children tend to be drawn into family and kin networks at their destination sites (Thorsen, 2009). A more complex scrutiny of a given child mobility situation therefore requires a range of new factors to be introduced into both the cost and benefit links of the equation.

If the A-side of the equation and the B-side of the equation no longer represent individuals but instead represent extended families and networks, the role of the child may come out as a piece in a larger puzzle. The piece can be significant or minor to the overall picture yet still affect the overall balance of the interhousehold relationship. The transfer of a child can serve to (re) initiate a relationship, as suggested by Bledsoe, or constitute one part among many in an ongoing exchange that may also involve cash, credit, loans, or a countless number of other payments, goods, or services. Taking in a child can be a complete win–win situation for the two households and even a win–win–win situation if the child is included as an independent actor. However, it will also often constitute a net cost or a net burden to one of the parties, or at least be perceived as such. A perceived cost can be compensated for by other parallel transfers or obligations from the biological parents or simply as social status incurred by the benefactor. When the child represents a net contribution to his or her new household, the biological parents may be compensated in the form of money, gifts, or services (like insurance). It is easy to see how all of these factors can create a much more complex equation from which it is difficult to determine who benefits the most.

Unequal Bargaining Powers

Some households exchanging children may be equal to each other with regard to bargaining power; and sometimes the social bonds of love, commitment, and responsibility may overrule the mere considerations of costs and benefits. However, this is not often the case. Several of the exploitation definitions presented earlier were concerned with the unequal bargaining powers of A and B and assume the bargaining powers of B to be inferior to those of A. Where social practices do not regulate and prevent the abuse of such inequity, the equation may easily become unfair.

Bledsoe's (1990) description of political patronage in Sierra Leone is perhaps one of the clearest examples of uneven bargaining powers between two parties. In short, she describes how social relationships form between influential families (patrons) and those in need of political or economic assistance (clients). The latter is granted, as "In exchange, clients work for patrons when required, give them important information, provide them with daughters as wives or children as servants, and so on" (ibid., p. 75). Structural social inequalities force the powerless to offer what they may have, including their children, to gain access to assistance from those who monopolize power and resources. The offering of a child may symbolize a token of collective submission; the poor family implicitly suggesting a patron–client relationship. The patron's promise of future protection in the form of political and economic assistance when needed may be invaluable to the client household. The equation shifts: the guarantee of future social protection is added onto B's side of the equation and subtracted from A's. In practice, such a guarantee may allow B's parents to take a new risk that may be highly rewarding and thereby improve their livelihoods. Indirectly, this will also help secure the future of B. With regard to security, an alliance with A may protect B's family from aggressors and conflict as the mere possibility of engaging in conflict with A's ally would be deterring (Bledsoe, 1990). This also implies that A cannot simply decide to take in any child—the risks involved with regard to the obligations incurred must be carefully considered.

A Case From Benin

While Bledsoe writes about Sierra Leone, I'd like to share a case from Benin that is in many ways illustrative of the complexities of the social relationships wherein child relocations take place. My acquaintance, a single mother living in one of the southern cities of the country, has taken in two girls that, by first glance, would fall into the suspected category of exploitation. The two get up early in the morning, sweep the compound, and then spend the day producing little items that they sell in the woman's store. In difficult times, she sends them to sell water on the street, then they go back home to cook and babysit. None of them are related to the woman, they both come from different towns quite far away, and they are not paid. They are not in school, while all three of her biological children are. She occasionally slaps them when she gets upset.

The background for the situation, however, confuses the picture in what I will argue is a fairly typical way, and so do the complications that arise: the woman is not rich and does not have a stable income. However, she has a house. Thus, as the motherless daughter of her sister's imprisoned husband needed a place to stay (after the sister had a mental breakdown), the family elderly decided, above her head, that the girl was to be sent to her. Although only 11 years old at the time, the child has been out of school for a long time working in a small bar, and the local schools turn out not to be very flexible with regard to late enrollments. Besides, the girl is not interested in studying.

The second girl is sent to the woman by her older brother, who lives in the northern part of the country. The girl dropped out of school in the second grade because the teacher rarely showed up to class. Instead, she has been working on the farm of the woman's brother. One day, the girl saw some other workers stealing the employer's seed and went to report this to him. As a reward to the loyal girl (and possibly to protect her from the retaliation of the perpetrators), he sent her south to his sister. In some ways, the brother appears to be taking on patron role vis-à-vis the girl's family, all of whom are working for him on his farm. Unlike the first girl, the second girl is extremely keen on learning.

The woman faces a difficult trade-off. For now, she spent almost all her income paying school tuition for her own three daughters. The only way she can pay for another, unacquainted (and unsolicited) child would be to take her own children out of the good school and send all the children to an inferior school, which she decides not to do. The daughters are her social security, and she needs to invest in them. However, the new girl quickly learns French from the other children in the household.

Around the same time, yet a third child is transferred to her household. This time, the child is a boy and is a relative—the son of another sister who has remarried and cannot bring along her son to her new husband. The family decides that the boy is to live with the woman. A brother is made responsible for paying his school fees, an obligation he later invents a reason to neglect. Officially, this boy is given to the woman's old mother, who is also a member of her household. In spite of going to school, the boy is considered her keeper, assistant, and companion, and when not in school, he is expected to stay at the house at all times to be available to her. While the other children are coming and going he is not allowed out to play with friends or do sports.

The equation of this household is obviously a complex one. The woman takes the money from her shop, where the products were partly produced by the two girls and also often sold by them. The returns from the shop are quite meager but still help her pay for the education of her own three daughters. She also enjoys all their housework that frees up her own time to look for business and her daughters' time to study. She gains the freedom of moving around, as babysitters are always available. In addition, she accumulates a social credit with the family heads and her brother in the north. Refusing to take in the children could easily have become a liability—services expected from close kin, consultation and participation in decision-making of importance could quickly have become withheld if she had not collaborated.

On the negative side, she got some new expenses. Her household has quite a fluctuating income, and in bad times, she is now bound to feed the six children rice instead of buying some chicken for her own three. She is not made of stone, and the education issue bothers her conscience, not so much for the first girl, but the second is clearly gifted and interested in learning. Her family no longer goes to restaurants, as this is a place where the difference between three and six children is noticeable. They have also stopped going on trips to nearby beaches, since they no longer fit into one car, and she feels uncomfortable taking only her own girls. In addition to this, she is starting to become aware of the social risks that she has taken on, something that is about to manifest in reality.

What does the equation look like from the side of the girls and their families? The first girl is virtually an orphan, while the second regularly provides support to her family in their home village. They have a reasonably comfortable life, especially compared to their previous homes but also compared to the other children in the same household. They sleep on the floor, but so do the family children on hot days. They get the same food and the same occasional slap. They do not go to school, but the northern girl has picked up a lot from the other children. Both feel they have improved their life situation a lot. The first girl worked in a bar before she came to the household and the second in the hot cotton fields. Both are thus protected from past risks: the bar girl from the clients and the farm girl from parasites and illnesses rampant in the rural areas. However, beading and housework does not do much to earn them a future marketable skill, and they do not get to save any money.

Then two things happen. The girls get older. The first girl finds a boyfriend on the street. He encourages her to steal from the households she has access to and give the goods to him. After a while, they are discovered. She flees back to the village of her paternal grandparents, and they later learn she is pregnant. Instead of being credited for taking care of the girl, the woman is now blamed for her sad destiny. Tension arises in the waters of a boat that cannot rock. Bad news also arrives from the north. The second girl was promised to a local boy a long time ago, and her future in-laws would now like them to get married. The girl is upset. The woman tries to mediate. Many social relationships that involve a number of people need careful management. And it goes wrong. The girl runs away, most probably toward Nigeria. Networks are harmed, both those of the woman and those of the brother in the north. And she becomes truly depressed about it all.

What did she gain from all this and what did she lose? And the girls? What were their costs and benefits?

Practical Consequences and Future Considerations

Perhaps the girls should be considered victims of trafficking. One could argue that they fit the simple child trafficking definition reasonably well. They certainly had few options in life that could have been a better investment in their future. What would have been the consequences of this labeling? In a legally functioning West African state, probably that they would have been sent back home, and possibly the woman would have been reprimanded by some authority. What would this have meant to the woman and the girls and their networks and futures? And should it matter?

There is a trap of cultural relativism in which the abuse and exploitation of children easily may become legitimized as cultural. Should we not, as a principle, agree that the criteria that define a trafficked or exploited child should be equal to a child in Norway and a child in Guinea Bissau? Perhaps it is not so much the technical definition as its political implication that is the problem at stake in a real-life situation: since trafficking and exploitation are considered crimes, legal responses seem inevitable. The problem of following the logics of legal responses to what is defined as trafficking or exploitation becomes obvious in a context where both child labor and child mobility are endemic and massively intertwined with a range of vital, informal social institutions. It resembles the establishing of children's right to parents and a home as legally binding in a poor, AIDS-ridden society. We agree about how things ought to be, but who deserves persecution and punishment when things are not as they should be?

In the West African setting, a traditional social practice of child circulation has largely become criminalized by the trafficking labeling, at least on paper. Technically speaking, quite correctly, as trafficking is defined as a crime and destined to be met by judicial policies and regulations. Simultaneously, poverty and poor education systems were pointed out as the main causes of the trafficking, but due to the legal labeling of the practice, investments were placed in legal projects rather than in poverty alleviation, social protection, and schools. Police were trained, laws were developed, and new papers and procedures were introduced to make border crossing more complicated for minors. And as it turned out, targeting was poor. For a period of time, all child travelers not accompanied by parents were indiscriminately suspected of being trafficking victims, they were persecuted, detained, and returned without much investigation into the reasons why they were out there and the situations causing them to be. Consequences were dramatic. Because as it turned out, the children kept traveling. Their helpers, however, were now suspected of intermediation, largely scaring off the good ones while leaving the field to less scrupulous people. On top of this, the children now had to obtain false papers and bribe border guards and police in order to move across borders (see Castle and Diarra, 2002; Dottridge, 2004; Kielland and Bjørkhaug, 2009; UNICEF, 2008). Definitions of child trafficking and exploitation may seem unquestionable, but there is still room for using sound judgment when it comes to action. As John Rawls advises, right action is what you get when you deduct the logical conclusions from theory and then test it against your gut: although logically sensitive, if it does not feel right, it probably isn't. The truth lies between the logics and the gut feeling in what Rawls (1993) calls a *reflexive equilibrium*.

Currently, this situation is more widely being acknowledged, and the international actors who have pushed for the labeling and policies are changing their approach. In line with the child agency discourse, relocating children are redefined from passive victims to actors on their own. The new label reflects this and the understanding of the diverse nature of these children as a group: they are "the children on the move." Children on the move are people with agency, but they are vulnerable. The new policy approaches aim to provide protection for these children rather than pursuing them and to prevent risky mobility rather than rescue. Preventing child mobility should not be done by force but by identifying the causes of why children leave home (and families let them) and addressing those causes (Dottridge, 2004). International charters and conventions set the normative standards: children should not be exploited and should, under normal conditions, be best off with family and kin. The issue is the place of legal and other means in the enforcement of such goals. In the end, the welfare of each child must remain a short-term pivotal concern.

Discussion Questions

1. What are the normative and practical implications of using the "child trafficking" term to label traditional social practices in a context like West Africa?
2. What do you think would be the practical consequences of a boycott of chocolate for the children who work on cocoa farms in the Ivory Coast? Would it still be right?
3. What is meant by the social construction of childhood, and how does this construction affect the way the international discourse addresses child labor and child mobility issues in a region like West Africa?
4. What is meant by child agency, and how are the two main forms of agency relevant to children in general and children in trafficking situations in particular?

5. What is meant by the intergenerational contract, and what may be the implication of such social commitments for children working away from home?
6. How is child trafficking defined differently from human trafficking, and why do you think this difference has developed?

Notes

1. Kabeer (2000) uses the term "intergenerational contract" to refer to the shared, although possibly conflicting, understandings between family members "as to what each owes and can expect from others within the family."
2. [T]he recruitment, transportation, transfer, harbouring or receipt of persons, by means of the threat or use of force or other forms of coercion, of abduction, of fraud, of deception, of the abuse of power or of a position of vulnerability or of the giving or receiving of payments or benefits to achieve the consent of a person having control over another person, for the purpose of exploitation. Exploitation shall include, at a minimum, the exploitation of the prostitution of others or other forms of sexual exploitation, forced labour or services, slavery or practices similar to slavery, servitude or the removal of organs.(Article 3, paragraph (a) of the UN Protocol to Prevent, Suppress and Punish Trafficking in Persons)
3. At this point, I would like to mention that children are commonly stated to be protected by the UN Convention for the Rights of the Child (CRC), in this context notably by Articles 35 and 36. It is interestingly often left out—and therefore worth stressing—that children also are human beings and therefore also covered by the Universal Declaration of Human Rights (in this case, Article 4). Globally, the Universal Declaration gives more extensive rights, and it is symptomatic that the CRC seem to replace it in the case of human children.
4. The source of this is my own personal conversations with the managers at Terre des Hommes, as I was working in Cotonou at the time of the incident.
5. In his dissertation work, Richard Akresh traces around 350 children from Burkina Faso to the Ivory Coast.
6. In fact, the story of Chaga brings about some unfortunate associations with the treatment of Africans in the very tale it refers to: *Charlie and the Chocolate Factory* (Dahl, 1964). Indeed, Willy Wonka travels to Africa to rescue the Oompa-Loompa tribe from their awful diet. He transports them to England in little boxes and keeps them locked up in the factory, where they work for up-keeping. They are mischievous like children but seemingly happy and singing all the time. The main difference—Roald Dahl was outrageous on purpose.

References

Ainsworth, M., 1992, *Economic Aspects of Child Fostering in Cote d'Ivoire* (LSMS Working Paper No. 92), Washington, DC: World Bank.

Akresh, R., 2009, "Flexibility of household structure: child fostering decisions in Burkina Faso", *Journal of Human Resources*, Vol. 44, No. 4, pp. 976–997.

Aries, P., 1960, L'Enfant et la Vie Familiale sous l'Ancien Régime, Paris: Plon; translated into English by Robert Baldick as Centuries of Childhood: A Social History of Family Life (1962), New York: Alfred A. Knopf.

Bales, K., 1999, *Disposable People, New Slavery in the Global Economy*. Berkeley, CA: University of California Press.

BBC, 2001, April 17, "Mystery surrounds child 'slave' ship." Available at: http://news.bbc.co.uk/2/hi/africa/1280991.stm

Benn, S., 1988, *A Theory of Freedom*. Cambridge: Cambridge University Press.

Bhalotra, S., 2003, "Child farm labor and the wealth paradox." *The World Bank Economic Review* 17 (2): 197–227, Washington DC.

Bledsoe, C., 1990, "No success without struggle: social mobility and hardship for Sierra Leone children", *Man* (N.S.), No. 25, pp. 70–88.

Bourdillon, M., Levison, D., Myers, W., and White, B., 2010, *Rights and Wrongs of Children's Work*. New Jersey, CT, and London: Rutgers University Press.

Castle, S. and A. Diarra, 2002, *The International Migration of Young Malians: Tradition, Necessity or Rite of Passage?* London: London School of Hygiene and Tropical Medicine.

Case, A., Paxson, C., and Ableidinger, J., 2002, *Orphans in Africa*. Princeton, NJ: Center for Health and Wellbeing Research Program in Development Studies, Princeton University.

CNN, 2001, April 14, "Benin searches for child slave ship." Available at: http://premium.edition.cnn.com/2001/WORLD/africa/04/14/child.slave.ship/index.html

Dahl, R. A., 1961, *Who Governs*. Newhaven, CT: Yale University Press.

De Certeau, M., 1984, *The Practice of Everyday Life*. Trans. Steven Rendall. Berkeley, CA: University of California Press (original title L'invention du quotidien. Vol. 1, Artsde faire 1980).

De Lange, A., 2006, *Going to Kompienga—A Study on Child Labour Migration and Trafficking in Burkina Faso's South-Eastern Cotton Sector*, Amsterdam: Report published by IREWOC and supported by Plan.

Dottridge, M., 2004, *Kids as Commodities: Child Trafficking and What to Do about It*. Lausanne, Switzerland: Terre des Hommes.

Giddens, A., 1984, *The Construction of Society: Outline of the Theory of Structuration*. Berkeley, CA: University of California Press.

Giddens, A., 1991, *Modernity and Self-Identity: Self and Society in the Late Modern Age*. Stanford, CA: Stanford University Press

Goody, E., 1982, *Parenthood and Social Reproduction: Fostering and Occupational Roles in West Africa*. Cambridge: Cambridge University Press.

Hartman, B., 2017, Chaga and the Chocolate Factory. Retrieved from https://www.tradeaid.org.nz/content/uploads/2017/01/Chaga.pdf

Hashim, I., and Thorsen, D., 2011, *Child Migration in Africa*. New York: Zed Books.

Hill, J. L., 1994, "Exploitation." *Cornell Law Review* 79, 631–699.

Honwana, A., 2006, *Child Soldiers in Africa*. Philadelphia, PA: University of Pennsylvania Press.

ILO, 2007, October 18, "Human trafficking in Africa: A regional and domestic response." Delivered at the Africa Regional Conference. Available at: www.slideshare.net/ahmedbashu/ilo-tecl-presentation-071018-e (accessed February 22, 2013).

Isiugo-Abanihe, U. C., 1985, 'Child fosterage in West-Africa', *Population and Development Review*, Vol. 11, No. 1, pp. 53–73.

Iversen, V., 2002a, 'Autonomy in child labour migrants', *World Development*, Vol. 30, No. 5, pp. 817–834.

Iversen, V., 2002b, *Idiosyncrasies of Child Labour in Peasant Households in Sub-Saharan Africa: Anthropological Observations and the Economics of Labour Obligations and Exchange.* UNICEF.

Kabeer, N., 2000, "Inter-generational contracts, demographic transitions and the quantity-quality tradeoff: Parents, children and investing in the future." *Journal of International Development* 12, 463–482.

Kielland, A., 2008, *Child Labour Migration in Benin; Incentive, Constraint or Agency?*, Bonn: VDM Verlag.

Kielland, A., 2009, "Child mobility as household risk management." *Forum for Development Studies* 36: 2, 257–274.

Kielland, A., and Bjørkhaug, I., 2009, "Child mobility in West Africa: Strategy, poverty or crime?" *Forum for Development Studies* 36: 2, 229–256.

Kielland, A., and Gaye, I., 2010, *Climate Change and the Role of Children in Household Risk Management Strategies in Rural Senegal.* Washington DC: World Bank.

Kielland, A. and M. Tovo, 2006, *Children at Work: Child Labour Practices in Africa.* Boulder, CO: Lynne Rienner.

Last, M., 2000, 'Children and the experience of violence: contrasting cultures of punishment in Northern Nigeria', *Africa*, Vol. 70, No. 3, pp. 359–339.

Levine, A., 1988, *Arguing for Socialism.* London: Verso.

Lovejoy, P. (Ed.), 2000, *Transformations in Slavery: A History of Slavery in Africa* (2nd edition). Cambridge: Cambridge University Press.

Lukes, S., 2005, *Power: A Radical View* (2nd edition). Basingstoke, UK: Palgrave Macmillan.

Moore, B., 1973, *Reflections on the Causes of Human Misery.* Boston, MA: Beacon Press.

Munzer, S., 1990, *A Theory of Property.* Cambridge: Cambridge University Press.

Organization of African Unity, 1999, African Charter on the Rights and Welfare of the Child. Available at: www1.umn.edu/humanrts/africa/afchild.htm.

Rawls, J., 1993, "Political Liberalism." In *The John Dewey Essays in Philosophy*, Vol. 4. New York: Columbia University Press.

Reiman, J., 1987, "Exploitation, force, and the moral assessment of capitalism: Thoughts on Roemer and Cohen." *Philosophy and Public Affairs* 16, 3–41.

Reynolds, P., 1991, *Dance Civet Cat.* London: Zed Books.

Roemer, J., 1986, "An Historical Materialist Alternative to Welfarism." In J. Elster and A. Hylland (Eds.), *Foundations of Social Choice Theory.* Cambridge: Cambridge University Press.

Serra, R., 2000, A Theoretical Framework for Child Fostering Arrangements in Sub-Saharan Africa. Available at: www.econ.unian.it/ricerca/convegni/atti_cnr/serra.pdf

Thorsen, D., 2007, "Junior-senior linkages in migration: Youngsters' perceptions of migration in rural Burkina Faso." In H. P. Hahn, and G. Klutepp (Eds.), *Cultures of Migration* (pp. 175–199). Berlin: LIT Verlag.

Thorsen, D. (2009, July) "L'échec de la famille traditionnelle ou l'étirement des relations familiales. L'exode des jeunes Burkinabés des zones rurales vers Ouagadougou et Abidjan." Migrations et Hommes.

UNICEF, 2008, *Evaluation of UNICEFs Sida-Funded Child Protection/Trafficking Programme in West and Africa.* www.unicef.org/wcaro/documents_publications_2759.html, accessed May 2, 2009.

Wertheimer, A., 2008, "Exploitation." The Stanford Encyclopedia of Philosophy (Fall 2008 Edition). Available at: http://plato.stanford.edu/entries/exploitation/ (accessed June 30, 2011)

Whitehead, A., Hashim, I., and Iversen, V. (2005) Child Migration, Child Agency and Inter-generational Relations in Africa and South Asia. Working Paper. Presented to "Children and Youth in Emerging and Transforming Societies—CHILDHOODS2005," 29 June–3 July, Oslo, Norway.

9

BLACK FEMALE BODIES AND HUMAN TRAFFICKING

TERRI COLLIN DILMORE

The purpose of this chapter is to highlight the intersectionality of race, systems of slavery, and trauma in the trajectories of human trafficking, with special consideration of the sexual exploitation of African-American women and girls. This chapter pays special attention to some of the historical vulnerabilities that continue to victimize women and children of color with respect to sexual exploitation. A review of the impacts of slavery and the continued commodification and criminalization of Black female bodies, the propagated myths about Black female bodies, and the unique vulnerabilities facing Black girls and women will be described in the following chapter.

Chapter Learning Objectives

- Understand the intersectionality between race, systems of slavery, gender, and stereotypes and the continued sexual exploitation of African-American girls and women.
- Understand the factors that contribute to making African-American women and girls more susceptible to sexual exploitation.

Historical Perspective of Slavery and the Commodification of Black Women and Girl Bodies

Within the context of an African-American Diasporic history, the sexual exploitation of Black women and girls has been proliferated by the "racialized and sexualized economies of slavery" (Winters, p. 8). During slavery,

DOI: 10.4324/9781003124672-11

Black women and girl bodies served both to fulfil the sexual desires of individual white oppressors and to act as vessels for the moral burden of sin of desire and sexuality in stark contrast to the dignity designated only to white women and girls. This positioning of the Black female body furthered "the racialized and sexualized power relationships of slavery" (Winters, 2016, p. 8) and began a process of criminalizing and dehumanizing Black femininity and Black female sexuality and experience for the sake of preserving the manufactured distinction of moral superiority to whites alone.

Black female bodies have historically been used by Western culture to represent hypersexuality and immorality and to justify emotional and physical abuse and discrimination. As Black bodies were assigned tasks of labor to serve the industry of their master, so too were they assigned the societal role of sexual vagrant—bearing the burden of sin and base animal instinct for their white oppressors. As the expression of this assigned burden, Black female bodies became embodied representations of the allegorical Jezebel—cultural symbols of the profane into which sin could be projected (Butler, 2015). Once assigned, that role was normalized and unrelentingly reinforced through a continuous cycle of denigration of Black female bodies through labor, physical abuse, forced breeding, and sexual exploitation. The psychological impact of this burdening and trauma at the individual level was devastating; the intergenerational legacy of that oppression is profound and touches all aspects of our society.

As Butler (2015) describes, the "construction of Black women as Jezebels" forced a perverse stereotype during and after slavery, that Black women and girls should be seen and treated as nameless bodies, with no personhood (absent of Ms., Mrs., or called by proper name), an invisible sexual object with no claim to their own desires or identities. This stereotype also belies the construct of the Black concubine, who also is objectified and seen as an appendage to the desires of the oppressor, the oppressor of the past and the present. Butler (2015) furthered that these dehumanizing representations of Black women and girls bled into the degrading representations of Black men as well, which together viewed both genders as sexual deviants only to serve the purpose of reproduction for the good of the American economy. The depths of this level of sexual exploitation of Black women, children, and men not only led to the loss of personal and familial identity but also to the fracture of the Black family, as Black men were treated as "breeders" not fathers or husbands, and women were treated as hosts waiting to be bred. This visual is a traumatic and devastatingly debased image of the Black body. However, even more devastating is the sad reality that this image continues to exist through cultural stereotypes and the practice of human trafficking.

The desires of Black children and women have historically been at the external valuation of others. Daina Berry (2017) describes how the monetary assessment of African-American women during slavery was based largely on their "age, skills and reproductive status" (p. 12). African-American women were not privy to the control of their own bodies, but their bodies served a breeding function used in sustaining and expanding the institution of slavery in the United States (p. 13). Through the sexual exploitation of Black women and girls perpetrated by slavery, the whole person was reduced to the itemized components of the body and the utility in which these parts could serve. The valuation of African-American women was based on the "individual buyer's needs and desires . . . that choice also meant that potential buyers put a price tag on enslaved children before conception" (p. 13). As Berry (2017) so accurately asserts, "the institution of slavery in the United States extended its reach into women's bodies" (p. 13). In this way, Black children entered the world not as human beings to be witnessed but as chattel, like their mothers, fathers, and grandparents before them, then to be processed, exploited, and sold. This legacy of slavery and the dynamics of sexual exploitation that it cultivated must be taken into account if we are to fully understand and begin to address issues around human trafficking of Black girls and women.

Sexual Exploitation and the Loss of Innocence in Girlhood

The United Nations Convention on the Rights of the Child establishes the definition of children and the rights they are afforded. The second clause of this declaration asserts,

> All children have all these [human] rights, no matter who they are, where they live, what language they speak, what their religion is, what they think, what they look like, if they are a boy or girl, if they have a disability, if they are rich or poor, and no matter who their parents or families are or what their parents or families believe or do. No child should be treated unfairly for any reason.

The ideal that this declaration aspires to stands in stark contrast to the lived experience of African-American children, who experience persistent discrimination and intergenerational trauma stemming from that which was inflicted on their enslaved ancestors. From birth, Black children observe, experience, and internalize those persistent patterns of discrimination, exploitation, and abuse, and it is in that context that they are forced to interpret their value and learn their role in society. Importantly for the subject of this chapter, the toxic objectification and sexual exploitation of Black women and girls that was established in slavery has continued into the present day as sexualization of Black women and girls. In this vein, through the intergenerational transmission of racialized sexual exploitation, Black girls have been forced to embody a kind of violence not of their making. Instead of being seen as innocent children, Black girls are typically viewed as hypersexual and aggressive and are not evaluated based on their inner attributes or their whole selves. All too often, sexual violence becomes the lived experience of Black girls, becoming more the rule than the exception throughout their childhood and extending into adulthood.

Some children seem to garner more sympathy than others. Why are only some children treated generously while others are not? Why are Black children, as compared to white children, systemically neglected or only viewed based on what they can do with their bodies versus who they are? The enduring narrative remains that the value of Black children lies not in them as persons but in them as commodifiable objects. This is particularly the case for Black girls, who have historically been prescribed a negative representation that is primarily positioned outside of their bodies. Black girls are generally undervalued, minimized, and neglected—their behaviors interpreted as aggressions rather than innocent childhood expressions. Words like "innocence" and "victim" are not usually within the vernacular when speaking of Black girls. This is particularly highlighted in the writing of Jasmine Philips, who uses critical race theory to depict the faulty ways in which Black girls are viewed, as she states, "It appears that for Black girls, however, the label of 'victim' is not only rebuttable but is also never presumed to begin with. Black girls consequently occupy a contested 'victim' position, regardless of whether they have been exploited by a trafficker or engaged in survival sex" (Philips, 2015, pp. 1645–1646; Holloway, 2014). This inherent bias, far from innocuous, manifests itself within the increased and sustained criminalization of their behavior (as seen in the juvenile justice system) as well as in the exploitation of their bodies.

In one critical examination on the adultification of Black girls, Epstein, Blake, and González (2017) speak to the classic stereotypes ascribed to them such as Jezebel, which highlight the "culturally rooted fantasies of Black girls" as highly sexual, promiscuous, and unbecoming, compared to the Madonna-like image assigned to their white female counterparts. These historical images of Black girls that have been transmitted from slavery continue to fuel the commodification of Black girl bodies in the form of human trafficking and continue to live in the collective unconscious in the form of implicit bias and myth-based characterizations of Black femininity. In a seminal study on the perceptions of Black girls, Epstein and colleagues (2017) sampled 325 adults from diverse ethnic backgrounds and asked about their perceptions of Black girlhood. The authors were interested to determine whether "adults assign Black girls' qualities that render them more like adults—and less innocent—than their white peers" (p. 7). Dr. Epstein and her colleagues found that across all four age brackets (i.e., 0–4, 5–9, 10–14, 15–19), collectively Black girls were perceived to be more adult than their white counterparts. More specifically, results revealed that study participants "perceived Black girls as needing less protection and nurturing than white girls, and that

Black girls were perceived to know more about adult topics and are more knowledgeable about sex than their white peers" (p. 7). These study findings not only suggest the implicit bias that the wider American public holds about Black girls but that race dictates whether someone is perceived as innocent or corrupted. Furthermore, the perception of Black girls in needing of less nurturance and having a knowledge about adult matters suggests that larger social systems designed to help children potentially harm Black children, especially when seen in this adult and unforgiven light. Dr. Epstein and Dr. Blake's research revealed that the stereotypes and implicit bias ascribed to Black girls traverse other inequities seen across social systems and continue to assign the blame of sexual exploitation to Black girls as opposed to placing it within the larger context of historical trauma and systematic racism. This structural failure perpetuates the subjugation and sexual defilement of Black girls, leaving them disproportionately vulnerable to exploitation and recruitment into the commercial sex trade.

Intersection Between Race, Structural Inequalities, and Perpetuation of Sexual Exploitation of Black Women and Girls

African-American women and girls are disproportionality at greater risk for sexual exploitation than any other racial group in the United States. The organization Rights For Girls (2019) noted that the incidence of Black girls involved in the domestic sex trafficking industry is disproportionately higher than any other racial category. Phillips (2015) noted that "in the United States, Black youth account for approximately 62 percent of minors arrested for prostitution offenses even though Blacks only make up 13.2 percent of the U.S. population" (Table 43: Arrests by Race, 2013, FBI). Rights For Girls reported that "In a two-year review of all suspected human trafficking incidents across the country, 40% of sex trafficking victims were Black" (Federal Bureau of Investigation, Crime in the United States, 2017). This same group further reported that even in cases in which the Black community is underrepresented, Black girls are disproportionately more likely to be trafficked. For example, they noted that in King County, Washington, "84% of child sex trafficking victims are female and 52% are Black, though Black children and adults together only comprise 7% of the general population. In Multnomah County, Oregon, approximately 95% of child sex trafficking victims are female and 27% of child sex trafficking victims are Black, though Black people comprise less than 6% of the population. In Louisiana, Black girls account for nearly 49% of child sex trafficking victims, though Black girls comprise approximately 19% of Louisiana's youth population" (Federal Bureau of Investigation, Crime in the United States, 2017; Bureau of Justice Statistics, Characteristics of Suspected Human Trafficking Incidents, 2008–2010).

These statistics show a pattern of overrepresentation in the sexual exploitation of Black girls and suggest the presence of social and racial inequalities that push black girls into a life of exploitation. One of the critiques of trafficking literature is that some of the research may overlook the underlying "structural inequalities that facilitate exploitation" (Blazek et al., 2019, p. 64). Blazek et al. (2019) assert that the roles of race, gender, and social inequalities "interact" to set the "structural conditions to shape life chances and experiences" that make Black girls and women more susceptible to sexual exploitation.

Research (Blazek et al., 2019; Phillips, 2015; Rights for Girls, 2019) has identified several factors that increase vulnerability to sexual exploitation for Black girls and women:

- Poverty
- History of neglect, physical, emotional, and sexual abuse; drug abuse
- Child welfare involvement and foster-care placement
- Low educational performance
- Community disorganization
- Early entry into the criminal justice system
- Criminalization of sexual behavior
- Inability to access mental health and other health care supports.

The relative role of these factors and their value for interpreting and predicting an individual's susceptibility to recruitment into the commercial sex trade are areas of active academic investigation. Better data and refined interpretation will serve to bring attention to the problem and focus efforts of education, advocacy, and intervention. However, the impact on the lives of individual Black girls and women and society as a whole is too great to justify waiting for better data and more nuanced interpretations. Enough is understood about the underlying causes and interdependencies of these factors, and there is a clear ethical imperative to act to proactively address these complex, intertwined, and intergenerational issues.

In defiance of intergenerationally established systemic discrimination, objectification, and exploitation, Black girls and women and the communities that support them are finding their voice. Black Lives Matter and other grassroots movements have spurred a dramatic increase in the "role of minority youth as leaders and spokespersons in the antitrafficking movement. Their voices defy stereotypes of Black sexuality and call upon legislators and advocates to address some of the unique vulnerabilities that kids of color face with respect to sex trafficking" (Butler, 2015). The confluence of increased awareness, advocacy, and action gives hope that the cycle of racial discrimination, sexual exploitation, and intergenerational subjugation of Black girls and women can be broken.

Discussion Questions

1. What role should government and social institutions play in breaking the cycles of intergenerational racialized trauma in Black girls and women?

2. Based on our understanding of the dynamics that predispose Black girls and women to sex trafficking, what interventions can be provided to help empower them and reshape the narrative of Black femininity and identity?

References

Berry, D. R. (2017). *The Price for Their Pound of Flesh: The Value of the Enslaved, from Womb to Grave, in the Building of a Nation*. Boston, MA: Beacon Press.

Blazek, M., Esson, J., & Smith, D. P. (2019). Relational geographies of human trafficking: Inequality, manoeuvring and im/mobility across space and time. *Transactions of the Institute of British Geographers, 44*(1), 63–78.

Bureau of Justice Statistics, Characteristics of Suspected Human Trafficking Incidents, 2008–2010 (2011, April). https://bjs.ojp.gov/library/publications/characteristics-suspected-human-trafficking-incidents-2008-2010

Butler, C. N. (2015). The racial roots of human trafficking. *UCLA Law Review, 62*, 1464.

Epstein, R., Blake, J., & González, T. (2017). *Girlhood interrupted: The erasure of Black girls' childhood*. http://dx.doi.org/10.2139/ssrn.3000695.

Federal Bureau of Investigation, Crime in the United States 2017, Tables 43B. Accessed from https://ucr.fbi.gov/crime-in-the-u.s/2019/crime-in-the-u.s.-2019/topic-pages/tables/table-43

Phillips, J. (2015). Black girls and the (im) possibilities of a victim trope: The intersectional failures of legal and advocacy interventions in the commercial sexual exploitation of minors in the United States. *UCLA Law Review, 62*, 1642.

Rights For Girls. (2019). Human Rights Project for Girls. Accessed March 10, 2021 from https://rights4girls.org/wp-content/uploads/r4g/2015/02/African-American-Girls-and-Trafficking.pdf

Winters, L. Z. (2016). *The mulatta concubine: Terror, intimacy, freedom, and desire in the Black transatlantic (Race in the Atlantic World, 1700–1900 Ser.)*. Athens, GA: University of Georgia Press.

SECTION III
THE ANTISLAVERY MOVEMENT

10

SEXUAL MINORITIES AND HUMAN TRAFFICKING

VULNERABILITIES AND CHALLENGES FACED BY AN OVERLOOKED POPULATION

CANDENCE WILLS

Chapter Learning Objectives

- Critically analyze the current limitations of human trafficking literature and research on nondominant victim frames.
- Explain the risk factors that allow sexual minorities to have increased vulnerability to human trafficking.
- Understand the nature of the relationship between law enforcement and sexual minorities and law enforcement responses to sexual minority victims of trafficking.
- Describe the unique challenges transgender trafficking victims face and limited avenues for support and help.

Brief Overview of Human Trafficking of Sexual Minorities

In recent years, human trafficking research expanded on the narrow focus of sex trafficking of women and girls to include other forms of trafficking and vulnerable populations. Human trafficking scholars have explored vulnerabilities of racial and ethnic minorities (Brunovskis & Surtees, 2010; Bryant-Davis & Tummala-Narra, 2017; Deer, 2009; Stumblingbear-Riddle et al., 2019), physical and mental disabilities (Franchino-Olsen et al., 2020; Reid, 2018), addiction and substance abuse (Stoklosa et al., 2017), and more

DOI: 10.4324/9781003124672-13

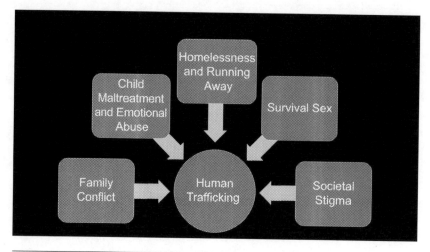

Figure 10.1   Risk factors for human trafficking related to sexual minority status

recently, sexual minorities (Atteberry-Ash et al., 2019; Boukli & Renz, 2019; Hogan & Roe-Sepowitz, 2020). While research interests have been more inclusive of various vulnerable groups outside of the traditional focus on women and girls, exploration into understanding the unique vulnerabilities of each group is still limited.

Gaining particular trafficking research attention are sexual minorities or those "whose sexual identity, orientation or practices differ from the majority of the surrounding society" and generally include lesbian, gay, bisexual, intersex, transgender, and gender nonbinary or nonconforming individuals (Liberties-K, 2001; Math & Seshadri, 2013). Often, human trafficking literature avoided sexual minorities in dominant victim narratives and frameworks. Hyperfocused on the sex trafficking of cis-gender girls and young women, migrants labor trafficking, and national security, early human trafficking framing impacted the scope of research and subsequent policies, programs, and services responding to victims (Boukli & Renz, 2019; Brennan, 2017; Chuang, 2014; Farrell & Fahy, 2009; Schwarz & Britton, 2015). Over 20 years after passing the initial Trafficking Victims Protection Act (TVPA), labor trafficking research gained little knowledge of forced labor beyond the exploitation of immigrants who are made vulnerable due to language, legal, and location barriers prohibiting access to legal protections and social services. Sex trafficking has largely been framed within a heterosexual context involving hetero men who take advantage of vulnerable girls and women through a "grooming" process, coercion, or trafficking across borders into a foreign country (Dempsey, 2010; Farr, 2005; Soderlund, 2005; Weitzer, 2007). While this does occur, the dominant narrative of trafficking and victims limits the understanding of trafficking situations beyond women and girls forced into sex trafficking.

Trafficking of sexual minorities is a growing area of human trafficking research that notably expands on homeless youth exploited in sex trafficking. More recent studies have focused on specific populations, such as transgender youth and young adult victims of human trafficking; however, sexual minorities are commonly treated as a monolith in research and grouped into one category. Without distinguishing between subpopulations of any diverse group, the findings then diminish the unique experiences and challenges of each subgroup. Studies acknowledging sexual minorities within the general population usually include minority gender or orientation categories to examine sexual minority outcomes as a subpopulation within a predominantly heterosexual study population. Many studies examine sexual minorities within the context of homeless youth and commercial sexual exploitation of children (CSEC), also termed domestic minor sex trafficking (DMST), finding that sexual minorities are more vulnerable to sexual exploitation and trafficking compared to heterosexual peers. Few studies move passed these initial findings that only begin to unravel the vulnerabilities of trafficked sexual minorities. Unfortunately, there is little available research on labor exploitation of sexual minorities, even though individuals identifying as LGBTI+ have been excluded from legal employment (Fehrenbacher et al., 2020; Martinez & Kelle, 2013).

Globally, identifying as a sexual minority is still considered taboo in many countries. According to the most recent ILGA State-sponsored Homophobia Report (2020), minority sexual orientations continues to be criminalized in 70 states, while laws banning gender non-conforming activities, such as crossdressing, specifically target gender expression and de facto criminalize transgender persons (ILGA World et al., 2020). Primarily due to the sensitive nature and safety of sexual minorities, research involving sexual minorities derives from progressive, LGBTI+ accepting countries where sexual minorities have stronger protections by law and openly identifying as a sexual minority is less stigmatizing and hazardous. With ethical and safety concerns for sexual minorities in many countries, a biased perspective appears in research regarding human trafficking of sexual minorities and is largely representative of experiences by those from the US, UK, and Canada. Although human trafficking research has been incorporating sexual minorities into studies, trafficking and forced exploitation of sexual minorities remains globally underresearched.

Risk Factors for Trafficking Vulnerabilities

Human trafficking literature identifies sexual minority status, both orientation and gender, as a risk factor for human trafficking. Several studies reveal an overrepresentation of sexual minorities among sexually exploited victims

(Chohaney, 2016; Choi, 2015; Choi et al., 2015; Dank et al., 2015); however, few studies venture into the underlying reasons as to *why* being a sexual minority serves as a risk factor and make the connection between vulnerability and victimization. Simply identifying as a sexual minority is not inherently the direct cause of being vulnerable to exploitation. Social issues, such as societal oppression and systematic inequality, collectively fail to protect those vulnerable from becoming victims. Compounding emotional instability or lack of support with societal oppression and stigma further increases vulnerability to victimization (Twis, 2020). The following sections describe risk factors that increase vulnerability of sexual minorities to trafficking victimization.

Family Conflict and Childhood Abuse

One of the most significant factors underlying contribution to increasing vulnerability to human trafficking for sexual minorities is familial conflict. Youth who identify as a sexual minority frequently face the unique challenge of family intolerance for their orientation or gender identity. Families may verbalize their disagreements with "lifestyles" of sexual minorities and LGBTI+ community as a whole. Those with stronger negative views toward sexual minorities go beyond verbal disagreements and clearly express intolerance or even hatred for the sexual minorities. Youth identifying as sexual minorities in intolerant households endure tumultuous relationships with their families (Chohaney, 2016; Choi et al., 2015; Hart et al., 2018). Even when youth are not open about their sexual identities, suspicion of youth identifying as a sexual minority or exhibiting behaviors that do not conform to traditional gendered roles and stereotypes can lead to similar family conflict. In a study by Chohaney (2016), the author noted that after controlling for informal social control, poor parental relationships play a significant role as a risk factor for sex trafficking. Further contributing to increased vulnerabilities to trafficking, hatred toward sexual minorities can escalate to LGBTI+ youth being kicked out of their homes by intolerant family members (Chohaney, 2016; Dank et al., 2015).

Dysfunctional family relationships due to strong intolerance toward sexual minorities can become abusive and further exacerbate vulnerabilities to trafficking. One study found that negative childhood experiences increase the likelihood of being victimized in trafficking (Reid, 2012, pp. 93–95). Although the study focused on the sexual exploitation of cis-gender girls, the findings can extend to sexual minorities. Reid (2012, p. 100) found that childhood maltreatment in the form of negative and abusive relationships with parents, particularly mothers, causes a chain of events, including abuse, attempts by youth to escape, drug abuse, and sexual denigration, that increases the possibility of becoming a trafficking victim and being sexual exploited.

Childhood maltreatment is more common among sexual minority youth than their heterosexual peers. In a US study of 2,917 adult participants, men who identify as either gay or bisexual reported higher rates of childhood trauma including emotional and physical maltreatment than the heterosexual men, while lesbian and bisexual women participants experienced higher rates of physical and more extreme forms of physical abuse in childhood compared to heterosexual women in the study (Corliss et al., 2002). Sexual minorities also have higher rates of adverse childhood experiences and maltreatment compared to heterosexual individuals in childhood (Andersen & Blosnich, 2013). Lesbian and bisexual women are also more likely to report physical and sexual abuse in childhood and adolescence compared to heterosexual women. In frequency, severity, and persistence, physical and sexual abuse is more commonly reported by women who identify as sexual minorities (Austin et al., 2008). Among sexual minority men, psychological distress is reportedly higher than heterosexual men attributable to stress from childhood abuse (Hart et al., 2018). The study also shows that the stress of childhood torment from being bullied for not conforming to masculine gendered roles further contributes to increased rates of adulthood distress among sexual minority men (Hart et al., 2018). Bontempo and d'Augelli (2002) find that youth identifying as sexual minorities have a greater risk for experiencing victimization in school than their heterosexual peers. Examining adolescents, Friedman et al. (2011) explain that those who identify as a sexual minority are more likely to have adverse childhood experiences including trauma, parent abuse, peer victimization, and sexual abuse compared to heterosexuals. They reveal that sexual minorities are 3.8 times more likely to experience sexual abuse, 1.2 times more likely to experience parental physical abuse, 1.7 times more likely to endure assault at school, and 2.4 times more likely to miss school because of fear. Childhood maltreatment through physical, emotional, and sexual abuse consistently associate with trafficking victimization.

While childhood maltreatment, including physical and sexual abuse, strongly relates to forced exploitation and human trafficking, the association between maltreatment and exploitation is weaker and less consistent than childhood emotional abuse. Examining physical, sexual, and emotional abuse among sexual minorities, childhood emotional abuse is the strongest predictor of psychological distress (Balsam et al., 2010). Childhood emotional abuse also strongly associates with DMST in a study with 273 youth and adults engaged in commercial sex or exploited in sex trafficking (Fedina et al., 2019). Roe-Sepowitz (2012) concludes that childhood emotional abuse, running away or missing from care, and survival sex strongly correlate with sexual exploitation, but only childhood emotional abuse remained significant related to CSEC at a younger age. These findings strengthen insight into how emotional abuse increases vulnerability to human trafficking. Sexual minority youth are already at a greater risk of experiencing emotional and

physical abuse at home and bullying victimization in school for not conforming to gendered norms. Childhood emotional abuse is a critical risk factor for
human trafficking among those identifying as sexual minorities.

Homelessness and Running Away

Runaway and homeless youth are especially vulnerable to exploitation
(Fong & Cardoso, 2010). Without resources or shelter, homeless youth are
forced to rely on those willing to take advantage of their vulnerable position
in order to meet their basic needs (Dank et al., 2015). Youth running away
from home often do so to escape or avoid harmful, difficult home environments. Factors youth may face such as trauma, abuse, neglect, assault, and
general dysfunctional home lives encourage youth to run away from home or
their caregivers.

Sexual minorities are overrepresented among youth experiencing homelessness (Choi et al., 2015; Dank et al., 2017; Hogan & Roe-Sepowitz, 2020;
Kattari & Begun, 2017; National Coalition for the Homeless, 2017). It is
estimated that between 20% and 40% of homeless and runaway youth
identify as LGBTI+ but are only 5% to 7% of the general youth population
(Forge et al., 2018; Quintana et al., 2010). As explained previously, sexual
minorities experience childhood maltreatment, family disfunction, and abuse
because of their LGBTI+ identity and run away from home in order to
escape their unstable or abusive family life. LGBTI+ youth may also be
enticed to leave unaccepting families in search of like-minded sexual minority
communities. Sexual minority youth are also more likely to be kicked out of
their homes by intolerant family members (Dank et al., 2015). In a study
composed of 20% sexual minority homeless youth, the most common reason
given for homelessness for both sexual and gender minorities is being forced
out by parents or running away because of their sexual minority status. Youth
also cite "family issues, poverty and lack of housing, forced out and ran away
for other issues, aging out of foster care, and abuse at home" as reasons for
homelessness (Choi et al., 2015). Duration of homelessness is also longer for
61% of LGBTI+ youth than heterosexual homeless youth and drastically
longer for nearly 80% of trans youth compared to their cis-gender heterosexual peers (Choi et al., 2015).

Consistently, studies on homeless youth explain that being homeless
increases the likelihood of becoming a victim of sexual exploitation and
human trafficking. Choi (2015) finds a strong association between youth
homelessness, including running away from home, and sexual exploitation.
Youth and adults involved in commercial sex are more likely to be victims of
sex trafficking if they had a history of running away. For adults in the commercial sex industry, running away from home remained a significant risk
factor for sex trafficking and is over five times greater for child trafficking
victims than non–child trafficking victims. In the same study, participants

reported overall high rates of running away, and this factor was particularly salient among sexual minority youth (Fedina et al., 2019).

Since sexual minority youth more commonly run away and experience homelessness compared to their cis-gender heterosexual peers, they have an elevated risk of trafficking victimization (Greeson et al., 2019; Morton et al., 2018). They may be more susceptible to trafficking and being sought by exploiters who offer a pseudo-family, security, and familial structure that could not be found at home (Chohaney, 2016). Sexual minority youth with low self-esteem may be targets for trafficking predators who make false promises of love, friendship, security, and excitement (Chohaney, 2016). The odds of being both sex trafficked and a sexual minority are 2.25 times higher compared to being a heterosexual young adult (Hogan & Roe-Sepowitz, 2020). Homeless sexual minorities may also be vulnerable to other forms of trafficking including forced begging, petty theft, and survival sex in order to meet their basic needs. In adulthood, those trafficked who have experienced homelessness as a minor or been trafficked as a minor also have greater difficulty integrating into licit markets and prosocial activities, thus continuing the vulnerability into adulthood (Chohaney, 2016).

Survival Sex
Sexual minority youth and young adults reportedly engage in survival sex to meet their basic needs, such as money, food, clothing, and shelter (Dank et al., 2015). Shelters and youth congregate care homes may discriminate against sexual minorities, particularly if they are faith-based organizations. The marginalized youth face stigma, homophobia, transphobia, harassment, and at times violence in foster care, shelters, health care facilities, social service agencies, and law enforcement (Dank et al., 2015). Trading sex for survival becomes the product of economic insecurity, combined with prior victimization, homelessness, and lack of resources.

Youth and young adults identifying as sexual minorities may have barriers to legal employment due to age if a minor, emotional trauma, and employer discrimination due to their gender identity or orientation. Barred from the licit economy, sexual minorities are more likely to resort to survival sex (Hogan & Roe-Sepowitz, 2020). Involvement in survival sex ranges from force to being "unexpectedly propositioned" to exchanging sex for money or needs. Sexual minority youth also enter commercial sex by voluntarily seeking opportunities and being introduced to commercial sex by friends or peers (Dank et al., 2015). Chohaney (2016) explains that engaging in survival sex and having friends involved in sex sales as either the procurer or the seller is strongly associated with increased the odds of being forced into minor sex trafficking. Hogan and Roe-Sepowitz (2020) also find that sexual minorities who were sex trafficked are more likely to report exchanging sex for money. Both studies further reveal that homeless sexual minorities exploited in sex trafficking report higher rates of challenging life experiences, suicide attempts, drug use, and risk-taking compared to sex trafficked heterosexual homeless young adults.

Survival sex increases risk for sexual exploitation and trafficking by exposing vulnerable individuals to potential exploiters, pimps, and traffickers. Interacting with buyers attracts more buyers, who will inevitably include sex traffickers wanting to prey off of the desperation and vulnerabilities of those engaging in survival sex (Chohaney, 2016). Exploiters may start out as protectors providing safety and security or acceptance and understanding as a sexual minority. LGBTI+ trafficking victims may also rely on a romantic partner for basic needs and seem complicit in their victimization (Boukli & Renz, 2019). In a comprehensive study on New York LGBTI+ youth and survival sex, 6% of youth trading sex started through a third-party exploiter. Although some youth agree to the exploiter's terms, others involuntarily or forcefully become the victim of an exploiter (Dank et al., 2015). Without access to shelters, employment, and resources, sexual minorities rely on survival sex and continue to be vulnerable to human traffickers willing to exploit them.

Transgender

Fear and bias toward transgender persons contribute to victimization of trans-identifying persons. Trans youth are often victimized in school through bullying, social isolation, and discrimination. As with all sexual minorities, transgender individuals face intolerance because of their gender identity, rejection by family and friends, and being kicked out of their homes, which increases their likelihood of homelessness. Trans persons are more likely to experience psychological symptoms, such as depression, substance abuse, and social marginalizing, due to their victimization. Parental disengagement, lack of support, and disbelief of gender dysphoria increase stress and contributes to adverse psychological outcomes, physical pain, and illness among gender nonconforming youth (Hammond et al., 2020).

Due to societal stigma, transgender persons are socially marginalized and excluded from legal employment and face greater vulnerability to trafficking than those who are cis-gender. Particularly vulnerable to victimization and human trafficking are trans people of color (POC). Intersecting minority statuses for POC sexual minorities attract discrimination from their minority orientation or gender identity along with their minority race. Intersectional minority statuses further increase the likelihood of having to rely on survival sex, as well as vulnerability to trafficking. Trans youth, especially trans youth of color, are at exceptionally high risk for engaging in survival sex and being exploited in sex trafficking (Morton et al., 2018).

Transgender immigrants are also more vulnerable to exploitation and trafficking. Many trans-identifying immigrants flee persecution and victimization in their home countries only to be preyed on by traffickers and exploiters in their host country. Depending on their visa and immigration status, transgender immigrants can be banned from employment in the licit economy and are economically forced into survival sex (Fehrenbacher et al., 2020). The compounding factors of being trans, POC, immigrant, and in poverty drastically increase the likelihood of trans persons becoming victims of trafficking, in particular forced sexual exploitation (Hammond et al., 2020; Meyer, 2003).

Transgender youth also report engaging in the sex trade in order to secure large amounts of funds necessary for costly procedures related to their trans identity (Dank et al., 2015). Trans youth engaged in the sex trade may be motivated to seek gender reassignment and gender-affirming surgeries, medical treatment, or hormone replacement therapies in order to transition. The unique challenges that transgender persons face including social stigma and costly medical care to transition make trans persons extraordinarily vulnerable to human trafficking and exploitation.

Responses to Trafficking of Sexual Minorities by Law Enforcement
Globally and in the US, there is a significant history of mistreatment and violence toward the LGBTI+ community by law enforcement that is still felt by sexual minority communities today. Law enforcement deliberately participated in entrapment plans and profiled sexual minorities. Events such as the stonewall riots on June 28, 1969, highlight the long and conflicting relationship between police and LGBTI+ community. Despite societal progress with the national legalization of same sex marriage, passing the Sheppard Baird Act federally protecting sexual minorities from discrimination and hate crimes, and the development of police sensitivity trainings, law enforcement have continue to overlook discrimination and crimes against sexual minorities (Israel et al., 2014).

Many people identifying as sexual minorities continue to fear law enforcement, as police officers and corrections officers have victimized sexual minorities (Buist & Lenning, 2016, p. 64; Mallory et al., 2015). Sexual minorities physically appear less conforming to traditional gendered expressions, including men looking or acting too feminine, women looking and acting too masculine or "butch," and trans persons not conforming to their gender assigned at birth face greater harassment and discrimination by law enforcement (Mallory et al., 2015). Fear of mistreatment at the hands of police further prevents sexual minorities from reporting their victimization.

Minors identifying as sexual minorities commit status offenses when running away from home in search of LGBTI+ communities in more socially progressive places. Although law enforcement may be more tolerant of sexual minorities in more sexually diverse and progressive places, youth who commit status offenses by running away from home can be criminally detained and forcibly returned to their home. Sexual minority youth seeking to escape abuse and familial intolerance encounter the same abuse that they left when forced to return. Alternatively, after being detained by law enforcement, they may be placed in congregate care facilities or foster care that do not meet the unique needs of sexual minorities youth who have experienced trauma and victimization by family members. The cycle of running, detention by police, and return to residential care or facilities instills fear of police in youth and avoidance of police even when victimized.

In instances when sexual minorities report victimization experiences, some report that their victimizations are not taken seriously, and they are brushed off as "crazy" or "freaks," only further enhancing the fear of mistreatment and distrust of law enforcement. Disbelief and disregard inhibit avenues for victims to seek help (Mallory et al., 2015). Police, when responding to victims of trafficking and sexual exploitation, have in some circumstances refused to take a police report or recognize a trafficked person as a victim because of their sexual minority status (Egyes, 2017, pp. 172–173). Transgender trafficked victims are more often perceived by law enforcement as offenders rather than victims when they are trafficked in forced labor and sexual exploitation compared to cis-gender women in similar victim circumstances. Law enforcement reportedly have instead met trans trafficked victims with brutality, violence, and further exploitation (Fehrenbacher et al., 2020). Situations of trafficking and forced exploitation are further perpetuated without protection and intervention by police.

Sexual minorities forced into sexual exploitation, forced labor, or forced criminality, including drug trade, forced begging and theft, or recruiting others to be exploited, may not be as easily recognized as victims by law enforcement. Law enforcement may be trained on human trafficking within their agencies; however, the trainings often focus largely on sex trafficking of children, namely girls, and women forced into prostitution (Boukli & Renz, 2019). Law enforcement perceptions of trafficking victims distorts the lens through which they detect different forms of exploitation and the context for where trafficking victimization occurs. Youth criminalized for engaging in criminal behaviors related to their trafficking victimization may encounter the juvenile justice and criminal justice systems.

Similarly, boys and young men are not as easily identifiable as victims compared to girls and young women (Boukli & Renz, 2019; Hodge & Sexton, 2020). When male victims experience forced sexual exploitation, sexual assault, or rape, both heterosexual and gay men may feel especially uncomfortable contacting police. Stigma still attached to male rape combined with identifying as a gay man often prohibits victims from seeking help for their victimization, especially from police, who are imbedded in a culture of hyper-masculinity. Too often, victims are blamed for their own victimization, and men, in particular gay-identifying men, are not seen as being worthy of the victim status (Rumney, 2009). Unfortunately, sexual minorities that want to reach out for help and expose their exploitation and abuse may not feel comfortable or confident that the police will help them in their time of need. The lack of trust in police contributes to ongoing exploitation.

Conclusion and Suggestions for Service Providers and Policies
While human trafficking research continues to grow and include various groups previously overlooked, information regarding the vulnerabilities of sexual minorities to trafficking victimization remains underresearched. Traditional perceptions of victims as predominantly vulnerable girls and young women trapped in sex trafficking is changing as our understanding of human trafficking, including types of trafficking and vulnerable populations, continues to evolve with each new study.

In recent years, research has shown that sexual minorities are significantly impacted by human trafficking. Sexual minorities are more vulnerable to trafficking victimization than their heterosexual peers. Identifying as a sexual minority is understood to increase vulnerability but is not inherently a risk factor for trafficking. Societal stigma, familial rejection, homelessness and poverty, and childhood abuse are risk factors that directly associate with human trafficking and mediate the relationship between identifying as a sexual minority and victim exploitation. Sexual minorities often face stigma and social marginalization globally. In progressive countries, identifying as a sexual minority can create barriers to legal employment opportunities, housing and shelter, service provision, and protection by law enforcement. In more traditional or socially conservative countries, sexual minorities may be socially shamed and ostracized, jailed, and murdered by the intolerant people or the state. Families also play a key role in the potential vulnerability of sexual minorities to human trafficking. Unstable or abusive families that express intolerance or hatred toward the LGBTI+ community and reject sexual minority family members increase the likelihood of sexual minorities being trafficked. Further, sexual minority youth are overrepresented among homeless and runaway youth due to being forced from their homes or running away from abusive households. Homeless LGBTI+ youth are more likely to engage in survival sex to meet their basic needs while homeless than heterosexual homeless youth and are more likely to report trafficking victimization.

Studies acknowledging sexual minorities as being particularly vulnerable further emphasize the need to continue research into the underlying reasons for heightened vulnerability. Specifically, studies should explore experiences of those who identify as transgender or gender nonconforming. Although the perception of the iconic victim in trafficking is changing in research and police are offered sensitivity and trafficking training that include more vulnerable groups, sexual minorities are often overlooked as victims. As noted in prior qualitative studies, sexual minorities, especially transgender persons, are too often dismissed or mistreated by law enforcement and viewed as offenders of criminal activities related to their trafficking experience rather than being viewed as trafficking victims forced into survival sex or criminal activities.

Provider Services

Those who identify as sexual minorities have compounding issues of being more vulnerable to human trafficking while having greater difficulties receiving services and treatment for their victimization (Schwarz & Britton, 2015). Most service providers for trafficked victims cater toward cis-gender girls, as they are most often identified by law enforcement. Trafficking victims and homeless youth further encounter being denied housing and services because of sexual minority status. Sexual minorities can also feel uncomfortable in a residential facility, especially if the facility is religiously affiliated. They may feel unsafe when placed in a residential facility that refuses to recognize gender identity over assigned gender at birth or targeted for their minority status. Overall, general social services most often cater to heteronormative populations. As such, specialized services that treat the unique needs of the sexual minorities, including transgender victims, are often limited or absent (Hammond et al., 2020).

The common initial reaction by law enforcement and providers is to stabilize the victim. This involves treating the immediate needs of the victim by arranging medical care, short-term housing, mental health care, and a forensic interview. Attention given to immediate care and stabilization is often at the expense of long-term rehabilitation efforts that focus on unique trauma and special needs of sexual minority, transgender, and male victims (Hammond et al., 2020). In these cases, targeted services are necessary to treat not just the victimization but the trauma of childhood emotional and physical abuse, rejection by family and friends, societal stigma, and marginalization because of sexual minority identity.

Policy Implications

With the implementation of the Strengthening Families Act of 2014, states have to recognize sexually exploited minors as child abuse victims and respond with child abuse protocols. While this is a remarkable step forward, the policies fall short of actually protecting youth and providing youth exploited victims the unique and necessary services for their exploitation. Consequently, policies fall short of expanding tailored protocols, resources, and services to youth who identify as sexual minorities.

Within sexual minorities, the various identity groups have unique needs that are not captured in current policies or provider-mandated care. There are also "red flags" or signs of trafficking victimization within the sexual minority subgroups that differ from commonly identified cis-gender girls and young women victims. Policies should be created that stipulate trainings for law enforcement, health care providers, and other first responders or professionals in direct contact with potential victims on the various behaviors exhibited by unique sexual minority populations that signal trafficking and exploitation.

Discussion Questions

1. How do families and relationships within families impact the likelihood of trafficking victimization among youth sexual minorities?
2. How do childhood abuse and maltreatment contribute to sexual minorities having increased vulnerability to human trafficking?
3. What can service providers do to reduce the likelihood and impact of trafficking victimization?
4. Why do many sexual minority victims of human trafficking avoid seeking help from law enforcement?
5. Why are sexual minorities more likely to engage in survival sex or become victims of sex trafficking?

Quiz/Exam Questions

1. Explain the risk factors that contribute to sexual minorities becoming vulnerable to exploitation and human trafficking.
2. Describe policies that can be implemented to prevent and protect sexual minorities from being victims of human trafficking.
3. Explain the unique challenges transgender persons face that increase their vulnerability to human trafficking.

References

Andersen, J. P., & Blosnich, J. (2013). Disparities in adverse childhood experiences among sexual minority and heterosexual adults: Results from a multi-state probability-based sample. *PLoS One, 8*(1), e54691.

Atteberry-Ash, B., Walls, N. E., Kattari, S. K., Peitzmeier, S. M., Kattari, L., & Langenderfer-Magruder, L. (2019). Forced sex among youth: accrual of risk by gender identity, sexual orientation, mental health and bullying. *Journal of LGBT Youth*, 1–21.

Austin, S. B., Jun, H.-J., Jackson, B., Spiegelman, D., Rich-Edwards, J., Corliss, H. L., & Wright, R. J. (2008). Disparities in child abuse victimization in lesbian, bisexual, and heterosexual women in the Nurses' Health Study II. *Journal of Women's Health, 17*(4), 597–606.

Balsam, K. F., Lehavot, K., Beadnell, B., & Circo, E. (2010). Childhood abuse and mental health indicators among ethnically diverse lesbian, gay, and bisexual adults. *Journal of Consulting and Clinical Psychology, 78*(4), 459.

Bontempo, D. E., & d'Augelli, A. R. (2002). Effects of at-school victimization and sexual orientation on lesbian, gay, or bisexual youths' health risk behavior. *Journal of Adolescent Health*, *30*(5), 364–374.

Boukli, A., & Renz, F. (2019). Deconstructing the lesbian, gay, bisexual, transgender victim of sex trafficking: Harm, exceptionality and religion—Sexuality tensions. *International Review of Victimology*, *25*(1), 71–90.

Brennan, D. (2017). Fighting human trafficking today: Moral panics, zombie data, and the seduction of rescue. *Wake Forest Law Review*, *52*(2), 477–496.

Brunovskis, A., & Surtees, R. (2010). Untold stories: Biases and selection effects in research with victims of trafficking for sexual exploitation. *International Migration*, *48*(4), 1–37.

Bryant-Davis, T., & Tummala-Narra, P. (2017). Cultural oppression and human trafficking: Exploring the role of racism and ethnic bias. *Women & Therapy*, *40*(1–2), 152–169. https://doi.org/ 10.1080/02703149.2016.1210964

Buist, C. L., & Lenning, E. (2016). Gender issues in corrections. In C. M. Hilinski-Rosick & J. P. Walsh (Eds.), *Issues in corrections: Research, policy, and future prospects* (pp. 57–79). Lanham, MD: Lexington Books.

Chohaney, M. L. (2016). Minor and adult domestic sex trafficking risk factors in Ohio. *Journal of the Society for Social Work Research*, *7*(1), 117–141.

Choi, K. R. (2015). Risk factors for domestic minor sex trafficking in the United States: A literature review. *Journal of Forensic Nursing*, *11*(2), 66–76.

Choi, S. K., Wilson, B. D., Shelton, J., & Gates, G. J. (2015). *Serving our youth 2015: The needs and experiences of lesbian, gay, bisexual, transgender, and questioning youth experiencing homelessness*. Los Angeles: The Williams Institute with the True Colors Fund.

Chuang, J. A. (2014). Exploitation creep and the unmaking of human trafficking law. *American Journal of International Law*, *108*(4), 609–649.

Corliss, H. L., Cochran, S. D., & Mays, V. M. (2002). Reports of parental maltreatment during childhood in a United States population-based survey of homosexual, bisexual, and heterosexual adults. *Journal of Child Abuse and Neglect*, *26*(11), 1165–1178.

Dank, M. L., Yahner, J., Madden, K., Bañuelos, I., Yu, L., Ritchie, A., Mora, M., & Conner, B. M. (2015). *Surviving the streets of New York: Experiences of LGBTQ youth, YMSM, and YWSW engaged in survival sex*. Washington, DC: Urban Institute.

Dank, M. L., Yahner, J., Yu, L., Vasquez-Noriega, C., Gelatt, J., & Pergamit, M. R. (2017). *Pretesting a human trafficking screening tool in the child welfare and runaway and homeless youth systems*. Washington, DC: Urban Institute.

Deer, S. (2009). Relocation revisited: Sex trafficking of native women in the United States. *William Mitchell Law Review*, *36*(2), 621–683.

Dempsey, M. M. (2010). Sex trafficking and criminalization: In defense of feminist abolitionism. *University of Pennsylvania Law Review*, *158*(6), 1729–1778.

Egyes, L. (2016). Borders and intersections: The unique vulnerabilities of LGBTQ immigrants to trafficking. In E. C. Heil & A. J. Nichols (Eds.), *Broadening the scope of human trafficking* (pp. 107–123). Durham, NC: Carolina Academic Press.

Farr, K. (2005). *Sex trafficking: The global market in women and children*. New York, NY: Worth Publishers.

Farrell, A., & Fahy, S. (2009). The problem of human trafficking in the US: Public frames and policy responses. *Journal of Criminal Justice*, *37*(6), 617–626.

Fedina, L., Williamson, C., & Perdue, T. (2019). Risk factors for domestic child sex trafficking in the United States. *Journal of Interpersonal Violence*, *34*(13), 2653–2673.

Fehrenbacher, A. E., Musto, J., Hoefinger, H., Mai, N., Macioti, P., Giametta, C., & Bennachie, C. (2020). Transgender people and human trafficking: Intersectional exclusion of transgender migrants and people of color from anti-trafficking protection in the United States. *Journal of Human Trafficking*, *6*(2), 182–194.

Fong, R., & Cardoso, J. B. (2010). Child human trafficking victims: Challenges for the child welfare system. *Evaluation and Program Planning, 33*(3), 311–316.

Forge, N., Hartinger-Saunders, R., Wright, E., & Ruel, E. (2018). Out of the system and onto the streets: LGBTQ-identified youth experiencing homelessness with past child welfare system involvement. *Child Welfare, 96*(2).

Franchino-Olsen, H., Silverstein, H. A., Kahn, N. F., & Martin, S. L. (2020). Minor sex trafficking of girls with disabilities. *International Journal of Human Rights in Healthcare, 13*(2), 97–108.

Friedman, M. S., Marshal, M. P., Guadamuz, T. E., Wei, C., Wong, C. F., Saewyc, E. M., & Stall, R. (2011). A meta-analysis of disparities in childhood sexual abuse, parental physical abuse, and peer victimization among sexual minority and sexual nonminority individuals. *American Journal of Public Health, 101*(8), 1481–1494.

Greeson, J. K., Treglia, D., Wolfe, D. S., & Wasch, S. (2019). Prevalence and correlates of sex trafficking among homeless and runaway youths presenting for shelter services. *Social Work Research, 43*(2), 91–100.

Hammond, I., Godoy, S., Kelly, M., & Bath, E. (2020). A transgender girl's experience: Sexual exploitation and systems involvement. *International Journal of Human Rights in Healthcare, 13*(2).

Hart, T. A., Noor, S. W., Vernon, J. R., Kidwai, A., Roberts, K., Myers, T., & Calzavara, L. (2018). Childhood maltreatment, bullying victimization, and psychological distress among gay and bisexual men. *The Journal of Sex Research, 55*(4–5), 604–616.

Hodge, J. P., & Sexton, L. (2020). Examining the blue line in the rainbow: The interactions and perceptions of law enforcement among lesbian, gay, bisexual, transgender and queer communities. *Journal of Police Practice, 21*(3), 246–263.

Hogan, K. A., & Roe-Sepowitz, D. (2020). LGBTQ+ homeless young adults and sex trafficking vulnerability. *Journal of Human Trafficking.* https://doi.org/10.1080/23322705.2020.1841985

ILGA World, Chiam, Z., Duffy, S., Gil, M. G., Goodwin, L., & Patel, N. T. M. (2020). *Trans legal mapping report 2019: Recognition before the law.* Geneva: International Lesbian Gay, Bisexual, Trans and Intersex Association [ILGA].

ILGA World, Mendos, L. R., Botha, K., Lelis, R. C., Peña, E. L. d. L., Savelev, I., & Tan, D. (Eds.). (2020). *State-sponsored homophobia 2020: Global legislation overview update.* Geneva: International Lesbian Gay, Bisexual, Trans and Intersex Association [ILGA]. https://ilga.org/downloads/ILGA_World_State_Sponsored_Homophobia_report_global_legislation_overview_update_December_2020.pdf

Israel, T., Harkness, A., Delucio, K., Ledbetter, J. N., & Avellar, T. R. (2014). Evaluation of police training on LGBTQ issues: Knowledge, interpersonal apprehension, and self-efficacy. *Journal of Police Criminal Psychology, 29*(2), 57–67.

Kattari, S. K., & Begun, S. (2017). On the margins of marginalized: Transgender homelessness and survival sex. *Affilia, 32*(1), 92–103.

Mallory, C., Hasenbush, A., & Sears, B. (2015). *Discrimination and harassment by law enforcement officers in the LGBT community.* https://williamsinstitute.law.ucla.edu/publications/lgbt-discrim-law-enforcement/

Martinez, O., & Kelle, G. (2013). Sex trafficking of LGBT individuals: A call for service provision, research, and action. *The International Law News, 42*(4). https://pubmed.ncbi.nlm.nih.gov/25342864

Math, S. B., & Seshadri, S. P. (2013). The invisible ones: Sexual minorities. *The Indian Journal of Medical Research, 137*(1), 4–6. https://pubmed.ncbi.nlm.nih.gov/23481045

Meyer, I. H. (2003). Prejudice, social stress, and mental health in lesbian, gay, and bisexual populations: Conceptual issues and research evidence. *Psychological Bulletin, 129*(5), 674.

Morton, M. H., Dworsky, A., Matjasko, J. L., Curry, S. R., Schlueter, D., Chávez, R., & Farrell, A. F. (2018). Prevalence and correlates of youth homelessness in the United States. *Journal of Adolescent Health*, *62*(1), 14–21. http://voicesofyouthcount.org/brief/national-estimates-of-youth-homelessness/

National Coalition for the Homeless. (2017). *LGBTQ homelessness*. http://nationalhomeless.org/wp-content/uploads/2017/06/LGBTQ-Homelessness.pdf

People's Union for Civil Liberties-K. (2001). *Human rights violations against sexuality minorities in India: A PUCL-K fact-finding report about Bangalore*. Karnataka, India: People's Union for Civil Liberties-K.

Quintana, N. S., Rosenthal, J., & Krehely, J. (2010). *On the streets: The federal response to gay and transgender homeless youth*. Washington, DC: Center for American Progress.

Reid, J. A. (2012). A girl's path to prostitution: Linking caregiver adversity to child susceptibility. El Paso, TX: LFB Scholarly Publishing.

Reid, J. A. (2018). Sex trafficking of girls with intellectual disabilities: An exploratory mixed methods study. *Sexual Abuse*, *30*(2), 107–131.

Roe-Sepowitz, D. E. (2012). Juvenile entry into prostitution: The role of emotional abuse. *Violence Against Women*, *18*(5), 562–579.

Rumney, P. N. S. (2009). Gay male rape victims: Law enforcement, social attitudes and barriers to recognition. *The International Journal of Human Rights*, *13*(2–3), 233–250.

Schwarz, C., & Britton, H. E. (2015). Queering the support for trafficked persons: LGBTQ communities and human trafficking in the heartland. *Social Inclusion*, *3*(1). https://doi.org/10.17645/si.v3i1.172

Soderlund, G. (2005). Running from the rescuers: New US crusades against sex trafficking and the rhetoric of abolition. *NWSA Journal*, 64–87.

Stoklosa, H., Stoklosa, J. B., & MacGibbon, M. (2017). Human trafficking, mental illness, and addiction: Avoiding diagnostic overshadowing. *AMA Journal of Ethics*, *19*(1), 23–34.

Stumblingbear-Riddle, G. P., Burlew, A. K., MaDore, M. R., Neville, H., & Joseph, G. (2019). Standing with our American Indian and Alaska Native women, girls, and two-spirit people: Exploring the impact of and resources for survivors of human trafficking. *Journal of Indigenous Research*, *7*(1), 1.

Twis, M. K. (2020). Risk factor patterns in domestic minor sex trafficking relationships. *Journal of Human Trafficking*, *6*(3), 309–326.

Weitzer, R. (2007). The social construction of sex trafficking: Ideology and institutionalization of a moral crusade. *Politics & Society*, *35*(3), 447–475.

11

DOMESTIC & FOREIGN POLICY RESPONSES TO THE PROBLEM OF HUMAN TRAFFICKING

SANDI DIMOLA AND ALLYSON M. LOWE

Chapter Learning Objectives

- Explain the U.S. State Department's three-pronged approach to combatting human trafficking.
- Identify and explain global and domestic challenges to eradicating trafficking in persons.
- Explain the role of the Trafficking in Persons report as a tool to combat human trafficking.
- Explain the efforts of various U.S. government agencies in prevention of human trafficking.Please check the headings sequence below chapter once.

Introduction

Human trafficking is a grave human rights abuse that threatens the social, economic, and political stability of all nations. Trafficking in persons promotes the disintegration of families and communities. It facilitates the economy of organized crime while depleting a country's human capital reserves. Trafficking undermines public health and creates opportunities for extortion and subversion among government officials (National Institute of Justice, "Overview of Human Trafficking and NIJ's Role," February 25, 2019, nij.ojp.gov:https://nij.ojp.gov/topics/articles/overview-human-trafficking-and-nijs-role).

DOI: 10.4324/9781003124672-14

The United Nations defines human trafficking as the "recruitment, transportation, transfer, harbor, or receipt of persons by improper means for an improper purpose including forced labor or sexual exploitation" (UN Office of Drugs and Crime, "Protocol to Prevent, Suppress, and Punish Trafficking in Persons, Especially Women and Children," www.unodc.org/unodc/en/organized-crime/intro/UNTOC.html#GA). The protocol was adopted in 2000 by the United Nations General Assembly and entered into force on December 25, 2003. As of May 2020, 176 parties have ratified the protocols.[1]

While trafficking victims are primarily women and children, the widening wealth gap between industrialized countries in the Global North and lesser-developed countries in the Global South has created a class of "economic refugees." Economic refugees are persons forced to leave their countries of residence to find work. These individuals often travel in irregular migration status,[2] which makes them vulnerable to forced labor and other forms of human commoditization across industry sectors.

Human trafficking can be accomplished through the use of threats, force, or other forms of coercion, deception, or abuse, including the retention of the victim's identity and travel documents. The practice can be fueled by the victim's economic insecurity, lack of language skills or legal status in the trafficked country, and fear for the safety of his or her family. The United Nations estimates approximately 2.5 million persons from 127 different countries are being trafficked around the world for forced labor, bonded labor, and forced prostitution. Human trafficking ranks third among the most lucrative global criminal ventures (U.S. Dept. of State, "Global Trafficking in Persons Report 2020," www.state.gov/wp-content/uploads/2020/06/2020-TIP-Report-Complete-062420-FINAL.pdf).

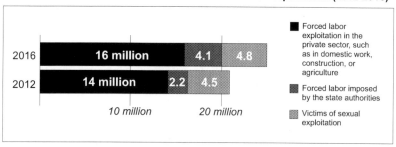

Global Number of Victims of Forced Labor or Sexual Exploitation (2012-2016)

Source: ILO & Walk Free Foundation, 2017 and ILO, 2012.

Figure 11.1   Global number of victims of forced labor or sexual exploitation (2012–2016)

Source: Adapted from ILO & Walk Free Foundation, 2017, and ILO, 2021

This chapter examines the United States' domestic and foreign policy initiatives directed toward the prevention of trafficking in persons. The chapter begins with an examination of the definition of "trafficked person" under United States and international law. The focus moves to a consideration of the U.S. State Department's four-pronged approach to combat trafficking: prevention, protection, prosecution, and partnerships; and concludes with a consideration of the efficacy of U.S. domestic and foreign policy initiatives within a human rights framework.

Domestic Policy Creation: The Trafficking Victims Protection Act

The terms "trafficking in persons," "human trafficking," and "modern slavery" refer to the act of "recruiting, harboring, transporting, providing, or obtaining a person for compelled labor or commercial sex acts through the use of force, fraud, or coercion." Human trafficking may involve—but does not require— the movement of persons. Therefore, persons may be considered trafficking victims in any of the following scenarios:

- Persons who are born into a condition of servitude
- Persons who are exploited in their places of residence
- Persons who are transported into exploitative situations
- Persons who previously consented to work for a trafficker or who participated in other criminal activity as a result of being a victim of trafficking

The common element in each of these situations is the traffickers' goal of exploiting and enslaving their victims through coercive and deceptive practices. Under U.S. law, the crime of trafficking in persons also encompasses ancillary criminal conduct surrounding forced labor, sex trafficking, and any other forms of compulsory service (Trafficking Victims Protection Act, 22 U.S.C. Sec. 7101, et. seq.).

Human trafficking became a topic of public concern in the 1990s. The disintegration of the former Soviet Union caused an increase in migration flows and a corresponding growth in transnational criminal organizations. Intelligence reports pointed to sex trafficking and forms of forced labor as some of these organizations' largest sources of profit. The first efforts to address trafficking in persons focused heavily on combating the sex trafficking of women and girls (Makei, 2013).

In 1994, the U.S. Department of State began to monitor human trafficking as part of the Department's annual "Country Reports on Human Rights Practices." These early monitoring efforts focused exclusively on sex trafficking of women and girls. As the understanding of human trafficking expanded, the U.S. government, in collaboration with various nongovernmental organizations, identified the need for specific legislation that would address how traffickers operate and provide the legal tools necessary to combat all forms of trafficking in persons.

The Trafficking Victims Protection Act (TVPA) of 2000 (22 USC Sections 7101, et. seq.) became the cornerstone of the State Department's efforts to combat human trafficking. This Act: classified human trafficking and related offenses as federal crimes; provided for mandatory restitution to victims of human trafficking; and created the "T" visa classification to allow trafficked persons to remain in the United States and assist in the prosecution of their traffickers. Since its initial passage, the TVPA has been reauthorized five times, with strong bipartisan support (P.L. 108–193). The first reauthorization provided trafficking victims with a federal civil right of action to pursue a civil lawsuit against their traffickers (18 U.S.C. Sections 1961–1968).

The Office to Monitor and Combat Trafficking in Persons (OMCTP) was created under the TVPA and operates as a division of the State Department. The OMCTP directs the United States' global efforts to fight human trafficking through a four-pronged approach that includes efforts to prevent trafficking, protect the victims, prosecute the traffickers, and partner with civil society organizations (Siskin & Wyler, 2013).

Prevention of Trafficking

The OMCTP's prevention efforts first centered on public-awareness campaigns launched in the United States and in countries that were traditional destinations for trafficked persons. These campaigns were also targeted to persons who were vulnerable to exploitation, such as children, migrant workers, and women. As the problem of trafficked persons continued to reach across borders and populations, the OMCTP entered into partnerships with various nongovernmental and civil society organizations to strengthen protections for these vulnerable populations. For example, the OMCTP worked with the ILO and labor organizations to examine labor recruitment programs to ensure protections were in place to guard against worker exploitation and worked with counterparts in other countries to assess and remediate vulnerabilities in the issuance of identity documents, such as birth certificates, passports, and national identity cards. The goal of these preventative efforts was to monitor global supply chains to ensure the free movement of persons and to reduce demand for goods made with forced labor. Additional efforts focused on international advocacy to reform laws that omit certain classes of workers from protection and to provide labor enforcement mechanisms in the industrial and service sectors, where trafficked victims are most likely to be found (Human Rights Watch, 2016).

Protection for Victims of Trafficking

Protection for victims of trafficking includes efforts to restore personal dignity and to provide opportunities to engage in productive work. The "T" visa classification, under the TVPA, allows identified victims of trafficking to remain in the United States to assist with prosecution of their traffickers.

Some victims who are trafficked into the United States enter the country in "irregular" migration status; that is, they enter without proper documentation and do not have a legally protected right, under U.S. immigration law, to remain in the United States. The lack of proper documentation and legal immigration status makes these persons especially vulnerable to their trafficker for as long as they remain in the United States. By contrast, some persons consent to be smuggled into the United States and later become victims of trafficking. In these instances, smuggled aliens become trafficking victims when their traffickers confiscate their immigration or identity documents. This is done to control the victim and often to extort money from his or her family members.

The person's lack of legal immigration status contributes to his or her unwillingness to seek help or to engage with law enforcement officials and to aid in the apprehension and prosecution of his or her trafficker. In response to this problem, the United States Immigration Service created the "T" visa. The T Visa is a temporary visa classification that is available to foreign nationals who have been trafficked into or who became trafficking victims while in the United States. Persons who are granted T Visa status may remain in the United States for up to four (4) years. The T Visa is a pathway to an application for permanent resident status if the individual is continually present in the United States for three years. The spouse and minor children of adult victims and the parents of victims who are under age 21 may also apply for this status. The T Visa status allows the trafficking victim and his or her family members to receive authorization to work in the United States. T Visa status may be extended beyond the initial four years if a federal, state, or local law enforcement official, prosecutor, judge, or other authority investigating or prosecuting activity relating to human trafficking certifies that the victim's presence in the United States is necessary to assist in the investigation or prosecution of a trafficking-in-persons case. Under the "T" visa, trafficking victims are able to engage in employment and access medical and social services without the fear of being detained or deported as a result of having entered the country illegally or because of crimes committed while a trafficked person.

The OMCTP, supported by measures under the TVPA, has led the United States' efforts to rescue victims from conditions of slavery, provide funding to support physical and psychological rehabilitation of victims, and assist former trafficking victims who desire to reconnect with family and to obtain "decent work."[3] The OMCTP ensures best practices are in place to allow victims to obtain identification documents (e.g. passports) and to obtain legal immigration status and provides protection for the victim's family members who may be threatened by the victim's trafficker.

The OMCTP's goal is to rehabilitate and repatriate a former trafficked person to his or her home country. Often, however, these people are unable or unwilling to return. When this happens, the OMCTP seeks to resettle the individual in a third country. In those instances, the OMCTP works with NGOs and civil society partners to ensure the third country will provide education, employment, and housing to encourage a stable and sustainable situation for a formerly trafficked person.

Prosecution of Traffickers

The TVPA recognizes that trafficking can be both a domestic and a transnational crime. Therefore, the act has established the following four minimum standards for the elimination of trafficking, which should be implemented whether the government is in a country of origin, transit, or destination of the trafficked person:

1. The government of the country should prohibit severe forms of trafficking in persons and punish acts of such trafficking.
2. For the knowing commission of any act of sex trafficking involving force, fraud, coercion, or in which the victim of sex trafficking is a child incapable of giving meaningful consent, or of trafficking t includes rape or kidnapping or which causes a death, the government of the country should prescribe punishment commensurate with that for grave crimes, such as forcible sexual assault.
3. For the knowing commission of any act of a severe form of trafficking in persons, the government of the country should prescribe punishment that is sufficiently stringent to deter and that adequately reflects the heinous nature of the offense.
4. The government of the country should make serious and sustained efforts to eliminate severe forms of trafficking in persons.(Trafficking Victims Protection Act of 2000, Div. A of Pub. L. No. 106–386, § 108, as amended)

Countries' compliance with the TVPA's standards is monitored by the OMCTP and reported annually in the Trafficking in Persons Report (TIP). The TIP analyzes efforts by individual countries to prosecute traffickers and provides a diagnostic analysis of global prevention efforts using the mandated minimum standards found in the TVPA (P.L. 106–386).

The OMCTP published its first TIP report in July 2001. The report included 82 country narratives, based on information received from embassies and consulates abroad. The information was obtained from governments and law enforcement officials, NGOs, U.S. agencies, and journalists, and included brief descriptions of each country's efforts to combat human trafficking. The report's production in the early years was a monumental task for the newly established TIP Office. It required the small staff to create simultaneously both a methodology for the report and processes for gathering data, drafting narratives, and assessing government efforts. Perhaps most challenging for the TIP Office and posts abroad were the effort to gather data from other governments, many of which had never developed systematic measures for collecting human trafficking data. In addition, the report would be the first of its kind to rank countries publicly on their efforts to combat human trafficking, a crime newly denounced by the international community (Council on Hemispheric Affairs, 2011).

At the time, inclusion in the report depended on whether there was evidence of a "significant number" of victims in a given country, though the U.S. Congress did not specify what it considered to be a "significant number." Once the drafters of the first report received reporting from all the U.S. embassies, which included information on the estimated number of victims in each country, they determined that 100 or more victims would be the threshold number, taking into account that for small countries, this would be a high threshold, but for large countries, a low one. The report pointed to a dearth of reliable information to explain the exclusion of so many countries and called attention to the need for more governments to develop mechanisms to detect and report on human trafficking.

Over the years, the TIP Report has become a roadmap for diplomatic engagement on the issue of human trafficking. U.S. diplomatic posts, as well as domestic agencies in the various countries, report on the instances of trafficking within a country and the government-led actions to combat this crime. Research is culled from meetings with government officials, representatives of local and international NGOs, journalists, academics, and survivors of trafficking. Countries are ranked in four tiers based on the extent of a government's actions to combat trafficking. The determination as to where a country falls in the TIP Report is based on the extent of a government's efforts to achieve compliance with the minimum standards for the elimination of human trafficking as provided in the Trafficking Victims' Protection Act and the Palermo Protocol[4] (U.N. General Assembly, *Protocol to Prevent, Suppress, and Punish Trafficking IN Persons, Especially Women and Children, Supplementing the United Nations Convention against Transnational Organized Crime*, 15 November 2000). Tier rankings reflect a cumulative assessment of the following criteria for each country:

- Enactment and enforcement of laws that prohibit severe forms of trafficking as defined in the Trafficking Victims Protection Act
- Vigorous prosecution of traffickers and sentencing penalties that provide a minimum of four (4) years imprisonment or other deprivation of liberty
- Proactive victim identification measures that provide guidelines to law enforcement and other first responders to aid in victim identification

- Government funding and partnerships that provide victims with access to physical and mental healthcare, counseling, and shelter
- Victim protection that includes alternatives to removal to countries in which victims would face retribution and that ensures safe and humane voluntary repatriation
- Government efforts to curtail practices that are contributing factors to human trafficking, such as retention of identity documents by employers and excessive recruitment fees charged by labor recruiters.(*Trafficking in Persons Report* 2020)

The OMCTP also makes recommendations to countries on the minimum criminal penalties that should be set for the crime of trafficking in persons. When assessing a government's antitrafficking efforts, the OMCTP suggests countries implement minimum criminal penalties consistent with the 2000 United Nations Convention of Transnational Organized Crime (A/RES/55/25). The convention imposes a minimum of four (4) years imprisonment or other deprivation of liberty. Sentencing judges are encouraged to consider the extent of an individual's involvement in trafficking, as well as sentences imposed for other grievous crimes, consistent with a particular country's laws.

Development of Civil Society Partnerships

Over the years, TIP Report country narrative lays out a justification for the tier ranking followed by prioritized recommendations for how the government can better meet the TVPA minimum standards. Department of State officials from U.S. embassies and consulates, as well as the TIP Office, use the TIP Report when they meet with foreign government officials across a variety of agencies to draw attention to human trafficking, discuss policy recommendations, and work toward solutions.

Beyond meetings with government officials, embassies find other ways to raise awareness about human trafficking, reinforce the TIP Report recommendations, and highlight promising practices. In many cases, these activities serve to empower NGOs and other local actors and to drive partnerships between governments and civil society.

Global Policy Creation Through U.S. Interagency Responses

Human trafficking impacts all persons in the United States, irrespective of nationality or immigration status. The 2015 report identified the United States as both a transit and a destination country for trafficked adults and children. It is estimated that approximately 17,500 persons are trafficked into the United States annually (U.S. Department of State, 2020, *Trafficking in Persons Report*). The most common destination for trafficked persons in America is servile labor, primarily in the domestic, agricultural, manufacturing, and janitorial sectors and in the various sex trades. Most criminal investigations and prosecutions for trafficking involve workers in the sex trades. The result is that other industries that rely on low-wage, large-scale influxes of human capital often escape detection.

(Begum, 2016)

Some suggest[5] targeted prosecutions in the sex industry have less to do with deliberate domestic policy initiatives and more with the composition of the victims of trafficking. For example, many persons who toil in non-sex industries are migrants, while workers in the sex trade tend to be children and adults who are U.S. citizens or permanent residents. The TVPA created two agencies to facilitate coordination on global antitrafficking policy across U.S. government offices: the President's Interagency Task Force to Monitor and Combat Trafficking and the Senior Policy Operating Group.

The President's Interagency Task Force to Monitor and Combat Trafficking (PITF) is a cabinet level entity that comprises 14 departments and agencies across the federal government, responsible for coordinating U.S. governmentwide efforts to combat trafficking in persons. PITF coordinates efforts from leaders in government, the private sector, and law enforcement, together with advocates and survivors of trafficking, to design best practices to strengthen federal efforts to combat human trafficking. The U.S. Advisory Council on Human Trafficking was created in May 2013 to provide trafficking survivors a formal voice in antitrafficking policy.

The Senior Policy Operating Group (SPOG) brings together federal departments and agencies to address various aspects of human trafficking, such as enforcement of criminal and labor laws, development of victim identification and protection measures, and support for innovation in data collection and research. This section will address examples of interagency cooperation designed to combat human trafficking.

Trafficking in the Global Supply Chain
The Departments of Homeland Security, Labor, and State are required to maintain lists of foreign products that have been produced by forced labor, child labor, indentured labor, forced or indentured child labor, and convict labor (E.O. 13126). These agencies have worked to combat trafficking in the global supply chain through a combination of efforts involving the foreign blacklist, foreign aid restrictions, and foreign trade preferences.

FOREIGN BLACKLIST
Certain specified goods and products are banned from import into the United States if produced, mined, or manufactured with the use of convict, forced, or indentured labor. Other specified goods and products are barred from being

used by U.S. federal contractors because they are likely to have been mined, produced, or manufactured by forced or indentured child labor. These restrictions are designed to discourage producers and manufacturers from viewing the United States as a destination market for consumer goods that were produced with forced or servile labor ("Notice of Final Determination Revising the List of Products Requiring Federal Contractor Certification as to Forced or Indentured Child Labor Pursuant to Executive Order 13126," *Federal Register*, Vol. 7, No. 64, April 3, 2012).

Foreign Aid Restrictions

Congress has enacted two provisions to deny certain types of foreign aid to countries that are not advancing the antitrafficking goals of the United States and the international community. One provision, originating in the TVPA, restricts the distribution of nonhumanitarian, non–trade-related foreign aid to governments that do not evidence progress in eliminating severe forms of trafficking in persons. Under this provision, countries that are ranked in the third or fourth tier of the Trafficking in Persons Report become ineligible to receive non-humanitarian, non–trade-related aid in the year following their ranking. The second provision, originating in the Child Soldiers Prevention Act of 2008, restricts U.S. military assistance to countries that are known to recruit or to use children in their armed forces and to countries that provide a haven to nongovernmental armed forces that recruit or use child soldiers (Child Soldiers Prevention Act, 4 U.S. Code § 401).

Foreign Trade Preferences

The U.S. government has implemented various unilateral trade preference programs designed to promote exports among selected developing countries and designate beneficiary countries to receive duty-free entry of specified products into the United States. Beneficiary countries may be designated (or removed) based on eligibility criteria specified in relevant authorizing legislation. The eligibility criteria for beneficial trade status require countries to express a commitment to worker rights, including prohibiting any form of compulsory labor and committing to the eradication of child trafficking. The rationale behind this approach is to use preferential trade status as an incentive for developing countries to become motivated to comply with international efforts to combat trafficking in persons. This work is undertaken by the U.S. Department of Labor in conjunction with the Office of the U.S. Trade Representative.

The Office of the U.S. Trade Representative works with the Department of Labor to negotiate trade agreements. These agreements include enforceable obligations to eliminate forced labor. The Trade Representative's Office also administers the trade preference programs that require countries to meet worker rights eligibility requirements, including taking steps to address forced labor. In September 2020, the U.S. Department of Labor released its annual "Findings on the Worst Forms of Child Labor." This report assessed foreign governments' efforts and provides suggested actions to combat the worst forms of child labor, including child trafficking, in 131 countries and territories. It also released the biennial "List of Goods Produced with Forced Labor and Child Labor." The purpose of this report was to advance supply chain accountability by providing information on goods made with forced and child labor by country of origin.

Child labor and forced labor in supply chains present serious and material risks to companies and industries. To help mitigate these risks, the U.S. Department of Labor has created an application known as "Comply Chain: Business Tools for Labor Compliance in Global Supply Chains." This application targets companies and industry groups seeking to develop robust social compliance systems for their global production. Comply Chain provides detailed guidance on the critical elements of social compliance, which includes engaging stakeholders and partners, assessing risks and impacts, developing a code of conduct, communicating and training across the supply chain, monitoring compliance, remediating violations, independent review, and reporting performance and engagement. The application contains

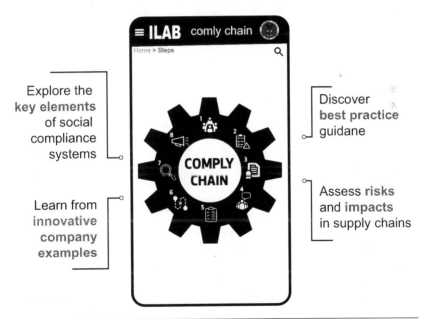

Figure 11.2   Global number of victims of forced labor or sexual exploitation (2012–2016)

Source: Adapted from ILO & Walk Free Foundation, 2017, and ILO, 2021

Estimated Proceeds per year from Human Trafficking

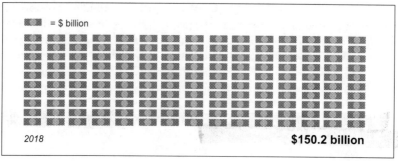

2018   **$150.2 billion**

Source: ILO (2014)

Figure 11.3 *Fast Fact:* In 2018 estimated worldwide profits from human trafficking reached (US)

Source: Adapted from ILO, 2014

examples of specific practices companies, industry groups, and multistake-holder initiatives have instituted to ensure goods are being produced without the use of forced or child laborers.

Economic Disruption of Human Trafficking

Human trafficking is an economically lucrative, transnational threat that preys on society's most vulnerable populations and poses significant harm to persons in every sector of the economy. The U.S. Department of the Treasury brings financial expertise to the fight against human trafficking. Treasury Department efforts follow the State Department's protocols to enact measures to prevent trafficking, protect the victims, and prosecute the traffickers.

Prevent Trafficking

Treasury has various tools and offices to support the mission of combating human trafficking, including anti–money laundering (AML) and sanctions authorities. The Office of Terrorism and Financial Intelligence integrates countering the financial operations of human trafficking networks into Treasury's strategy to safeguard the financial system and combat illicit threats. This work is undertaken through Treasury's Office of Terrorist Financing and Financial Crimes, the Office of Foreign Assets Control, and the Financial Crimes Enforcement Network. These offices work with federal agencies, as well as state and local law enforcement groups, to identify transactions that are markers for human trafficking and to eliminate the financial incentive of trafficking.

The Treasury Department also works with the multilateral development banks[6] to integrate anti–human trafficking provisions into their project development and social safeguards into their procurement processes. On January 9, 2019, President Trump signed into law the Trafficking Victims Protection Reauthorization Act of 2017.[7] The law requires the U.S. Executive Director of each multilateral development bank to work to develop anti–human trafficking provisions in their bank's project development, procurement, and evaluation policies.

The Treasury Department takes action against human traffickers both at home and abroad. The Office of Terrorist Financing and Financial Controls develops policy, initiatives, and strategies that are deployed by other offices within the Treasury Department. For example, the Internal Revenue Service and the Office of Foreign Assets Control collect and analyze financial intelligence and data to identify human traffickers and their networks, disrupt and disable the financial underpinnings of these networks, and support law enforcement investigations. These offices apply financial sanctions and oversee a range of sanctions programs that can target human trafficking, including several country programs focused on human rights and corruption. These programs also target activities that typically occur with human trafficking, including narcotics trafficking, human rights abuse and corruption, malicious cyberenabled activities, terrorism, and transnational organized crime. As a result of U.S. financial sanctions, U.S. persons are generally prohibited from engaging in dealings with a blocked, or designated, person, and the designated person's property and interests in property are blocked.

Protect Trafficked Persons

One challenge many formerly trafficked persons face is the lack of identity documents, such as a birth certificate or driver's license. Identity documents are required to access financial services, such as checking accounts, in almost every country. The U.S. Treasury Department has been leading efforts to support a risk-based approach to the use of responsible digital identity solutions to help survivors of human trafficking to access the financial services systems.

Treasury continues to identify and track the activities of human traffickers with data made available through Bank Secrecy Act reporting requirements and other sources. The Treasury Department's Financial Crimes Enforcement Network publishes an advisory on human trafficking to help financial institutions identify the movement of human traffickers' funds and to support law enforcement investigations that use financial intelligence. In 2018, the network updated its Suspicious Activity Report (SAR) form to include a checkbox for financial institutions to identify potential suspicious activity related to human trafficking. This update facilitated the reporting of suspicious activity potentially tied to human trafficking in a more comprehensive way. The update also allowed law enforcement to more easily identify potential perpetrators or enablers of human trafficking. The Treasury Department received 6,672 suspicious activity reports from August 2018 through December 2019 from financial institutions reporting suspicious activities involving human trafficking.[8]

Prosecute Traffickers

The Internal Revenue Service's Criminal Investigation (IRS-CI) division is the law enforcement arm of the Internal Revenue Service. The Criminal Investigations division partners with the Department of Justice, as well as federal, state, local, tribal, and foreign law enforcement agencies, to investigate labor trafficking and sex trafficking cases from a financial perspective. Criminal Investigation agents identify and trace cash, electronic funds, virtual currency, real estate, and other assets generated by human trafficking in order to build criminal cases within their jurisdiction and potentially seize and ultimately forfeit those criminal proceeds, which may then be returned to the victims in the form of restitution. For example, the Criminal Investigations division partnered with the Oregon Anti-Trafficking Coordination Team Oregon, Homeland Security, the Federal Bureau of Investigations (FBI), the Diplomatic Security Service, and the Department of Labor Wage and Hour Division to investigate and prosecute individuals involved in an "investor visa" scam. The scam involved fraudulently obtained investor visas that were used to bring Thai nationals into the United States to work at various Thai restaurants. Once the victims arrived, the defendants confiscated their passports and documents, exploited and coerced the victims' labor, and profited from this degrading crime. The defendants were guilty of trafficking, visa fraud, and filing false tax returns.[9]

Treasury has demonstrated its resolve to identify and hold accountable human rights abusers, facilitators of human trafficking, and corrupt actors who undermine peace, stability, and the rule of law. In December 2019, TFI hosted its inaugural Partnership to Combat Human Rights Abuse and Corruption event, bringing together over 100 NGOs, industry, and government partners to combat human rights abuse and corruption through enhanced information sharing and coordination on illicit finance and corruption networks. Treasury led a panel discussion on information sharing models with financial institutions and NGOs on combating human trafficking.

Partner to Combat Human Rights Abuses & Corruption

The Treasury Department's Office of Terrorist Financing and Financial Crimes headed the U.S. delegation to the Financial Action Task Force and worked with the task force and its global network to start a typologies project on combating money laundering through human trafficking and migrant smuggling crimes. The Financial Action Task Force sets global standards for anti–money laundering and combating the finance of terrorism to promote greater understanding of human trafficking, exchange information to identify and disrupt networks, and coordinate efforts of law enforcement and inter-agency partners. Treasury's Terrorist Financing and Financial Crimes Division collaborates with the task force and its global network to raise awareness of this issue and encourage governments to adopt practices including enhancing public–private partnerships and mechanisms to utilize risk indicators aimed at identifying and targeting financial flows associated with human trafficking. Treasury also works through the Task Force's global network to promote the inclusion of human trafficking when countries are conducting their national risk assessments for money laundering and terrorist financing.

Challenges to Implementing Effective Antitrafficking Policy

While there is a general consensus among U.S. government agencies on the need for decisive action to curb human trafficking, civil society and victims' advocates have raised important questions about the overall effectiveness of the United States' antitrafficking policies. This section will discuss those concerns.

Institutional commitments against human exploitation have had a long existence in local, national, regional, and global laws and policies. Since trafficking can involve the movement of persons across international borders, one of the most important policy concerns is migration policy. The United Nations Office on Drugs and Crime identified poverty, political instability, social unrest, and crisis as drivers for the crime of trafficking in persons. Populations that are socially, politically, and economically marginalized within countries are particularly vulnerable to becoming trafficking victims (UNODC, *An Introduction to Human Trafficking*, 2008). Economic and political disparities between countries in the Global North and the Global South have contributed to an increase in the movement of persons who are "economic refugees"; that is, persons who travel from an impoverished country of residence to find work in more prosperous countries. The economic refugee is a class that has no legal recognition in the migration laws of most countries. Economic refugees often enter countries in irregular migration status and are therefore vulnerable to promises of employment that turn into situations of forced labor.

The International Labour Organization (ILO) considers any of these practices to constitute forced labor:

- Restriction of deductions and deception in wage payments
- Sanctions or disciplinary measures that result in an obligation to work or that are used as a worker's ability to terminate an employment contract
- Threats of violence and intimidation
- Debt bondage, illegal wage punishment for participation in a strike

- Compulsory overtime above the limit permitted in national law and collective agreements
- Restriction of freedom of movement
- Retention of identity documents (against the will of workers and workers not having access to their documents)
- Threats of dismissal and denunciation in the case of irregular migrant workers (International Labor Organization, 2012).

There is a gendered aspect to migration that has increased the likelihood of women becoming victims of trafficking. For example, in the period from 1960 through the mid-1980s, 95% of female migrants were migrating with a spouse or following to join one. This pattern has changed. During the period from the mid-1980s to the present, 95% of females migrate alone. While some of these women are migrating to continue their education or to accept a job in the professional sector, most of the women who migrated without a spouse or family member migrated to work in an industry with a propensity to "employ" trafficked victims or to escape gendered cultural practices, such as forced marriage or circumcision. Research from the World Bank documents that almost half of the world's migrants are women and girls. Women comprise 47% of the world's migrants (Rubiano-Matulevih and Beegle, "Women and Migration: Exploring the Data." World Bank. December 19, 2018). Women migrating alone are more likely to become victims of trafficking. The United Nations' International Office for Migration has identified the need to construct solutions that will take into account migration vulnerabilities and risks associated with gender (www.iom.int).

United States immigration processes are also contentious. The "T" visa was created to provide an immigration mechanism for trafficking victims to remain temporarily in the United States in order to assist in investigations and prosecutions and to provide humanitarian protection to the victims. Critics of this process argue that the emphasis on aiding law enforcement is more important than aiding the victims. Critics point to a controversial aspect of the T Visa's continued-presence provision, which provides that federal agents may require a victim to remain in the United States against his or her wishes if the victim's departure is considered prejudicial to the interests of the United States. Approximately 184 NGOs have reported incidents of law enforcement officers telling victims that they risk losing their benefits if they do not cooperate. Victims' advocacy organizations also contend it has been challenging getting law enforcement to recognize reluctant victims for protection purposes.

Many analysts have asserted that the overall impact of the TIP report as a diplomatic tool to raise international human trafficking awareness depends upon the credibility of the State Department's annual country assessments. Furthermore, some argue that there has been inconsistent application of the minimum standards mandated by the TVPA, which impacts the credibility of the country assessments. The methodology used to sector countries into the various tiers has been criticized as spurious. While it is difficult to determine what standards make a country eligible for Tier 1 classification, the Tier 2 "watch list" has become a catchall for countries that should have received Tier 3 classification. According to the GAO, in addition to a lack of clarity in the tier ranking process, the narratives in the *Trafficking in Persons Report* are incomplete and, thus, the report's usefulness is diminished. In response, the State Department has acknowledged that the report needs to be more comprehensive but believes it is necessary to ensure the report is concise.

International cooperation is required in order to stop international trafficking. Incentives and sanctions may be needed to influence the policies of other governments. Some of the incentives include financial and technical assistance, while sanctions include the threat of withholding certain forms of assistance. Critics of this approach, however, argue that sanctions are effective when they are transparent and evenly applied. The United States' aid restrictions do not meet these criteria. For example, aid cuts are often only applied to countries already subject to other diplomatic restrictions, and threatening other countries with sanctions may actually encourage them to become less open to working with the United States. Conversely, most countries depend on good political and economic relations with the United States. Those countries fear the public humiliation that comes with a Tier 3 designation as much as they fear actual aid restrictions.

In 2008, Congress added a new requirement to the TIP country rankings process, in which Tier 2 Watch List countries would become at risk of being automatically downgraded to the Tier 3 category after two consecutive years on the Tier 2 Watch List. There are concerns that bilateral relationships may be negatively affected as more countries are listed as Tier 3 and thus subject to aid restrictions.

Finally, when the high politics of diplomacy and international reporting have reached their natural limits, local communities have attempted grassroots or "bottom-up" responses to trafficking policies including local NGO development, police training, and adoption of international provisions at municipal levels, such as the Cities for CEDAW movement in the United States. None of these avenues alone is sufficient to combat trafficking, and together, they represent a patchwork of domestic and international responses to which many pieces remain to be completed.

Discussion & Action

A. Efforts by the Office to Monitor & Combat Trafficking in Persons to end human trafficking include prevention, protection of victims, prosecution of offenders, and development of partnerships with civil society organizations. Identify one civil society partnership (in your community, your state, or nationally), and find a comparable international organization and answer the following:

1. What are the strengths and challenges of these partnerships?
2. What type of institutional support is required is make these partnerships work?
3. What are some of the barriers to creating or continuing civil society partnerships?

Advocacy Exercises
50 FOR FREEDOM
The International Labour Organization's (ILO) Protocol on Forced Labor could restore hope and freedom to millions of people trapped in modern slavery. But first, it has to be ratified by countries around the world. The ILO's goal was to persuade at least 50 countries to ratify the Protocol on Forced Labor by the end of 2019. Check the website for 50 for Freedom to see how many countries have ratified the protocol and add your name to show your support: https://50forfreedom.org

Cities for CEDAW
Cities for CEDAW (Convention on the Elimination of All Forms of Discrimination Against Women) was organized to protect the rights of women and girls by encouraging cities to pass legislation that incorporates the principles of CEDAW in municipal governance and ordinances. Various organizations have developed the Cities for CEDAW Campaign to help persons take action in their cities. A toolkit is available at: www.citiesforcedaw.org/get-involved/. Read through the toolkit and consider what steps you would take to begin the campaign in your city or town. Then draft a letter to the editor of your newspaper or testimony that you would deliver at a city council hearing to make the case for your city to become a CEDAW city. Provide some specific examples of how CEDAW will benefit your city.

Join the Fight Against Human Trafficking
Anyone can join in the fight against human trafficking. Here are 10 ideas to consider acting on (www.state.gov/20-ways-you-can-help-fight-human-trafficking/):

*   Learn the indicators of human trafficking. The Department of Homeland Security's Blue Campaign has a list of signs that indicate a person may be a trafficking victim: www.dhs.gov/blue-campaign/indicators-human-trafficking.
*   If you are in the United States and believe someone may be a victim of human trafficking, call the 24-hour National Human Trafficking

Hotline at 1-888-373-7888 or report an emergency to law enforcement by calling 911. Trafficking victims, whether or not U.S. citizens, are eligible for services and immigration assistance.

- Be a conscientious and informed consumer. Find out more about who may have picked your tomatoes or made your clothes at ResponsibleSourcingTool.org, or check out the Department of Labor's List of Goods Produced by Child Labor or Forced Labor. Encourage companies to take steps to prevent human trafficking in their supply chains and publish the information, including supplier or factory lists, for consumer awareness.
- Volunteer and support antitrafficking efforts in your community.
- Meet with and/or write to your local, state, and federal elected officials to let them know you care about combating human trafficking and ask what they are doing to address it.
- Be well informed. Set up a web alert to receive current human trafficking news. Also, check out CNN's Freedom Project for more stories on the different forms of human trafficking around the world.
- Host an awareness-raising event to watch and discuss films about human trafficking. For example, learn how modern slavery exists today; watch an investigative documentary about sex trafficking; or discover how forced labor can affect global food supply chains. Alternatively, contact your local library and ask for assistance identifying an appropriate book and ask them to host the event.
- Organize a fundraiser and donate the proceeds to an antitrafficking organization.
- Encourage your local schools or school district to include human trafficking in their curricula and to develop protocols for identifying and reporting a suspected case of human trafficking or responding to a potential victim.
- Use your social media platforms to raise awareness about human trafficking, using the following hashtags: #endtrafficking, #freedomfirst.

Exam Questions
1. Explain and provide at least one (1) example of how the following factors contribute to the problem of human trafficking:

   a. Globalization
   b. Economic disparities
   c. Migration
   d. Organized crime
   e. Gender disparities
   f. Human rights abuses

2. In her paper, *A Human Rights Life Course Approach*, Dr. Angela Reed argues we must move from thinking about trafficking as random acts of victimization and toward an understanding of the systemic oppression that causes vulnerability over the course of a person's life (Reed, 2009, 2014. *A Human Rights Life Course Approach*). How might social, political, economic, and cultural forces contribute to making a person or a group of persons vulnerable to becoming trafficking victims?

Notes

1. www.unodc.org/unodc/en/treaties/CTOC/signatures.html
2. Irregular migration status refers to entering a country either without the proper documentation or with forged documentation. It is a term that is used in place of "illegal alien" to recognize that a person is not illegal.
3. The International Labour Organization (ILO) defines decent work as work in which persons toil in conditions that are safe and humane.
4. The Palermo Protocol is an international agreement to address the crime of trafficking in persons, especially women and children, on a transnational level. It creates global language and legislation to define trafficking, prevent trafficking, assist victims, and establish a framework for judicial cooperation and exchange of information among countries.
5. United Nations Office on Drugs and Crime.
6. A multilateral development bank (MDB) is an international financial institution chartered by two or more countries for the purpose of encouraging economic development in poorer nations. MDBs provide financial and technical support to developing countries to help them strengthen economic management and reduce poverty.
7. Trafficking Victims Protection Reauthorization Act of 2017, S. 1862 (115th), Jan. 2, 2019.
8. www.fincen.gov/reports/sar-stats
9. *United States of America v. Veraphon Phatanakitjumroon*, 3:18-cr-00036-BR (2018).

References

Begum, R. (2016). *Migrant Domestic Workers: Overworked and Under-protected*. Retrieved from http://www.hrw.org/news/2016/06/15/migrant-domestic-workers-overworked-and-underprotected/

Council on Hemispheric Affairs. (2011). *The Trafficking in Persons Report: Who Is the United States to Judge?* Retrieved from www.coha.org/the-trafficking-in-persons-report-who-is-the-united-states-to-judge/

Human Rights Watch. (2016). *Exploitation, Forced Labor, & Trafficking*. Retrieved from www.hrw.org/topic/trudovye-migranty/exploitation-forced-labor-trafficking

International Labor Organization. (2012). *Global Estimates of Forced Labor: Results and Methodology* (International Labor Organization, Special Action Program to Combat Forced Labor Publication No. SAP-FL, Geneva, ILO, 2012, v.1). Geneva, Switzerland: International Labor Office.

Makei, Vladimir. (2013). Human trafficking in the post-cold war era: A comprehensive approach. *Journal of International Affairs*. School of International & Public Affairs, Columbia University.

National Institute of Justice. (2019, February 25). *Overview of Human Trafficking and NIJ's Role*. Retrieved from https://nij.ojp.gov/topics/articles/overview-human-trafficking-and-nijs-role

"Notice of Final Determination Revising the List of Products Requiring Federal Contractor Certification as to Forced or Indentured Child Labor Pursuant to Executive Order
13126," 7(64), April 3, 2012 (77 FR 20051).

Reed, A. (2009). United in a bright future: Giving voice to trafficked women. Asia Pacific
NGO Forum on Beijing+15: Weaving Wisdom, Confronting Crises, Forging the
Future. Miriam College, Quezon City, Philippines.

Reed, A. (2014). *Exploiting vulnerability: A study of the lives of Filipino women who have
been trafficked into sex work* (PhD Dissertation). School of Global Urban and Social
Studies, RMIT University.

Rubiano-Matulevih, E., and Beegle, K. (2018, December 19). *Women and Migration:
Exploring the Data.* World Bank. https://blogs.worldbank.org/opendata/women-and
-migration-exploring-data

Siskin, A., and Wyler, L. S. (2013). *Trafficking in Persons: U.S. Policy and Issues for Congress.*
(Congressional Research Service Publication No. 7–5700, RL34317). Washington,
DC: Congressional Research Service.

Trafficking Victims Protection Act, 22 U.S. Code § 7101.

United Nations' Office of Drugs and Crime. (2008). *Human Trafficking: A Crime that
Shames Us All* (United Nations' Global Initiative to Fight Human Trafficking, Publication No. V.07–88925). Vienna, Austria: Vienna International Centre.

(USAID Office of Women in Development). Washington, DC: U.S. Agency for International Development.

U.S. Department of State. (2020). *Global Trafficking in Persons Report* (U.S. Department of
State Publication Office of the Under Secretary for Civilian Security, Democracy, and
Human Rights). Washington, DC: U.S. Government Printing Office.

12

VICTIM PROTECTION POLICY IN A LOCAL CONTEXT

A CASE STUDY

PATRIZIA TESTAÌ

Chapter Organization and Structure

This chapter focuses on antitrafficking policies by presenting a case study of the ways in which grassroots organizations and NGOs play a role within specific local contexts where antitrafficking law is applied. The case study is Italy and Article 18 of the Italian immigration law passed in 1998, which grants a residence permit for "reasons of social protection" to migrant women who are defined as victims of trafficking by state authorities and social actors. The importance of this case study consists in the fact that Article 18 has provided Italy with an antitrafficking policy, which gives central importance to the protection of victims, as a social aspect to be treated independently from juridical considerations, such as the value of victims as witnesses to prosecute traffickers.

The chapter pays particular attention to the institutional process and aspects of the law related to the meaning of "slavery" and its applicability to migrant women engaged in prostitution and to the selective criteria operating within the protection system in order to distinguish between victims and nonvictims. It also aims to shed some light on the meaning of social integration as either acquisition of citizenship rights or simply as a process of "redemption" from prostitution and regaining of an identity as a nonprostitute woman. By doing so, the chapter will critically assess the working of victim protection as an instrument for re-gaining citizenship rights. In particular, the social integration process of trafficked prostitutes into Italian society through Article 18 will be problematized to the extent that it is achieved through a social and institutional process that first marks them as "victims" and "sexual slaves" and then

DOI: 10.4324/9781003124672-15

recasts them into the domestic field of servile labor via a rehabilitation process, which turns them into domestic workers still subject, or at risk to being subjected, to considerable exploitation.

The chapter is based on the results of a doctoral field research that the author undertook between spring 2005 and summer 2006 in three Italian cities where social protection programs under Article 18 were applied. Prior to this research, however, the author had accumulated substantial background first-hand information on a local level in Catania (Sicily), where she was involved in a sexually transmitted diseases (STD) prevention project carried out by the local branch of the NGO Italian League Fighting against AIDS (LILA) and the local health authority.

The study offers an analysis of social protection programs as applied in each of the three research sites studied, which were Catania, in the Sicilian region, Lecce, in the Puglia region, and Rome, in the Latium region. Quantitative and qualitative interview data will be provided, particularly about specific sex market contexts and local approaches to prostitution and social protection. Although the original study was based on interviews with both key actors working in social protection programs and migrant women working as prostitutes and migrant women who were administratively identified as "victims of trafficking" and who were accepted to access social protection programs, for the purpose of this chapter, I will report only interview extracts with key actors. These qualitative data will reveal the importance of questions of moral meaning in social protection programs and of the way in which "slavery" and "trafficking" get conflated with prostitution, of the tension between repressive aspects (immigration and crime control), and human rights aspects (protection of victims) within projects under Article 18, and finally of the way in which citizenship is linked to sexuality and gender.

The chapter is divided into two parts: the first part will give an overview of the international and national (Italian) contexts of trafficking law and of the principle of victim protection within the law. It will highlight specific differences between the international and the national approaches to victim protection. The second part will present the three local contexts studied, with a particular attention to the ways in which antitrafficking policy is affected by local administrative approaches toward prostitution and to the ways in which "slavery" is treated as a concept describing prostitution and trafficking.

This chapter will enhance students' understanding of the combination of legal aspects and social outcomes implied in the victim protection system. In particular, it will offer students the opportunity to reflect on the following issues.

Chapter Learning Objectives

- Understand the international legal definition of trafficking and how it is translated and applied in national and local policies.
- Recognize the concept of victims' protection and its configuration in antitrafficking law and applied in antitrafficking policies.
- Understand how the links between the concepts of trafficking, slavery, sexual exploitation, and prostitution are worked out and how they lead to a particular understanding and application of antitrafficking policies, especially on a local level.
- Describe how grassroots activities and organizations, including religious organizations, shape specific antitrafficking campaigns and policies.
- Understand how, in practice, the principle of victim protection is influenced by particular definitions of trafficking.

In particular, the chapter will point out that a particular definition of trafficking as sexual exploitation and as a crime affecting migrant women and girls working in prostitution has opened the way for antitrafficking campaigns and policies that have migrant women as main targets, who are thus considered not as agents of migratory experiences and projects but simply as casualties of migration/trafficking. At the end of this discussion, the students will reflect on possible alternatives to protection policies as not linked to the idea of turning "prostitutes" into "good domestic workers" or to get testimony from them in order to combat trafficking-linked migration but inspired by a genuine human rights approach, which would not link protection to witnesses' testimony but would effectively give them access to a range of services that will help them overcome the abuse suffered and to find long term socioeconomic integration that is not necessarily tied to the domestic field.

From a theoretical point of view, the chapter will illustrate how antitrafficking policies are influenced by particular theoretical frameworks dominating the discourse of trafficking. In particular, the linking of trafficking–prostitution–slavery reflects radical feminist theorizing of prostitution as a form of slavery, viewed in terms of women's subordination to men as a consequence of patriarchal forms of power affecting societies across all geographical and cultural contexts. This theorizing of prostitution as a modern form of slavery linked to global migratory movements and projects pursued by women from poorer countries has also been embraced by moralizing actors and policy makers, such as catholic organizations and the political right, which have traditionally had opposite political aims and agenda to feminist ones.

There are also gender implications from trafficking being linked, in policy terms, to prostitution, and these are:

- Antiprostitution laws that affect negatively the life and work of migrant and nonmigrant women involved in prostitution and even women who are not involved in prostitution.
- Anti-immigration and emigration laws that affect negatively women, both those in destination countries and those in emigration countries.

Trafficking and the Protection of Victims: The International and National Context

The principle of "victim protection" was established in Italy through Article 18 of the Italian immigration law (Law Decree n. 286/1998), which grants a residence permit for "reasons of social protection" to foreign individuals who are administratively defined as victims of trafficking. This principle is not unique to the Italian context, as it had already been established in the international arena and was part of a wider debate on trafficking in persons.

Italy took an active role in this debate, and it was in fact under pressure of the Italian delegation that, during the works of an ad hoc group for the drafting of the United Nations (UN) Convention Against Transnational Organized Crime and of the additional Protocol against Trafficking, the slavery offence was included among the crimes involved in trafficking, and the protection and assistance of victims was proposed as part of the strategies to combat trafficking (Spiezia et al., 2002). The final document signed in Palermo, 2000, known also as the Palermo Protocol, is the present international instrument against trafficking and, in it, the latter is defined in terms of exploitation, including "the exploitation of the prostitution of others or other forms of sexual exploitation, forced labor or services, slavery or practices similar to slavery, servitude or the removal of organs" (United Nations, 2000, Article 3, paragraph a). Article 6, Section II, of the same document provides specifically that each state shall ensure the assistance and protection of victims of trafficking in persons. The inclusion of "sexual exploitation" within the scope of trafficking and "exploitation of the prostitution of others" and their interpretation, within the trafficking discourse, as forms of modern slavery, is particularly relevant, since, as we shall see, Article 18, as an antitrafficking policy, also established a link between trafficking, prostitution, sexual exploitation, and slavery practices.

On a UN level, it was in particular the American-based Coalition Against Trafficking in Women (CATW), together with the European Women's Lobby (EWL) and the International Abolitionist Federation (IAF), that pressed for an inclusion of sexual exploitation within the Palermo Protocol and for prostitution as the main sector of exploitation for women and girls within trafficking. This concept of trafficking as sexual exploitation has left

Figure 12.1 Map of Italy

ample room for single states (and Italy is one of them, as we shall see) to interpret antitrafficking policy as antiprostitution policy (see Doezema, 2002; Ditmore and Wijers, 2003). However, another, more moderate feminist lobbying bloc, called Human Rights Caucus and comprising the International Human Rights Law Group (IHRLG) and the Global Alliance Against Trafficking in Women (GAATW), pressed for a delinking of trafficking and prostitution, maintaining that trafficking occurs in other labor contexts and for a limitation of trafficking to cases where force and coercion were used, arguing that prostitution can be a freely chosen "legitimate labour" (Doezema, 2002; Ditmore and Wijers, 2003; Raymond, 2002). The result is an ambiguous definition of trafficking that, while formally accepting a gender-neutral language and including exploitation in sectors different than prostitution as instances of trafficking, gives special attention, in practice, to trafficking for the purpose of sexual exploitation/prostitution, popularly considered as a particularly degrading form of slavery.

As for the protection of victims of trafficking, although Article 25 of the Convention Against Transnational Crime addresses the protection of victims and their rights to compensation, the provision is not mandatory for states in any sense. By the same token, Article 7 of the UN Convention invites state parties to provide for legislation or other instruments that will allow victims of trafficking to remain in their territory, temporarily or permanently in appropriate cases, but with no obligations within the letter of the article.

In 2004, the European Commission also provided for a Council Directive on short-term-stay permits issued to victims of trafficking and to those who have been subject to an action to facilitate illegal immigration and who cooperate with relevant authorities.[1] In this directive, the aim of protecting and assisting the victims is entirely secondary to that of strengthening instruments to combat illegal immigration (Curtol et al., 2004). It is clearly stated that protection and assistance are linked to the victim's usefulness for the purpose of investigations, evaluated by the competent authority, her willingness to cooperate, and the fact that she has severed all relations with those suspected of the given offence. Although progress was made on a European Union (EU) level, with the Convention on Action against Trafficking in Human Beings in 2005,[2] in general, we can say that in victim protection policy, both the EU and the UN treat protection as part of a strategy to obtain cooperation from the victims and therefore within a repressive framework. Meanwhile, there is no universally recognized standard for the rights of victims to receive assistance and protection (Brusca, 2011; Shinkle, 2007).

In Italy, the protection of victims of trafficking is provided for in Article 18 of the immigration law that, under Section III entitled "Dispositions of humanitarian character," establishes that:

> When, during police operations, investigations or proceedings related to the criminal offence provided for in article 3 of the law 20 February 1958, n. 75, or to the criminal offences provided for in article 380 of the penal code, or during interventions of local authorities' social services, there are [. . .] situations of violence or of severe exploitation against a foreign person, and there emerge concrete dangers for his/her safety, as a result of his/her efforts to escape the control of an association dedicated to one of the above mentioned crimes, or of statements given in the course of preliminary investigations or during trial [. . .], the Chief police officer [*Questore*] [. . .] grants a special residence permit to allow the foreign person [. . .] to participate in a programme of assistance and social integration.[3]

While this piece of law does not mention "sexual exploitation" in its text, it nevertheless refers to prostitution as one of the crimes of which the "foreign person" may be victim. Law n. 75/58 (mentioned in the text quoted) is in fact the law that regulates prostitution in Italy, and Article 3 provides for the punishment of third-person involvement in the exercise of prostitution and makes brothel-keeping punishable. N. 6 of Article 3 in particular, punishes anyone who induces a person to move to another state or within it for the purpose of prostitution; in other words, it refers to "trafficking for the purpose of prostitution."[4] Article 380 of the penal code, on the other hand, refers to a range of criminal offences, among which is "reduction to slavery" and organized crime.[5]

It has been noted by some that Article 18 is situated between a witness protection measure and an "amnesty" law to regularize specific migrant groups, in particular women "victims of trafficking." In the mind of the legislator, it was this second aspect that distinguished Article 18 on a European level, since it stressed "not so much the protection of the witness, to guarantee the genuine nature of his/her statements, but rather the legalization of a foreign person (generally a woman) victim of trafficking-related crimes" (Petrini and Ferraris, 2002, p. 53). Article 18 allowed for an antitrafficking policy that, while providing for punishments against perpetrators (by collecting testimonies from victims), it stressed the humanitarian character of the law (by providing for protection and assistance for the victims). The uniqueness of Article 18 as a victim protection measure, then, is that it can effectively separate the aspect of protection from the aspect of repression by allowing a foreign person to obtain a residence permit for reasons of social protection even if she (since in most cases the person is a woman) refuses to act as a witness of trafficking-related crimes, the central preoccupation being the victim's safety and protection in front of a concrete danger. Even if we make a comparison with other countries where similar measures have been applied, the Italian system remains the most advanced in terms of the central attention given to the humanitarian aspect of trafficking and in providing for a program of integration that allows for a permanent settlement within Italian society. Thus, Belgium, in its legislation against trafficking in human beings passed on April 13, 1995, also provided for a temporary residence permit for reasons of social protection to victims of trafficking and that this permit be transformed into permanent residence rights, but this is allowed only if the victim cooperates with police investigations and if investigations lead to good results (i.e., they must lead to the conviction of traffickers; Pearson, 2002, p. 90).[6] For a victim to access Article 18 protection programs, on the other hand, it is sufficient that she has integrated into Italian society during her "rehabilitation" process (Pearson, 2002; Mancini, 2007).

More recently, it has been noted that the emphasis posed on "situations of violence or severe exploitation" means that Article 18 is different from other similar antitrafficking provisions because it does not apply exclusively to irregular (i.e., undocumented) foreigners who are found to be victims of trafficking, but it can apply also to foreigners who have a regular residence permit (Mancini, 2007). This point was made clear in 2006 by a legal provision (Law Decree n. 300/2006)[7] that establishes that nationals of new member states of the EU who did not need a visa and had a regular residence permit could access social protection programs under Article 18 of the immigration law if they were found in the conditions described by the same law article. This was certainly the case of many women from Romania, who, by 2004 (the year of the fifth enlargement process within the EU), did not need a residence permit but could still access Article 18 protection and assistance programs. As noted by David Mancini, the delinking of Article 18 from residence status makes victim protection in Italy a truly humanitarian instrument that would benefit those (even EU, and therefore even Italian, citizens) who are victims/witnesses of serious crimes and, as such, are entitled to protection, assistance, and social integration through state-funded projects in which the voluntary sector and social services are also actively involved (Mancini, 2007).

In spite of this good legislative framework, the application of Article 18 can be quite difficult, as it can be influenced by a number of factors, namely the regional context where programs take place, the role of the voluntary sector in general and, in particular, religious actors active in social protection projects, and the priorities of local governments in relation to immigration control and prostitution policies. In terms of Article 18's relation to prostitution, we should consider, for example, that Article 18 has allowed for a kind of policy orientation operational in Italy since the early 1990s, when many NGOs, both religious and lay, began to work in the field of migrant prostitution, giving basic assistance and protection to migrant prostitutes. The grassroots activities carried out by these NGOs created the ground for a policy framework that reflected a mixture of progressive instances of migrants' and women's rights groups on the one hand and religious groups' and ordinary people's preoccupation with street migrant prostitution, viewed as the most degrading form of slavery, on the other. Behind the antitrafficking campaigns and projects, there were a variety of interpretations as to the target-people involved (prostitutes, sex workers, victims of trafficking), the type of problem (prostitution, trafficking, exploitation, and slavery), methods (rigid/institutional control, flexible/harm-reduction/empowerment method), and aims (eradication of prostitution, management of social conflicts linked with migrant street prostitution).

Antitrafficking Policies and Local Approaches to Prostitution and Slavery
INTRODUCTION: ARTICLE 18, SLAVERY, AND PROSTITUTION IN
LOCAL CONTEXTS

Over the past 10 years, Italian antitrafficking policies have been influenced by the domestic discourse around (migrant) prostitution, which has become an important area for consensus-building within local politics. On the other hand, local governments have also been influenced by the various religious and nonreligious groups working around migrants', women's, and sex workers' rights. These groups have pressed for specific, often ideologically driven (but also driven by the mere need for funding), approaches to prostitution, going from conservative (usually deploying the metaphor of slavery to describe migrant prostitution), through to preventive (e.g., harm-reduction approaches) and sex workers' rights measures (based on the principle that prostitution can be freely chosen as "work") (Prina, 2002; Picciolini, 2000).

These approaches have caused the discourse concerning prostitution to be polarized in a way that, as noted by Prina, can be summarized on the lines of the scheme shown in Table 12.1.

While local policies have been affected by the different rhetoric used by the different actors operating on a grassroots level, the concept of slavery has been adopted by all groups (religious and nonreligious) as a metaphor to describe the condition of virtually all migrant women involved in prostitution. To signify the importance of slavery as a dominant category within antitrafficking policies, in 2003, the legislator intervened to modify the penal code just in those articles concerning the crime of slavery-like offences by introducing Article 223 that, indeed, defined trafficking essentially in terms of "reduction to slavery" and "servitude." Although the intent was to apply the

Table 12.1   Representation of Actions and Rhetoric on Prostitution in Italy

Actions toward	*Considered as . . .*	*For the purpose of . . .*
Individuals	Exploited, victims of trafficking	Redemption, salvation, social reintegration
	Migrant prostitutes with no rights	Support to get legalized and to acquire citizenship rights, promotion of autonomy processes
Social phenomena	Evil	Eradication
	Social problems causing conflicts	"Management" of problems and mediation of social conflicts

Source: Adapted from Prina (2002, p. 506)

slavery offence in trafficking cases, in practice, the slavery crime was difficult to demonstrate, and the law on prostitution was more often applied in cases investigated through Article 18. In spite of the difficulty of slavery as a viable legal category, women who were protected through Article 18 were described as slaves. This in turn transformed Article 18 and the social assistance and protection programs provided through it into an "emancipation" and "redemption" machine, in such a way that all actors working in social protection programs were tied to institutional requirements related to a variety of considerations, such as:

1. The selection phase, linked to a definition of "victim" that accords with the slavery rhetoric and that rests on the victim's willingness to "change her life."
2. The role of denunciation, which acquires the status of "proof" of a radical change on the part of the victim and her willingness to change her life.
3. The aims of social programs, with an emphasis on a "moral reconstruction" of the person on the one hand and the suppression/eradication of prostitution as the manifestation of "trafficking" and as a form of slavery on the other.
4. The instruments adopted, with an accent on institutional control (for example, through community accommodation—flight houses—as opposed to autonomous accommodation,[8] thus substituting "support" with "control."
5. The work solution, oriented toward "niche" labor markets (e.g., domestic work) rather than towards effective integration in the wider employment market and using women's personal resources and effective training schemes.

Next, we shall look at how victim protection policy took place in the three research sites, with attention paid to the above mentioned dynamics between repressive and protection aims and to the question of social control linked to the listed institutional requirements.

The Three Research Contexts

The three sites where research was conducted offer different sex market contexts in terms of the numbers and types of groups involved in street prostitution, in terms of the migrant groups involved in social protection programs, the types of organizations in charge of protection projects, and the degree of local government involvement and its role within the projects.

Catania

Catania is the second Sicilian city, after Palermo, affected by migrant street prostitution. Over the last seven years, there have been changes to the way in which migrant prostitution is practiced, the groups involved, and the policy adopted by the local government. Until 1999, most migrant prostitution was practiced in flats and houses within the town's historical "red light district" area, where since the late 1980s, Italian women and transsexual people have worked together with women and transsexual people from Latin America, mainly the Dominican Republic and Colombia. From the early 1990s, Latin American women were joined also by Nigerian women, so that by 1999–2000, the local LILA estimated a total of 270 prostitutes in the area, of which 240 were migrant. Most migrant sex workers were from the Dominican Republic (96) and from Colombia (89), followed by African women (51).[9] At the end of 2000, a massive roundup by the local police led to the removal of all migrant prostitutes from the area and the repatriation of some of them, with the consequence that those who remained were then forced to work in the streets outside the traditional sex market area and in the roadways outside the city centre. From this moment on, there were more African women and girls involved in street sex work, whereas many Latin American women in the city alternated street work with work in flats. So, during August 2003–June 2004, the LILA mobile street unit estimated a total of 82 migrant prostitutes working in the roadways outside the city centre, of which 51 were African (from Nigeria, Ghana, Togo, Benin), 20 Latin American (from Colombia and from the Dominican Republic), six Romanian, and five Albanian.[10]

The authorities in Catania have not approached prostitution as a potential site of slavery and exploitation; rather, they left the market to operate unregulated during the 1980s and 1990s apart from a few symbolic raids, which were followed, from December 2000, by a politics of repression that led to mass repatriation. Within this new repressive policy framework, while the metaphor of slavery has been used more heavily than before by both the police and judiciary authorities and the voluntary actors involved in protection programs, residence permits for social protection have been rare (the local police records show only two permits from the year 2000, one of which was a renewal of a residence permit issued in another locality).

There are two groups mainly active in social protection, one adopting a nonreligious approach based on "women's rights" principles; the second is a Catholic group, working on the principle that all prostitution is slavery and, as such, must be eliminated. The two groups work separately and cooperate with different police authorities, although they both work with migrant prostitutes who operate in the same Catania area. All relevant institutions in Catania, namely the municipality, the local health service, in particular the transcultural psychiatric service, and the police have established cooperative relationships with the Catholic group, whereas relationships with the non-Catholic group have been less cooperative, partly because the Catholic group enjoys more credit nationwide due to the popularity gained by its former director through television programs and the press.

The fact that the municipality has established more positive relationships of cooperation with the Catholic group means that social protection programs have assumed a specific approach based on the principle of a "life change" undertaken by those women who were taken into care by the group. This, in turn, meant that the route to social integration for many women and girls who accessed social protection programs in Catania was marked by a "moral" approach to antitrafficking policy that, while giving primary importance to a "new life" initiated within a family or religious environment where they were "educated" to new values linked to "real affection" and "real, hard work," as opposed to "commercial love" and the "easy way to money," gave less importance to the acquisition of citizenship rights in the form of a residence permit and a work contract that would allow them economic independence. This approach to protection programs for victims of trafficking is also translated, in the case of Catania, in an antitrafficking policy, which, during the selective phase, may not give importance to the victim's cooperation as a witness of "trafficking crimes." In other words, it was not important for the victim to report the names of her "traffickers" or exploiters prior to her access to protection projects, as we can see from an interview extract with the representative of the religious group in Catania:

> It is not necessary that women make a report with names of traffickers. Often they don't want to do this out of fear . . . for us the most important thing in the first contact is not to speak about residence permit, but to make friendship . . . many of the girls did not obtain the residence permit but they managed to exit prostitution with our help. What we ask girls is to stay in families where they are treated like daughters. We don't force them. We ask them "do you have a mother and a father? . . . What would they say if they knew what you do in Italy?" This question makes them unsettled.[11]

The methods of victim protection used in Catania were based on "rehabilitation" and reeducation to an "honest" life within community/family accommodation and within religious institutes where girls were closely controlled, where their mobile phones were taken from them to prevent them from "falling back" into prostitution.

As to the prostitution–trafficking–slavery link, from the interview with the judge of the Catania court, it emerged that, although antitrafficking operations originally were initiated because there was a suspicion that people were smuggled from Sri Lanka to be exploited in agriculture and in domestic service, Article 18 was applied only to prostitution cases:

> As far as our experience is concerned, I must say that the crime of
> reduction into slavery was always linked to sexual exploitation, not to
> other sectors . . . We have found some cases of ordinary crime com-
> mitted by some ethnic groups against people in the same groups, like
> money extortion and things like that, but not really something like
> slavery . . .

Article 18 is applied in cases of migrant prostitutes because the most striking cases were found among people who were exploited in prostitution but
also because in many cases where people are found in exploitative situations
(domestic work, agriculture), they left their country voluntarily, and this
makes the application of Article 18 impossible.[12]

To summarize, we can say that in Catania, the tension between the government's desire to control immigration and its commitment to protect wom-
en's human rights is played out at the expense of the latter; that women's
search for citizenship rights through a residence permit granted under Article
18 is frustrated by the predominantly religious approach adopted by the local
group, for which the aim of "getting a woman off the street" prevails over that
of granting her real residence rights. Finally, the combined local government,
courts', and NGO's interest exclusively in prostitution suggests that here, as
in most parts of Italy, (migrant) prostitution is seen as a serious problem
linked to "trafficking" and "slavery" and that persons subject to exploitation
and abuse in other sectors, such as domestic work, agriculture, construction,
stand little chance of being identified or assisted as victims of trafficking.

Lecce

The first interesting aspect of this research site is its special nature as a border
city, situated as it is along the coastal area near Albania (the nearby Otranto
is only 70 km from Vilonia), from where boats approached the Italian eastern
coast, leaving, from the second half of the 1990s up to 2002, thousands of
people from Eastern Europe, mainly Moldavia, Ukraine, and Romania, on its
shores. The second important aspect of Lecce concerns the role of the local
detention centre (Centro di Permanenza Temporanea e Assistita, CPTA) as
a collector of undocumented migrant people and potential victims of trafficking and smugglers. The centre, which was closed in 2005 for overcrowding
and because basic human rights were found to be routinely violated, was
co-funded by the Regina Pacis Foundation, a church agency, and the Minis-
try of Home Affairs. The Regina Pacis Foundation was also responsible for
the social protection project for victims of trafficking, which used part of the
detention centre premises as a "protected house" for women and girls who
accessed protection projects. Although there was another project in Lecce,
run and promoted by the Lecce province and based on nonreligious, women's
rights values, it was, like in Catania, the church-funded Regina Pacis

Foundation that maintained a special, privileged, relation with the prosecutor's office and the local police headquarter (*questura*). However, unlike in Catania, this cooperation produced, between 1999 and 2002, a total of 150 residence permits for social protection granted mainly to women and girls from Moldavia (Orfano and Ferraris, 2002, p. 281), making Lecce a case of high production of residence permits for social protection in a context of low incidence of migrant street prostitution. As reported by Orfano and Ferraris:

> the high number of residence permits issued is linked to the peculiarity of the Lecce area, on the one hand, as a territory of shipping of clandestine migrants, and, on the other, as a collector of applications of residence permits linked to facts of exploitation of prostitution which have taken place . . . in other geographic contexts.
>
> (Ibid., p. 285)

Unlike what happens in the great majority of projects for victim protection in Italy, in Lecce, victims were not contacted by social operators while they were working in the street during their outreach work[13] but by the police in the detention centre where they were brought as soon as they arrived in the nearby port towns. Among the residence permits issued by the Questura in Lecce, there were, therefore, those granted to women who had worked as prostitutes in other Italian cities or in other transit areas outside Italy.

Given this premise about Lecce, the question arises on the specific approach adopted here by the various institutions involved, in particular, how they went about identifying victims and how they established the link between trafficking, prostitution, and slavery. The following interview extract with the prosecutor in Lecce clarifies this point:

> The women who arrived here in order to be exploited in prostitution were easily identifiable because our experience led us to understand this and also they spoke against their traffickers . . . Our criterion really was based simply on the fact that these women were young, they were in groups, and so it was assumed that they were transported here to be sexually exploited . . . they had all been sexually exploited abroad . . . there was evidence that there had been violence, although not from the country of origin, as normally these women voluntarily left their country.[14]

While the Lecce case is usually cited as one in which a purely social approach to victim protection is applied, meaning that women are not asked to report or give testimony in trial against their traffickers, in actual fact, the Lecce "system" consists of a mixture of social and judicial approach whereby, after a first contact between the woman and the volunteers of the detention centre, a second phase is initiated with the woman's decision to report against those who "brought" them in Italy to be exploited in prostitution.

To summarize, Lecce, like Catania, has a predominantly moral approach to antitrafficking policy, since the great bulk of social protection offered here is provided by the Regina Pacis Foundation, an agency linked to the church. However, unlike Catania, Lecce was characterized by a high number of residence permits issued under Article 18 and benefiting predominantly women and girls coming from Eastern Europe who were identified within the Regina Pacis detention centre as "victims of trafficking." Prostitution was considered by the local administration and institutions as a serious and real problem related to "trafficking" and slavery, as the interview with the prosecutor indicates:

> I think 90% of trafficking concerns exploitation in prostitution. It is true that there are cases of trafficking concerning labour exploitation in general, and in fact in Italy 16 residence permits with article 18 were granted to men who were not working in prostitution. The new law on trafficking has also given more importance to cases of trafficking concerning labour exploitation, but in my experience in Lecce most cases were about prostitution not because of a deliberate interest in prostitution, but because obviously trafficking did involve mainly prostitution.[15]

This leaves Lecce in the paradoxical position of having a high number of residence permits, which would suggest a greater openness to granting citizenship rights not only to women exploited in prostitution but also to women exploited in the domestic sector (two cases registered by the nonreligious project run by the Provincia authority). On the other hand, like in Catania (without wanting to generalize for the rest of Italy), an "unholy" relationship exists between the religious-based operation of protection programs and citizenship rights granted to women who are institutionally defined as "sexual slaves." In Lecce, in fact, as in Catania, social protection programs acquire a moral meaning that gives a great deal of importance, again, to "rehabilitation" to a "new" life that "breaks" with the previous prostitution experience. This is illustrated by the volunteer interviewed in the Regina Pacis center:

> It's easy to take a woman off the street, but it's difficult to rehabilitate her . . . she is an empty woman, deprived of her femininity, so she has to regain the ability to take care of her body, her hygiene, her sexuality . . . they are people who've lost any guideline.
>   . . . Once the women accept to enter the protection programme they would be asked to sign their commitment to adhere to the rules of the programme and to take all responsibilities . . . if in the course of the

programme they adopted a behaviour which was incompatible with the programme itself [i.e., to go back to the streets], there would be the revocation of their residence permit.[16]

As to the tension between "repressive" and "human rights" approaches from the part of the authorities, Lecce has not been affected by a policy of rounding up and massive deportation, as there was in Catania, but the absence of such policies is due more to the absence of a local street sex market than to a tilting of the balance in favour of a "human rights" commitment. On the whole, however, women and girls detained in the Regina Pacis center were treated as real or potential sexual slaves, or "victims of sexual exploitation," as the interview suggests, but not as participants in criminal offences. In Lecce, perhaps more than in the other two research sites, social protection programs were characterized by a marked paternalistic approach towards migrant women prostitutes, for whom the metaphor of slavery was widely used in a way that reduced their roles as the programs' beneficiaries to mere objects of a disciplinary project which aimed to redefine their identities as women, workers, daughters, and mothers in opposition to an identity as prostitutes.

Rome

Rome is different from the two other sites for the particular organization of protection programs around the municipality that coordinates all the groups involved and has decision-making power over individual programs in terms of funding, supervision, and services provided. The main characteristic of this research site is the great number and variety of groups, both religious and nonreligious, and projects involved in protection programs, using a variety of methods, from rehabilitation on the same line followed in Catania and Lecce through to "emancipation" according to women's rights conceptions and prevention through a harm-reduction philosophy. In spite of this variety, however, programs are all influenced by the institutional control of the municipality and also of the prosecutor's office, whose discretionary power over granting residence permits remains crucial, in spite of its peripheral role under the letter of the law. In relation to the relationship between the migrant sex market and the antitrafficking policy pursued under Article 18 programs, we have in Rome quite the reverse of what happens in Lecce. According to data elaborated by the Parsec action-research group in 1996–1998, the Rome metropolitan area attracts 50 percent of the total prostitution market in Italy, with 3,000 to 3,500 units out of a total of 5,537 to 6,989 units (Carchedi, 2000, p. 165). Within the Roman market, there are all the national groups represented throughout Italy, with a predominance of Eastern European women coming mainly from Moldavia, Romania, Albania, and ex-USSR countries, and women from Nigeria. With respect to the

discrepancy between the large prostitution market and the low level of prosecutorial activities carried out by the Rome court, we have to remember
that Rome, like Lecce, is also a transit area for migrants heading towards
other cities, and it is perhaps for this reason that here, "there were far more
proceedings for smuggling of migrants than for trafficking in persons"
(Curtol et al., 2004, p. 116). The municipality in Rome acted both as a
funding agency and as a promoter of projects of social protection, and this
made the whole system of social protection under Article 18 a lot more
structured around a central authority, which provided all groups involved
with funds, services, training, and expertise. However, relationships
between the municipality and the various NGOs and grassroots organizations involved were not always smooth, and, according to one informant,
NGOs sometimes lamented that the central administration adopted its own
selective criteria and often denied protected houses to women already taken
in care by them.

With regard to the links between trafficking, slavery, and prostitution,
I will quote what the judge in Rome told me, as it well illustrates the difficulty of "slavery" as a legal category but at the same time its constant association with prostitution:

> I'm involved in offences related to illegal immigration, exploitation of
> prostitution and introduction of women to be exploited in prostitution,
> not trafficking and reduction in slavery as such, although the women
> exploited are kept in conditions similar to slavery and are in actual fact
> prisoners of these exploiters. But it's not easy to contest an offence dis-
> ciplined in the penal code, like reduction to slavery, through Article
> 18 . . . I mean, within the anti-Mafia District Direction, once the slav-
> ery offence is contested it gets easily linked to prostitution related
> offences and exploitation of prostitution, so they are not two separate
> things altogether.[17]

As to the importance given to denunciation as a prerequisite for access to
protection programs, people working in the Rome project pointed out that
this was a problem and made Article 18 very limited in its application.
I report here what a female psychologist of a nonreligious group working in
the Rome project told me:

> In Rome it's impossible right now to apply for a residence permit under
> Article 18 without a full report. In reality it's always been like this, but in
> the past it had happened that if there were particularly dangerous groups
> involved and it was too risky for the girl to denounce them, the police
> would agree that they would use only our information leaving the girl

outside the actual legal proceeding. This wouldn't happen anymore . . . They treat the granting of a residence permit as a reward for the woman who collaborates with the judiciary and the police. In other words the report with names of exploiters is essential. The last amendments to the law have led to an ever more rigid interpretation of Article 18, more than in any other city. As a consequence, if a girl who has already accessed Article 18 programmes goes to the police to have her residence permit renewed, she will have her fingerprints taken, then if they find out there was a past deportation order for her in their files, they will stop her and keep her in custody for a night. So, after she has started a social protection programme, she is suddenly treated like a criminal.[18]

Within the Rome project, access to social protection programs concerned a total number of 40 women as in June 2002, of whom three abandoned programs and two decided to repatriate after a long wait for residence permits (Minguzzi, 2002). Of the 35 women in protection programs who had been monitored by the municipality office during June 2002, two were without residence permits, whereas among the residence permits granted to the other women, 22 were for work reasons, eight were for social protection, and two were for family reunion (ibid., p. 172). It is further reported that only 15 women with residence permits for work reasons have maintained their jobs when the project was concluded, whereas the rest, including those with no residence permit at all, had experienced precarious and discontinuous work. Among the reasons for this precariousness and discontinuity, the research carried out within the Rome municipality mentions women's difficulty to adapt to a work environment and lifestyles which they perceived as different and "to the difficulty of accepting job offers which they perceived as unfavourable" (ibid.), with work in the black economy and long "apprenticeship" periods during which women work irregularly, and work contracts which are extremely "volatile" and underpaid (ibid., pp. 172–173). In terms of the types of work that are normally available for women who complete protection programs, domestic and care work remains the most common solution in Rome, as in the rest of Italy.[19] However, as it was reported by the project coordinator of the municipality office, "there are some of them [women] who decide to get married and get a little job or no job at all." Another crucial weakness with regard to the job opportunities afforded by social protection programs is the absence of trade unions as economic actors, which, as a female psychologist in Rome pointed out, "leaves a lot of room for risks of labour exploitation."

In terms of the tension between "repressive" and "human rights" approaches used by the municipality, the accent on cooperation between the victim and judicial authorities as expressed by the psychologist above, means, among other things, that women are less and less treated like victims of human rights violation, more and more as penal subjects (e.g., witnesses in antitrafficking operations, illegal migrants when found with an expired residence permit). We should also consider that, although the municipality was keen to present its project in lay, nonmoralizing terms, the "religious" aspect emerged also in this research site, where a number of Catholic institutions and associations were involved in social protection programs. This, together with the "repressive" evolution of protection programs mentioned above, suggests that in Rome, as in Catania and in Lecce, victim protection was applied according to a "rehabilitation" principle which, again, marginalized the economic (i.e., work) and legal (residence rights) aspects of integration and privileged the ethical aspect, centred, again, on the regaining of an identity as "good" woman, in opposition to an identity as "prostitute," as the following interview extract illustrates:

> She [the woman] is a destroyed person . . . She has no point of reference, she lost her dignity . . . so we really have to help her to become conscious of what happened to them, their experience of prostitution, to understand its meaning, how they found themselves in this situation, and then restart life as it was before . . .
>
> The important thing in this process is to regain a sense of childhood, innocence, and all positive things they did before the bad experience. So it's important to understand and to forgive what they've done.[20]

In this rehabilitation process, the distinction between a "real victim" and a "fallen" woman is important, and the justice system has an important role in the application of "sexual" criteria for selecting a victim, as one of my interviewees, a female flight house coordinator in a nonreligious group in Rome, pointed out:

> In practice the women who enter Article 18 programmes have the feeling of being judged on a moral level, they begin to feel a sense of guilt, to feel dirty . . . I have observed some pre-trial hearings, where the woman had to testify in front of the public prosecutor who questioned her . . . in these circumstances some questions are really terrifying, like "before you worked as a prostitute did you have sexual relations with men? How many sexual relations? With how many men?" . . . this is the way they see whether the women are responsible of their prostitution or not . . . the lawyers or judges ask these kinds of questions in order to help the woman, because in this way they demonstrate through legal proceedings the real innocence of the woman.[21]

Conclusions

Discourse and policies on trafficking in human beings have tended, on an international level, to link trafficking to "sexual exploitation" and exploitation for prostitution purposes. Within single states, there have been tensions with respect to "humanitarian" (victims protection) versus "repressive" (i.e., immigration and prostitution control) aspects of antitrafficking policies, with some states emphasizing the former, others the latter. With the introduction of Article 18 of the immigration law passed in 1998, Italy has approached antitrafficking policy decidedly—if only rhetorically—as a humanitarian issue and, in consequence, has emphasized the protection of victims.

Field research in three Italian cities shows that social protection programs have been influenced by an antitrafficking campaign which, in Italy as elsewhere, was centred on the old image of the victim—that is the migrant/"trafficked" prostitute—as powerless and in need to be restored to mainstream society's values regarding sexuality and work. In other words, in order to gain protection and assistance and to be able to stay and work permanently within the country, a victim of trafficking is to abide by some institutional requirements related to her decision to "break" with the exploitative environment (i.e., break with prostitution) and to "change life."

As interview data in the three research sites confirmed, prostitution was regarded as the main site of exploitation in "trafficking" and a form of slavery linked to organized crime. It emerged that, in spite of the difficulty of "slavery" as a legal category to be used in prosecutions, it was nevertheless used in key actors' narratives about who was a "victim of trafficking." Research also shows that religious groups play an important role in interpreting Article 18 according to a "redemption" from the experience of prostitution and to a disciplinary approach which effectively prevents the "risk" of falling back into prostitution and is oriented towards "good" (female) sexuality (e.g., as wife or mother) and "good" work (e.g., as domestic worker).

Religious/redemptive, as opposed to principles of emancipation as economic autonomy, the focus on prostitution as a form of slavery, and the evolution towards a judiciary/witness approach to Article 18, as opposed to a social/human rights protection approach, mean that in the three cities where research was conducted, repressive principles prevailed over human rights principles. While the granting of a permanent residence permit is never straightforward and tends to depend on the victims' willingness to cooperate with the judiciary system, the process of social integration to which the granting of permanent residence and work rights is subordinated under Article 18 is often turned into a form of social control. Women who are defined as "victims" are subjected to paternalistic measures designed to turn them into "good women" and "good workers," rather than into individuals whose citizenship rights are recognized also by being enabled to gain economic independence through a wide range of work opportunities.

Finally, the evolution of the immigration law, in particular amendments made in 2002 with Law 189/2002 (the so-called Bossi-Fini Law), together with other law provisions under the rubric of security and public order (see note 1), have led to a further restriction of migrants' rights concerning entry, residence, and many other aspects, and which can be summarized in the provision of making the residence permit tied up to the existence of a work contract. This has impacted negatively on the condition of those women who obtained a residence permit under the system of victim protection established by Article 18 and whose work contract is not renewed by their employer.

Discussion Questions

1. What are the main obstacles to establish an effective victim protection policy on an international level?
2. On the basis of the case study presented in this chapter, how do you understand the tension between repression and protection within the Italian national context of victim protection policy?
3. In what ways is the principle of victim protection influenced by gender issues?
4. What did this case study show in terms of local policy and the nexus trafficking–prostitution–immigration?

Notes

1. Directive 2004/81/EC: "On the residence permit issued to third-country nationals who are victims of trafficking in human beings or who have been the subject of an action to facilitate illegal immigration who cooperate with the competent authorities." European Commission. Official Journals, OJ L 261, 6/08/2004. http://eur-lex.europa.eu/LexUriServ/LexUriServ.do?uri=CELEX:32004L0081:EN:HTML.
2. Council of Europe Convention on Action against Trafficking in Human Beings. Warsaw 16.V.2005. http://conventions.coe.int/Treaty/EN/Treaties/Html/197.htm.
3. Law Decree 25 July 1998, n. 286, *Testo unico delle disposizioni concernenti la disciplina dell'immigrazione e norme sulla condizione dello straniero*, www.parlamento.it/leggi/deleghe/98286dl.htm. For a further discussion on the impact of Article 18 as an anti-trafficking/antislavery law see Virgilio (2001).
4. See Virgilio, 2002, p. 78.
5. While Article 18 includes "reduction to slavery" as one of the crimes of which a foreigner may be victim, the Italian legislation provided in 2003 for a specific law against trafficking in persons and against slavery (Law n. 228/2003, which modified the penal code in those articles dealing with slavery and the slave trade). Law n. 228 of 2003 also provides, in Article 13, for assistance and protection programmes, but only for victims of slavery or slavery-like practices, whereas in Article 18, it is sufficient that a

foreigner is found in "situations of violence" or "serious exploitation." In practice, Article 18 has made it easier for the judiciary authorities to prosecute and convict persons involved in trafficking-related crimes. For further reading, see the research by Pearson, 2002, p. 142. For a comparison with Article 13 of Law 228 against trafficking, see Mancini (2007).

6. See also *Articolo 18: tutela delle vittime del traffico di esseri umani e lotta alla criminalità (l'Italia e gli scenari europei. Rapporto di ricerca.* Chapter 4, "La dimensione comparativa,"2.5 Belgium, pp. 393–422.

7. The general title of the law is "Prorogation of terms provided for by legislative dispositions." See Mancini (2007).

8. According to data from the Equal Opportunities Department related to the monitoring of 42 protection projects carried out throughout Italy from March 2001 to March/April 2002, 1,194 women were lodged in flight houses, 428 women were lodged in autonomous housing, 190 in families, and 203 were lodged in other types of accommodation, including semi-autonomous lodging (47), community centres, and friends. See Barberi (2004, p. 78).

9. Part of the results of the pilot research conducted by the local LILA are published in Nigro et al. (2006).

10. These are unpublished data from the street unit operators of the local LILA.

11. Representative of religious group, Catania.

12. Judge1, Catania.

13. For the modality of contacts with victims of trafficking see Barberi (2004). See also Pearson (2002), in particular chapter 9 on the Italian case.

14. Judge1, Lecce.

15. Judge1, Lecce.

16. Volunteer of religious project, Lecce.

17. Judge1, Rome.

18. Female psychologist2, nonreligious group, Rome.

19. Barberi (2004) reports that "the greatest difficulty [. . .] consists in inserting people into a 'normal' occupational sector, that is a productive activity, whereas in reality they are 'parked' in pseudo-jobs consisting in most cases in domestic work," p. 80.

20. Female psychologist2, religious group, Rome.

21. Female flight house coordinator1, nonreligious group, Rome.

References

Barberi, A. (2004) "Analisi conclusiva dei dati relativi al monitoraggio dei progetti di protezione sociale." In A. Barberi (Ed.), *Azioni in favore del reinserimento sociolavorativo delle vittime della tratta. European Conference, Turin, October 24–25 2003.* Rome: Presidenza del Consiglio dei Ministri. Available at: www.pariopportunita.gov.it/Pari_Opportunita/UserFiles/Il%20Dipartimento/versioneinternet[2].pdf

Brusca, C. S. (2011) "Palermo protocol: The first ten years after adoption." *Global Security Studies, 2*(3), 9–21.

Carchedi, F. (2000) "Le iniziative in atto e la prospettiva di un intervento integrato." In F. Carchedi, A. Piccolini, G. Mottura, and G. Campani (Eds.), *I colori della notte. Migrazioni, sfruttamento sessuale, esperienze di intervento sociale.* Milan, Italy: FrancoAngeli.

Curtol, F., Decarli, S., Di Nicola, A., and Savona, E. U. (2004) "Victims of human trafficking in Italy: A judicial perspective." *International Review of Victimology, 11*, 111–141.

Ditmore, M., and Wijers, M. (2003) "The negotiations on the UN protocol on trafficking in persons." *Nimesis, 4.* Available at: www.bayswan.org/traffick/NEMESIS_Ditmore. pdf (accessed July 7, 2021).

Doezema, J. (2002) "Who gets to choose? Coercion, consent, and the UN Trafficking protocol." *Gender and Development, 10,* 20–27.

Mancini, D. (2007) "La protezione sociale ex art. 18 del dlgs 286/1998 svincolata dallo status di cittadinanza: l'art. 6, comma 4 del decreto legge 300/2006." In *FiloDiritto. La legge—il diritto—le risposte.* Available at: www.filodiritto.com/index.php?azione=visualiz za&iddoc=543

Minguzzi, C. (2002) "Risultati: indicatori quantitativi e qualitativi del Progetto." In C. Minguzzi (Ed.) *Il futuro possibile. Tratta delle donne, inserimento social, lavoro.* Rome: Comune di Roma.

Nigro, L., Larocca, L., Celesia, B. M., Montineri, A., Sjoberg, J., Caltabiano, E., and Fatuzzo, F. (2006) "Prevalence of HIV and other sexually transmitted diseases among-Colombian female sex workers living in Catania, Eastern Sicily." *Journal of Immigrant Health, 8,* 319–323.

Orfano, I., and Ferraris, V. (2002) "Lecce." In *Articolo 18: tutela delle vittime del traffico di esseri umani e lotta alla criminalità (l'Italia e gli scenari europei). Rapporto di ricerca.* Martinsicuro, Italy: On the Road.

Pearson, E. (2002) *Human Traffic, Human Rights: Redefining Victims Protection.* London: Antislavery International.

Petrini, D., and Ferraris, V. (2002) "Analisi dell'art. 18 nel quadro della legislazione sull'immigrazione e della lotta alla criminalità organizzata. Storia e premialità dell'istituto e dei suoi antecedenti." In *Articolo 18: tutela delle vittime del traffico di esseri umani e lotta alla criminalità (l'Italia e gli scenari europei). Rapporto di ricerca.* Martinsicuro, Italy: On the Road.

Picciolini, A. (2000) "Il quadro normativo italiano sul problema del traffico internazionale finalizzato alla prostituzione e allo sfruttamento sessuale delle donne." In F. Carchedi, A. Piccolini, G. Mottura, and G. Campani (Eds.), *I colori della notte. Migrazioni, sfruttamento sessuale, esperienze di intervento sociale.* Milan, Italy: FrancoAngeli.

Prina, F. (2002) "I progetti e le forme di implementazione della norma: modelli organizzativi, sistemi di significato, articolazione della prassi." In *Articolo 18: tutela delle vittime del traffico di esseri umani e lotta alla criminalità (l'Italia e gli scenari europei). Rapporto di ricerca.* Martinsicuro, Italy: On the Road.

Raymond, J. G. (2002) "The new UN trafficking protocol." *Women's Studies International Forum, 25,* 491–502.

Shinkle, W. (2007) "Preventing human trafficking: An evaluation of current efforts." In *Policy Brief: Transatlantic Perspectives on Migration. Institute for the Study of International Migration, Walsh School of Foreign Service.* Washington DC: Georgetown University.

Spiezia, F., Frezza, F., and Pace, N. M. (2002) *Il traffico e lo sfruttamento di esseri umani. Primo commento alla legge di modifica alla normativa in materia di immigrazione ed asilo.* Milan, Italy: Giuffré.

United Nations (2000, November 15) *Protocol to Prevent, Suppress and Punish Trafficking in Persons, especially Women and Children, supplementing the United Nations Convention Against Transnational Organised Crime.* Available at: http://unodc.org/documents/ treaties/UNTOC/Publications/TOC%20Convention/TOCebook-e.pdf (accessed July 7, 2021).

Virgilio, M. (2001) "Libertà sessuale e nuove 'schiavitù.'" In L. Fioravanti (Ed.), *La tutela penale della persona. Nuove frontiere, difficili equilibri*. Milan, Italy: Giuffrè.

Virgilio, M. (2002) "L'articolo 18 nel quadro della legislazione penale di contrasto della criminalità contro le persone migranti." In *Articolo 18: tutela delle vittime del traffico di esseri umani e lotta alla criminalità (l'Italia e gli scenari europei). Rapporto di ricerca*. Martinsicuro, Italy: On the Road.

13

INTERNATIONAL DEVELOPMENT AND GLOBALIZATION ISSUES THAT CONTRIBUTE TO TRAFFICKING IN PERSONS

GABRIELLE SINNOTT AND LYNSIE CLOTT

Introduction

Human trafficking is a transboundary concern that is intersectional in nature. Many factors such as population, refugees, migration, economics, and politics influence human trafficking practices. This chapter aims to assess and examine problems associated with human trafficking through the discipline of international human development studies. In 2000, Kofi Annan, Secretary-General of the United Nations, proclaimed, "trafficking of persons . . . is one of the most egregious violations of human rights which the United Nations now confronts"(Annan, 2000). Twenty-one years later, human trafficking is still one of the most criminal and grievous violations of human rights.

The chapter will begin by addressing concerns about globalization that foster human trafficking. Also examined will be the contribution that population, climate change, poverty, and gender inequality, among other topics, make to human trafficking practices. This chapter will evaluate conflict, political instability, and social violence while also exploring the role of consumerism, resource scarcity, and supply chain management. Lastly, this chapter will identify technology's advancements and hindrances in human trafficking around the world.

DOI: 10.4324/9781003124672-16

Chapter Learning Objectives

- Understand the implications that globalization has on human trafficking.
- Be able to explain the effect of population growth and migration on trafficking in persons.
- Identify risks that victims of human trafficking might face in areas where there is conflict, political instability, or government corruption.
- Analyze the current and future impact of climate change on trafficking in persons.
- Understand the impacts of consumerism, resource scarcity, and supply chain management on trafficking in persons.
- Demonstrate knowledge of how trafficking in persons disproportionately impacts women and girls.
- Understand the advantages and hindrances of technology and trafficking in persons.

Globalization

Globalization is the growing connectedness and interdependence of countries' economies, cultures, and populations through international trade, travel, and technology. New technologies like electronic mail, cell phones, and online banking services allow for immediate global communications and instant capital mobility. The commercialization of the flight industry paired with Wi-Fi has made travel around the world cheap and effortless. The new global economy is defined by deregulation of trade, enhanced communication technologies, and international borders' openness; as the world becomes globalized, the wealth disparity between the rich and poor increases. The inequalities between developing and developed countries are a product of inequitable economic growth that results in vulnerable communities. The globalization of the world economy has increased people's movement across borders, whether it be for travel, migrating, or seeking asylum. In regions where vulnerabilities are prevalent, traffickers can exploit the weaknesses in the movement of people. As the world becomes more globalized and saturated with technological opportunities, traffickers can take advantage of individuals through open borders, ease of travel, and conflict zones to prey on the most vulnerable.

The asymmetrical growth and development from globalization has created a system with structured exploitation, from what clothes one wears to the food one eats. Globalization has set the stage for a new global industry, one in which human trafficking provides the labor, and the free flow of money, goods, and services provides the demand. Unprecedented demand, production, and movement of goods worldwide have resulted in unsustainable practices and abuse of human labor. Coffee harvested in Africa and Latin America and South America, and Indonesia surface in various coffee shops across the United States and Europe, while cotton harvested by child laborers in Uzbekistan makes an appearance through several clothing markets in Russia, China, and Korea (U.S. Department of Labor, 2019). Seafood bought and sold in the United States is caught halfway across the globe off the coast of Thailand, Burma, Vietnam, and Indonesia, a sector flooded with migrant forced labor (International Labor Organization, 2021). Shampoo, Conditioner, and soap may contain palm oil harvested by the use of forced labor in Myanmar, Malaysia, or Ecuador (Verité Inc., 2020a). Precious materials like gold, cobalt, coltan, and diamonds used in producing cell phones and jewelry have left thousands of children and adults in the Democratic Republic of the Congo and Liberia vulnerable to forced and exploitative labor (U.S. Department of Labor, 2020). All citizens are part of the epidemic of human trafficking, whether it be directly participating or through consumption.

Poverty and Lack of Opportunity

Today, nearly 729 million people have been pushed into extreme poverty, living on less than $1.90 a day, due to the effects of COVID-19, climate change, and conflict (The World Bank, 2020). Half of the world's poor, about 368 million, reside in just five countries: India, Nigeria, Democratic Republic of Congo, Ethiopia, and Bangladesh (Katayama & Wadhwa, 2019). According to the United Nations, Economic and Social Council of 2017, 42 percent of the sub-Saharan Africa population live on less than $1.90 a day (United Nations, Department of Social and Economic Affairs, 2018). While human trafficking does not discriminate between industrialized and developing countries, vulnerable communities face serious growth and many human development and security issues.

Poverty is one of the leading causes of human trafficking. Severe poverty and lack of opportunity put pressure on people and communities to engage in risky behavior. Families living in extreme poverty may resort to migrant labor to make ends meet. Without transparent procedures and with high risk with the potential of high rewards, many individuals find themselves in debt bondage. According to the International Labor Organization's "Global Estimates of Modern Slavery" 2017, nearly half of all victims of forced labor imposed by private actors were being held using debt bondage tactics (International

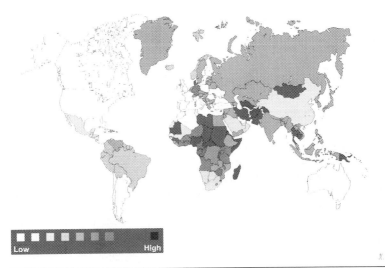

Figure 13.1 Global slavery index 2018—Prevalence of slavery

Labor Office, 2017). United Nations Secretary-General António Guterres remarks on the impact of poverty on vulnerable communities:

> Slavery manifests itself today through descent-based servitude, forced labor, child labor, domestic servitude, forced marriage, debt bondage, trafficking in persons for the purpose of exploitation, including sexual exploitation, and the forced recruitment of children in armed conflict. Poor and marginalized groups, in particular racial and ethnic minorities, indigenous peoples and migrants, are disproportionally affected by contemporary forms of slavery.

Traffickers use fees for visas, placement, and travel as a means of controlling victims. The fees increase over time as interest compounds on every penny the victim owes. Additionally, traffickers may charge for medical expenses, protection services, food, clothing, and shelter. Most victims never receive any medical attention or protection services, yet their debt continues to grow. Traffickers utilize growing debt as a method of control over their victims to scare them into servitude.

"Poverty, the lack of economic alternatives, illiteracy, and the discrimination that people from minority groups suffer leave them with no other option than to take a loan or advance from employers or recruiters to meet basic needs, in exchange for their work or the work of their families" (Bhoola, Special Rapporteur, 2016).

Human trafficking and debt bondage arise in countries with dysfunctional labor markets, poor labor enforcement, and dismal opportunities and employment. Traffickers prey on poor and otherwise vulnerable people by luring them into fraudulent employment contracts and assuring of them greater returns if they work abroad or in a separate area of the country. Unfortunately, these are false promises; instead, they become victims of human trafficking, unpaid and enslaved (Council on Foreign Relations, 2019b).

Population, Migration, and Refugees

The role of population trends in human security has been a subject of long-standing importance. Many of the planet's underlying problems—from climate change to resource scarcity, from conflict to displacement, from poverty to economics, and from immigration to human trafficking—are all a result of a booming world population. Fears of overpopulation and carrying capacity are real: the world's population has exponentially increased from 2.6 billion in 1950 to nearly 7.9 billion in 2021, with a projected increase to 9.7 billion in 2050 (United Nations, 2020). Population growth is only going to continue pushing the planet's carrying capacity to its limit and exacerbate many global problems, including the problem of human trafficking.

With an increase in population comes an increase in conflict over resources, migrant smuggling, and vulnerable communities' migration. Human trafficking is often confused with migrant smuggling, and while there are similarities between the two, there are just as many differences. The most crucial difference is that of consent—victims of human trafficking do not consent to travel or move to different countries or cities. The line blurs when an individual who consents to immigration smuggling may end up in dangerous or forced trafficking situations en route and upon arrival. Once individuals are deceived or coerced into a situation through control, they are no longer a migrant but a trafficking victim (United Nations Office on Drugs and Crime, 2020). Human trafficking is considered a crime against an individual, whereas migrant smuggling is a crime against the state (The Inter-Agency Coordination Group against Trafficking in Persons, 2016).

In areas where population growth is not matched with viable employment opportunities, vulnerable individuals may find themselves in potential human trafficking situations. Looking for meaningful employment in distant cities or countries leaves refugees and migrants, among others, at risk for severe human rights violations. Refugees already face harsh living conditions and limited resources and are more susceptible to discrimination in transit and the destination country and to human rights violations (Council on Foreign Relations, 2019a). Once victims arrive at their destination country, they remain in areas with high immigrant populations, so they blend in and do not attract attention. Adding to the problem of identifying trafficking victims, law enforcement agents who encounter forced labor are likely to mistake it for illegal immigration and treat the victims as criminals (Lankford, 2010, p. 14).

Conflict, Political Instability, Government Corruption, and Child Soldiers

Areas devastated by war, plagued with government corruption and political instability, alongside societal violence, create the perfect environment to exploit vulnerable people. War and societal violence may contribute to mass displacement and migrants, leaving orphans and children increasingly vulnerable to human trafficking (United Nations Office on Drugs and Crime, n.d.). Official corruption and government participation make it exponentially challenging to apprehend traffickers, especially when officials are involved in trafficking efforts. According to the Department of State's Trafficking in Persons (TIP) Report 2020, they reported on a corruption case in Colombia:

> In 2019, in a case dating back to 2014, authorities convicted one complicit official for the sex trafficking of a 14-year-old girl. [Colombian] Officials from the inspector general's office noted judicial leniency towards public officials involved in trafficking crimes.
>
> (Colombia—United States Department of State, 2020)

An excerpt from the Department of State, Office to Monitor and Combat Trafficking in Persons, 2020 Trafficking in Persons report:

Afghanistan

Most Afghan trafficking victims are children forced to work in carpet making, brick kilns, domestic servitude, commercial sex, begging, poppy cultivation and harvesting, salt mining, transnational drug smuggling, and truck driving. Some Afghan families force their children into labor with physical violence or knowingly sell their children into sex trafficking, including bacha bazı. Opium-farming families sometimes sell their children to settle debts with opium traffickers, and some drug-addicted parents subject their children to sex trafficking or force them into labor, including begging. Some orphanages run by NGOs and overseen by the government subjected children to trafficking . . . In 2019, 165 boys in Logar province reported widespread sexual abuse by government teachers, principals, and local law enforcement, including

> requiring children to have sex in exchange for passing grades and sub-
> jecting boys to sex trafficking in bacha bazı. Some boys who reported
> sexual abuse and sex trafficking to police reported police officers then
> raped them.

Corruption within government agencies results in failure to investigate cases, failure to prosecute traffickers and slaveholders, and governments receiving bribes to withhold information. Victims who frequently see traffickers bribe officials, see officials partaking in trafficking, or see women used as a payment in kind are much less likely to trust government or immigration officials. The corrupt relationship between the traffickers and government officials allows human trafficking to remain a high-profit, low-risk interaction (Polaris, 2020). Trafficking situations not only happen within the context of corruption, but political instability exacerbates this relationship and strains development initiatives. The cost of police officers, training, prosecution services, criminal courts, welfare and social costs for victims, public and mental health costs, and a plethora of other resources are directed toward combating trafficking and victims, which may delay the promotion of other development and societal initiatives (United Nations Office on Drugs and Crime, 2008).

In conflict areas, it is not unusual for military personnel or peacekeeping troops to have inappropriate relationships with women trafficked for sexual exploitation. The Department of State's Trafficking in Persons (TIP) Report 2020 identified exploitation facilitated by UN peacekeepers over twelve years:

> Between 2007 and 2019, the UN received 1,033 allegations of sexual
> exploitation and abuse, including instances of sex trafficking, by UN
> peacekeeping mission members. During the 13-year stabilization mis-
> sion in Haiti, peacekeepers allegedly coerced women and girls into sex
> in exchange for necessities such as food. Reports implicate UN person-
> nel from 13 countries.
>
> (United States Department of State, 2020)

In some instances, brothels were operating so close to US military bases that allegations were made that the army was operating its own houses of prostitution. It has even been alleged that the army has protected establishments where women trafficked for sexual exploitation have been housed and "employed." Further investigations insisted that they did not find any substance to the claim that US troops were protecting or facilitating activity at local brothels. The report stated concerns with the army's relationship to these establishments and that signs of trafficking had been ignored (Fisanick, p. 100). The same investigation also determined that women working in these establishments were victims of trafficking. It was also concluded that victims had suffered physical abuse, and their identity documentation, such as passports and visas, had been confiscated.

In regions where civil wars and corruption are prevalent, too many children are forced to work as child soldiers. These children are often orphaned by war, abducted, or forced to leave their families to fight. While some children are forced to fight, others may have joined the conflict in return for food, vengeance for relatives that have been killed, or because they believe the armed forces are their best chance at survival (Bleasdale, 2013). In many cases, these children may be as young as six or seven years old and may not comprehend the actions they are forced to take. Child soldiers may act as cooks, guards, messengers, porters, servants, wives, sex slaves, and spies. They may also be forced to participate in direct conflict, ordered to walk into minefields ahead of other soldiers, and used in suicide missions. Child soldiers who survive the conflict are likely to experience deep psychological trauma far after the conflict ends.

Climate Change and Deforestation

An enormous amount of resources and attention put on the relationship between impoverished communities and human trafficking, much less is spent on the impacts of climate change. Climate Change increases human insecurity in a region by way of intense natural disasters that strain overall livelihoods. Unexpected natural disasters in areas where communities do not have the resources to cope result in an influx of climate migrants. Climate migration may also increase in surrounding areas where resource-based livelihoods are prevalent, such as rising sea levels or warming ocean waters (International Organization for Migration, 2016).

Verité, a nonprofit working to empower laborers, conducted a case study on the intersection of environmental degradation and human trafficking in the Kachin region of Myanmar. Their study illustrates their findings of forced labor, exploitive work, and child labor by interviewing eighteen banana plantation workers on nine banana plantations. The report notes the banana plantation creates "vulnerabilities for local communities due to associated deforestation, land conflict, and the unregulated use of pesticides." While the sample size may not reflect national-level data, more resources must be allocated to understanding the intersection of environmental degradation and human trafficking. In turn, academics, nonprofits, and private-sector groups need to inform policymakers and lawmakers by disseminating prescient research and analysis and creating applicable laws to improve livelihoods.

In 2020 alone, intense flooding in Western and Central Africa impacted 1.7 million people through the destruction of goods, crops, and fields and exacerbated already food insecure areas (United Nations Office for the Coordination of Humanitarian Affairs, 2020a). In Southeast Asia, Super Typhoon Goni made rainfall in the Philippines. With winds that neared 225 kph and gusts of 280 kph, Filipino water systems, agriculture and food systems, and infrastructure were severely impacted (International Federation of Red Cross and Red Crescent Societies, 2020). In Central America, over 2.5 million people were impacted by Hurricane Eta through rains and flooding that left thousands of communities in rubble with heightened food insecurity (United Nations Office for the Coordination of Humanitarian Affairs, 2020b). The World Bank estimates by 2050, "Sub-Saharan Africa, South Asia, and Latin America could see more than 140 million people move within their countries' borders" due to the impacts of climate change (The World Bank, 2021a). Without any money or specialized skills and with limited access to employment, climate migrants become susceptible to human trafficking.

Many rural communities and migrants rely on forests to support their livelihood. Large-scale agribusiness in banana, coffee, or palm oil plantations has facilitated deforestation through illegal logging and clearance of land to develop new plantations. When land is precious, human trafficking is more prevalent because of the need for cheap labor. Agricultural and plantation workers are vulnerable to trafficking because of the nature of work, the difficulty of enforcing labor standards, and quota-based work systems. Many rural and indigenous communities in Southeast Asia, Sub-Saharan Africa, and South America depend on small-scale agriculture for income and food security. When large-scale agribusinesses such as banana and palm oil plantations destroy their livelihoods, migrants and rural workers who lack other options remain in sectors that result in environmental degradation, forest loss, and poor working conditions (Verité Inc., 2020b).

Consumerism and Supply Chain Management

As the world population increases, so too does consumption. The majority of the world's largest economies are corporations, not governments, and corporate influence is unquestionably prominent in our lives. The current economic climate involving constant consumption and overwhelming corporate control creates an idyllic setting for traffickers to prey on the world's poorest and most vulnerable populations. With the consumption growth, there is often a parallel growth in demand for cheap labor and cheap products. Agricultural products like palm oil, among other precious resources, have been known to host forced laborers in their supply chains. Palm oil, a global agricultural product, is used in more than 50 percent of consumer goods, including lipsticks, soaps, oil-based products, and biofuels (Rainforest Action Network, 2018). To keep costs low for consumers, companies may force laborers to harvest palm oil through tactics like debt bondage. Because the harvest of palm oil seeds is several steps away from the final consumer good, ensuring the supply chain is free from forced labor is a tenuous job.

Consumers may not be aware they contribute indirectly to slave labor by purchasing products several steps up the supply chain. When supply chains are not readily monitored and contain multiple production levels, it becomes more difficult to identify victims in labor trafficking situations. In recent years, several countries, including the United Kingdom in 2015 and Australia in 2018, have passed their Modern Slavery Acts. Both countries' Modern Slavery Acts have identified the need for supply chain transparency in legislation and have employed enforcement mechanisms to check on businesses. On the consumer side, one can be confident that they are not supporting slave labor or human trafficking if the products they purchase are certified fair trade or slave labor free. Images such as the one that follows are sometimes used to alert consumers of fair trade or slave-labor-free products.

Gender Inequality and Sexism

While poverty and economics are significant causes of human trafficking, they do not fully explain the frequency of trafficking in women and girls. In these cases, gender inequality is also an important issue. "Violence against women and girls makes its hideous imprint on every continent, country, and culture," said United Nations Secretary-General Ban Ki-moon (2007). Gender inequality has saturated human trafficking statistics, as women and girls are disproportionately affected by modern slavery. According to the International Labour Organization, 71 percent of the overall total, or nearly 28.7 million women and girls, are victims of modern slavery practices (International Labour Organization, 2017). Women in much of the world lack full support for fundamental functions of daily life. As Antonio Gutuerres notes,

> Women and girls already account for more than 70 percent of detected human trafficking victims, and today are among the hardest hit by the pandemic. With previous downturns showing that women face a harder time getting paid jobs back in the aftermath of a crisis, vigilance is especially important at this time.
>
> (Gutuerres, 2020)

In 2016, an estimated 16 million people were in forced-labor situations, comprised of 9.2 million (57.6 percent) women and 6.8 million (42.4 percent) men. Types of forced labor included domestic workers, construction, agriculture, and fishing, among others. Women and girls are disproportionately represented in other forms of trafficking, such as forced marriage and sexual exploitation. Forced marriage may arise through deception from family members, cultural tradition, emotional and psychological blackmail, physical abuse, or even death. Nearly 15.4 million people lived in a forced marriage in 2016, with 88 percent of victims being women and girls (International Labor Organization, 2017, p. 11). Women face cultural and social barriers that impede their participation in political life, and in many nations, women are not considered equal to men under the law. Because of this, many women and girls, especially in vulnerable communities, may not have access to litigation services they desire and remain in the marriage out of fear and lack of opportunity. Effective policy and legislation to combat human trafficking must reflect gender inequality while prioritizing women's high-risk profiles.

Technology

In the twenty-first century, new technologies are harnessed to complete a plethora of tasks. From ordering takeout to translating documents, there has been a surge of information technology systems that have worked to make our lives easier, yet this has also hindered and advanced anti–human trafficking initiatives.

The intersection of information technologies, social media, and human trafficking has given traffickers a whole new platform to exploit, coerce, and sell victims. From posting on Facebook of high earning potential to communicating through WhatsApp of opportunities, traffickers are innovative and will use technology services to their advantage (Polaris, 2018). In the United States, out of the 543 active criminal sex trafficking cases in 2017, 7.6% (35) of the internet-based commercial sex cases involved Facebook, 6.3% (29) were posted on Craigslist.com, and 331 (72.3%) of cases involved advertisements posted on Backpage.com (Feehs & Richmond, 2017). Besides social media platforms, traffickers may also use financial systems to support their endeavors. Wiring money to separate bank accounts, using their victims' resources to destroy their credit, and forcing their victims to take out large loans to pay for their recruitment fees are among several ways traffickers utilize financial systems. With little money or support to leave a trafficking situation, many victims are unable to escape.

Tech Against Trafficking

One coalition, Tech Against Trafficking, is a collaborative network including AT&T, Amazon, Microsoft Corporation, BT, and Salesforce.org that work with "civil society, law enforcement, academia, technologists, and survivors to advance and scale the use of technology to prevent, disrupt, and reduce human trafficking and increase and expand survivors' access to resources." Tech Against trafficking does this by developing a coalition of antislavery experts, researching human trafficking issues, testing current technologies' success, and creating innovative solutions.

Technology has undoubtedly aided traffickers, but coalitions of technology companies, government agencies, and several nonprofits have been working with information technology systems and communities to prevent and eradicate human trafficking. Data trends and mapping, awareness-raising and education, and payment security, among other types of intervention, are commonly used to identify cases of human trafficking and deter potential trafficking situations (OSCE, 2020). Stop the Traffik, a nonprofit based in the UK, uses an intelligence-based approach to identify hotspots and show trends of trafficking to collect data that will be used in prevention methods. In collaboration with financial service organizations, law enforcement agencies, businesses, and community members, Stop the Traffik can raise awareness and support resilient initiatives to aid vulnerable communities. From January 2019 to August 2020, Stop the Traffik trained 1,300 people across four countries and nine campaigns and ultimately reached over 1.9 million people (Stop the Traffik, 2020). While Stop the Traffik is just one example of a nonprofit using technology to combat trafficking, other government agencies, financial institutions, and private-sector businesses are also taking measures to identify, deter, and prevent human trafficking.

Future Consideration, Research, and Activism Suggestions

Human trafficking is a multifaceted and complicated issue with several root causes—poverty, lack of education, and gender inequality. While education and adequate livelihood opportunities are ways to help people out of poverty, other social, cultural, and geographic considerations may also hinder progress. We must assess human trafficking holistically with a human rights–centered approach to prevent and deter future violations.

As consumers, we must be more aware of the products we purchase. We can boycott companies known to support slave labor, and we can seek out certified fair-trade or slave-labor-free products. By doing so, we are not only

Figure 13.2 Tech against trafficking coalition—Theory of progress

standing up for the world's most vulnerable people, but we are also sending a message to corporations—we are telling them that they must be vigilant about the source of their products and supplies.

Addressing one issue associated with human trafficking may create more hindrances, but there is hope. Government action, social and community development, advocacy, and awareness can help promote antitrafficking initiatives and alleviate modern slavery. Educational campaigns, providing countries, communities, and victims with more resources to prevent trafficking, are the first steps in creating a world without slavery.

Discussion Questions

1. How does globalization impact trafficking in persons?
2. How do poverty and lack of opportunity exacerbate human trafficking?
3. How have increased population, migration, and refugees impacted human trafficking?
4. Please explain the relationship between government corruption and political instability with trafficking in persons.
5. What are the impacts of climate change on human trafficking?
6. Discuss the effects of consumerism and resource scarcity and how they influence trafficking in persons.
7. What role does gender inequality play in human trafficking?
8. Why is human trafficking hard to identify within global supply chains?
9. How can technology aid traffickers? How can technology advance antitrafficking initiatives?

References

Annan, K. (2000, December). *UNODC—address by The secretary-general, MR. Kofi Annan, at the*. Retrieved February 23, 2021, from www.unodc.org/unodc/en/about-unodc/speeches/speech_2000-12-12_1.html

Bhoola, U. (2016, September 15). Debt bondage remains the most prevalent form of forced Labour worldwide—New UN report. Retrieved February 27, 2021, from www.ohchr.org/EN/NewsEvents/Pages/DisplayNews.aspx?NewsID=20504

Bleasdale, M. (2013). *Child soldiers*. Retrieved February 27, 2021, from www.hrw.org/topic/childrens-rights/child-soldiers#

Colombia—United States Department of State. (2020, December 1). Retrieved February 27, 2021, from www.state.gov/reports/2020-trafficking-in-persons-report/colombia/

Council on Foreign Relations. (2019a, December 30). *Fleeing home: Refugees and human trafficking*. Retrieved February 27, 2021, from www.cfr.org/blog/fleeing-home-refugees-and-human-trafficking

Council on Foreign Relations. (2019b). *Modern slavery*. Retrieved February 27, 2021, from www.cfr.org/modern-slavery#!/section2/item-5

Feehs, K. E., & Richmond, J. C. (2017). *Federal human trafficking report*. Retrieved from www.traffickingmatters.com/wp-content/uploads/2018/05/2017-Federal-Human-Trafficking-Report-WEB-Low-Res.pdf

Gutuerres, A. (2020, July 30). *World day against trafficking in persons—statements*. Retrieved February 27, 2021, from www.unodc.org/endht/en/statements.html

International Labour Office (ILO). (2017). *Global estimates of modern slavery: Forced labor and forced marriage*. Retrieved from www.ilo.org/wcmsp5/groups/public/@dgreports/@dcomm/documents/publication/wcms_575479.pdf

Impact Report 2019–2020 Stop the Traffik. (2020) Retrieved February 27, 2021, from www.stopthetraffik.org/report/impact-2019-2020/

International Federation of Red Cross and Red Crescent Societies. (2020, December 3). *Philippines: Floods and typhoons 2020 (Typhoon goni) Operation Update Report n° Mdrph041 — Philippines*. Retrieved February 27, 2021, from https://reliefweb.int/report/philippines/philippines-floods-and-typhoons-2020-typhoon-goni-operation-update-report-n

International Labor Organization. (2021). *Forced labour and human trafficking in fisheries (forced labour, modern slavery and human trafficking)*. Retrieved February 23, 2021, from www.ilo.org/global/topics/forced-labour/policy-areas/fisheries/lang--en/index.htm

International Labour Office (ILO). (2017). *Global estimates of modern slavery: Forced labor and forced marriage*. Retrieved from www.ilo.org/wcmsp5/groups/public/@dgreports/@dcomm/documents/publication/wcms_575479.pdf

International Organization for Migration. (2016). *The climate change—Human trafficking nexus*. Retrieved February 27, 2021, from https://publications.iom.int/system/files/pdf/mecc_infosheet_climate_change_nexus.pdf

Katayama, R., & Wadhwa, D. (2019, January 19). *Half of the world's poor live in just 5 countries*. Retrieved February 23, 2021, from https://blogs.worldbank.org/opendata/half-world-s-poor-live-just-5-countries

Lankford, R. D. Jr. (Ed.). (2010). *Slavery today*. Detroit, MI: Greenhaven Press.

OSCE Office of the Special Representative and Coordinator for Combating Trafficking in Human Beings and Tech against Trafficking, Leveraging innovation to fight Trafficking in human beings: A comprehensive analysis of technology tools (2020, May). Retrieved February 27, 2021, from www.osce.org/files/f/documents/9/6/455206_1.pdf

Polaris. (2018, July). *On-ramps, intersections, and exit routes: A roadmap for systems and industries to prevent and disrupt human trafficking*. Retrieved from https://polarisproject.org/wp-content/uploads/2018/08/A-Roadmap-for-Systems-and-Industries-to-Prevent-and-Disrupt-Human-Trafficking-Social-Media.pdf

Polaris. (2020). *Human trafficking*. Retrieved February 27, 2021, from https://humantraffickinghotline.org/type-trafficking/human-trafficking

Rainforest Action Network. (2018, August 27). *Palm oil fact sheet*. Retrieved February 27, 2021, from www.ran.org/palm_oil_fact_sheet/

The Inter-Agency Coordination Group against Trafficking in Persons. (2016, October). *What is the difference between trafficking in persons and smuggling of migrants?* Retrieved from http://icat.network/sites/default/files/publications/documents/UNODC-IB-01-draft4.pdf

The World Bank. (2020). *COVID-19 to add as many as 150 million extreme poor by 2021*. Retrieved February 27, 2021, from https://www.worldbank.org/en/news/press-release/2020/10/07/covid-19-to-add-as-many-as-150-million-extreme-poor-by-2021

The World Bank. (2021a). *Groundswell: Preparing for internal climate migration*. Retrieved February 27, 2021, from www.worldbank.org/en/news/infographic/2018/03/19/groundswell—preparing-for-internal-climate-migration

The World Bank. (2021b). *Poverty overview*. Retrieved February 23, 2021, from www. worldbank.org/en/topic/poverty/overview#1

U.S. Department of Labor. (2019). *Findings on the worst forms of child labor—UZBEKI STAN*. Retrieved February 23, 2021, from www.dol.gov/agencies/ilab/resources/ reports/child-labor/uzbekistan

U.S. Department of Labor. (2020). *2020 list of goods produced by child labor or forced labor*. Retrieved February 23, 2021, from www.dol.gov/sites/dolgov/files/ILAB/child_labor_ reports/tda2019/2020_TVPRA_List_Online_Final.pdf

United Nations. (2020). *Population*. Retrieved February 27, 2021, from www.un.org/en/ sections/issues-depth/population/

United Nations, Department of Social and Economic Affairs. (2018). *Frontier technologies for sustainable development*. Retrieved February 23, 2021, from www.un.org/develop-ment/desa/dpad/wp-content/uploads/sites/45/publication/WESS2018_full_web.pdf

United Nations Office for the Coordination of Humanitarian Affairs. (2020a, September 25). *West and Central Africa: Flooding situation as of 25 September 2020 – NIGER*. Retrieved February 27, 2021, from https://reliefweb.int/report/niger/west-and-central-africa -flooding-situation-25-september-2020

United Nations Office for the Coordination of Humanitarian Affairs. (2020b, November 9). *Latin America & The Caribbean—Weekly Situation Update (2–8 November 2020) as of 9 NOVEMBER 2020—honduras*. Retrieved February 27, 2021, from https://reliefweb.int/ report/honduras/latin-america-caribbean-weekly-situation-update-2–8-november-2020 –9-november-2020

United Nations Office on Drugs and Crime. (2008). *An introduction to human trafficking: Vulnerability, impact and action*. Retrieved from www.unodc.org/documents/human-trafficking/An_Introduction_to_Human_Trafficking_-_Background_Paper.pdf

United Nations Office on Drugs and Crime. (2020). *Human trafficking and migrant smug-gling*. Retrieved February 27, 2021, from www.unodc.org/e4j/en/secondary/human-trafficking-and-migrant-smuggling.html

United Nations Office on Drugs and Crime. (n.d.). *Electronic toolkit chapter 9 prevention of trafficking in persons*. Retrieved February 27, 2021, from www.unodc.org/unodc/en/ human-trafficking/2008/electronic-toolkit/electronic-toolkit-chapter-9-prevention-of-trafficking-in-persons.html

United States Department of State. (2007, June 12). *U.S. Department of State 2007 traffick-ing in persons report – Jamaica*. Retrieved from https://www.refworld.org/docid/467be3 ba23.html

United States Department of State. (2020, June). *Trafficking in persons report 20th edition*. Retrieved from www.state.gov/wp-content/uploads/2020/06/2020-TIP-Report-Com plete-062420-FINAL.pdf

Verité Inc. (2020a, June 18). *Palm oil commodity Atlas research page with a map*. Retrieved February 23, 2021, from www.verite.org/project/palm-oil-3/

Verité Inc. (2020b, August). Exploring Intersections of Trafficking in Persons Vulner-ability and Environmental Degradation in Forestry and Adjacent Sectors. Retrieved from www.verite.org/wp-content/uploads/2020/08/Burma-Case-Studies-Summary-Report-%E2%80%93-Verit%C3%A9-Forestry.pdf

14

THE HUMAN SECURITY FRAMEWORK

A DIFFERENT APPROACH TO PREVENTING AND COMBATTING HUMAN TRAFFICKING

LAURA GOODING AND LYNSIE CLOTT

Chapter Learning Objectives

- Understand the origins of the traditional realist security approach and the human security approach and the differences between them.
- Define human security and name the three fundamental freedoms associated with it.
- Explain the four analytical principles of human security and how they apply to human trafficking.
- Understand why and how human trafficking is a human security threat.
- Learn the three primary realist security policy responses to human trafficking and how these responses differ from a human security approach.
- Describe the added value of a human security approach to trafficking over traditional realist security.
- List concrete human security recommendations to address human trafficking.

DOI: 10.4324/9781003124672-17

Overview of Security Studies Frameworks
Realism and the Traditional Security Approach

Among international relations theories, realism remains one of the most dominant frameworks both in and out of the classroom. Realism is still widely accepted and utilized among governments and foreign officials, and as a result, understanding this framework is critical for understanding modern international policy and debates. The modern realist security paradigm refers to a concept of security that grew out of the mid-20th century after the failure of international cooperation following the First World War, the collapse of the League of Nations, and the outbreak of World War II. Realist security views the international system through an anarchical lens and sees the nation state as the primary actor. Because the international arena is anarchical, states prioritize their own interests in international relations, always focusing on maintaining their own power. In realism, states can never be sure of other states' intentions, and therefore, external threats from beyond a state's borders are the primary concern. The focus and subject of protection is the nation-state itself rather than the people that make up the nation state. Under this framework, it is presumed that if the state is secure, so too are its citizens (Ionescu, 2007, p. 218). While realism has historically reigned as the dominant theoretical framework in security studies, other non-traditional security frameworks—specifically human security—have gained traction among many international affairs programs, scholars, and practitioners.

The Origins of the Human Security Approach

Human security originated from international actors recognizing that not all citizens enjoy security in realist or state-centric security policies. The nation-state alone is incapable of guaranteeing protection from the wide range of globalized threats and often fails to respect human rights of all its citizens (Ionescu, 2007, pp. 220–221). In 1992, United Nations (UN) Secretary General Boutros Boutros-Ghali and expert human rights practitioners called for the development and use of a "bottom-up" security framework that would better address the types of severe, pervasive, and chronic threats many individuals around the world face by using a multidimensional and collaborative approach. Two years later, human security was first articulated by the UN Development Program in its 1994 Human Development Report with the purpose of expanding security frameworks beyond traditional or state-centric security and shift the focus from the nation-state to the individual (Tadjbakhsh & Chenoy, 2007, pp. 9–38).

At this point, human security was in its infancy. There was no consensus on a precise definition, only broad elements that could be generally agreed upon. Today, practitioners, activists, and policy makers agree on many foundational elements of the human security framework, but its definition and analytical tools remain contested. Broadly speaking, human security approaches work to combat insecurities, which can be defined as any legitimate concerns or threat to people in their everyday lives and the ways in which they view their security. The primary disagreements in human security focus on the issue of breadth, as a person may perceive security as protection from poverty, unemployment, disease, crime, hunger, armed conflict, political repression, and environmental dangers or any other threat that prevents them from enjoying freedom from fear, freedom from want, and freedom to live in dignity (Tadjbakhsh & Chenoy, 2007, pp. 39–57). According to Friman and Reich (2007), the fact that human security came out of the policy community instead of the academic one explains the lack of rigorous analytical precision and consistency (Friman & Reich, 2007, p. 138). Scholars have since joined the debate in an effort to elicit clarity and build consensus.

Exploring the Human Security Approach

The United Nations Commission on Human Security definition of human security:

> to protect the vital core of all human lives in ways that enhance human freedoms and human fulfilment. . . . It means protecting people from critical (severe) and pervasive (widespread) threats and situations. It means using processes that build on people's strengths and aspirations. It means creating political, social, environmental, economic, military and cultural systems that together give people the building blocks of survival, livelihood and dignity.
>
> (Commission on Human Security, 2003, p. 4)

The fundamental freedoms stated in this definition are freedom from fear, freedom from want, and freedom to live in dignity. In regard to human trafficking or any human security threat, obstruction of these freedoms is both a contributing factor and a result. Freedom from fear refers to threats such as terrorism, conflict, and violence, along with the measures designed to protect civilian populations from direct violence, famine, and disease as a result of these threats. Its sentiments are also captured in the global political commitment of "responsibility to protect," an international norm adopted unanimously by the UN in 2005 that aims to protect populations from genocide, war crimes, crimes against humanity and ethnic cleansing. Freedom-from-want issues are the complex socioeconomic and political vulnerabilities such as extreme poverty, hunger, high unemployment, infant mortality, disease epidemics, limited access to potable water, and urban overcrowding issues. While these threats are broad, they are also a very destructive force. The meaning of freedom to live in dignity is less clear than the first two freedoms, mainly due to its breadth and amorphous structure. It stresses the importance of rule of law or ensuring civil and political human rights to all (Friman & Reich, 2007, pp. 139–140).

The 1994 UN *Human Development Report* categorized the primary threats to human security into economic, food, health, environmental, personal, community, and political insecurity (Table 14.1). This framework is a helpful starting point when applying the human security framework to real-world security issues. A paradigm shift to a more human security focused strategy is needed because these types of threats transcend national borders, weaken the national security of all nation-states, and ultimately challenge our ability to protect people globally.

When it comes to international affairs, there are three disciplinary silos in which practitioners, policy makers, and scholars primarily operate: national security, human rights, and development. According to the UN Commission, the human security approach was created to be inherently interdisciplinary—it attempts to incorporate the "human elements" of these three silos into one approach. In addition, human security recognizes the importance of collaborating with civil society actors in the protection of individuals.

Following these goals, human security is identified by the following four analytical principles: (1) people centered, (2) comprehensive, (3) context specific, and (4) prevention oriented (UN Human Security Unit, 2016). The people-centered focus is human security's essence and where it deviates most from realist security. By placing the individual instead of the nation-state at the center of analysis, human security is concerned with:

Table 14.1   Types of human insecurities and possible root causes

Type of Insecurity	Root Causes
Economic Insecurity	Persistent poverty, unemployment, lack of access to credit and other economic opportunities
Food Insecurity	Hunger, famine, sudden rise in food prices
Health Insecurity	Epidemics, malnutrition, poor sanitation, lack of access to basic health care
Environmental Insecurity	Environmental degradation, resource depletion, natural disasters
Personal Insecurity	Physical violence in all its forms, human trafficking, child labor
Community Insecurity	Interethnic, religious and other identity-based tensions, crime, terrorism
Political Insecurity	Political repression, human rights violations, lack of rule of law and justice

Source: United Nations Human Security Unit, 2016

[. . .] how people live and breathe in a society, how freely they exercise their many choices, how much access they have to market and other social opportunities- and whether they live in conflict or in peace. Human security [. . .] allows us to focus on the protection and the security of the human individual and the community rather than on the state and its territorial integrity.

(Ionescu, 2007, pp. 220–221)

The comprehensive aspect of human security indicates that it aims to tackle the full range of insecurities that individuals face, drifting away from a focus exclusively on violent conflicts to a more holistic and multisectoral approach that creates solutions for both the short and long term. Context-specific approaches seek to account for local, regional, national, and international factors that might be affecting security. Contextualization acknowledges that security threats vary across communities and that a one-size-fits-all policy will never be effective broadly. The prevention-oriented principle of human security seeks to address root causes of war, conflict, terrorism, and violence, specifically extreme poverty, discrimination, and civil and political oppression. These create unstable environments and vulnerability among people. It is in these respects that human security is significant in the fight against trafficking in persons (Ionescu, 2007, pp. 220–221). A human security framework is the best approach for prioritizing and producing effective policies to protect vulnerable populations from the risk of being trafficked.

Realist Security Model as the Primary Lens for Human Trafficking

Since realist security is still the dominant framework, it has significantly shaped current human trafficking policy. The government's antitrafficking response is primarily "a criminal justice type that focuses on prohibition (criminalizing) and control (securitization)" (Ionescu, 2007, p. 216).

In the first study of its kind, all printed articles from 2000 to 2005 on human trafficking from major media sources in the United States (*New York Times* and *Washington Post*), United Kingdom (*Times of London* and *Guardian*), and Canada (*Toronto Star* and *Globe and Mail*) were compiled and analyzed for various content. When reviewing mentioned causes of human trafficking stated in these articles, the results exposed the realist security influence (Brysk & Choi-Fitzpatrick, 2012, pp. 54–55).

The most commonly mentioned set of causes, cited in 40 percent of the articles, was criminal activity, including forms of force, fraud, or coercion. Trafficking activity perpetrated by organized crime networks was mentioned specifically in 26 percent of the articles. The next most cited causes were poverty and lack of economic opportunities (13 percent), war and political violence (9 percent), corruption by government officials (8.5 percent), and the selling of victims by family members (7.5 percent). The ranking of causes provides support for the hypothesis that the dominant narrative when discussing the causes of trafficking has been the "crime frame."

(Brysk & Choi-Fitzpatrick, 2012, p. 62)

The study revealed several additional key findings: (1) media coverage of human trafficking increased dramatically after 2002; (2) media focused on sex trafficking significantly more than any other type of trafficking; and (3) media sources for the articles were almost entirely from government and law enforcement officials who framed the problem as a result of organized crime and recommended enhanced law enforcement, legal measures, and assistance for victims (Brysk & Choi-Fitzpatrick, 2012, pp. 67–68).

Another study that utilized interviews with human trafficking advocates in the U.S. on news articles surrounding human trafficking found that media portrayal of trafficking often only focuses on parts of the story, usually the more sensationalized parts, and that "this may encourage public support for simplistic solutions to human trafficking that do not properly address the multiple systems and complexities of the problem, such as cycles of poverty and abuse that may limit access to resources, opportunities, and education" (Houston-Kolnik et al., 2020, pp. 1115–1116).

The most discernable evidence, though, that realist security is the primary lens through which policymakers understand and address human trafficking is evident in the three popularized policy responses: (1) securitizing borders to prevent illegal migration, (2) targeting organized crime, and (3) addressing prostitution. The realist security approach relies heavily on the immigration and criminal justice systems as "front-line" entities responsible for protecting U.S. citizens from dangerous foreigners and criminals that could exacerbate the threat of human trafficking.

Securitizing Borders to Prevent Illegal Migration

Globalization and neoliberal economic policies have resulted in poor socio-economic and health outcomes for many people across the world, especially those residing in the Global South. Such policies have resulted in extreme poverty, inequality, discrimination, high rates of unemployment, destabilized governments and economies, crime, and the deprioritization of education for women and girls. These are known as "push factors," and they motivate individuals to relocate in search of a better life for themselves. Migrants flow to more developed nations, usually those that have benefited from globalization, where they have greater opportunities, real or perceived. These opportunities are commonly referred to as "pull factors." Because traffickers target people who are in desperate situations, particularly those seeking employment, migrants and potential migrants are particularly vulnerable to the predation of human traffickers. This is especially true if they are in close proximity to a destination country and lax border control, because traffickers can make higher profits in these areas. The conundrum for most Western developed nations is how to exploit the economic perks associated with the free trade of goods, jobs, and money across borders while restricting the movement of people (Ionescu, 2007, p. 211).

While the realist security lens acknowledges that push and pull factors drive the supply and demand of trafficked persons, its policy solutions almost exclusively include measures that (1) reinforce border security, (2) tighten visa policies, (3) reduce the number of visas, and (4) increase the penalties against foreign visitors and workers caught breaking the law (Brysk & Choi-Fitzpatrick, 2012, pp. 89–90). These policy responses are not surprising since traditional security assumes that migrants inherently represent a national threat and that human trafficking is a transnational crime that states must confront by enforcing stricter immigration laws and border controls. There is also the potential for politicians to use the threat of human trafficking as a guise to propose and enact restrictive immigration legislation motivated by xenophobia. Destination countries' restrictive immigration policies coupled with strict border control lead to higher rates of human trafficking. If governments limit legal and safe avenues for a healthy flow of migration, desperate people

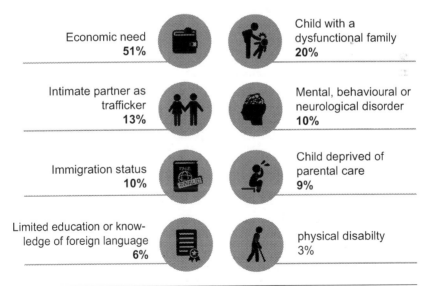

Economic need **51%**		Child with a dysfunctional family **20%**	
Intimate partner as trafficker **13%**		Mental, behavioural or neurological disorder **10%**	
Immigration status **10%**		Child deprived of parental care **9%**	
Limited education or knowledge of foreign language **6%**		physical disabilty **3%**	

Figure 14.1   Factors that human traffickers take advantage of when targeting victims

Source: Based on UN Global Trafficking in Persons Cases 2020

are forced to use illegal methods of migrating, putting them into the dangerous hands of smugglers and traffickers.

Dissimilar to the traditional security approach, a human security approach to human trafficking would be: (1) people centered, (2) comprehensive, (3) context specific, and (4) prevention oriented. A government using this approach would collaborate with multiple stakeholders from various sectors including civil society actors to ensure that the protection of individuals is prioritized over the state and to better understand and address the complexities of the push and pull factors of trafficking persons into and/or out of their borders. This approach would lead to the creation of a people-centered preventive measure rather than a reactionary policy on migration.

Since human security merges the three international affairs silos of national security, human rights, and development, policy recommendations regarding migration would advise governments of human trafficking destination countries to enact clear and consistent border control measures in tandem with increasing access to employment and guest worker visa programs and the number of visas issued. Other human security recommendations advise governments to meet with neighboring destination and transit countries' officials to devise context-specific measures that better address underlying push and pull factors.

When the U.S. government enacted the Trafficking Victims Protection Act (TVPA) in 2000, many human rights activists and human security practitioners viewed it as indicative that our government turned towards and possibly even embraced a human security approach to human trafficking. TVPA calls for many "victim-centered" provisions such as:

1. enhanced criminal penalties for traffickers and trafficking-related offenses
2. prohibition of charging and prosecuting survivors of trafficking who committed illegal acts as a consequence of being trafficked
3. increased protections for child victims of human trafficking
4. access to federal benefits and services
5. temporary or permanent residence in the U.S. for survivors and their families through a T Visa with the condition that they assist law enforcement and district attorneys with investigation and prosecution of their traffickers
6. preventive efforts to reduce the demand and vulnerability to trafficking predictors (ex. human trafficking education programs and public awareness campaigns)

Authors Brysk and Choi-Fitzpatrick (2012) are not convinced that TVPA represents an honest shift to a human security approach. They highlight contraction between the U.S. government's official discourse on human trafficking being a human rights violation and its subsequent policy actions. The authors proceed with a critical analysis of the TVPA and whether its provisions truly align with the human rights or human security approach:

But the review of core provisions of the TVPA raise questions of the extent to which the Act represents a progressive departure from the more typical security-oriented response to trafficking . . . In the United States, the language of "human rights" and "human rights violations" is usually reserved for discussions of other states. [. . .] the government's construction of trafficking as externally driven and ignores how the physical and psychological integrity of international "others" has too often been sacrificed in the name of US security.

(Brysk & Choi-Fitzpatrick, 2012, pp. 86–87)

Under the TVPA, the federal government is required to prioritize the prosecution of trafficking offenses and the protection, not punishment, of victims who committed criminal acts while being trafficked. For foreign-born victims, these crimes usually involve illegal or undocumented entry into the U.S. As mentioned, the protections afforded to foreign victims include the T Visa, work authorization, and access to federal social service benefits such as Temporary Assistance for Needy Families (TANF), Medicaid, Supplemental Nutrition Assistance Program (SNAP), and Women Infants and Children (WIC). However, these protections are contingent on the individual's willingness to assist in every reasonable way in the investigation and prosecution of their trafficking, with the exception of those under the age of 18. In the years following the passage of TVPA in 2000, foreign-born survivors who did not want to cooperate with law enforcement due to circumstances such as fear of retaliation from traffickers faced detention and deportation.

In the last few years of the Obama administration, federal law enforcement (FBI) and national security (Homeland Security) agencies abandoned the requirement that foreign-born survivors cooperate with law enforcement to receive any protections or assistance. This practice demonstrated an honest effort on the part of the U.S. government to be victim centered and signaled a genuine shift toward embracing the human security approach. A reauthorization of TVPA expanded on its recommended prevention and protection strategies to include education and income-generating programs. In addition, the Justice for Victims of Trafficking Act was passed in 2015 and included the creation of a survivor-led U.S. Advisory Council on Human Trafficking. The adoption of TVPA, its reauthorizations, and recent use of victim-centered practices among federal agents clearly demonstrated the U.S. government's desire and intentions to embrace a more victim-centered approach.

President Trump demonstrated his commitment to a more realist security approach by way of his executive orders on immigration and human trafficking. He prioritized strict immigration and border control, as well as prosecution, as means of national security, in particular detaining immigrants who under previous administrations would have been released while their cases were being reviewed. Though controversial, this included separating many children from their parents during case processing under a "zero tolerance" immigration policy announced by the Department of Justice in 2018. The Trump administration also promoted a "Remain in Mexico" policy, which sent asylum seekers back across the border into Mexico to await the adjudication of their cases. In 2020, President Trump signed an executive order on the anniversary of the TVPA designating additional funding toward the prosecution of traffickers; however, antitrafficking practitioners know that an immigration and prosecution focus only exacerbates sex- and labor-exploitive cases involving foreign-born victims. It discourages them from seeking help for fear of legal punishment and their traffickers' ability to retaliate against them if they do seek help.

The traditional realist security approach's concentration on eliminating external threats is partially to blame for the U.S. government's slow response to recognize, accept, and react to cases of localized and interstate domestic minor sex trafficking (DMST). According to research by the Polaris Project, the majority of identified trafficking victims in the U.S. are children (Polaris, 2019). DMST is not a new threat, but the government only recently turned its attention and resources to addressing it. Due to its contradiction to the realist security mindset, acknowledging that internal threats are a primary human trafficking danger to minors was likely difficult for many policy makers who are accustomed to thinking in a realist framework.

Targeting Human Trafficking Organized Criminal Networks

The second of the three popularized policy responses to human trafficking under the realist security paradigm is overemphasizing its connection to organized crime and targeting these criminal networks as a means to curtail human trafficking.

Human trafficking was officially established as an organized crime threat by the UN Convention Against Transnational Organized Crime (UNCTOC) in 2000, which defined an organized criminal group as:

> a structured group of three or more persons, existing for a period of time and acting in concert with the aim of committing one or more serious crimes . . . in order to obtain, directly or indirectly, a financial or other material benefit.
>
> (UNODC, 2000, Article 2a)

U.S. and international policies that sprang out of the UNCTOC focus on creating and implementing stricter anticrime legislation aimed at dismantling organized criminal networks with centralized and hierarchical structure. Under the UN Trafficking Protocol that came out of the UNCTOC in 2000, state parties are required to fulfill measures meant to prevent, detect, and punish trafficking in persons. These included:

1. criminalizing trafficking under domestic law
2. strengthening border control agencies
3. providing training to law enforcement and immigration authorities to better intercept organized criminal activities
4. ensuring that travel or identity documents issued by the state are secure and not easily altered or replicated(UNODC, 2000, Articles 5–12)

The consequence of attaching the Trafficking Protocol to the UNCTOC is that human trafficking is often viewed as primarily an organized criminal activity under international law, shifting the focus away from protecting victims and toward law enforcement. Under international human rights law, states are obliged to ensure their citizens are empowered to exercise and enjoy the full spectrum of human rights. Viewing human trafficking through the lens of criminal activity fails to take into account the structural factors that lead to victim's vulnerability and susception to trafficking in the first place, resulting in less effective antitrafficking policies overall.

With regard to protecting and assisting human trafficking survivors, the Trafficking Protocol serves as a guide by providing suggestions to state parties. This open-ended structure affords states discretion in fulfilling rights and crafting victim-centered measures, which has become a major source of criticism among human security specialists (Brysk & Choi-Fitzpatrick, 2012, pp. 91–92). For example, the Trafficking Protocol states:

> Each party shall *consider* implementing measures to provide for the physical, psychological and social recovery of victims of trafficking, such as housing, counseling, medical assistance, and employment and training opportunities.
> (UNODC, 2000, Article 6, Section III, emphasis mine)

This lack of a prioritization of trafficked individuals' human rights demonstrates what the realist security framework is missing and what human security can add to anti–human trafficking efforts. Since human security integrates all three international affairs silos, it does not advocate for abandoning measures that curb organized crime. Combatting organized crime is an important piece of the complex puzzle that is eliminating human trafficking. However, the problem with the realist security approach is its overemphasis on targeting organized crime. This leads to the prioritization of high-profile crackdowns against major trafficking networks, the investigations of which are time consuming and expensive. Law enforcement agencies are pressured to prosecute human trafficking cases successfully to demonstrate their progress toward eliminating trafficking, which can result in cherry-picking cases that are easier to prosecute. Additionally, the focus on organized crime specifically diverts attention and funds away from prevention strategies and policies that aim to reduce the demand and supply of vulnerable people to be trafficked. It also ignores other actors who facilitate trafficking or are traffickers such as family members, friends, family farms, domestic and international companies (in agriculture, construction, textiles, etc.), restaurants and hotels, employment recruitment agencies, UN peacekeepers and military personnel, law enforcement and/or border control officers, individual pimp/madam traffickers, and families who have private domestic servants.

The unintended consequences of focusing so heavily on fighting organized crime networks are the development of new routes, driving operations underground, displacing sex trafficking from large to small cities and rural towns, and shifting operations from clubs to private apartments/homes and from the street to the dark net (Friman & Reich, 2007, p. 148). Human trafficking is a lucrative business, one that criminals won't give up so easily—in 2014, the International Labour Organization (ILO) estimated that human trafficking generates $150 billion (USD) annually in illegal profits (ILO, 2012). In order to keep up operations, traffickers are evolving, becoming increasingly sophisticated at evading detection or leaving insufficient evidence behind for successful prosecution. Law enforcement has to consistently work to catch up to the evolving operations of the traffickers. It is especially difficult for law enforcement to seize a well-organized trafficking group that has versatile operations and uses advanced technology to communicate and coordinate. But while technology facilitates traffickers' criminal enterprises, it could also soon be their downfall. The U.S. government and law enforcement agencies have been facilitating partnerships with technology experts and companies to outsmart traffickers. These collaborations have yielded technology that has aided law

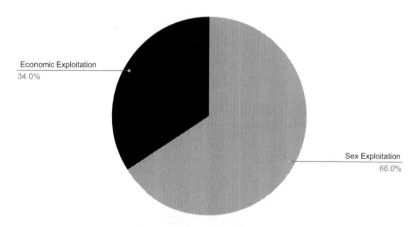

Figure 14.2   ILO estimates of human trafficking profits by sector

enforcement in taking down interstate pimp/madam trafficking rings by helping to target the traffickers rather than targeting and arresting trafficking victims in raids or sting operations.

Debating, Legislating, and Enforcing Prostitution Laws
The last of the three popularized policy responses to human trafficking under the realist security paradigm is overfixation on combatting prostitution as a means to end human trafficking. The result is in an ongoing debate about the nature of prostitution and how to legislate and enforce prostitution laws as a means to curb human trafficking.

While prostitution is closely connected to human trafficking, conflating the two is inaccurate. Recall, trafficking in persons requires elements of force, fraud, or coercion. If a person is engaging in a commercial sex act without the presence of one of these three elements, it is prostitution. That being said, there have been many cases in which a person enters the commercial sex industry in prostitution and later experiences force, fraud, or coercion, at which point, they become a trafficking victim.

Prostitution has been heavily analyzed by scholars, feminists, activists, and policy makers. The primary debate revolves around whether prostitution and the commercial sex industry should be legalized or not. While many have joined these deliberations, the main policy options lack intricacy or precision. The three formulaic policy options consistently presented are: (1) implement a complete moratorium on prostitution and stigmatize the commercial sex industry, as the United States has done, (2) legalize and regulate the industry, like the Netherlands and Germany, or (3) decriminalize the solicitation of prostitution but not the purchase of sex or management of sex, thereby targeting clients instead of sex workers, like Sweden did 15 years ago.

These three models have been adopted by many other countries. A nation's decision on which policy would be most effective should be influenced by careful analysis of the push and pull factors within the region, its geographical positioning, the commercial sex industry market flow in the region, and various laws and policies of its neighbors. Far more often, though, policy decisions are drawn from the nation's political stances towards commercial sex, women's rights, and, for more developing countries, their level of reliance on

Table 14.2 The Three Dominant Policy Responses

Models	Selling Sex	Buying Sex	Organizing Sex
Prohibition	Illegal	Illegal	Illegal
Legalization	Legal	Legal	Legal
Neoabolitionism	Legal	Illegal	Illegal

U.S. foreign aid. Through the TIP Report, the U.S. government is able to withhold foreign aid from countries who legalize and/or are explicitly permissive of prostitution. This incentivizes more countries to adopt strict laws criminalizing the commercial sex industry. As countries have since followed suit, adopting one of these three policies, the fierce battle to prove which model is superior at eliminating human trafficking has taken center stage.

The problem with the first policy option, prohibition, is that it has failed to prevent or even curb human trafficking up to this point. In fact, the unintended consequences of such aggressive criminalization are driving prostitution deeper underground and making it more dangerous for victims. In 2019 alone, the National Human Trafficking Hotline identified 22,326 individual survivors of human trafficking. Due to the nature of the crime, this number is very likely only a small portion of the actual number of victims in the U.S. each year. In addition, criminalizing prostitution makes life more difficult for survivors. Arrest records make it harder for sex workers to find alternative employment or take advantage of social services that could help them exit the industry, and the looming threat of incarceration makes it riskier for workers to report violence and abuse from clients, managers, or even law enforcement (Yale Global Health Justice Partnership, 2020).

Following the second policy path of legalization has also proven to be ineffective.

A study published in 2012 used UNDOC data for 150 countries to analyze the effect legalization of prostitution has on human trafficking. Cho et al. analyze the legalization of prostitution from an economic perspective, looking at the relationship between the scale effect of legalizing prostitution, which leads to an expansion of the prostitution market and thus an increase in human trafficking, and the substitution effect, which reduces demand for trafficked prostitutes by favoring legal prostitutes already living in the country (Cho et al., 2013). The study found that the scale affect overshadows the substitution effect, with the results demonstrating that, on average, countries with legalized prostitution experience a higher degree of reported human trafficking inflows (Cho et al., 2013) In addition to increasing demand, preexisting trafficking organizations continue to exist deep underground along with illegal sex workers to meet the demand market for cheap sex from those customers who do not wish to pay the high-prices of the "government-regulated" red-light districts (Ionescu, 2007, p. 217).

Sweden's policy of criminalizing the purchasers of commercial sex, known as the Prohibition of Purchase of Sexual Services Act, went into effect January 1, 1999. Upon its decriminalization of prostitution, Sweden was lauded for creating a progressive policy that showed true promise of ending human trafficking and violence against women in the commercial sex industry. For some, the jury is still out on the effectiveness of the Swedish model, while others have noted that it has not moved the needle on reducing human trafficking. Studies have shown that while levels of street sex work declined when the law was introduced, there is no convincing evidence that overall levels of prostitution or human trafficking in Sweden have decreased since 1999 (Levy & Jakobsson, 2014). Other studies have shown that criminalizing the purchase of sex has had a similar effect to criminalizing prostitution, pushing the industry underground and making sex workers engage in higher-risk sexual services due to having less choice of clients and bargaining power with clients who are fearful of arrest (Levy & Jakobsson 2014). Nevertheless, Sweden's approach still receives praise for its efforts to help people in prostitution with an "exit" strategy.

From a human security perspective, it comes as no surprise that none of these "one-size-fits-all" policies have yielded the desired outcomes. Research in this area is limited, as there are few researchers who have committed to sound social research methods in the area of understanding people in prostitution, and even less so on johns or pimps/madams. Psychologist Dr. Melissa Farley led a team of researchers to study the lives of 854 people working in prostitution in nine countries (Canada, Colombia, Germany, Mexico, South Africa, Thailand, Turkey, United States, and Zambia) to better understand their circumstances and how they entered the commercial sex industry. Farley's research identified alarming trends in violence for individuals in prostitution:

- 71% had experienced physical assaults in prostitution
- 62% had been raped in prostitution
- 89% stated that they wished to leave prostitution but did not have other options
- 60% to 90% had been sexually assaulted as children

Farley also points out that women who experienced extreme violence are underrepresented in these studies, resulting in conservative estimates (Farley, 2003, p. 6).

However, not all people in prostitution are or appear to be acting under the threat of force or coercion. This makes it difficult to discern human trafficking from voluntary prostitution, especially from the perspective of law enforcement. This is why law enforcement in the U.S. frequently relies on sting operations. In sting operations, because law enforcement frequently acts as the "john," these operations are inherently biased to target victims. Law enforcement officers hope that during these prostitution "roundups," they are able to identify trafficking victims, who are then offered legal, financial, and social assistance. This ignores the violence and victimization experienced by most in prostitution (Farley, 2003, p. 1). For those who are arrested but not identified as being trafficked (because there is either no or not enough evidence of force, fraud, or coercion), law enforcement operates with the hope that being arrested will "break through" to these women and men in prostitution and set them back on the right path. They are then released back to the world with the same conditions that originally pushed or forced them into prostitution. In most cases, individuals arrested for prostitution are not afforded the same treatment or benefits as trafficking victims. Prostitution exit programs in the U.S. are almost nonexistent, with the exception of a handful of faith-based and civil society organizations distributed unevenly across the country.

A human security approach to understanding the link between human trafficking and prostitution begins with the four principles of human security. It must be (1) people centered, (2) comprehensive; (3) context specific, and (4) prevention oriented. Being primarily people centered, a human security policy response would focus on the physical, psychological, and/or sexual injury perpetrated against the trafficked person, regardless of their immigration or criminal status. Criminal justice and prosecution efforts would target johns and traffickers. Greater efforts to understand the complex and context-specific causes that pushed or forced a person into prostitution would be prioritized. A human security approach aiming to end human trafficking and violence against people in prostitution would highlight and address gender inequality, incest and childhood sexual assault, poverty and homelessness, economic policy, domestic violence, drug and alcohol addiction, demand, and how cultures normalize prostitution and commercial sex.

The focus on debating, legislating, and enforcing laws on prostitution consumes much of the attention, time and effort, resources, and funds, which could be put to better use by:

- Exploring, researching, and creating alternative policy models.
- Researching the link between human trafficking and prostitution, johns, and pimps.
- Stimulating the private sector, like technology companies, to create innovative partnerships, tools, and approaches to reduce demand.
- Investing funds to build up less economically developed communities.
- Increasing funding for more specialized training to identify dysfunctional families and physical and sexual abuse.
- Funding local social service agencies to enhance services and resources available to struggling parents and children.
- Investing in and developing therapeutic foster family systems over group homes.
- Developing exit programs that offer a variety of services and empowerment measures like providing skill building, mental and emotional support, employment, and financial aid to make exiting "the life" a viable option.

The Insufficiency of a Realist Security Approach to Human Trafficking

Human trafficking is a global human rights challenge that is best addressed through the expansion of rights and protections geared toward the empowerment of women, children, and vulnerable populations. It is also a global human development challenge that must be approached through policies and development programs that target structures that exacerbate poverty, inequality, displacement of people, and other conditions that prevent people in source countries from enjoying the full range of human security through freedom from want and freedom to live in dignity.

International organizations and agencies such as the United Nations Office on Drugs and Crime, the International Office on Migration, the U.S. Department of State, and the European Union all argue in favor of multifaceted and integrated responses to prevent, protect, and prosecute human traffickers. They have vocally advocated for the principles of freedom from fear and freedom from want. However, in practice, policy and enforcement responses are still rooted in realist security. Prevention efforts that do get proposed and employed are insufficient to address underlying push and pull factors. They also often overlook critical and effective prevention mechanisms like education programs, support for economic development, or programs aimed at enhancing gender equality (Friman & Reich, 2007, p. 146).

With regard to prevention and protection efforts, realist security has failed to understand the complexity of labor and sexual exploitation cases and to evaluate them within the context of economic, sociocultural, political, and international influences. It does not account for the fact that many trafficking victims are hesitant to identify themselves as such because they have fled from worse conditions, including environmental devastation, armed conflict, and chronic and severe socioeconomic or political threats. Some victims do receive an exploitive level of payment for their labor in wealthier cities, regions, or countries, which can be preferable to the conditions they left. These cases are very difficult and frustrating for law enforcement and civil society actors to detect and assist; often, victims do not want to report their situations or cooperate for fear of deportation or losing what little income they do receive from their traffickers (Ionescu, 2007, pp. 218–219). Some human trafficking experts and law enforcement officers believe that this form of victimization may be more common than deception or forced labor, especially among foreign-born victims.

Sadly, the realist security approach has limited human trafficking prevention responses to curtailing immigration, organized crime, and prostitution. The consequences of this narrower scope mean that realist security has failed to adequately ensure individuals' rights and well-being. Policy options are not people centered or rights focused, and are, therefore, ineffective approaches for eliminating human trafficking. If the U.S. and international communities are going to effectively prevent and combat human trafficking, then human trafficking must be framed and broadly perceived as, first and foremost, a human rights violation. The development of responses that embrace the human security framework and follow its four principles is key. There must be increased collaboration and dedication to researching complex and interacting conditions of vulnerability and creating policy outcome indicators to denote progress in order to ensure security and protection for those most at risk (Clark, 2003, p. 260).

The Added Value of the Human Security Approach to Human Trafficking
Individual security and national security should be congruent with our values and commitment to human rights and development. Human security is the only security framework to incorporate all three international affairs silos in order to ensure freedoms, rights, and dignity. If the goal is to collectively eliminate human trafficking, there is an acute need for the U.S. government and the global community to shift their analyses of human trafficking and their approaches to policy responses. The human security approach recognizes that the answer resides in the empowerment of vulnerable people by providing services and socioeconomic support without any strings attached (Ionescu, 2007, pp. 218–219). Security studies and policy both benefit from the interdisciplinary, comprehensive, and context-specific principles of human security. This approach is capable of capturing and accounting for a variety of variables and the ways in which they interact.

Critics of human security disparage the approach for being too imprecise and broad in scope, making it impractical for policymakers. However, its breadth and interdisciplinary nature is a source of strength when studying and designing effective policies and implementation protocols. Human security enables policymakers and practitioners to analyze and design tailored measures that are more responsive to the various forms of human trafficking and survivors' needs. Policy responses for labor trafficking of foreign-born male adults should be different from cases involving the commercial sex exploitation of a domestic transgender minor. The debate on immigration, organized crime, and prostitution paralyzes progress on human trafficking. Scholars and practitioners point to human security as the best route to avoid these rhetoric and policy pitfalls. Human security has become a rallying cry, uniting diverse entities on a number of threats including human trafficking (Friman & Reich, 2007, p. 153).

Recommendations and Conclusion
Human security specialists use the four principles as an analytical tool to understand threats like human trafficking and to design appropriate policy measures to address and eliminate the threat. While there is no human

security prescriptive formula that can be implemented to magically eradicate human trafficking, what human security does provide is a framework for guiding our analysis and policy responses while accounting for context (geography, demographics, economy and politics of the regions, available actors, root causes, etc.). Governments should invest in human security research institutes and provide incentives for researchers to focus on human trafficking through grant programs. In addition, governments should invest in human trafficking institutes that use integrative research methods, advise policy makers, and provide advice or direct assistance to survivors. There are a few of these institutes in the U.S., usually tied to a university; however, they are underfunded.

The recommendations that follow are not intended to discredit or criticize current ongoing efforts. Instead, they are meant to serve as building blocks to help policy makers evaluate the comprehensiveness of current approaches and provoke the types of thought and discussions necessary for a security paradigm shift.

The recommended ***People-Centered*** responses include but are not limited to:

- Identify and research the vulnerable populations (runaway or street youth, abused children, unemployed parents, children, single mothers, rejected LGBT youth, undereducated women, etc.)
- Involve the affected populations and community(ies) when gathering data on needs/vulnerabilities and capacities of the affected.
- Identify how root causes of human trafficking impact individuals.
- Develop empowerment strategies based on capacities needed. Do not make their decisions for them; instead, provide them with support and allow them to make educated choices.
- Strengthen the resilience of individuals and communities.
- Develop open labor and migration policies that would allow migrants to gain an income that ensures the survival and security of their families.
- Convince destination countries to steer clear of focusing on prosecution of migrant or prostitute/sex worker strategies as these are very harmful.

The recommended ***Comprehensive*** responses include but are not limited to:

- Holistic analysis of human trafficking as a threat.
- Wide-spectrum consideration of human trafficking threats and vulnerabilities within and across communities (local, national, regional, and international factors).
- Cross-community involvement of all stakeholders such as government development agencies, private sector, employers' and workers' organizations, and the target populations are necessary to provide access to comprehensive protection and assistance programs.

- Comprehensive development of a strategy that addresses both the supply and demand sides of trafficking.
- Monetary support for local coalitions in urban and rural areas, not just in the largest metropolitan cities.
- In source countries, effective polices that address and alleviate poverty, unemployment, and discrimination as well as ensure equal opportunity and access to education and vocational training.

The recommended *Context-Specific* responses include but are not limited to:

- Ensure that human trafficking analysis incorporates context-specific local information.
- Include community perception of the threats and vulnerabilities in addition to other qualitative indicators.
- Highlight potential mismatch between domestic and/or international policies and the priority security needs of the affected community(ies).
- Identify gaps in the existing security infrastructure.
- Develop cooperative programs within source countries to reduce the flow of migration and subsequently the pool of vulnerable people upon whom traffickers can prey.

The recommended *Prevention-Oriented* responses include but are not limited to:

- Identify root causes of human trafficking including structural violence and the push and pull factors.
- Identify the primary protection and empowerment gaps so as to develop sustainable solutions.
- Prioritize trafficking prevention over reactive policy measures to combat trafficking.
- Cease and desist government actions and policies to prevent human trafficking that impede migratory freedom or freedom to travel or infringe on protections for refugees in destination countries.
- Focus on empowerment measures that build upon local capacities (UN Human Security Unit, 2009, p. 15).

Human security is the best approach to eliminating human trafficking because it combines and builds on the strengths of national security, human rights, and human development approaches. Its principles are clear and provide scholars and practitioners with guidelines for studying and responding to human trafficking. Human security is a comprehensive people-centered framework that aims to address structural causes of human trafficking through context-specific preventive and protective policies developed by multiple stakeholders—including those it proposes to protect. Prevention policy goals transcend tackling immigration and organized crime, and protection policy would prioritize rescuing victims, not returning them to the same or worse conditions from which they left. Trafficking is a complex issue, and our policy framework needs to be able to navigate that complexity. This is where human security outpaces other security or international affairs approaches. Only an integrated, multilateral, and multidisciplinary perspective of human trafficking enables us to develop the tools and responses necessary to work toward the elimination of trafficking in persons.

Chapter Discussion Questions

1. How is the focus (or subject) of protection in human security different from that in realist security studies?
2. Why is human trafficking considered a human security threat?
3. How can a realist security immigration policy response exacerbate human trafficking and differ from a human security approach?
4. What are the consequences of attaching the Trafficking Protocol to the UN Convention on Transnational Organized Crime? What are the consequences of the realist security approach's overemphasis on targeting organized crime?
5. What are the three common global prostitution policy responses to human trafficking?
6. What are the dangers of governments and law enforcement using a prosecution-focused approach and tactics such as antiprostitution/antitrafficking sting operations?
7. What are some of the human security policy recommendations for addressing human trafficking?

References

Brysk, A., & Choi-Fitzpatrick, A. (2012). *From human trafficking to human rights: Reframing contemporary slavery.* Philadelphia, PA: University of Pennsylvania Press.

Cho, S.-Y., Dreher, A., & Neumayer, E. (2013). Does legalized prostitution increase human trafficking? *World Development, 41,* 67–82. https://doi.org/10.1016/j.worlddev.2012.05.023.

Clark, M. (2003). Trafficking in persons: An issue of human security. *Journal of Human Development, 4*(2), 247–263.

Commission on Human Security. (2003). *Human security now.* Retrieved from https://reliefweb.int/sites/reliefweb.int/files/resources/91BAEEDBA50C6907C1256D19006A9353-chs-security-may03.pdf

Farley, M. (2003). Prostitution and the invisibility of harm. *Women & Therapy, 26*(3–4): 247–280.

Friman, R., & Reich, S. (2007). *Human trafficking, human security, and the Balkans*. Pittsburgh, PA: University of Pittsburgh Press.

Houston-Kolnik, J. D., Soibatian, C., & Shattell, M. M. (2020). Advocates' experiences with media and the impact of media on human trafficking advocacy. *Journal of Interpersonal Violence, 35*(5–6), 1108–1132.

International Labor Organization. (2012). *ILO global estimate of forced labor 2012: Results and methodology*. Retrieved from www.ilo.org/wcmsp5/groups/public/—ed_norm/—declaration/documents/publication/wcms_182004.pdf

Ionescu, M. (2007). A human security approach to anti-trafficking policies in the EU: Tackling the structural sources of vulnerability [Doctoral dissertation].

Levy, J., & Jakobsson, P. (2014). Sweden's abolitionist discourse and law: Effects on the dynamics of Swedish sex work and on the lives of Sweden's sex workers. *Criminology & Criminal Justice, 14*(5), 593–607. https://doi.org/10.1177/1748895814528926

Polaris. (2019). *2019 data report, the U.S. national human trafficking hotline*. Retrieved from https://polarisproject.org/wp-content/uploads/2019/09/Polaris-2019-US-National-Human-Trafficking-Hotline-Data-Report.pdf

Tadjbakhsh, S., & Chenoy, A. (2007). *Human security: Concepts and implications*. New York: Routledge.

UN Human Security Unit. (2009). Human security in theory and practice: An overview of the human security concept and the United Nations Trust Fund for Human Security. *United Nations Trust Fund for Human Security*. Retrieved from www.un.org/humansecurity/sites/www.un.org.humansecurity/files/human_security_in_theory_and_practice_english.pdf

UN Human Security Unit. (2016). *Human security handbook. United Nations Trust Fund for Human Security*. Retrieved from www.un.org/humansecurity/wp-content/uploads/2017/10/h2.pdf

UN Office on Drugs and Crime. (2000). *UN convention against transnational organized crime and the protocols thereto*. Retrieved from www.unodc.org/documents/treaties/UNTOC/Publications/TOC%20Convention/TOCebook-e.pdf

Yale Global Health Justice Partnership. (2020). *The harmful consequences of sex work criminalization on health and rights*. Retrieved from https://law.yale.edu/sites/default/files/area/center/ghjp/documents/consequences_of_criminalization_v2.pdf

15

TECHNOLOGY AND HUMAN TRAFFICKING

EMILY KENNEDY

Chapter Overview

The purpose of this chapter is to evaluate the human trafficking problem as it represents itself online, with a lens of technology innovation. The chapter will cover the evolving history of sex trafficking online in the United States, how the Internet and technology play a role in both preventing and facilitating human trafficking, common myths around human trafficking that technology can help us understand and dispel, and review the potential opportunities and challenges for artificial intelligence (AI) and related technologies to help accelerate the fight against human trafficking.

Chapter Learning Objectives

- Understand how the Internet plays a role in facilitating modern human trafficking.
- Know the history of how the Internet and technology have been used to both facilitate and prevent human trafficking.
- Be able to dispel commonly-held myths around human trafficking and the Internet.
- Understand the role that AI and the Internet can play in preventing and combating human trafficking as well as the challenges technology brings.
- Be aware of emerging technologies that have the potential to combat human trafficking.

DOI: 10.4324/9781003124672-18

Evolving Platforms Where Victims Are Advertised

In recent years, technology has played an increasing role in the spread of human trafficking as well as the fight against it. This has been especially true for sex trafficking in the United States. The platforms that host this activity are numerous and varied. Contrary to popular belief, the current majority of this activity is not hidden on the dark web or other esoteric websites; hundreds of thousands of sex ads are posted every day in the United States, in plain sight on the public web on many common and easy-to-find classifieds websites (Marinus Analytics, n.d.-b).

Before the Internet's popularity, most traffickers advertised their victims on the streets, often known as "tracks." This provided law enforcement with a physical place to observe and find potential victims. They could do stings on "johns"—those who purchase sex—with police officers posing as prostitutes on the street (Hardesty & D'Auria, 2020) or combat trafficking from the supply side by identifying the victims and traffickers themselves. But since the advent of the Internet, sex advertisement has largely moved online. Lauren Hersh, former prosecutor and chief of the Kings County District Attorney's Office Sex Trafficking Unit, says, "Pimps are turning to the Internet. They're not putting the girls on the street so much" (Kristof, 2012c).

This benefits both at-will sex workers and traffickers alike. It is important to note that not all those working in the sex industry are victims of sex trafficking; the vast majority are at-will sex workers in the industry of their own volition, while a smaller subset are victims of sex trafficking. At-will sex workers benefitted from the migration of sex advertisements to the Internet because it broadened their potential customer base, provided more opportunities to screen customers, and opened up opportunities for online sex work. The move online also benefitted traffickers by making it easier for them to maintain their own anonymity, broaden the customer base to which they would advertise their victims, and evade detection by law enforcement. It became common for traffickers to move their victims across state lines, further frustrating efforts to recover victims (Dickinson & Holmes, 2011). In short, the Internet became a tool for traffickers to expand their reach for advertising and selling while maintaining anonymity and physical security.

The migration to online sex advertisement made law enforcement's job of finding sex traffickers and recovering victims much more difficult. Not only were the victims no longer in plain sight, they were hidden behind a computer screen, with traffickers often managing the ads. Traffickers became harder to find because they would advertise online and frequently travel across cities and states to disorient their victims and make it less likely that they would reach out for help (Polaris, n.d.; Dickinson & Holmes, 2011). There were a number of websites on which this activity grew, but one of the first prominent platforms was Craigslist.

Craigslist

Craigslist was founded by Craig Newmark in 1995 as a way for his community to stay connected for local events (Craigslist, n.d.-a). Craigslist was one of the first well-known online classifieds websites and became incorporated as a for-profit corporation in 1999. Although it was expanded to become a medium for buying and selling, Craigslist prided itself on its "relatively non-commercial nature" (Craigslist, n.d.-b). This is a surprising self-characterization, however, because when Craigslist opened its Erotic Services section—later renamed Adult Services—Craigslist creators found a lucrative niche within their own business. The Erotic Services section became a place where individuals—both at-will sex workers and traffickers—could post advertisements selling sex, and Craigslist would charge a small amount of money for each post. Craigslist's Adult Services section was ultimately shut down voluntarily after accusations that it had become a platform for child sex trafficking; it was one of the first websites of its kind to be associated with sex trafficking. Craigslist was projected to bring in $36 million from these sex ads in just *one* year by the money it made from charging users to post (Stone, 2010).

The shutdown of Craigslist's Adult Services section is one of the first examples of the fluidity of this form of online advertising; after it was closed, according to AIM Group, prostitution ads online decreased by more than 50 percent (Kristof, 2012d). But in the month after the Adult Services section closed, the traffic at Backpage—a similar online classifieds website—increased by half a million visitors. According to Quantcast, a web traffic analysis company, Backpage then became the number-one website in the United States for facilitating escort ads at that time (Stoeffel, 2011). The quick shift from Craigslist to Backpage demonstrated the ability of this activity to easily flow from one place to another; when one site was shut down, many sellers simply moved to other venues.

Although Craigslist was ultimately closed voluntarily, one might wonder why Craigslist could not be prosecuted for facilitating posts that advertise illegal activity. Because of how Section 230 of the Communications Decency Act of 1996 was written at that time, Craigslist, as provider of the advertising service, could not be treated as the publisher or speaker of what its users wrote. The act stated: "No provider or user of an interactive computer service shall be treated as the publisher or speaker of any information provided by another information content provider" (Communications Decency Act of 1996, 1996). These are appropriate protections for online classifieds providers, but they result in a vacuum of accountability for illegal services advertised on the Internet, especially those that exploit the vulnerable. The Communications Decency Act would prove to be controversial and much discussed by experts in the coming years.

Backpage

Backpage—an enterprise owned by Village Voice Media (Kristof, 2012c)—operated under a goal similar to that of Craigslist. On its "About" page on the website, it answered the question of "Why Backpage?" with the response: "Because other people want what you have, and they might have what you want" (Village Voice Media, n.d.). Operating out of Phoenix, AZ, and Dallas, TX, Backpage offered a similar feel to Craigslist of a friendly community website. Backpage tapped into the same lucrative business that Craigslist had found: facilitating escort ads. According to a consulting company at the time, AIM Group, Backpage made more than $22 million per year from its ads for sex (both ads selling the services of at-will sex workers and those selling trafficking victims) (Aim Group, 2010), and in 2012, it hosted about 70 percent of the total online ads for prostitution in the United States (Kristof, 2012d). Backpage ultimately went on to make an estimated $500 million from sex ads since 2004 (Billeaud, 2018). Former prosecutor Lauren Hersh termed Backpage "a great vehicle for pimps trying to sell girls" (Kristof, 2012c). *New York Times* journalist Nicholas Kristof commented on the evolution of Village Voice Media: "Paradoxically, Village Voice began as an alternative newspaper to speak truth to power. It publishes some superb journalism. So it's sad to see it accept business from pimps in the greediest and most depraved kind of exploitation" (Kristof, 2012d).

Trafficking on Backpage was a proven problem, not just an anecdotal one. In March 2012, Kristof reported, "arrests were made in 22 states for trafficking of under-age girls who had been marketed on Backpage" (Kristof, 2012b). As the most popular website for escort ads in the United States at the time—and for the following six years—activity grew immensely on Backpage. Researchers saw potential in the ability to use that activity to help law enforcement find and recover victims of sex trafficking. Research on Backpage and its potential to help law enforcement was begun at a number of universities, including at Carnegie Mellon University in 2011 by researchers in the Dietrich College of Humanities and Social Sciences and the Robotics Institute's Auton Lab, who initially observed hundreds of posts on Backpage per day (Kennedy, 2012). Researchers ultimately spun the work out of the university into the Pittsburgh-based software company Marinus Analytics, which furthered the research to productize AI-based tools to combat human trafficking. As Backpage grew in popularity, escort ad activity boomed accordingly; Marinus Analytics observed as many as 133,000 ads *per month* in the United States in 2018 (Tarinelli, 2018).

In response to Kristof's criticism, the *Village Voice* wrote a piece defending its actions; it also wrote opinion pieces criticizing other efforts to bring awareness to sex trafficking in the United States (Stoeffel, 2012). Writing about a girl who was trafficked on Backpage at the age of 12, Kristof said, "Backpage cooperates with police and tries to screen out ads for underage girls, but that didn't help Brianna" (Kristof, 2012a). He pointed out the fact that despite efforts to quell trafficking, the problem was still real; and Backpage, facilitating 70 percent of U.S. ads for sex (Aim Group, 2012), enabled a major share of the problem (Kristof, 2012a).

How Technology Can Be an Effective Tool to Combat Sex Trafficking
The Challenges of Using the Internet to Combat Human Trafficking
One of the biggest problems stemming from the Internet's role in sex trafficking was the vast firehose of data that it produced, an amount far too large and complex for law enforcement to use effectively to find victims. In the late 2000s, human trafficking detectives had no dedicated investigative software to analyze data for these cases. More savvy detectives would typically try to cobble together various tools such as TinEye (an image search tool), Google Search to look for misspellings or other idiosyncrasies in online ads that might help uncover a trail of activity, and Excel spreadsheets to track data compiled in their investigations. These piecemeal methods proved unable to stand up to the complexity of these cases and the edge afforded to traffickers by the Internet.

Specifically, the ease with which traffickers could remain anonymous—behind a computer screen rather than waiting in a car in eyesight of their victim on the street—made it more difficult for detectives to find them. The sheer volume of the daily ads, from tens to hundreds of thousands of ads per day, made it extremely difficult to identify victims in the data. Many easy-to-use technologies served to help traffickers, such as the ability to buy a cheap burn phone and quickly and conveniently recycle phone numbers used to advertise their victims, further compounding this complexity. Finally, where the Internet made it easier for traffickers to move their victims across city and state lines and easily connect with new potential customers online, it made it harder for detectives to track traffickers across these geographic boundaries.

Software Platforms for Human Trafficking Investigations
In the 2010s, many different organizations developed software platforms to alleviate these challenges. Researchers at Carnegie Mellon University developed and deployed Traffic Jam to law enforcement in 2013, an AI-based software platform for sex trafficking investigations. It utilized a wide variety of AI, from machine learning to image processing. Traffic Jam was then brought to a larger law enforcement user base by software company Marinus Analytics. Traffic Jam's mission was to help law enforcement analyze the hundreds of thousands of online sex ads that occur daily in the United States, Canada, and the United Kingdom to help find and recover victims and dismantle organized criminal networks (Wu, 2020). It was also used by non-profits like the National Center for Missing & Exploited Children (Marinus

Analytics, n.d.-a) to process the approximately 10,000 child sex trafficking reports they receive every year and identify whether any of these children were advertised online for sex. In 2019, Traffic Jam assisted with the identification of 3,800 victims of sex trafficking (Kennedy, 2020; Marinus Analytics, n.d.-b).

Traffic Jam leverages AI to find patterns in the data that aid in victim recovery and help reveal massive organized criminal networks. For example, the tool can identify trafficking rings operating across cities and states and help prioritize leads for critical resource planning. Traffic Jam narrows the scope of relevant information to an amount that is manually digestible by humans so that investigators know what data is important to dig deeper into for their case. It brings to light the most potentially actionable leads for an investigation and often cuts down investigative time from months to days, for a fraction of the cost of a full-time equivalent. In addition to helping find missing kids, Traffic Jam also helps law enforcement identify organized crime groups exploiting dozens or even hundreds of victims. As a result of leads generated using AI-based tools, organized crime rings can be dismantled, such as one that was indicted in early 2019 for trafficking Chinese foreign nationals for sex in 12 U.S. cities and Toronto. The sting operation came from a lead originating in Traffic Jam, and it resulted in the successful takedown of nearly 500 website domains and computer systems that logged more than 30,000 customer phone numbers (Kennedy, 2020; U.S. Attorney's Office District of Oregon, 2019).

In similar fashion, nonprofit organization Thorn released Spotlight in 2014 (Boorse, 2016) to assist law enforcement in finding child sex trafficking victims. Spotlight is a software tool for investigations, deployed in the United States and Canada, and has helped in the identification of an average of 3,700 victims per year (Thorn, n.d.).

Other Notable Technology Efforts to Combat Human Trafficking

There have been numerous other technology tools created to accelerate the fight against human trafficking and assist with prevention and intervention. "Many trafficking victims cannot just pick up the phone and call for help, because of extreme isolation or constant monitoring by their traffickers" (Polaris, 2013) said Bradley Myles, executive director of Polaris. "The ability to send a silent text message could mean the difference between escape and continued exploitation" (Polaris, 2013). In 2013, cloud communications company Twilio partnered with Thorn, the Salesforce Foundation, and Polaris to create the BeFree shortcode project (Thorn, 2014). An SMS text sent to the BeFree shortcode (233733) would be rerouted to the National Human Trafficking Hotline (operated by Polaris). The goal of this was to provide a discreet way for victims to reach out for help without being detected by their traffickers, who would likely monitor their browser history and other online activity. The project estimated that the BeFree short code was able to double the opportunity for victims to ask for help (Thorn, 2014).

Another group focused on preventing human trafficking by intervening at the point of victim grooming. Often, victims are groomed by traffickers—building trust and connection—for months or even years before they are exploited. Polaris identified through a survivor survey that 26 percent of respondents stated they were groomed via social media. Bark is an online monitoring tool for parents designed to help prevent online-based problems by monitoring children's phones for content such as cyberbullying, suicide, depression, violence, and exploitation (Bark, n.d.). Bark also helps address the problem of grooming of children for human trafficking by monitoring their devices for grooming or abuse language, as well as alerting parents when apps known to be more likely to be used for grooming are downloaded (Zapal, 2019). Similar applications to help intervene before vulnerable people are groomed or trafficked continue to be developed.

Dispelling Common Sex Trafficking Myths

Sex trafficking is a hot-button topic, and therefore, there is much conversation amongst politicians, the media, and the public about it, especially with the Internet's increase in popularity since the 2000s. The Internet and technology have both served to amplify facts about sex trafficking as well as disseminate falsehoods; these technologies can serve as powerful tools to help us better understand the problem and disprove myths that often circulate in the public discourse.

Myth #1: The Super Bowl Is the #1 Event for Human Trafficking in the United States

> "The Super Bowl is the greatest show on Earth, but it also has an ugly underbelly. It's commonly known as the single largest human trafficking incident in the United States."—Texas Attorney General Greg Abbott, USA Today, 2011 (Goldberg, 2013)
>
> " . . . the dirty little secret is that the Super Bowl actually is one of the highest levels of human sex trafficking activity of any event in the country."—Sen. John Cornyn (R-Tex.), news conference, Jan. 27, 2015 (Lee, 2015)
>
> "The Super Bowl has become one of the largest venues for sex trafficking in the country."—Sen. Amy Klobuchar (D-Minn.), news release, Jan. 17, 2014 (Lee, 2015)

Beginning around the early 2010s, politicians began to believe that one of our most beloved American pastimes, the Super Bowl, was actually harboring a gritty, terrible secret as the most popular human trafficking event in the U.S.

every year. This was unconscionable and inspired much public outcry by poli-ticians and media, collaborations with the NFL to crack down on this activ-ity, and efforts to legislate policies like the Stop Exploitation Through Trafficking Act (SETT) by Senator Amy Klobuchar and Cindy McCain (Klobuchar, 2013).

This discussion brought the topic of sex trafficking to the forefront of the public's mind and inspired increased action and awareness, but statements about the Super Bowl being the "single largest human trafficking incident" (Goldberg, 2013) were largely based on anecdotal evidence. Researchers from the Carnegie Mellon Auton Lab and Marinus Analytics explain why this is important:

> . . . there has been no discernible evidentiary basis for the claim that the Super Bowl is the biggest day for human trafficking in the United States each year. Support has been largely anecdotal. Many opponents of this belief have pointed out that there is a lack of data to establish the hypothetical connection between the Super Bowl and sex traffick-ing. Relying on hearsay and popular belief for decision-making may result in misappropriation of resources in anti-trafficking efforts. Attempting to alleviate this issue, we propose a data-driven approach to analyzing sex trafficking, especially as it is carried on during—and perhaps in response to—large public events such as the Super Bowl.
>
> (Miller et al., 2016)

These researchers produced a study comparing the Super Bowl to 33 other large public events to determine whether the increase in activity around the Super Bowl was statistically significant compared to other large events. The study analyzed more than 32 million online escort advertisements in the cities where events were located and around the time period that the events took place. The study included the Super Bowl as well as other popular events, such as South by Southwest, the Consumer Electronics Show, and the Ken-tucky Derby (Miller et al., 2016).

While there *was* a statistically significant increase in activity around the Super Bowl, it was not on the magnitude that would have been expected based on the politicians' claims. In addition, the study identified events that did not get the same attention as the Super Bowl to actually have *larger* sta-tistically significant increases in activity—such as the Memorial Day motor-cycle rally in Myrtle Beach and industry conferences. According to NBC News, the "study suggested that an annual Memorial Day weekend gathering in Myrtle Beach, South Carolina, topped the Super Bowl in terms of 'exceed-ance'—the percentage increase from the number of sex-related personals ads expected on a historical basis vs. the number actually recorded surrounding the event" (Saliba & Euronews, 2016).

It is highly important that researchers and experts analyzing this activity pay more attention to the *statistical significance* rather than simple activity totals from one day to the next, as simple totals cannot show how meaningful a conclusion is. Activity totals—e.g., comparing the total number of ads the day *before* an event to the total number of ads *the day of* the event—give a limited view, while statistical significance can tell us how *meaningful*—or outside of normal trends—that increase or decrease in activity is. As Dr. Tom Redman, data quality expert, explains, "Statistical significance helps quantify whether a result is likely due to chance or to some factor of interest" (Gallo, 2016). *Harvard Business Review* elaborates, "When a finding is significant, it simply means you can feel confident that it's real, not that you just got lucky (or unlucky) in choosing the sample" (Gallo, 2016).

Clear knowledge and use of these concepts are crucial to ensuring real impact is made on societal problems. A misunderstanding of how to take a data-driven approach to human trafficking efforts could mean that lawmakers, researchers, law enforcement, and first responders who overcommit resources and attention to the Super Bowl are missing other occurrences of large-scale sex trafficking activity. Since resources are limited for supporting human trafficking investigations and responses, the study suggests that attention brought to human trafficking based on anecdotal evidence is not nearly as useful as data-driven statistics that can help responders understand where best to allocate their resources. As the Carnegie Mellon study states, "Reliance on quantitative evidence accessible through data-driven analysis can inform wise resource allocation, guide good policies, and foster the most meaningful impact" (Miller et al., 2016).

Myth #2: Viral Scandals Bring Awareness to Human Trafficking and Help the Cause

Not only has human trafficking become a household topic, with many churches, schools, and government agencies bringing resources to the issue, it has also gone viral in many anecdotal stories of potential trafficking and scandals of large organizations believed to facilitate trafficking. When working to solve societal problems, impact is just as important as intention. Ensuring statistics are accurate and details behind viral stories are true is crucial to ensuring a positive impact on the cause.

The Internet can be an extremely powerful tool for disseminating fact-based research, creating awareness for human trafficking, and inspiring the next generation of abolitionists, but it can be even more easily used to recklessly share false information. While the general public often sees these stories and scandals as helping the cause by bringing awareness, they can actually be extremely harmful when they spread false information and create more noise for investigators and others doing the real work on the front lines to combat human trafficking. Two specific cases put this fact into clear relief.

The Ikea Kidnapper

In 2017, Diandra Toyos, a mother of three, was browsing an Ikea store with her children when she noticed a middle-aged man watching her children. She continued to observe him and believed he and another man were following her and her children. She found a store employee, and the men stopped following them; soon after, she wrote a Facebook post about this encounter, claiming, "I am also sure that we were the targets of human trafficking" (Earl, 2017). The post rapidly went viral and was shared more than 105,000 times. Although this post brought attention to the problem of human trafficking, it did so with misleading information stemming from this anecdotal story written by the average civilian. As human trafficking expert witness Dr. Kimberly Mehlman-Orozco stated about the incident, "Anything is possible. It's just highly improbable" (Earl, 2017). She went on to say:

> These types of stories perpetuate misinformation, which leads to people being misinformed about how human trafficking happens in real life. It's not like a Hollywood movie. People aren't coming up and kidnapping victims like in the movie *Taken*.
>
> (Earl, 2017)

In reality, trafficking victims are often groomed for *years* by a trafficker before exploitation begins; traffickers are typically on the lookout for vulnerable populations, e.g., children who often run away from home, have already been abused at home, or have been in the foster care system (National Center for Missing & Exploited Children, n.d.; Perna, 2020). As CBS News reported, "Mehlman-Orozco has conducted over 2,000 interviews with human traffickers and victims, and she says she's never heard of a situation where someone was trafficked or kidnapped from a public place like IKEA" (Earl, 2017).

It is crucially important that the information that goes viral—or that is generally shared—about human trafficking is accurate; instead of stoking public fear and panic about very rare instances of trafficking, accurate information will inform people of the most common ways that trafficking takes place and useful tips that readers can apply to their everyday lives to make a difference; not doing so can actually create more problems for victims. Child sex trafficking expert and former U.S. National Human Trafficking Hotline Manager at Polaris Lara Powers explained that the Facebook post:

> . . . so misrepresents the dangers, warning signs and risks associated with sex trafficking that its readers and likers may now try to protect kids by watching for the wrong things in the wrong places. They may miss real sex trafficking as it happens; they may miss the opportunity to

extend a lifeline to child who needs their help. What people *don't understand* about sex trafficking can prove lethal to kids.

(emphasis added) (Powers, 2017)

Ms. Powers went on to give actionable advice about how the public could use accurate online data to their advantage to bring awareness and combat human trafficking:

If you want to protect your children, listen to the messages of those who know this crime best. Pay attention to statistical reports, seek out the interest groups who are working on this issue, look at the evidence presented by survivors. Don't let the understandable sympathy engendered by a scary story blind you to what sex trafficking is really about.

(Powers, 2017)

Similarly, David Finkelhor, Director of the Crimes Against Children Research Center at the University of New Hampshire, explained:

Child abduction rarely occurs in a crowded public venue like that, where help would be easy to muster. [Moreover] most sex-trafficking lures and abductions are of teenagers. Parents should spend their worry time on other perils.

(Skenazy, 2017)

Clearly, it is important to check viral anecdotal stories with the experts and spend time on efforts that bring awareness to accurate information. But what about when the story that goes viral is an accusation against a well-known furniture company? What are the effects of an accusation that completely lacks evidence?

The Wayfair Scandal

In mid-2020, a conspiracy theory went viral on Twitter and other websites claiming that a popular company that sells furniture online, Wayfair, was trafficking children for sex through sale of expensive items like storage cabinets. A number of claims were presented as "evidence," such as the fact that names of the furniture pieces had the same names as children who had gone missing in the United States, that expensive pillows were priced at $10,000 because they were associated with child trafficking, and that if an Internet user were to search the SKU (stock-keeping unit) numbers of Wayfair items in the Russian search engine Yandex, the results would yield pictures of young women, who were presumed to be the victims. The claims went viral online and were further touted by QAnon followers (Brown, 2020; Evon, 2020). Here is an example of one online post that went viral from Twitter user @Bri_taughtyou:

So wayfair has third party vendors that are HUMAN SEX TRAF-
FICKING on their website. There are items like throw pillows,
cabinets etc. priced at 10–20,000 dollars and named after missing girls.
PLEASE BE CAREFUL!!

(Brown, 2020)

As these claims went viral, they were quickly debunked. The names of furniture items corresponding with names of missing children was not surprising;
in the FBI's National Crime Information Center, there were greater than
400,000 entries for missing children in 2019 alone (Evon, 2020). The expensive pillows were overpriced due to a glitch on the website, according to
Wayfair (Spring, 2020). Finally, the curious occurrence of SKU numbers
bringing up photos of young women on Yandex was debunked as being
related to Wayfair trafficking children when it was discovered that any random string of numbers searched in Yandex would bring up the same search
result (Whalen, 2020; Spring, 2020).

Since this incident was such an extreme case of an unproven conspiracy
theory going viral, it spurred the public to talk about human trafficking once
again. But what were the effects? One might assume that "any press is good
press," and even if a theory about sex trafficking is inaccurate, it is benefitting
the cause by bringing more attention to it. This has been proven to be untrue.
After the Wayfair conspiracy began to go viral online, the National Human
Trafficking Hotline, operated by Polaris, became overwhelmed with reports
related to this conspiracy (Polaris, 2020a). Polaris stated:

> While Polaris treats all calls to the Trafficking Hotline seriously, the
> extreme volume of these contacts has made it more difficult for the
> Trafficking Hotline to provide support and attention to others who are
> in need of help . . . none of the reports we have received involving
> Wayfair contained any information beyond what has been widely
> shared online. Nor have any of these reports been made by someone
> who has a specific connection to any alleged missing children.
>
> (Polaris, 2020a)

Polaris also explained that, in addition to "overwhelming services meant for
victims" (Polaris, 2020b), viral and unproven stories like these can also hurt
bystanders and victim survivors when they are involuntarily pulled into situations that do not involve them:

> The Wayfair theory has already resulted in online harassment and pri-
> vacy intrusions of people mistakenly believed to be victims, as well as
> broad sharing of online sexual abuse material of actual victims who
> have not been connected in any way to Wayfair. This harm is real for

survivors who want to maintain their privacy, victims who are being re-exploited by broader distribution of their abuse materials, or bystanders whose lives can be overwhelmed by the actions of potentially well-meaning online communities.

(Polaris, 2020b)

Finally, stories like the Wayfair conspiracy and the viral Ikea post "distract from the more disturbing but simple realities of how sex trafficking actually works, and how we can prevent it" (Polaris, 2020b). Experts and organizations who have worked in this space for many years provide numerous resources and studies on these issues that can actually help the public grow their awareness of human trafficking and are much more useful to a proactive and impactful response to the problem (Polaris, 2020b).

Myth #3: Passing Legislation to Regulate Advertisement Platforms Will Eradicate Sex Trafficking for Good

To understand this myth, we must first better understand Section 230 of the Communications Decency Act, arguably "one of the most important pieces of internet legislation ever created" (Romano, 2018). As was afore-mentioned in the Craigslist case, the key language states that "No provider or user of an interactive computer service shall be treated as the publisher or speaker of any information provided by another information content provider." This has served for years, since the advent of the Internet, as a pro-tection for tech companies and Internet service providers (ISPs)—including social media companies like Twitter and Facebook—by not holding them accountable for the content that is created or posted by third-party users of those platforms. It was thought that these companies should not be held accountable for the behavior of their users and that accountability could make it cost prohibitive for companies to monitor every single piece of activity on their platforms.

When sex trafficking on websites like Craigslist and Backpage was becom-ing much more prominent in the 2010s, lawmakers began pursuing options for holding these websites liable for content posted on online platforms and ISPs that facilitated the exploitation of victims of sex trafficking. In the case of Backpage, it was ultimately proven that the owners of the site not only knew that sex trafficking exploitation was happening via their platform but that they were helping to further facilitate it (Riviera et al., 2017). This was followed shortly by the release of the *I Am Jane Doe* (Mazzio, n.d.) documen-tary, which showed how Backpage was used to exploit minors for sex and argued that the part of Section 230 that gave safe harbor to these websites should be amended. Lawmakers took to a bipartisan effort to legislate accountability for websites that might host any type of sex trafficking activity (Romano, 2018).

These efforts culminated in the ultimate seizure and shut down of Backpage by the United States Department of Justice on April 6, 2018. This caused a massive disruption to the online sex trafficking space, with sex workers and traffickers alike looking for new places to advertise and detectives scrambling to reorient active cases that had been based primarily on Backpage (Oberhaus, 2018). Experts in the online data space saw the Backpage shutdown to be a major disruption but not an end to online sex trafficking. Emily Kennedy, CEO of Marinus Analytics, said in a statement shortly after the seizure of Backpage:

> Because it is a black market, human trafficking is an ever-evolving crime. Traffickers are constantly innovating and—as they have in the past—will move to new websites and platforms where they can publicly advertise, to capitalize on this billion-dollar industry.
>
> (Marinus Analytics, 2018)

Days after the Backpage shutdown, a new bill was signed into law (Allow States and Victims to Fight Online Sex Trafficking Act of 2017, 2018). After years of legislative movement, lawmakers ultimately settled on H.R. 1865, also known as the Allow States and Victims to Fight Online Sex Trafficking (FOSTA) and Stop Enabling Sex Traffickers Act (SESTA), together known as FOSTA-SESTA (Allow States and Victims to Fight Online Sex Trafficking Act of 2017, 2018). It was a combination of multiple pieces of legislation, including the previously mentioned Stop Exploitation Through Trafficking Act (SETT) brought forth by Senator Klobuchar. FOSTA-SESTA stated that platforms and ISPs would not be liable for third-party content on their platforms, *except* in cases of sex trafficking. Specifically, it says:

> (Sec. 2) This bill expresses the sense of Congress that section 230 of the Communications Act of 1934 was not intended to provide legal protection to websites that unlawfully promote and facilitate prostitution and websites that facilitate traffickers in advertising the sale of unlawful sex acts with sex trafficking victims. Section 230 limits the legal liability of interactive computer service providers or users for content they publish that was created by others.
>
> (Sec. 3) The bill amends the federal criminal code to add a new section that imposes penalties—a fine, a prison term of up to 10 years, or both—on a person who, using a facility or means of interstate or foreign commerce, owns, manages, or operates an interactive computer service (or attempts or conspires to do so) to promote or facilitate the prostitution of another person.
>
> (Allow States and Victims to Fight Online Sex
> Trafficking Act of 2017, 2018)

There were immediate concerns about the implications of this change for a number of groups, in particular for sex workers as well as small innovative companies. The concern by sex worker groups was that making it more difficult for them to advertise on online platforms would make it harder to screen potential customers and maintain anonymity as desired and could put their physical safety in jeopardy. There were also concerns that FOSTA-SESTA did not distinguish sex trafficking from at-will sex work and that the two would be conflated and had the potential to put sex workers at risk. One sex worker, Melissa Mariposa, responded to the passage of FOSTA-SESTA by creating the sex worker–run website Red Umbrella Hosting as a replacement for sites like Backpage. She stated:

> If sex workers lose their storefront and safety tools, two things are going to happen. Number one, the predators will come out to play. Number two, prostitution is going to be pushed right back on the street and in hotel bars by women who will no longer want to see internet clientele and would rather take the risks freelancing. This will create more victims than it helps.
>
> (Valens, 2018)

Another major concern about the implications of FOSTA-SESTA was the level of effort that would be required to enforce it. While massive technology companies would likely have the resources to deploy AI-based and manual review processes to monitor the data for potentially exploitative activity, many believed that young startups would not have the resources needed to comply with such a law. Aaron Mackey, staff attorney at the Electronic Frontier Foundation, explained, "It's important to think about what Section 230 does and what it would open up . . . . What I worry about isn't Facebook or Google's ability to comply, but it's what does that mean for the next set of innovators, for people thinking about how to organize online and in different ways" (Quinn, 2017). Not only would these websites need to be able to monitor the activity on their sites, it was also feared that they would need "a 'team of lawyers' with knowledge of all state and federal trafficking laws that could make them subject to lawsuits or criminal prosecutions" (Quinn, 2017).

Despite these concerns, FOSTA-SESTA had bipartisan support, backing from big tech companies like Facebook, IBM, and Oracle (Samuels, 2018), and broad public praise (Portman, 2018). When passed in the Senate in March 2018, it was passed with a vote of 97 to 2, with only one abstention (Allow States and Victims to Fight Online Sex Trafficking Act of 2017, 2018); it was signed into law later that April.

While many companies and their lawyers scrambled to determine the implications of the new law in the following months, lawmakers went on to praise the success of the bill. Lawmakers took to claiming victory in the fight against sex trafficking. Three months after FOSTA-SESTA passed, one of the bill's sponsors, Missouri Representative Ann Wagner, said, "We have shut down nearly 90% of the online sex-trafficking business and ads" (Markowicz, 2019). Tom Dart of Cook County in Illinois, another proponent of the bill, said, "This legislation will give victims and survivors of sex trafficking the justice they deserve from companies that unabashedly destroy lives for financial gain—this is something for which we've long been fighting. We're already seeing significant results from the Senate passage alone" (Dar, 2018).

It took months for the dust to settle before experts could actually measure what the effects of these two massive events in the sex trafficking space had been; it became clear that it had caused a major disruption. Sex ads on websites other than Backpage plummeted immediately, and much of the online space went silent for a few months. But months later, activity began to pick up again. Marinus Analytics identified an estimated 133,000 advertisements posted on Backpage daily in the month *before* it was shut down, and—somewhat surprisingly—activity on other websites *grew* to approximately 146,000 sex ads per day, just six months after the shutdown (Tarinelli, 2018).

This demonstrates the severe whack-a-mole aspect of this problem; even though the biggest website, Backpage, was shutdown, the activity quickly dispersed to other websites, both old and new. Many new websites popped up to capitalize on the billion-dollar opportunity of hosting sex ads online and were not deterred by the new FOSTA-SESTA law. For example, the website CityXGuide was explicitly created to "[take] over from where Backpage left off" (CBS Dallas/Fort Worth, 2020). Its owner, Wilhan Martono, created multiple sites and "allegedly registered the domain names for several of the sites just one day after the FBI shut down Backpage.com," ultimately "[netting] more than $21 million off a suite of illicit websites promoting prostitution and sex trafficking" (CBS Dallas/Fort Worth, 2020). Like its predecessor, CityXGuide was also ultimately seized and shut down by the Department of Homeland Security, and it was identified to have been used to advertise multiple minor victims.

Although there is a fairly low barrier to entry to launch and promote a new website like Backpage or CityXGuide, U.S. Attorneys' offices and federal agencies like DOJ, FBI, and DHS consistently seek to shut them down, demonstrating the ever-evolving and fleeting nature of sex trafficking online (CBS Dallas/Fort Worth, 2020). "As soon as DOJ shut down one despicable site, another popped up to take its place," said U.S. Attorney Erin Nealy Cox. "Like the owners of Backpage, this defendant made millions facilitating the online exploitation of women and children. The Justice Department will not rest until these sites are eliminated and their owners held accountable for their crimes" (CBS Dallas/Fort Worth, 2020).

In response, many of these websites continue to develop new strategies to avoid the plight of Backpage:

Margie Quin, an assistant professor at Cumberland University in Tennessee, said an escort website could start selling ads for the American market after setting up operations overseas in a country that does not work well with the U.S. Such a move could weaken the ability to extract evidence and prosecute a case, said Quin, a former assistant special agent in charge at the Tennessee Bureau of Investigation. As long as demand is still around, the crime will still be committed.

(Tarinelli, 2018)

Although both the shutdown of Backpage and the passage of FOSTA-SESTA received widespread praise from law enforcement, tech companies, and victim advocates like, the move also ultimately made it even harder for law enforcement to find this fragmented activity so they can locate victims (Tarinelli, 2018). This made AI-based tools even more crucial to the human trafficking fight. As Marinus Analytics stated in response to the events: "Websites and platforms will inevitably shift, but our Artificial Intelligence capabilities flexibly adapt to new data sources as they emerge over time. Marinus Analytics maintains our mission to keep law enforcement on the cutting edge with advanced capabilities" (Marinus Analytics, 2018). AI-based software tools like Marinus Analytics' Traffic Jam became even more important because of their ability to aggregate fragmented data into one place and find patterns across differing data sources to help law enforcement locate and recover victims and dismantle organized criminal networks (Tarinelli, 2018).

Future solutions are needed to prevent and identify advertisement of victims online, especially when it comes to international laws and collaboration across multiple countries, as it is extremely easy for platforms to move their servers outside of U.S. jurisdiction and render whatever U.S. laws are passed—like FOSTA-SESTA—moot. In addition, since the online space will always be an evolving space and sites will continue to come up and be taken down, an increased focus is needed on using the data available online to (1) distinguish human trafficking victims from at-will sex workers, (2) analyze that data using AI to find and locate sex trafficking victims, and (3) develop advanced AI to identify more complex groups that operate within the organized crime landscape.

Emerging Challenges to Combating Human Trafficking Online

The Internet and emerging AI technologies provide both increasing challenges and opportunities for solutions to the problem of human trafficking. The Internet has caused human trafficking to be a rapidly evolving space, with new problems and shifts in the landscape popping up frequently. There are also many experts and innovators fighting on the front lines by researching and developing new technology to address these emerging threats.

The Move to Encrypted Apps

In recent years, online exploitation has expanded from publicly available personals and escort advertisements to the extremely private world of encrypted applications, particularly those that are accessible via mobile phone. Traffickers often use apps to groom potential victims—especially minors that tend to frequent new apps—for future exploitation; this grooming can take months or even years. The discussion over the use of these encrypted apps for exploitation has sparked an ongoing debate about the tension between justice and privacy.

Messaging systems—such as Facebook-owned WhatsApp—are among those commonly used by traffickers due to their encryption protection. "Traffickers advertise online, track victims by cellphones and use encrypted messaging systems to communicate with accomplices, experts say, fueling debate between human rights advocates who value protection against authorities concerned that encryption hampers law enforcement and enables criminals" (Wulfhorst, 2017). Law enforcement and prosecutorial experts claim the limits that encryption places on access to data could have distinct negative impacts for victims. Cyrus Vance, New York County District Attorney, explains, "It has in some cases very significantly adversely affected our ability to solve cases and to get justice for victims" (Wulfhorst, 2017).

Conversely, Human Rights Watch Executive Director Ken Roth argues the number of crimes that would be enabled by getting rid of encryption would outweigh the benefit of the crimes that would be solved. He said, "Yes, there are a handful of crimes that are going to be solved . . . but think about the crimes that are going to be committed. There are reams of hackers out there, criminal and governmental. And they're going to win" (Wulfhorst, 2017).

President Obama commented on encryption in 2016, arguing for law enforcement and technology innovators alike to take a nuanced view. He compared the use of encryption in devices now to the balances that the United States has struck with privacy in the past with respect to violent and serious crimes:

> All of us value our privacy, and this is a society that is built on a Constitution and a Bill of Rights and a healthy skepticism about overreaching government power. Before smartphones were invented and to this day, if there is probable cause to think that you have abducted a child, or that you are engaging in a terrorist plot, or you are guilty of some serious crime, law enforcement can appear at your doorstep and say we have a warrant to search your home and they can go into your bedroom and into your bedroom drawers and rifle through your underwear to see if there's any evidence of wrongdoing.
>
> (Constine, 2016)

President Obama then went on to describe his view that an absolutist stance on this matter should not be taken:

> My conclusion so far is that you cannot take an absolutist view on this. So if your argument is strong encryption, no matter what, and we can and should, in fact, create black boxes, then that I think does not strike the kind of balance that we have lived with for 200, 300 years. And it's fetishizing our phones above every other value. And that can't be the right answer.
>
> (Superville, 2016)

Obama went on to explain that an ideal scenario would be to create a key to unlock the encryption that is governed by U.S. law and accessible to the smallest number of people possible in the smallest number of situations possible. In response, California Representative Darrell Issa said, "There's just no way to create a special key for government that couldn't also be taken advantage of by the Russians, the Chinese or others who want access to the sensitive information we all carry in our pockets every day" (Superville, 2016).

This debate is extremely applicable to the dialogue around human trafficking, which is a violent crime itself. The government, its citizens, the technology companies that create these apps, and the legislative bodies that make laws around them must decide whether the ability to intervene in extreme cases of violent crime is worth creating encryption keys, and if so, how those keys would be managed. As it stands now, encryption in apps such as WhatsApp is limiting human trafficking detectives' ability to intervene in cases of exploitation, find evidence of abuse, and prevent recruitment and grooming of vulnerable potential victims. Cross-sector collaboration is crucial to solving this problem in a way that preserves the majority of privacy while also enabling justice to be served to violent offenders.

Increase in Streaming of Child Sexual Abuse Material

Along with the Internet bringing an increase in online ads, it has also provided other methods for exploitation of the vulnerable. In particular, the streaming of child sexual abuse material (CSAM) has exploded in recent years. "Particularly with the advent of live-streaming technology, the Internet is now a convenient tool for abusers, who wish to pursue the gratification they experience from child abuse from the comforts of their own home while avoiding the risk inherent in physically trafficking children" (Buchanan, 2020). These abusers are termed "virtual offenders"; despite the fact that they are not physically abusing a child, they are benefitting from the abuse of a child, and that demand fuels the abuse of more children in the future, typically overseas. "Prosecutors usually charge virtual offenders under federal child pornography statutes, 18 U.S.C. Sections 2251 and 2252. These statutes criminalize the production and receipt, respectively, of child pornography" (Buchanan, 2020).

The streaming of CSAM content is much more difficult to track and prevent than other, more physically present methods of exploitation. "These abuse materials and livestreams are created to satisfy the online demand of child sex offenders who pay for, direct and view the abuse from the comfort of their homes in the U.S., Australia, Canada, UK, and Europe" (Tanagho, n.d.). This content is ephemeral, as livestreamed content is only available while it is live, and then becomes hard—if not impossible—to track. Groups that harbor this content are often on common social media platforms and can be hard to find, as they typically must be infiltrated by undercover officers (Tanagho, n.d.).

There are a number of steps that are needed to ensure an effective response to this problem. Electronic service providers (ESPs) must make it a priority to detect this activity on their platforms, and technology companies must participate in cross-sector collaboration and data sharing. These organizations can benefit from strong partnerships with nongovernmental organizations (NGOs) that can help them identify risk profiles and patterns that may indicate this type of activity is taking place. Finally, since this exploitation is often motivated by greed, money service businesses (MSBs) must be aware of these issues to be able to identify and take action when suspicious transfers of money potentially related to CSAM are detected. Further innovation is needed by researchers and tech companies to develop algorithms that can automatically identify CSAM in images and videos at scale (Tanagho, n.d.).

The Potential of AI to Revolutionize the Human Trafficking Response
Graph Networks to Identify Organized Crime

There are technologies with massive potential to make a game-changing impact on the way we respond to trafficking in the Internet age. Graph databases are a way of organizing data so that patterns can be more quickly and easily connected across millions of datapoints. They also have the potential to help investigators identify large, organized criminal groups in online escort advertisement data. This has historically been a difficult problem (Amazon Science, 2020). As Prem Viswanathan, Data Scientist at Amazon Web Services explains:

> Identifying an ad posted by an organized crime network is challenging. First, most of the ads posted on the Internet don't have structured data. To analyze information effectively, it is necessary to sift through the text of every ad to pull out relevant information like the location, date of posting, images, social media handles and other pertinent information.
>
> (Amazon Science, 2020)

In addition, investigators need to be able to view often-fragmented connections that would reveal a hidden organized crime network in the data. Graph networks—also known as "knowledge graphs"—are critical to help solve this problem. Viswanathan explains how this works in Traffic Jam, the AI-based software for human trafficking investigations:

> Traffic Jam sifts through the information contained in these large number of nodes to uncover suspicious patterns. Consider an example of two ads that have different images, and posted from different locations, but share the same phone number. If you combine text indicators of potential human trafficking to these signals, you arrive at a movement pattern that analysts might identify as problematic, and surface to law enforcement for further review.
>
> (Amazon Science, 2020)

This technology also helps investigators view patterns in the data through a social network analysis lens, highlighting which phone numbers or images are extremely valuable to an investigation: in a case in which you might have hundreds of phone numbers, the ability to do this with the click of a button is game changing. This has huge potential to impact the success of larger investigations involving massive organized crime groups. Marinus Analytics CEO Cara Jones explains the benefits: "Using the knowledge graph and associated sub-graphs, we are now able to capture four times as much information as previously possible. More importantly, we are able to analyze data and identify potential crime groups in real-time, even as new information comes in" (Amazon Science, 2020).

Natural Language Processing and Machine Learning to Improve Survivor Outcomes

Technology innovation is not only useful for investigations; there is also potential for the area of survivor restoration and recovery. Organizations are seeing possibility in natural language processing (NLP) and machine learning (ML) developments to accelerate the capabilities of victim aftercare services. In particular, analysts at McKinsey & Company worked with a survivor aid organization to analyze over 10,000 anonymized survivor support records (McKinsey & Company, n.d.). As McKinsey & Company explains:

> The work included digitally analyzing more than 250,000 services offered to the survivors and some 100,000 paragraphs of case-worker notes. McKinsey experts used a combination of machine learning, natural language processing, and journey analytics mapping to understand the drivers of survivors' recovery and ways to raise the likelihood that they could quickly regain their lives.
>
> (McKinsey & Company, n.d.)

Although the human interaction between a case worker and a survivor cannot be replaced by technology, studying past successful interactions can help organizations better understand best practices that result in optimal outcomes for survivors. In particular, this study identified that

> having case workers meet in person with survivors and initiate support within 30 days improved the chances of successful outcomes by more than 50 percent. The team also found that survivors' accounts of the recovery process, documented through natural language processing, could help determine specific events associated with positive or negative sentiments. Furthermore, the research identified risk factors that could indicate a higher likelihood to drop out or take longer to recover, such as age, risk of losing housing, or risk of harm by perpetrators.
>
> (McKinsey & Company, n.d.)

Analyses such as these highlight the importance of human and AI collaboration. These technologies are not meant to replace the work and expertise of a case worker, but they can amplify the impact each human can have in the life of a survivor. They also help identify best practices across large datasets of interactions and help organizations identify which services are the most impactful, further increasing likelihood of case success (McKinsey & Company, n.d.).

Blockchain to Identify Human Trafficking in Supply Chains

Blockchain is another technology with great potential to disrupt the human trafficking problem. Forced labor is a form of human trafficking that often does not get nearly as much media attention and press coverage as sex trafficking but is actually more prevalent globally. Forced labor is "work that is performed involuntarily and under the menace of any penalty. It refers to situations in which persons are coerced to work through the use of violence or intimidation, or by more subtle means such as manipulated debt, retention of identity papers or threats of denunciation to immigration authorities" (International Labour Organization, n.d.). Where sex trafficking involves an estimated *4.8 million* people, an estimated *24.9 million* people are exploited in forced labor globally (International Labour Organization, n.d.).

When "blockchain" is mentioned, most people think of cryptocurrency, but its capabilities extend far beyond digital currency. "Blockchain is essentially a decentralised, cryptographically secured, immutable database that . . . enables users to make transactions or share data without the need for an intermediary" (Mekong Club, n.d.). This removes the need for centralized organizations—like banks, in the case of cryptocurrency—to moderate, track, and police transfers of money or information. "It is impossible for one party to add information to the chain without the consensus of the group, and all

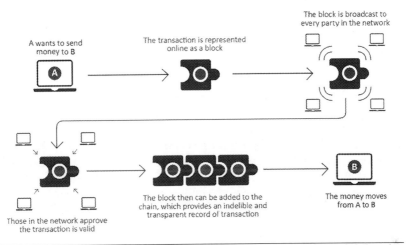

Figure 15.1   Domonstration of how money or data are transferred and recorded through a blockchain

Source: Mekong Club, n.d.

records remain on the blockchain unchanged to be viewed by participants at any time" (Mekong Club, n.d.). These capabilities have huge implications for the future of technology, in an age where "data is the new oil of the digital economy" (Toonders, 2015). Figure 15.1 demonstrates how money or data are transferred and recorded through a blockchain.

This capability of the blockchain to monitor transfers of data with "transparency, trackability, accountability and integrity" (Mekong Club, n.d.) is crucial for solving problems of human trafficking, especially when it comes to forced labor in the supply chain. Supply chains often do not provide clear accountability of what is happening throughout the process; in the case of human trafficking, when humans might be abused in forced labor to create one component of a phone or other item, this ability to track the process in an honest and accountable way is highly important. All parties would have the capability to know where each component in the supply chain comes from and be able to investigate where the component travels through the process if it is believed to be created through forced labor. In addition, "identity documents and employment contracts stored in a format that cannot be changed or accessed for illegitimate purposes provide greater security to those vulnerable to exploitation" (Mekong Club, n.d.).

There are limitations to this technology, such as figuring out how to track products physically that are represented in the blockchain, the logistics and cost of recording this data in the blockchain, the requirements of collaboration among parties for the blockchain to work, and ensuring the data inputted to the blockchain is itself accurate. Private companies, nongovernmental organizations, and international bodies like the United Nations are collaborating on projects to implement blockchain tools, and despite the logistical challenges, it has real potential to create practical solutions to the problem of human trafficking and forced labor globally.

Conclusion

This chapter gave a thorough background of the Internet and technology's roles in both facilitating and preventing modern human trafficking and demonstrated how this history is continuously evolving. It covered a number of common myths around human trafficking and the Internet and gave recommendations for how these myths can be dispelled using data-driven approaches. It explained the role AI can play in the fight against human trafficking and showed specific examples of how emerging technologies are making a specific and tangible impact as well as the potential challenges that technology brings. Socially conscious innovation is extremely important to ensuring that the next generation of AI is able to fight human trafficking effectively and measurably and that we use technology for good to create the change we want to see in the world.

Discussion Questions

1. Do you think additional legislation like FOSTA-SESTA would help or hurt efforts to investigate sex trafficking? What are the pros and cons of trying to approach the problem from a legislative perspective?
2. What are the pros and cons of prioritizing an enforcement or investigative perspective of solving human trafficking (as opposed to legislative or demand-focused approaches)?
3. What are some practical ways that the general public can check facts about human trafficking before disseminating them online?
4. If you were the head of a government agency, what things would you take into account to ensure your agency was effectively using limited resources to address human trafficking? What kinds of data would you want to take into account?
5. There is a tension between justice and privacy when it comes to encryption. If you were in charge of legislation over encryption, would you err on the side of providing limited keys for use in cases of extreme violence? Or would you err on the side of complete encryption and protection of privacy?

References

Aim Group. (2010, October 19). *Backpage replaces Craigslist as prostitution-ad leader.* Retrieved November 17, 2020, from https://web.archive.org/web/20101025083817/http://aimgroup.com/blog/2010/10/19/backpage-replaces-craigslist-as-prostitution-ad-leader/

Aim Group. (2012, February 24). *Sites set combined record for online prostitution-ad revenue.* Retrieved November 17, 2020, from https://web.archive.org/web/20120304042857/http://aimgroup.com/blog/2012/02/24/sites-set-combined-record-for-online-prostitution-ad-revenue/

Allow States and Victims to Fight Online Sex Trafficking Act of 2017, 18 U.S.C. § 1591, 1595, 2421A and Chapter 117 (2018).

Amazon Science. (2020, August 11). *How Marinus analytics uses knowledge graphs powered by Amazon Neptune to combat human trafficking.* Retrieved November 18, 2020, from www.amazon.science/latest-news/how-marinus-analytics-uses-knowledge-graphs-powered-by-aws-neptune-to-combat-human-trafficking

Bark. (n.d.). *About Bark.* Retrieved November 18, 2020, from www.bark.us/about

Billeaud, J. (2018, April 9). *Feds: Backpage.com made $500M from prostitution-related ads.* Retrieved November 23, 2020, from https://apnews.com/article/53c6b38cb0174b5caaa0ce598762511b

Boorse, K. (2016, November 25). *Spotlight helps law enforcement identify victims of sex trafficking faster.* Retrieved November 18, 2020, from www.thorn.org/blog/spotlight-helps-identify-sex-trafficking-victims-faster/

Brown, M. (2020, July 22). *Fact check: Home goods retailer Wayfair is not involved in child sex trafficking.* Retrieved November 18, 2020, from www.usatoday.com/story/news/factcheck/2020/07/22/fact-check-wayfair-not-involved-child-sex-trafficking/5460739002/

Buchanan, Z. (2020, February 21). *Offenders without borders: How technology is globalizing child sex trafficking.* Retrieved November 18, 2020, from www.traffickingmatters.com/offenders-without-borders-how-technology-is-globalizing-child-sex-trafficking/

CBS Dallas/Fort Worth. (2020, June 19). *Prostitution, sex trafficking website that took over for Backpage shut down; owner indicted.* Retrieved November 18, 2020, from https://dfw.cbslocal.com/2020/06/19/prostitution-sex-trafficking-website-backpage-shut-down-owner-indicted/

Communications Decency Act of 1996, 47 U.S. Code § 230. (1996). Retrieved from www.law.cornell.edu/uscode/text/47/230

Constine, J. (2016, March 11). *Obama: 'We don't want government to look into everyone's phones willy-nilly'.* Retrieved November 18, 2020, from https://techcrunch.com/2016/03/11/obama-says-we-dont-want-government-to-look-into-everyones-phones-willy-nilly/?_ga=2.167736382.1896676371.1605135247–1779358488.1605135247

Craigslist. (n.d.-a). *Craigslist: About craig Newmark.* Retrieved November 17, 2020, from https://web.archive.org/web/20120504152907/www.craigslist.org/about/craig_newmark

Craigslist. (n.d.-b). *Craigslist: About factsheet.* Retrieved November 17, 2020, from https://web.archive.org/web/20120504152905/www.craigslist.org/about/factsheet

Dart, T. (2018, March 23). *Sheriff supported anti-sex trafficking bill passes U.S. senate.* Retrieved November 18, 2020, from www.cookcountysheriff.org/sheriff-supported-anti-sex-trafficking-bill-passes-u-s-senate/

Dickinson Goodman, J., & Holmes, M. (2011, October 30). *"Can we use RSS to catch Rapists?" Poster finished!* Retrieved November 17, 2020, from http://jessicadickinsongoodman.com/2011/10/30/can-we-use-rss-to-catch-rapists-poster-finished/

Earl, J. (2017, March 30). *Mom's warning about "human trafficking" at IKEA goes viral; what you need to know.* Retrieved November 18, 2020, from www.cbsnews.com/news/moms-warning-about-human-trafficking-at-ikea-goes-viral/

Evon, D. (2020, July 10). *Is Wayfair trafficking children via overpriced items?* Retrieved November 18, 2020, from www.snopes.com/fact-check/wayfair-trafficking-children/

Gallo, A. (2016, February 16). *A refresher on statistical significance.* Retrieved November 18, 2020, from https://hbr.org/2016/02/a-refresher-on-statistical-significance

Goldberg, E. (2013, February 3). *Super bowl is single largest human trafficking incident in U.S.: Attorney general.* Retrieved November 18, 2020, from www.huffpost.com/entry/super-bowl-sex-trafficking_n_2607871?guccounter=1

Hardesty, G., & D'Auria, R. (2020, January 23). *How a 'John sting' targets the demand side of human sex trafficking.* Retrieved November 18, 2020, from www.police1.com/investigations/articles/how-a-john-sting-targets-the-demand-side-of-human-sex-trafficking-ok78G6yG9UGytZCv/

International Labour Organization. (n.d.). *What is forced labour, modern slavery and human trafficking.* Retrieved November 18, 2020, from www.ilo.org/global/topics/forced-labour/definition/lang--en/index.htm

Kennedy, E. (2012, April). *Predictive patterns of sex trafficking online.* Retrieved November 18, 2020, from http://shelf1.library.cmu.edu/HSS/2012/a1471388.pdf

Kennedy, E. (2020, July 28). *Testimony of Emily Kennedy before United States House of Representatives.* Retrieved November 18, 2020, from www.congress.gov/116/meeting/house/110942/witnesses/HHRG-116-SY21-Wstate-KennedyE-20200728.pdf

Klobuchar, U. (2013, November 19). *Klobuchar, Cornyn, Heitkamp, Kirk introduce bipartisan legislation to crack down on sex trafficking.* Retrieved November 18, 2020, from www.klobuchar.senate.gov/public/index.cfm/2013/11/klobuchar-cornyn-heitkamp-kirk-introduce-bipartisan-legislation-to-crack-down-on-sex-trafficking

Kristof, N. (2012a, April 18). *Not quite a teen, yet sold for sex.* Retrieved November 18, 2020, from www.nytimes.com/2012/04/19/opinion/kristof-not-quite-a-teen-yet-sold-for-sex.html

Kristof, N. (2012b, April 31). *The secret owners behind a prostitution website.* Retrieved November 18, 2020, from https://kristof.blogs.nytimes.com/2012/03/31/the-secret-owners-behind-a-prostitution-website/

Kristof, N. (2012c, January 26). *How pimps use the web to sell girls.* Retrieved November 17, 2020, from www.nytimes.com/2012/01/26/opinion/how-pimps-use-the-web-to-sell-girls.html

Kristof, N. (2012d, March 17). *Where pimps peddle their goods.* Retrieved November 17, 2020, from www.nytimes.com/2012/03/18/opinion/sunday/kristof-where-pimps-peddle-their-goods.html

Lee, M. (2015, January 29). *A bipartisan fail over claims there was a 300 percent increase in 'escort' ads during the Dallas Super Bowl.* Retrieved November 18, 2020, from www.washingtonpost.com/news/fact-checker/wp/2015/01/29/a-bipartisan-fail-over-claims-there-was-a-300-percent-increase-in-escort-ads-during-the-dallas-super-bowl/

Marinus Analytics. (2018, April 9). *Marinus Analytics statement on Backpage.* Retrieved November 18, 2020, from www.marinusanalytics.com/articles/2018/4/9/marinus-analytics-statement-on-backpage

Marinus Analytics. (n.d.-a). *Partnerships.* Retrieved November 18, 2020, from www.marinusanalytics.com/partnerships

Marinus Analytics. (n.d.-b). *Traffic jam.* Retrieved November 18, 2020, from www.marinusanalytics.com/traffic-jam

Markowicz, K. (2019, July 14). *Congress' awful anti-sex-trafficking law has only put sex workers in danger and wasted taxpayer money.* Retrieved November 18, 2020, from www.businessinsider.com/fosta-sesta-anti-sex-trafficking-law-has-been-failure-opinion-2019–7

Mazzio, M. (n.d.). *I am Jane Doe film*. Retrieved November 18, 2020, from www.iamjane doefilm.com/

McKinsey & Company. (n.d.). *Harnessing the power of AI to improve recovery for survivors of human trafficking*. Retrieved November 18, 2020, from www.mckinsey.com/business-functions/mckinsey-analytics/how-we-help-clients/noble-intelligence/harnessing-the-power-of-ai-to-improve-recovery-for-survivors-of-human-trafficking

Mekong Club. (n.d.). *Using blockchain to combat modern slavery*. Retrieved November 18, 2020, from https://themekongclub.org/wp-content/uploads/2018/04/Blockchain-for-Modern-Slavery_For-web.pdf

Miller, K., Kennedy, E., & Dubrawski, A. (2016, February 16). *Do public events affect sex trafficking activity?* Retrieved November 18, 2020, from https://arxiv.org/abs/1602.05048

National Center for Missing & Exploited Children. (n.d.). *Child sex trafficking*. Retrieved November 19, 2020, from www.missingkids.org/theissues/trafficking

Oberhaus, D. (2018, April 6). *The FBI just seized Backpage.com*. Retrieved November 19, 2020, from www.vice.com/en/article/j5avp3/fbi-seized-backpage-sex-trafficking

Perna, B. (2020, February 4). *Grooming in the digital age*. Retrieved November 19, 2020, from www.missingkids.org/blog/2020/grooming-in-the-digital-age

Polaris. (2013, March 28). *Texting increases human trafficking victims' access to help*. Retrieved November 18, 2020, from https://polarisproject.org/press-releases/texting-increases-human-trafficking-victims-access-to-help/?fbclid=IwAR226dxqfWF-b4JDgc-dXn0WXAJ4UuiQgwNKuICTccmy-B1ShNzhlN96vE8

Polaris. (2020a, July 20). *Polaris statement on Wayfair sex trafficking claims*. Retrieved November 18, 2020, from https://polarisproject.org/press-releases/polaris-statement-on-wayfair-sex-trafficking-claims/

Polaris. (2020b, July 22). *How unproven trafficking stories spread online and why stopping them matters*. Retrieved November 18, 2020, from https://polarisproject.org/blog/2020/07/how-unproven-trafficking-stories-spread-online-and-why-stopping-them-matters/

Polaris. (n.d.). *Sex trafficking at truck stops*. Retrieved November 23, 2020, from https://humantraffickinghotline.org/sites/default/files/Sex%20Trafficking%20at%20Truck%20Stops%20AAG.pdf

Portman, R. (2018, March 21). *Anti-trafficking advocates, law enforcement, tech praise senate passage of the stop enabling sex traffickers act*. Retrieved November 18, 2020, from www.portman.senate.gov/newsroom/press-releases/anti-trafficking-advocates-law-enforcement-tech-praise-senate-passage-stop

Powers, L. (2017, April 3). *Op-Ed: Why a mom's Facebook warning about human traffickers hurts sex-trafficked kids*. Retrieved November 18, 2020, from www.latimes.com/opinion/op-ed/la-oe-powers-ikea-mom-sex-trafficking-20170331-story.html

Quinn, M. (2017, September 18). *Tech community fighting online sex trafficking bill over fears it will stifle innovation*. Retrieved November 18, 2020, from www.washingtonexaminer.com/tech-community-fighting-online-sex-trafficking-bill-over-fears-it-will-stifle-innovation

Riviera, G., Jesko, J., Hawkins, S., & Millman, J. (2017, January 13). *Emotional senate hearing finds Backpage.com complicit in underage sex trafficking as victim's families testify*. Retrieved November 18, 2020, from https://abcnews.go.com/US/emotional-senate-hearing-finds-backpage-complicit-underage-sex/story?id=44762342

Romano, A. (2018, April 13). *A new law intended to curb sex trafficking threatens the future of the internet as we know it*. Retrieved November 18, 2020, from www.vox.com/culture/2018/4/13/17172762/fosta-sesta-backpage-230-internet-freedom

Saliba, E., & Euronews. (2016, February 16). *Study takes look at how big events fuel U.S. sex trafficking.* Retrieved November 18, 2020, from www.nbcnews.com/news/us-news/study-takes-new-look-how-big-events-fuel-u-s-n519071

Samuels, B. (2018, April 11). *Trump signs online sex trafficking bill.* Retrieved November 18, 2020, from https://thehill.com/policy/technology/382664-trump-signs-online-sex-trafficking-bill

Skenazy, L. (2017, March 29). *Get a grip, crazy moms: Your kids won't get kidnapped at Ikea.* Retrieved November 18, 2020, from https://nypost.com/2017/03/29/get-a-grip-crazy-moms-your-kids-wont-get-kidnapped-at-ikea/

Spring, M. (2020, July 15). *Wayfair: The false conspiracy about a furniture firm and child trafficking.* Retrieved November 18, 2020, from www.bbc.com/news/world-53416247

Stoeffel, K. (2011, April 26). *Village voice media getting down and dirty with escort ads.* Retrieved November 17, 2020, from https://observer.com/2011/04/village-voice-media-getting-down-and-dirty-with-escort-ads/

Stoeffel, K. (2012, March 27). *The Backpage backlash: Nicholas Kristof on 'egregious capitalism' at the village voice.* Retrieved November 23, 2020, from https://observer.com/2012/03/the-backpage-backlash-nicholas-kristof-on-egregious-capitalism-at-the-village-voice/

Stone, B. (2010, April 26). *Sex ads seen adding revenue to craigslist.* Retrieved November 17, 2020, from www.nytimes.com/2010/04/26/technology/26craigslist.html

Superville, D. (2016, March 11). *Obama says 'dangers are real' in debate over encryption.* Retrieved November 19, 2020, from https://apnews.com/article/40552a43b82446628e9a2a4f2bfde075

Tanagho, J. (n.d.). *Online Sexual Exploitation of Children: Hidden in Plain Sight.* Retrieved November 18, 2020, from www.ijm.org/stories/online-sexual-exploitation-of-children-hidden-in-plain-sight

Tarinelli, R. (2018, November 29). *Online sex ads rebound, months after shutdown of Backpage.* Retrieved November 18, 2020, from https://apnews.com/article/159434f052eb40dd87b9dd9b65da53f5

Thorn. (2014, May 8). *The fight against child sexual exploitation, powered by a text message.* Retrieved November 18, 2020, from www.thorn.org/blog/fight-child-sexual-exploitation-powered-text-message/

Thorn. (n.d.). *Spotlight helps find kids faster.* Retrieved November 18, 2020, from www.thorn.org/spotlight/

Toonders, J. (2015, August 7). *Data is the new oil of the digital economy.* Retrieved November 18, 2020, from www.wired.com/insights/2014/07/data-new-oil-digital-economy/

U.S. Attorney's Office District of Oregon. (2019, January 16). *Nationwide sting operation targets illegal Asian brothels, six indicted for racketeering.* Retrieved November 18, 2020, from www.justice.gov/usao-or/pr/nationwide-sting-operation-targets-illegal-asian-brothels-six-indicted-racketeering

Village Voice Media. (n.d.). *About backpage.com.* Retrieved November 17, 2020, from https://web.archive.org/web/20120504004931/www.backpage.com/classifieds/AboutUs

Valens, A. (2018, April 02). *This sex worker-run site is fighting back against SESTA.* Retrieved November 18, 2020, from www.dailydot.com/irl/sex-worker-sesta-hosting-service/

Whalen, A. (2020, July 10). *Kids shipped in armoires? The person who started the Wayfair conspiracy speaks.* Retrieved November 18, 2020, from www.newsweek.com/wayfair-child-trafficking-conspiracy-theory-cabinets-scandal-1517013

Wu, J. (2020, April 14). *AI is helping us combat the economic problem of human trafficking.* Retrieved November 18, 2020, from www.forbes.com/sites/cognitiveworld/2020/04/14/

ai-is-helping-us-combat-the-economic-problem-of-human-trafficking/?sh=
29215ec3752c

Wulfhorst, E. (2017, April 25). *Technology use by sex traffickers fuels debate between privacy and security*. Retrieved November 18, 2020, from www.reuters.com/article/us-trafficking-conference-technology/technology-use-by-sex-traffickers-fuels-debate-between-privacy-and-security-idUSKBN17R2UI

Zapal, H. (2019, January 11). *National human trafficking awareness day*. Retrieved November 18, 2020, from www.bark.us/blog/bark-supports-national-human-trafficking-awareness-day/

16

THE ROLES AND RESPONSIBILITIES OF US FINANCIAL INSTITUTIONS IN COMBATTING HUMAN TRAFFICKING

MARY ONUFER

Introduction

The ultimate goal of every business is to derive profit from providing goods and services. Unfortunately, the business of human trafficking is a very lucrative enterprise. Individuals who engage in human trafficking do so purely to derive profit. The International Labor Organization reports that globally, human trafficking creates profits of $150 billion per year (ILO, n.d.). The US Treasury Department reports:

> Human trafficking poses a grave threat to the rule of law and endangers the safety and security of citizens in the United States and around the world. In addition to its enormous human cost, human trafficking is estimated to generate billions in illicit revenue each year, making it one of the most profitable crimes in the world. Treasury's 2020 National Strategy for Combating Terrorist and Other Illicit Financing identified money laundering linked to human trafficking as one of the most significant illicit finance threats facing the United States (The US Treasury, n.d.).

Money laundering, by simple definition, is the process by which criminals move large amounts of cash or property through traditional financial systems in ways that hide the true source or destination of the illegally derived funds so that they appear to be legitimate (ACAMS, n.d.c).

DOI: 10.4324/9781003124672-19

Given the risk that the flow of illicit funds from various fraudulent and illegal activities through financial institutions poses to the global and US financial systems, the US government has enacted laws and taken several steps to engage financial institutions as partners in the pursuit of detecting and controlling these crimes. There are specific parameters in regard to the tracking of those funds related to human trafficking. In this chapter we will review the basic tenets of money laundering, The Bank Secrecy Act, the Federal Crimes Enforcement Network (FinCen), and the FinCen Advisories that require financial institutions to "follow the money" in the effort to track, detect, and report the illicit funds generated by traffickers for investigation and prosecution by various law enforcement agencies. We will also discuss the role of compliance and corporate social responsibility in financial institutions in regard to human trafficking.

Chapter Learning Objectives

- Understand the basic tenets of money laundering in general.
- Understand the laws and advisories that define and outline the expectations for financial institutions to track and report red flags of suspected human trafficking financial transactions.
- Analyze the response of financial industries.

Money Laundering

Money laundering can be generally defined as the actions taken by criminals to take illegal profits and make them appear as legitimate funds that they can invest or spend (ACFE, 2020). It is not an activity that only human traffickers participate in, but criminals engaged in illicit activities worldwide are looking to disguise their illegal funds as legitimate. Money laundering is big business. Due to the fact that laundering is a global endeavor where criminals carefully use strategies to avoid tracking and reporting structures, it is a challenge to estimate the exact dollar amount. Using various methods, the United Nations estimates that the amount of money laundered on a global level is between 2% and 5% of the world GDP, a figure that amounts to trillions of dollars. As reported previously, illicit profits from human trafficking are estimated at $150 billion (United Nations, n.d.).

The process of money laundering takes place in three distinct stages with various strategies, all designed to hide the source of the illicit funds and make those funds appear legitimate.

1. Placement—This is the first step in the process where the criminal introduces the cash in the financial system. Criminals are most vulnerable at this point, as the profit is tied directly to the crime. Various methods can be used:

    Smurfing—Breaking up large amounts of cash into smaller amounts under the reportable limit of $10,000
    Smuggling—Taking large amounts of cash outside of the country
    Loan or credit card repayment
    Foreign currency exchanges—changing cash into a foreign currency
    Funneling money through legitimate purchases or gambling
    Blending illegal money with legitimate sale receipts through a cash-based business
    False invoicing through legitimate companies (trade based)

2. Layering—The second step in the process is where the illegal funds are separated and diffused in multiple ways to again hide the source and confuse law enforcement. Different methods are:

    Multiple wire transfers
    Converting to digital currencies and transferred through multiple wallets
    Converting to monetary instruments
    Purchasing of assets
    Loan-back arrangements

3. Integration—The last step in the process is where the money comes back to the criminal from what appears to be legitimate sources with no ties to the original funds such as:

    Real estate investment
    Purchase of securities and investments
    Purchase of high value luxury items(All Banking Alerts, 2018)

The Bank Secrecy Act

The Bank Secrecy Act (BSA) is formally known as The Currency and Foreign Transactions Reporting Act of 1970. It is also referred to as the "anti–money laundering" law (FinCen, n.d.a). In essence the law requires financial institutions to:

- Keep records of cash purchases of negotiable instruments
- File reports of cash transactions exceeding $10,000
- Report suspicious activities that might signify money laundering, tax evasion, or other criminal activities including human trafficking

The act has been amended several times to improve the reach of the law and to increase cooperation between the financial industry and law enforcement to help stem the flow of illegal funds throughout our banking systems. This includes provisions established in the US Patriot Act of 2001. After the Patriot Act, the five pillars for compliance within the industry require:

1. Internal policies that are clearly written in regard to money laundering and procedures put into place to help deal with any type of suspicious activities, including reporting.
2. Establishment of an anti-money laundering (AML) officer within the institution to make sure that internal policies and procedures are clear, in place, and being followed. Depending on the size of the institution, the AML officer may oversee an entire department or may be the only employee dedicated to AML.
3. Training on AML matters is required for employees
4. Customer due diligence (CDD) processes must be exercised in the effort to "know your customer." Each institution must have processes in place to verify the identity of their customers.
5. Independent testing of AML systems in place are necessary and provide an unbiased review of risk and compliance for the institution.(ACAMS, n.d.b)

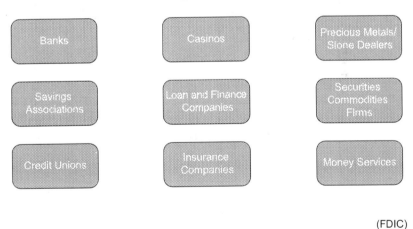

(FDIC)

Figure 16.1   Institutions responsible for compliance under the Bank Secrecy Act

Source: FDIC, n.d.

The US Department of the Treasury and the Financial Crimes Enforcement Network (FinCen)

The Treasury Department is authorized by the BSA to "issue regulations requiring banks and other financial institutions to take a number of precautions against crime" (FinCen, n.d.a). As a bureau of the Treasury Department, FinCen operationalizes the intent and goals set forth in the BSA. FinCen's duties include:

- Issues and interprets regulations authorized by statute;
- Supports and enforces compliance with those regulations;
- Supports, coordinates, and analyzes data regarding compliance examination functions delegated to other federal regulators;
- Manages the collection, processing, storage, dissemination, and protection of data filed under FinCen's reporting requirements;
- Maintains a governmentwide access service to FinCen's data and networks users with overlapping interests;
- Supports law enforcement investigations and prosecutions;
- Synthesizes data to recommend internal and external allocation of resources to areas of greatest financial crime risk;
- Shares information and coordinates with foreign financial intelligence unit (FIU) counterparts on AML/Combatting Finance Terrorism (CFT) efforts; and
- Conducts analysis to support policy makers; law enforcement, regulatory, and intelligence agencies; FIUs; and the financial industry (FinCen, n.d.a).

The establishment of FinCen through the BSA provided a centralized resource for both law enforcement and financial institutions with the intent to increase support and information sharing in the effort to combat money laundering in general and human trafficking specifically. FinCen works in partnership with other financial regulatory agencies that have jurisdiction over the various financial institutions, including the Federal Deposit Insurance Corporation (FDIC), the Office of the Controller of the Currency (OCC), the Federal Reserve, and the Securities and Exchange Commission (SEC). While authorized to enforce compliance, the bureau takes a proactive approach by providing guidance and support to financial institutions. Information and support are provided on how to interpret the statutes and direct efforts toward creating a risk-based approach to protecting the institution and its customers. How much risk is there that illegal funds might be funneled through their accounts? What is the potential that customers may be victims of human traffickers or paying for services offered by them? Compliance for financial institutions is rooted within the five pillars of AML mentioned previously. Institutions that choose to be noncompliant can be charged civilly or criminally, lose their charters, and be assessed large fines and penalties. Foreign financial institutions that do not comply risk receiving fines and penalties and losing their ability to operate in the US. Over the last few years, individual financial officers have also been charged and fined for their deliberate actions to subvert AML requirements at their institutions (NAFCU, n.d.).

In 2014, FinCen issued a specific advisory on human trafficking that provided information to financial institutions on what constituted different forms of human smuggling and trafficking. The advisory outlined red-flag indicators to be recognized and reported on. The advisory was updated in 2018 and 2020. Banks in particular have the opportunity to report on behaviors exhibited in the front lines of their establishments that indicate an individual who may be the victim of a trafficker. It is important to note that FinCen warns that indicators of human trafficking may also be the result of other illegal activity, and institutions are required to do their due diligence in investigating and reporting. In 2018, the advisory was updated to expand the list of red flags.

Table 16.1   FinCen Red Flags

	FinCen Red Flags 2014, 2018
	A third party speaks on behalf of the customer (a third party may insist on being present and/or translating)
	A third party insists on being present for every aspect of the transaction
	A third party attempts to fill out paperwork without consulting the customer
	A third party maintains possession and/or control of all documents or money
	A third party claims to be related to the customer but does not know critical details
	A prospective customer uses or attempts to use third-party identification (of someone who is not present) to open an account
	A third party attempts to open an account for an unqualified minor
	A third party commits acts of physical aggression or intimidation toward the customer

(Continue)

Table 16.1 (Continue)

A customer shows signs of poor hygiene, malnourishment, fatigue, signs of physical and/or sexual abuse, physical restraint, confinement, or torture
A customer shows lack of knowledge of their whereabouts, cannot clarify where they live or where they are staying, or provides scripted, confusing, or inconsistent stories in response to inquiry
Customers frequently appear to move through and transact from different geographic locations in the United States. These transactions can be combined with travel and transactions in and to foreign countries that are significant conduits for human trafficking.
Transactions are inconsistent with a customer's expected activity and/or line of business in an apparent effort to cover trafficking victims' living costs, including housing (e.g., hotel, motel, short-term rentals, or residential accommodations), transportation (e.g., airplane, taxi, limousine, or rideshare services), medical expenses, pharmacies, clothing, grocery stores, and restaurants, to include fast food eateries
A customer frequently makes cash deposits with no Automated Clearing House (ACH) payments
An individual frequently purchases and uses prepaid access cards. A customer's account shares common identifiers, such as a telephone number, email, and social media handle, or address, associated with escort agency websites and commercial sex advertisements
Frequent transactions with online classified sites that are based in foreign jurisdictions
A customer frequently sends or receives funds via cryptocurrency to or from dark-net markets or services known to be associated with illicit activity. This may include services that host advertising

Table 16.1   (Continue)

	content for illicit services or sell illicit content or financial institutions that allow prepaid cards to pay for cryptocurrencies without appropriate risk-mitigation controls
	Frequent transactions using third-party payment processors that conceal the originators and/or beneficiaries of the transactions
	A customer avoids transactions that require identification documents or that trigger reporting requirements

Suspicious Activity Reports (SAR)

When a financial institution suspects that a customer is engaged in illegal activities and/or receives indicators through data collection, they are required to complete an electronic suspicious activity report or SAR. It is expected that the information reported in the SAR has been fully vetted by the institution and provides as much supporting documentation and information as possible to aid law enforcement in the investigation process.

The filing of a SAR is not required to be disclosed to the suspect as otherwise required by the Right to Financial Privacy Act and may be shared with law enforcement and other financial institutions. SAR filings are "protected by the safe harbor provisions applicable to both voluntary and mandatory suspicious activity reporting by financial institutions" (FinCen, n.d.b). Law enforcement may use the information reported in the SAR for investigation but not prosecution. In other words, a SAR cannot be subpoenaed. It is expected that law enforcement will investigate and collect evidence to prepare for arrest and prosecution of the actor(s). Disclosure of SAR information outside of law enforcement and financial institutions is considered illegal (FinCen, n.d.b).

In 2018, human trafficking received its own checkbox on the SAR form, which was a victory for activists and financial institutions. Previously a bank filing a SAR for suspected human trafficking would select "other" and then write a description. This small checkbox took an act of Congress but now facilitates timely investigation of suspected trafficking activity. SARS are required to be filed within 30 days of the suspicious activity, but many times, discovery may lead to further investigation of past events to be included as well.

Once a SAR is filed, it is vetted by a FinCen fusion center, where it is evaluated and then distributed to the proper agencies for investigation. Agencies that might be involved in the investigation of suspected trafficking activities are Health and Human Services (HHS), Homeland Security, IRS, FBI, and other appropriate Department of Justice agencies. It is estimated that a SAR will be disseminated in 30 to 60 days, while the investigation may take six to nine months or more to build a case for prosecution. The SAR and the funneling of the SAR through one agency has encouraged discussion and collaboration between all entities in the efforts to combat human trafficking.

Financial Industries
Financial industries are under close scrutiny by governmental agencies due to the fact that they handle the flow of money and negotiables for individuals, business entities, and the government. The health and security of the US and global financial systems depend on the ability and willingness of all financial institutions to follow the rules set forth in our banking and commerce laws and comply with FinCen directives. Compliance in the financial industries can be an expensive undertaking, and the extent to which an institution can comply may be within the confines of its size and ability to do so. However, failure to comply can result in the loss of a bank's charter, sizable fines, and, more recently, the possibility of criminal prosecution for bank employees who blatantly disregard regulations.

While compliance is required by law, many banks see compliance in the area of human trafficking as part of their corporate social responsibility. The concept of corporate social responsibility and its effect on profit have been widely discussed, but it is basically understood to be a company's responsibility to its shareholders, customers, employees, community, and the environment to engage in ethical practices and decision-making. Failure to do so may result in a lack of trust and damage to the institution's reputation as well as the loss of profits.

The BSA and FinCen advisories on human trafficking clearly define behaviors and activities for financial institutions to follow. Each institution's response will be different, and they may report to a different regulatory agency depending on the activities engaged in and the size of their operations. Larger banking organizations may have an AML director or an entire AML department and report to the OCC. Smaller institutions may have one person who serves as AML director and reports to the FDIC. Size or ability does not preclude an organization from compliance; rather, each must demonstrate a clear intent to follow the laws and guidelines provided.

What is the process for filing a SAR report in regard to human trafficking and how does a suspected case get reported? The AML officer at each institution is tasked with making sure that policies and processes are in place that clearly define the actions an employee must take when faced with a possible situation of trafficking and how to report it. Front-line workers are required to perform due diligence when opening accounts to verify the identity of the customer. Tellers may encounter a situation in that process that clearly indicates red flags. Those red flags are reported within a defined structure to the AML director or unit for further investigation.

The rise of big data and tools to handle large data sets have helped financial institutions that have the ability to set rules and parameters within their databases to search for red flags and indicators to produce reports for AML officers for investigation. Some parameters set up within the data may look for large amounts of money being spent in areas that are common to victims of human trafficking like hotels, transportation, video streaming services, food, and lingerie. Others may be set up to look for funnel accounts. Once these reports are generated, it is again the responsibility of the AML officer to investigate and determine whether to file a SAR and/or to take action by freezing or shutting down the account. Due diligence is important at this stage because the decision made can put the bank at risk from both the customer side and regulatory issues. Unfortunately, most bank accounts that are flagged are those of a trafficking victim, not the trafficker. The financial institution may not want to shut the account down or freeze it to avoid ultimately causing more damage to the victim. However, as FinCen warns, indicators that point to possible human trafficking may be indicators of other criminal activity. The need for predetermined policies and procedures to help guide the AML director in exhausting all areas of investigation, including researching open sources, are critical to making the decision to report via a SAR. Measured decision making is important for compliance and avoiding risk.

In other cases, an alert AML director or department may become aware of a major crime investigation or arrests that give them cause to go back and search their records to determine if the suspect was a customer. If yes, the same process of investigating and due diligence should be followed to determine the action needed.

At times when financial reporting crosses into the realm of the victimization of humans, the stakes are high and the roles of those involved share a common concern for getting it right, not just from a risk or compliance angle but from a social responsibility perspective as well. There are professional organizations that support those working in the field. The Association for Certified Anti-money Laundering (ACAMS), the Association for Certified Fraud Examiners (ACFE, n.d.), the Association of Certified Financial Crimes Specialists (ACFCS, n.d.), and the American Banking Association (ABA, n.d.) all provide training, support, and certifications for professionals in the industry. ACAMS offers a free course, Fighting Modern Slavery and Human Trafficking, for members and nonmembers (ACAMS, n.d.b)

The financial services industry has for the most part taken its role seriously by following the money and has become an important partner in combatting human trafficking. From a Polaris report (2018) on the role of the financial industry:

> Federal laws, including the Bank Secrecy Act (BSA) and the USA PATRIOT Act, mandate that financial institutions monitor for and report suspected illegal activity. The handling of funds generated by human trafficking can constitute money laundering. This legal obligation—unique to the finance industry—has led to the creation of robust systems to detect suspicious activities associated with human trafficking, money laundering, and related financial crime. These systems have in turn led to actionable information for law enforcement to launch investigations and identify potential perpetrators. Because financial crimes are not as reliant on victim testimony as other offenses, pursuing traffickers from a money laundering angle can be an effective method to obtain justice in situations in which the victims are too scared or traumatized to cooperate. Thanks to the leadership and commitment of many in the financial services industry, traffickers' motivating force—greed—has been turned into a powerful weapon against them (Polaris, 2018).

The profit derived from human trafficking, the predicate crime to money laundering, remains staggering. Combatting these criminals takes cooperation from governments, businesses, financial industries, and society. While the financial sector has the tools and the motivation to be an active partner in combatting human trafficking, motivated criminals will continue to search for ways to anonymize their criminal activities and financial transactions. This will continue to be a challenge for law enforcement and the financial industry. Hopefully, the collaboration and information sharing established through the BSA and FinCen will continue to evolve in ways to counter new evasive criminal tactics and continue to fight against human traffickers and their activities.

Discussion Questions

1. What do you think prompts most financial institutions to create AML officers and/or departments? Are they motivated by fear of being found not in compliance or by a genuine concern for corporate social responsibility?

2. Do you think that there are different motivations for institutions to be AML compliant in general as opposed to anti–human trafficking efforts specifically? Why?
3. Do you believe that financial institutions can really be strong partners in the effort to combat trafficking?
4. Do you believe the BSA, FinCen, and human trafficking advisories are compelling enough to encourage compliance?
5. How do you think other human trafficking laws, statutes, and acts can work in conjunction with the BSA and FinCen advisories to strengthen the fight against trafficking?

References

ABA. (n.d.). *The United Voice of America's Banks*. Aba.org
ACAMS. (n.d.-a). *About ACAMS*. www.acams.org/en/about#about-us-c4ffaef2
ACAMS. (n.d.-b). *Beyond the five pillars*. www.acamstoday.org/beyond-the-five-pillars-taking-a-holistic-approach-to-aml/
ACAMS. (n.d.-c). *What is the definition of money laundering?* www.acams.org/en/resources/aml-glossary-of-terms#a-9799feca
ACFCS. (n.d.). *ACFCS preparing for the future of financial crime today*. www.acfcs.org/
ACFE. (2020). *Fraud examiners manual*. ACFE.
ACFE. (n.d.). *Association of certified fraud examiners*. www.acfe.com/
All Banking Alerts. (2018). *What is money laundering?* http://allbankingalerts.com/what-is-money-laundering-three-methods-or-stages-in-money-laundering/
FDIC. (n.d.). *The bank secrecy act*. www.fdic.gov/regulations/resources/director/virtual/bsa.pdf
FinCen. (n.d.a). *FinCens mandate from Congress*. www.fincen.gov/resources/statutes-regulations/fincens-mandate-congress
FinCen. (n.d.b). *Suspicious activity report supporting documentation*. www.fincen.gov/resources/statutes-regulations/guidance/suspicious-activity-report-supporting-documentation
International Labor Organization. (n.d.). *ILO says forced labour generates annual profits of US$ 150 billion*. www.ilo.org/global/about-the-ilo/newsroom/news/WCMS_243201/lang--en/index.html
NAFCU. (n.d.). *BSA/AML violations can cost you*. www.nafcu.org/compliance-blog/bsaaml-violations-can-cost-you
Polaris. (2018). *A roadmap for systems and industries to prevent and disrupt human trafficking–financial services industry*. https://polarisproject.org/wp-content/uploads/2018/08/A-Roadmap-for-Systems-and-Industries-to-Prevent-and-Disrupt-Human-Trafficking-Financial-Industry.pdf
The US Treasury. (n.d.). *The role of the treasury*. https://home.treasury.gov/about/general-information/role-of-the-treasury
United Nations. (n.d.). *Money laundering*. www.unodc.org/unodc/en/money-laundering/overview.html

17

LAW ENFORCEMENT CONSIDERATIONS FOR HUMAN TRAFFICKING

BRADLEY W. ORSINI

Introduction

Human trafficking is a crime that has gone largely unnoticed and unreported in the United States. Within the last 10 years, efforts to address this issue have increased among federal, state, and local law enforcement agencies. Resources allocated to these agencies have been primarily dedicated to efforts in support of understanding the crime, identifying the perpetrators and victims, and developing significant intelligence bases and robust investigative programs about the problem. This chapter addresses law enforcement considerations when investigating human trafficking organizations or attempting to identify a victim. The emphasis is on the responsibility of law enforcement agencies to recognize indicators of human trafficking and to coordinate intelligence-gathering efforts with local and national groups working on this issue.

Chapter Learning Objectives

- Understand human trafficking as a crime through a law enforcement lens.
- Understand unique investigative considerations and techniques germane to the crime of human trafficking.
- Know the indicators of human trafficking.

DOI: 10.4324/9781003124672-20

Law Enforcement Definition of Human Trafficking

The Federal Bureau of Investigation (FBI) has long been involved in the battle to confront and eradicate human slavery in the United States. The FBI works with other federal, state, and local law enforcement agencies to identify and investigate organized groups that engage in human trafficking. The FBI also enlists the help of nongovernmental organizations (NGOs) and civic groups to help identify victims of human trafficking.

Predominantly, the FBI investigates human trafficking within its Civil Rights Program. The FBI Civil Rights Program is made up of four subprograms, which are briefly described here.

- **Hate crimes** are those crimes that are motivated by a bias against the victim, such as skin color, ethnicity, country of origin, or religion. In 2009, the Matthew Shepard and James Byrd Jr. Hate Crimes Prevention Act added sexual orientation, gender, gender identity, and disabilities to the list of biases that constitute hate crimes.
- **Color of law violations** involve actions taken by someone acting under the authority of the law—local, state, or federal. Examples include use of excessive force by law enforcement agencies or correctional officers or allegations of sexual assault and theft.
- **FACE Act violations** are crimes committed against individuals who seek to obtain or provide reproductive health care services. These crimes include blockades, assaults, threatening phone calls or mail, assaults, and murders.
- **Human trafficking** includes forced physical labor, forced household service, and sex trafficking involving international victims or adult U.S. citizens. (Sex trafficking of U.S. children is handled by the FBI's Crimes Against Children program.)

Currently, human trafficking takes up approximately 16 percent of manpower of the Civil Rights Program.

It is important to note that trafficking of minors may also be investigated by members of the FBI's Violent Crime Program. Both of these programs are housed within the FBI's Criminal Investigative Division. Human trafficking is divided between adult and minor victims because although the crime is the same, the law is very different for minors, and investigating an incident that involves minors takes special training and expertise.

The basic definition of human trafficking is when force, threats of force, physical restraints or threats of physical restraints; serious harm or threats of serious harm to any person; abuse or threatened abuse of the law or legal process; or any scheme, plan, or pattern intended to cause fear of serious harm to any person are used to compel an individual for labor, services, or commercial sex acts. When this exploitation involves a minor, according to federal law, the sex trafficking of children does not require the element of force, fraud, or coercion; but the perpetrator must knowingly benefit from the commercial sex act of a minor or knowingly or recklessly disregard the age of the minor or have had reasonable opportunity to observe the minor.

The conditions under which human trafficking occurs are not always straight forward and easily identified. To clarify further, the FBI breaks down and investigates human trafficking under the following three categories:

- sex trafficking;
- forced labor;
- domestic servitude.

Sex Trafficking

Approximately 50 percent of FBI human trafficking investigations are sex trafficking cases. These are the types of cases most people think about when they hear the words "human trafficking." The commercial sex trade in the United States and the world is systemic and incredibly lucrative. Sex trafficking can take place in the form of street prostitution, brothels, and massage parlors. Commercial sex trafficking can involve women, men, and children who are United States citizens and those who are brought into the United States from all over the world. Many of the individuals are lured into the country under false pretenses and promises. The traffickers begin a psychological pattern of coercion designed to keep the victims under their control. Another means of coercion is "debt bondage," which is a method employed to keep the victim under control. The traffickers convince the victim that they are indebted and owe a payment for entry into the United States. Over time, it may or may not be realized by the victim that the debt may never be paid. It should be noted, despite common misperceptions, that United States citizens are not immune to sex trafficking.

Forced Labor

Forced labor investigations make up approximately 35 percent of all human trafficking cases across the country. The agriculture industry makes up the majority of these investigations in using migrant workers for unskilled labor with the cultivating and harvesting of crops. Other industries that may enter into human trafficking are construction, landscaping, factory, food processing, and hotel/resort cleaning jobs throughout the United States. Victims may be forced to live in inhumane conditions, may have excessive work hours, and may be exploited further by nonpayment from employer. As with sex trafficking, forced labor victims may live in inhumane conditions and be sheltered together. Many times, if the victims have immigration documentation, it may be confiscated by their employer.

Domestic Servitude

Domestic servitude encompasses approximately 15 percent of human trafficking investigations worked by the FBI. These cases are usually singular in nature, and the victim is kept in a private home. Routinely, the victim is subjected to mental and physical harm by the trafficker to keep them under control. Many cases result in the victims also being sexually assaulted by the trafficker.

The term "human trafficking" may seem confusing to some. The word "trafficking" implies transportation of victims, and that is not required for most federal statutes in which the cases are investigated under the human trafficking program. Human trafficking is different than alien smuggling, which does require transportation of humans across an international border. Law enforcement agencies should understand the fundamental differences between human trafficking and alien smuggling. The differences are:

More specifically, smuggling usually involves a one-time interaction, the focus is the transportation of the individual, the crime is against the sovereignty/border, and the person is complicit. With human trafficking, the victim is held for a term, the focus is the denial of liberty, the crime is against the civil rights of the victim, and the victim is not complicit but coerced.

Law Enforcement and Human Smuggling in the United States

The United States has always been a destination for millions of people in search of freedom and economic opportunity. However, the very characteristics that make the U.S. attractive for immigrants converge to create an environment that is conducive for those willing to engage in exploitative practices. Human trafficking is a very lucrative industry. It has been identified as one of the most lucrative criminal acts committed in the United States, resulting in billions of dollars of profit for perpetrators.

How can law enforcement combat human trafficking? What legal mechanisms are in place for law enforcement officers to use? In 1865, the 13th

Table 17.1 Trafficking Smuggling

Trafficking	Smuggling
No movement required	Must involve illegally moving across borders
Focus is compelled labor, service, or commercial sex	Focus is transporting or harboring illegal alien
Victim is a person	Crime is against integrity of border/ victim is a country
Victim can be a citizen, documented migrant, or undocumented	

Amendment to the U.S. Constitution abolished slavery and involuntary servitude. The 13th Amendment states, "Neither slavery nor involuntary servitude, except as punishment for crime whereof the party shall have been duly convicted, shall exist in the United States. Congress shall have power to enforce this article by appropriate legislation."

In October 2000, the Trafficking Victims Protection Act (TVPA) of 2000 was enacted. Prior to this law, no comprehensive federal law existed to protect victims of trafficking or to prosecute their traffickers. TVPA updated federal antislavery statutes. The goals of TVPA are prevention, protection, and prosecution:

- Prevent trafficking overseas and provide education and public awareness.
- Protect victims and help them rebuild their lives in the United States with federal and state support. The law established the T Visa, which allows victims of trafficking to become temporary residents of the United States. The T Visa signifies a shift in immigration policy. The law also makes victims of trafficking eligible for the Witness Protection Program.
- Prosecution, wherein the law strengthened the prosecution and punishment of traffickers, making human trafficking a federal crime with severe penalties. TVPA addressed the subtle means of coercion used by traffickers to bind their victims in servitude, including psychological coercion, trickery, and the seizing of documents.

The Trafficking Victims Protection Reauthorization Act (TVPRA) of 2003 renewed the U.S. government's commitment to combatting human trafficking. The TVPRA provides resources and initiatives to assist victims of human trafficking. In December 2008, the TVPRA of 2008 further enhanced federal law through inclusion of language to address human trafficking conspiracy, as well as anyone who benefits by receiving anything of value knowing that the venture engaged in a human trafficking violation.

The FBI's Civil Rights Program launched a Human Trafficking Initiative in 2004 to establish a proactive approach to aggressively investigate human trafficking. The FBI's goal was to take a multiagency approach to identify human trafficking that may affect communities across the country. Each of the 56 FBI field offices was tasked with recommended actions to be implemented.

Some of the recommendations were as follows:

- Conduct a threat assessment to determine the nature and scope of human trafficking problems within each field office. This entailed a thorough research of existing intelligence reports gathered, existing information on investigations (past and present), contact with other federal, state, and local law enforcement agencies, and contact with community-based groups.

- Join or establish, if appropriate, a task force or working group. This group, which will include members of state and local law enforcement agencies as well as community-based groups, will enhance the intelligence base for all of law enforcement to enact on the threat of human trafficking.
- Outside of the task force or working group, establish liaison contacts with NGOs, community-based organizations, and churches and other civic groups. These groups are uniquely positioned to provide information on potential victims and possible case referrals.
- Aggressively investigate the human trafficking cases once the matter has been predicated as a viable case that will have an impact on the trafficking organization.

In order to advance this initiative, it was imperative that the FBI implement all of the above strategies to build a robust intelligence base to identify the true nature of trafficking in each of the 56 field offices. In particular, training has been key in increasing awareness for law enforcement agencies as well as the community as a whole. Community awareness is critical to enhance the extent to which everyday citizens are able to report to law enforcement bodies any issues that may even have the appearance of human trafficking. Following the receipt of a tip, it is incumbent upon law enforcement agencies to aggressively investigate. This initiative has had success since its inception and has increased awareness of the growing problem throughout the entire United States. Some of the success can be noted as follows:

- The number of human trafficking cases identified has nearly doubled.
- The number of prosecutions and convictions quadrupled from 2004 to 2009.
- In 2010, the FBI's 56 field offices participated in approximately 70 working groups dedicated to addressing human trafficking. The groups are important to showcase law enforcement efforts to consolidate resources to leverage the number of agents and officers working on the human trafficking threat. The groups were involved in approximately 60 percent of the human trafficking cases that resulted in an indictment in 2009 and 2010.

Law enforcement utilizes many different statutes to prosecute offenders of human trafficking. Many states have their own statutes that relate to human trafficking. This chapter will focus on the federal statutes enacted in which the FBI, other federal law enforcement agencies, and the working groups and task forces utilize to prosecute offenders. These federal statutes are explained in detail in the Federal Criminal Codes and Rules, 2011 edition under Chapter 77.

The applicable federal statutes regarding human trafficking matters are: Title 18, United States Code (U.S.C.), Sections 1584 and 1589 to 1594 (inclusive). The federal government gets its authority to enforce violations of all of these statutes through the 13th Amendment except Title 18, U.S.C., Section 1591. Although slavery was fraught with sexual misconduct, this misconduct was not the primary purpose, and therefore was not protected by the 13th Amendment. Title 18, U.S.C., Section 1591 must prove interstate commerce. A more detailed explanation of the statutes appears in the box on the following pages.

Within the peonage and slavery statutes, federal law provides a separate conspiracy provision under Title 18, U.S.C. 1594. Generally, conspiracy can be described as when two or more people conspire to commit any of the stated offenses.

The legal statutes stated here are not inclusive of the statutes law enforcement can utilize to investigate human trafficking. However, they are listed for the sole reason that they are the most prevalent and relevant to human trafficking issues. It should be noted that each statute has numerous elements of which law enforcement must demonstrate the occurrence in order to charge a subject. It is extremely important that law enforcement agencies continually consult with prosecuting attorneys to ensure the investigation is yielding the best possible evidence to meet the elements of each statute in order to prosecute offenders.

Challenges of Investigating Human Trafficking

Law enforcement faces many challenges when it comes to human trafficking. As previously discussed, human trafficking can go largely unnoticed in a community. For example, a seemingly innocent business front can be passed by countless individuals on a daily basis without anyone noticing. As it relates to sex trafficking, most business establishments are not labeled and go "under the radar" with the general public. Law enforcement and other professionals who might come into contact with victims (i.e., nurses, doctors, other health care professionals, psychologists, counselors, social workers, etc.) should be constantly vigilant and understand the indicators of human trafficking in their area of responsibility. The indicators of trafficking can be broken down into two categories. One relates to human trafficking indicators to be aware of in victims, and the other are indicators for a business that houses trafficked victims.

Title 18, United States Code

Title 18, United States Code (U.S.C.), 1584, Sale Into Involuntary Servitude:

---

a. Whoever knowingly and willfully holds to involuntary servitude or sells into any condition of involuntary servitude, any other person for any term, or brings within the United States any person so held, shall be fined under this title or imprisoned not more than 20 years, or both. If death results from the violation of this section, or if the violation includes kidnapping or an attempt to kidnap, aggravated sexual abuse or the attempt to commit aggravated sexual abuse, or an attempt to kill, the defendant shall be fined under this title or imprisoned for any term of years or life, or both.

b. Whoever obstructs, attempts to obstruct, or in any way interferes with or prevents the enforcement of this section, shall be subject to the penalties described in subsection (a).

Title 18, U.S.C., 1589, Forced Labor:

a. Whoever knowingly provides or obtains the labor or services of a person by any one of, or by any combination of, the following means—

1. by means of force, threats of force, physical restraint, or threats of physical restraint to that person or another person;

2. by means of serious harm or threats of serious harm to that person or another person;

3. by means of the abuse or threatened abuse of law or legal process; or

4. by means of any scheme, plan, or pattern intended to cause the person to believe that, if that person did not perform such labor or services, that person or another person would suffer serious harm or physical restraint.

b. Whoever knowingly benefits, financially or by receiving anything of value, from participation in a venture which has engaged in the providing or obtaining of labor or services by any of the means described in subsection (a), knowing or in reckless disregard of the fact that the venture has engaged in the providing or obtaining of labor or services by any of such means, shall be punished as provided in subsection (d).

c. In this section:

1. The term "abuse or threatened abuse of law or legal process" means the use or threatened use of a law or legal process, whether administrative, civil, or criminal, in any manner or for any purpose for which the law was not designed, in order to exert pressure on another person to cause that person to take some action or refrain from taking some action.

2. The term "serious harm" means any harm, whether physical or nonphysical, including psychological, financial, or reputational harm, that is sufficiently serious, under all the surrounding circumstances, to compel a reasonable person of the same background and in the same circumstances to perform or to continue performing labor or services in order to avoid incurring that harm.

Title 18, U.S.C., 1590, Trafficking With Respect to Peonage, Slavery, Involuntary Servitude, or Forced Labor:

a. Whoever knowingly recruits, harbors, transports, provides, or obtains by any means, any person for labor or services in violation of this chapter shall be fined under this title or imprisoned not more than 20 years, or both. If death results from the violation of this section, or if the violation includes kidnapping or an attempt to kidnap, aggravated sexual abuse, or the attempt to commit aggravated sexual abuse, or an attempt to kill, the defendant shall be fined under this title or imprisoned for any term of years or life, or both.

b. Whoever obstructs, attempts to obstruct, or in any way interferes with or prevents the enforcement of this section, shall be subject to the penalties under subsection(a).

Title 18, U.S.C., 1591, Sex Trafficking of Children or by Force, Fraud, or Coercion:

a. Whoever knowingly—

1. in or affecting interstate or foreign commerce, or within the special maritime and territorial jurisdiction of the United States, recruits, entices, harbors, transports, provides, obtains, or maintains by any means a person; or

2. benefits, financially or by receiving anything of value, from participation in a venture which has engaged in an act described in violation of paragraph (1), knowing, or in reckless disregard of the fact, that means of force, threats of force, fraud, coercion described in subsection (e) (2), or any combination of such means will be used to cause the person to engage in a commercial sex act, or that the person has not attained the age of 18 years and will be caused to engage in a commercial sex act, shall be punished as provided in subsection (b).

Title 18, U.S.C., 1592, Unlawful Conduct With Respect to Documents in Furtherance of Trafficking, Peonage, Slavery, Involuntary Servitude, or Forced Labor:

a. Whoever knowingly destroys, conceals, removes, confiscates, or possesses any actual or purported passport or other immigration document, or any other actual or purported government identification document of another person—

  1. in the course of a violation of section 1581, 1583, 1584, 1589, 1590, 1591, or 1594(a);

  2. with intent to violate section 1581, 1583, 1584, 1589, 1590, or 1591; or

  3. to prevent or restrict or to attempt to prevent or restrict, without lawful authority, the person's liberty to move or travel, in order to maintain the labor or services of that person, when the person is or has been a victim of a severe form of trafficking in persons, as defined in section 103 of the Trafficking Victims Protection Act of 2000, shall be fined under this title or imprisoned for not more than 5 years, or both.

b. Subsection (a) does not apply to the conduct of a person who is or has been a victim of a severe form of trafficking in persons, as defined in section 103 of the Trafficking Victims Protection Act of 2000, if that conduct is caused by, or incident to, that trafficking.

c. Whoever obstructs, attempts to obstruct, or in any way interferes with or prevents the enforcement of this section, shall be subject to the penalties described in subsection (a).

Title 18, U.S.C., 1593A, Benefitting Financially From Peonage, Slavery, and Trafficking in Persons:

Whoever knowingly benefits, financially or by receiving anything of value, from participation in a venture which has engaged in any act in violation of section 1581(a), 1592, or 1595(a), knowing or in reckless disregard of the fact that the venture has engaged in such violation, shall be fined under this title or imprisoned in the same manner as a completed violation of such section.

Some of the indicators of trafficking in victims are as follows:

• absence of contact with friends or family;
• psychological manipulation and control used in workplace;

- no access to identification documents or bank accounts/money;
- inhumane living and working conditions;
- provided with drugs to increase dependence;
- communication and movements always monitored;
- confined in living accommodation by locks and fences;
- lives in a general atmosphere of violence;
- provides inconsistent accounts of where they have been with a lack of knowledge about city they currently reside in;
- subject to arbitrary penalties, rules, and control;
- show signs of physical restraint, sexual/physical abuse, confinement, malnourishment, or torture;
- not allowed to speak for themselves when questioned;
- dishonest when questioned by law enforcement agencies about involvement in the trafficking situation;
- is frequently moved to or rotated through multiple locations in a short amount of time;
- owes a large and/or increasing debt and is unable to pay it off;
- works excessively long and unusual hours and is unpaid or paid very little through tips;
- has been sexually assaulted or abused by an employer or someone who forces them to work;
- recruited on false promises concerning the nature and conditions of the work;
- unable to take breaks or days off or has unusual work restrictions;
- has unexplained work injuries or signs of untreated illness or disease.

Business that engages in human trafficking can also display signs that may indicate the presence of human trafficking. Some of the indicators are as follows:

- a business that caters to males only;
- a business that is opened at unusual hours;
- a business that opened with no real advertisement;
- if the business does advertise, it may only do so in the personals section of the newspaper;
- a business with no real signage; name may be painted on building;
- a business that cannot be viewed from the outside, for example, windows covered.

It is important to keep in mind that the indicators stated here are nothing more than a guide for law enforcement officers to use in their day-to-day activities. The presence of one or even two indicators does not mean that human trafficking is present. Indicators should be utilized to identify areas for further investigation. As law enforcement starts to identify the presence of human trafficking, other investigative problems arise. Many of the victims and subjects of human trafficking are international, and law enforcement may encounter a language barrier. This issue may result in a delay of investigative efforts and a proper interview of the initial complainant or victim. Law enforcement agencies may not have the ability to provide a sworn officer who speaks the language necessary. The next hurdle to overcome is for law enforcement to solicit the services of a qualified translator. Law enforcement officers have to ensure that the translator is not only qualified but has the ability to work with law enforcement so that facts are interpreted and exactly what is being said is communicated. Law enforcement agencies have to be vigilant for an interpreter who may not be used to working with law enforcement and may not translate precisely what the officer is asking the victim or witness. Sometimes, field-expedient methods are used by law enforcement officers to gather information from a witness/victim on the scene. This may entail the officer utilizing a community member or someone close to the victim/witness. Law enforcement should follow up, when possible, with an interview with a qualified translator.

Another issue that may arise with the victim or witness is cultural issues. Many international groups that immigrate to the United States have an inherent distrust of law enforcement. This distrust may lead to ineffective interviews of individuals without gathering a full understanding of the problem. Witnesses/victims may mislead law enforcement to cover for subjects. They also may have a larger fear of the perpetrators than they have of law enforcement, which will leave law enforcement with no real guidance or influence on the victim/witness to tell the truth. Law enforcement officers' ability to understand the cultural issues of a particular group in their area of responsibility is crucial for a successful relationship with the community as a whole. As talked about earlier, when human trafficking is worked in a task force/working group setting, law enforcement has already established contacts and liaison in the affected com munities. A pre-established relationship with the community that may already be affected by human trafficking is built into the system.

A common scenario that law enforcement deals with on a daily basis is that of the immigration concerns of the victims/witnesses. These valid concerns provide enormous hurdles for law enforcement and the victims/witnesses of the investigation. Law enforcement agencies recognize the need to coordinate the investigative efforts with Immigration Custom Enforcement (ICE) early on in an investigation. Law enforcement as "one entity" has to discuss these issues and work together to bring a successful conclusion to the investigation. Federal law makes allowances for victims and witnesses who are "out of status" within the United States. Law enforcement will work with federal prosecutors to obtain visas to allow victims and witnesses to stay during the course of an investigation and prosecution of the human trafficking subjects. As discussed earlier, the TVPA provides the mechanism for law enforcement groups to utilize a special visa to protect these victims from deportation and aid in prosecution.

As these investigations mature and grow, additional issues may arise with subjects having involvement in foreign countries. Sometimes, these issues can be addressed through a multiagency investigation in collaboration with federal agencies that have the ability to conduct overseas investigations. For example, the FBI has legal attachés throughout the world. A legal attaché has the ability to facilitate investigative efforts within a foreign country once proper approvals have been obtained. This can aid significantly in addressing a human trafficking organization at its root when that organization has its origins outside of the United States.

Investigative Techniques and Training

Law enforcement investigations can be broken down into two categories: "reactive" and "pro-active" investigations. Generally, law enforcement throughout the country investigates crimes in a "reactive" fashion. That is, a complaint is made by a citizen, and the police respond and start the investigation. This is an everyday occurrence and will never change. Law enforcement is charged with the responsibility of protecting the public and responding to incidents and crimes in progress when they occur.

With regard to human trafficking, many of the cases are dealt with in a "reactive" manner. Victims may report the crime, or a witness may bring forth information regarding a possible human trafficking crime. In many instances, law enforcement may learn of a human trafficking crime while responding to other complaints, such as a domestic violence call.

Law enforcement's best avenue to combat and diminish the threat of human trafficking is to work the criminal threat using a "proactive" approach when possible. That is, law enforcement agencies should attempt to work the investigation in a covert manner as long as possible to get to the core organizational structure of the group being investigated. Many criminal organizations are investigated in this manner. Human trafficking organizations should be no different.

When practical, law enforcement investigations should focus efforts in the following areas to achieve a proactive approach to combat human trafficking:

- intelligence gathering;
- intelligence sharing;
- physical surveillance techniques;
- consensual monitoring;
- utilization of cooperating witnesses;
- possible utilization of an undercover scenario.

These law enforcement techniques are not unique and are in fact quite common. Law enforcement should start out by building a strong intelligence base to garner as much information on the human trafficking organization as possible. As discussed earlier, working human trafficking in a task force/working group maximizes law enforcement's ability to quickly gather information from numerous sources. It may be as simple as information from your community-based group or a local law enforcement official reporting possible indicators of human trafficking. This intelligence can then be exploited by checking public records, Internet checks, and law enforcement intelligence data basis. As the information is obtained, law enforcement officers have the ability to share intelligence with other agencies to possibly verify or strengthen intelligence obtained.

When information is vetted and determined credible, law enforcement agencies have the ability to investigate the matter fully. At this point, physical surveillance may be deployed to ascertain movements of subjects and/or victims. An example of this could be the established surveillance of a "massage parlor" where law enforcement developed possible intelligence that led to numerous indicators of human trafficking. A physical surveillance can be established to determine the possible movements of victims to/from the business. It could also show that the victims may be housed at the business establishment. Photographs at a physical surveillance location can possibly provide pictures of subjects and victims of human trafficking. These photographs can be used throughout the investigation and a potential prosecution of subjects.

Sometimes, a covert investigation is conducted utilizing cooperating witnesses or informants. These individuals may have direct access to the subjects, victims, or business or may have been involved in the criminal acts themselves. Law enforcement investigations are always very careful in utilizing the cooperating witness/informant and needs to assess their motivation before using them in a covert manner. Agencies have to be vigilant in their efforts to corroborate informant information. The rationale to continually assess informant information is to ensure the intelligence furthers the investigation and not the motives of the informant. If the informant's information can be proven credible, the investigation can move forward, and further intelligence and evidence can be obtained.

Where feasible, cooperating witnesses/informants can obtain evidence through the use of consensual monitoring of conversations with subjects. It should be noted that every state has its own laws on the utilization of consensual monitoring, and law enforcement should be aware of these laws and seek appropriate approval to use the investigative technique. Numerous considerations should be evaluated prior to conducting a consensual conversation with an informant and a subject. This investigative technique needs to be closely monitored by law enforcement authorities to ensure proper procedures and stay within the bounds of state laws. The informant should be thoroughly instructed on what they can and cannot do or say during the conversation. If successful, invaluable evidence can be obtained through this technique. Law enforcement, hopefully, will gather evidence and determine any safety issues for victims. The safety of victims is paramount, and it should be noted that the ultimate rescue of victims should take priority over the case in chief.

When possible, law enforcement groups should consider the deployment of an undercover operation. When a human trafficking organization is identified, law enforcers need to keep in mind the complexities of the organization and try to gather evidence that will expose the root of the organization. An undercover operation may be the best way to gather evidence deep into the organization. As the human trafficking organization operates under a veil of secrecy, the undercover law enforcement official can gather evidence while the crime is occurring. Ultimately, this may be the best evidence to use to convict the subjects. Also, by deploying an undercover operation, law enforcers can control the investigation much better than with the utilization of a cooperating witness/informant.

With the use of this technique, it is possible to design a scenario to best infiltrate the organization and allow investigating officers to explore the extent of the criminal activity. It will be important to penetrate the organization to identify as many subjects as possible and determine if there is any nexus to interstate or international subjects. Furthermore, an undercover operation can assess the full extent of victims' health and safety and aid in devising a plan for their ultimate rescue.

When an investigation turns from the "covert" stage to "overt," law enforcers can investigate in a more traditional manner. One of the significant aspects of this part of the investigation is the determination of the financial aspects of the human trafficking organization. This can involve many facets, and dependent on the size of the organization, law enforcement should seek financial records of these organizations. The records should include, but not be limited to: banking records, real estate holdings, and corporate records.

As discussed before, law enforcement has the ability to leverage considerable resources to investigate criminal organizations. When it relates to human trafficking, there is no one technique that will work with every type of trafficking subject. It should be assessed on a case-by-case basis to determine the best investigative methods necessary to investigate and prosecute subjects and to rescue victims.

While on the topic of investigative techniques, it goes without saying that training should be a continuous process within law enforcement. When law enforcement investigators become aware of possible human trafficking within their domain, they should react accordingly. The quick reaction and adjustment to specific situations is where training becomes critical.

Training should be designed and implemented in a three-pronged approach:

- training of law enforcement officers only;
- training of NGOs and community-based groups; and
- training of both law enforcement and NGOs/community-based groups.

Training for law enforcement should focus on elements of human trafficking laws and methods to collect evidence to meet those elements. There is also a need to educate law enforcement professionals in how to identify human trafficking indicators. Awareness of human trafficking issues is critical in order for law enforcement agencies to recognize and accept the threat as real.

Law enforcement groups should identify and liaise with NGOs and community-based groups that have a special interest or can impact a human trafficking investigative program. Once identified, a presentation can be conducted on human trafficking laws and methods in which these groups can aide law enforcement.

Finally, bringing law enforcement agencies and NGOs/community groups together can have a significant impact on building a productive coalition to combat human trafficking. During these meetings, strategies can be designed and relationships fostered to gather as much intelligence on the threat of human trafficking as possible. Law enforcement professionals will build a base of support to aid in every aspect of investigating and prosecuting subjects. They will also put mechanisms in place to support rescued victims. Conversely, NGOs/community-based groups will have an outlet to provide information when they develop any intelligence of human trafficking. The collaboration between law enforcement and NGOs/community-based groups will ultimately lead toward exposing and eradicating human trafficking organizations.

Victim Considerations for Law Enforcement
As stated before, human trafficking investigations offer unique challenges to law enforcement. Officers balance investigative activities while having to keep in mind the safety and well-being of any potential victim of human trafficking. Law enforcement has a duty and a moral obligation to protect these victims and keep them from further harm. Law enforcers need to continually assess investigative activities to determine the nature and extent of physical harm to victims.

Early on in any human trafficking investigation, there should be consultation with victim advocates to determine the best courses of action once a victim is rescued. The paramount consideration is the physical and mental health of the victim. Victims should be examined as soon as possible to determine any health issues. Law enforcers need to be particularly aware of this and take necessary precautions to protect themselves from the possible threat of any communicable diseases from victims.

Other considerations may involve the inability for law enforcement officers to communicate with victims because of language barriers. They may have to go outside their agency to acquire an individual to interpret. Financial concerns may arise, as there may be a need to facilitate the feeding, clothing, and lodging of victims.

With international victims, consultation with ICE and the United States Citizenship and Immigration Services is advisable in order to discuss immigration issues. These agencies provide law enforcement the tools necessary to work with victims on immigration issues. For international victims, the fear of being deported may overwhelm and limit their cooperation in an investigation. These agencies ensure the victims' rights are met under federal regulation as it relates to human trafficking victims.

As stated before, federal law provides a wide array of services and protections for victims of severe forms of trafficking. The FBI has established the Office of Victim Assistance to ensure that the victims of federal crimes have access to the rights and assistance to which they are entitled. Throughout the FBI, there are over 100 "victim specialists," most of whom are licensed social workers. The primary role of the victim specialist is ensuring the provision of basic victim's rights, crisis intervention, comprehensive direct services, and appropriate referrals. The victim specialist can also provide access to Emergency Victim Assistance Funds and the identity of additional victim assistance resources.

FBI special agents routinely consult with the victim specialist during the course of a human trafficking investigation. Victim specialists help bridge the gap between law enforcement authorities and victims, giving law enforcers the tools necessary to strengthen the relationship. These strong relationships are necessary for a successful investigation and aid the victim in healing. The victim specialists are also trained to conduct forensic interviews of children who may have been traumatized by sex trafficking exploitation.

Conclusions

Human trafficking is tantamount to modern-day slavery. As demonstrated, law enforcement has many obstacles to overcome in the battle to fight this horrific crime and violation of humanity. Discussed in this chapter were the law enforcement definitions and types of human trafficking law enforcement officers investigate; the background of human trafficking as it pertains to law enforcement and the federal statutes law enforcement authorities utilize to investigate this crime; the challenges law enforcement faces; investigative techniques and the importance of continuous training; and victim considerations for those involved in law enforcement. Successful resolutions can be achieved as law enforcers become more aware of the nature and extent of this criminal violation. Public awareness, law enforcement training, liaison with NGOs, coalitions, and task forces make up the necessary formula for successful identification, investigation, and combat of human trafficking.

Discussion Questions

1. What programs fall under the Civil Rights Program in the FBI?
2. How are human trafficking and smuggling different from each other?
3. What are some law enforcement considerations when investigating human trafficking cases?

SECTION IV

SUPPORTING SURVIVORS AND PROGRAMMING CONSIDERATIONS

18

Combatting Sex Trafficking Through the Prosecution of Traffickers

Michael J. Frank and G. Zachary Terwilliger

In this chapter, we discuss the use of criminal prosecution as a means to combat human trafficking. We discuss the mechanisms by which traffickers exploit victims for money, recruit and maintain victims, the tools they use to market victims to customers, and how they deter victims from escaping their clutches. It also analyses the common attributes of traffickers and the facets of sex trafficking that inhibit investigation and prosecution of sex trafficking.

> **Chapter Learning Objectives**
>
> - Understand the primary motivation of sex traffickers.
> - Describe the basic operation of sex trafficking ventures in the United States, including the means by which traffickers recruit, maintain, and market victims.
> - Explore how victim vulnerability pervades almost all aspects of a "successful" sex trafficking scheme.
> - Examine the different roles and the division of labor between traffickers and victims.
> - Recognize some of the root causes of sex trafficking in the United States.

DOI: 10.4324/9781003124672-22

- Consider how the relationship between traffickers and victims develops and can hinder investigation and prosecution of trafficking crimes.

Money may or may not be the root of all evil, but it certainly motivates sex traffickers. Trafficking of human beings occurs because it is profitable for the traffickers. Sex traffickers sell victims only when they benefit financially from the trafficking, and trafficking will persist as long as traffickers continue to enjoy pecuniary gains from this activity. One means to combat trafficking, therefore, is to deny traffickers the monetary benefits of trafficking. This can be accomplished a number of ways, but the most common means is prosecution in criminal courts. A successful criminal prosecution results in the imprisonment of a trafficker, which, at least temporarily, precludes a trafficker from enjoying the fruits of his crime. In addition, imprisonment exacts its own costs from traffickers and inhibits trafficking while the traffickers are incarcerated. Trafficking laws in the United States also require a trafficker to forfeit any profits derived from trafficking and requires restitution for victims. Accordingly, criminal prosecution is one weapon in the fight against trafficking.

To minimize the risk that innocent people are mistakenly prosecuted and punished, American law wisely has created rules and standards that must be met before the law will punish a criminal. These include the requirement that guilt be established beyond a reasonable doubt, the right to a jury trial, and the right to be confronted by one's accusers, to name but a few of the safeguards. Traffickers, like other criminals, have learned how to evade detection of their crimes by law enforcement and minimize their risk of prosecution while maximizing profits. The prosecution of trafficking cases entails a constant battle between investigators and prosecutions on the one hand and traffickers on the other.

Inside American Sex Trafficking

In the sex trafficking context, the prostitution of women and girls entails a number of advantages, including a ready supply of "product," low overheads, a large customer base, and the fact that a sex trafficking venture requires only minimal skill to operate. Because traffickers are motivated by the desire for profits, they see sex trafficking as a great opportunity to generate revenue.

Substantial Profits and Minimal Startup Costs

Perhaps the greatest attraction of sex trafficking as an illicit revenue source is its low startup costs. With as little as $100 of investment capital, a sex trafficker operating in the United States can quickly recoup this investment and reap substantial profits. To get started, a trafficker only needs a single victim to prostitute, and victims usually can be had for nothing or a tiny fraction of the profits. It helps if the trafficker has alcohol or drugs to inebriate the victim, as well as a cellular telephone that customers can call, but even these simple tools are not essential. A hotel room is valuable insofar as traffickers use hotels for "dates" (as commercial sexual assignations are typically called). But sex traffickers have been known to prostitute victims in cars, abandoned houses, automobile repair shops, or borrowed apartments. Traffickers sometimes persuade customers to rent hotel rooms for sex acts with a victim. Once a customer is done and gone, the trafficker can use the room for sex acts with subsequent customers. Sex traffickers also promote "outcalls," which entail taking a victim to a customer's house or apartment for the sex acts. Outcalls require transportation of the victim, but they save traffickers the expense of renting hotel rooms or operating a brothel. Sex traffickers, therefore, can get started with little or no investment capital.

Once initiated, a sex trafficking venture quickly becomes profitable. Traffickers may charge as little as $30 for 15 minutes of sex (the price varies from market to market), but others charge as much as $250 or higher for "extras" or "fetishes." The level of profitability depends on the number of customers and the amount each customer is charged, but in many parts of the United States, there is a large customer base willing to pay substantial sums for sex. A single victim can easily generate at least $500 per day even in suburban areas, and frequently much more. Consider also that because the trafficking proceeds are typically paid in cash, and thus are difficult to trace, traffickers typically pay no taxes on this income. Assuming a trafficker incurs $100 per day in overhead (for condoms, a cheap hotel room, Internet advertisements, food for the victim, drugs, and cellular telephone service), that still leaves a trafficker with $400 per day profit, and that entails prostituting only one victim. If two victims are prostituted from the same hotel room, the additional overhead is negligible, while the profits double. Add a third victim (which is fairly typical), and a trafficker can easily generate profits in excess of $1,000 per day, tax free. Although many sex trafficking victims are prostituted six or seven days per week, assuming three victims are prostituted only 300 days per year, a trafficker can reap over $300,000 per year, tax free.

Risk Minimization

Besides providing an opportunity for substantial profits, sex trafficking frequently allows traffickers to minimize various risks that they would face in operating other criminal ventures. These include the risk of death or injury from violence, the risk of detection by the police, and the risk of successful prosecution.

Sex trafficking usually does not require traffickers to engage in violent acts toward anyone other than the victims, and even these can be minimized through the intimidation and manipulation of victims. Most victims are simply too fearful to resist a trafficker openly, so traffickers often can control victims without resorting to violence. Furthermore, when instances of sex trafficking "require" the use of violence, traffickers are less likely to be on the receiving end of the violence, in contrast to the danger of being harmed during drug transactions or extortion attempts. Thus, running a sex trafficking operation usually poses significantly less risk of injury from violence than does narcotics distribution, loan sharking, extortion, or other crimes that traffickers might find profitable. In committing those crimes, criminals face a substantial risk that their victims will be armed. That makes those endeavors more dangerous than sex trafficking, because sex trafficking victims typically are unarmed.

Furthermore, although traffickers may beat victims as a means of controlling them, any such beatings are likely to occur away from prying eyes and sympathetic individuals who might report this violence to the police. Also, victims frequently are not in a position to resist with force, retaliate with violence, or report their victimization to the police (at least while they are under a trafficker's control). Most female victims also lack the upper-body strength needed to inflict significant injury on their traffickers, and they usually do not have access to firearms that might level the playing field. This further reduces the risk of violence to traffickers. Thus, whatever violence a trafficker elects to inflict on a victim is unlikely to result in publicly observable confrontations or injuries that could garner police attention. Reducing the level of violence required to earn a profit, therefore, also minimizes the risk of discovery by law enforcement agents, who are more likely to be called when a violent confrontation ensues.

The nature of the "product" (i.e., the victims) distributed by sex traffickers also does not lend itself to police detection. Consider that when the police encounter a drug trafficker and find a quantity of narcotics in the trafficker's possession, the unlawful nature of the narcotics usually is readily apparent. When the drug distributor is prosecuted, the patent unlawfulness of his wares leaves the distributor with only the defense of lack of knowledge: "The drugs are not mine and I did not know that they were in my car, bag, pocket, etc." But such a defense can be easily defeated in most cases because distributors will have demonstrated the requisite *mens rea* (i.e., the knowledge of intent required to establish criminal liability) through prior transactions, the quantity and location of the narcotics, testimony of customers, false exculpatory statements, or through admissions by the distributor. In short, it is not difficult for law enforcement agencies to determine when a drug trafficker is in possession of unlawful substances such as narcotics, and once discovered, the available defenses are extremely limited. This makes it more likely that such crimes will result in the arrest and successful prosecution of the perpetrator.

In contrast, a trafficker found to be in possession of a sex trafficking victim may look innocuous to even a well-trained investigator. After all, there is nothing particularly suspicious about young men having young women or teenage girls in their presence, and "possession" of a victim versus accompanying a victim is not readily discernable. When encountered by the police, the trafficker and the victim may appear to be dating, or they could be friends or even relatives. A police officer making a traffic stop, therefore, has no reason to believe that women or girls he sees in a vehicle with a man are victims of trafficking. Even if he suspects something is amiss, unless a victim confirms this, the officer will have no articulable facts upon which to make an arrest. And most victims will either be too intimidated by, fearful of, or infatuated with a trafficker to say anything, even if a patrol officer conducts a private interview of a victim. Without a victim willing or able to report the crime, sex trafficking often goes undetected. Thus, for this reason too, sex trafficking is a much less dangerous endeavor than most other means that criminals use to generate income.

Assuming, however, that the police are somehow able to determine that a person is a sex trafficker, law enforcement agents still need probable cause to make an arrest, and the prosecution must marshal sufficient evidence to prove each elements of sex trafficking beyond a reasonable doubt. Thus, for example, to prove in federal court that a person was involved in sex trafficking a minor, the prosecution would have to show that the defendant: (1) knowingly recruited, enticed, harbored, transported, provided, obtained, or maintained a victim or benefitted financially from participation in a venture which sex trafficked a victim; (2) the defendant did so knowing or in reckless disregard of the fact that the victim would be caused to engage in a commercial sex act; (3) the defendant knew that the victim was under the age of eighteen years, recklessly disregarded this fact, or had a reasonable opportunity to observe the victim; and (4) the sex trafficking had some minimal effect on interstate commerce. Notably, there is no need for the government to show that a minor victim was coerced or forced to perform sex acts, but the burden of proving these elements beyond a reasonable doubt is substantial. Except in "stings" in which a fictitious victim is used to lure traffickers or sex customers, the prosecution of sex trafficking necessarily requires at least minimal cooperation from the victim. But because such cooperation is frequently lacking, that too makes sex trafficking less risky for criminals than the commission of other remunerative crimes.

Theoretically, prosecutors could establish the essential elements of sex trafficking of a child without the testimony of the victim. For example, if there were video footage of the sex acts and the payment for the act, this might be sufficient evidence. But it is uncommon to find such video evidence. It is also possible to establish the elements of sex trafficking of a child through the testimony of a sex customer (that he paid for sex and engaged in a commercial sex act or attempted to do so). But most sex customers lack the moral fiber that would induce them to tell the truth absent some further inducement (such as immunity from prosecution). Furthermore, an underage victim could still testify falsely for the defense that she prostituted herself and was not being prostituted by anyone else. If believed, this would also result in a sex trafficker's acquittal.

Most sex traffickers are happy to prostitute both minors and adults; after all, both result in money in the traffickers' pockets. Although consent is not a defense to sex trafficking minors, under federal law in the United States, true consent (i.e., consent not vitiated by fraud or unlawful coercion) is a defense to the trafficking of adults. Thus, when adults are trafficked, the prosecution must show that the defendants used force, fraud, or coercion to cause the victims to submit to sex acts with customers. That is, the prosecution must demonstrate that a defendant (1) knowingly; (2) in or affecting interstate or foreign commerce; (3) enticed, recruited, harbored, transported, provided, obtained, or maintained by any means a person; (4) knowing or in reckless disregard of the fact that force, fraud, or coercion would be used to cause such person to engage in a commercial sex act.

Additionally, a defendant is criminally liable when he has aided and abetted some other person in sex trafficking or benefitted financially from participating in a sex trafficking venture. Sex trafficking of juveniles is also often accomplished by using force, fraud, and coercion, but the government need not prove that force, fraud, and coercion were used by a defendant in order to convict a defendant of the crime of sex trafficking of a child. Still, because the statute imposes a mandatory minimum sentence of fifteen years of imprisonment when sex trafficking is accomplished via force, fraud, or coercion, the prosecution has incentive to prove this element even in the sex trafficking of minors. It would be extremely difficult to prove that force, fraud, or coercion induced acts of prostitution without the testimony of the victim.

Because sex trafficking of adults requires the government to prove that the victim was coerced in some way to perform the commercial sex acts, if an adult victim refuses to testify that she was coerced and instead falsely claims that she was voluntarily performing commercial sex acts, the government cannot establish the defendant's guilt beyond a reasonable doubt. When the victims are juveniles, the prosecution does not need to establish that the victims were coerced, but generally, the prosecution still needs a victim to testify that she was prostituted by the defendant or defendants. As noted, theoretically, this could also be accomplished through testimony from sex customers who had commercial sex with a juvenile, but even when such testimony is obtained, the victim could sabotage such a prosecution by falsely claiming that she was prostituting herself and that the defendants were merely present when she was doing so. Mere presence of a crime or mere association with criminals is not sufficient to establish guilt. Therefore, testimony from sex trafficking victims is crucial to the prosecution of sex trafficking cases.

Because of fear that a trafficker will retaliate for truthful testimony or because of loyalty or love for a trafficker, victims commonly claim that they were not coerced or, in the case of juvenile victims, that they were prostituting themselves or had never engaged in sex acts. Indeed, many victims are willing to commit perjury to help their traffickers avoid being convicted of sex trafficking (and the government usually cannot establish that perjury was committed without the victim telling the truth or the trafficker admitting his conduct). For many traffickers, therefore, inducing victims to lie to the police or a jury—or to refuse to say anything—is relatively simple.

The Operation of a Sex Trafficking Venture

The operation of a sex trafficking venture is rather simple. As noted, it requires only victims who can be sexually exploited by traffickers and customers willing to pay for sex acts with the victims. Those are the essential ingredients of sex trafficking. Because the recruitment of victims is vital to any sex trafficking endeavor, a consideration of recruitment mechanisms is helpful to understanding sex trafficking.

Victim Recruitment Mechanisms

Sex trafficking is a labor-intensive endeavor in the sense that it requires girls and women who can be prostituted. The victims' bodies are the commodity that the sex traffickers sell for money. Without these commodities, sex traffickers cannot operate. Many regular sex customers also express a preference for having sex with a variety of victims, and they will patronize traffickers who can accommodate their desire for variety. A ready supply of prostitutable females, therefore, is essential to a successful sex trafficking operation. Unfortunately, there seems to be no shortage of vulnerable women and girls.

Most victims of sex trafficking come from troubled or what were once called "broken" homes. That is, most victims come from single-parent or no-parent residences, which leaves them vulnerable to a host of evils. Typically, it is the father who is absent from the victims' lives, and it is well known among law enforcement personnel that victims from father-absent households are more likely to become victims of sex trafficking and other crimes. There are a number of reasons for this, including the fact that mothers of victims have less time and resources to protect their daughters from the traffickers than two-parent families can. These mothers also lack a spouse with whom they can share parental duties.

But the key vulnerability of victims from fatherless homes is a psychological one. Deprived of any meaningful relationship with their fathers, many female victims crave attention from strong male figures. They cannot fathom why their fathers take no interest in them, and they often seek a substitute in male traffickers who express a keen interest in the victims. Indeed, many victims will endure violent abuse from traffickers because this abuse is sometimes mixed with affection or at least attention, and the victims often believe that any attention from a man is better than none. When suspended from school or having dropped out, many victims also have plenty of time on their hands. Brimming with emotional troubles and unfulfilled emotional needs, many victims fail to realize that they have large targets on their backs, which are readily visible to sex traffickers.

Also, many victims are "followers" rather than leaders. They may be withdrawn from their peers and lack the assertiveness to tell traffickers "no." Most are not running with a "popular crowd," despite longing to fit in somewhere, which also makes them vulnerable to traffickers who exploit this longing. Sex traffickers can quickly size up potential victims, ascertain their vulnerabilities, and exploit them. To those victims deprived of parental attention and discipline, traffickers can quickly become objects of affection for victims.

It is no accident that traffickers frequently require the victims whom they prostitute to refer to the trafficker as "daddy." Many sex traffickers recruit victims with implicit promises of fatherly attention and care. Indeed, many traffickers require victims to compete with one another for "daddy time" and sexual favors from "daddy." Some victims will perform extra or dangerous sex acts and take on extra customers in an effort to raise more money and thus please "daddy." Many traffickers will promise victims that prostituting will help them create "a family," which, as mentioned, is something many victims crave. Traffickers often will enforce isolation of victims so that the trafficker takes on the roles of the victim's mother, father, and siblings. This ensures that all of the victims' emotional attachments are to the trafficker. This also ensures that the victims have no refuge should they ever desire to leave the trafficker. When isolated from friends and family, victims starved for any form of relationship will, over time, develop a relationship with the trafficker that substitutes for a family relationship. Most importantly, many such victims develop a loyalty to their sex traffickers much like they would otherwise develop with their parents. Is it any wonder, therefore, that investigators and prosecutors face an uphill battle in convincing victims to cooperate in the prosecution of traffickers?

Traffickers employ a variety of means to recruit victims, but essentially, they employ both carrots and sticks to entice and motivate victims. That is, they use incentives to encourage recruitment and "good" behavior and impose penalties to punish disloyalty and "bad" behavior. Common recruitment/ motivation mechanisms are those of the so-called wealthy traffickers, Romeo/ finesse traffickers, gorilla traffickers, drug-supplier traffickers, and creditor traffickers. Each provides a different means of recruiting and maintaining victims. Because victims and their feelings for their traffickers change over time, and some victims may be vulnerable to some types of coercion but not other types, not all of these means are employed with all victims. Nor are any of these five methods mutually exclusive. Traffickers may end up using all of these mechanisms (and others) to control a single victim. For example, when wooing a victim fails or is insufficiently swift, a trafficker may resort to gorilla-trafficker behavior.

Wealthy/Successful Traffickers and Online Recruitment
Sex trafficking victims, among others, generally are attracted to wealthy and successful men, or at least men who appear wealthy and successful. The standards for "wealth" and "success" are relative, however. Because many sex trafficking victims come from homes afflicted by poverty, they may have a particularly strong attraction to wealthy men who can provide for a victim's physical needs and even small luxuries that are beyond a victim's financial means. Even victims from middle-class backgrounds recognize the advantages that wealth entails and are not immune to the allure of riches. Traffickers exploit this attraction and desire for wealth. If victims could see the reality of prostitution and the hardships that it will entail, they would quickly run from traffickers before becoming ensnared by their false promises. For that reason, traffickers often hide behind a patina of wealth and success when recruiting victims.

As one court described a group of traffickers: "To persuade underage females to prostitute for them, the Defendants (and other traffickers charged in the indictment) presented a vision of ostentatious living, promising fame and fortune. Traffickers perpetrated this myth with their own flamboyant dress, flashy jewelry, and exotic, expensive cars" (*United States v. Pipkins*, 378 F.3d 1281, 1285 (11th Cir. 2004)). Traffickers often employ a flashy exterior to attract victims and to trick them into thinking that they will enjoy a luxurious life if they consent to being prostituted. Some traffickers post photographs of the cash they've made from prostitution on their Facebook pages and other social media. They do this both as a status symbol and as a means of luring potential victims. Sadly, many victims are dazzled by the flashy jewelry, expensive cars, stacks of cash, and false promises of a glamorous life.

Traffickers also exploit the Internet to recruit victims. Sometimes, recruiting starts on Facebook or other social media with a message to a potential victim that she looks pretty or lonely. Other traffickers are more direct and open with an invitation: "Do you want to make some money?" There are at least three major advantages of using the Internet for recruitment.

First, traffickers can recruit a larger number of victims because they need not take the time and effort to meet each potential recruit. Rather, recruitment can occur from anywhere traffickers can get an Internet connection. Prior to exploitation of the Internet, traffickers were limited to making personal contact with potential recruits, which can be time-consuming.

Second, traffickers can exploit a larger geographic area via the Internet than is possible by personal introductions. Many traffickers are transient because this allows them to stay one step ahead of the police. Through Internet recruiting, they need not have familiarity with a particular city in order to recruit victims. They can also vary their destinations depending on their level of successful recruiting in a particular area. For example, if a trafficker is corresponding with a number of potential recruits in Detroit, he might alter his itinerary to move closer to Detroit in the hope that he will soon be recruiting a new victim in that area. Traffickers also no longer need to take cross-country trips to recruit victims unless and until they have a commitment from a victim via the Internet. That minimizes the number of wasted trips.

Third, Internet recruitment allows traffickers to maintain anonymity as they recruit victims and misrepresent their identities. With the assistance of the Internet and social media, traffickers can falsely present themselves not only as successful but as females of a similar age and background as the targeted victims. Teenage girls can be duped into thinking that they are communicating with a young girl like themselves. Traffickers know that potential victims would be more cautious and skeptical if they knew the true identities of those with whom they are corresponding.

Fourth, online recruiting permits traffickers to misrepresent them as being rich and successful. Traffickers often do this with victims who are already being trafficked. Many victims are marketed to customers via online advertisements, such as those found on www.backpage.com and similar sites. These advertisements usually include a telephone number at which customers ostensibly can contact the victims for sex. Traffickers call or send text messages to these telephone numbers, looking for victims who want to leave their traffickers. Once traffickers connect with a potential victim, they start reeling them in with lies, misrepresentations, and false promises. Online recruitment allows a trafficker to lead off with a rich/successful trafficker persona. If that fails, traffickers are happy to switch tactics and utilize other fictions to lure victims. One of the most common is the Romeo/finesse trafficker persona.

Romeo/Finesse Traffickers

Among the "carrots" that traffickers offer potential victims are promises of romance and devoted attention from a man. Because many victims were raised in homes devoid of a nurturing male presence and often don't know what a loving male–female relationship looks like, victims are particularly susceptible to promises of a romantic relationship and loving attention from a man. Sex traffickers who recruit by feigning love for or romantic interest in the victims are sometimes known as "Romeo" or "suave" traffickers. They use romance as a means to gain the trust of girls and women and then exploit that trust for the traffickers' financial benefit. Once a victim is hooked, many Romeo traffickers explicitly tell their victims: "If you love me, you'll make money for me." As in many real romances, the Romeo figure often makes vague promises of future wealth and bliss. The first step toward this dream coming true, according to the trafficker, is earning some quick cash from prostitution. This request/demand is usually made with whatever promises are deemed necessary to motivate the victim.

Some Romeo traffickers will purchase expensive clothes or jewelry for a victim as a means of furthering the myth of love. Many a victim has been trapped by a feeling that they must reciprocate by selling their bodies and giving the proceeds to the trafficker. As long as the victims continue to generate significantly more money than the trafficker spends on the victims, even expensive gifts are worthwhile investments. Furthermore, because many victims have never had a man give them a present, insignificant trinkets often suffice. Still others are satisfied with being permitted to have their hair and fingernails professionally "done." Still other victims are content merely with a little attention from a man and compliments that they are good, loyal, beautiful, or loved . . . so long as they continue to earn money.

When necessary, traffickers readily promise that the commercial sex is only a temporary means to realize their common dreams and that once they have made "enough" money, the prostitution can stop. In other cases, victims are so desperate or addicted that traffickers have no need to make promises of future happiness. Being with the Romeo trafficker suffices, at least for a while. Tragically, some victims come to accept that commercial sex will be their lifelong occupation.

Because Romeo traffickers sometimes employ a certain style and finesse to attract and control victims, they are also sometimes known as "finesse traffickers" (although the wealthy/successful type of trafficker may also be considered a "finesse" trafficker). A finesse trafficker, however, does not always use romance to control victims, nor do finesse traffickers always use a veneer of success and wealth to entice victims. For example, a finesse trafficker may plainly state to a victim that he is down on his luck or is running from the police as a means to gain sympathy from victims. That sympathy will then be exploited to induce the victims to perform commercial sex acts. Talented finesse traffickers with charisma and a convincing shtick can attract followers without ever having to claim that they are in love with their victims and without the trappings of success employed by "wealthy" pimps. Therefore, while many Romeo traffickers and wealthy/successful-type traffickers could accurately be described as "finesse" traffickers, not every finesse trafficker is a Romeo trafficker or a wealthy/successful type trafficker.

Gorilla Pimps

Violent traffickers who gain control over victims via threats and acts of violence are frequently known as "gorilla pimps" or "gorilla traffickers." It is important to note that many gorilla traffickers do not reveal their violent tendencies when they initiate contact with potential victims. More frequently, they initially attempt to recruit victims using a Romeo or finesse method. But when that fails, or when victims are no longer beguiled by those lies, traffickers sometimes show that they are truly violent criminals willing to inflict bodily harm with little provocation. Many trafficking victims have suffered substantial injuries at the hands of gorilla traffickers. There are no accurate records as to how many of these beatings have resulted in death. Some traffickers even brag that they are "gorilla pimps" as a means of gaining status and to instill fear in victims. From a sex trafficker's perspective, this brutality and having a reputation of being a gorilla trafficker effectively communicate to other victims: "Obey or you'll be beaten." Indeed, traffickers are known to batter victims in front of other trafficking victims to demonstrate their power and to engender fear in other victims. Gorilla traffickers understand the value of beatings and the fact that a little violence goes a long way toward inducing compliance.

Even those traffickers who are insufficiently violent to warrant the label "gorilla trafficker" are aware of psychological controls that can be employed on victims. For example, traffickers frequently refer to their victims as "ho" and "bitch," which implicitly communicates to victims that they have no value or identity except as a sex worker. In contrast, victims typically are required to refer to the trafficker as "daddy" and to treat him with honor and respect.

Traffickers also impose a laundry list of rules that implicitly instruct victims that they are simply chattel and must remain subservient to their trafficker. For example, many victims are not permitted to look a trafficker in the eye, must walk behind their traffickers, most obey any orders from their traffickers, must submit to any sex act with the trafficker (whenever he desires sex), and are not allowed to keep the money they earn. All of these things reinforce in the victims' minds that the trafficker is superior to them and must be obeyed. Traffickers have also been known to force victims to undergo abortions, both as a means of demonstrating the trafficker's power over the lives of others and because the demands of pregnancy and childcare would reduce the trafficker's profits. Still other traffickers intentionally impregnate victims so that they will forever be tied to the trafficker through their children.

Drug-Supplier Traffickers

Nearly all traffickers supply their victims with drugs and alcohol as a means of numbing the victims and keeping them compliant. Indeed, traffickers know quite well that performing multiple commercial sex acts day after day takes a toll on the victims' minds and bodies. Drugs are a means of coping with the abuse that they suffer daily and the shame many of them feel. Drugs, therefore, are an essential tool of the trade, as the victims in the *United States v. Edwin Barcus* case stated:

Some of the women and girls found it difficult to have sex with strange men repeatedly. Barcus and other members of the child exploitation enterprise provided the girls and women whom they prostituted with alcoholic beverages, such as vodka and beer, and narcotics, such as marijuana, cocaine, and MDMA . . . —which in its crystalline form is commonly known as "Molly," and in its pill form is commonly known as "Ecstasy." The alcohol and narcotics made the girls more vulnerable and susceptible to being prostituted, and Barcus sometimes told the girls that these substances would "loosen up" and "calm" the women and girls and would help the girls to have sexual relations with the customers . . . Sometimes Barcus poured "Molly" directly into the mouths of girls whom Barcus prostituted.

United States v. Edwin Barcus, No. 1:13-CR-95
(E.D. Va. March 13, 2013), Statement of Facts 22

Indeed, in light of the stresses inherent in being trafficked to a large quantity of men, many victims are able to cope only by being drunk or high. That is, many victims will submit to sex acts when numbed by intoxicants but could not do so if fully sober. As one victim testified, she was given drugs because "you can't do a date sober."

Beyond merely numbing victims with drugs, traffickers have been known to target for recruitment women with drug addictions or victims who likely can be turned into addicts. This is no accident. Traffickers know that addicts are already enslaved to one master, and it is simple to induce an addict to accept a second master (the trafficker) who has a ready supply of drugs. Just as some traffickers exploit victims' craving for a family and fatherly love, drug-supplier traffickers have learned to exploit a craving for mind-altering substances. Once a trafficker learns a victim's weakness, he will use this vulnerability to gain control. That is exactly what happened in *United States v. Warren*, where a victim's drug supplier assumed the role of her trafficker. As the court of appeals described it:

At trial, witness Larisha Duncan testified she lived in Minnesota and was a prostitute who regularly purchased drugs from Warren. Duncan testified that when she told Warren she was a prostitute in 2004 or 2005, he expressed interest in splitting her earnings. Duncan testified that in May 2008, she moved into a house her mother was renting from Warren. After that time, Warren generally knew when Duncan went to prostitution appointments and how much she earned from those appointments because he was often present when Duncan scheduled her prostitution appointments, drove her to the appointments, or asked her how much she was earning from the appointments. Duncan referred to these appointments as "dates" throughout her testimony. Duncan testified that Warren sometimes paid for her to post online ads and book hotel rooms for her prostitution services, and that he started demanding she give him all her prostitution earnings in exchange for drugs. On several occasions when Duncan failed to give Warren all her prostitution earnings, he either beat her or withheld drugs.

United States v. Warren, 491 F. App'x 775, 776–77
(8th Cir. 2012)

Many sex traffickers began their criminal careers as drug traffickers. Often, they find sex trafficking to be less dangerous and more lucrative than the sale of narcotics. They bring to their new occupation their drug connections and experiences, including a ready band of suppliers. Traffickers will sometimes brag to potential recruits that they have access to all kinds of drugs and can get the victims whatever they need. Although most addicts are not choosy when they are in the throes of withdrawal, many addicted victims have a preference for certain types of substances. To the extent that victims have addictions to or a preference for specific substances, a trafficker with access to a wide variety of narcotics is usually better situated to satisfy such victims and thereby successfully recruit and retain them. For example, a ready supply of heroin might not be the ideal substance to use with a victim addicted to pain pills, especially if a trafficker is making his initial pitch to a victim. A trafficker with a ready supply of pills might have the upper hand in recruiting this victim.

Once a trafficker has some control of the addicted victim, it is rather easy to motivate the victim to become or remain profitable: threaten to take away the substance a victim craves. Indeed, if mere threats do not motivate the victim, it is easy enough to stop giving the drugs to the victim until she is in the throes of withdrawal and detoxification. Once that process begins, victims are extremely pliable and can be induced to do almost anything to make the pain of detoxification stop. Addicted victims, therefore, carry within themselves another vulnerability that traffickers are happy to exploit.

Furthermore, even victims who are not per se "addicts" can be motivated by drugs. Many traffickers have been known to induce victims to earn more with promises of drugs. As noted, most victims cannot continue to perform commercial sex acts without "medicating" themselves with alcohol or narcotics. In light of this need, drugs make a suitable reward for the cash that victims provide to traffickers. Especially because these narcotics help to ensure that victims will continue to submit to sex acts with customers. The drugs provided by traffickers typically cost only a fraction of the revenue that the victims generate. With enough victims, traffickers can obtain narcotics at a wholesale price. This further allows them to reduce overhead and increase profits.

CREDITOR TRAFFICKERS

Sex traffickers have also been known to use debts incurred by victims or their families to induce victims to perform commercial sex acts. Like an addiction, a victim with a debt has a vulnerability that traffickers can exploit. Peonage trafficking, as it is sometimes called, is often successful because of the power that unpaid debts give to creditor traffickers. Traffickers are notorious for using debt bondage with great frequency on impoverished victims, particularly those from Mexico, Central America, and Asia. Frequently, this is done in conjunction with smuggling a victim into the United States. That is, traffickers will sometimes smuggle victims into the United States themselves or pay smuggling networks to perform this task. Some victims are told in advance that they will be prostituted to reimburse the trafficker the costs he incurred in arranging for the smuggling. Many victims, however, agree to be smuggled into the United States based on false promises of employment as waitresses, cleaners, or kitchen staff, without the traffickers even mentioning a smuggling debt. Once the victims arrive in the United States, however, they are informed that they have incurred a smuggling debt and that the only way to pay off the debt is to submit to paid sex acts. For example, in *United States v. Garcia-Gonzalez*, the court of appeals described how the defendant made use of debts incurred by two minor victims to coerce them into prostitution:

> Garcia arranged for C.M. and her sister, B.Y., to leave Honduras with no money or clothes besides what they were wearing, under false pretenses that they would be working in a restaurant. C.M. was seventeen years old and B.Y. was fifteen years old when they were smuggled into the United States. On the day that C.M. and B.Y. arrived in United States, Garcia took them to buy revealing clothing for their jobs in his bar, where customers paid for the sisters to drink alcohol. Garcia kept and applied all wages earned to the sisters' smuggling debt. Garcia and his employees constantly monitored the sisters, and Garcia threatened that he would harm the sisters' family if they tried to escape. C.M. testified that Garcia told her that the only way she could make money was through having sex with customers. Garcia proposed that the sisters engage in prostitution, told them how much to charge for sex, and arranged the sexual encounters.
>
> *United States v. Garcia-Gonzales*, 714 F.3d 306, 313
> (5th Cir. 2013)

For some victims, the debts continue to accrue even after they are in the United States. That is, some traffickers continue to add to the debts expenses for food or "rent" that the victims are incurring while residing in the United States. Oftentimes, traffickers inflate these amounts to ensure that they can keep the victims for at least for a few years. Still other traffickers will loan money to women unlikely to be able to make repayment, and when payment are not made, demand that the victims submit to prostitution. Other traffickers will transfer this control over victims to another set of traffickers in exchange for a fee, usually the amount of the victim's debt plus a portion of the profits the trafficker likely will earn from the victims. Thus, victims are truly sold by traffickers to other traffickers. Undoubtedly, creative traffickers will continue to utilize variations of the creditor–debtor relationship to control victims.

Techniques for Retaining Victims

Many of the techniques that traffickers use in recruiting victims can be employed to retain victims. Retention of victims is extremely important to traffickers insofar as their profits are tied to the number of victims that can be prostituted. Most traffickers also invest at least some time, energy, and money into recruiting and "training" victims, and the longer they can retain victims the larger the return on their investments. For that reason, under "traditional" rules of pimping, victims are prohibited from leaving their traffickers, although some permutations of this rule allow victims to pay a "choose up" fee, which permits a victim to leave one trafficker for another trafficker. This simply creates a Hobson's choice for the victims; they are free to pick whichever trafficker seems less undesirable. Under these same traditional "rules" of pimping, competitor traffickers can take possession of a victim if she is "out of pocket," that is, noncompliant. But, again, this simply entails substituting the fist of one trafficker for another.

Some sex traffickers simply prohibit victims from leaving for the obvious reason that this will result in greater profits for the trafficker. To back up their commands not to depart, many traffickers explicitly tell victims that if they leave, they and/or their families will be killed or beaten. Other traffickers, particularly those trafficking juvenile victims, do not rigorously enforce this "no exit" rule, but they also do not make it easy for victims to leave and often will make efforts to isolate victims and hinder relationships with anyone who might assist a victim in departing. Perhaps because of the criminal penalties that sex trafficking minors entails, some traffickers are more liberal in allowing victims to leave for a period of time to return to their families or friends. Their thinking is that if they allow the victims some freedom of movement, these victims will be less likely to realize the extent of their exploitation and will come back to the trafficker after brief absences. This practice, of course, is also designed to maximize profits under the theory that it is better to allow the victims some brief respite rather than lose them altogether. Other traffickers, however, prefer to completely isolate victims and thereby preclude any absences.

Although initially, some victims may acquiesce in their exploitation, at some point, most victims want to escape the ordeal. Indeed, most victims quickly discover that a life of prostitution is not glamorous, traffickers are not romantic or kindhearted, prostitution entails substantial dangers, and there are many incentives to flee such a life. Because the traffickers' business model requires a steady supply of victims to prostitute, the traffickers have an equally strong incentive to ensure that victims do not depart. The traffickers, therefore, utilize various mechanisms to retain the labor they need to remain profitable.

When a victim is successfully recruited via promises of love, the Romeo trafficker typically continues the fake romance for as long as possible. As mentioned, many such victims will discover that the relationship is sham and is motivated only by greed. When that happens, the traffickers often must resort to other carrots and sticks to prevent the victims from leaving. Traffickers have become very creative in this department. Their methods include providing drugs to the victims (either to numb the victims or cause them to become addicted). They also isolate victims and prevent them from forming friendships and relationships that might provide them with a means of escape.

Other times, traffickers will use delaying tactics, such as promising victims that they must stay until they make $10,000, and then they can leave. Of course, once the $10,000 is earned, the traffickers frequently renege and impose a new amount or additional conditions. Some traffickers, for example, require victims to help recruit a replacement before they will be permitted to leave. Traffickers have also been known to hold a victim's property and identification documents until the victim produces sufficient money to "ransom" them. Traffickers also beat victims into submission and threaten beatings and violence to prevent departures. Traffickers are also well known for threatening to kill or harm members of a victim's family (*United States v. Taleek Swinney*, No. 1:13-CR-422 (E.D. Va. November 4, 2013)). Many traffickers explicitly inform victims that their families will be harmed if the victim even attempts to escape. Traffickers also use rape as a means of controlling, demoralizing, and punishing victims to ensure that they never depart. They have also been known to threaten revealing to the victims' friends and family that the victims were engaging in commercial sex acts. When all else fails, traffickers may promise to let the victim leave . . . tomorrow or next week, all the while knowing that this is simply a tactic to keep the victim for as long as possible.

Because retaining victims is vital to the success of trafficking ventures, traffickers often employ guards to prevent escape. For example, many traffickers will post a guard outside of the hotel room where a victim is housed and prostituted. Sometimes it is a trafficker himself, or other times, the most senior prostitute (sometimes known as the "bottom bitch") performs this function, or sometimes a member of a trafficker's gang will stand guard. Traffickers may claim that this is done to protect the victims and ensure that competitors don't "steal" them or their earnings, but the presence of a guard necessarily inhibits escape and reminds the victims that they are under constant surveillance. Such surveillance is often sufficient to destroy any hope of escape that victims may secretly harbor.

When traffickers lack the personnel to stand guard (or choose not to stand guard themselves to minimize observation by the police), they usually require victims to send frequent reports via text messages. That is, they often require victims to send a text message at every step in the process: receipt of a call from a customer; arrival of the customer; payment by the customer (including the amount paid); and the departure of the customer. Traffickers will punish victims who fail to text them after each event, so victims have a strong incentive to comply with these rules. Some traffickers will also perform surprise checks on victims to ensure that they are complying with this reporting requirement and are not withholding proceeds from the trafficker. Accordingly, through fear, traffickers can cause victims to perform self-surveillance, thus freeing the trafficker to perform other tasks.

Marketing the Victims
Customers willing to part with their money are essential to all businesses, including those in the sex trade. But sex trafficking entails a unique dilemma regarding marketing and advertising the victims. On the one hand, traffickers must inform potential customers that victims are available for commercial sex, lest the customers not patronize them. On the other hand, traffickers must hide the trafficking from the police, because both trafficking and prostitution are unlawful. This creates an obvious problem. If there is too much secrecy, customers will never learn about the opportunity to have sex with the victims. Too much notoriety, however, will invite unwanted attention from law enforcement personnel, which could result in the arrest and prosecution of the traffickers, not to mention the rescue of the victims. Traffickers use a variety of means to walk a middle path between these two extremes.

INTERNET ADVERTISING
As noted, many traffickers advertise their victims on a variety of Internet sites, the most common one being www.backpage.com. Because of the anonymity permitted by the Internet, traffickers can easily create and post these advertisements with minimal risk. Traffickers use prepaid debit cards to pay backpage.com's fee, so these payments generally cannot be traced to a trafficker. Although the advertisements usually include photographs of women (usually dressed in lingerie and in sexually suggestive poses), traffickers frequently harvest photographs from other advertisements on www.backpage.com and usually don't use the real photographs of the women and girls they are trafficking. The advertisements contain a telephone number that

customers can call to arrange a "date" with the victim. As a further hindrance to law enforcement, many traffickers use prepaid cellular telephones and periodically throw away these phones.

Some traffickers train the victims to answer the telephone calls from customers seeking sex, although others prefer to have trusted and experienced women answer the calls, sometimes the trafficker's "bottom bitch." This has two advantages. First, an experienced woman may be better at determining whether the caller is an undercover police officer. Second, because the initial negotiations are conducted over the telephone (usually in code), this allows the trafficker to know the amount the customer is likely to pay. If the trafficker knows the amount the customer is supposed to pay, when a victim fails to turn over that amount to the trafficker, the trafficker will know that she is withholding money.

Whether it is a victim or another woman who answers the calls, the trafficker will instruct them to be vigilant for undercover law enforcement personnel posing as customers. One common technique to screen for law enforcement personnel is to ask the caller his occupation. If the caller hesitates, the recipient of the call often will hang up. Most victims are instructed to ask if the caller is affiliated with law enforcement, apparently under the mistaken belief that police officers are obliged to confess their employment by a law enforcement agency. Victims are also told never to explicitly discuss sex over the telephone in case the call is being recorded. Another common technique is to demand that the customer send a "dick pic" that is, a photograph of his penis. This practice is based on the trafficker's belief that an undercover police officer will not send a photograph of his penis, and therefore, anyone who sends a photograph is a legitimate customer.

If the caller sounds like a legitimate sex customer, he is instructed to go to a location near the hotel (or apartment) where the sex is to take place. Once there, he calls again and will be told which hotel. The customer usually is not provided the hotel room number yet. Instead, he is instructed to call back once he has arrived at the hotel. There is a reason for this: once traffickers know that a customer is on his way to the hotel, they can begin their surveillance to see if the customer arrives with multiple cars or with someone in his car, thus signaling that the customer is really an undercover police officer.

Once at the hotel, the customer typically calls and states that he is at the hotel. The customer is usually asked to describe himself and the car he drove to further confirm that he is alone and so that the surveillance personnel can correctly identify him. Assuming the customer does not raise any alarms, only then is he provided with the number of the room to which he is supposed to go for the commercial sex. The trafficker's surveillance of the customer continues for as long as possible to ensure that he is not an undercover officer and does not communicate the room number to an arrest team. Once the customer is in the room, the surveillance continues, since the customer may be wearing a body wire, and an arrest team may arrive while the customer is in the hotel room. Victims are also instructed to touch the customer's genitalia or to require the customer to disrobe before discussing prices. This is done based on the belief that an undercover officer will reveal that he is an undercover officer rather than allow this to happen.

DIRECT SOLICITATION OF CUSTOMERS

Some traffickers decline to use the Internet to solicit customers. There are a number of reasons for this. Some are risk averse and realize that advertisements will eventually garner police attention. Other traffickers do not use the Internet because the customers they seek to service are illegal aliens who may not have ready access to the Internet or may not know which Internet sites to use. These traffickers are still able to make substantial profits without utilizing the Internet to advertise their business. Instead, they use other mechanisms to solicit customers. One method is to drive around to sites where illegal aliens are known to congregate and inform these potential customers that the traffickers have girls available for sex. Sometimes they even take the victims along to entice customers by letting them have a firsthand look at "the merchandise." Sometimes eager customers may have commercial sex right in the car, but more commonly, they are given a telephone number to call if they are interested in purchasing sex.

Other advertising mechanisms include handing out business cards (typically in the Spanish language) that advertise sporting goods, flowers, plumbing, automobile repair, or some other innocuous occupation. When handing out the cards, however, the potential customer is informed that they should call the telephone number if they want sex. Of course, in the event that the police or some uninformed person (such as a wife or girlfriend) found one of the cards, they would presume that the cards were advertising a legitimate business. From the trafficker's perspective, this system of advertising is superior to the Internet, because it helps insulate the sex trafficking from detection. Business cards are also much less expensive than Internet advertisement insofar as www.backpage.com charges around $8 to $12 per advertisement, and many traffickers post multiple advertisements throughout a day. The key drawbacks to using business cards include the fact that customers may lose them, and the trafficker must keep the telephone number listed on the business cards, lest the information on the cards become obsolete.

Still other traffickers have been known to take victims door to door in neighborhoods populated largely by immigrants, including illegal aliens. If a male answers the door and appears like a potential customer, the trafficker will then offer the victim for sexual services. To outsiders, it would seem that this method is quite risky, insofar as one of the residents could easily call the police and report the venture. Yet despite using this method to prostitute primarily underage girls, few people ever call the police to report this crime. Certain cultures believe that girls as young as 12 are old enough for sexual activities, and some members of those cultures who reside in the United States believe that there is little or nothing wrong with prostituting teenage girls. Apparently the traffickers have correctly foreseen that "apartment-to-apartment" advertisement bears only minimal risk. In such neighborhoods, traffickers are free to traffick underage girls with relative impunity.

Customer Relations

Like any other business, traffickers must have a mechanism to handle "customer relations" issues, such as "problem" customers or thieves posing as customers. Many trafficking victims are raped or beaten by customers. Sex customers have been known to become violent with little or no provocation. If a victim is in "the game" (as sex trafficking is called in some circles) long enough, they are likely to be raped or beaten by customers, including customers who want sexual services that some victims are unwilling to provide.

Many victims also encounter customers who rob them, typically while threatening to kill the victims. In stealing these funds, the thieves usually are not shy about harming victims, especially those who resist or are too slow in handing over the cash. From the traffickers' perspective, such robberies are worse than the victims being beaten or raped. After all, the traffickers do not care about the pain suffered by victims (unless it prevents the victim from working), but robberies deny the traffickers the very purpose of their trafficking: profits. Many traffickers, therefore, will beat victims who "allowed" themselves to be robbed. Indeed, because most traffickers impose a monetary quota that victims must meet, any robbery of a victim will usually entail the victim not meeting the quota and, therefore, punishment at the hands of the trafficker.

Rival traffickers also try to "steal" victims so that they, in turn, can prostitute these victims. From the traffickers perspective, the only thing worse than losing a day's profits is losing a stream of income. A loss of even one victim can substantially reduce profits, so traffickers that can prevent such losses will be able to maintain a higher level of profitability than rivals who cannot thwart such losses.

Because victims are typically afraid of the police or choose to avoid any entanglements with law enforcement personnel, many of these rapes, robberies, and kidnappings go unreported. Indeed, that is one of the reasons thieves and violent customers target these victims: they know that there is only a small chance that these crimes will be reported to the police. Because traffickers cannot obtain police protection without revealing the nature of their criminal conduct, they have no incentive to report rapes or robberies to the police and instead must fend for themselves.

Conclusion

The aggressive prosecution of sex traffickers can be an effective means of disabling traffickers and dismantling their ventures. It becomes even more effective to the extent that prosecution causes traffickers to disgorge their profits and compensate victims for some of the pain that they endured. But the prosecution of traffickers almost always must start with victims willing to report their exploitation, which usually occurs (if ever) only after a trafficker no longer controls a victim. As the discussion indicates, traffickers take great care to prevent the detection and prosecution of their crimes. But every victim, disgruntled accomplice, and arrested trafficker is a potential source of information for the police. Although prosecution of traffickers can never undo the harm done to victims, it can result in the punishment of traffickers. This, in turn, can deter both the trafficker who was prosecuted and other traffickers who are deterred by the punishments imposed.

Beyond disabling traffickers during their period of incarceration, prosecution can help prevent harm to potential victims who otherwise would have been trafficked. It can also provide victims with the knowledge that somebody cares about their plight. Although this may seem inconsequential on the surface, the belief of many victims is that nobody cares about the trauma they suffered, and it makes no difference whether they are trafficked again. Such feelings of despair inhibit victims from making a fresh start and feed into the defeatism that traffickers try to inculcate in victims. Finally, a successful prosecution of a trafficker can provide a victim with a feeling of safety and the knowledge that they can begin rebuilding their lives without having to worry about their trafficker reappearing or retaliating. That alone is something worth fighting for.

Discussion Questions

1. Is sex trafficking a victim-centric or economic crime or both?
2. Given the lack of barriers to entry into trafficking versus the substantial barriers to detection, what tools can we give law enforcement and/or prosecutors to level the playing field?

3. What role does the family unit play in both preventing and perpetuating the trafficking of a victim?
4. Is there a way to increase a victim's incentives to report her exploitation?
5. Would the legalization of prostitution effect sex trafficking?
6. What other means might be employed to deter trafficking?

19

MENTAL HEALTH CARE

HUMAN TRAFFICKING AND POSTTRAUMATIC STRESS DISORDER

VERONICA M. LUGRIS, MARY C. BURKE, SHANNON WHITE AND TINA KROLIKOWSKI

Traffickers engage in modern-day slavery through both sexual exploitation and forced labor. They are able to succeed in this lucrative criminal activity by threatening and coercing vulnerable children and adults who then experience a lack of control over their safety or freedom. Unable to protect themselves, trafficking victims often become submissive in order to survive, so that regardless of whether threats made are acted upon, the perpetrator maintains psychological control over the victim, often with devastating, long-lasting emotional consequences, including posttraumatic stress disorder (PTSD). This chapter will address PTSD as a potential mental health concern for victims of human trafficking.

Chapter Learning Objectives

- Know the DSM 5 definition of trauma.
- Know the criteria and four symptom clusters of PTSD.
- Know the preschool subtypes.
- Understand the variety of ways in which symptoms may manifest in victims of human trafficking.
- Understand potential neurobiological correlates of PTSD.

DOI: 10.4324/9781003124672-23

- Understand important treatment considerations when working with traumatized victims of human trafficking.

Trauma is defined as an experience that threatens one's sense of safety and security and may or may not involve physical harm. Generally, trauma is experienced as either a single or a repeating event that overwhelms an individual's coping mechanisms and interferes with one's ability to integrate and make sense of emotions and thoughts related to the experience. According to the *Diagnostic and Statistical Manual of Mental Disorders 5* (American Psychiatric Association, 2013), a traumatic event is one that involves "exposure to actual or threatened death, serious injury, or sexual violence" (p. 271). To meet diagnostic criteria, a person does not necessarily have to have experienced the event themselves; they may have witnessed the event, learned about how it has happened to a close family member or a friend, or may have repeated or extreme exposure through media to the trauma. A wide variety of events can be characterized as traumatic. Examples include naturally occurring or human-made catastrophic events such as dangerous storms and war or interpersonal violence such as intimate partner violence, rape, and emotional or physical abuse. Trafficking victims are among those individuals for whom captivity and threatened death, serious injury, and/or sexual violence are repeated, which increases their risk of developing PTSD.

Traumatic Bonding or Stockholm Syndrome

Traumatic bonding, which is more commonly known as Stockholm Syndrome, frequently occurs in human trafficking and other similar contexts. Individuals who are held captive (e.g., kidnapping, sex trafficking, etc.) or are victims of sexual abuse are susceptible to forming bonds with their captors. Traumatic bonding is viewed as an adaptive, unconscious survival strategy and arises from a combination of feelings in the survivor/victim including gratitude and fear (Deshpande & Nour, 2013). "Stockholm Syndrome" was coined in 1973 after the robbery of a bank in Stockholm, Sweden, in which the employees showed concern for their captors even after their release (De Fabrique et al., 2007). It is believed that the simultaneous experiences of fear (for one's safety) and thankfulness (for not exacting harm) result in victims forming a loyalty to their captors. Graham, Rawlings, and Rigsby (1994) identified four precursors to Stockholm Syndrome, including:

- an awareness of threat
- a perceived kindness from the captor
- seclusion from outside influence
- the belief that they must form a relationship with the captor to ensure safety

The resulting relationship leads the victim to be grateful toward the captor simply for allowing them to live (De Fabrique et al., 2007; Deshpande & Nour, 2013). The bonding process exists to preserve the self during extremely distressing events (De Fabrique et al., 2007). From this perspective, as noted earlier, traumatic bonding is viewed as an adaptive coping mechanism (Jameson, 2010).

Particularly vulnerable to PTSD are trafficking victims who experience severe physical and sexual assaults. Given that 70 percent of trafficking victims are trafficked for sexual exploitation, and sexual assault is a traumatic experience, these victims are likely to experience PTSD or posttraumatic stress symptoms (PTSS). Furthermore, more than 70 percent of trafficking victims are women and girls, and research suggests that women are more vulnerable to PTSD than men (Ditlevsen & Elklit, 2012; Seedat, Stein, & Carey, 2005) and that PTSD symptoms last longer in women than in men (Breslau, 2009; Breslau et al., 1998). It is important to note that the degree to which a person experiences PTSS after a sexual assault is extremely variable. Studies suggest that two weeks after a sexual assault, 94 percent of women will present with some degree of PTSS, while one in three women will meet full criteria for PTSD postrape.

The distinction between PTSS and PTSD is an important one. To warrant a diagnosis of PTSD, one must meet full criteria as specified by the *Diagnostic and Statistical Manual of Mental Disorders 5*. If one experiences symptoms of PTSD that are subthreshold, this is referred to as PTSS or "partial PTSD." The symptom criteria for PTSD are presented in four clusters. These clusters are intrusion, avoidance, negative alterations in cognition or mood, and heightened arousal. In order to meet the full criteria for PTSD, a person must present with each of these symptoms.

Intrusion symptoms include memories of the event that are involuntary, intrusive, and distressing. Distressing dreams, dissociative reactions, distress at exposure to triggers of the event, and physiological reactions to trauma cues are also included in this cluster. Avoidance is the next symptom set. This is characterized by efforts to avoid thoughts or feelings associated with the trauma and/or efforts to avoid external reminders that activate memories of the event.

Negative alterations in cognition or mood are a symptom cluster that was recently added to the DSM-5. This refers to a broad range of symptoms including an inability to remember aspects of the event, exaggerated negative beliefs about oneself, others, or the world, distorted cognitions of guilt, negative emotional state, anhedonia, feelings of detachment, and inability to experience positive emotions.

The final cluster, hyperarousal or hyperreactivity, is evidenced by irritability, recklessness, exaggerated startle response, problems with concentration, and sleep disturbance.

To meet a PTSD diagnosis, the duration of the four latter criteria must persist more than one month, and in some cases may last throughout a lifespan, causing significant distress or impairment in social, occupational, or other areas of functioning. Complicating early and accurate diagnosis is the fact that individuals may not exhibit PTSD for months or years following the traumatic event, only to be triggered by a situation that resembles the original trauma.

A recent diagnostic addition to the DSM-5 is PTSD for Children Six Years and Younger. This diagnosis was added to appreciate that children often have different sequelae of psychological trauma than adults. The main differences in these diagnoses are (1) traumatic experience cannot include media exposure, (2) intrusive memories may not appear distressing but may be expressed through play, (3) content of dreams though frightening, may appear to be unrelated to a traumatic event, and (4) the avoidance cluster and the negative cognitions cluster have been collapsed into one category.

Often, a person diagnosed with PTSD also meets criteria for other diagnoses, including mood and anxiety disorders, alcohol or substance abuse and dependence, or personality disorders, potentially complicating treatment (Alexander et al., 2005; Breslau, 2009; Caren et al., 2019; Raymond et al., 2002; Zimmerman et al., 2006; Zimmerman, 2003).

The Complexity of Human Trafficking and PTSD

Herman (1997) suggests that current PTSD criteria fail to consider the complexity of symptoms present in individuals exposed to prolonged violence, such as domestic abuse, sexual abuse, and torture, all commonly seen in trafficking victims. Herman proposes an alternative formulation that takes into account somatization, dissociation, and pathological changes in identity. The state of the science reflects a trend toward a greater understanding of the complexity of trauma, and the DSM-5 has begun to capture these more complicated traumatic reactions with specifiers under the PTSD diagnosis of dissociative symptoms. Survivors of more complex trauma, such as trafficking victims, are also at risk for self-destructive and risk-taking behaviors as well as revictimization (Courtois, 2008).

It is essential to consider that current PTSD diagnostic criteria reflect Western culture and worldview, limiting our understanding of the impact of cultural influences on trauma experience, specifically concerning trafficking victims from non-Western societies. Culture is a significant variable, given that there are approximately 11.7 million in bonded labor in the Asia-Pacific region, 3.7 million in Africa, 1.8 million in Latin America and the Caribbean, 1.6 million in Central and South-Eastern Europe and the Commonwealth of Independent States, 1.5 million in Developed Economies and the European Union, and 600,000 in the Middle East (ILO, 2012). Furthermore, countries of origin are primarily in South Asia, Southeast Asia, Latin America and the Caribbean, former Soviet republics, eastern Europe, and Africa. In contrast, countries of destination primarily include the United States, Japan, Canada, and many countries in western Europe, emphasizing the need for culturally sensitive approaches to working with traumatized trafficking survivors in our sphere, if not elsewhere in the world.

Healthy family or social support networks can mitigate the risks of PTSD in trafficking victims. However, while the Trafficking Victims Protection Act (2000) clarifies that all the risk factors for severe PTSD are present in the human trafficking experience, the mitigating factors that might help prevent the long-term mental health consequences, such as family and social supports, are generally absent.

Complex Posttraumatic Stress Disorder

Although not an official diagnosis classified in the *Diagnostic and Statistical Manual of Mental Disorders* (DSM-5), complex posttraumatic stress disorder (C-PTSD) is classified in the International Statistical Classification of Diseases and Health Problems (ICD-11). Accordingly, various researchers denote that C-PTSD shares similarities to, while at the same time being distinguished from, Posttraumatic Stress Disorder (PTSD). C-PTSD is not only akin to PTSD but to other DSM-5 diagnoses—Somatization Disorder, Borderline Personality Disorder, and Dissociative Identity Disorder (Herman, 1997). The distinctive quality of C-PTSD is that the individual who has been subjected to sexual exploitation via the human trafficking industry experiences profound issues within their core identity—core identity distortion in tandem with an impaired ability to emotionally self-regulate (Brewin et al., 2017). Even though the C-PTSD criteria have yet to be approved by the American Psychiatric Association (APA) for inclusion in the DSM-5, it is currently recognized by notable organizations—the National Health Service and the United States Department of Veterans Affairs (VA).

Because a sex trafficking victim's impairment is numerous and traumatically complex, it is crucial to understand their intricate issues. Courtois (2008) clarifies the magnitude of complicatedness stemming from complex trauma, in that it transpired over the span of months and/or years. Consequently, survivor-victims of sex trafficking typically suffer from C-PTSD, as the repeated abuse they incur is profoundly interpersonal and intimate.

Gattuso (2018) asserts that victim-survivors of ongoing trauma—sexual exploitation and trafficking—present with symptomology such as flashbacks that are profoundly intense. The ongoing nature of trauma for victim-survivors delineates C-PTSD from PTSD in that, it is a disorder resulting from extreme stress that continually interrupts an individual's life (Gattuso, 2018). In essence, it is a highly complex and advanced form of PTSD. It exists as a multifaceted disorder that affects an individual's entire cognitive, emotional, and mental processes.

Courtois (2008) delineates seven crucial symptoms of complex posttraumatic stress disorder (C-PTSD):

- Impairments in the ability to emotionally self-regulate;
- Modifications in attentiveness and individualism;
- Diminishing ability to self-examine/self-evaluate;
- Variance in the evaluation of the offender;
- Somatoform disorders; affective disorders;
- Dissimilarities in the observation/discernment of others;
- Variance in constructs of meanings.(Courtois, 2008)

Neurobiological Correlates of PTSD

Over the past two decades, neuroscience has begun to uncover the neurobiological changes that correlate with symptoms of traumatic stress disorders. Under normal circumstances, the human brain has evolved to effectively assess different stimuli, discriminate what is truly life-threatening, and respond quickly. While threat activates the autonomic nervous system (ANS), exposure to more extreme forms of threat, such as that found in human trafficking, significantly impacts individuals' ability to modulate sympathetic and parasympathetic nervous systems in the ANS, failing to organize an effective response to threat. Instead of a fight-or-flight response, immobilization ensues (Kozlowska et al., 2015; Van der Kolk, 2006). A clear example of this is the conditioned behavioral response of immobilization that follows inescapable shock in laboratory animals.

The traumatization of trafficking victims occurs in a context of repetitive and unrelenting boundary violations and loss of agency, self-regulation, and social support. Such conditions lead traumatized trafficking victims to develop a mechanistic compliance or resigned submission, not unlike the response demonstrated in laboratory animal subjects, even in situations where one might expect them to react differently.

Neurobiological findings show that trauma entails a fundamental dysregulation of arousal modulation at the brainstem level. Traumatized victims suffer from baseline autonomic hyperarousal and lower resting heart rate compared to controls, suggesting that they have increased sympathetic and decreased parasympathetic tone (Schneider & Schwerdtfeger, 2020; Cohen et al., 2002; Sahar et al., 2001). These biological changes can have a long-lasting impact on a traumatized trafficking victim's personality, such as losing the ability to regulate emotions or manage even small amounts of stress. They may exhibit chronic states of irritability or anger. For some, dissociation may become the primary way of coping, and they may be unable to account for significant periods of time. Victims may also become "dissociated" from their emotions so as to seem emotionally numb.

Many traumatized victims become chronically overwhelmed by their emotions and are unable to use their affective states as guides to adaptive action. They frequently fail to identify their feelings and may freeze when responding (Van der Kolk, 2006). When they try to attend to their internal process, they often report becoming overwhelmed by intrusive imagery and distressing physical and emotional feelings triggered by their traumatic experiences. Traumatized victims also tend to struggle with a clear sense of self and often report negative body image, potentially leading them to ignore physical concerns. Thus, a lack of emotional attunement may cause traumatized victims to neglect their needs and/or the needs of others.

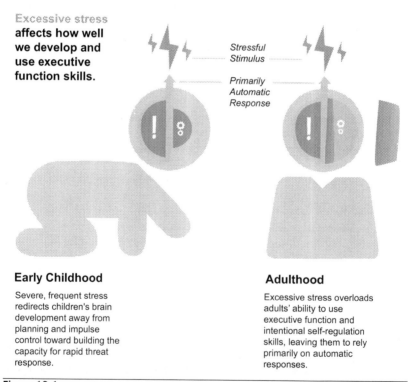

Excessive stress **affects how well we develop and use executive function skills.**

Stressful Stimulus

Primarily Automatic Response

Early Childhood

Severe, frequent stress redirects children's brain development away from planning and impulse control toward building the capacity for rapid threat response.

Adulthood

Excessive stress overloads adults' ability to use executive function and intentional self-regulation skills, leaving them to rely primarily on automatic responses.

Figure 19.1

Biological changes in the brain's cortical regions may cause loss of cognitive abilities so that a traumatized trafficking victim may experience difficulty remembering, organizing, planning, or thinking. Alternatively, a constant emotional state of numbness may lead to depression, lack of energy, and a sense of hopelessness. One of the most robust findings of neuroimaging studies of traumatized people is that under stress, the higher brain areas involved in "executive functioning" (i.e., planning for the future, anticipating the consequences of one's actions, and inhibiting inappropriate responses) become less active (Markowitsch et al., 2000; Shin et al., 2001; Harvard University, 2021).

Neurological studies of trauma survivors show changes in cognitive abilities, such as preferential use of the right hemisphere, inhibition of left frontal cortical areas of the brain, activation of the limbic area, and diminished hippocampus volume. There is also comprehensive literature showing dysregulation in various neurotransmitter and neurohormonal systems, including the hypothalamic-pituitary axis, catecholamines, serotonin, and opioid systems (Van der Kolk, 2006; Kozlowska et al., 2015).

Reminders of traumatic experiences activate brain regions that support intense emotions and decrease activation in the central nervous system (CNS) regions involved in integrating sensory input with motor output, modulating physiological arousal, and communicating experience into words. Traumatized research participants show cerebral blood flow increases in the right medial orbitofrontal cortex, insula, amygdala, and anterior temporal pole and a relative deactivation in the left anterior prefrontal cortex, specifically in Broca's area, the expressive speech center in the brain, the area necessary to communicate what one is thinking and feeling (Hull, 2002; Lanius et al., 2001; Lindauer et al., 2004; Rauch et al., 1996; Van der Kolk, 2006).

Neuropsychology and neuroimaging research report findings that traumatized individuals have problems with sustained attention and working memory, which causes difficulty in performing tasks with focused concentration and being fully engaged in the present. This is most likely the result of a dysfunction of frontal–subcortical circuitry and deficits in corticothalamic integration (Clark et al., 2003; Vasterling et al., 1998; Van der Kolk, 2006; Hoffman, 2013). Such dysregulation helps to explain how traumatized trafficking victims may either lash out or appear stunned in the context of minor challenges, leaving witnesses to question the validity of victims' responses.

Specifically, neuroimaging studies of people with PTSD have found decreased activation of the medial prefrontal cortex (mPFC) (Devinsky et al., 1995; Markowitsch, 2000; Shin et al., 2001; Hughes et al., 2011). The medial prefrontal comprises the anterior cingulate cortex (ACC) and medial parts of the orbitofrontal prefrontal cortices. The ACC specifically has consistently been implicated in PTSD. The ACC plays a role in the experiential aspects of emotion as well as in the integration of emotion and cognition.

The mPFC plays a role in the extinction of conditioned fear responses by exerting inhibitory influences over the limbic system, thereby regulating the generalization of fearful behavior, by attenuating peripheral sympathetic and hormonal responses to stress, and in the regulation of the stress hormone cortisol by suppressing the stress response mediated by the HPA. The fact that the mPFC can directly influence emotional arousal has enormous clinical significance, since it suggests that activation of interoceptive awareness can enhance control over emotions and allow traumatized victims to overcome their conditioned immobilization (Van der Kolk, 2006; Rodrigues et al., 2009).

A dearth exists in the literature that might determine the longitudinal impact of trauma after successful treatment. Research has found positive changes in the anterior cingulate and amygdala of patients with PTSD after a successful response to cognitive-behavioral therapy (CBT). Future research may uncover the potential for psychotherapy to positively affect neurobiology posttrauma.

Maslow's Hierarchy of Needs

As previously outlined in Chapter 1, from the perspective of how the trafficker utilizes Maslow's model, a trauma-informed approach will now be explicated while employing the same model. Children who have been sexually exploited/trafficked are especially prone to experience complex mental health issues—self-harm, suicide attempts, and other long-term mental health concerns (Laser-Maira, Peach, & Hounmenou, 2019). Because child sex trafficking denotes exhaustive covert processes in regard to how and where it occurs, researchers have experienced roadblocks in understanding the extent to which children are exploited (Greenbaum & Crawford-Jakubiak, Committee on Child Abuse and Neglect, 2015). In 2020, an estimate of almost 5,000 children were assumed to be exploited for trafficking in the United Kingdom, a 10% increase from the previous year (The National Referral Mechanism, 2020). Therefore, in knowing that these results are mere estimates in one global location in comparison to the entirety of global estimates, it is imperative for mental health professionals to utilize Maslow's model in tandem with current treatment considerations and interventions.

First and foremost, mental health and other social service providers should seek to swiftly assist victim-survivors with their most fundamental, basic needs—food, shelter-rest, clothing, and assistance to obtain proper identification (Hardy et al., 2013; Hom & Woods, 2013). However, resources are difficult to locate, especially when services are culturally insensitive, resulting in the victim-survivor feeling more fear due to the obstacles they may encounter in the process (Clawson et al., 2008; Domoney et al., 2015; Ijadi-Maghsoodi et al., 2018; Powell et al., 2018). Extremely long waitlists for services may

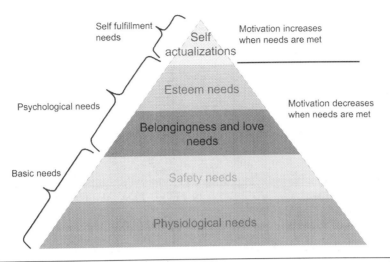

Figure 19.2 Maslow's hierarchy of needs

Source: Adapted from Maslow, 1943

further complicate and delay much-needed services to victim-survivors (Domoney et al., 2015).

Many children and adult victim-survivors feel trapped within the sex trade conglomerate due to their marginalized state and other aspects of vulnerability associated with basic physiological needs—experiences of sexual abuse, lack of education, and chronic homelessness, to name a few (Clawson et al., 2008; Dank et al., 2015; Greenbaum & Crawford-Jakubiak, Committee on Child Abuse and Neglect, 2015; Laser-Maira et al., 2018; Naramore et al., 2017; Roe-Sepowitz, 2012; Steiner et al., 2018). Accordingly, the all-encompassing abuse that victim-survivors have experienced repeatedly requires a holistic framework to adequately address their needs, which should include service coordination that is all-inclusive (Laser-Maira et al., 2019).

As there are numerous ways to devise unique treatment plans for victim-survivors, a beneficial origination point would be to conceptualize each survivor-victim's case via the vantage point of Maslow's Hierarchy of Needs. Additionally, it is crucial that all mental health service providers maintain an awareness of the chronic threats to safety that victim-survivors often encounter from unmet needs that emerge from their past and/or current connection to traffickers (Laser-Maira et al., 2019). Victim-survivors' need for belongingness is a vital aspect of their overall wellbeing, so mental health providers and evaluators must be culturally sensitive and inclusive. Clinicians should seek to assist victim-survivors from a framework akin to Maslow's Hierarchy of Needs to restore them with the self-actualizing state in mind. Therefore, if one's needs are not sufficiently addressed in a hierarchical fashion, then self-actualization may not be attainable.

Treatment Considerations

Ethnicity can impact the way individuals seek assistance, identify their problems, consider psychological difficulties, experience their trauma, and understand recovery. Many cultures do not distinguish psychological, emotional, and spiritual reactions from physical ones. Just as therapy can be commonplace in Western culture, individuals from other cultures may turn to folk healing, religious interventions, or other forms of treatment to support psychological wellness (Williamson & Hood, 2011; Williamson, Dutch, & Clawson, 2008).

It is recommended that treatment be individualized to focus on the traumatized trafficking survivor's needs and capabilities while considering safety and affect regulation as foundational to the work. Part of creating safety and a sense of self-determination includes

- informed patient consent,
- the assessment of motivation for treatment,
- clarification of treatment expectations,
- education about the therapy process in ways that are demystifying, and
- communication of a sense of hope.

Initial sessions typically assess for prior traumatic experiences, comorbid symptoms, and availability of resources. When inquiring about prior traumas, it is essential not to assume that disclosure will be forthcoming, even when there is a history of trauma present. Some traumatized trafficking survivors may only disclose later, as trust develops in the therapy relationship.

Trauma that is acknowledged can be assessed as part of a battery of psychological tests that include validated measures of PTSD, such as the Clinician-Administered PTSD Scale (CAPS) (Blake et al., 1996), the Impact of Event Scale-Revised (IES—R) (Weiss & Marmar, 1997), the Detailed Assessment of Posttraumatic Stress (DAPS) (Briere, 2001), and the Posttraumatic Stress Diagnostic Scale (PDS) (Foa, 1995). These tools can help the therapist identify the traumatized trafficking survivor's preferred psychological defenses, self-regulation, and relational capacities. Two other recommended instruments offer information useful in assessing more complex trauma, such as that found in trafficking victims. They are the Trauma Symptom Inventory (TSI), which assesses domains of the self and relations with others (Briere, 1995; Briere et al., 1995), and the Structured Interview for Disorders of Extreme Stress (SIDES), developed for the DSM-IV field trial (Pelocovitz et al., 1997; Zlotnick & Pearlstein, 1997). Also helpful is the Inventory of Altered Self Capacities (IASC) (Briere, 2000b), which assesses difficulties in relatedness, identity, and affect regulation, the Cognitive Distortion Scales (CDS) (Briere, 2000a) and the Trauma and Attachment Belief Scale (Pearlman, 2003), both of which assess cognitions. Measures of dissociation include the Dissociative Experiences Scale (DES) (Bernstein & Putnam, 1986; Carlson & Putnam, 1993), which can be enhanced by the Multiscale Dissociation Inventory (MDI) (Briere, 2002a) and the Somatoform Dissociation Scale (SDQ-20) (Nuenhuis, 2000), and the Structured Clinical Interview for DSM-IV Dissociation Disorders, SCIDD (Steinberg, 1994). Clinicians should consider using self-report measures or paper-and-pencil assessments with individuals that have a history of trauma, as this may be less threatening than clinical interviews (Center for Substance Abuse Treatment, 2014). Other common practices include assessing for suicidality or thoughts of suicide and making sure the client is grounded before ending sessions (Center for Substance Abuse Treatment, 2014).

Regardless of whether or not treatment includes psychological testing, it is paramount from the beginning for the therapist to emphasize safety in the therapy relationship. Part of this includes teaching traumatized trafficking patients how they may exercise self-determination during sessions and ways to contain emotions that may spill over in the following sessions.

Neurobiological findings suggest that it may be useful for traumatized trafficking survivors to learn to regulate their physiological arousal through mindfulness training techniques (Lazer et al., 2005; Rockinson-Szapkiw, 2017). Mindfulness training allows the traumatized trafficking patient to become a careful observer of one's inner experience and to notice one's breath, gestures, thoughts, feelings, bodily sensations, and impulses that arise.

Traumatized trafficking individuals need to experience that it is safe to have feelings and sensations. If they learn to attend to their inner experience, traumatized trafficking victims can appreciate that bodily experiences are always in flux, and they, themselves, can exert greater agency in their present experiences.

By learning to attend to nontraumatic stimuli in the present, traumatized trafficking individuals can learn to release themselves from reliving their past traumas, and they can practice reengaging their ability to protect themselves. Thus, the therapist helps the traumatized trafficking survivor gain control over extreme affective responses that may seem out of place, self-destructive thoughts and behaviors, addictions, and dissociative episodes.

While self-attunement is a fundamental building block in physiological self-regulation, interpersonal trauma often results in fear of intimacy. Engaging a traumatized trafficking individual in a therapy relationship may trigger shame and memories of betrayal. On the other hand, a strong working alliance of empathic attunement can provide opportunities to resolve past attachments and improve self- and relational capacities. Furthermore, connecting affectively with traumatic memories in the context of a supportive therapeutic relationship helps to provide resolution (Fosha, 2003; Murphy et al., 2019;

Neborsky, 2003; Schore, 2003; Solomon & Siegel, 2003). The goal is not to trigger the emergence of new memories, although that is a possibility when the trauma is addressed more directly (Caffaro, 2017; Gold & Brown, 1997). Connecting effectively with traumatic memories includes grief work that creates space for the traumatized patient to mourn losses associated with the experience. The goal is to emerge from the therapeutic experience with decreased PTSD and comorbid symptoms, increased self-attunement and self-regulatory skills, improved self-care, a greater sense of agency, adaptive interpersonal capacities, and a sense of hope and planning for the future.

Evidence-based techniques founded on research that show them effective are recommended, although this does not mean that other treatment modalities may not be sufficient, just less studied due to the complexity of variables involved. Examples of evidence-based techniques that have been shown to be effective with traumatized populations include CBT (Rauch & Cahill, 2003; Ursano et al., 2004) and cognitive processing therapy (CPT) (Resick & Schnicke, 1992), and attention to trauma-based cognitions can help decrease cognitive symptomatology related to a negative sense of self (Jehu et al., 1985; Roth & Batson, 1997).

CBT combines cognitive and behavioral approaches to change dysfunctional thoughts, feelings, and behaviors through techniques such as exposure therapy, thought stopping, and breathing regulation. Exposure therapy entails confronting a specific source of anxiety through progressively intense exposure until habituation is reached. Exposure therapy can take place in imaginal or in vivo formats. Thought stopping and breathing regulation are self-explanatory.

CPT is based around the concept of understanding how trauma impacts a client's life. CPT aims to help clients overcome the self-blame, changes in belief systems, overgeneralizations, and distortions resulting from trauma. Before processing the trauma in depth, the client is taught to label emotions and, like CBT, recognize the connections between events, thoughts, and feelings. The three primary goals of CPT are to remember and accept the trauma without avoidance of memories or emotions, allow natural emotions to be experienced in totality, and work toward more balanced beliefs instead of insincere maladaptive emotions (Resick et al., 2014). Importantly, the therapist works to teach the clients to question thoughts and assumptions related to the trauma so that they can act as their own therapist after termination.

Eye movement desensitization and reprocessing (EMDR) (Merlis, 2018; Shapiro & Solomon, 1995) is another empirically validated treatment for trauma survivors that uses rapid eye movement to induce bilateral stimulation to decrease traumatic imagery and negative emotions (Bradley et al., 2005; Rauch & Cahill, 2003; Ursano et al., 2004).

CBT has been found to have long-term effectiveness 8 to 14 years following treatment in patients with comorbid anxiety (McIntosh et al., 2004).

Benefits have been found in other populations as well, such as decreasing psychological distress in individuals with comorbid anxiety and depression who previously experienced heart failure (Slaughter & Allen, 2020). A combination of CBT and interpersonal therapy that focuses on the correlation between relationships and mood has been found to be useful for comorbid depression (Karasu et al., 2000; McIntosh et al., 2004; Weersing et al., 2006).

CBT, motivational enhancement therapy, behavioral therapy, 12-step groups, and interpersonal therapy are evidence-based treatments for comorbid substance-related disorders. In addition, self-help books, brief interventions, skill building, case management, and group, marital, and family therapy can also help (Gill & Cordisco Tsai, 2020; Kleber et al., 2006; Pascual-Leone et al., 2017).

Motivational enhancement therapy uses motivation to form decisions and plans for change (Miller, 2003). Twelve-step groups use group support under the rubric of acceptance of a higher power to help with long-term recovery (Nowinski, 2003). Treatment that focuses on managing substance abuse or dependence without addressing the underlying trauma will have less successful outcomes, and patients are more likely to relapse (Alexander et al., 2005). Further, it is important to utilize safety planning, especially if the traffickers still pose a significant risk or if the individual has engaged in behaviors that jeopardize their health (Pascual-Leone et al., 2017).

Despite existing research on the psychological effects of trauma, more evidence-based research is needed on trafficking populations. Many non-Western cultures have healing traditions that activate and use physical movement and breath, such as yoga, chi gong, and tai chi, all of which claim to regulate emotional and physiological states. Clinically proven pharmacological treatments for PTSD include selective serotonin reuptake inhibitors (SSRIs) and serotonin-norepinephrine reuptake inhibitors (SNRIs) (Bernardy & Friedman, 2015). There is evidence to suggest that SSRIs can work in conjunction with psychotherapy to improve PTSD and comorbid symptoms related to anxiety and mood disorders (Seedat et al., 2005; Ursano et al., 2004; Weersing et al., 2006). The Veterans Affairs Clinical Practice Guidelines echo the recommendation of SSRIs to treat PTSD, and as an alternative for those who do not respond well to SSRIs, they recommend tricyclic antidepressants (TCAs) or monoamine oxidase inhibitors (MAOIs) under the care of a healthcare professional and in concert with psychotherapy.

Diagnosis of PTSD in children has been less studied than in adults (Pfefferbaum, 1997; La Greca et al., 2010). Research on younger sexually abused children shows CBT to be more effective than other approaches (Putnam, 2003; Ramchandani & Jones, 2003; Trask, Walsh, & Dilillo, 2011). Psychological treatment should consider that sexually abused children often have long-term symptoms and/or later onset, and they may not benefit from long-term therapy (Putnam, 2003; Ramchandani & Jones, 2013; Hall & Hall, 2011). Notably, a review of research on children receiving psychotherapy posttrauma found improvements across all forms of therapy (including CBT; exposure-based, psychodynamic, and narrative therapy; supportive counseling; and EMDR) were greater than control in reducing PTSD symptoms (Gilles et al., 2013; Dorsey, 2016).

If we are to have successful outcomes, it is just as important to understand what does not work to understand what does work in treating traumatized trafficking individuals. One example of what has been shown to be countertherapeutic and potentially increase PTSD is psychological debriefing shortly after the traumatic event (Ursano et al., 2004). Further, clinicians must ensure that clients do not prematurely discontinue treatment by engaging in efficacious yet gratifying techniques (Corrigan & Hull, 2015).

Regardless of the technique(s) selected, the pace and intensity of treatment should match the client's capabilities. Briere (2002b) has cautioned therapists about the need to work within what he calls the "therapeutic window," or the client's ability to feel without repeating familiar destructive behaviors such as dissociation, self-injury, alcohol/substance abuse, and suicidality.

Treatment is not formulaic, meaning it needs to consider the individual's needs, and the techniques described should be selected, taking this individuality into consideration. For some, it may require more sessions than for others; still, for others, they may only complete part of the work. The option to return to therapy when needed is also advisable, as transitions and life changes and stressors may trigger prior traumas, albeit at a likely decreased level of symptomatology. Finally, termination (i.e., ending) can potentially trigger feelings of grief, fear, and abandonment. Thus, it is best when termination can be collaborative and clearly demarcated and processed.

Closing

Human trafficking survivors are subjected to various degrees of stress, maltreatment, and abuse. The impact of these experiences can be lifelong and have a significant impact on the well-being and quality of life of the survivor. To that end, it is essential that consideration of the mental health needs is at the fore of work with survivors. Attention to trauma and other mental health concerns when planning treatment is essential, as are considerations of cultural factors. Finally, ongoing research on the mental health needs of the survivor is necessary to ensure provision of quality care.

Discussion Questions

1. What are the criteria associated with a PTSD diagnosis?
2. What are some of the therapeutic approaches useful for working with traumatized trafficking victims? What do you see as the benefits and drawbacks of each?
3. What does it mean to work within the "therapeutic window"?
4. Neurobiological findings suggest that it may be useful for traumatized trafficking survivors to learn to regulate their physiological arousal through techniques such as mindfulness training (Lazer et al., 2005). What are some of the benefits of mindfulness training for victims?

References

Alexander, K. W., Quas, J. A., Goodman, G. S., Ghetti, S., Edelstein, R. S., Redlich, A. D., Cordon, I. M., & Jones, D. P. H. (2005). Traumatic impact predicts long-term memory for documented child sexual abuse. *Psychological Science, 16*(1), 33–40.

American Psychiatric Association. (2013). *Diagnostic and statistical manual of mental disorders* (5th ed.). https://doi.org/10.1176/appi.books.9780890425596

Blake, D. D., Weather, F. W., Nagy, L. M., Kaoupek, D. G., Charney, D. S., & Keane, T. M. (1996). *The Clinician-Administered PTSD Scale (CAPS)*. Boston, MA: National Center for PTSD, Boston VA Medical Center.

Bernstein, E. M., & Putnam, F. W. (1986). Development, reliability, and validity of a dissociation scale. *Journal of Nervous and Mental Disease, 174*, 727–735.

Bernardy, N. C., & Friedman, M. J. (2015). Psychopharmacological strategies in the management of posttraumatic stress disorder (PTSD): What have we learned? *Current Psychiatry Reports, 17*, 20. https://doi.org/10.1007/s11920-015-0564-2

Bradley, R., Greene, J., Russ, E., Dutra, L., & Westen, D. (2005) A multidimensional meta-analysis of psychotherapy for PTSD. *American Journal of Psychiatry, 162*, 214–227.

Breslau, N. (2009). The epidemiology of trauma, PTSD, and other posttrauma disorders. *Trauma, Violence, & Abuse, 10*(3), 198–210. https://doi.org/10.1177/1524838009334448

Breslau, N., Kessler, R. C., Chilcoat, H. D., Schultz, L. R., Davis, G. C., & Andreski, P. (1998). Trauma and posttraumatic stress disorder in the community: The 1996 detroit area survey of trauma. *Archives of General Psychiatry, 55*(7), 626–632. https://doi.org/10.1001/archpsyc.55.7.626

Brewin, C., Cloitre, M., Hyland, P., Shevlin, M., Maercker, A., & Bryant, R. (2017). A review of current evidence regarding the ICD-11 proposals for diagnosing PTSD and complex PTSD. *Clinical Psychology Review, 58*, 1–15. https://doi.org/10.1016/j.cpr.2017.09.001

Briere, J. (1995). *Psychological assessment resources. Trauma symptom inventory (TSI) professional manual*. Odessa, FL: Psychological Assessment Resources.

Briere, J. (2000a). *Cognitive distortions scale (CDS)*. Odessa, FL: Psychological Assessment Resources.

Briere, J. (2000b). *Inventory of altered self capacities (LASC)*. Odessa, FL: Psychological Assessment Resources.

Briere, J. (2001). *DAPS—Detailed assessment of posttraumatic stress professional manual*. Odessa, FL: Psychological Assessment Resources.

Briere, J., Elliot, D., Harris, K., & Cotman, A. (1995). Trauma symptom inventory: Psychometrics and association with childhood and adult victimization in clinical samples. *Journal of Interpersonal Trauma, 10,* 387–401.

Caffaro, J. (2017). Treating adult survivors of sibling sexual abuse: a relational strengths-based approach. *Journal of Family Violence, 32*(5), 543–552. https://doi.org/10.1007/s10896-016-9877-0

Caren, J. B., Mark, A. F., Eva, M., Tamas, K., & Marin, V. (2019). A review of epigenetics of PTSD in comorbid psychiatric conditions. *Genes, 2,* 140–140. https://doi-org.carlow.idm.oclc.org/10.3390/genes10020140

Carlson, E. B., & Putnam, W. (1993). An update on the Dissociative Experiences Scale. *Dissociation, 6,* 16–27.

Center for Substance Abuse Treatment (US). (2014). *Trauma-informed care in behavioral health services.* Substance Abuse and Mental Health Services Administration (US). https://pubmed.ncbi.nlm.nih.gov/24901203/

Clark, C. R., McFarlane, A. C., Morris, P., Weber, D. L., Sonkkilla, C., Shaw, M., Marcina, J., Tochon-Danguy, H. J., & Egan, G. F. (2003). Cerebral function in posttraumatic stress disorder during verbal working memory updating: A positron emission tomography study. *Biological Psychiatry, 53*(6), 474–481. https://doi-org.carlow.idm.oclc.org/10.1016/S0006-3223(02)01505-6

Clawson, H. J., Dutch, N. M., Salomon, A., & Grace, L. G. (2009). *Study of HHS programs Serving human trafficking victims. Final report.* Washington, DC: U.S. Department of Health & Human Services.

Clawson, H. J., Salomon, A., & Grace, L. G. (2008). *Treating the hidden wounds: Trauma treatment and mental health recovery for victims of human trafficking.* Washington, DC: U.S. Department of Health & Human Services.

Cohen, J. A., Perel, J. M., DeBellis, M. D., Friedman, M. J., & Putnam, F. W. (2002). Treating traumatized children: Clinical implications of the psychobiology of posttraumatic stress disorder. *Trauma, Violence, & Abuse, 3*(2), 91–108. https://doi.org/10.1177/15248380020032001

Corrigan, F., & Hull, A. (2015). Neglect of the complex: Why psychotherapy for posttraumatic clinical presentations is often ineffective. *BJPsych Bulletin, 39*(2), 86–89. https://doi.org/10.1192/pb.bp.114.046995

Courtois, C. (2008). Complex trauma, complex reactions: Assessment and treatment. *Psychological Trauma: Theory, Research, Practice, and Policy, 5*(1), 86–100. https://doi.org/10.1037/1942-9681.S.1.86

Dank, M., Yahner, J., Madden, K., Bañuelos, I., Yu, L., Ritchie, A., Mora, M., & Conner, B. (2015). *Surviving the streets of New York: Experiences of LGBTQ youth, YMSM, and YWSW engaged in survival sex.* Washington, DC: Urban Institute.

De Fabrique, N., Romano, S. J., Vecchi, G. M., & Van Hasselt, V. B. (2007). Understanding Stockholm syndrome. *FBI Law Enforcement Bulletin, 76*(7), 10–15.

Deshpande, N., & Nour, N. (2013). Sex trafficking of women and girls. *Reviews in Obstetrics and Gynecology, 6*(1), 22–27. https://doi.org/10.3909/riog0214

Devinsky, O., Morrell, M. J., & Vogt, B. A. (1995). Contributions of anterior cingulate cortex to behaviour. *Brain: A Journal of Neurology, 118,* 279–306.

Ditlevsen, D. N., & Elklit, A. (2012). Gender, trauma type, and PTSD prevalence: A re-analysis of 18 Nordic convenience samples. *Annals of General Psychiatry, 11*(1), 26–31. https://doi-org.carlow.idm.oclc.org/10.1186/1744-859X-11-26

Domoney, J., Howard, L. M., Abas, M., Broadbent, M., & Oram, S. (2015). Mental health service responses to human trafficking: A qualitative study of professionals' experiences of providing care. *BMC Psychiatry, 15*(289), 1–9. https://doi.org/10.1186/s12888-015-0679-3

Dorsey, S., McLaughlin, K. A., Kerns, S., Harrison, J. P., Lambert, H. K., Briggs, E. C., Revillion Cox, J., & Amaya-Jackson, L. (2017). Evidence base update for psychosocial treatments for children and adolescents exposed to traumatic events. *Journal of Clinical Child and Adolescent Psychology*, *46*(3), 303–330. https://doi.org/10.1080/15374416.201 6.1220309

Foa, E. B. (1995). *The Posttraumatic Diagnostic Scale (PDS) manual.* Minneapolis, MN: National Computer Systems.

Fosha, D. (2003). Dyadic regulation and experimental work with emotion and relatedness in trauma and disorganized attachment. In M. F. Solomon & D. J. Siegel (Eds.), *Healing trauma: Attachment, mind, body, and brain* (pp. 221–281). New York: Norton.

Gattuso, R. (2018). Complex PTSD: How a new diagnosis differs from standard PTSD. *Talk Space*. Retrieved from http://talkspace.com/blog/2018/03/complex-ptsd-versus-standard-ptsd/

Graham, D., Rawlings, E. I., & Rigsby, R. K. (1994). *Loving to survive: Sexual terror, men's violence, and women's lives* (Ser. Feminist crosscurrents). New York: New York University Press.

Greenbaum, J., Crawford-Jakubiak J., & Committee on Child Abuse and Neglect. (2015). Child sex trafficking and commercial sexual exploitation: Health care needs of victims. *Pediatrics*, *135*(3), 566–574. https://doi.org/10.1542/peds.2014-4138

Gill, M., & Cordisco Tsai, L. (2020). Building core skills among adult survivors of human trafficking in a workplace setting in the Philippines. *International Social Work*, *63*(4), 538–544. https://doi.org/10.1177/0020872818819043

Gilles, D., Taylor, F., Gray, C., O'Brien, L., & D'Abrew, N. (2013) Psychological therapists for the treatment of post-traumatic stress disorder in children and adolescents (Review). *Evidence-Based Child Health: A Cochrane Review Journal*, *8*(3), 1004–1116.

Gold, S. N., & Brown, L. S. (1997). Therapeutic responses to delayed recall: Beyond recovered memory. *Psychotherapy: Theory, Research, Practice, Training*, *34*, 182–191.

Hall, M., & Hall, J. (2011). *The long-term effects of childhood sexual abuse: Counseling implications.* Retrieved from http://counselingoutfitters.com/vistas/vistas11/Article_19.pdf

Hardy, V., Compton, K., & McPhatter, V. (2013). Domestic minor sex trafficking: Practice implications for mental health professionals. *Journal of Women and Social Work*, *28*(1), 8–18. https://doi.org/10.1177/0886109912475172

Harvard University: Center on the Developing Child. (2021). *The science of adult capabilities.* Retrieved from https://developingchild.harvard.edu/science/deep-dives/adult-capabilities/

Herman, J. (1997). *Trauma and recovery: The aftermath of violence--From domestic abuse to political terror.* Retrieved from https://archive.org/details/traumarecovery00herm_0Hoffmann, M. (2013). The human frontal lobes and frontal network systems: An evolutionary, clinical, and treatment perspective. *International Scholarly Research Notices*, *2013*, 892459. https://doi.org/10.1155/2013/892459

Hom, K. A., & Woods, S. J. (2013). Trauma and its aftermath for commercially sexually exploited women as told by front-line service providers. *Issues in Mental Health Nursing*, *34*(2), 75–81. https://doi.org/10.3109/01612840.2012.723300

Hughes, K. C., & Shin, L. M. (2011). Functional neuroimaging studies of post-traumatic stress disorder. *Expert Review of Neurotherapeutics*, *11*(2), 275–285. https://doi.org/10.1586/ern.10.198

Hull, A. M. (2002). Neuroimaging findings in post-traumatic stress. *The British Journal of Psychiatry*, *181*(2), 102–110. https://doi.org/10.1017/S000712500016180X

Ijadi-Maghsoodi, R., Bath, E., Cook, M., Textor, L., & Barnert, E. (2018). Commercially sexually exploited youths' health care experiences, barriers, and recommendations: A qualitative analysis. *Child Abuse Neglect*, 334–341. https://doi.org/10.1016/j.chiabu.2017.11.002

International Labour Organization. (2012). *ILO Global estimate of forced labour results and methodology*. Retrieved from www.ilo.org/wcmsp5/groups/public/—ed_norm/—decla ration/documents/publication/wcms_182004.pdf

Jameson, C. (2010). The "short step" from love to hypnosis: A reconsideration of the Stockholm Syndrome. *Journal for Cultural Research*, *14*(4), 337–355. https://doi. org/10.1080/14797581003765309

Jehu, D., Klassen, C., & Gazan, M. (1995) Cognitive restricting of distorted beliefs associated with childhood sexual abuse. *Journal of Social Work and Human Sexuality*, *4*, 49–69.

Karasu, T. B., Gelenberg, A., Merriam, A., & Wang, P. (2000, April). *Practice guideline for treatment of patients with major depressive disorder* (2nd ed.). Arlington, VA: American Psychiatric Association.

Kleber, H. D., Weiss, R. D., Anton, R. F., Jr., George, T. P., Greenfield, S. F., et al. (2006, August). *Practice guideline for the treatment of patients with substance use disorders* (2nd ed.). Arlington, VA: American Psychiatric Association.

Kozlowska, K., Walker, P., McLean, L., & Carrive, P. (2015). Fear and the defense cascade: Clinical implications and management. *Harvard Review of Psychiatry*, *23*(4), 263–287. https://doi.org/10.1097/HRP.0000000000000065

La Greca, A., Boyd, B., Jaycox, L., Kassam-Adams, N., Mannarino, A., Silverman, W., Tuma, F., & Wong, M. (2008). Children and trauma: Update for mental health professionals. *American Psychological Association*, 1–7. Retrieved from www.apa.org/pi/ families/resources/children-trauma-update

La Greca, A. M., Silverman, W. K., Lai, B., & Jaccard, J. (2010). Hurricane-related exposure experiences and stressors, other life events, and social support: Concurrent and prospective impact on children's persistent posttraumatic stress symptoms. *Journal of Consulting and Clinical Psychology*, *78*, 794–805.

Lanius, R. A., Williamson, P. C., Densmore, M., Boksman, K., Gupta, M. A., Neufeld, R. W., Gati, J. S., & Menon, R. S. (2001). Neural correlates of traumatic memories in posttraumatic stress disorder: A functional MRI investigation. *The American Journal of Psychiatry*, *158*(11), 1920–1922. https://doi.org/10.1176/appi.ajp.158.11.1920

Laser-Maira, J., Huey, C., Castro, O., Ehrlich, K., & Nicotera, N. (2018). Human trafficking in Peru: Stakeholder perceptions of how to combat human trafficking and help support its survivors. *Journal of Sociology and Social Work*, *6*(1), 34–40.

Laser-Maira, J., Peach, D., & Hounmenou, C. (2019). Moving towards self-actualization: A trauma-informed and needs-focused approach to the mental health needs of survivors of commercial child sexual exploitation. *International Journal of Social Work*, *6*, 27. https://doi.org/10.5296/ijsw.v6i2.15198

Lazer, S. W., Kerr, C. E., Wasserman, R. H., Gray, J. R., Grieve, D. N., Treadway, M. T., McGarvey, M., Quinn, B. T., Dusek, J. A., Benson, H., Rauch, S. L., Moore, C. I., & Fischi, B. (2005). Meditation experience is associated with increased cortical thickness. *Neuroreport*, *16*, 1893–1897.

Lindauer, R. J. L., Booij, J., Habraken, J. B. A., Uylings, H. B. M., Olff, M., Carlier, I. V. E., Den Heeten, G., Van Eck-Smit, B. L. F., & Gersons, B. P. R. (2004). Cerebral blood flow changes during script-driven imagery in police officers with posttraumatic stress disorder. *Biological Psychiatry*, *56*(11), 853–861. https://doi-org.carlow.idm.oclc. org/10.1016/j.biopsych.2004.08.003

Markowitsch, H. J. (2000). Repressed memories. In E. Tulving (Ed.), *Memory, consciousness, and the brain: The Tallinn Conference* (pp. 319–330). Philadelphia, PA: Psychology Press.

Maslow, A. H. (1943). A theory of human motivation. *Psychological Review*, *50*(4), 370–396.

McIntosh, A., Cohen, A., Turnbill, N., Esmonde, L., Dennis, P., Eatock, J., Feetam, C., Hague, J., Hughes, I., Kelly, J., Kosky, N., Lear, G., Owens, L., Ratcliffe, J., &

Salkovskis, P. (2004, December). *Clinical guidelines and evidence review for panic disorder and generalized anxiety disorder.* Sheffield and London: University, National Collaborating Centre for Primary Care.

Merlis, D. T. (2018). Eye movement desensitization and reprocessing (EMDR) therapy, third edition: Basic principles, protocols, and procedures. *Journal of EMDR Practice & Research, 12*(2).

Miller, W. R. (2003) *Motivational enhancement therapy: Description of counseling approach.* Bethesda, MD: National Institute on Drug Abuse.

Murphy, D., Elliott, R., & Carrick, L. (2019). Identifying and developing therapeutic principles for trauma-focused work in person-centered and emotion-focused therapies. *Counselling & Psychotherapy Research, 19*(4), 497–507. https://doi-org.carlow.idm.oclc.org/10.1002/capr.12235

Naramore, R., Bright, M. A., Epps, N., & Hardt, N. S. (2017). Youth arrested for trading sex have the highest rates of childhood adversity: A statewide study of juvenile offenders. *Sexual Abuse, 29*(4), 396–410. https://doi.org/10.1177/1079063215603064

Neborsky, R. J. (2003). A clinical model for the comprehensive treatment of trauma using an affect experiencing attachment theory approach. In M. F. Solomon & D. J. Siegel (Eds.), *Healing trauma: Attachment, mind, body, and brain* (pp. 282–321). New York: Norton.

Nowinski, J. (2003, June 18). *Twelve-step facilitation.* Bethesda, MD: National Institution on Drug Abuse.

Nuenhuis, E. (2000). Somatoform dissociation: Major symptoms of dissociative disorders. *Journal of Trauma and Dissociation, 1,* 7–32.

Pascual-Leone, A., Kim, J., & Morrison, O. (2017). Working with victims of human trafficking. *Journal of Contemporary Psychotherapy, 47*(1), 51–59. https://link.springer.com/content/pdf/10.1007/s10879-016-9338-3.pdf

Pearlman, L. A. (2003). *Trauma and Attachment Belief Scale (TABS) manual.* Los Angeles, CA: Western Psychological Services.

Pelocovitz, D., Van Ker Kolk, B. A., Roth, S., Mandel, F. S., Kaplan, S., & Resick, P. A. (1997). Development of a criteria set and a structured interview for disorders of extreme stress (SIDES). *Journal of Traumatic Stress, 10,* 3–17.

Pfefferbaum, B. (1997, November). Posttraumtic stress disorder in children: A review of the past 10 years. *Journal of the American Academy of Child and Adolescent Psychiatry, 36*(11), 1503–1511.

Powell, C., Asbill, M., Louis, E., & Stoklosa, H. (2018). Identifying gaps in human trafficking mental health service provision. *Journal of Human Trafficking, 4*(3), 256–269.

Putnam, F. W. (2003, March). Ten-year research update review: Child sexual abuse. *Journal of the American Academy of Child and Adolescent Psychiatry, 42*(3), 269–278.

Ramchandani, P., & Jones, D. P. H. (2013). Treating psychological symptoms in sexually abused children. *The British Journal of Psychiatry, 183,* 484–490.

Rauch, S. A., & Cahill, S. P. (2003). Treatment and prevention of posttraumatic stress disorder. *Primary Psychiatry, 10*(8), 60–65.

Rauch, S. L., van der Kolk, B. A., Fisler, R. E., Alpert, N. M., Orr, S. P., Savage, C. R., Fischman, A. J., Jenike, M. A., & Pitman, R. K. (1996). A symptom provocation study of posttraumatic stress disorder using positron emission tomography and script-driven imagery. *Archives of General Psychiatry, 53*(5), 380–387.

Raymond, J. G., D'Cunha, J. D., Dzuhayatin, S. R., Hynes, H. P., Rodriguez, Z. R., & Santos, A. (2002). *A comparative study of women trafficked in the migration process: Patterns, profiles and health consequences of sexual exploitation in five countries (Indonesia, the Philippines, Thailand, Venezuela and the United States).* Coalition Against Trafficking in Women. Retrieved from https://catwinternational.org/wp-content/uploads/2019/09/CATW-Comparative-Study-2002.pdf

Resick, P. A., Monson, C. M., & Chard, K. M. (2014). *Cognitive processing therapy: Veteran/military version: Therapist and patient materials manual.* Washington, DC: Department of Veterans Affairs.

Resick, P. A., & Schnicke, M. K. (1992). Cognitive processing therapy for sexual assault victims. *Journal of Consulting and Clinical Psychology, 60,* 748–756.

Rockinson-Szapkiw, A. J., Spaulding, L. S., Justice, J. M. S., & Owens, D. (2017). Identify, intervene, and advocate: Human services workers' role in youth sex trafficking. *Journal of Human Services, 37*(1), 63–76.

Rodrigues, S., Ledoux, J., & Sapolsky, R. (2009). The influence of stress hormones on fear circuitry. *Annual Review of Neuroscience, 32,* 289–313. https://doi.org/10.1146/annurev.neuro.051508.135620

Roe-Sepowitz, D. E. (2012). Juvenile entry into prostitution: The role of emotional abuse. *Violence against Women, 18*(5), 562–579. https://doi.org/10.1177/1077801212453140

Roth, S., & Batson, R. (1997). *Naming the shadows: A new approach to individual and group psychotherapy for adult survivors of childhood incest.* New York: Free Press.

Sahar, T., Shalev, A. Y., & Porges, S. W. (2001). Vagal modulation of responses to mental challenge in posttraumatic stress disorder. *Biological Psychiatry, 49*(7), 637–643. https://doi-org.carlow.idm.oclc.org/10.1016/S0006-3223(00)01045-3

Schneider, M., & Schwerdtfeger, A. (2020). Autonomic dysfunction in posttraumatic stress disorder indexed by heart rate variability: A meta-analysis. *Psychological Medicine, 50*(12), 1937–1948. https://doi.org/10.1017/S003329172000207X

Schore, A. N. (2003). *Affect regulation and the repair of the self.* New York: Norton.

Seedat, S., Stein, D. J., & Carey, P. D. (2005). Post-traumatic stress disorder in women. *CNS Drugs, 19*(5), 411–427.

Seedat, S., Stein, M. B., & Forde, D. R. (2005). Association between physical partner violence, posttraumatic stress, childhood trauma, and suicide attempts in a community sample of women. *Violence and Victims, 20*(1), S.87–98.

Shapiro, F., & Soloman, R. M. (1995). Eye movement desensitization and reprocessing: Neurocognitive information reprocessing. In G. Everly (Ed.), *Innovations in disaster and trauma psychology.* Elliot City, MD: Chevron Publishing.

Shin, L. M., Whalen, P. J., Pitman, R. K., Bush, G., Macklin, M. L., Lasko, N. B., Orr, S. P., McInerney, S. C., & Rauch, S. L. (2001). An fMRI study of anterior cingulate function in posttraumatic stress disorder. *Biological Psychiatry, 50*(12), 932–942. https://doi.org/10.1016/S0006-3223(01)01215-X

Slaughter, C., & Allen, C. (2020). Cognitive behavioural therapy for co-morbid anxiety and depression in heart failure: A case report. *The Cognitive Behaviour Therapist, 13.* https://doi-org.carlow.idm.oclc.org/10.1017/S1754470X20000197

Solomon, M., & Siegel, D. (2003). *Healing trauma: Attachment, mind, body, and brain.* New York: Norton.

Steinberg, M. (1994). *Interviewer's guide to the structured clinical interview for DSM-IV Dissociative Disorders-Revised (SCID-D-R).* Washington DC; American Psychiatric Press.

Steiner, J. J., Kynn, J., Stylianou, A. M., & Postmus, J. L. (2018). Providing services to trafficking survivors: Understanding practices across the globe. *Journal of Evidence-Informed Social Work, 15*(2), 151–169.

The National Referral Mechanism (NRM). (2020). In 2020, more children as ever identified as potential victims of trafficking. Retrieved from www.ecpat.org.uk/news/2020-more-children-than-ever-identified-potential-victims-of-trafficking

Trask, E. V., Walsh, K., & Dilillo, D. (2011). Treatment effects for common outcomes of child sexual abuse: A current meta-analysis. *Aggression and Violent Behavior, 16*(1), 6–19. https://doi.org/10.1016/j.avb.2010.10.001

Ursano, R. J., Bell, C., Eth, S., Friedman, M., Norwood, A., et al. (2004, November). *Practice guideline for the treatment of patients with acute stress disorder and posttraumatic stress disorder.* Arlington, VA: American Psychiatric Association.

Van der Kolk, B. A. (2006). Clinical implications of neuroscience research in PTSD. *Annals of the New York Academy of Sciences, 1071*(1), 277–293. https://doi-org.carlow. idm.oclc.org/10.1196/annals.1364.022

Vasterling, J. J., Brailey, K., Constans, J. I., & Sutker, P. B. (1998). Attention and memory dysfunction in posttraumatic stress disorder. *Neuropsychology, 12*(1), 125–133. https:// doi.org/10.1037/0894-4105.12.1.125

Weersing, V. R., Iyengar, S., Kolko, D. J., Birmaher., B., & Brent, D. A. (2006). Effectiveness of cognitive-behavioral therapy for adolescent. *Behavior Therapy, 37*, 36–48.

Weiss, D. S., & Marmar, C. R. (1997). The Impact of Event Scale—Revised. In J. P. Wilson & T. M. Keane (Eds.), *Assessing psychological trauma and PTSD* (pp. 399–411). New York: The Guilford Press.

Williamson, E., Dutch, N., & Clawson, H. (2008). *National symposium on the health needs of human trafficking victims: Post-symposium brief.* Washington, DC: Office of the Assistant Secretary for Planning and Evaluation, US Department of Health and Human Services.

Williamson, W. P., & Hood, R. (2011). Spirit baptism: A phenomenological study of religious experience. *Mental Health, Religion & Culture, 14*(6), 543–559. https://doi-org. carlow.idm.oclc.org/10.1080/13674676.2010.493860

Zimmerman, C. (2003). *The health risks and consequences of trafficking in women and adolescents: Findings from a European study.* London: London School of Hygiene & Tropical Medicine.

Zimmerman, C., Hossain, M., Yun, K., Roche, B., Morison, L., & Wattts, C. (2006). *Stolen smiles, a summary: On the physical and psychological health consequences of women and adolescents trafficked in Europe* (Ser. Open access e-resources). London: London School of Hygiene & Tropical Medicine.

Zlotnick, C., & Pearlstein, T. (1997). Validation of the structured interview for disorders of extreme stress. *Comprehensive Psychiatry, 38*, 243–247.

20

ADDRESSING THE PROBLEM

COMMUNITY-BASED RESPONSES AND COORDINATION

JUDY HALE

While many governments have made great strides in addressing the issue of human trafficking over the past two decades, community-based or "grass-roots" efforts have often been more effective at providing immediate responses of prevention and service delivery to victims. The necessity of community organizing and the critical role of collaboration among multiple professional communities will be described. This chapter will provide an overview of the good practices evident in inclusive, broad-based responses to human trafficking in communities as well as at the national level, focusing on antitrafficking work within the United States.

> "Combating human trafficking requires a comprehensive, multidisciplinary effort . . . . Coordinated federal efforts that incorporate state, local, and tribal entities; the private sector; civil society; survivors; religious communities; and academia are essential to an integrated response to human trafficking that leverages resources and amplifies results."[1]

Chapter Learning Objectives

- Understand key roles of the "3 Ps:" preventing, protecting, and prosecuting, and the "4th P" of partnerships.

DOI: 10.4324/9781003124672-24

- Understand frameworks for inclusive, broad-based responses to human trafficking.
- Learn to what is and what is not effective in antitrafficking partnerships.
- Understand the fundamentals of effective community-based responses to human trafficking.

Community-Based Responses and Coordination in Antitrafficking Work

The field of work that encompasses antitrafficking in human beings, also often referred to as "countertrafficking," has evolved from both the bottom up and the top down. An example of bottom-up responses in the U.S. (and other countries) is that local women's shelters and women's organizations have identified victims of domestic servitude and domestic violence at the hands of American husbands met online through international dating services. Another bottom-up example is that agricultural and other categories of labor organizers have discovered migrant laborers forced to work in dangerous and toxic conditions without pay, health care, or freedom of movement.

An example of a top-down response is the United Nations Protocol to Prevent, Suppress, and Punish Trafficking in Persons, Especially Women and Children, Supplementing the United Nations Convention Against Transnational Organized Crime, also known as the Palermo Protocol, which requires all states that are a party to the convention to promulgate national legislation within a specific period of time. The UN, which has the broadest reach of any law-making body on our planet, has designed this international law to address the issue at the international, regional, and national levels, with laws cascading down in some legal systems to state, county, and occasionally city levels.

- **Coordination** is the organization of different people, programs, and/or activities to work together effectively for a common goal or effect; it involves collaboration and cooperation.
- **Collaboration** is working together to achieve a common goal by sharing knowledge, learning, and building consensus.
- **Cooperation** is the process of working or acting together to the same end, creating greater-than-the-sum-of-its-parts outcomes and results; it entails assistance and ready compliance with requests.

Coordination, collaboration, and cooperation enable actors to better accomplish mutual goals and has long been a model of good practice in various other fields, including law enforcement, social services, community and

Figure 20.1   The UN protocol to prevent, suppress and punish trafficking in persons especially women and children, supplementing the United Nations Convention against Transnational Organized Crime (2000)

international development, social change, and legislative reform. While similar, these terms describe different aspects of successful antitrafficking work. Hounmenou discusses how coalitions "are helpful in implementing community-based projects in areas such as community health, homelessness, and violence . . . [Coalitions] increase the capacity of individuals and groups . . . and help individuals achieve objectives beyond the scope of any one individual or organization."[2]

Barriers to antitrafficking work at the policy and legal levels, as well as the service provision level, include the greater flexibility of traffickers, endemic poverty, structural inequality and discrimination, violence and social fragmentation, lack of funding and training for antitrafficking efforts, and corruption and infrastructure problems in source, transit, and destination countries. Jurisdictional issues can be a barrier for law enforcement responses to human trafficking. Lack of coordination and scarce resources between various groups working against trafficking often compound these issues, including barriers to effective collaborative work.

Challenges or barriers to coalitions and other collaborative work can include identifying an appropriate lead agency or entity with the organizational "capacity, resources, and [ability] to attract broad-based participating in the community" and to lead and manage a coalition; the issues that arise from competition among agencies for funding and other scarce resources; the issues around identifying common goals, addressed in the preceding paragraph; and reluctance to participate in a coalition by members who could potentially strengthen the group with their membership,[34] for example, reluctance because of disagreements or lack of resources including time. Hounmenou notes that government can provide the needed leadership and resources to coordinate nongovernment and government coalitions,[5] and Jones and Lutze acknowledge that coordination is desired within antitrafficking organization, but a lack of planning and coordination is a barrier to collaboration.[6]

In terms of identifying a common goal, the UN definition and the U.S. national definitions of trafficking include a full spectrum of labor, servitude, and other activities as well as forced prostitution and sexual exploitation involving force, fraud and coercion for adults, and any sexual exploitation of a child. Finding common ground or a common working definition for the purposes of joint activities and projects is fundamental to effective collaboration. Complete agreement, on the other hand, is not a prerequisite to effective joint endeavors.

Different professions and organizations may have distinct approaches that can create barriers to coordination. For example, many antitrafficking advocates believe categorically that all prostitution is trafficking, while others see prostitution as more varied, recognizing that in some situations, people working in the commercial sex trade are able to control the conditions of their labor and even advocate for regulation to achieve safer working conditions and ensure legal recourse for abuse and victimization. Unfortunately, end-demand efforts and the criminalization of sex work often increase harms to people involved in commercial sexual exchanges, "[w]hether someone's involvement in sex work is because of choice, circumstances, or coercion."[7] Differing viewpoints on issues such as prostitution and sex work do not have to preclude common goals, although sometimes differing viewpoints do inhibit collaboration in antitrafficking efforts.[8]

However, the benefits of navigating through the challenges of finding common ground to prevent human trafficking, to identify and provide services to victims, and to prosecute traffickers and stop individuals from further victimizing more people well outweighs the challenges. Hounmenou discusses the benefits of coalitions, looking at "how organizations with diverse structures can work together against human trafficking" by improving "victims' access to services through developing referral relationships, learning from the experiences of others, and collaboration among service providers and law enforcement to coordinate a diversity of services" as well as disrupting networks of traffickers and providing increased resources for antitrafficking professionals and victims.[9]

One administrative and strategic planning tool for improving coordination, collaboration, and cooperation, whether a group has been working together for a longer time or is just beginning to work together, is the Strengths, Weaknesses, Opportunities, Threats (SWOT) analysis. A SWOT analysis looks at internal strengths and weaknesses and external opportunities and threats to assess a program or set of activities. For example, a SWOT analysis of coordination in addressing human trafficking can provide an at-a-glance assessment of key issues and is a strong tool for quick analysis without requiring the resources needed for research or empirical data collection and analysis.

Table 20.1   Sample SWOT Analysis of Coordination to Address Human Trafficking

Internal Strengths	*Internal Weaknesses*
• Better information sharing • Faster response by various service providers for identified victims • Greater extension of outreach to identify victims and potential victims • Safer outcomes for identified victims, increased likelihood of testifying in court • Increase convictions of traffickers	• Can take more time, especially to establish • Many actors requires professional coordination by central agency or leadership from a relevant authority • Differing definitions, professional goals/objectives, data sets, and philosophical and moral perspectives may create barriers to collaboration • This model usually fails to address root causes of trafficking (racism and other forms of oppression, structural inequality, lack of safe migration)
External Opportunities	*External Threats*
• Increased reach, scope, and authority with multiple actors and agencies • Increased opportunity for funding due to multiple actors and because of funding trends favoring collaborative efforts • Increased potential to prevent, protect, and prosecute by improving partnerships • Streamlined investigations and enhanced victim support	• Could potentially be infiltrated by traffickers • Due to broad spectrum of professionals, could be difficult to unify on specific issues and some professionals may be limited for certain activities (e.g., law enforcement cannot lobby for better laws to enforce in order to assist in prevention, identification, prosecution, or partnerships) • Criticism of certain efforts as disempowering for victims can hinder coordination and funding

Multidisciplinary approaches offer benefits that can be more robust when combined. Both top-down and bottom-up approaches have developed effective mechanisms to address human trafficking through prevention, prosecution, protection, partnerships, and other strategies.[10] Both have been proven capable of cultivating different forms of coordination among varied actors. Broad coordination among many entities in both governmental and community-based responses can include a diverse array of professionals. In broad partnerships, it is possible to achieve a great deal more than any individual or even individual field, i.e., only law enforcement, only social services, or only faith communities, could accomplish. A major strength of community responses to trafficking is that they help develop partnerships that can more effectively identify, assist, prosecute, protect, and prevent trafficking. See the box insert for a list of professionals, agencies, organizations, and groups that could contribute to robust antitrafficking efforts.

Services needed to prevent trafficking, identify and assist victims, and prosecute traffickers can include many different professions and entities.[11]

- all levels of government
- academic and policy organizations
- antiexploitation, union, labor, and workers' rights groups
- case management services
- child and youth services
- community outreach organizations to vulnerable groups
- employment offices and agencies
- educational, vocational, and workforce development institutions and agencies
- faith or religious leaders and communities
- family assistance and support services
- grant makers
- housing, homeless, and women's or domestic violence shelters
- human rights groups
- immediate needs including food, clothing, cash assistance, and public benefits
- immigration and asylum professionals and migration experts
- GBTQIA+ activists and organization
- language, translation, and interpretation professionals
- legal aid, prosecutors, and law enforcement professionals
- medical, dental, mental health and counseling, and public health professionals
- sexual assault services

- substance abuse services
- victims' services organizations
- women's rights groups
- youth workers

Coordination among many actors should be based on the actual rather than the perceived needs of victims and potential victims. Individual trafficking victims often have different needs at different times, from identification through reintegration and ongoing support needs, including medical, psychological, legal, social, housing, cash, and vocational assistance. Recognizing and addressing victims' needs can play a crucial role in gaining a victim's cooperation in prosecution (if the survivor chooses to seek justice through the legal system), which in turn improves the likelihood of convicting traffickers.

In addition, working with victims and vulnerable populations significantly improves prevention schemes, which may range from education about risks and national hotlines to local and regional or statewide task force–type coordination groups, to broad economic empowerment and employment projects and socioeconomic reform to alleviate risk factors and enhance social, economic, and human security. Listening to victims is essential, and many task forces, working groups, and coalitions addressing human trafficking have begun to involve trafficking survivors in their work.[12]

Collaborative work with victims must also be trauma-informed. Trauma-informed means understanding the diverse effects that trauma has on victims. The U.S. Department of Justice Office for Victims of Crime Training and Technical Assistance Center calls a trauma-informed approach "imperative" in working with human trafficking victims, including "understand[ing] trauma, and how trauma affects victims' response to services and the criminal justice process, and the individual task force members' response to victims."[13] Polaris has reported on trauma-informed work that has significantly improved outcomes for victims of trafficking, who experience a variety of forms of trauma.[14]

Good Practice

Best practices or good practices are generally accepted and informally or formally standardized techniques, methods, or processes that have been proven to be effective by other professionals or colleagues in the same or related fields. Even when these practices may not be completely adaptable to every organization, situation, or culture, they can still hold valuable lessons. Thus the term **good practice** is used, because the word "best" indicates one superior way of carrying out an activity or program, and this does not allow for organizational, contextual, or cultural variations. In antitrafficking work, partnerships and collaboration are a good practice.[15]

Here is an illustration of a good practice in antitrafficking coordination:

A Good Practice—Listening to Survivors

An example of a good practice is the United States Advisory Council on Human Trafficking. This council "provides a formal platform for trafficking survivors to advise and make recommendations on federal antitrafficking policies to the President's Interagency Task Force to Monitor and Combat Trafficking in Persons. Each member is a **survivor** of human trafficking, and together they represent a diverse range of backgrounds and experiences."[16]

The "3Ps" and Partnerships: The Fourth "P"

U.S. antitrafficking law is centered on the "3Ps" of prevention, protection, and prosecution. In 2009, U.S. Secretary of State Hillary Rodham Clinton added a "fourth P" of partnership "as a pathway to achieve progress on the 3Ps in the effort against modern slavery."[17] Multidisciplinary approaches to antitrafficking work are based on the principle that effective strategies require systematic and coordinated services from a wide variety of professionals. Meaningful, multidisciplinary partnerships have the potential to "bring about fundamental or systemic change, moving beyond mere mitigation of human trafficking" to reduce and prevent trafficking.[18]

Multidisciplinary partnerships can enhance antitrafficking work in a variety of ways. The more people who are working to raise awareness, the better able they are to identify the most hidden victims of human trafficking. By working collaboratively with community groups, social services, and culturally competent interpreters, law enforcement is better able to correctly identify victims and avoid deportation, abuse, and further trauma. Collaboration enables law enforcement to appropriately investigate trafficking cases and support victim witnesses and their families in a way that is safe and not harmful to victims or their families. By working together, social service professionals help victims to feel safer; the victims may receive a variety of social services and support, which can help them navigate the criminal justice system in the prosecution of traffickers, where possible; and law enforcement is then better able to obtain convictions and stop traffickers.

Collaboration among diverse professional fields enables task forces, working groups, and coalitions to develop, implement, and improve effective, worthwhile prevention and victim reintegration programs and to inform strong, appropriate laws at various levels, from international and national to state and local. Indeed, "purposeful partnership" to combine prosecution, prevention, and protection "by partnering those who are law-enforcement minded and those who are victim-oriented is the most effective way . . . to attack the trafficking problem in practice."[19]

Combating human trafficking requires the expertise, resources, and efforts of many individuals and entities. It is a complex, multifaceted challenge requiring a comprehensive response of government and nongovernment entities in such areas as human rights, labor and employment, health and social services, and law enforcement. Creating a positive impact requires partnerships among all these entities.

> The power of a successful anti-human collaborative effort can transform the limitations of a singular agency or organization into a strong, strategic multidisciplinary team with substantially improved capacity to impact the problem.[20]

Partnerships increase the effectiveness of antitrafficking efforts by bringing together diverse experiences, amplifying messages, and leveraging resources, thereby accomplishing more together than any one entity or sector would be able to accomplish alone.[21] Examples of existing partnerships that governments currently use to facilitate prosecution, prevention, and protection include:

- task forces among law enforcement agencies that cooperate to share intelligence, work across jurisdictions, and coordinate across borders;[22]
- alliances between governments and business associations that seek to create protocols and establish compliance mechanisms, including monitoring and improvements, for slavery-free supply chains;[23] and
- coalitions of multiple levels of law enforcement, social services, medical providers, and other governmental agencies and nongovernmental organizations working together.[24]

Outside of governmental efforts, partnerships include coalitions of nongovernmental organizations (NGOs) coming together for purposes of advocacy, service provision, and information sharing, and networks of survivors whose experiences inform the broader trafficking movement. Collaboration between government and nongovernment entities is essential for effective antitrafficking efforts.

While there is broad agreement on the purpose and benefits of a partnership approach to human trafficking, good practices are still emerging for proven, successful strategies for coalitions. Gerassi, Nichols, and Michelson have noted benefits of coalition work, including "opportunities for practitioners to expand community awareness and provide training, to build referral networks with other service providers, to coordinate services, and to engage in cross-disciplinary collaboration."[25] Jones and Lutze found that collaborative interagency work needed funding, clear leadership, and training especially for law enforcement policies and procedures; they also found that competition for funding could hinder collaboration.[26] Many victims, once liberated or deported home, are returned to the same circumstances from which they were trafficked. Their situation now compounded by the trauma of their trafficking experience, they often try to migrate again to do what they set out to do in the first place: improve their and their families' lives. Trafficking victims who are not repatriated but sent home within their own country are similarly returned to the same situations from which they were trafficked, leaving them vulnerable to further exploitation if they are not connected with supportive services. Social service provision plays a key role in victim rehabilitation to reduce or eliminate repeated vulnerability—victims who "try again" and think they can "do better this time," or victims who are "rescued" and returned to the same underlying circumstances that left them vulnerable to trafficking in the first place.

NGOs and other human service or social service providers can ensure that victims feel safe and understand the value of participating in legal proceedings as well as have economic options and alternatives to being retrafficked or accepting risky smuggling or migration opportunities. All of this can further help law enforcement develop stronger cases to gain more convictions. This will both stop the traffickers who are convicted and send a clear message of the negative repercussions of engaging in human trafficking for profit. However, deeper structural changes are needed for prevention to meaningfully address the vulnerabilities that lead to trafficking.[27]

Formal partnerships with law enforcement and government actors often increase the reputation or legitimacy of NGOs and social services, which thereby increases their ability to obtain and maintain funding to provide services. Formal partnerships also increase public trust of government and law enforcement partners in many contexts. For example, the U.S. Department of Health and Human Services funds the Polaris Project to operate a national hotline.[28] This fosters mutual trust and formalizes lines of communication between the two partners. Perhaps most of all, people with uncertain or illegal documentation status in the U.S. are more comfortable to call the nongovernmental hotline for information and assistance, because they are not reporting themselves to the government but seeking assistance from a concerned, compassionate nongovernmental organization. This is especially important because traffickers often threaten deportation or criminal charges to coerce foreign national and U.S. citizen victims' complicity.[29]

- **Task Force:** A temporary group organized for a defined task or activity.[30]
- **Coalition:** An alliance formed by a group of individuals or organizations with diverse expertise and at least some overlapping interests, who cooperate in joint endeavors and collaborate in a "working alliance" for a specific common cause or goal that they could not accomplish separately.[31] Coalitions may be temporary or ongoing, although they generally exist for a longer period of time than a task force and may be viewed as permanent or long term. A coalition's mandate or activities may be broader and more flexible in scope than a task force.

Governments and community-based organizations both play important but different roles in responding to human trafficking. Community-based responses lead the way in antitrafficking work in many countries, including the U.S. Think of an elephant and a mouse: a mouse, like a community group, can be nimble on the ground and change direction quickly. An elephant, like a government, takes time to change direction.[32] As trafficking in persons has come to the attention of more people over the past two decades, small groups and organizations have been better able to quickly identify and assist victims. Sometimes community groups, which do not directly know about or seek to identify and assist victims of trafficking in particular, identify victims by chance. Members of a community are often best able to identify and address problems in their community, especially problems that seem hidden. One example is domestic abuse victims who met their partner through an international matchmaking organization and are identified and assisted by a faith community or a women's rights or domestic violence organization. Another example is labor organizers and union outreach workers who have identified agricultural and manufacturing workers in forced-labor and trafficking situations.

The processes of governments—drafting legislation, creating enforcement mechanisms, providing budgets, hiring and training staff—are often inherently slow and cumbersome. Nonetheless, these are necessary processes for effective antitrafficking efforts. Governments can provide the laws to protect victims and prosecute offenders by providing a legal framework and, in many countries, by providing funding for antitrafficking work domestically and sometimes also abroad. In fact, governments often rely on nongovernment and community actors to inform the process in developing appropriate, effective legal and administrative frameworks to address trafficking in persons.

This is especially important to realize in an antitrafficking context, where a community may have very little awareness of resources, and local professionals, especially in legal and law enforcement roles, can be unaware of human trafficking problems in a particular community. It is also important to include members of local communities in national and local antitrafficking endeavors.

Working from common definitions, policies, and procedures is essential to effective coordination for identifying and assisting victims, prosecuting traffickers, and meaningful prevention efforts. Common definitions in raising awareness of the root causes of trafficking must be integrated into efforts to address poverty, conflict, instability, economic crisis, inequality, all forms of discrimination, and cultural tolerance of violence against women, people of color, transgender and gender nonconforming persons, youth, and other vulnerable groups of people.

Risks to Community-Based Responses and Antitrafficking Work

Antitrafficking efforts without a common framework of definitions and laws will be hindered in efforts to engage in effective work. Moreover, analysis by practitioners and academics has noted that antitrafficking efforts, if not carried out thoughtfully, have the potential to worsen conditions for victims as well as other migrants. As one example, Busza, Castle, and Diarra identified that efforts to reduce or stop human trafficking often harmed both voluntary migrants and human trafficking victims.[33] Busza et al. found that antitrafficking efforts aimed at increasing regulation at border crossings can effectively create barriers to migration and leave many migrants, including trafficking victims, further marginalized and therefore vulnerable to exploitation. Another finding was that ending funding for organizations that did not "explicitly support the eradication of all sex work" removed financial support for local organizations that support sex workers to improve their safety.[34]

Another example is criminalization of an activity in which victims are forced to engage, which can increase the negative repercussions for victims if they have to change to more dangerous activities, such as when street begging becomes illegal, or added risks if they continue, including risks of incarceration, fines, and a criminal record. A well-documented example is how two federal U.S. laws, Fight Online Sex Trafficking Act (FOSTA) and Stop Enabling Sex Traffickers Act (SESTA), have caused economic harm and decreased safety for consenting sex workers in the U.S. by criminalizing ways that many consenting sex workers used online platforms to generate business and screen clients for safety.[35]

The issue of conflating trafficking with prostitution is another example of the potential for complexity and disagreement in definitions and motivations within antitrafficking work. In addition to the previous discussion on prostitution and sex work, many activists and experts express concern about defining human trafficking as only prostitution, or only prostitution of women and children, because human trafficking also encompasses male sex trafficking victims, as well as male, female, trans, nonbinary, adult, and child victims of myriad forms of nonsexual exploitation and mixed sexual and non-sexual forms of exploitation across all industries.[36] A narrow definition excludes vast numbers of victims from policies and assistance, which is a great disservice to these victims.

This also causes confusion between trafficking and prostitution. While many people working in sexual industries are coerced to greater or lesser extents, programs should focus on those who are not able to leave this work behind due to force and coercion. Many, albeit perhaps a minority, of the people working in sex industries are able to control the conditions and hours of their work, accept or decline clients, influence and keep their wages, and can change their work if and when they choose. These sex workers are not victims of trafficking involving force, fraud, and coercion, and their choices are not for anyone else to control or vilify.

Susie Bright points out that some antitrafficking advocates are "too eager to close down every manifestation of sex work," insinuating antisex rather than antitrafficking motivations among antitrafficking actors, who often refer to themselves as abolitionists.[37] These are examples of ways that differing definitions and approaches can conflict and hinder antitrafficking efforts.

Good Practices to Establish or Improve an Antitrafficking Coalition

Good practices will vary from community to community and country to country; however, the following are elements to consider in developing or improving an antitrafficking task force or coalition.

- Do no harm.[38] This includes not intervening to "rescue" a person without appropriate preparation for their safety; not assuming that a person is a victim because they are involved in certain categories of work; and not assuming that a perceived victim would self-identify as a victim.
- Maintain a victim-centered, trauma-informed approach.[39]
- Work with local migrant, immigrant, and international groups to learn about communities in your area and take their concerns into consideration.
- Establish a common working definition for the purposes of common action and planning. Everyone does not have to agree completely, but they have to agree to a common definition for the purposes of working together.[40]
- Hold meetings at a regular meeting time and place that is accessible to all attendees, or identify other forums for a regular exchange of information and for building professional, collegial relationships.

- Have regular facilitator/s. Facilitators can rotate or share duties as co-facilitators or co-chairs. Keep in mind that it is helpful for leaders and all participants to maintain consistency in the leadership as well as to change leadership before the obligations become too onerous for any one person.
- Structure the meetings. Structure can take many forms based on the needs and interests of the group and can change over time. Some examples include: every participant speaking briefly to report on activities; gathering information via email, web form, or paper for a shared matrix of activities (which is also good for record keeping); taking turns to present to or train other members on specific issues and specialized activities; inviting specialists or experts from local, state, and national organizations to present on new or less-understood topics.
- Based on identified needs in your region, engage in ongoing education to increase understanding of domestic victims, underage victims of human trafficking including LGBTQIA+ youth, minority and immigrant groups in your area who may be trafficking victims.
- Develop and improve mechanisms for collaborative efforts across disciplines (nongovernmental organizations and law enforcement) and jurisdictions (local, state, federal, and/or international) and consider a statewide organizational structure for improved services.
- Identify, when possible, an existing agency to facilitate coordination rather than creating a new entity.
- Seek ways to increase and improve efforts for prevention, protection, prosecution including identification and investigation, partnership, and data collection and reporting.
- Listen and cooperate. Find the common ground among potential collaborators, and find ways to work together. Where there is no common ground, do not force collaboration.
- Read and research. Learn about and share information to improve the cultural competency or cultural humility of members and the coalition or group as a whole. Educate yourself about the culture of the area or region for which coordination is needed, as well as the culture from which potential victims are or may be. Be aware that many victims are from minority groups, whose languages and cultures may be quite different from majority groups within their area or country of origin.
- Document your work. Documentation and data are some of the best ways to obtain or maintain funding for your work and to recruit more partners. Find a professional or an agency to partner with that has the capacity and competency to document the work of a coalition or coordinating body. Use either an agency that performs this work or a person with relevant training and experience; many universities are now studying antitrafficking efforts and could be excellent partners in this regard. Google documents are excellent for small, unfunded or underfunded

groups to share information, resources, tips, and contact information with service providers and other partners.

- Volunteer or fundraise. Research several antitrafficking organizations and identify one that has needs you can meet. Many of these organizations have developed multiple and creative grassroots awareness-raising and fundraising endeavors. Traffickers are infinitely creative in the ways they both use and circumvent laws to fit their profit motive; antitraffickers need to apply creativity to their efforts as well.

Case Study Resources

A rich resource of case studies on human trafficking, including analytical profiles of trafficking by world region, is Dr. Louis Shelley's *Human Trafficking: A Global Perspective* (2010). Similarly, Amanda D. Clark's *Framing the Fight Against Human Trafficking: Movement Coalitions And Tactical Diffusion* (2019) describes how "many different anti-trafficking organizations have worked together as a coalition to influence anti-trafficking public policy," and "came together . . . because they found a common ground . . . human rights."[41]

Conclusion

Each country, region, and community may develop different responses to human trafficking. The types of trafficking that exist or that are identified in an area shape the antitrafficking responses, as do the resources available and the knowledge and capacity that local people have to address this complex and dangerous issue. Not all antitrafficking initiatives are exemplary, yet all contribute to increasing safety for vulnerable people, to upholding the law, and to the observance of fundamental human rights. By assessing resources and identifying opportunities for collaboration, people in villages, towns, cities, and governments can work together to make their home, their community, and their country a better and safer place to live for every person.

Discussion Questions

- What are elements of positive, constructive coordination?
- What are barriers to coordination in many countries and cultures?

- How does coordination of various antitrafficking actors enhance the overall response to trafficking and the experience of victims once identified?
- What is the importance of community-based responses and community groups to antitrafficking work?
- Why is trauma-informed work important to assisting victims of human trafficking?
- Using news reports, build a case study illustrating how a community or community partnership has identified and assisted a victim or group of victims of human trafficking.
- Why is partnership important to any level of anti–trafficking-in-persons work?
- Describe some of the benefits of taking a coordinated approach in carrying out antitrafficking work.
- If you are hired to lead an antitrafficking initiative (in the U.S., your own country, or another country), what are your first steps, and from whom do you seek input?

Notes

1. U.S. Department of State, *Federal Response on Human Trafficking*, available at https://www.state.gov/humantrafficking/ (last accessed February 20, 2021).
2. Hounmenou, Charles., A statewide coalition's input in human trafficking policy implementation: Member organizations' involvement and perceptions. *Journal of Human Trafficking* (2021) 7:1, pp. 69–87 at 70–91.
3. UN, *Protocol to Prevent, Suppress and Punish Trafficking in Persons Especially Women and Children, Supplementing the United Nations Convention against Transnational Organized Crime* (2000), available at www.ohchr.org/en/professionalinterest/pages/protocoltraffickinginpersons.aspx (last accessed February 20, 2021).
4. Hounmenou, A statewide coalition's input in human trafficking policy implementation, pp. 69–87 at 71.
5. Ibid.
6. Jones, Tonisha R. & Faith E. Lutze, Anti-human trafficking interagency collaboration in the state of Michigan: An exploratory study. *Journal of Human Trafficking* (2016) 2:2, pp. 156–174 at 165. DOI: 10.1080/23322705.2015.1075342.
7. Lutnick, A., The "prioritizing safety for sex workers policy": A sex worker rights and anti-trafficking initiative. *Anti-Trafficking Review*, (2019) 12, pp. 140–154, available at www.antitraffickingreview.org, at p. 144 and generally
8. Lutnick, The "prioritizing safety for sex workers policy".
9. Hounmenou, A statewide coalition's input in human trafficking policy implementation, pp. 69–87 at 72.
10. See e.g., Gerassi, Lara, Andrea Nichols & Erica Michelson, Lessons learned: Benefits and challenges in interagency coalitions addressing sex trafficking and commercial sexual exploitation. *Journal of Human Trafficking* (2017) 3:4, pp. 285–302.

11. List partially developed from U.S. Department of Justice, Office of Justice Programs, Office for Victims of Crime Training and Technical Assistance Center (OVCT-TAC), *Human Trafficking Task Force e-Guide: Strengthening Collaborative Responses. Forming a Task Force,* available at https://www.ovcttac.gov/taskforceguide/eguide/2-forming-a-task-force/ (last accessed February 20, 2021), and Hounmenou, A statewide coalition's input in human trafficking policy implementation, pp. 69–87 at 77.

12. Here are two national examples in the U.S.:
     U.S. Department of State, Federal Response on Human Trafficking, *Survivor Leadership*, available at www.state.gov/humantrafficking-survivor-leadership/ (last accessed February 20, 2021), and Polaris Project, *Centering Survivors*, available at https://polarisproject.org/centering-survivors/ (last accessed February 20, 2021).

13. U.S. Department of Justice, Office of Justice Programs, Office for Victims of Crime Training and Technical Assistance Center (OVCTTAC), *Human Trafficking Task Force e-Guide: Strengthening Collaborative Responses: Using a Trauma-Informed Approach,* available at www.ovcttac.gov/taskforceguide/eguide/4-supporting-victims/41-using-a-trauma-informed-approach/ (last accessed February 20, 2021),

14. Polaris is a leading U.S. anti-trafficking non-governmental organization. Polaris, *Promising Practices: An Overview of Trauma-Informed Therapeutic Support for Survivors of Human Trafficking,* November 2015, available at https://polarisproject.org/wp-content/uploads/2019/09/Sanar-Promising-Practices.pdf (last accessed February 20, 2021).

15. For a discussion of using the terms "good practices" vs. "best practices" including a collection of additional articles, see Garfield, Stan., *Proven Practices Process: Don't Call It "Best Practice."* available at www.linkedin.com/pulse/proven-practices-process-stan-garfield/ (last accessed February 20, 2021).

16. U.S. Department of State, Federal Response on Human Trafficking. *Survivor Leadership*, available at www.state.gov/humantrafficking-survivor-leadership/ (last accessed February 20, 2021).

17. U.S. Department of State, Office to Monitor and Combat Trafficking in Persons, *Factsheet: The 3Ps: Prevention, Protection, Prosecution* (June 27, 2011), available at https://2009-2017.state.gov/j/tip/rls/fs/2011/167228.htm (last accessed February 20, 2021).

18. Lagon, Mark P., Traits of transformative anti-trafficking partnerships. *Journal of Human Trafficking* (2015) 1, pp. 21–38 at 22–23.

19. Sheldon-Sherman, Jennifer A.L., The missing "P": Prosecution, prevention, protection, and partnership in the trafficking victims protection act. *Penn State Law Review*, (2012) 117:2, pp. 443–501 at 501.

20. U.S. Department of Justice, Office of Justice Programs, Office for Victims of Crime Training and Technical Assistance Center (OVCTTAC), *Human Trafficking Task Force e-Guide.*

21. See e.g. U.S. Government Accountability Office, *Human Trafficking: A Strategic Framework Could Help Enhance the Interagency Collaboration Needed to Effectively Combat Trafficking Crimes* (July 2007); Gerassi et al., Lessons learned.

22. A federal U.S. example is U.S. Department of Justice, *Department of Justice Components.* Last updated October 2020, available at www.justice.gov/humantrafficking/department-justice-components (last accessed February 20, 2021); an international example is Interpol, *Partnerships against Human Trafficking,* available at www.interpol.int/en/Crimes/Human-trafficking/Partnerships-against-human-trafficking (last accessed February 20, 2021).

23. Examples include U.S. Chamber of Commerce, *Institutions against Human Trafficking,* available at www.uschamber.com/issues/labor/task-force-eradicate-human-trafficking/institutions-against-human-trafficking (last accessed February 20, 2021); UN GIFT,

Human Trafficking and Business: Good Practices to Prevent and Combat Human Trafficking, 2010, available at www.ilo.org/wcmsp5/groups/public/—ed_norm/—declaration/documents/publication/wcms_142722.pdf (last accessed February 20, 2021); and Task Force on Human Trafficking in Fishing in International Waters. *Report to Congress.* (January 2021) available at www.state.gov/report-on-human-trafficking-in-fishing-in-international-waters/ (last accessed February 2021).

24. One example is Operation T.E.N. (Trafficking Ends Now), *see* U.S. Attorney's Office Western District of Pennsylvania, *U.S. Attorney Brady Announces Coalition Dedicated to Ending Human Trafficking*, July 22, 2020, available at www.justice.gov/usao-wdpa/pr/us-attorney-brady-announces-coalition-dedicated-ending-human-trafficking (last accessed February 20, 2021).

25. Gerassi et al., Lessons learned, pp. 285–302 at 290–292.

26. Jones & Lutze, Anti-human trafficking interagency collaboration in the state of Michigan, pp. 156–174 at 164–165.

27. See e.g., Chuang, Janie, Beyond a snapshot: Preventing human trafficking in the global economy. *Indiana Journal of Global Legal Studies* (2006) 13:1, Article 5.Rothman, E. F., Stoklosa, H., Baldwin, S. B., Chisolm-Straker, M., Kato Price, R., Atkinson, H. G., & HEAL Trafficking, Public health research priorities to address US human trafficking. *American Journal of Public Health* (2017) 107:7, pp. 1045–1047.U.S. Dept. of Human Services, Administration for Family and Children, Family & Youth Services Bureau, *Issue Brief: Human Trafficking Prevention—Strategies for Runaway and Homeless Youth Settings* (November 2020), available at www.acf.hhs.gov/sites/default/files/documents/fysb/acf_issuebrief_htprevention_10202020_final_508.pdf (last accessed February 20, 2021).

28. Polaris Project funding for the U.S. Dept. of Health and Human Services, available at https://taggs.hhs.gov/Detail/RecipDetail?arg_RecipId=JT2qqf206ITM%2Bl6LwRpiYw%3D%3D (last accessed February 20, 2021).

29. U.S. Dept. of Homeland Security, Immigration and Customs Enforcement, *Human Trafficking*, available at www.ice.gov/features/human-trafficking (last accessed February 20, 2021).

30. Office for Victims of Crime Training and Technical Assistance Center, *Human Trafficking Task Force e-Guide*, available at www.ovcttac.gov/taskforceguide/eguide/ (last accessed February 20, 2021); a U.S. federal example is the President's Interagency Task Force to Monitor and Combat Trafficking in Persons (PITF), available at www.state.gov/the-presidents-interagency-task-force/#:~:text=The%20President's%20Interagency%20Task%20Force%20to%20Monitor%20and%20Comba t%20Trafficking,government%2Dwide%20efforts%20to%20combat (last accessed February 20, 2021).

31. Hounmenou, A statewide coalition's input in human trafficking policy implementation, pp. 69–87.

32. Thanks to Ana Revenco of La Strada Moldova for the elephant and mouse metaphor.

33. Busza, Joanna, Sarah Castle & Aisse Diarra, Trafficking and health: Attempts to prevent trafficking are increasing the problems of those who migrate voluntarily. *BMJ* (2004) 328, pp. 7452–1369–71 at 1369.

34. Busza et al., Trafficking and health, p. 1371.

35. See e.g., Chamberlain, Lura, FOSTA: A hostile law with a human cost, *Fordham Law Review,* (2019) 87, p. 2171, available at: https://ir.lawnet.fordham.edu/flr/vol87/iss5/13, and Blunt, D. & A. Wolf, Erased: The impact of FOSTA-SESTA and the removal of Backpage on sex workers. *Anti-Trafficking Review*, (2020) 14, pp. 117–121, https://doi.org/10.14197/atr.201220148.

36. "Human trafficking frequently involves multiple forms of abuse, including deception, coercion, extortion, threats, and, for many, physical or sexual violence." Kiss, L., & C.

Zimmerman, Human trafficking and labor exploitation: Toward identifying, implementing, and evaluating effective responses. *PLoS Medicine* (2019) 16:1, p. e1002740.

37. Susie Bright's Journal, *Trafficking Panic!—Junk Science Meets Sex Police* (2011), available at https://susiebright.blogs.com/susie_brights_journal_/2011/04/stop-bogus-sex-trafficking-panics-the-junk-science-is-appalling.html (last accessed February 20, 2021).

38. See e.g., Countryman-Roswurm, Karen, Rise, unite, support: Doing "no harm" in the anti-trafficking movement. *Slavery Today Journal* (2015) 2:1, pp. 1–22.

39. For more information on trauma-informed work with victims and vulnerable people, two starting points are:Office for Victims of Crime Training and Technical Assistance Center, *Using a Trauma Informed Approach*, available at www.ovcttac.gov/taskforceguide/eguide/4-supporting-victims/41-using-a-trauma-informed-approach/ (last accessed February 20, 2021); and CDC, *6 Guiding Principles to a Trauma-Informed Approach*, available at www.cdc.gov/cpr/infographics/6_principles_trauma_info.htm (last accessed February 20, 2021).

40. See e.g., Jones & Lutze, Anti-Human Trafficking Interagency Collaboration in the State of Michigan.

41. Bishop, Johanna P., Book review: Framing the fight against human trafficking. *Humanity & Society* (2020) 44:2, pp. 233–239 at 234.

INDEX

Note: Page numbers in *italic* indicate a figure and page numbers in **bold** indicate a table on the corresponding page.

Printed in the United States
by Baker & Taylor Publisher Services